right whale, ringtail, Sangreal,   tittletale, tooth and nail,

Springfield, Massachusetts, U.S.A.

Merriam-Webster's
Rhyming
Dictionary

Second Edition

Merriam-Webster, Incorporated
Springfield, Massachusetts, U.S.A.

A GENUINE MERRIAM-WEBSTER

The name Webster alone is no guarantee of excellence. It is used by a number of publishers and may serve mainly to mislead an unwary buyer.

Merriam-Webster™ is the name you should look for when you consider the purchase of dictionaries or other fine reference books. It carries the reputation of a company that has been publishing since 1831 and is your assurance of quality and authority.

Preface to the Second Edition

This new edition of MERRIAM-WEBSTER'S RHYMING DICTIONARY contains over 67,000 rhyming words, about 12,000 more than the first edition. These additions naturally include words that have come into common use since the earlier book's publication— words such as *busk, blog, perp, kludge, out-there, reboot, dreadlocked, fearmonger,* and *jaw-dropper.* But most of the additions are not actually new to the language. For the first time, almost all the rhyming two-, three-, four-, and five-word entries found in *Merriam-Webster's Collegiate Dictionary* have been entered in this dictionary. The result is that, for example, at the entry **y** you will find not only the rhyming word *eye* but also *evil eye, black eye,* and *see eye to eye*—not to mention *big lie, black tie, junior high, on the fly,* and *kiss good-bye.* At **ar** you will find not only *car* but also *prowl car, cable car,* and *funny car*—not to mention *film noir, North Star, fern bar,* and *air guitar.* At **are⁴** you will find not only *air* but also *dead air, hot air, in the air,* and *breath of fresh air*—not to mention *big hair, no fair, easy chair, lion's share, then and there,* and *wear and tear.* And at **ine¹** you will find not only *line* but also *punch line, fault line, conga line, draw the line, firing line,* and *toe the line*—not to mention *high sign, ice wine, cloud nine, gold mine,* and *knotty pine.*

The first edition's basic organization has been retained. Of the various methods that rhyming dictionaries have employed to organize their contents over the years, the one used here has proved at least as readily graspable as any other— probably even for users who have been too impatient to read the Explanatory Notes. Its method does not require numbered categories or a separate index; and since all rhymes are arranged by number of syllables, the user with a precise metrical slot to fill is spared unnecessary effort in finding the ideal candidate.

As in the first edition, many uncommon words have been included, though most highly technical and obscure words have been omitted, as have most words whose only meanings are vulgar, offensive, or obscene. The rhyming lists include acronyms and initialisms (*BVD, VIP*), contractions (*don't, won't*), first names (*Jeanne, Dean*), geographical and biographical names (*Denmark, Menlo Park; Mozart, Earhart*), irregular plurals (*libretti, amoretti*), and irregular verb inflections (*bought, sought*). They also direct the user to nouns, verbs, and adjectives with standard inflections that might be overlooked; for example, the entry **ix**[1] lists such rhyming words as *Styx*, *transfix*, and *crucifix*, but also sends users to **ick**, where nouns and verbs with regular inflections (*licks*, *sidekicks*, *cherry-picks*, etc.) can be found.

    We hope this revision, with its intuitive ease of use and its significantly enhanced word lists, will prove to be the tool of first resort for a new generation of poets and lyricists.

This edition, like most Merriam-Webster publications, can be considered the product of a collective effort, since it builds on the previous edition and the latter's own predecessor, *Webster's Compact Rhyming Dictionary*, and thus on the work of those works' editors, particularly Julie A. Collier, David B. Justice, and Mary Wood Cornog. The current revision was undertaken by C. Roger Davis and Mark A. Stevens.

Explanatory Notes

Rhyming Sounds

Words in this book are gathered into entries on the basis of their rhyming sound, which begins with the vowel sound in the last stressed syllable. This syllable may receive either primary or secondary stress; that is, a word may be listed at a given entry because the rhyming sound begins either with the word's most strongly accented syllable or with a following syllable that is only somewhat accented.

The actual rhyming sounds have one, two, or three syllables. (The rhyming words themselves are of widely varying lengths, though rarely of more than six syllables, since long words can be extremely difficult to work with and are rarely found in lyrics and rhymed poetry.) One-syllable rhyming sounds are found in one-syllable words, such as *wand* \wänd\ (rhyming sound \änd\), and in words where the primary or secondary stress falls on the final syllable, as in *despond* \di-'spänd\. Two-syllable rhymes are found in words where the last syllable with primary or secondary stress is the next-to-last syllable, as in *Torah* \'tôr-ə\ (where the rhyming sound is \ôr-ə\, as in *aurora* and *grandiflora*). Three-syllable rhymes are found in words where the third syllable from the end is accented, as in *charity* \'char-ət-ē\ (where the rhyming sound is \ar-ət-ē\, as in *barbarity* and *solidarity*).

Main Entries and Cross-References

Main entries consist of a boldface entry form, a pronunciation, and a list of rhyming words separated by bullets (•) into syllable groupings.

To find a rhyme for a given word, you need to know only the spelling of the word, including its rhyming sound. The entry form is usually the most common spelling of the rhyming sound shown in the pronunciation. If, for instance, you were seeking a word to rhyme with *guess*, you would look up **ess** (the spelling of *guess*'s rhyming sound) and find the following entry:

> **ess** \es\ bless, cess, chess,
> cress, dress, ess, fess, guess,
> Hess, Hesse, jess, less, loess, . . .

If you had been seeking a rhyme for *evanesce*, you might instead have looked up **esce** and found the cross-reference entry

esce \es\ see ESS

When the same spelling is used for more than one rhyming sound, superscript numbers are used to distinguish them. Thus, someone seeking a rhyme for *give* would look up **ive** and find the following entries:

ive[1] \īv\ chive, Clive, dive, drive, five, gyve, hive, I've, jive, live, ...

ive[2] \iv\ give, live, sheave, shiv, sieve, spiv • forgive, misgive, ...

ive[3] \ēv\ see EAVE[1]

Since the rhyming sound in *give* is pronounced \iv\, the second entry is the appropriate one.

Because many words have more than one standard pronunciation, some words appear in more than one list, and not every word on every list will rhyme for every person.

An explanation of the pronunciation symbols is found on page x.

Unlisted Rhyming Words

In order to save space, regularly inflected forms of words have not been included in the lists of rhymes. Inflected forms are forms created by adding grammatical endings to the base word. For instance, the base word *arm*, a noun, is made plural by adding *-s* to form *arms*, and the base word *walk*, a verb, forms its past tense by adding *-ed* to form *walked*. To find a rhyme for *arms* or *walked*, the user must go to the entry where the base word is listed.

Inflected forms often share their rhyming sound with other words that are not inflected, as when *docks* and *socks* (inflected) share the rhyming sound of *lox* and *paradox* (uninflected). In such cases, only the uninflected forms are usually listed, but an italic note at the end of the entry indicates where the base forms of the inflected words can be found:

> **ox** \äks\ box, cox, fox, Fox,
> Knox, lox, ox, pax, phlox, pox . . .
> —*also* -s, -'s, *and* -s' *forms of
> nouns and* -s *forms of verbs listed
> at* ock[1]

Such notes have been added whenever three or more rhyming words could be created by adding endings to the base words at the entry. If only one or two such rhymes could be created, the note is generally omitted and the inflected forms are simply added to the list.

     The other class of rhyming words that may not be actually listed consists of derived words. A derived word, like an inflected word, is one to which an ending has been added, but a derived word generally represents a different part of speech from its base word. For instance, when -*ly* is added to the adjective *quick*, the derived word, *quickly*, is an adverb, and when -*ness* is added to the adjective *glad*, the derived word, *gladness*, is a noun. There is no entry for a rhyming sound if all the words that would be on the list are derived words created by adding a suffix to words drawn from another list. Thus, there is no entry for **usely** because the only rhyming words (*doucely, loosely, sprucely, abstrusely, diffusely, obtusely, profusely*) are adverbs formed by adding -*ly* to adjectives found at **use**[1]. If, however, any of the rhyming words are not derived forms, a complete list is given. Thus, the entry **eanly** is included because among the adverbs at the entry there is also the adjective *queenly*, and, for the purposes of this book, adjectives ending in -*ly* are not treated as regular derived forms.

Pronunciation Symbols

ə	banana, collide, abut	n	no, own
ᵊ	preceding \l\ and \n\, as in battle, mitten, and eaten; following \l\, \m\, \r\, as in French table, prisme, titre	ⁿ	preceding vowel or diphthong is pronounced with the nasal passages open, as in French un bon vin blanc \œⁿ-bōⁿ-vaⁿ-blä^ⁿ\
ər	further, merger, bird	ŋ	sing \'siŋ\, finger \'fiŋ-gər\, ink \'iŋk\
a	mat, gag, sap		
ā	day, fade, aorta	ō	bone, know, beau
ä	bother, cot, father	ȯ	saw, all, caught
au̇	now, loud, Faust	ȯi	coin, destroy
b	baby, rib	p	pepper, lip
ch	chin, nature \'nā-chər\	r	red, car, rarity
d	did, adder	s	source, less
e	bet, peck, help	sh	shy, mission, machine, special
ē	fee, easy, media	t	tie, attack, late
f	fifty, phone, rough	th	thin, ether
g	go, big	th	then, either
h	hat, ahead	ü	rule, fool, union \'yün-yən\, few \'fyü\
i	tip, banish, active		
ī	site, buy, deny	u̇	pull, would, book
j	job, gem, judge	v	vivid, give
k	kin, cook, ache	w	we, away
ḵ	German ich, Buch	y	yard, cue \'kyü\, mute \'myüt\
l	lily, pool	z	zone, raise
m	murmur, dim	zh	vision, azure \'a-zhər\
		-	mark of syllable division

a

a¹ \ä\ aah, ah, baa, bah, blah, Blois, bra, dah, droit, fa, Fra, ha, Jah, Kwa, la, ma, moi, na, nah, pa, pas, qua, Ra, rah, schwa, shah, ska, spa, ta, Váh • à bas, aba, Accra, aha, Allah, amah, Armagh, Artois, ayah, Bekaa, blah-blah, Borgia, bourgeois, brava, Casbah, chamois, Chang-sha, Chechnya, Chita, chutzpah, compas, Degas, dolma, Dubois, Dumas, Dunois, éclat, fa la, faux pas, fellah, Fermat, feta, foie gras, gaga, galah, Galois, goombah, grandma, grandpa, ha-ha, halvah, Hama, hoo-ha, hoopla, Hsia, hurrah, huzzah, isba, Issa, Konya, Luda, Makah, Marat, markka, Maurois, mirepoix, mudra, Murat, Oita, oompah, opah, orgeat, Oujda, quinoa, pai-hua, paisa, Para, pasha, patois, pooh-bah, prutah, pya, Sanaa, sangfroid, selah, Seurat, Shema, Shoah, sola, sol-fa, supra, Syrah, ta-ta, tola, Tonghua, Ufa, Utah, Valois, Vaudois, viva, voilà, wah-wah, whoopla • abaca, Abdullah, Adana, agora, ahimsa, Akita, aliya, aloha, Antalya, assignat, Astana, Aymara, baccarat, baklava, Bogotá, brouhaha, cervelat, Chippewa, coup d'état, Cumaná, Delacroix, Directoire, entrechat, feria, guarana, habdalah, haftarah, haniwa, Heredia, inshallah, Karbala, Kashiwa, koruna, Kostroma, la-di-da, Libera, ma-and-pa, Machida, Malinois, Mardi Gras, Masséna, Modena, moussaka, Omaha, Oshawa, Ottawa, pakeha, panama, Panama, Paraná, parashah, pas de trois, persona, pietà, podesta, polenta, polynya, port de bras, Québécois, reseda, rufiyaa, Shangri-la, tempura, ulema, usquebaugh • Alma-Ata, ayatollah, caracara, con anima, coureur de bois, hispanidad, hors de combat, je ne sais quoi, Karaganda, ménage à trois, phenomena, res publica, sursum corda, tamandua • mousseline de soie, pâté de foie gras • Afars and the Issas, exempli gratia

a² \ā\ see AY¹

a³ \o\ see AW¹

aa¹ \a\ see AH³

aa² \ä\ see A¹

aachen \ä-ḵən\ Aachen, lochan

1

aag \äg\ see OG¹

aal¹ \äl\ see AIL

aal² \ol\ see ALL

aal³ \äl\ see AL¹

aam \äm\ see OM¹

aan \an\ see AN⁵

aans¹ \äns\ see ANCE²

aans² \änz\ see ONZE

aard \ärd\ see ARD¹

aari \är-ē\ see ARI¹

aaron \ar-ən\ see ARON²

aarten \ärt-ᵊn\ see ARTEN

aas \äs\ see OS¹

aatz \ätz\ see OTS

ab¹ \äb\ see OB¹

ab² \äv\ see OLVE²

ab³ \ab\ ab, blab, cab, crab, Crabbe, dab, drab, fab, flab, gab, grab, jab, lab, Lab, Mab, nab, scab, slab, stab, tab • Ahab, backstab, baobab, Cantab, confab, Moab, prefab, Punjab, Rajab, rehab, she-crab, smack-dab • bafflegab, baobab, minilab, pedicab, taxicab

aba \äb-ə\ aba, baba, Kaaba, Labe, PABA, Saba, Sabah • casaba, djellaba, indaba • Ali Baba, Orizaba, Sorocaba • jaboticaba

abah \äb-ə\ see ABA

abala \ab-ə-lə\ Kabbalah • parabola

abalist \ab-ə-ləst\ cabalist • diabolist

abard \ab-ərd\ clapboard, scabbard, tabard—also -ed forms of verbs listed at ABBER²

abatis \ab-ət-əs\ abatis, habitus

abbalah \ab-ələ\ see ABALA

abbard \ab-ərd\ see ABARD

abbas \ab-əs\ see ABBESS

abbat \ab-ət\ see ABIT

abbed¹ \ab-əd\ crabbed, rabid

abbed² \abd\ blabbed, stabbed—also -ed forms of verbs listed at AB³

abber¹ \äb-ər\ see OBBER

abber² \ab-ər\ blabber, clabber, crabber, dabber, drabber, gabber, grabber, jabber, slabber, stabber, yabber • backstabber, land-grabber, rehabber • bonnyclabber

abbess \ab-əs\ abbess • Barabbas

abbet \ab-ət\ see ABIT

abbey \ab-ē\ see ABBY

abbie¹ \äb-ē\ see OBBY

abbie² \ab-ē\ see ABBY

abbin \ab-ən\ see ABIN

abbit \ab-ət\ see ABIT

abbitry \ab-ə-trē\ see ABBITTRY

abbitt \ab-ət\ see ABIT

abbittry \ab-ə-trē\ Babbittry, rabbitry

abble¹ \äb-əl\ bauble, bobble, cobble, gobble, hobble, Kabul, nobble, obol, squabble, wabble, wobble

abble² \ab-əl\ Babel, babble, brabble, dabble, drabble, gabble, grabble, habile, rabble, Schnabel, scrabble • bedabble, hardscrabble • psychobabble, technobabble

abblement \ab-əl-mənt\ babblement, rabblement

abbler \ab-lər\ babbler, dabbler, gabbler, grabbler, rabbler, scrabbler • psychobabbler

abbly \ab-lē\ see ABLY

abbot \ab-ət\ see ABIT

abby \ab-ē\ abbey, Abby, blabby, cabbie, crabby, flabby, gabby, grabby, scabby, shabby, tabby, yabby • Punjabi

abe¹ \āb\ babe, mabe, nabe • astrolabe

abe² \ab\ see AB

abe³ \ä-bə\ see ABA

abel \ā-bəl\ see ABLE

aben \äb-ən\ see OBIN

aber¹ \ā-bər\ see ABOR

aber² \äb-ər\ see OBBER

abes \ā-bēz\ see ABIES

abi¹ \äb-ē\ see OBBY

abi² \əb-ē\ see UBBY

abi³ \ab-ē\ see ABBY

abia \ā-bē-ə\ labia, Swabia • Arabia • Bessarabia • Saudi Arabia

abian \ā-bē-ən\ Fabian, gabion, Swabian • Arabian • Bessarabian

abid \ab-əd\ see ABBED

abies \ā-bēz\ rabies, scabies, tabes • antirabies—*also* -s, -'s, *and* -s' *forms of nouns listed at* ABY

abile \ab-əl\ see ABBLE²

abilis \äb-ə-ləs\ obelus • annus mirabilis

abin \ab-ən\ cabin, rabbin

abion \ā-bē-ən\ see ABIAN

abit \ab-ət\ abbot, babbitt, Babbitt, Cabot, habit, rabbet, rabbit, sabbat • cohabit, inhabit, jackrabbit

abitant \ab-ət-ənt\ habitant • cohabitant, inhabitant

abitus \ab-ət-əs\ see ABATIS

able \ā-bəl\ Abel, able, Babel, Bebel, cable, fable, Froebel, gable, label, Mabel, sable, stable, table • disable, enable, instable, pin-table, retable, round table, timetable, turn-table, unable, unstable, worktable • thermostable

abled \ā-bəld\ fabled, gabled —*also* -ed *forms of verbs listed at* ABLE

ablis \ab-lē\ see ABLY

ably \ab-lē\ chablis, drably, scrabbly

abola \ab-ə-lə\ see ABALA

abolist \ab-ə-ləst\ see ABALIST

abor \ā-bər\ caber, labor, neighbor, saber, tabor, weber, Weber • belabor, zeitgeber

aborer \ā-bər-ər\ laborer, taborer

abot \ab-ət\ see ABIT

abra \äb-rə\ sabra, Sabra • candelabra

abre \äb\ see OB[1]

abul \äb-əl\ see ABBLE[1]

abular \ab-yə-lər\ fabular, tabular • vocabular • acetabular

abulous \ab-yə-ləs\ fabulous • fantabulous

abulum \ab-yə-ləm\ pabulum • incunabulum

aby \ā-bē\ baby, gaby, maybe • crybaby, grandbaby

ac[1] \ak\ see ACK[2]

ac[2] \äk\ see OCK[1]

ac[3] \ȯ\ see AW[1]

aca[1] \äk-ə\ see AKA[1]

aca[2] \ak-ə\ Dhaka, paca • alpaca, malacca, Malacca, sifaka • portulaca • Strait of Malacca

acable \ak-ə-bəl\ see ACKABLE

acao \ō-kō\ see OCO

acas \ak-əs\ Bacchus, fracas, Gracchus, rachis • Caracas

acca[1] \ak-ə\ see ACA

acca[2] \äk-ə\ see AKA[1]

accent \ak-sənt\ accent • relaxant

acchanal \ak-ən-ᵊl\ see ACONAL

acchic \ak-ik\ bacchic • halakic, stomachic, tribrachic • amphibrachic

acchus \ak-əs\ see ACAS

accid \as-əd\ see ACID

accio \ä-chē-ō\ bocaccio, Boccaccio, carpaccio, Masaccio

acco[1] \ak-ə\ see ACA

acco[2] \ak-ō\ see AKO[2]

acculus \ak-yə-ləs\ sacculus • miraculous

ace[1] \ās\ ace, base, bass, brace, case, chase, dace, face, grace, Grace, lace, mace, Mace, Naas, pace, place, plaice, prase, race, res, space, Thrace, trace, vase, Wace • abase, airspace, Alsace, ambsace, apace, backspace, best-case, biface, birthplace, blackface, boldface, bookcase, bootlace, braincase, briefcase, clubface, crankcase, cyclase, debase, deface, disgrace, displace, dogface, doughface, efface, embrace, emplace, encase, enchase, enlace, erase, euclase, firebase, fireplace, footpace, footrace, foreface, freebase, gyrase, half-space, hard case, headspace, hydrase, Jerez, kinase, lactase, lightface, lipase, lyase, maltase, manes, millrace, milreis, misplace, mutase, notecase, null-space, nutcase, outface, outpace, outrace, paleface, postface, Quilmes, reface, replace, retrace, scapegrace, shoelace, showcase, showplace, slipcase, smearcase, someplace, staircase, subbase, subspace, suitcase, surbase, tailrace, tenace, typeface, ukase, unbrace, unlace, watchcase, wheelbase, whey-face, whiteface, workplace, worst-case • about-face, aerospace, anyplace, boniface, bouillabaisse, carapace, catalase, cellulase, common-place, contrabass, cyberspace, database, diabase, diastase, double-space, elastase, everyplace, hydrolase, hydrospace, hyperspace, interface, interlace, interspace, invertase, kilobase, lemures, lowercase, marketplace, oxidase, pillowcase, reductase, Samothrace, single-space, steeplechase, thoroughbass, thoroughbrace, triple-space, uppercase • rarae aves • in medias res • Aguascalientes

ace² \ā-sē\ see ACY

ace³ \äs\ see OS¹

ace⁴ \as\ see ASS³

ace⁵ \äch-ē\ see OTCHY

ace⁶ \äs-ə\ see ASA¹

aceable \ā-sə-bəl\ placeable, traceable • displaceable, effaceable, embraceable, erasable, persuasible, replaceable, unplaceable, untraceable • ineffaceable, irreplaceable

acean \ā-shən\ see ATION¹

aced \āst\ based, baste, chaste, faced, geest, haste, laced,

mayest, paste, taste, waist, waste • bald-faced, barefaced, bold-faced, distaste, dough-faced, foretaste, impaste, lambaste, lightfaced, moonfaced, pie-faced, po-faced, posthaste, rad waste, retaste, self-paced, shamefaced, shirtwaist, snail-paced, slipcased, stone-faced, straight-faced, straitlaced, toothpaste, two-faced, unchaste, unplaced, white-faced • aftertaste, brazen-faced, double-faced, Janus-faced, hatchet-faced, open-faced, pantywaist, poker-faced, thorough-paced • scissors-and-paste—*also* -ed *forms of verbs listed at* ACE¹

aceless \ā-sləs\ baseless, faceless, graceless, laceless, placeless, spaceless, traceless

aceman \ā-smən\ baseman, placeman, spaceman

acement \ā-smənt\ basement, casement, placement • abasement, debasement, defacement, displacement, effacement, embracement, emplacement, encasement, enlacement, misplacement, outplacement, replacement • bargain-basement, self-effacement

acence \ās-ᵊns\ see ASCENCE¹

acency \ās-ᵊn-sē\ adjacency, complacency, subjacency • self-complacency

acent \ās-ᵊnt\ nascent • adjacent, complacent,

complaisant, subjacent
• circumjacent, superjacent, uncomplacent

aceor \ā-sər\ see ACER[1]

aceous \ā-shəs\ see ACIOUS

acer[1] \ā-sər\ baser, bracer, chaser, facer, pacer, placer, racer, spacer, tracer • debaser, defacer, disgracer, effacer, embraceor, embracer, eraser, freebaser, replacer, subchaser • Odoacer, steeplechaser

acer[2] \as-ər\ see ASSER

acery \ās-rē\ tracery • embracery

acet[1] \ā-sət\ hic jacet, non placet

acet[2] \as-ət\ asset, facet, tacet, tacit

acewalking \ās-wȯ-kiŋ\ racewalking, spacewalking

acey \ā-sē\ see ACY

ach[1] \äk\ Bach, Mach, saugh • Cranach, Pesach, pibroch, shtetlach • Auerbach, Eisenbach, Offenbach

ach[2] \äk\ see OCK[1]

ach[3] \ak\ see ACK[2]

ach[4] \ach\ see ATCH[4]

acha \äch-ə\ cha-cha, dacha, gotcha, kwacha • focaccia, viscacha

achary \ak-ə-r-ē\ see ACKERY[2]

ache[1] \āk\ see AKE[1]

ache[2] \ash\ see ASH[3]

ache[3] \äch-ē\ see OTCHY

ache[4] \ach-ē\ see ATCHY

acheal \ā-kē-əl\ brachial, tracheal • endotracheal

ached \acht\ attached, detached • unattached • semidetached —*also* -ed *forms of verbs listed at* ATCH[4]

acher \ā-kər\ see AKER[1]

achet \ach-ət\ see ATCHET

achi \äch-ē\ see OTCHY

achial \ā-kē-əl\ see ACHEAL

achian \ā-shən\ see ATION[1]

achic \ak-ik\ see ACCHIC

aching \ā-kiŋ\ see AKING[1]

achio[1] \ash-ō\ mustachio, pistachio

achio[2] \ash-ē-ō\ mustachio, pistachio

achm \am\ see AM[2]

achment \ach-mənt\ see ATCHMENT

achne \ak-nē\ see ACNE

acho \äch-ō\ macho, nacho • gazpacho, muchacho, quebracho

achou \ash-ü\ see ASHEW

achsen \äk-sən\ see OXEN

acht \ät\ see OT[1]

achtsman \ät-smən\ see OTSMAN

achy \ā-kē\ see AKY

acia \ā-shə\ Dacia, fascia, geisha, Thracia • acacia, Alsatia, Croatia, crustacia, cymatia, Dalmatia, ex gratia, Galatia, rosacea, Sarmatia • prima facie • exempli gratia

acial \ā-shəl\ facial, glacial, racial, spatial • abbatial, bifacial, biracial, englacial, palatial, primatial, subglacial, transracial • interfacial, interglacial, interracial, multiracial • maxillofacial

acian \ā-shən\ see ATION[1]

acias \ā-shəs\ see ACIOUS

acid \as-əd\ acid, Chasid, flaccid, Hasid, jassid, placid • Abbasid, antacid, diacid, nonacid, subacid • hyperacid

acie \ā-shə\ see ACIA

acient \ā-shənt\ see ATIENT

acier[1] \ā-shər\ see ASURE[1]

acier[2] \ā-zhər\ see AZIER

acile \as-əl\ see ASSEL[2]

acing \ā-siŋ\ bracing, casing, facing, lacing, racing, spacing, tracing • catfacing, effacing • all-embracing, interfacing, letterspacing, self-effacing —also -ing forms of verbs listed at ACE[1]

acious \ā-shəs\ gracious, spacious, Statius • audacious, bodacious, capacious, ceraceous, cetaceous, cretaceous, crustaceous, curvaceous, drupaceous, edacious, fallacious, flirtatious, fugacious, hellacious, Helvetius, herbaceous, Horatius, Ignatius, loquacious, mendacious, micaceous, mordacious, pomaceous, predaceous, pugnacious, rapacious, rosaceous, sagacious, salacious, sebaceous, sequacious, setaceous, tenacious, testaceous, tufaceous, ungracious, veracious, vexacious, vinaceous, vivacious, voracious • arenaceous, carbonaceous, contumacious, disputatious, efficacious, farinaceous, fieri facias, foliaceous, gallinaceous, orchidaceous, ostentatious, perspicacious, pertinacious, scire facias, solanaceous, violaceous • inefficacious

acis \as-ē\ see ASSY

acist \ā-səst\ see ASSIST

acit \as-ət\ see ACET[2]

acity[1] \as-tē\ see ASTY[2]

acity[2] \as-ət-ē\ audacity, capacity, edacity, fugacity, loquacity, mendacity, opacity, predacity, pugnacity, rapacity, sagacity, sequacity, tenacity, veracity, vivacity, voracity • efficacity, incapacity, perspicacity, pertinacity • overcapacity

acive \ā-siv\ see ASIVE

ack[1] \äk\ see OCK[1]

ack[2] \ak\ back, black, Braque, clack, claque, crack, flack, flak, hack, jack, Jack, knack, lac, lack, lakh, mac, Mac, Mack, pack, plaque, quack, rack, sac, Sac, sack, sacque, shack, slack, smack, snack, stack, tach, tack, thwack, track, Wac, wack, whack, wrack, yak • aback, ack-ack, alack, amtrac, Anzac, arrack, Arak, attack, backpack, backtrack, Balzac, bareback, blackjack, blowback, blue-black, bootblack, bootjack, brushback, bushwhack, buyback, callback, calpac, carjack, champac, cheapjack, Coalsack, coatrack, cognac, come back, comeback, cookshack, Cormack, cossack, crackback, crookback, cut back, cutback, Dayak, dieback, Dirac, draw back, drawback, fall back, fallback, fastback, fast-track, fatback, feedback, finback, fireback, flapjack, flareback, flashback, fullback, gimcrack, giveback, graywacke, greenback, gripsack, guaiac, halfback, half-track, hardback, hardhack, hardtack, hatchback, hayrack, haystack, hijack, hogback, hold back, holdback, hopsack, horseback, humpback, hunchback, Iraq, jam-pack, jet-black, Kanak, Karnak, kayak, Kazak, kickback, knapsack, knickknack, Kodak, kulak, kyack, laid-back, lampblack, leaseback, linac, macaque, man jack, manpack, Micmac, mossback, muntjac, Muzak, notchback, offtrack, one-track, outback, packsack, payback, pitch-black, play back, playback, plow back, plowback, pullback, quillback, racetrack, ransack, repack, restack, rickrack, roll back, rollback, roorback, rucksack, runback, sad sack, scatback, serac, set back, setback, shellac, shellback, shoeblack, shoepac, sidetrack, six-pack, skewback, skipjack, skyjack, slapjack, slotback, Slovak,

smokejack, smokestack, snap back, snapback, snowpack, softback, sumac, swayback, sweepback, swept-back, switchback, tailback, tarmac, thornback, throw back, throwback, thumbtack, ticktack, tieback, tie tack, tombac, touchback, tow sack, trictrac, tripack, unpack, Welsbach, wetback, whaleback, wingback, wisecrack, wolf pack, woolpack, woolsack, yashmak, Yurak, zwieback
• almanac, amberjack, anorak, antiblack, anticrack, applejack, Arawak, Armagnac, Aurillac, back-to-back, birdyback, bivouac, black-on-black, brainiac, bric-a-brac, camelback, canvasback, cardiac, carryback, celiac, coeliac, cornerback, Cousin Jack, crackerjack, cul-de-sac, diamondback, fiddleback, fishyback, Frontenac, GayLussac, gunnysack, hackmatack, haversack, high-lowjack, huckaback, hydrocrack, iliac, ipecac, Kodiak, ladderback, leatherback, lumberjack, maniac, medevac, Merrimack, minitrack, mommy track, moneyback, multipack, multitrack, nunatak, Nunivak, off-the-rack, otomac, paperback, Pasternak, pickaback, piggyback, Pontiac, portapak, postattack, quarterback, razorback, retropack, running back, sandarac, Sarawak, Sazerac, silverback, singletrack, Skaggerak, snapperback, solonchak, steeplejack,

stickleback, superflack, supplejack, Syriac, tamarack, tenure-track, theriac, tokamak, turtleback, umiak, Unimak, Union Jack, zodiac • Adirondack, ammoniac, amnesiac, Aniakchak, biofeedback, celeriac, counterattack, demoniac, elegiac, insomniac, Monterey Jack, paranoiac, simoniac, tacamahac • Anglophiliac, aphrodisiac, coprophiliac, Dionysiac, dipsomaniac, egomaniac, hemophiliac, hypochondriac, intracardiac, kleptomaniac, melancholiac, monomaniac, mythomaniac, necrophiliac, neophiliac, nymphomaniac, paraphiliac, pedophiliac, pyromaniac, Rhodesian Ridgeback, sacroiliac, sal ammoniac • bibliomaniac, erotomaniac, megalomaniac

ackable \ak-ə-bəl\ packable, placable, stackable • implacable

ackage \ak-ij\ package, trackage • prepackage, repackage

ackal \ak-əl\ see ACKLE

acked \akt\ see ACT

acken \ak-ən\ blacken, bracken, flacon, slacken • Arawakan

ackened \ak-ənd\ blackened —*also* -ed *forms of verbs listed at* ACKEN

acker \ak-ər\ backer, clacker, cracker, hacker, jacker, knacker, lacquer, packer, racker, sacker, slacker, smacker, stacker, tacker, tracker, whacker • attacker, backpacker, bushwhacker, carjacker, comebacker, fast-tracker, firecracker, graham cracker, greenbacker, hijacker, kayaker, linebacker, nutcracker, racetracker, ransacker, safecracker, shellcracker, skyjacker, unpacker, wise-cracker • Rickenbacker, simulacre, soda cracker • counterattacker—*also* -er *forms of adjectives listed at* ACK[2]

ACKERAY \ak-ə-rē\ see ACKERY

ackerel \ak-rəl\ see ACRAL

ackery \ak-ə-rē\ flackery, quackery, Thackeray, Zachary • gimcrackery

acket \ak-ət\ bracket, jacket, packet, placket, racket • bluejacket, bush jacket, dust jacket, flak jacket, life jacket, mess jacket, rejacket, strait-jacket, wave packet • bomber jacket, dinner jacket, Eton jacket, Norfolk jacket, water jacket, yellowjacket

ackey \ak-ē\ see ACKY

ackguard \ag-ərd\ see AGGARD

ackie \ak-ē\ see ACKY

acking \ak-iŋ\ backing, blacking, cracking, packing, sacking, smacking, tracking, whacking • bushwhacking, kayaking, linebacking, meatpacking, nerve-racking, safecracking, skyjacking • antihijacking—*also* -ing *forms of verbs listed at* ACK[2]

ackish \ak-ish\ blackish, brackish, quackish

ackle \ak-əl\ cackle, crackle, grackle, hackle, jackal, macle, rackle, shackle, spackle, tackle • debacle, gang-tackle, ramshackle, unshackle • block and tackle, tabernacle

ackly \ak-lē\ blackly, crackly, hackly, slackly • abstractly, compactly, exactly • inexactly • matter-of-factly

ackman \ak-mən\ Blackmun, hackman, packman, trackman • attackman

ackney \ak-nē\ see ACNE

ackneyed \ak-nēd\ see ACNED

acko \ak-ō\ see AKO²

acksman \ak-smən\ see AXMAN

ackson \ak-sən\ see AXON

acky \ak-ē\ ackee, Bacchae, hackie, Jackie, khaki, lackey, tacky, wacky • Nagasaki, ticky-tacky

acle¹ \ik-əl\ see ICKLE

acle² \äk\ see OCK¹

acle³ \äk-əl\ see OCKLE

acle⁴ \ak-əl\ see ACKLE

acne \ak-nē\ acne, hackney, Hackney • Arachne, chloracne

acned \ak-nēd\ acned, hackneyed

aco \äk-ō\ see OCCO

acon¹ \ā-kən\ see AKEN¹

acon² \ak-ən\ see ACKEN

aconal \ak-ən-ᵊl\ bacchanal • diaconal

acque¹ \ak\ see ACK²

acque² \äk\ see OCK¹

acquer \ak-ər\ see ACKER

acques \äk\ see OCK¹

acral \ak-rəl\ mackerel, sacral • horse mackerel, jack mackerel, king mackerel • ambulacral, lumbosacral • craniosacral

acre¹ \ā-kər\ see AKER¹

acre² \ak-ər\ see ACKER

acrum \ak-rəm\ sacrum • ambulacrum, simulacrum

act \akt\ act, backed, bract, cracked, fact, packed, pact, stacked, tact, tracked, tract • abstract, attract, class act, coact, compact, contact, contract, crookbacked, detract, didact, diffract, distract, enact, entr'acte, epact, exact, extract, half-tracked, humpbacked, hunchbacked, impact, infract, intact, mossbacked, outact, playact, protract, react, redact, refract, retract, sex act, subtract, swaybacked, transact, unbacked • abreact, artifact, cataract, chain-react, counteract, cross-react, eye contact, inexact, interact, nonabstract, noncontact, nonimpact, overact, paperbacked, postimpact, precontact, razor-backed, reenact, riot act, subcompact, subcontract, tesseract, underact, vacuum-packed, ventifact • autodidact, cutthroat contract, matter-of-fact, overreact, semiabstract, social contract, ultracompact, underreact • yellow-dog contract— *also* -ed *forms of verbs listed at* ACK²

actable \ak-tə-bəl\ actable, tractable • abstractable, attractable, compactible, contractible, distractible, exactable, extractable, intractable, retractable, unactable

actance \ak-təns\ attractance, reactance

actant \ak-tənt\ attractant, reactant, surfactant • interactant

acte¹ \äkt\ see OCKED

acte² \akt\ see ACT

acted \ak-təd\ fracted • abstracted, impacted—*also* -ed *forms of verbs listed at* ACT

acter \ak-tər\ see ACTOR

actery \ak-trē\ see ACTORY

actible \ak-tə-bəl\ see ACTABLE

actic \ak-tik\ lactic, tactic • apractic, atactic, climactic, didactic, galactic, syntactic • ataractic, chiropractic, geotactic, hypotactic, isotactic, malolactic, nondidactic, parallactic, paratactic, phonotactic, phototactic, phyllotactic, prophylactic • anaphylactic, anticlimactic, autodidactic, extragalactic, intergalactic, intragalactic, stereotactic

actical \ak-ti-kəl\ practical, tactical • didactical, impractical, syntactical

actice \ak-təs\ cactus, practice • group practice, malpractice, sharp practice • cataractous, family practice

actics \ak-tiks\ tactics • didactics, syntactics • phonotactics—*also* -s, -'s, *and* -s' *forms of nouns listed at* ACTIC

actile \ak-tᵊl\ dactyl, tactile • contractile, protractile, refractile, retractile • polydactyl, pterodactyl

acting \ak-tiŋ\ acting • exacting, self-acting—*also* -ing *forms of verbs listed at* ACT

action \ak-shən\ action, faction, fraction, taction, traction • abstraction, attraction, bolt-action, class action, coaction, compaction, contraction, cross action, detraction, diffraction, distraction, exaction, extraction, impaction, inaction, infraction, job action, live-action, olfaction, protraction, reaction, redaction, refraction, retraction, stop-action, subtraction, transaction • abreaction, benefaction, cause of action, chain reaction, common fraction, complex fraction, counteraction, dark reaction, direct action, interaction, liquefaction, malefaction, overaction, petrifaction, police action, proper fraction, putrefaction, rarefaction, retroaction, satisfaction, simple fraction, single-action, stupefaction, tumefaction • alarm reaction,

decimal fraction, dissatis-
faction, improper fraction,
overreaction, photoreaction,
self-satisfaction, semiabstrac-
tion • affirmative action, angle
of refraction

actional \ak-shnəl\ factional,
fractional, tractional
• abstractional, contractional,
redactional, transactional
• interactional

actious \ak-shəs\ factious,
fractious

active \ak-tiv\ active, tractive
• abstractive, attractive,
coactive, contractive, detrac-
tive, distractive, extractive,
impactive, inactive, proactive,
protractive, reactive, refractive,
subtractive, bioactive • coun-
teractive, cross-reactive,
hyperactive, interactive,
neuroactive, nonreactive,
overactive, psychoactive,
putrefactive, retroactive,
surface-active, unattractive,
vasoactive • radioactive

actly \ak-lē\ see ACKLY

actor \ak-tər\ actor, factor,
tractor • abstractor, attractor,
coactor, cofactor, compactor,
contractor, detractor, enactor,
exactor, extractor, fudge factor,
g-factor, impactor, infractor,
load factor, protractor, reactor,
redactor, refractor, retractor,
subtracter, transactor
• benefactor, chiropractor,
malefactor, multifactor,
subcontractor • bioreactor,
campylobacter

actory \ak-trē\ factory
• olfactory, phylactery,
refractory • calefactory,
manufactory, satisfactory
• dissatisfactory, unsatisfactory

actous \ak-təs\ see ACTICE

actress \ak-trəs\ actress,
benefactress

actual \ak-chəl\ actual, factual,
tactual • contractual
• artifactual, counterfactual

acture \ak-chər\ facture, fracture
• contracture, freeze fracture,
stress fracture • compound
fracture, greenstick fracture,
manufacture, simple fracture
• remanufacture

actus \ak-təs\ see ACTICE

actyl \ak-təl\ see ACTILE

acular \ak-yə-lər\ macular
• oracular, spectacular,
spiracular, tentacular,
vernacular • tabernacular,
unspectacular

aculate \ak-yə-lət\ maculate
• ejaculate, immaculate

aculous \ak-yə-ləs\ see ACCULUS

acy \ā-sē\ Basie, lacy, pace,
précis, racy, spacey, Stacy,
Thrace, Tracy • O'Casey,
Scorsese • Pergolesi, prima
facie, Sulawesi, Veronese

acyl \as-əl\ see ASSEL²

ad¹ \ä\ see A¹

ad² \äd\ see OD¹

ad³ \ad\ ad, add, bad, bade,
brad, cad, chad, Chad, clad,
dad, fad, gad, Gad, glad, grad,

had, lad, mad, pad, plaid, rad, sad, scad, shad, tad, Thad, trad • Akkad, aoudad, Baghdad, Belgrade, Carlsbad, caudad, comrade, Conrad, crash pad, crawdad, doodad, dorsad, dryad, dyad, egad, farad, Flagstad, footpad, forbade, gonad, granddad, heptad, hexad, horn-mad, ironclad, keypad, launchpad, maenad, Mashad, monad, mouse pad, Murad, naiad, nicad, nomad, NORAD, notepad, pentad, pleiad, postgrad, reclad, scratch pad, Sinbad, tetrad, thinclad, touch pad, triad, triclad, Troad • armor-clad, Ashkhabad, cephalad, chiliad, ennead, Galahad, hebdomad, helipad, Hyderabad, Iliad, kilorad, laterad, legal pad, Leningrad, lily pad, mediad, oread, overplaid, Pythiad, Stalingrad, superadd, Trinidad, undergrad, Volgograd • Ahmadabad, Allahabad, bromeliad, gesneriad, hamadryad, hispanidad, jeremiad, Kaliningrad, Kirovograd, Marienbad, microfarad, olympiad, seminomad, Upanishad

ada¹ \äd-ä\ Dada • Marmolada • aficionada

ada² \äd-ə\ nada, sadhe, tsade • Agada, Agade, Aggada, armada, cicada, gelada, Granada, Haggadah, Jumada, Masada, Nevada, panada, posada, ramada, tostada • autostrada, empanada, enchilada, Ensenada, intifada, Kakinada, Theravada, Torquemada, yada yada • aficionada, carne asada, piña colada, Ponta Delgada • cascara sagrada, Sierra Nevada

ada³ \äd-ə\ Ada, Veda • armada, cicada, Grenada, Ikeda • alameda, ayurveda • Avellaneda

adable \äd-ə-bəl\ gradable, tradable, wadable • abradable, degradable, evadable, persuadable, upgradable • nondegradable • bio-degradable, photodegradable

adah \äd-ə\ see ADA²

adal \äd-ᵊl\ see ADDLE

adam \ad-əm\ Adam, madam • macadam • tarmacadam

adan¹ \ad-n\ see ADDEN

adan² \äd-n\ see ODDEN

adant \äd-ᵊnt\ cadent • decadent

add \ad\ see AD³

adden \ad-ᵊn\ Fadden, gladden, madden, sadden • Aladdin, Ibadan, McFadden

adder \ad-ər\ adder, bladder, ladder, madder • air bladder, fish ladder, gallbladder, puff adder, stepladder, swim bladder • Jacob's ladder
—*also -er forms of adjectives listed at* AD³

addie \ad-ē\ see ADDY

addik \äd-ik\ see ODIC

addin \ad-ᵊn\ see ADDEN

adding \ad-iŋ\ cladding, madding, padding—*also* -ing *forms of verbs listed at* AD[3]

addish[1] \äd-ish\ see ODDISH

addish[2] \a-dish\ see ADISH

addison \ad-ə-sən\ Addison, Madison

addle \ad-əl\ addle, paddle, raddle, saddle, spraddle, staddle, straddle • astraddle, dog paddle, foresaddle, gonadal, packsaddle, sidesaddle, skedaddle, unsaddle • English saddle, fiddle-faddle, western saddle

addler[1] \äd-lər\ see ODDLER

addler[2] \ad-lər\ saddler, paddler, straddler • skedaddler

addo \ad-ō\ see ADOW

addock[1] \ad-ik\ see ADIC[2]

addock[2] \ad-ək\ Braddock, haddock, paddock, shaddock

addy[1] \ad-ē\ baddie, caddie, caddy, daddy, faddy, laddie, paddy • forecaddie, granddaddy, tea caddy • finnan haddie

addy[2] \äd-ē\ see ODY[1]

ade[1] \ād\ Ade, aid, aide, bade, blade, braid, cade, clade, fade, glade, grade, jade, lade, laid, made, maid, paid, raid, rayed, shade, spade, stade, staid, suede, they'd, trade, wade, Wade • abrade, afraid, aggrade, air raid, arcade, Band-Aid, barmaid, Belgrade, blockade, bondmaid, brides-maid, brigade, brocade, cascade, Cascade, charade, clichéd, cockade, corrade, cross-trade, crusade, decade, degrade, dissuade, downgrade, evade, eyeshade, fair-trade, first aid, forebade, gainsaid, glissade, grenade, handmade, handmaid, homemade, housemaid, inlaid, invade, Kincaid, limeade, low-grade, man-made, mermaid, milkmaid, navaid, nightshade, nursemaid, old maid, outlaid, parade, persuade, pervade, plain-laid, pomade, postpaid, repaid, sacheted, scalade, sea-maid, self-made, shroud-laid, souffléed, stockade, sunshade, switchblade, tirade, torsade, twayblade, twice-laid, unbraid, unlade, unmade, unpaid, upbraid, upgrade, waylaid • accolade, Adelaide, ambuscade, aquacade, autocade, balustrade, barricade, bastinade, cable-laid, cannonade, carronade, cavalcade, centigrade, chambermaid, chiffonade, colonnade, countertrade, custom-made, dairymaid, defilade, enfilade, escalade, escapade, esplanade, everglade, foreign aid, fusillade, gallopade, gasconade, grant-in-aid, hawser-laid, hearing aid, intergrade, legal aid, lemonade, marinade, marmalade, masquerade, medicaid, meter maid, motorcade, orangeade, orthograde, overtrade, palisade, panty raid, pasquinade, plantigrade, promenade, ready-made, renegade, retrograde, serenade, stock-in-trade, tailor-made, unafraid, underlaid, visual aid • fanfaronade, harlequinade, overpersuade, rodomontade—*also* -ed *forms of verbs listed at* AY[1]

ade[2] \äd\ *see* OD[1]

ade[3] \ad\ *see* AD[3]

ade[4] \äd-ə\ *see* ADA[2]

aded \äd-əd\ bladed • arcaded, brocaded, cockaded • colonnaded—*also* -ed *forms of verbs listed at* ADE[1]

adeless \äd-ləs\ fadeless, gradeless, shadeless

adely \ad-lē\ *see* ADLY

aden[1] \äd-ᵊn\ Aden, laden, maiden • handmaiden, menhaden • overladen

aden[2] \äd-ən\ Aden • Wiesbaden • Baden-Baden

adent \äd-ᵊnt\ *see* ADANT

ader \äd-ər\ aider, blader, braider, cheder, fader, grader, heder, Nader, nadir, raider, seder, shader, spader, trader, wader • abrader, blockader, crusader, day trader, degrader, dissuader, evader, fair trader, free trader, horse trader, invader, parader, persuader, upbraider • escalader, gasconader, masquerader, promenader, serenader—*also* -er *forms of adjectives listed at* ADE[1]

ades[1] \äd-ēz\ ladies, Hades • quaker-ladies

ades[2] \ādz\ AIDS, Glades • Cascades • antitrades, Everglades • jack-of-all-trades— *also* -s, -'s, *and* -s' *forms of nouns and* -s *forms of verbs listed at* ADE[1]

adge \aj\ badge, cadge, hajj, Madge • film badge

adger \aj-ər\ badger, cadger

adh \äd\ *see* OD[1]

adhe[1] \äd-ə\ *see* ADA[2]

adhe[2] \äd-ē\ *see* ODY[1]

adia \äd-ē-ə\ stadia • Acadia, arcadia, Arcadia, palladia

adial \äd-ē-əl\ radial • biradial • interstadial

adian \äd-ē-ən\ radian • Acadian, Akkadian, arcadian, Arcadian, Barbadian, Canadian, circadian, Grenadian, Orcadian, Palladian • French Canadian, milliradian, Trinidadian

adiant \äd-ē-ənt\ gradient, radiant

adic[1] \äd-ik\ Vedic • tornadic

adic[2] \ad-ik\ Braddock, haddock, paddock • balladic, Cycladic, dyadic, faradic, haggadic, hexadic, maenadic, monadic, nomadic, sporadic, tetradic, tornadic, triadic, Troadic • Iliadic • seminomadic

adie \äd-ē\ *see* ADY

adient \äd-ē-ənt\ *see* ADIANT

adies \äd-ēz\ *see* ADES[1]

ading \äd-iŋ\ braiding, lading, shading • arcading, degrading, unfading—*also* -ing *forms of verbs listed at* ADE[1]

adir \ād-ər\ see ADER

adish \ad-ish\ caddish, faddish, maddish, radish • horseradish

adison \ad-ə-sən\ see ADDISON

adist[1] \òd-əst\ sawdust • haggadist

adist[2] \äd-əst\ see ODEST

adium \ād-ē-əm\ radium, stadium • caladium, palladium, vanadium

adle \ād-ᵊl\ cradle, dreidel, ladle, wedel

adley \ad-lē\ see ADLY

adly \ad-lē\ badly, Bradley, gladly, madly, sadly • comradely

adness \ad-nəs\ badness, gladness, madness, sadness

ado[1] \äd-ō\ bravado, Salado • camisado, carbonado, cruzado, Manado, mikado, passado, stoccado, strappado • avocado, bastinado, Colorado, Coronado, desperado, El Dorado, hacendado • amontillado, zapateado • aficionado, incommunicado, Llano Estacado

ado[2] \ād-ō\ dado, credo • Alfredo, crusado, gambado, Laredo, strappado, teredo, tornado • barricado, bastinado, camisado, carbonado, desperado, El Dorado, Oviedo • fettuccine Alfredo

ados \ā-dəs\ see ADUS

adow \ad-ō\ Caddo, Hadow, shadow • eye shadow, foreshadow, rain shadow • overshadow

adrate \äd-rət\ see ODERATE

adre \ad-rē\ see ADERY

adrian \ā-drē-ən\ Adrian, Adrienne, Hadrian

adrienne \ā-drē-ən\ see ADRIAN

adt \ät\ see OT[1]

adual \aj-əl\ see AGILE

adus \ā-dəs\ Padus • Barbados—*also* -s, -'s, *and* -s' *forms of nouns listed at* ADA[3]

ady \ād-ē\ Brady, cedi, glady, lady, Sadie, shady • bag lady, first lady, forelady, landlady, milady, old lady, pink lady, saleslady • dragon lady, leading lady, painted lady

ae[1] \ā\ see AY[1]

ae[2] \ē\ see EE[1]

ae[3] \ī\ see Y[1]

aea \ē-ə\ see IA[1]

aean \ē-ən\ see EAN[1]

aedal \ēd-ᵊl\ see EEDLE

aedile \ēd-ᵊl\ see EEDLE

aedra \ē-drə\ see EDRA

aegis[1] \ā-jəs\ see AGEOUS

aegis[2] \ē-jəs\ see EGIS

ael \āl\ see AIL

aeli \ā-lē\ see AILY

aelic[1] \äl-ik\ see OLIC[1]

aelic² \al-ik\ see ALLIC

aemon \ē-mən\ see EMON¹

aen \än\ see ANT¹

aena¹ \ä-nä\ scena • faena

aena² \ē-nə\ see INA²

aenia¹ \ē-nē-ə\ see ENIA¹

aenia² \ē-nyə\ see ENIA²

aens \äⁿs\ see ANCE¹

aeon \ē-ən\ see EAN¹

aera \ir-ə\ see ERA²

aere¹ \er-ē\ see ARY¹

aere² \ir-ē\ see EARY

aerial¹ \er-ē-əl\ see ARIAL

aerial² \ir-ē-əl\ see ERIAL

aerie¹ \ā-rē\ aerie, aery, faerie, fairy

aerie² \er-ē\ see ARY¹

aerie³ \ir-ē\ see EARY

aero¹ \er-ō\ see ERO²

aero² \ar-ō\ see ARROW²

aeroe¹ \ar-ō\ see ARROW²

aeroe² \er-ō\ see ERO²

aery¹ \ā-rē\ see AERIE¹

aery² \er-ē\ see ARY¹

aesar \ē-zər\ see EASER²

aese \ā-zə\ see ESA²

aestor \ē-stər\ see EASTER

aestus \es-təs\ see ESTIS

aet \āt\ see ATE¹

aetor \ēt-ər\ see EATER¹

aeum \ē-əm\ see EUM¹

aeus \ē-əs\ see EUS¹

af \af\ see APH

afe¹ \āf\ chafe, kef, safe, strafe, waif • fail-safe, unsafe, vouchsafe • bathyscaphe, supersafe

afe² \af\ see APH

afel \äf-əl\ offal, waffle • falafel, pantofle, rijsttafel • Belgian waffle

afer \ā-fər\ chafer, strafer, wafer • cockchafer

aff \af\ see APH

affable \af-ə-bəl\ affable, laughable

affe \af\ see APH

affed \aft\ see AFT²

affer¹ \äf-ər\ see OFFER¹

affer² \af-ər\ chaffer, gaffer, Kaffir, kafir, laugher, quaffer, sclaffer, staffer, zaffer • paragrapher, polygrapher

affia \af-ē-ə\ raffia, agraphia

affic \af-ik\ see APHIC

affick \af-ik\ see APHIC

affir \af-ər\ see AFFER²

affish \af-ish\ raffish, giraffish

affle¹ \äf-əl\ see AFEL

affle² \af-əl\ baffle, raffle, snaffle

affron \af-rən\ saffron • Biafran

affy \af-ē\ chaffy, daffy, Safi, taffy

afic \af-ik\ see APHIC

afir \af-ər\ see AFFER²

afran \af-rən\ see AFFRON

aft¹ \äft\ toft, waft
• gemeinschaft, gesellschaft
—*also* -ed *forms of verbs listed
at* OFF¹

aft² \aft\ aft, craft, daft, draft,
graft, haft, kraft, raft, shaft, Taft,
waft • abaft, aircraft, butt shaft,
campcraft, camshaft, crank-
shaft, downdraft, driveshaft,
engraft, handcraft, indraft,
kingcraft, life raft, redraft,
regraft, rockshaft, scoutcraft,
seacraft, skin graft, spacecraft,
stagecraft, statecraft, trade-
craft, updraft, witchcraft,
woodcraft • allograft, antidraft,
autograft, countershaft, fore-
and-aft, handicraft, homograft,
Hovercraft, isograft, landing
craft, overdraft, rotorcraft,
turboshaft, understaffed,
watercraft, xenograft • anti-
aircraft, heterograft—*also* -ed
forms of verbs listed at APH

aftage \af-tij\ graftage, waftage

after \af-tər\ after, crafter, dafter,
drafter, grafter, laughter, rafter,
wafter • hereafter, thereafter
• fore-and-after, handicrafter,
hereinafter, thereinafter

aftness \af-nəs\ daftness,
Daphnis, halfness

aftsman \af-smən\ craftsman,
draftsman, raftsman • hand-
craftsman • handicraftsman

afty \af-tē\ crafty, drafty

ag \ag\ ag, bag, brag, crag, dag,
drag, fag, flag, gag, hag, jag,
lag, mag, nag, quag, rag, sag,
scag, scrag, shag, slag, snag,
sprag, stag, swag, tag, wag,

YAG, zag • air bag, beanbag,
black-flag, blue flag, brown-
bag, chin-wag, dirtbag,
dishrag, dog tag, do-rag,
fleabag, flight bag, gasbag,
grab bag, greylag, handbag,
hangtag, ice bag, jet lag, kit
bag, mailbag, mixed bag,
outbrag, phone tag, postbag,
price tag, ragbag, ragtag,
ratbag, red flag, retag, sand-
bag, schoolbag, scumbag,
seabag, sight gag, sleazebag,
Sontag, sweet flag, tea bag,
time lag, tote bag, washrag,
white flag, wigwag, windbag,
workbag, zigzag • ballyrag,
barracks bag, basic slag, body
bag, bullyrag, carpetbag, dilly
bag, ditty bag, doggie bag,
duffel bag, garment bag, heavy
bag, litterbag, lollygag,
punching bag, saddlebag,
scalawag, shopping bag,
shoulder bag, sleeping bag,
tucker-bag, water bag
• Bermuda bag, capture the
flag, overnight bag, radio-tag,
telephone tag

aga¹ \äg-ə\ quagga, raga, saga
• anlage, Gonzaga, vorlage
• 's Gravenhage, Zuloaga

aga² \ā-gə\ Frege, Vega
• bodega, omega • rutabaga

aga³ \eg-ə\ *see* EGA¹

aga⁴ \ȯ-gə\ *see* AUGA

agan \ā-gən\ *see* AGIN

agar¹ \ā-gər\ Eger, Hagar, jaeger

agar² \äg-ər\ *see* OGGER¹

agar³ \əg-ər\ *see* UGGER¹

agary \ag-ə-rē\ see AGGERY

agate \ag-ət\ see AGGOT

age¹ \äj\ dodge, lodge, raj, stodge, wodge • barrage, collage, corsage, dislodge, garage, hodgepodge, Karaj, massage, swaraj • camouflage, Sanandaj • espionage • counterespionage

age² \äzh\ plage • assuage, barrage, collage, corsage, dressage, frottage, garage, gavage, lavage, massage, ménage, mirage, montage, moulage, portage, potage, treillage, triage • arbitrage, assemblage, badinage, bon voyage, bricolage, cabotage, camouflage, colportage, curettage, decoupage, empennage, enfleurage, entourage, fuselage, Hermitage, maquillage, moyen-âge, persiflage, repechage, reportage, sabotage, vernissage • décolletage, espionage, photomontage, rite de passage • counterespionage

age³ \āj\ age, cage, gage, Gage, gauge, mage, page, phage, rage, sage, stage, swage, wage • assuage, backstage, bird-cage, broad-gauge, coon's age, dark age, downstage, encage, end stage, engage, enrage, forestage, front-page, greengage, ice age, Iron Age, new age, offstage, onstage, Osage, outrage, presage, rampage, restage, rib cage, road rage, roll cage, school age, soundstage, space-age, substage, teenage, thrust stage, uncage, upstage • batting cage, center stage, clary sage, disengage, golden age, legal age, mental age, middle age, multistage, ossifrage, overage, reengage, report stage, saxifrage, scarlet sage, underage • coming-of-age, minimum wage

age⁴ \āg\ see EG¹

age⁵ \äzh\ see EIGE¹

age⁶ \äg-ə\ see AGA¹

ageable \ā-jə-bəl\ gaugeable, stageable • unassuageable

aged \ājd\ aged, gauged • broad-gauged, engaged, unpaged • middle-aged—*also* -ed *forms of verbs listed at* AGE³

agel \ā-gəl\ bagel, Hegel, plagal, Pregl, Schlegel, vagal • finagle, inveigle • vasovagal, wallydraigle

ageless \āj-ləs\ ageless, wageless

agen¹ \ā-gən\ see AGIN

agen² \ä-gən\ see OGGIN

agenous \aj-ə-nəs\ see AGINOUS

ageous \ā-jəs\ aegis • ambagious, courageous, contagious, outrageous, rampageous, umbrageous • advantageous, noncontagious • disadvantageous

ager¹ \ā-jər\ gauger, major, Major, pager, stager, wager • New Ager, presager, teenager

• Canis Major, golden-ager, middle-ager, preteenager, Ursa Major—*also* -er *forms of adjectives listed at* AGE³

ager² \äg-ər\ *see* OGGER¹

agey \ā-jē\ *see* AGY

agga \äg-ə\ *see* AGA¹

aggar \äg-ər\ *see* OGGER¹

aggard \ag-ərd\ blackguard, haggard, laggard

agged \ag-əd\ cragged, jagged, ragged

agger \ag-ər\ bagger, bragger, dagger, dragger, gagger, jagger, lagger, nagger, sagger, stagger, swagger, wagger
• brown bagger, footdragger, four-bagger, one-bagger, sandbagger, three-bagger, two-bagger • carpetbagger, cloak-and-dagger, double dagger

aggery \ag-ə-rē\ jaggery, staggery, waggery • carpet-baggery

aggie \ag-ē\ *see* AGGY²

agging \ag-iŋ\ bagging, flagging, lagging, nagging • brown bagging, foot-dragging, unflagging • carpetbagging—*also* -ing *forms of verbs listed at* AG

aggish \ag-ish\ haggish, waggish

aggle \ag-əl\ draggle, gaggle, haggle, raggle, straggle, waggle • bedraggle • raggle-taggle

aggly \ag-lē\ scraggly, straggly, waggly

aggot \ag-ət\ agate, faggot, fagot, maggot

aggy¹ \äg-ē\ *see* OGGY¹

aggy² \ag-ē\ aggie, baggy, braggy, craggy, draggy, jaggy, quaggy, ragi, scraggy, shaggy, snaggy, staggy

agh \ä\ *see* A¹

agi¹ \äg-ē\ *see* OGGY¹

agi² \ag-ē\ *see* AGGY²

agian \ā-jən\ *see* AJUN

agic \aj-ik\ magic, tragic
• choragic, pelagic
• hemorrhagic, macrophagic

agile \aj-əl\ agile, fragile, gradual, vagile

agin \ā-gən\ fagin, pagan, Reagan, Sagan • Copenhagen

aginal \aj-ən-ᵊl\ paginal, vaginal
• imaginal

aging \ā-jiŋ\ aging, raging, staging • unaging—*also* -ing *forms of verbs listed at* AGE³

aginous \aj-ə-nəs\ collagenous, farraginous, viraginous
• cartilaginous, mucilaginous, oleaginous

agion \ā-jən\ *see* AJUN

agious \ā-jəs\ *see* AGEOUS

aglia \äl-yə\ *see* AHLIA¹

aglio \al-yō\ intaglio, seraglio

agm \am\ *see* AM²

agma \ag-mə\ magma
• syntagma

agman \ag-mən\ bagman, flagman, swagman

agna \än-yə\ see ANIA[1]

agne \än\ see ANE[1]

agnes \ag-nəs\ Agnes • Albertus Magnus

agnum \ag-nəm\ magnum, sphagnum

agnus \ag-nəs\ see AGNES

ago[1] \äg-ō\ lago • Chicago, farrago, galago, imago, virago • Asiago, Calinago, Santiago, solidago

ago[2] \ə-gō\ sago • farrago, galago, imago, lumbago, plumbago, sapsago, Tobago, virago • solidago, San Diego • Tierra del Fuego

ago[3] \äŋ-gō\ see ONGO

agon \ag-ən\ dragon, flagon, lagan, wagon • bandwagon, chuck wagon, green dragon, jolt-wagon, Pendragon, snapdragon, spring wagon, tea wagon • battlewagon, coaster wagon, covered wagon, paddy wagon, station wagon, water wagon • Komodo dragon • Conestoga wagon

agonal \ag-ən-ᵊl\ agonal • diagonal, heptagonal, hexagonal, octagonal, pentagonal, tetragonal

agora \ag-ə-rə\ agora • mandragora

agoras \ag-ə-rəs\ Protagoras, Pythagoras • Anaxagoras

agot \ag-ət\ see AGGOT

agrance \ā-grəns\ flagrance, fragrance

agrancy \ā-grən-sē\ flagrancy, fragrancy, vagrancy

agrant \ā-grənt\ flagrant, fragrant, vagrant • conflagrant

agster \ag-stər\ dragster, gagster

agua \äg-wə\ Inagua, majagua, Managua, piragua • Aconcagua, Nicaragua

ague[1] \āg\ see EG[1]

ague[2] \äg\ see OG[1]

aguey \eg-ē\ see EGGY

agus \ā-gəs\ magus, Tagus, tragus • choragus, Las Vegas • Simon Magus

agy \ā-jē\ cagey, Meiji, stagy

ah[1] \ä\ see A[1]

ah[2] \ȯ\ see AW[1]

ah[3] \a\ baa, nah • pas de chat

aha \ä-hä\ aha, Baja, Naha, Praha

aham \ā-əm\ see AHUM

ahd \äd\ see OD[1]

ahdi \äd-ē\ see ODY[1]

ahdom \äd-əm\ see ODOM

ahib \äb\ see OB[1]

ahl \äl\ see AL[1]

ahler \äl-ər\ see OLLAR

ahlia[1] \äl-yə\ dahlia • passacaglia

ahlia[2] \ä-lē-ə\ see ALIA[1]

ahma[1] \äm-ə\ see AMA[1]

ahma[2] \am-ə\ see AMA[2]

ahman[1] \äm-ən\ see OMMON

ahman[2] \am-ən\ see AMMON

ahn \än\ see ON[1]

ahms \ämz\ see ALMS

ahnda \än-də\ see ONDA

ahr \är\ see AR[3]

ahru \ä-rü\ see ARU

aht \ät\ see OT[1]

ahua \ä-wə\ see AWA[1]

ahum \ä-əm\ Graham, mayhem, Nahum • Te Deum

ahveh \ä-vā\ see AVE[1]

ai[1] \ā\ see AY[1]

ai[2] \ē\ see EE[1]

ai[3] \ī\ see Y[1]

ai[4] \öi\ see OY

ai[5] \ä-ē\ see AII

a'i \ī\ see Y[1]

aia[1] \ä-ə\ Freya • Aglaia, cattleya, Hosea, Isaiah, Judea, Nouméa • Adygeya, Himalaya, Kilauea, Mauna Kea, Meghalaya

aia[2] \ī-ə\ see IAH[1]

aiad[1] \ä-əd\ naiad, pleiad

aiad[2] \ī-əd\ see YAD

aiah \ä-ə\ see AIA

aias \ä-əs\ see AIS[1]

aic \ä-ik\ laic • alcaic, Altaic, archaic, Chaldaic, deltaic, Hebraic, Incaic, Judaic, Mishnaic, Mithraic, mosaic, Mosaic, Passaic, prosaic, Romaic, spondaic, stanzaic, trochaic, voltaic • algebraic, Aramaic, Cyrenaic, faradaic, formulaic, pharisaic, Ptolemaic • apotropaic, paradisaic, photomosaic, Ural-Altaic

aica \ā-ə-k-ə\ Judaica • Cyrenaica

aical \ä-ə-kəl\ laical • pharisaical • paradisaical

aice \ās\ see ACE[1]

aich \āk\ see AIGH

aiche \esh\ see ESH[1]

aicos \ā-kəs\ see ECAS

aid[1] \ād\ see ADE[1]

aid[2] \ed\ see EAD[1]

aid[3] \ad\ see AD[3]

aida \ī-də\ see IDA[2]

aide[1] \ād\ see ADE[1]

aide[2] \īd-ē\ see IDAY

aiden \ād-ᵊn\ see ADEN

aider \ād-ər\ see ADER

aiding \ād-iŋ\ see ADING

aido \ī-dō\ see IDO[1]

aids \ādz\ see ADES[2]

aiety \ā-ət-ē\ see AITY

aif \āf\ see AFE[1]

aig \āg\ see EG[1]

aiga \ī-gə\ taiga • Auriga

aight \āt\ see ATE[1]

aighten \āt-ᵊn\ see ATEN[1]

aightly \āt-lē\ see ATELY[1]

aign \ān\ see ANE[1]

aigne \ān\ see ANE[1]

aignment \ān-mənt\ see AINMENT

aiian \ä-yən\ zayin • Hawaiian

aijin \ī-jēn\ gaijin, hygiene

aik \īk\ see IKE²

aika \ī-kə\ see ICA¹

ail \āl\ ail, ale, baal, bail, bale, Bâle, brail, braille, Braille, dale, Dale, drail, fail, flail, frail, Gael, gale, Gale, Gayle, grail, hail, hale, Hale, jail, kale, mail, male, nail, pail, pale, quail, Quayle, rail, sail, sale, scale, shale, snail, stale, swale, tael, tail, taille, tale, they'll, trail, vail, vale, veil, wail, wale, whale, Yale • abseil, airmail, all hail, assail, avail, bake sale, bangtail, bewail, blackmail, blacktail, bobtail, broadscale, broadtail, bucktail, bud scale, canaille, cattail, chain mail, Clydesdale, coattail, cocktail, contrail, curtail, derail, detail, doornail, dovetail, downscale, ducktail, e-mail, entail, exhale, fan mail, fantail, female, fife rail, fire sale, fishtail, folktale, foresail, foxtail, fresh gale, full-scale, gapped scale, Glendale, gray scale, greenmail, guardrail, Hallel, handrail, hangnail, headsail, hightail, hobnail, horntail, horsetail, impale, inhale, junk mail, light rail, Longueuil, lugsail, mainsail, mare's tail, Mondale, moon snail, outsail, oxtail, pass-fail, percale, pigtail, pintail, pinwale, plate rail, portrayal, pot ale, presale, prevail, rattail, regale, renail, resale, rescale, retail, right whale, ringtail, Sangreal,

Scottsdale, sea kale, sei whale, shavetail, shirttail, skysail, slop pail, small-scale, snail mail, soft hail, sperm whale, split rail, springtail, spritsail, square sail, staysail, strong gale, surveil, swordtail, taffrail, tag sale, telltale, third rail, thumbnail, timescale, toenail, toothed whale, topsail, travail, treenail, trysail, unnail, unveil, upscale, ventail, voice mail, wage scale, wagtail, wassail, whiptail, white sale, whitetail, white whale, whole gale, wholesale, yard sale • abigail, Abigail, altar rail, antimale, armored scale, audit trail, aventail, Beaufort scale, beavertail, betrayal, bill of sale, bristletail, button quail, Chippendale, Chisholm Trail, clapper rail, coffin nail, Corriedale, cottontail, countervail, Coverdale, defrayal, direct mail, disentail, draggle-tail, express mail, fairy tale, farthingale, fingernail, flickertail, forestaysail, gaff-topsail, galingale, garage sale, ginger ale, Holy Grail, HO scale, humpback whale, Irish mail, killer whale, macroscale, martingale, microscale, monorail, montadale, nano-scale, nightingale, Nightingale, old wives' tale, overscale, paper trail, pilot whale, ponytail, press of sail, purple scale, Richter scale, romeldale, rummage sale, scissortail, sliding scale, solar sail, studding sail, Sunnyvale, supersale, swallowtail, tattletale, tooth and nail, tripletail, trundle-tail, vapor trail, yellowtail • certified mail, chromatic scale, eightpenny nail, Fort Lauderdale, moderate gale, Oregon Trail, registered mail, Santa Fe Trail, self-betrayal, sixpenny nail, tenpenny nail • electronic mail, ragtag and bobtail • economy of scale

ailable \ā-lə-bəl\ bailable, mailable, sailable, salable, scalable • assailable, available, resalable, unsalable • unassailable, unavailable

ailand \ī-lənd\ see IGHLAND

ailant \ā-lənt\ see ALANT

aile \ī-lē\ see YLY

ailed \āld\ mailed, nailed, sailed, scaled, tailed, veiled • detailed, engrailed, hobnailed, pigtailed, ring-tailed, unveiled • ponytailed, swallow-tailed —also -ed forms of verbs listed at AIL

ailer \ā-lər\ alar, bailer, bailor, baler, hailer, jailer, mailer, Mailer, malar, nailer, railer, sailer, sailor, scalar, scaler, tailer, tailor, Taylor, trailer, wailer, waler, whaler • blackmailer, curtailer, derailleur, detailer, e-mailer, entailer, e-tailer, house trailer, inhaler, loud-haler, retailer, self-mailer, wassailer, wholesaler • motor sailer, semitrailer—also -er forms of adjectives listed at AIL

ailey \ā-lē\ see AILY

ailful \āl-fəl\ see ALEFUL

ailie \ā-lē\ see AILY

ailiff \ā-ləf\ bailiff, caliph

ailing \ā-liŋ\ failing, grayling, mailing, paling, railing, sailing, tailing, veiling, whaling • boardsailing, prevailing, retailing, self-mailing, unfailing • parasailing, unavailing—also -ing forms of verbs listed at AIL

aille¹ \āl\ see AIL

aille² \ī\ see Y¹

aille³ \īl\ see ILE¹

aille⁴ \ä-yə\ see AYA¹

ailles \ī\ see Y¹

ailleur \ā-lər\ see AILER

ailment \āl-mənt\ ailment, bailment • curtailment, derailment, entailment, impalement

ailor \ā-lər\ see AILER

ails \ālz\ see ALES

ailsman \ālz-mən\ see ALESMAN

aily \ā-lē\ Ailey, bailey, Bailey, bailie, daily, Daley, Daly, gaily, grayly, paly, scaly, shaley, wally • Bareilly, Bareli, Disraeli, Israeli, shillelagh • motte and bailey, triticale, ukulele

aim \ām\ see AME¹

aima \ī-mə\ see YMA

aimable \ā-mə-bəl\ see AMABLE

aiman \ā-mən\ see AMEN¹

aimant \ā-mənt\ see AYMENT

aiment \ā-mənt\ see AYMENT

aimer \ā-mər\ blamer, claimer, flamer, framer, gamer, maimer, namer, tamer • acclaimer, declaimer, defamer, disclaimer, exclaimer, inflamer, nicknamer, proclaimer • Hall of Famer —*also* -er *forms of adjectives listed at* AME[1]

aimless \ām-ləs\ see AMELESS

ain[1] \ā-ən\ see AYAN[1]

ain[2] \ān\ see ANE[1]

ain[3] \en\ see EN[1]

ain[4] \in\ see IN[1]

ain[5] \īn\ see INE[1]

ain[6] \aⁿ\ see IN[4]

aina \ī-nə\ see INA[1]

ainable \ā-nə-bəl\ stainable, trainable • attainable, containable, distrainable, explainable, maintainable, obtainable, restrainable, retrainable, sustainable • ascertainable, inexplainable, unattainable, uncontainable, unobtainable

ainder \ān-dər\ attainder, remainder

aine[1] \ān\ see ANE[1]

aine[2] \en\ see EN[1]

ained \ānd\ brained, caned, craned, drained, grained, maned, pained, paned, stained, strained, vaned, veined • birdbrained, bloodstained, close-grained, coarse-grained, contained, crackbrained, cross-grained, edge-grained, harebrained, ingrained, lamebrained, left-brained, mad-brained, membraned, restrained, right-brained, tearstained, unfeigned, unstained, untrained • featherbrained, multipaned, rattlebrained, scatterbrained, self-contained, unexplained, unrestrained—*also* -ed *forms of verbs listed at* ANE[1]

ainer \ā-nər\ caner, drainer, feigner, gainer, grainer, Mainer, planar, planer, seiner, stainer, strainer, trainer, veiner • abstainer, campaigner, complainer, container, co-planar, cordwainer, detainer, distrainer, entrainer, explainer, lupanar, maintainer, no-brainer, obtainer, ordainer, profaner, restrainer, retainer, sailplaner, sustainer, Trakehner • aqua-planer, entertainer—*also* -er *forms of adjectives listed at* ANE[1]

ainful \ān-fəl\ baneful, gainful, painful • disdainful

aininess \ā-nē-nəs\ braininess, graininess

aining \ā-niŋ\ veining • complaining, sustaining, weight training • self-explaining, self-sustaining, uncomplaining— *also* -ing *forms of verbs listed at* ANE[1]

ainish \ā-nish\ brainish, Danish, swainish

ainless \ān-ləs\ brainless, grainless, painless, stainless

ainly \ān-lē\ mainly, plainly, sanely, thegnly, vainly • germanely, humanely, inanely, insanely, mundanely, profanely, ungainly, urbanely • inhumanely

ainment \ān-mənt\ arraignment, attainment, containment, detainment, detrainment, enchainment, entrainment, ordainment, refrainment • ascertainment, edutainment, entertainment, infotainment, preordainment, self-containment • biocontainment

aino \ī-nō\ see INO[1]

ains \ānz\ Keynes, reins • cremains, Great Plains, remains—*also* -s, -'s, *and* -s' *forms of nouns and* -s *forms of verbs listed at* ANE[1]

ainsman \ānz-mən\ plainsman, reinsman

aint \ānt\ ain't, faint, feint, mayn't, paint, plaint, quaint, saint, taint, 'tain't • acquaint, attaint, bepaint, complaint, constraint, distraint, greasepaint, impaint, oil paint, repaint, restraint, war paint • head restraint, patron saint, plaster saint, self-restraint, unconstraint, unrestraint • Latter-Day Saint, luminous paint, passive restraint, prior restraint

ain't \ānt\ see AINT

ainting \ān-tiŋ\ oil painting, sandpainting, wall painting • action painting, finger painting, underpainting—*also* -ing *forms of verbs listed at* AINT

aintly \ānt-lē\ faintly, quaintly, saintly

ainy \ā-nē\ Beni, brainy, grainy, rainy, veiny, zany • Dunsany, Eugénie, Gallieni, Khomeini • Allegheny

ainz \īnz\ see INES[3]

aipse \āps\ see APES

air[1] \er\ see ARE[4]

air[2] \īr\ see IRE[1]

aira \ī-rə\ see YRA

aird \erd\ see AIRED

aire[1] \er\ see ARE[4]

aire[2] \ir\ see EER[2]

aire[3] \īr\ see IRE[1]

aired \erd\ caird, haired, laird • fair-haired, impaired, longhaired, misleared, prepared, shorthaired, unpaired, wirehaired • multilayered, underprepared, unimpaired —*also* -ed *forms of verbs listed at* ARE[4]

airer \er-ər\ see EARER[1]

aires[1] \er\ see ARE[4]

aires[2] \ar-ēs\ see ARES[2]

airess[1] \er-əs\ see ERROUS

airess[2] \ar-əs\ see ARIS[2]

airie \er-ē\ see ARY[1]

airing \er-iŋ\ see ARING[1]

airish \er-ish\ see ARISH[1]

airist \er-əst\ see ARIST

airly \er-lē\ barely, fairly, ferlie, rarely, sparely, squarely • debonairly, unawarely

airn \ern\ see ERN[1]

airo \ī-rō\ see YRO¹

airs \erz\ theirs • backstairs, downstairs, nowheres, somewheres, upstairs • kick upstairs, unawares • foreign affairs, musical chairs—*also* -s, -'s, *and* -s' *forms of nouns and* -s *forms of verbs listed at* ARE⁴

airy¹ \er-ē\ see ARY¹

airy² \ā-rē\ see AERIE¹

ais¹ \ā-əs\ dais, Gaius, Laius • Isaias • Menelaus

ais² \ā\ see AY¹

aisal¹ \ā-zəl\ see ASAL²

aisal² \ī-səl\ see ISAL¹

aisance \ās-ᵊns\ see ASCENCE¹

aisant \ās-ᵊnt\ see ACENT

aise¹ \āz\ see AZE¹

aise² \ez\ see AYS¹

aisement \āz-mənt\ see AZEMENT

aiser¹ \ā-zər\ see AZER

aiser² \ī-zər\ see IZER

aisian \ā-zhən\ see ASION

aisin \āz-ᵊn\ see AZON

aising \ā-ziŋ\ blazing, braising, glazing, hazing, phrasing • amazing, appraising, barn raising, fund-raising, hair-raising, hell-raising, house-raising, stargazing, trailblazing • crystal gazing, double glazing, navel-gazing • consciousness-raising—*also* -ing *forms of verbs listed at* AZE¹

aisle \ī\ see ILE¹

aisley \āz-lē\ paisley, nasally

aisne \ān\ see ANE¹

aisse \ās\ see ACE¹

aisson \ās-ᵊn\ see ASON¹

aist¹ \ā-əst\ see AYEST

aist² \āst\ see ACED

aist³ \āst\ see OST¹

aisy \ā-zē\ see AZY

ait¹ \ā\ see AY¹

ait² \āt\ see ATE¹

ait³ \īt\ see ITE¹

ait⁴ \at\ see AT⁵

aite \īt\ see ITE¹

aited \āt-əd\ see ATED

aiten \āt-ᵊn\ see ATEN¹

aiter \āt-ər\ see ATOR

aith \āth\ eighth, faith, Faith, saithe, scathe, wraith • Galbraith, good faith, unfaith • interfaith • article of faith

aithe \āth\ see AITH

aithless \āth-ləs\ faithless, scatheless

aiti \āt-ē\ see ATY

aitian \ā-shən\ see ATION¹

aiting \āt-iŋ\ see ATING

aitly \āt-lē\ see ATELY¹

aitor \āt-ər\ see ATOR

aitorous \āt-ə-rəs\ see ATERESS

aitour \āt-ər\ see ATOR

aitress \ā-trəs\ traitress, waitress

aity \ā-ət-ē\ deity, gaiety, laity • corporeity, spontaneity, synchroneity • diaphaneity,

homogeneity, simultaneity
• contemporaneity, extempo-
raneity, heterogeneity

aius¹ \ā-əs\ see AIS¹

aius² \ī-əs\ see IAS¹

aiva \ī-və\ see IVA¹

aive \āv\ see AVE²

aix \ā\ see AY¹

aize \āz\ see AZE¹

aj \äj\ see AGE¹

aja¹ \ä-hä\ see AHA

aja² \ī-ə\ see IAH¹

ajan \ā-jən\ see AJUN

ajj \aj\ see ADGE

ajor \ā-jər\ see AGER¹

ajos \ā-əs\ see AIS¹

ajun \ā-jən\ Cajun, Trajan
• contagion, Pelagian, reagin

ak¹ \äk\ see OCK¹

ak² \ak\ see ACK²

aka¹ \äk-ə\ Dhaka, kaka, paca,
taka • Lusaka, maraca,
medaka, Melaka, moussaka,
Oaxaca, Osaka, pataca,
Tanaka • Mbandaka,
saltimbocca, Toyonaka • Lake
Titicaca • Cabeza de Vaca

aka² \ak-ə\ see ACA²

akable \ā-kə-bəl\ breakable,
makable, shakable
• mistakable, nonbreakable,
unbreakable, unslakable
• unmistakable

akan¹ \äk-ən\ see AKEN²

akan² \ak-ən\ see ACKEN

akar \äk-ər\ see OCKER

ake¹ \āk\ ache, bake, Blake,
brake, break, cake, crake,
drake, Drake, fake, flake, hake,
jake, Jake, lake, make, quake,
rake, sake, shake, sheikh,
slake, snake, spake, stake,
steak, strake, take, wake, Wake
• air brake, awake, backache,
beefcake, beefsteak, betake,
blacksnake, bull snake,
canebrake, caretake, cheese-
cake, cheesesteak, clambake,
club steak, corncrake, cube
steak, cupcake, daybreak, disc
brake, drum brake, earache,
earthquake, fair shake, fast
break, firebreak, firedrake, fish
cake, flank steak, forsake,
friedcake, fruitcake, green
snake, grubstake, hand brake,
handshake, headache, heart-
ache, heartbreak, hoecake,
hotcake, housebreak, intake,
jailbreak, keepsake, king snake,
lapstrake, mandrake, Mars-
quake, milk snake, mistake,
moonquake, muckrake,
namesake, newsbreak,
oatcake, oil cake, opaque,
outbreak, outtake, Pan-Cake,
pancake, partake, pound cake,
prebake, pump fake, rat snake,
remake, retake, rewake, rock
brake, seaquake, sea snake,
seedcake, sheldrake, short-
cake, snowflake, sponge cake,
sweepstake, Swiss steak, tea
cake, toothache, unmake,
uptake, wheat cake, windbreak,
wind shake, youthquake
• aerobrake, bellyache, coaster
brake, coffee break, coral

snake, Crater Lake, double take, garter snake, give-and-take, Great Bear Lake, Great Salt Lake, Great Slave Lake, griddle cake, halterbreak, hognose snake, johnnycake, kittiwake, make-or-break, marble cake, microquake, minute steak, overtake, parking brake, patty-cake, piece of cake, plumber's snake, put-and-take, rattlesnake, Reindeer Lake, silver hake, station break, stomachache, undertake, wapentake, water snake, wedding cake, wideawake • chicken-fried steak, golden handshake, radiopaque, Salisbury steak, semiopaque, tension headache, upside-down cake • Delmonico steak, emergency brake, Lady of the Lake, potato pancake

ake² \ak\ see ACK²

ake³ \äk-ē\ see OCKY

aked \ākt\ awaked, half-baked, ringstraked, sunbaked—*also* -ed *forms of verbs listed at* AKE¹

akeless \ā-kləs\ brakeless, wakeless

aken¹ \ā-kən\ bacon, Bacon, Dakin, Macon, shaken, taken, waken • awaken, betaken, forsaken, mistaken, partaken, retaken, rewaken, unshaken, well-taken • godforsaken, overtaken, undertaken

aken² \äk-ən\ kraken • Arawakan

aker¹ \ā-kər\ acre, baker, breaker, faker, fakir, laker, maker, nacre, quaker, Quaker, raker, saker, shaker, taker, waker • backbreaker, bookmaker, caretaker, carmaker, comaker, dressmaker, drugmaker, earthshaker, filmmaker, gill raker, glassmaker, groundbreaker, grubstaker, hatmaker, haymaker, heartbreaker, homemaker, housebreaker, icebreaker, jawbreaker, kingmaker, lawbreaker, lawmaker, mapmaker, matchmaker, mistaker, Mount Baker, muckraker, mythmaker, noisemaker, oddsmaker, pacemaker, peacemaker, phrasemaker, platemaker, playmaker, Poundmaker, printmaker, rainmaker, sailmaker, saltshaker, shirtmaker, shoemaker, snowmaker, stavesacre, steelmaker, strikebreaker, tastemaker, tiebreaker, toolmaker, trailbreaker, watchmaker, windbreaker, winemaker, wiseacre • automaker, Basket Maker, bellyacher, boilermaker, circuit breaker, coffee maker, Diefenbaker, market maker, merrymaker, moneymaker, moviemaker, papermaker, pepper shaker, simulacre, troublemaker, undertaker, Wanamaker • cabinetmaker, holidaymaker, mover and shaker, policymaker—*also* -er *forms of adjectives listed at* AKE¹

AKER² \AK-ər\ see ACKER

akery \ā-krē\ bakery, fakery

akes \āks\ jakes • cornflakes, Great Lakes, sweepstakes

• ducks and drakes—*also* -s, -'s, *and* -s' *forms of nouns and* -s *forms of verbs listed at* AKE[1]

ake-up \ā-kəp\ break up, breakup, make up, makeup, rake up, shake-up, shake up, take-up, take up, wake-up

akey \ā-kē\ see AKY

akh \äk\ see OCK[1]

aki[1] \äk-ē\ see OCKY

aki[2] \ak-ē\ see ACKY

akian \äk-ē-ən\ see OCKIAN

akic \ak-ik\ see ACCHIC

aking[1] \ā-kiŋ\ aching, making, waking • backbreaking, bookmaking, breathtaking, caretaking, dressmaking, earthshaking, filmmaking, glassmaking, groundbreaking, heartbreaking, housebreaking, lawbreaking, lawmaking, leave-taking, lovemaking, map-making, matchmaking, mythmaking, noisemaking, pacemaking, painstaking, pathbreaking, peacemaking, phrasemaking, printmaking, rainmaking, snowmaking, stocktaking, strikebreaking, toolmaking, watchmaking, world-shaking • merrymaking, moneymaking, moviemaking, papermaking, troublemaking, undertaking • cabinetmaking, policymaking—*also* -ing *forms of verbs listed at* AKE[1]

aking[2] \ak-iŋ\ see ACKING

ako[1] \äk-ō\ see OCCO

ako[2] \ak-ō\ Sacco, shako, wacko • tobacco

aku \äk-ü\ Baku, raku • Bunraku, gagaku, nunchaku

akum \ā-kəm\ vade mecum • shalom aleichem

aky \ā-kē\ achy, braky, cakey, flaky, laky, shaky, snaky • headachy

al[1] \äl\ Baal, Bâle, col, dal, doll, kraal, loll, moll, nal, pol, quoll, rale, sol, Sol, Taal, toile, Vaal • Algol, atoll, austral, Baikal, Bhopal, cabal, Cabral, cantal, Chagall, chorale, grand mal, gun moll, hamal, jacal, mistral, narwhal, Natal, Nepal, nopal, Pascal, petrol, quetzal, Rampal, real, rial, riyal, Rizal, Shawwal, tical, timbale, Transvaal • à cheval, aerosol, Emmenthal, femme fatale, folderol, Heyerdahl, parasol, pastorale, Portugal, protocol, Provençal, Senegal, Simmental, urial, Wuppertal • entente cordiale, Neanderthal, procès-verbal, sublittoral • succès de scandale

al[2] \el\ see EL[1]

al[3] \ól\ see ALL

al[4] \al\ Al, gal, Hal, pal, rale, sal, Val • banal, cabal, canal, Chagall, chorale, copal, corral, decal, fal-lal, grand mal, joual, La Salle, Laval, locale, mescal, morale, nopal, pall-mall, pascal, Pascal, percale, quetzal, salal, serval, vinal • bacchanal, caracal, chaparral, femme fatale, musicale, pastorale, pedocal, rationale, retinal, Seconal • Guadalcanal, sublittoral

ala[1] \äl-ä\ à la, Allah, gala

ala[2] \äl-ə\ Allah, gala, olla, tala, wallah • cabala, cantala, Chapala, chuckwalla, cicala, corolla, Douala, halala, Kampala, koala, Lingala, marsala, Messala, nyala, tambala, Tlaxcala, Uppsala, Valhalla • ayotollah, Guatemala

ala[3] \ä-lə\ ala, gala • Venezuela, zarzuela

ala[4] \al-ə\ Allah, gala, Galla • cavalla, impala, Valhalla • Caracalla

alaam \ä-ləm\ Balaam, golem, Salem • Winston-Salem

alable \ā-lə-bəl\ see AILABLE

alace \al-əs\ see ALIS[2]

alad \al-əd\ see ALID[2]

alam \äl-əm\ see OLUMN

alamine \al-ə-mən\ allemande, calamine

alan \al-ən\ see ALLON

alance \al-əns\ balance, valance • imbalance, outbalance, rebalance, trial balance, unbalance • counterbalance, overbalance, platform balance

alant \ā-lənt\ assailant, bivalent, covalent, exhalant, inhalant, surveillant, trivalent • multi-valent, polyvalent, univalent

alap \al-əp\ see ALLOP[2]

alar \ā-lər\ see AILER

alary[1] \al-rē\ see ALLERY

alary[2] \al-ə-rē\ calorie, gallery, Mallory, Malory, salary, Valerie, Valéry • rogues' gallery • intercalary, kilocalorie

alas \al-əs\ see ALIS[2]

alate \al-ət\ see ALLET[2]

alcon[1] \o-kən\ see ALKIN[1]

alcon[2] \al-kən\ falcon, gyrfalcon, grimalkin • peregrine falcon

ald[1] \old\ auld, bald, scald, skald, Wald, walled • close-hauled, keelhauled, kobold, piebald, ribald, skewbald, so-called, sunscald • Archibald, Buchenwald, coveralled, Grindelwald, Grünewald, overalled, Rosenwald—*also* -ed *forms of verbs listed at* ALL

ald[2] \olt\ see ALT

alder \ol-dər\ alder, balder, Balder, Calder

aldi \ol-dē\ Bartholdi, Vivaldi • Frescobaldi, Garibaldi

aldron \ol-drən\ cauldron, chaldron

ale[1] \ā-lē\ see AILY

ale[2] \āl\ see AIL

ale[3] \äl\ see AL[1]

ale[4] \al\ see AL[4]

ale[5] \äl-ē\ see OLLY[1]

ale[6] \al-ē\ see ALLY[4]

alea \ā-lē-ə\ see ALIA[1]

aleck[1] \el-ik\ see ELIC[2]

aleck[2] \al-ik\ see ALLIC

aled \āld\ see AILED

aleful \āl-fəl\ baleful, wailful

aleigh[1] \äl-ē\ see OLLY[1]

aleigh² \ȯl-ē\ see AWLY

alem \ä-ləm\ see ALAAM

alement \āl-mənt\ see AILMENT

alen \ä-lən\ see OLLEN⁵

alence \ā-ləns\ valence
• covalence, surveillance
• polyvalence

alends \al-ənz\ see ALLANS

alent¹ \al-ənt\ see ALLANT

alent² \ā-lənt\ see ALANT

alep \al-əp\ see ALLOP²

aler¹ \ā-lər\ see AILER

aler² \äl-ər\ see OLLAR

alerie \al-ə-rē\ see ALARY²

alery \al-ə-rē\ see ALARY²

ales¹ \ālz\ sales, Wales • entrails,
Marseilles • New South Wales,
Prince of Wales, cat-o'-nine-
tails—*also* -s, 's, *and* s' *forms
of verbs listed at* AIL

ales² \äl-əs\ see OLIS

alesman \ālz-mən\ bailsman,
dalesman, salesman, talesman

alet \al-ət\ see ALLET²

alette \al-ət\ see ALLET²

aley \ā-lē\ see AILY

alf \af\ see APH

alfa \al-fə\ see ALPHA

alfness \af-nəs\ see AFTNESS

algia \al-jə\ neuralgia, nostalgia

ali¹ \äl-ē\ see OLLY¹

ali² \al-ē\ see ALLY⁴

ali³ \ȯ-lē\ see AWLY

ali⁴ \ā-lē\ see AILY

alia¹ \ā-lē-ə\ Australia, azalea,
battalia, realia, regalia, vedalia,
Westphalia • bacchanalia,
coprolalia, echolalia, genitalia,
glossolalia, inter alia, Luper-
calia, marginalia, penetralia,
saturnalia, Orientalia
• paraphernalia

alia² \al-yə\ dahlia • battalia, et
alia • passacaglia

alian¹ \ā-lē-ən\ alien • Australian,
Daedalian, Deucalion, Hegelian,
mammalian, Pygmalion, Uralian
• bacchanalian, Lupercalian,
madrigalian, saturnalian
• Episcopalian, sesquipedalian,
tatterdemalion

alian² \al-yən\ see ALLION

alic \al-ik\ see ALLIC

alice \al-əs\ see ALIS²

alid¹ \äl-əd\ see OLID

alid² \al-əd\ ballad, pallid, salad,
valid • cobb salad, corn salad,
invalid • Caesar salad, Waldorf
salad

alie \äl-yə\ see AHLIA¹

alien \ā-lē-ən\ see ALIAN¹

aling \ā-liŋ\ see AILING

alinist \äl-ə-nəst\ see OLONIST

alinn \al-ən\ see ALLON

alion¹ \ā-lē-ən\ see ALIAN¹

alion² \al-yən\ see ALLION

aliph \ā-ləf\ see AILIFF

alis¹ \ā-ləs\ see AYLESS

alis² \al-əs\ Alice, balas, callous, callus, chalice, Dallas, gallus, malice, palace, Pallas, phallus, talus, thallous, thallus • oxalis, prothallus • digitalis • hemerocallis • aurora borealis, Corona Borealis

alist \al-əst\ ballast, callused, gallused • cabalist, sodalist

ality¹ \äl-ət-ē\ jollity, polity, quality • equality, frivolity • coequality, inequality

ality² \al-ət-ē\ anality, banality, brutality, carnality, causality, centrality, duality, extrality, fatality, feudality, finality, formality, frontality, frugality, legality, lethality, locality, mentality, modality, morality, mortality, nasality, natality, neutrality, nodality, orality, plurality, primality, rascality, reality, regality, rurality, sodality, tonality, totality, venality, vitality, vocality • abnormality, actuality, amorality, animality, atonality, axiality, bestiality, bilinguality, bimodality, bipedality, cardinality, classicality, coevality, comicality, commonality, communality, conjugality, cordiality, corporality, criminality, criticality, cyclicality, ethicality, externality, factuality, farcicality, fictionality, functionality, generality, geniality, hospitality, ideality, illegality, immorality, immortality, informality, integrality, internality, irreality, joviality, lexicality, liberality, lineality, literality, logicality, lognormality, marginality, musicality, mutuality, nationality, notionality, nuptiality, optimality, parfocality, partiality, personality, physicality, practicality, principality, prodigality, punctuality, quizzicality, rationality, seasonality, sensuality, sexuality, siege mentality, sociality, spaciality, speciality, subnormality, surreality, technicality, temporality, textuality, topicality, triviality, typicality, unmorality, unreality, verticality, virtuality, whimsicality • asexuality, bisexuality, bunker mentality, collegiality, colloquiality, commerciality, conceptuality, conditionality, congeniality, connaturality, connubiality, conventionality, conviviality, corporeality, dimensionality, directionality, effectuality, emotionality, essentiality, eventuality, exceptionality, extensionality, grammaticality, horizontality, illogicality, impartiality, impersonality, impracticality, inhospitality, instrumentality, intentionality, irrationality, monumentality, municipality, originality, pansexuality, paranormality, polytonality, potentiality, proportionality, provinciality, sentimentality, spirituality, split personality, substantiality, supernormality, theatricality, transexuality, universality • artificiality, confidentiality, consequentiality, constitutionality, homosexuality, hypersexuality, immateriality, individuality, intellectuality, intersexuality, superficiality, territoriality, two-dimensionality, uncongeniality, unconventionality, virtual reality

alium \al-ē-əm\ see ALLIUM

alius \ā-lē-əs\ alias
• Sibelius,Tiselius, Vesalius

alk \ȯk\ auk, balk, Bloch, calk, caulk, chalk, gawk, hawk, Koch, Kock, Salk, Sauk, squawk, stalk, talk, walk • back talk, Bartók, Black Hawk, bemock, boardwalk, cakewalk, catwalk, chalktalk, cornstalk, cross talk, crosswalk, duckwalk, eyestalk, fast-talk, fish hawk, French chalk, goshawk, Gottschalk, jaywalk, langue d'oc, Languedoc, leafstalk, marsh hawk, Mohawk, moonwalk, nighthawk, Norfolk, Norwalk, outtalk, outwalk, pep talk, racewalk, ropewalk, shoptalk, sidewalk, skywalk, sleepwalk, small talk, space walk, Suffolk, sweet-talk, trash talk • baby talk, belle epoque, catafalque, chicken hawk, double-talk, happy talk, Kitty Hawk, pillow talk, power walk, sparrow hawk, widow's walk, tomahawk

alkan \ȯl-kən\ see ALKIN[1]

alker \ȯ-kər\ balker, caulker, gawker, hawker, squawker, stalker, walker • cakewalker, deerstalker, floorwalker, jayhawker, jaywalker, nightwalker, ropewalker, sleepwalker, spacewalker, streetwalker, trackwalker, trash-talker • double-talker

alkie \ȯ-kē\ balky, chalky, gawky, gnocchi, pawky, stalky, talkie, talky • Milwaukee • walkie-talkie • Winnipesaukee

alkin[1] \ȯ-kən\ Balkan, malkin • grimalkin

alkin[2] \al-kən\ see ALCON[2]

alking \ȯ-kiŋ\ caulking, walking • racewalking, spacewalking, streetwalking—*also* -ing *forms of verbs listed at* ALK

alkland \ȯk-lənd\ see AUCKLAND

alky \ȯ-kē\ see ALKIE

all[1] \ȯl\ all, awl, ball, bawl, brawl, call, caul, crawl, doll, drawl, fall, gall, Gaul, hall, Hall, haul, kraal, mall, maul, moll, pall, Paul, pawl, Saul, scall, scrawl, shawl, small, Sol, spall, sprawl, squall, stall, tall, thrall, trawl, wall, y'all, yauld, yawl • ALGOL, and all, Antall, appall, Argall, argol, air ball, ashfall, at all, atoll, AWOL, baseball, Baikal, beach ball, beanball, befall, Bengal, bestball, birdcall, blackball, Bokmål, bookstall, boxhaul, box stall, bradawl, brick wall, broomball, catcall, catchall, cell wall, close call, COBOL, cold call, cornball, Cornwall, crown gall, cue ball, cure-all, curveball, deadfall, de Gaulle, dewfall, dodgeball, downfall, downhaul, drywall, duck call, eight ball, enthrall, eyeball, fair ball, fastball, fireball, fire wall, floodwall, foosball, football, footfall, footstall, footwall, forestall, forkball, foul ball, four-ball, fourth wall, free-fall, gadwall, game ball, glycol, golf ball, Goodall, goofball, googol, guildhall, hair ball, handball, hardball, headstall, heelball, highball, holdall, house call, icefall, infall, install, John Paul, jump ball, keelhaul, know-all, landfall, Landsmål, line-haul, line squall, lowball, Maillol, meatball, menthol, mess hall, miscall, mothball, Naipaul, naphthol, Nepal, nightfall, nutgall, oddball, outfall, outhaul, paintball, pinball, pitfall, plimsoll, pratfall, prayer shawl, pub crawl, puffball, punchball, pushball, rainfall, rainsquall, recall, rial, Riksmål, riyal, rockfall, roll call, root-ball, rorqual, Saint Paul, save-all, screwball, seawall, short-haul, shortfall, sick call, sidewall, sleazeball, slimeball, snowball, snowfall, softball, sour ball, speedball, spitball, Stendhal, stickball, stonewall, stone wall, stoopball, strip mall, T-ball, tea ball, tell-all, three-ball, toll call, town hall, trackball, Tyrol, Udall, Walsall, what all, whip stall, Whitehall, whitewall, windfall, windgall, withal, withdrawal, you-all • above all, aerosol, after all, alcohol, all in all, altar call, barbital, basketball, body wall, borough hall, buckyball, butanol, butterball, buttonball, cannonball, carryall, caterwaul, cattle call, Chinese wall, city hall, climbing wall, conference call, cortisol, overall, coverall, crystal ball, curtain call, Demerol, disenthrall, Donegal, entresol, ethanol, evenfall, free-for-all, gasohol, girasole, gopher ball, Grand Guignol, haute école, hiring hall, judgment call, know-it-all, knuckleball, Komsomol, matzo ball, Mendenhall, methanol, minié ball, music hall, Montreal, Nembutal, off-the-wall, overall, overcall, overhaul, paddleball, parasol, Parsifal, party wall, Pentothal, preinstall, protocol, racquetball, reinstall, Seconal, Senegal, shopping mall, study hall, superball, tattersall, tetherball, therewithal, timolol, uninstall, urban sprawl, volleyball, wailing wall, wake-up call, wall-to-wall, warts-and-all, waterfall, wherewithal • cholesterol, Costa del Sol, hole-in-the-wall, Mariupol', Massif Central, medicine ball, Neanderthal, nonaerosol, Sevastopol, total recall, Transalpine Gaul, Vincent de Paul • be-all and end-all

all² \äl\ see AL¹

all³ \al\ see AL⁴

alla¹ \äl-ə\ see ALA²

alla² \al-ə\ see ALLOW⁴

allable \ȯ-lə-bəl\ callable, spallable • recallable

allace \al-əs\ see OLIS

allacy \al-ə-sē\ fallacy, jalousie

allad \al-əd\ see ALID²

allage \al-ə-jē\ see ALOGY²

allah¹ \äl-ä\ see ALA¹

allah² \äl-ə\ see ALA²

allah³ \al-ə\ see ALLOW⁴

allan \al-ən\ see ALLON

allans \al-ənz\ calends, Lallans—
also -s, -'s, and -s' forms of
nouns listed at ALLON

allant \al-ənt\ callant, gallant,
talent • topgallant • fore-
topgallant

allas \al-əs\ see ALIS²

allasey \äl-ə-sē\ see OLICY

allast \al-əst\ see ALIST

alle¹ \al\ see AL⁴

alle² \al-ē\ see ALLY⁴

alle³ \äl-ē\ see OLLY

alled \ȯld\ see ALD

allee \al-ē\ see ALLY⁴

allemande \al-ə-mən\ see
ALAMINE

allen¹ \ȯ-lən\ fallen, stollen
• befallen, chapfallen,
chopfallen, crestfallen,
downfallen, tarpaulin, unfallen

allen² \al-ən\ see ALLON

aller¹ \ȯ-lər\ baller, bawler,
brawler, caller, crawler, drawler,
faller, hauler, mauler, scrawler,
squaller, trawler • b-baller,
broomballer, fastballer, fire-
baller, footballer, forestaller,
installer, night crawler, pub
crawler, recaller, softballer,
stonewaller • basketballer,
knuckleballer, melon baller

aller² \al-ər\ pallor, valor

alles \ī-əs\ see IAS¹

allet¹ \äl-ət\ see OLLET

allet² \al-ət\ ballot, callet, mallet,
palate, palette, pallet, sallet,
shallot, valet • short ballot
• Hospitalet, secret ballot

alley \al-ē\ see ALLY⁴

alli \al-ē\ see ALLY⁴

alliard \al-yərd\ galliard, halyard

allic \al-ik\ Gaelic, Gallic, malic,
phallic, salic, Salic, thallic
• cephalic, italic, mandalic,
medallic, metallic, sialik, smart
aleck, Uralic, Vandalic, vocalic
• bimetallic, genitalic, homo-
thallic, intervallic, ithyphallic,
nonmetallic, postvocalic,
prevocalic • intervocalic,
semimetallic

allid \al-əd\ see ALID²

allie \al-ē\ see ALLY⁴

alling \ȯ-liŋ\ balling, calling,
drawling, falling, galling,
hauling, mauling, Pauling,
stalling • appalling, infalling,
name-calling—*also* -ing forms
of verbs listed at ALL¹

allion \al-yən\ scallion, stallion
• battalion, Italian, medallion,
rapscallion • tatterdemalion

allis¹ \al-əs\ see ALIS²

allis² \al-ē\ see ALLY⁴

allis³ \äl-əs\ see OLIS

allish \ȯ-lish\ Gaulish, smallish,
tallish

allit \ä-lət\ see OLLET

allith¹ \äl-əs\ see OLIS

allith² \äl-ət\ see OLLET

allium \al-ē-əm\ allium, gallium,
pallium, thallium, Valium

allment \ȯl-mənt\ enthrallment, forestallment, installment

allo \äl-ō\ see OLLOW[1]

allon \al-ən\ Alan, Allen, gallon, lallan, Tallinn, talon

allop[1] \äl-əp\ see OLLOP

allop[2] \al-əp\ gallop, galop, jalap, salep, Salop, scallop, shallop
  • bay scallop, escallop, sea scallop

allor \al-ər\ see ALLER[2]

allory[1] \al-rē\ see ALLERY

allory[2] \al-ə-rē\ see ALARY[2]

allot \al-ət\ see ALLET[2]

allous \al-əs\ see ALIS[2]

allow[1] \el-ō\ see ELLO

allow[2] \äl-ə\ see ALA[2]

allow[3] \äl-ō\ see OLLOW[1]

allow[4] \al-ō\ aloe, callow, fallow, hallow, mallow, sallow, shallow, tallow, Yalow • marshmallow, rose mallow, unhallow

allowed \al-ōd\ hallowed
  • unhallowed

allows \al-ōz\ gallows
  • Allhallows—*also* -s, -'s, *and* -s' *forms of nouns listed at* ALLOW[5]

alls \ȯlz\ Angel Falls
  • Cumberland Falls, Niagara Falls, Shoshone Falls, Yellowstone Falls • Victoria Falls, Yosemite Falls—*also* -s, -'s, *and* -s' *forms of nouns and* -s *forms of verbs listed at* ALL

allsy \ȯl-zē\ see ALSY

allus \al-əs\ see ALIS[2]

allused \al-əst\ see ALIST

ally[1] \ā-lē\ see AILY

ally[2] \äl-ē\ see OLLY[1]

ally[3] \ȯ-lē\ see AWLY

ally[4] \al-ē\ alley, bally, challis, dally, galley, gally, Halley, mallee, pally, rally, sallie, sally, Sally, Schally, tally, valley
  • Aunt Sally, bialy, blind alley, crevalle, Death Valley, finale, Nepali, tomalley, trevally
  • Central Valley, dillydally, Great Rift Valley, gally, Mexicali, shilly-shally, teocalli, Tin Pan Alley • Imperial Valley, lily of the valley, Yosemite Valley

allyn \al-ən\ see ALLON

alm \äm\ see OM[1]

alma \al-mə\ Alma, halma

almar \äm-ər\ see OMBER[1]

almer \äm-ər\ see OMBER[1]

almily \äm-ə-lē\ see OMALY

almish \äm-ish\ see AMISH[1]

almist \äm-ist\ palmist, psalmist
  • Islamist

almody \äm-əd-ē\ see OMEDY

almon \am-ən\ see AMMON

almoner \äm-ə-nər\ see OMMONER

alms \ämz\ alms, Brahms, Psalms—*also* -s, -'s, *and* -s' *forms of nouns and* -s *forms of verbs listed at* OM[1]

almy \äm-ē\ see AMI[1]

alo \äl-ō\ see OLLOW[1]

aloe \al-ō\ see ALLOW[5]

alogist¹ \äl-ə-jəst\ see OLOGIST

alogist² \al-ə-jəst\ analogist, dialogist, mammalogist • genealogist

alogy¹ \äl-ə-jē\ see OLOGY

alogy² \al-ə-jē\ analogy, hypallage, mammalogy, tetralogy • mineralogy

alom \äl-əm\ see OLUMN

alon \al-ən\ see ALLON

alop \al-əp\ see ALLOP²

alor¹ \äl-ər\ see OLLAR

alor² \al-ər\ see ALLER²

alorie¹ \al-rē\ see ALLERY¹

alorie² \al-ə-rē\ see ALARY²

alory¹ \al-rē\ see ALLERY

alory² \al-ə-rē\ see ALARY²

alousie \al-ə-sē\ see ALLACY

alp \alp\ alp, salp, scalp

alpa \al-pə\ salpa • catalpa • Tegucigalpa

alpel \al-pəl\ see ALPAL

alpha \al-fə\ alpha • alfalfa

alque¹ \ȯk\ see ALK

alque² \alk\ calque, talc • catafalque

als \älz\ see OLS

alsa \ȯl-sə\ balsa, salsa

alse \ȯls\ false, waltz

alsey \ȯl-zē\ see ALSY

alsy \ȯl-zē\ ballsy, Halsey, palsy

alt \ȯlt\ Balt, fault, Galt, gault, halt, malt, Olt, salt, smalt, vault, volt, Walt • asphalt, assault, basalt, Chennault, cobalt, cross vault, default, desalt, exalt, fan vault, foot fault, gestalt, Great Salt, no-fault, pole vault, rock salt, Schwarzwald, stringhalt • comma fault, double fault, garlic salt, single malt, somersault, table salt • pepper-and-salt • San Andreas Fault, sexual assault

alta \äl-tə\ Malta, Salta, Volta, Yalta

altar \ȯl-tər\ see ALTER

alter \ȯl-tər\ altar, alter, falter, halter, palter, Psalter, salter, vaulter, Walter • defaulter, desalter, exalter, Gibraltar, pole-vaulter

altery \ȯl-trē\ see ALTRY

alti¹ \əl-tē\ Balti • difficulty

alti² \ȯl-tē\ see ALTY

altic \ȯl-tik\ Baltic • asphaltic, basaltic, cobaltic, systaltic • peristaltic

alting \ȯl-tiŋ\ halting, salting, vaulting—*also* -ing *forms of verbs listed at* ALT

altless \ȯlt-ləs\ faultless, saltless

alto \al-tō\ alto • contralto, rialto, Rialto • Palo Alto

alton \ȯlt-ᵊn\ Alton, dalton, Dalton, Galton, Walton

altry \ȯl-trē\ paltry, psaltery

alty \ȯl-tē\ Balti, faulty, malty, salty, vaulty

altz \óls\ see ALSE

alu \äl-ü\ Yalu • Tuvalu

alue \al-yü\ value • book value, cash value, devalue, disvalue, face value, fair value, misvalue, par value, place value, revalue, transvalue • market value, overvalue, undervalue

alus[1] \ā-ləs\ see AYLESS

alus[2] \al-əs\ see ALIS[2]

alve[1] \äv\ see OLVE[2]

alve[2] \alv\ salve, valve • ball valve, bivalve, check valve, slide valve • mitral valve, safety valve, univalve • inequivalve

alve[3] \av\ calve, halve, have, salve

alver \al-vər\ salver, salvor • quacksalver

alvin \al-vən\ Alvin, Calvin

alvor \al-vər\ see ALVER

aly \al-ē\ see ALLY[4]

alyard \al-yərd\ see ALLIARD

alysis \al-ə-səs\ analysis, catalysis, dialysis, paralysis • cryptanalysis, metanalysis, self-analysis • microanalysis

am[1] \äm\ see OM[1]

am[2] \am\ am, bam, cam, cham, clam, cram, dam, damn, damned, drachm, dram, DRAM, flam, gam, Graham, gram, ham, Ham, jam, jamb, lam, lamb, Lamb, ma'am, Pam, pram, ram, RAM, Sam, SAM, scam, scram, sham, slam, spam, swam, tam, tram, wham, yam • air dam, Annam, ashram, Assam, dirham, Edam, ngram, exam, flimflam, goddamn, grandam, grand slam, hard clam, iamb, imam, logjam, madame, Mailgram, milldam, nizam, Priam, program, quondam, surf clam, tam-tam, thiram, trigram, webcam, whim-wham, ziram • Abraham, aerogram, Amsterdam, anagram, Birmingham, Boulder Dam, cablegram, centigram, Christogram, chronogram, cofferdam, cryptogram, decagram, deprogram, diagram, diaphragm, dithyramb, epigram, fluid dram, giant clam, hard-shell clam, hexagram, histogram, Hohokam, hologram, Hoover Dam, kilogram, logogram, mammogram, milligram, Minicam, monogram, nomogram, oriflamme, pentagram, phonogram, pictogram, reprogram, Rotterdam, scattergram, self-exam, skiagram, Smithfield ham, soft-shell clam, sonogram, subprogram, Surinam, telegram, tetradrachm, thank-you-ma'am, tinker's damn, Uncle Sam • ad nauseam, angiogram, audiogram, cardiogram, Grand Coolee Dam, heliogram, ideogram, in personam, microprogram, New Amsterdam, Omar Khayyám, Virginia ham • parallelogram

ama[1] \äm-ə\ Brahma, comma, drama, Kama, lama, llama, mama, momma, squama, Rama • Bahama, pajama,

Toyama • Atacama, closet drama, cyclorama, Dalai Lama, diorama, docudrama, Fujiyama, Fukuyama, Matsuyama, melodrama, monodrama, Mount Mazama, music drama, Okayama, Panchen Lama, panorama, photodrama, psychodrama, Sugiyama, Suriname, Wakayama, Yokohama • Fuji-no-Yama

ama² \äm-ə\ Brahma, drama, gamma, grama, mamma • da Gama, Manama, Miami, pajama • Alabama, anadama, cyclorama, diorama, docudrama, melodrama, monodrama, panorama, photodrama, psychodrama

amable \ā-mə-bəl\ blamable, claimable, framable, nameable, tamable • irreclaimable

aman¹ \ā-mən\ see AMEN¹

aman² \äm-ən\ see OMMON

amant¹ \ā-mənt\ see AYMENT

amant² \am-ənt\ see AMENT²

amas \am-əs\ see AMICE

amash \äm-ish\ see AMISH¹

amateur \am-ət-ər\ see AMETER

amatist \am-ət-əst\ dramatist • epigrammatist, melodramatist

amba \äm-bə\ gamba, mamba, samba, Zomba • Lobamba • Cochabamba • viola da gamba

ambar¹ \äm-bər\ see OMBER²

ambar² \am-bər\ amber, Amber, camber, clamber, sambar, timbre

ambe \am-bē\ see AMBY

ambeau \am-bō\ see AMBO

amber¹ \am-bər\ see AMBAR²

amber² \am-ər\ see AMMER

ambia \am-bē-ə\ Gambia, Zambia • Senegambia

ambit \am-bət\ ambit, gambit

amble¹ \äm-bəl\ see EMBLE¹

amble² \am-bəl\ amble, bramble, gamble, gambol, ramble, scramble, shamble • preamble, unscramble • skimble-skamble

ambler \am-blər\ ambler, gambler, rambler, scrambler • unscrambler

ambo \am-bō\ crambo, jambeau, sambo • Ovambo

ambol \am-bəl\ see AMBLE²

ambray \am-brē\ see AMBRY

ambry \am-brē\ ambry, chambray

ambulant \am-byə-lənt\ ambulant • somnambulant

amby \am-bē\ crambe • namby-pamby

ame¹ \ām\ aim, blame, came, claim, dame, fame, flame, frame, game, hame, kame, lame, maim, name, same, shame, tame, wame • A-frame, acclaim, aflame, airframe, ball game, became, big game, big-name, board game, brand name, byname, code name, cross-claim, declaim, defame, disclaim, endgame, enframe, exclaim, first name, forename, freeze-frame, grandame, head game, inflame, last name, mainframe, mind game, misname, nickname, no-name, pen name, place-name, postgame, pregame, prename, proclaim, quitclaim, reclaim, reframe, rename, selfsame, shell game, skin game, space frame, surname, time frame, trade name, war game • all the same, arcade game, Burlingame, counterclaim, domain name, family name, given name, Hall of Fame, just the same, maiden name, Niflheim, overcame, parlor game, singing game, spinning frame, waiting game • baptismal name, name of the game, video game

ame² \äm\ see OM¹

ame³ \am\ see AM²

ame⁴ \äm-ə\ see AMA¹

ameable \ā-mə-bəl\ see AMABLE

amed \āmd\ famed, named • ashamed, forenamed, unashamed—*also -ed forms of verbs listed at* AME¹

ameful \ām-fəl\ blameful, shameful

amel \am-əl\ see AMMEL

ameless \ām-ləs\ aimless, blameless, nameless, shameless, tameless

amely \ām-lē\ gamely, lamely, namely, tamely

amen¹ \ā-mən\ bayman, Bremen, caiman, Cayman, Damon, drayman, flamen, Haman, layman, shaman, stamen, Yemen • examen, Grand Cayman, gravamen, highwayman, velamen

amen² \äm-ən\ see OMMON

ameness \ām-nəs\ gameness, lameness, sameness, tameness • selfsameness

ament¹ \ā-mənt\ see AYMENT

ament² \am-ənt\ ament, clamant

amer \ā-mər\ see AIMER

ames \āmz\ Eames, James • fun and games • Olympic Games —*also -s, -'s, and -s' forms of nouns and -s forms of verbs listed at* AME¹

ameter \am-ət-ər\ amateur • decameter, diameter, heptameter, hexameter, octameter, parameter, pentameter, tetrameter

amfer¹ \am-pər\ see AMPER²

amfer² \am-fər\ camphor, chamfer

ami¹ \äm-ē\ balmy, commie, mommy, palmy, qualmy, swami, Tommy • gourami, Khatami, Lomami, pastrami, Sagami, salami, tatami, tsunami, umami • Lake Ngami, origami

ami² \am-ə\ see AMA⁴

ami³ \am-ē\ see AMMY

amia \ā-mē-ə\ lamia, zamia • Mesopotamia

amic¹ \ō-mik\ see OMIC²

amic² \am-ik\ gamic • Adamic, agamic, balsamic, ceramic, dynamic • adynamic, cleistogamic, cryptogrammic, cycloramic, dioramic, exogamic, panoramic, phonogrammic, polygamic, undynamic • aerodynamic, biodynamic, hydrodynamic, hypothalamic, ideogramic, photodynamic, psychodynamic, thermodynamic • electrodynamic, magnetodynamic

amice \am-əs\ amice, camas, chlamys, Lammas

amics \äm-iks\ see OMICS

amie¹ \ā-mē\ Amy, Jamie, Mamie, ramie • cockamamy

amie² \am-ē\ see AMMY

amil¹ \äm-əl\ see OMMEL¹

amil² \am-əl\ see AMMEL

amily \am-lē\ family • profamily, stepfamily • antifamily, blended family, interfamily, multifamily • nuclear family

amin \am-ən\ see AMMON

amina \am-ə-nə\ lamina, stamina

aminal \am-ən-ᵊl\ laminal • foraminal

aminant \am-ə-nənt\ contaminant, examinant

aminar \am-ə-nər\ see AMINER²

amine \am-ən\ see AMMON

aminer¹ \äm-ə-nər\ see OMMONER

aminer² \am-ə-nər\ laminar • examiner • cross-examiner, gewürztraminer, trial examiner

aming \ā-miŋ\ flaming, framing, gaming—*also* -ing *forms of verbs listed at* AME¹

amish¹ \äm-ish\ Amish, qualmish, quamash • schoolmarmish

amish² \am-ish\ Amish, famish

amist \äm-əst\ see ALMIST

amity \am-ət-ē\ amity • calamity

amlet \am-lət\ camlet, hamlet, Hamlet, samlet

amma \am-ə\ see AMA⁴

ammable \am-ə-bəl\ flammable • inflammable, nonflammable, programmable • diagrammable

ammal \am-əl\ see AMMEL

ammany \am-ə-nē\ see AMMONY

ammar \am-ər\ see AMMER

ammas \am-əs\ see AMICE

ammatist \am-ət-əst\ see AMATIST

amme \am\ see AM²

ammel \am-əl\ camel, mammal, stammel, Tamil, trammel • enamel

ammer \am-ər\ clamber, clammer, clamor, clamour, crammer, dammar, gammer, glamour, grammar, hammer, jammer, lamber, rammer, scammer, shammer, slammer, spammer, stammer, yammer • clawhammer, drop hammer, enamor, flimflammer, jackhammer, programmer, sledgehammer, trip-hammer, windjammer • ball-peen hammer, deprogrammer, katzenjammer, monogrammer, ninnyhammer, Rotterdammer, water hammer, yellowhammer

ammes \äm-əs\ see OMISE

ammie \am-ē\ see AMMY

ammies \am-ēz\ jammies—*also* -s, -'s, *and* -s' *forms of nouns listed at* AMMY

amming \am-iŋ\ damning
• programming, windjamming
• counterprogramming—*also* -ing *forms of verbs listed at* AM[2]

ammock \am-ək\ drammock, hammock, mammock

ammon \am-ən\ Ammon, Brahman, famine, gamin, gammon, mammon, salmon
• backgammon, examine, thiamine • cross-examine

ammony \am-ə-nē\ scammony, Tammany

ammy \am-ē\ chamois, clammy, gammy, Grammy, hammy, jammy, mammy, ramie, Sammy, shammy, whammy
• Miami • double whammy

amn \am\ see AM[2]

amned \am\ see AM[2]

amning \am-iŋ\ see AMMING

amois \am-ē\ see AMMY

amon[1] \ā-mən\ see AMEN[1]

amon[2] \äm-ən\ see OMMON

amor \am-ər\ see AMMER

amorous \am-rəs\ amorous, clamorous, glamorous

amos \ā-məs\ see AMOUS

amour \am-ər\ see AMMER

amous \ā-məs\ Amos, famous, ramus, shamus, squamous
• biramous, mandamus
• ignoramus, Nostradamus

amp[1] \ämp\ see OMP[1]

amp[2] \äⁿ\ see ANT[1]

amp[3] \amp\ amp, camp, champ, clamp, cramp, damp, gamp, gramp, guimpe, lamp, ramp, samp, scamp, stamp, tamp, tramp, vamp • arc lamp, black damp, boot camp, break camp, C-clamp, chokedamp, death camp, decamp, encamp, firedamp, flashlamp, floor lamp, food stamp, glow lamp, headlamp, off-ramp, on-ramp, preamp, revamp, sunlamp, tax stamp, time-stamp, unclamp, work camp • afterdamp, aide-de-camp, discharge lamp, labor camp, minicamp, postage stamp, rubber-stamp, safety lamp, smoking lamp, trading stamp, writer's cramp

ampean[1] \äm-pē-ən\ pampean, tampion

ampean[2] \am-pē-ən\ see AMPION[2]

amper[1] \äm-pər\ see OMPER

amper[2] \am-pər\ camper, chamfer, damper, hamper, pamper, scamper, stamper, tamper, tramper • top-hamper
• happy camper

amphor \am-fər\ see AMFER[2]

ampi[1] \äm-pē\ see OMPY

ampi² \am-pē\ see AMPY

ampian \am-pē-ən\ see AMPION²

ampion¹ \äm-pē-ən\ see AMPEAN¹

ampion² \am-pē-ən\ campion, champion, Grampian, pampean, tampion

ample \am-pəl\ ample, sample, trample • ensample, example, subsample • for example • counterexample

ampler \am-plər\ sampler, trampler

ampo \äm-pō\ see OMPO

ampos \am-pəs\ see AMPUS

ampsia \am(p)-sē-ə\ eclampsia • preeclampsia

ampus \am-pəs\ Campos, campus, grampus • noncampus • hippocampus, intercampus, multicampus

ampy \am-pē\ campy, crampy, scampi, trampy, vampy

ams \amz\ Jams—*also* -s, -'s, *and* -s' *forms of nouns and* -s *forms of verbs listed at* AM²

amson \am-sən\ damson, Samson

amster \am-stər\ hamster, lamster, scamster

amsun \äm-sən\ Hamsun, Thompson

amulus \am-yə-ləs\ famulus, hamulus

amus¹ \ā-məs\ see AMOUS

amus² \äm-əs\ see OMISE

amy \ā-mē\ see AMIE¹

amys \am-əs\ see AMICE

an¹ \äⁿ\ see ANT¹

an² \än\ see ON¹

an³ \ən\ see UN

an⁴ \aŋ\ see ANG²

an⁵ \an\ an, Ann, ban, bran, can, clan, Dan, fan, Fan, flan, Jan, Klan, man, Mann, nan, Nan, pan, Pan, panne, plan, ran, scan, San, Shan, span, Stan, tan, van, Van • adman, afghan, Afghan, aidman, ape-man, ashcan, Bataan, bedpan, began, best man, Bhutan, birdman, boardman, boss man, brainpan, brogan, caftan, caiman, cancan, capstan, captan, CAT scan, caveman, Cayman, Cèzanne, chessman, Cheyenne, chlordan, Chopin, claypan, clubman, Cohan, cooncan, corban, cowman, Cruzan, C-Span, cyan, deadman, deadpan, deskman, Dian, Diane, Diann, Dianne, dishpan, divan, doorman, dustpan, fantan, Fezzan, fibranne, flight plan, flyman, foreran, FORTRAN, freedman, freeman, frogman, gagman, game plan, Georgeann, glucan, G-man, Gosplan, Greenspan, hardpan, headman, he-man, iceman, inspan, Iran, japan, Japan, jazzman, Joann, Joanne, Kazan, kneepan, Koran, Kurgan, leadman, Leanne, legman, liege man, life span, liftman, loran, Luanne, madman, main man, Malan, Mandan, man's man, Marfan,

mailman, merman, Milan, milkman, newsman, oilcan, oilman, oil pan, old man, one-man, outman, outran, pavane, pecan, plowman, point man, postman, Poznan, preman, pressman, propman, Queen Anne, Qur'an, ragman, rattan, reedman, reman, rodman, Roseanne, routeman, Roxanne, Ruthann, Saipan, salt pan, sampan, sandman, Saran, saucepan, scalepan, school-man, sea fan, sedan, sideman, snowman, soundman, soutane, spaceman, Spokane, spray can, stewpan, stickman, stockman, straight man, straw man, strongman, stuntman, Sudan, suntan, Susanne, Suzanne, T-man, TACAN, taipan, Tarzan, test ban, tin can, tisane, toucan, trainman, trashman, trepan, triptan, Tristan, tube pan, unman, vegan, Walkman, weight man, wingspan, wise man, yardman, yes-man • advance man, Alcoran, allemande, also-ran, Ameslan, anchorman, Andaman, as one man, astrakhan, Astrakhan, ataman, Athelstan, attackman, automan, balmacaan, Bantustan, bartizan, Belmopan, black-and-tan, bogeyman, boogeyman, businessman, Caliban, camera-man, caravan, catalan, cattle-man, Civitan, colorman, cornerman, counterman, counterplan, countryman, courtesan, cutoff man, dairy-man, defenseman, detail man, everyman, exciseman, express-man, family man, fancy-dan, fancy man, fellowman, frying pan, funnyman, gamelan, garageman, garbageman, Hamadan, handyman, har-mattan, hatchet man, Hindustan, hotelman, in the can, Isle of Man, Java man, jerrican, Juliann, Julianne, Kazakhstan, Ku Klux Klan, Kurdistan, Kyrgyzstan, leading man, man-for-man, man-to-man, Marianne, master plan, middleman, minivan, minute-man, Monaghan, moneyman, mountain man, muscleman, Occitan, ombudsman, Omdur-man, overman, overran, Pakistan, Parmesan, partisan, pattypan, Peking man, Peter Pan, Piltdown man, pivotman, plainclothesman, Port Sudan, Powhatan, Ramadan, rather than, repairman, rewrite man, Ryazan, safetyman, sandwich man, selectman, serviceman, shandrydan, Shantyman, shovelman, signalman, spick-and-span, superman, tallyman, tamarin, Teheran, teleman, teleran, to a man, triggerman, trimaran, turbofan, Turkistan, vacuum pan, warming pan, weatherman, workingman, yataghan, Yucatan
• Afghanistan, angry young man, arrière-ban, attention span, Baluchistan, bipartisan, catamaran, catch-as-catch-can, cavalryman, committee-man, deliveryman, dirty old man, flash in the pan, Kalimantan, medicine man, newspaperman, orangutan,

radioman, salary man,
Tajikistan, Turkmenistan,
Uzbekistan, watering can

an⁶ \än-yə\ see ANIA¹

an⁷ \äng\ see ONG¹

an⁸ \änt\ see ANT²

ana¹ \än-ə\ Aa, ana, anna, Anna,
bwana, Dona, donna, Donna,
fauna, Ghana, Kana, Lana,
Lonna, mana, Yana
• Bechuana, Botswana,
chicana, Fergana, gymkhana,
iguana, jacana, lantana, liana,
Madonna, mañana, nagana,
nirvana, piranha, Purana, ruana,
Tijuana, Tirane, Toscana,
zenana • Africana, belladonna,
epifauna, French Guiana,
Guadiana, Haryana, Hinayana,
hiragana, ikebana, Ludhiana,
Mahayana, marijuana,
parmigiana, pozzolana, prima
donna, Rajputana, Rosh
Hashanah, Tatiana • Americana,
fata morgana, Lincolniana,
Ljubljana, nicotiana, Shakespeareana, Victoriana

ana² \ā-nə\ ana, Dana, Lana
• Africana, cantilena, Cartagena
• nicotiana, Shakespeareana

ana³ \an-ə\ ana, Anna, canna,
manna, Ghana, Hannah, Lana,
nana • banana, bandanna,
cabana, Diana, Fermanagh,
goanna, Guiana, Guyana,
gymkhana, Havana, hosanna,
Joanna, Montana, savanna,
Savannah, sultana, Susanna
• Africana, French Guiana,
Indiana, Juliana, Mariana,
poinciana, Pollyanna, Santa

Ana • Americana, fata
morgana, Louisiana, nicotiana,
Shakespeareana, Victoriana

aña \än-yə\ see ANIA¹

anacle \an-i-kəl\ see ANICAL

anage \an-ij\ manage, tannage
• mismanage, stage-manage
• micromanage

anagh \an-ə\ see ANA³

anah¹ \ō-nə\ see ONA¹

anah² \än-ə\ see ANA¹

anal \ān-əl\ anal, banal

analyst \an-əl-ist\ analyst,
annalist, panelist • cryptanalyst
• microanalyst, psychoanalyst,
systems analyst

anan \an-ən\ see ANNON

anape \an-ə-pē\ see ANOPY

anary¹ \ān-rē\ see ANERY

anary² \an-rē\ see ANNERY²

anate \an-ət\ see ANNET

anative \an-ət-iv\ sanative
• explanative

anbe \am-bē\ see AMBY

anc¹ \aⁿ\ see ANT¹

anc² \aŋ\ see ANG²

anc³ \aŋk\ see ANK

anca \aŋ-kə\ Bangka, Khanka
• barranca • Casablanca,
lingua franca, Salamanca

ance¹ \äⁿs\ jouissance, nuance,
outrance, Provence, Saint-
Saëns, séance • à outrance,
diligence, Fort-de-France, Ile
de France, Mendès-France,

ordonnance, par avance, renaissance • guerre à outrance, insouciance, mésalliance, par excellence • concours d'elegance • pièce de résistance

ance² \äns\ Hans, nonce, sconce • brisance, ensconce, faience, nuance, response, séance • Afrikaans, complaisance, fer-de-lance, nonchalance, provenance, renaissance • pièce de résistance

ance³ \ans\ chance, dance, France, glance, lance, Lance, manse, prance, stance, trance, trans, Vance • advance, askance, barn dance, bechance, break-dance, by chance, clog dance, closed stance, enhance, entrance, expanse, finance, freelance, lap dance, line dance, main chance, mischance, New France, outdance, Penzance, perchance, romance, Romance, round dance, sand dance, side-glance, snake dance, square dance, step dance, sun dance, sweatpants, sword dance, tap dance, tea dance, toe dance, war dance • at first glance, ballroom dance, belly dance, circumstance, complaisance, contra dance, country-dance, fer-de-lance, fighting chance, game of chance, happenchance, happenstance, in advance, Liederkranz, open stance, Port-au-Prince, prefinance, refinance, smarty-pants, song and dance, underpants—*also* -s,

-'s, *and* -s' *forms of nouns and* -s *forms of verbs listed at* ANT⁵

anceable \an-se-bel\ see ANSIBLE

anced \anst\ canst • circumstanced • underfinanced—*also* -ed *forms of verbs listed at* ANCE³

ancel \an-sel\ cancel, chancel, handsel • expansile, precancel

anceler \an-sler\ canceler, chancellor • lord chancellor, vice-chancellor

ancellor \an-sler\ see ANCELER

ancement \an-sment\ advancement, enhancement, entrancement • self-advancement

ancer \an-ser\ answer, cancer, dancer, glancer, lancer, prancer • advancer, break-dancer, clog dancer, enhancer, free-lancer, lap dancer, line dancer, lung cancer, merganser, nondancer, romancer, ropedancer, square dancer, sword dancer, tap dancer • anticancer, ballroom dancer, belly dancer, gandy dancer, geomancer, necromancer, rhabdomancer, taxi dancer • Tropic of Cancer

ances \an(t)-ses\ see ANCIS

ancet \an-set\ lancet • Narragansett

anch¹ \änch\ see AUNCH¹

anch² \ònch\ see AUNCH²

anch³ \anch\ blanch, Blanche, branch, ranch, stanch • dude ranch, rebranch • avalanche, olive branch

anche¹ \äⁿsh\ tranche • carte blanche, revanche

anche² \anch\ see ANCH³

anche³ \an-chē\ see ANCHY

ancher¹ \ȯn-chər\ see AUNCHER

ancher² \an-chər\ ceinture, rancher

anchi \an-chē\ see ANCHY

anchion \an-chən\ see ANSION

anchor \aŋ-kər\ see ANKER

anchoress \aŋ-krəs\ see ANKEROUS

anchy \an-chē\ branchy • Comanche

ancial \an-chəl\ see ANTIAL

ancis \an(t)-səs\ Frances, Francis, Aransas—*also -s, -'s, and -s' forms of nouns and -s forms of verbs listed at* ANCE³

anck \äŋk\ see ONK¹

anco \äŋ-kō\ see ONCO

ancolin \aŋ-klən\ see ANKLIN

ancor \aŋ-kər\ see ANKER

ancorous \aŋ-krəs\ see ANKEROUS

ancre \aŋ-kər\ see ANKER

ancrous \aŋ-krəs\ see ANKEROUS

anct \aŋt\ see ANKED

ancy \an-sē\ chancy, fancy, Nancy • unchancy • chiromancy, geomancy, hydromancy, necromancy, pyromancy, rhabdomancy, sycophancy • oneiromancy

and¹ \äⁿ\ see ANT¹

and² \änd\ see OND¹

and³ \and\ and, band, bland, brand, canned, gland, grand, hand, land, manned, NAND, rand, Rand, sand, Sand, stand, strand • armband, at hand, backhand, backland, badland, bandstand, barehand, benchland, blackland, brass band, broadband, brushland, bushland, cabstand, cloudland, coastland, co-brand, command, cowhand, crash-land, cropland, crown land, dead hand, deckhand, demand, disband, dockhand, dockland, downland, dreamland, dryland, duneland, expand, farmhand, farmland, fenland, field hand, filmland, firebrand, firsthand, flatland, forehand, four-hand, free hand, freehand, gangland, glad-hand, Gotland, grandstand, grassland, handstand, hardstand, hatband, headband, headstand, heartland, heathland, homeland, home stand, hour hand, Iceland, in hand, inkstand, inland, Inland, iron hand, jack stand, jug band, kickstand, Kokand, Lapland, left-hand, longhand, lymph gland, mainland, marshland, misbrand, newsstand, nightstand, northland, noseband, off-brand, offhand, oil gland, old hand, on hand, outland, outstand, parkland, passband, pineland, playland, proband, Queensland, quicksand, rangeland, remand, repand, Rheinland, Rhineland, ribband, right-hand, rimland, ring stand, roband, Saarland, salt gland, scabland, screenland, scrubland, seastrand, shorthand, sideband, softland, southland, spaceband, stagehand, steel band, summand, swampland, sweatband, sweat gland, tar sand, Thailand, thirdhand, tideland, trainband, unhand, unmanned, waistband, washstand, wasteland, watchband, wave band, wetland, whip hand, wildland, withstand, wristband, X band • ampersand, Arnhem Land, baby grand, bear a hand, beforehand, behindhand, bellyband, belly-land, borderland, bottomland, cap in hand, concert grand, confirmand, contraband, countermand, Damavand, Dixieland, ductless gland, eldest hand, fairyland, fatherland, Ferdinand, force one's hand, forestland, four-in-hand, garage band, gastric gland, Gelderland, graduand, Graham Land, hand in hand, hand-to-hand, hand to hand, helping hand, high command, hinterland, Holy Land, Krugerrand, la-la land, lotusland, meadowland, minute hand, motherland, Nagaland, narrowband, no-man's-land, on demand, one-man band, one-night stand, operand, ordinand, out of hand, overhand, overland, parlor grand, pastureland, promised land, prostate gland, public land, Queen Maud Land,

radicand, reprimand, Rio Grande, rubber band, running hand, Samarkand, saraband, secondhand, sleight of hand, Swaziland, tableland, Talleyrand, taxi stand, timberland, Togoland, try one's hand, underhand, undermanned, understand, wonderland, Zululand • adrenal gland, analysand, back of one's hand, Bechuanaland, chain of command, cloud-cuckoo-land, digestive gland, endocrine gland, fantasyland, Franz Josef Land, head-in-the-sand, mammary gland, misunderstand, multiplicand, pineal gland, Prince Rupert's Land, Somaliland, Sudetenland, to beat the band, vacationland, videoland, Witwatersrand • invisible hand, Matabeleland, never-never land • Alice-in-Wonderland—*also* -ed *forms of verbs listed at* AN⁵

and⁴ \än\ see ON¹

and⁵ \änt\ see ANT²

anda¹ \an-de\ Ganda, panda • Amanda, Luanda, Luganda, Miranda, red panda, Uganda, veranda • giant panda, jacaranda, memoranda, propaganda

anda² \än-de\ see ONDA

andable \an-de-bel\ mandible • commandable, demandable, expandable • understandable

andaed \an-ded\ see ANDED

andal \an-dᵊl\ see ANDLE

andaled \an-dᵊld\ handled, sandaled • well-handled—*also* -ed *forms of verbs listed at* ANDLE

andall \an-dᵊl\ see ANDLE

andalous \an-dləs\ see ANDLESS²

andam \an-dəm\ see ANDUM

andant \an-dənt\ see ANDENT

andar \ənd-ər\ see UNDER

andarin \an-drən\ mandarin • alexandrine, salamandrine

ande¹ \ən\ see UN

ande² \an\ see AN⁵

ande³ \an-dē\ see ANDY

ande⁴ \and\ see AND³

ande⁵ \än-dē\ see ONDA

anded \an-dəd\ banded, branded, candid, handed, landed, stranded • back-handed, bare-handed, cleanhanded, crossbanded, forehanded, four-handed, freehanded, ham-handed, hardhanded, high-handed, ironhanded, left-handed, light-handed, offhanded, one-handed, red-handed, right-handed, shorthanded, sure-handed, three-handed, two-handed, unbranded, verandaed • doublehanded, empty-handed, evenhanded, heavy-handed, openhanded, overhanded, singlehanded, underhanded—*also* -ed *forms of verbs listed at* AND³

andel \an-dᵊl\ see ANDLE

andem \an-dəm\ see ANDUM

andent \an-dənt\ candent, scandent, demandant

ander¹ \en-dər\ see ENDER

ander² \än-dər\ see ONDER¹

ander³ \an-dər\ bander, brander, candor, dander, gander, grandeur, lander, pander, sander, slander, strander, zander • auslander, backhander, blackhander, bystander, commander, demander, expander, flatlander, germander, glad-hander, goosander, grandstander, inlander, Leander, left-hander, Lysander, mainlander, meander, outlander, philander, pomander, right-hander, scrimshander, soft-lander, Uitlander • Africander, alexander, Alexander, calamander, coriander, gerrymander, oleander, salamander, single-hander, wing commander • Anaximander—*also* -er *forms of adjectives listed at* AND³

anderous \an-drəs\ see ANDROUS

anders \an-dərz\ Flanders • Bouvier des Flandres, golden alexanders—*also* -s, -'s, *and* -s' *forms of nouns and* -s *forms of verbs listed at* ANDER³

andery \an-drē\ see ANDRY

andes \an-dēz\ Andes—*also* -s, -'s, *and* -s' *forms of nouns and* -s *forms of verbs listed at* ANDY

andeur¹ \an-dər\ see ANDER³

andeur² \an-jər\ see ANGER⁴

andhi \an-dē\ see ANDY

andi \an-dē\ see ANDY

andible \an-də-bəl\ see ANDABLE

andid \an-dəd\ see ANDED

anding \an-diŋ\ branding, standing • commanding, crash landing, crossbanding, freestanding, hardstanding, long-standing, outstanding, upstanding • belly landing, dead-stick landing, mind-expanding, notwithstanding, pancake landing, three-point landing, understanding • instrument landing, misunderstanding—*also* -ing *forms of verbs listed at* AND³

andish \an-dish\ blandish, brandish, standish, Standish • outlandish

andist \an-dest\ contrabandist, propagandist—*also* -est *forms of adjectives listed at* AND³

andit \an-dət\ bandit, pandit

andle \an-dəl\ candle, dandle, Handel, handle, Randall, sandal, scandal, vandal • foot-candle, manhandle, mishandle, panhandle, stickhandle • coromandel, Coromandel, Roman candle, votive candle

andled \an-dəl\ see ANDALED

andler \an-lər\ candler, chandler, handler • ball handler, panhandler, stickhandler

andless \an-ləs\ see ANLESS

andly \an-lē\ see ANLY²

andment \an-mənt\ commandment, disbandment

ando \an-dō\ commando, Fernando, Orlando • San Fernando

andom \an-dəm\ see ANDUM

andor \an-dər\ see ANDER³

andra \an-drə\ Sandra • Cassandra • Alexandra, pachysandra

andrea \an-drē-ə\ see ANDRIA

andrel \an-drəl\ mandrel, mandrill, spandrel

andres \an-dərz\ see ANDERS

andria \an-drē-ə\ Andrea • Alexandria

andrill \an-drəl\ see ANDREL

andrine \an-drən\ see ANDARIN

andros \an-drəs\ see ANDROUS

androus \an-drəs\ Andros • slanderous • gynandrous, meandrous • polyandrous

andry \an-drē\ commandery, misandry, monandry • polyandry

ands \anz\ Badlands, Lowlands • Canyonlands • laying on of hands

andsel \an-səl\ see ANCEL

andsman \anz-mən\ bandsman, clansman, Klansman, landsman

andsome \an-səm\ see ANSOM

andum \an-dəm\ fandom, grandam, random, tandem • memorandum • quod erat demonstrandum

andy \an-dē\ Andy, bandy, brandy, Brandy, candy, dandy,

handy, Handy, Kandy, pandy, randy, Randy, sandhi, sandy, Sandy, shandy • ear candy, eye candy, hard candy, jim-dandy, rock candy, unhandy • cotton candy, penny candy, Rio Grande • modus operandi

ane¹ \ān\ ain, Aisne, ane, Bain, bane, blain, Blaine, brain, Cain, cane, chain, crane, Crane, Dane, deign, drain, Duane, fain, fane, feign, gain, grain, Jane, Kane, lane, Lane, main, Maine, mane, pain, Paine, pane, plain, plane, quean, rain, reign, rein, sain, sane, seine, Seine, skein, slain, Spain, sprain, stain, stane, strain, swain, thane, thegn, train, twain, Twain, vain, vane, vein, wain, wane, Wayne, Zane • abstain, again, air lane, airplane, amain, arcane, arraign, attain, Bahrain, Bassein, Beltane, biplane, birdbrain, Biscayne, block plane, bloodstain, boat train, brain drain, bugbane, campaign, champagne, champaign, Champlain, checkrein, chicane, chilblain, choke chain, chow mein, cinquain, cocaine, Cockaigne, Coltrane, coxswain, complain, constrain, contain, cordwain, cowbane, crackbrain, demesne, deplane, destain, detain, detrain, devein, disdain, distain, distrain, dogbane, domain, drivetrain, dumb cane, edge-grain, Elaine, emplane, enchain, engrain, enplane, entrain, ethane, explain, eyestrain, fast lane, fleabane,

floatplane, floodplain, food chain, forebrain, Fort Wayne, Gawain, germane, Great Dane, grosgrain, Haldane, half plane, Helene, henbane, hindbrain, house-train, humane, Hussein, Igraine, immane, inane, ingrain, insane, jack plane, lamebrain, left brain, lightplane, lo mein, long-chain, Loraine, Lorraine, maintain, marchpane, membrane, memory lane, methane, midbrain, migraine, Montaigne, montane, moraine, mortmain, Moulmein, mundane, neck-rein, New Spain, obtain, octane, ordain, pertain, plain-Jane, profane, propane, ptomaine, purslane, quatrain, raise Cain, refrain, remain, restrain, retain, retrain, right brain, romaine, sailplane, sea-lane, seaplane, seatrain, split-brain, sustain, tailplane, tearstain, terrain, terrane, Touraine, towplane, triplane, Ukraine, unchain, urbane, vervain, vicereine, villein, volplane, warplane, wave train, wolfsbane • acid rain, aeroplane, appertain, aquaplane, Aquitaine, ascertain, avellane, Bloemfontein, bullet train, cell membrane, cellophane, Charlemagne, Charles's Wain, chatelain, chatelaine, counterpane, daisy-chain, down the drain, entertain, featherbrain, focal plane, foreordain, frangipane, free throw lane, gravy train, Gunter's chain, gyroplane, high-octane, hurricane, hydroplane, hyperplane, inclined plane, inhumane,

Kwajalein, La Fontaine, London plane, marocain, Mary Jane, mise-en-scène, monoplane, multigrain, multilane, neutercane, novocaine, overlain, overtrain, paravane, paper-train, peneplain, pollen grain, Port of Spain, port-wine stain, power train, preordain, pursuit plane, rattlebrain, reattain, rhizoplane, rocket plane, sandhill crane, scatterbrain, shaggymane, Spanish Main, sugarcane, suzerain, take in vain, Tamburlaine, Tamerlane, tangent plane, terreplein, toilet train, tramontane, transmontane, unit train, urethane, wagon train, water main, weather vane, whooping crane, windowpane, yellow rain • abyssal plain, Alsace-Lorraine, auf Wiedersehen, balletomane, capital gain, Cartesian plane, convertiplane, demimondaine, elecampane, extramundane, Gangetic Plain, intermontane, Lake Pontchartrain, legerdemain, mucous membrane, public domain, Salisbury Plain, ultramontane • eminent domain, Serengeti Plain

ane² \an\ see AN⁵

ane³ \än-ə\ see ANA¹

ane⁴ \än\ see ON¹

anea \ā-nē-ə\ see ANIA²

anean \ā-nē-ən\ see ANIAN²

aned \änd\ see AINED

anee \an-ē\ see ANNY

aneful \ān-fəl\ see AINFUL

anel \an-ᵊl\ see ANNEL

anelist \an-ᵊl-əst\ see ANALYST

aneous \ā-nē-əs\ cutaneous, extraneous, spontaneous • instantaneous, miscellaneous, simultaneous, subcutaneous • contemporaneous, extemporaneous

aner¹ \ā-nər\ see AINER

aner² \än-ər\ see ONOR¹

anery \ān-rē\ granary, chicanery

anet \an-ət\ see ANNET

aneum \ā-nē-əm\ see ANIUM

aney \ȯ-nē\ see AWNY¹

anford \an-fərd\ Sanford, Stanford

ang¹ \äŋ\ see ONG¹

ang² \aŋ\ bang, bhang, clang, dang, fang, Fang, gang, gangue, hang, pang, prang, rang, sang, slang, spang, sprang, stang, tang, twang, whang, yang • bang-bang, big bang, birth pang, blue tang, chain gang, cliff-hang, Da Nang, defang, ginseng, go hang, harangue, linsang, meringue, mustang, orang, parang, Pinang, press-gang, probang, shebang, slam-bang, straphang, trepang, whizbang • antigang, boomerang, charabanc, give a hang, intergang, overhang, parasang, rhyming slang, siamang, yin and yang • interrobang, orangutan

ang³ \óŋ\ see ONG²

anga \äŋ-gə\ see ONGA

angar \aŋ-ər\ see ANGER²

ange¹ \äⁿzh\ blancmange, mélange

ange² \änj\ change, grange, mange, range, strange • arrange, Brooks Range, chump change, derange, downrange, estrange, exchange, free-range, gearchange, home range, long-range, outrange, sea change, short-range, shortchange, small change • base exchange, Bismarck Range, Cascade Range, counterchange, disarrange, driving range, interchange, omnirange, post exchange, prearrange, rearrange, stock exchange, Teton Range, Wasatch Range • Alaska Range, Aleutian Range, bill of exchange, dynamic range, foreign exchange, Mesabi Range, radio range, Taconic Range • Great Dividing Range, Menominee Range

ange³ \anj\ flange • phalange

angel \aŋ-gəl\ see ANGLE

angell \aŋ-gəl\ see ANGLE

angement \änj-mənt\ arrangement, derangement, estrangement • disarrange-ment, prearrangement, rearrangement

angency \an-jən-sē\ plangency, tangency

angent \an-jənt\ plangent, tangent • cotangent

anger¹ \ān-jər\ changer, danger, granger, manger, ranger, stranger • arranger, bush-ranger, endanger, estranger, exchanger, lone ranger, shortchanger • forest ranger, heat exchanger, interchanger, money changer, Texas Ranger • dog in the manger

anger² \aŋ-ər\ banger, clanger, clangor, clangour, ganger, hangar, hanger, Langer, languor, Sanger, twanger • cliff-hanger, coat hanger, haranguer, headbanger, straphanger • paperhanger

anger³ \aŋ-gər\ anger, clangor

anger⁴ \an-jər\ grandeur • phalanger

angi \aŋ-ē\ see ANGY²

angible \an-jə-bəl\ frangible, tangible • infrangible, intangible, refrangible

angie \an-ē\ see ANGY²

anging¹ \ān-jiŋ\ bushranging, unchanging, wide-ranging—also -ing forms of verbs listed at ANGE²

anging² \aŋ-iŋ\ hanging • cliff-hanging, paperhanging—also -ing forms of verbs listed at ANG²

angle \aŋ-gəl\ angle, bangle, dangle, jangle, mangel, mangle, spangle, strangle, tangle, wangle, wrangle • embrangle, entangle, face angle, Mount

Wrangell, pentangle, quadrangle, rectangle, right angle, round angle, straight angle, triangle, untangle, wide-angle • disentangle • Bermuda Triangle

angled \aŋ-gəld\ angled, tangled • newfangled, oldfangled, right-angled, star-spangled—*also* -ed *forms of verbs listed at* ANGLE

anglement \aŋ-gəl-mənt\ tanglement • embranglement, entanglement • disentanglement

angler \aŋ-glər\ angler, dangler, jangler, mangler, strangler, wangler, wrangler • entangler

angles \aŋ-gəlz\ Angles, strangles—*also* -s, -'s, *and* -s' *forms of nouns and* -s *forms of verbs listed at* ANGLE

anglian \aŋ-glē-ən\ Anglian, ganglion

angling \aŋ-gliŋ\ angling, gangling—*also* -ing *forms of verbs listed at* ANGLE

anglion \aŋ-glē-ən\ see ANGLIAN

angly \aŋ-glē\ gangly, jangly, tangly

ango \aŋ-gō\ mango, tango • Durango, fandango

angor¹ \aŋ-ər\ see ANGER²

angor² \aŋ-gər\ see ANGER³

angorous \aŋ-ə-rəs\ clangorous, languorous

angour \aŋ-ər\ see ANGER²

angster \aŋ-stər\ gangster, prankster

anguage \aŋ-gwij\ language, slanguage • sign language, tone language, trade language • body language, machine language, metalanguage, paralanguage, protolanguage

angue \aŋ\ see ANG²

anguer \aŋ-ər\ see ANGER²

anguish \aŋ-gwish\ anguish, languish

anguor \aŋ-ər\ see ANGER²

anguorous \aŋ-ə-rəs\ see ANGOROUS

angus \aŋ-gəs\ Angus, Brangus • Black Angus

angy¹ \ān-jē\ mangy, rangy

angy² \aŋ-ē\ tangy, twangy • Ubangi • collieshangie

anha \än-ə\ see ANA¹

anhope \an-əp\ see ANNUP

ani¹ \än-ē\ ani, Bonnie, bonny, Connie, Donnie, fawny, johnny, rani, Ronnie, tawny, afghani, Fulani, Galvani, Irani, Omani • chalcedony, Kisangani, maharani, Modigliani, Nuristani, Pakistani, quadriphony, Rafsanjani, Rajasthani • mulligatawny • Liliuokalani

ani² \an-ē\ see ANNY

ania¹ \än-yə\ Agana, España, lasagna, Titania • Emilia-Romagna

ania² \ā-nē-ə\ mania • gazania, Germania, Hispania, Hyrcania,

Tasmania, titania, Titania, Urania • Acarnania, Anglomania, Aquitania, collectanea, dipsomania, egomania, hypomania, kleptomania, Lithuania, Mauretania, Mauritania, miscellanea, monomania, Mount Lucania, mythomania, nymphomania, Oceania, Pennsylvania, Pomerania, pyromania, Transylvania • balletomania, bibliomania, decalcomania, erotomania, megalomania—*also words listed at* ANIA³

ania³ \än-yə\ Campania, Catania, Hispania, Titania • Aquitania, malaguena • Tripolitania—*also words listed at* ANIA²

anian¹ \än-ē-ən\ Kiwanian, Turanian • Araucanian

anian² \ā-nē-ən\ Albanian, Dardanian, Iranian, Jordanian, Romanian, Rumanian, Sassanian, Turanian, Ukrainian, Uranian, vulcanian • Lithuanian, Pennsylvanian, Pomeranian, Ruritanian, subterranean • Indo-Iranian, Mediterranean

aniard \an-yərd\ lanyard, Spaniard

anic \an-ik\ manic, panic, tannic • Balkanic, Brahmanic, Britannic, cyanic, firemanic, galvanic, Germanic, Hispanic, Koranic, mechanic, melanic, organic, Romanic, satanic, shamanic, Sudanic, sultanic, titanic, tympanic, volcanic, aldermanic, Alemannic

• councilmanic, epiphanic, inorganic, messianic, oceanic, Ossianic, pre-Hispanic, talismanic, theophanic • Aristophanic, Indo-Germanic, megalomanic, Rhaeto-Romanic, suboceanic, transoceanic

anical \an-i-kəl\ manacle, panicle, sanicle • botanical, mechanical, tyrannical, puritanical

anice \an-əs\ SEE ANISE

anicle \an-i-kəl\ SEE ANICAL

anics \an-iks\ annex • mechanics—*also* -s, -'s, *and* -s' *forms of nouns and* -s *forms of verbs listed at* ANIC

anid¹ \ā-nəd\ canid, ranid • tabanid

anid² \an-əd\ canid, ranid • Sassanid

aniel¹ \an-ᵊl\ SEE ANNEL

aniel² \an-yəl\ SEE ANUAL

anigan \an-i-gən\ SEE ANNIGAN

anikin \an-i-kən\ SEE ANNIKIN

animous \an-ə-məs\ animus • magnanimous, unanimous • pusillanimous

animus \an-ə-məs\ SEE ANIMOUS

anion¹ \än-yən\ SEE ONYON¹

anion² \an-yən\ banyan, canyon • Black Canyon, Bryce Canyon, companion, Grand Canyon, Hells Canyon • Waimea Canyon

anis \an-əs\ SEE ANISE

anise \an-əs\ anise, Janice, Janis, stannous • johannes, Johannes, pandanus, titanous • Scipio Africanus

anish¹ \ā-nish\ see AINISH

anish² \an-ish\ banish, clannish, mannish, planish, Spanish, tannish, vanish • Pollyannish

anist \än-əst\ see ONEST

anister \an-ə-stər\ banister, canister, ganister

anite \an-ət\ see ANNET

anity \an-ət-ē\ sanity, vanity • humanity, inanity, insanity, profanity, urbanity • Christianity, churchianity, inhumanity • superhumanity

anium \ā-nē-əm\ cranium • geranium, germanium, titanium, uranium • succedaneum

ank \aŋk\ bank, blank, brank, clank, crank, dank, drank, flank, franc, frank, Frank, hank, lank, plank, prank, rank, sank, shank, shrank, spank, stank, swank, tank, thank, yank, Yank • Burbank, claybank, Cruikshank, drop tank, drug tank, embank, eye bank, Firbank, flag rank, foreshank, gangplank, greenshank, land bank, left-bank, nonbank, outflank, outrank, pickthank, point-blank, redshank, sandbank, sheepshank, snowbank, state bank, think tank, West Bank • antitank, central bank, data bank, Dogger Bank, draw a blank, Georges Bank, interbank, Jodrell Bank, mountebank, national bank, piggy bank, reserve bank, riverbank, walk the plank • clinkety-clank

anka¹ \äŋ-kə\ concha, tanka • Sri Lanka

anka² \aŋ-kə\ see ANCA

ankable \aŋ-kə-bəl\ bankable, frankable

anked \aŋt\ shanked, tanked • spindle-shanked, sacrosanct—*also* -ed *forms of verbs listed at* ANK

ankee \aŋ-kē\ see ANKY

anken \aŋ-kən\ flanken, Rankine

anker \aŋ-kər\ anchor, banker, canker, chancre, flanker, franker, hanker, rancor, ranker, spanker, tanker, thanker • co-anchor, sea anchor, sheet anchor, unanchor, West Banker • supertanker—*also* -er *forms of adjectives listed at* ANK

ankerous \aŋ-krəs\ anchoress, cankerous, chancrous, rancorous • cantankerous

ankh \äŋk\ see ONK¹

ankie \aŋ-kē\ see ANKY

ankine \aŋ-kən\ see ANKEN

ankish \aŋ-kish\ crankish, Frankish, prankish

ankle \aŋ-kəl\ ankle, rankle

ankly \aŋ-klē\ blankly, dankly, frankly, lankly, rankly

anks \aŋs\ see ANX

ankster \aŋ-stər\ see ANGSTER

anky \aŋ-kē\ cranky, hankie, lanky, skanky, swanky, Yankee • hanky-panky

anless \an-ləs\ handless, manless, planless

anley \an-lē\ see ANLY[2]

anli \an-lē\ see ANLY[2]

anly[1] \än-lē\ fondly, thrawnly, wanly

anly[2] \an-lē\ blandly, grandly, manly, Stanley • Osmanli, unmanly

ann[1] \an\ see AN[5]

ann[2] \än\ see ON[1]

anna[1] \än-ə\ see ANA[1]

anna[2] \an-ə\ see ANA[3]

annage \an-ij\ see ANAGE

annah \an-ə\ see ANA[3]

annalist \an-əl-əst\ see ANALYST

annan \an-ən\ see ANNON

anne \an\ see AN[5]

anned \and\ see AND[3]

annel \an-əl\ channel, Daniel, flannel, panel, scrannel • bank channel, impanel • Bashi Channel, Bristol Channel, canton flannel, English Channel

annequin \an-i-kən\ see ANNIKIN

anner \an-ər\ banner, canner, fanner, lanner, manner, manor, planner, scanner, spanner, tanner, vanner • CAT scanner, deadpanner, grand manner, japanner, PET scanner, self-tanner • caravanner, city planner

annery[2] \an-rē\ cannery, granary, tannery

annes \an-əs\ see ANISE

anness \än-nəs\ fondness, wanness

annet \an-ət\ gannet, granite, Janet, planet • pomegranate

annexe \an-iks\ see ANICS

annibal \an-ə-bəl\ cannibal, Hannibal

annic \an-ik\ see ANIC

annie \an-ē\ see ANNY

annigan \an-i-gən\ brannigan • shenanigan

annikin \an-i-kən\ cannikin, manikin, mannequin, pannikin

annin \an-ən\ see ANNON

annish \an-ish\ see ANISH[2]

annon \an-ən\ cannon, canon, Shannon, tannin • Buchanan, Clackmannan, colcannon, Dungannon, loose cannon • water cannon

annous \an-əs\ see ANISE

anns \anz\ see ANS[4]

annual \an-yəl\ see ANUAL

annular \an-yə-lər\ annular, cannular, granular

annulate \an-yə-lət\ annulate, annulet • campanulate

annulet \an-yə-lət\ see ANNULATE

annum \an-əm\ see ANUM[2]

annup \an-əp\ sannup, stanhope

anny \an-ē\ Annie, canny, cranny, Danny, fanny, granny,

Lanny, nanny • afghani, ca'canny, kokanee, uncanny • frangipani, Hindustani, hootenanny

ano¹ \än-ō\ Ciano, guano, Kano, llano, mano, mono • Bolzano, Chicano, Lugano, Marrano, Milano, Nagano, piano, Pisano, Romano, Serrano, soprano • altiplano, Capistrano, grand piano, Ilocano, Lake Albano, Lake Lugano, stride piano, thumb piano, trebbiano, Vaticano, Verrazano • boliviano, fortepiano, mano a mano, mezzo piano, mezzo-soprano, player piano, upright piano

ano² \ā-nō\ ripieno, volcano

ano³ \an-ō\ Hispano, piano, soprano • fortepiano, mezzo-soprano

anon¹ \an-ən\ see ANNON

anon² \an-yən\ see ANION²

anopy \an-ə-pē\ canape, canopy

anor \an-ər\ see ANNER

anous \an-əs\ see ANISE

anqui \aŋ-kē\ see ONKY

ans¹ \äns\ see ANCE²

ans² \änz\ see ONZE

ans³ \ans\ see ANCE³

ans⁴ \anz\ banns, Hans, sans, trans • Sextans—*also* -s, -'s, *and* -s' *forms of nouns and* -s *forms of verbs listed at* AN⁵

ans⁵ \aⁿ\ see ANT¹

ansard \an-sərd\ see ANSWERED

ansas¹ \an(t)-səs\ see ANCIS

ansas² \an-zəs\ Kansas • Arkansas

anse \ans\ see ANCE³

ansea \än-zē\ see ANZY

anser \an-sər\ see ANCER

anset \an-sət\ see ANCET

ansett \an-sət\ see ANCET

ansible \an-sə-bəl\ danceable • expansible

ansile \an-səl\ see ANCEL

ansing \an-siŋ\ Lansing—*also* -ing *forms of verbs listed at* ANCE³

ansion \an-chən\ mansion, scansion, stanchion • expansion

ansk \änsk\ Bryansk, Gdansk, Luhans'k, Murmansk, Saransk

ansman \anz-mən\ see ANDSMAN

ansom \an-səm\ handsome, hansom, ransom, transom • king's ransom, unhandsome • over-the-transom

anst \anst\ see ANCED

answer \an-sər\ see ANCER

answered \an-sərd\ answered, Hansard, mansard • unanswered

ansy \an-zē\ pansy, tansy • chimpanzee

ant¹ \äⁿ\ Caen, Gant • arpent, beurre blanc, croissant, en banc, L'Enfant, Mont Blanc, riant, roman, Rouen, savant, versant • accouchement, aide-de-camp, au courant, battement, bien-pensant, ci-devant, contretemps, debridement, denouement, en passant, fainéant, insouciant, Maupassant, Mitterand, Orléans, Perpignan, rap-prochement, revenant, se tenant, soi-disant, vol-au-vent • arrondissement, chateau-briand, Chateaubriand, Clermont-Ferrand, idiot savant, ressentiment, sauvignon blanc

ant² \änt\ aunt, can't, daunt, flaunt, font, fount, gaunt, taunt, vaunt, want, wont • avant, avaunt, bacchant, bacchante, Balante, Beaumont, bouffant, brisant, courante, détente, entente, Fremont, gallant, grandaunt, piedmont, Pied-mont, piquant, romaunt, Rostand, savant, sirvente, Vermont • bon vivant, com-mandant, complaisant, confidant, debridement, debutant, debutante, dilettante, John of Gaunt, intrigant, nonchalant, poste restante, restaurant, symbiont • dicynodont, subdebutante

ant³ \ənt\ see ONT¹

ant⁴ \ȯnt\ see AUNT¹

ant⁵ \ant\ ant, aunt, brant, cant, can't, chant, grant, Grant, hant, Kant, pant, plant, rant, scant, shan't, slant • aslant, bacchant, bacchante, bezant, courante, decant, descant, discant, displant, eggplant, enceinte, enchant, explant, extant, face-plant, fire ant, formant, gallant,

Gallant, gas plant, grandaunt, houseplant, ice plant, implant, incant, jade plant, land grant, leadplant, levant, Levant, musk plant, pieplant, pissant, plainchant, pourpoint, preplant, recant, red ant, replant, savant, seed plant, snow plant, sup-plant, transplant, white ant • adamant, commandant, complaisant, confidant, confidante, cormorant, corposant, Corybant, covenant, demipointe, dilettante, disenchant, gallivant, hiero-phant, interplant, pitcher plant, power plant, rubber plant, spider plant, sycophant • century plant, flowering plant • Gregorian chant

anta \ant-ə\ anta, manta • Atlanta, infanta, vedanta • Atalanta

antage \ant-ij\ vantage • advantage • coign of vantage, disadvantage

antain \ant-ᵉn\ see ANTON²

antal¹ \änt-ᵉl\ see ONTAL¹

antal² \ant-ᵉl\ see ANTLE

antam \ant-əm\ bantam, phantom

antar \ant-ər\ see ANTER²

antasist \ant-ə-səst\ see ANTICIST

ante¹ \än-tä\ Brontë, Dante • andante, Asante, infante, volante • Alicante • Belo Horizonte

ante² \änt\ see ANT²

ante³ \ant\ see ANT⁵

ante⁴ \änt-ē\ see ANTI¹

ante⁵ \ant-ē\ ante, canty, chantey, pantie, scanty, shanty, slanty • andante, Ashanti, Chianti, infante • non obstante, penny-ante, vigilante • pococurante, status quo ante

antean \ant-ē-ən\ Dantean • Atlantean, post-Kantian

anteau \an-tō\ see ANTO²

anted \an-təd\ disenchanted— *also -ed forms of verbs listed at* ANT⁵

antel \ant-ᵊl\ see ANTLE

antelet \ant-lət\ mantelet, plantlet

anter¹ \änt-ər\ see AUNTER¹

anter² \ant-ər\ antre, banter, canter, cantor, chanter, granter, grantor, plantar, planter, ranter, scanter • decanter, enchanter, implanter, instanter, levanter, supplanter, transplanter, trochanter • covenanter, covenantor, disenchanter, tam-o'-shanter, Tam o' Shanter

antes \an-tēz\ Cervantes—*also -s, -'s, and -s' forms of nouns and -s forms of verbs listed at* ANTE⁵

antey \ant-ē\ see ANTE⁵

anth \anth\ hydranth • amaranth, coelacanth, perianth, tragacanth • globe amaranth

antha \an-thə\ Samantha • polyantha, pyracantha

anther \an-thər\ anther, panther • Black Panther

anthropy \an-thrə-pē\ lycanthropy, misanthropy, philanthropy

anthus \an-thəs\ Canthus, Xanthus • acanthus, ailanthus, dianthus • agapanthus, amianthus, polyanthus, Rhadamanthus

anti¹ \änt-ē\ Brontë, flaunty, jaunty, monte, Monte, Monty, vaunty • andante, Ashanti, Chianti • three-card monte

anti² \ant-ē\ see ANTE⁵

antial \an-chəl\ financial, substantial • circumstantial, consubstantial, insubstantial, nonfinancial, transsubstantial, unsubstantial

antian¹ \änt-ē-ən\ see ONTIAN

antian² \ant-ē-ən\ see ANTEAN

antic¹ \änt-ik\ see ONTIC

antic² \ant-ik\ antic, frantic, mantic • Atlantic, bacchantic, gigantic, pedantic, romantic, semantic, Vedantic • corybantic, geomantic, hierophantic, necromantic, North Atlantic, sycophantic, transatlantic, unromantic

anticist \ant-ə-səst\ fantasist • Atlanticist, romanticist, semanticist

antid \ant-əd\ mantid • Quadrantid—*also -ed forms of verbs listed at* ANT⁵

antie \ant-ē\ see ANTE⁵

antine \ant-ᵊn\ see ANTON²

anting[1] \ant-iŋ\ anting, canting, planting • enchanting • disenchanting—*also* -ing *forms of verbs listed at* ANT[5]

anting[2] \ent-iŋ\ see UNTING

antis \ant-əs\ cantus, mantis, Santos • Atlantis

antish \ant-ish\ dilettantish, sycophantish

antle \ant-ᵉl\ cantle, mantel, mantle, quintal • dismantle, Fremantle, quadrantal • consonantal, covenantal, overmantel

antlet \ant-lət\ see ANTELET

antling \ant-liŋ\ bantling, scantling • dismantling

anto[1] \än-tō\ Squanto • bel canto, Taranto, Toronto • Esperanto

anto[2] \an-tō\ canto, panto • coranto, Otranto, portmanteau • Esperanto

antom \ant-əm\ see ANTAM

anton[1] \änt-ᵉn\ see ONTON

anton[2] \ant-ᵉn\ Anton, canton, Canton, plantain, Scranton, Stanton • adamantine

antor \ant-ər\ see ANTER[2]

antos[1] \an-təs\ see ANTIS

antos[2] \än-təs\ Santos • Propontis

antra \ən-trə\ tantra, yantra

antre \ant-ər\ see ANTER[2]

antry \an-trē\ chantry, gantry, pantry • butler's pantry

ants \ans\ see ANCE[3]

antua \anch-wə\ mantua • Gargantua

antus \ant-əs\ see ANTIS

anty \ant-ē\ see ANTE[5]

anual[1] \an-yəl\ annual, Daniel, spaniel • biannual, field spaniel, Nathaniel • cocker spaniel, semiannual, springer spaniel, water spaniel

anual[2] \an-yə-wəl\ annual, manual, Manuel • biannual, bimanual, Emmanuel, Immanuel • semiannual • Victor Emmanuel

anuel \an-yəl\ see ANUAL[2]

anular \an-yə-lər\ see ANNULAR

anulate \an-yə-lət\ see ANNULATE

anum[1] \ā-nəm\ granum, paynim • arcanum

anum[2] \an-əm\ per annum, solanum

anus[1] \ā-nəs\ see AYNESS

anus[2] \an-əs\ see ANISE

anx \aŋs\ Manx, thanks • break ranks, Fairbanks, Grand Banks, phalanx • Outer Banks—*also* -s, -'s, *and* -s' *forms of nouns and* -s *forms of verbs listed at* ANK

any[1] \ā-nē\ see AINY

any[2] \en-ē\ see ENNY

anyan \an-yən\ see ANION[2]

anyard \an-yərd\ see ANIARD

anyon \an-yən\ see ANION[2]

anz \ans\ see ANCE[3]

anza¹ \än-zə\ kwanza, Kwanzaa
• Sancho Panza

anza² \an-zə\ stanza, zanza
• bonanza, Carranza, organza
• Sancho Panza
• extravaganza, heroic stanza

anzaa \än-zə\ see ANZA¹

anzee \an-zē\ see ANSY

anzer \än-sər\ see ONSOR

anzo \än-zō\ gonzo, garbanzo

anzy \än-zē\ bronzy, Ponzi, Swansea

ao¹ \ā-ō\ see EO¹

ao² \ō\ see OW¹

ao³ \au̇\ see OW²

aoedic \ēd-ik\ see EDIC¹

aoighis \äsh\ see ECHE¹

aole \au̇-lē\ see OWLY²

aône \ōn\ see ONE¹

aori \au̇r-ē\ see OWERY

aos¹ \au̇s\ see OUSE²

aos² \ā-äs\ chaos, Laos

aotian \ō-shən\ see OTION

aow \au̇\ see OW²

ap¹ \äp\ see OP¹

ap² \əp\ see UP

ap³ \ap\ cap, chap, clap, crap, flap, frap, gap, gape, hap, knap, lap, Lapp, map, nap, nape, nappe, pap, rap, sap, scrap, slap, snap, strap, tap, trap, wrap, yap, Yap, zap
• ASCAP, backslap, backwrap, bitmap, blackcap, bootstrap, burlap, Carnap, catnap, cell

sap, claptrap, death cap, death trap, dunce cap, dewlap, dognap, earflap, entrap, enwrap, firetrap, flatcap, foolscap, gelcap, giddap, gift wrap, gun lap, heeltap, hubcap, ice cap, jockstrap, kidnap, kneecap, lagniappe, light trap, livetrap, love tap, madcap, mantrap, mayhap, mishap, mobcap, mousetrap, mud flap, nightcap, on tap, pace lap, pinesap, rattrap, recap, redcap, remap, riprap, road map, root cap, sand trap, satrap, shiplap, shrink-wrap, skullcap, skycap, snowcap, spark gap, speed trap, steel-trap, stopgap, toe cap, unsnap, unstrap, unwrap, verb sap, watch cap, whitecap, wind gap, winesap, wiretap, word wrap • afterclap, baseball cap, beat the rap, blacklight trap, blasting cap, body wrap, booby trap, contour map, cradle cap, gangsta rap, giddyap, gimme cap, ginger-snap, handicap, inky cap, leghold trap, medigap, on the map, overlap, photomap, rattletrap, relief map, service cap, shoulder strap, spinal tap, stocking cap, thinking cap, thunderclap, Tonle Sap, tourist trap, verbum sap, water gap, weather map, wentletrap
• Venus flytrap

apa¹ \äp-ə\ grappa, Joppa, papa, poppa, tapa • Jalapa
• jipijapa

apa² \ap-ə\ kappa, tapa
• Harappa • Phi Beta Kappa

apable \ā-pə-bəl\ capable,
drapable, shapable
• escapable, incapable
• inescapable

apal \ā-pəl\ see APLE

apas \äp-əs\ Chiapas—*also* -s,
-'s, *and* -s' *forms of nouns
listed at* APA[1]

apboard \ab-ərd\ see ABARD

ape[1] \āp\ ape, cape, chape,
crape, crepe, drape, gape,
grape, jape, nape, rape, scape,
scrape, shape, tape • agape,
broomrape, cloudscape, date
rape, duct tape, escape, fox
grape, gang rape, great ape,
landscape, man ape, misshape,
moonscape, North Cape, red
tape, reshape, sea grape,
seascape, shipshape, snow-
scape, streetscape, take shape,
townscape, transshape,
undrape, waveshape • Barbary
ape, bias tape, cityscape,
Eastern Cape, fire escape,
friction tape, masking tape,
ticker tape, waterscape,
Western Cape, xeriscape,
audiotape • acquaintance rape,
adhesive tape, anthropoid ape,
bent out of shape, magnetic
tape, stereotape, videotape
• statutory rape

ape[2] \ap\ see AP[3]

ape[3] \äp-ē\ see OPPY

ape[4] \ap-ē\ see APPY

aped \āpt\ bell-shaped, pear-
shaped—*also* -ed *forms of
verbs listed at* APE[1]

apel \ap-əl\ see APPLE

apelin \ap-lən\ see APLAIN

apen \ā-pən\ capon, shapen
• misshapen, unshapen

aper \ā-pər\ aper, caper, draper,
gaper, japer, paper, raper,
scraper, shaper, taper, tapir,
vapor • bond paper, crepe
paper, curlpaper, endpaper,
escaper, flypaper, glasspaper,
graph paper, laid paper,
landscaper, newspaper,
notepaper, reshaper, rice
paper, sandpaper, skyscraper,
tar paper, term paper, wall-
paper, wastepaper, waxed
paper, white paper, wove paper
• Bible paper, blotting paper,
butcher paper, carbon paper,
filter paper, funny paper, litmus
paper, tissue paper, toilet
paper, tracing paper, writing
paper

aperer \ā-pər-ər\ paperer,
taperer, vaporer

apery \ā-prē\ drapery, japery,
napery, papery, vapory
• sandpapery

apes \āps\ traipse
• jackanapes— *also* -s, -'s,
and -s' *forms of nouns and*
-s *forms of verbs listed at*
APE[1]

apey \ā-pē\ crepey, grapy, kepi,
scrapie

aph \af\ caff, calf, chaff, daff,
gaff, gaffe, graph, half, laugh,
quaff, raff, sclaff, staff, staph,
Waf, waff • agrafe, bar graph,
behalf, carafe, chiffchaff,
cowlstaff, digraph, distaff,
Falstaff, flagstaff, Flagstaff,

giraffe, half-staff, horselaugh, kenaf, line graph, mooncalf, paraph, pikestaff, riffraff, tipstaff • allograph, autograph, barograph, bathyscaphe, cenotaph, chronograph, circle graph, cryptograph, epigraph, epitaph, half-and-half, hectograph, holograph, homograph, hygrograph, kymograph, lithograph, logograph, micrograph, monograph, pantograph, paragraph, phonograph, photograph, pictograph, polygraph, quarterstaff, seismograph, serigraph, shadowgraph, shandygaff, spectrograph, sphygmograph, telegraph, thermograph, typograph, understaff • cardiograph, choreograph, heliograph, ideograph, mimeograph, oscillograph, pseudepigraph, radiograph

aphael \af-ē-əl\ see APHIAL

aphe[1] \āf\ see AFE[1]

aphe[2] \af\ see APH

apher \af-ər\ see AFFER[2]

aphia \af-ē-ə\ see AFFIA

aphial \af-ē-əl\ Raphael • epitaphial

aphic \af-ik\ graphic, maffick, sapphic, traffic • digraphic, edaphic, serafic, triaphic • allographic, autographic barographic, biographic, calligraphic, cartographic, chronographic, demographic, epigraphic, epitaphic, ethnographic, geographic, hectographic, holographic, homographic, hydrographic, lithographic, logographic, mammographic, monographic, orthographic, pantographic, paragraphic, phonographic, photographic, pictographic, pornographic, seismographic, stenographic, stratigraphic, telegraphic, topographic, typographic, • bibliographic, choreographic, hagiographic, iconographic, lexicographic

aphical \af-i-kəl\ graphical • biographical, cartographical, cosmographical, crypto-graphical, epigraphical, ethnographical, geographical, orthographical, petrographical, topographical, typographical

aphics \af-iks\ graphics • demographics, micro-graphics, psychographics, reprographics, supergraphics

aphnis \af-nəs\ see AFTNESS

aphora \a-fə-rə\ anaphora, cataphora

api \äp-ē\ see OPPY

apid \ap-əd\ rapid, sapid, vapid

apie \ā-pē\ see APEY

apin \ap-ən\ see APPEN

apine \ap-ən\ see APPEN

apir \ā-pər\ see APER

apis \ā-pəs\ Apis • Priapus, Serapis

apist \ā-pist\ rapist • escapist, landscapist

aplain \ap-lən\ capelin, chaplain, Chaplin, sapling

aple \ā-pəl\ maple, papal, staple • red maple, rock maple, sugar maple • antipapal

aples \ā-pəlz\ Naples—*also* -s, -'s, *and* -s' *forms of nouns and* -s *forms of verbs listed at* APLE

apless \ap-ləs\ hapless, napless, sapless, strapless

aplin \ap-lə-n\ *see* APLAIN

aply \ap-lē\ *see* APTLY

apnel \ap-nᵊl\ grapnel, shrapnel

apo \äp-ō\ capo • da capo, gestapo, Mount Apo

apolis \ap-ə-lis\ Annapolis, Decapolis, Pentapolis • Minneapolis • Indianapolis

apon \ā-pən\ *see* APEN

apor \ā-pər\ *see* APER

aporer \ā-pər-ər\ *see* APERER

apory \ā-prē\ *see* APERY

apour \ā-pər\ *see* APER

app \ap\ *see* AP³

appa¹ \äp-ə\ *see* APA¹

appa² \ap-ə\ *see* APA²

appable \ap-ə-bəl\ flappable, mappable • recappable, unflappable

appalli \äp-ə-lē\ *see* OPOLY

appe \ap\ *see* AP³

apped \apt\ *see* APT

appen \ap-ən\ happen, lapin, rapine

apper¹ \äp-ər\ *see* OPPER

apper² \ap-ər\ capper, clapper, dapper, flapper, knapper, lapper, mapper, rapper, sapper, scrapper, snapper, strapper, tapper, trapper, wrapper, yapper, zapper • backslapper, bootstrapper, catnapper, didapper, dognapper, dust wrapper, kidnapper, knee-slapper, petnapper, red snapper, thigh slapper, wiretapper • gangsta rapper, handicapper, snippersnapper, understrapper, whippersnapper

appet \ap-ət\ lappet, tappet

apphic \af-ik\ *see* APHIC

appie \äp-ē\ *see* OPPY

appily \ap-ə-lē\ happily, scrappily, snappily • unhappily

appiness \ap-ē-nəs\ happiness, sappiness, scrappiness, snappiness • unhappiness

apping \ap-iŋ\ capping, mapping, strapping, trapping, wrapping • kneecapping, petnapping • spirit rapping —*also* -ing *forms of verbs listed at* AP³

apple \ap-əl\ apple, chapel, dapple, grapple, scrapple • crab apple, love apple, mayapple, oak apple, pineapple, star apple, thorn apple • Adam's apple, antechapel, lady apple

apps \aps\ *see* APSE

appy \ap-ē\ crappy, flappy, gappy, happy, nappy, pappy, sappy, scrappy, snappy, strappy, zappy • satrapy, serape, slaphappy, unhappy • triggerhappy aps \aps\ see APSE

apse \aps\ apse, chaps, craps,
lapse, schnapps, taps, traps
• collapse, elapse, perhaps,
prolapse, relapse, synapse,
time-lapse—*also* -s, -'s, *and* -s'
forms of nouns and -s *forms of
verbs listed at* AP³

apt \apt\ apt, napped, rapt
• adapt, black-capped, coapt,
dewlapped, enrapt, inapt,
snowcapped, unapt, untapped
• periapt—*also* -ed *forms of
verbs listed at* AP³

apter \ap-tər\ captor, chapter,
raptor • adapter • oviraptor
• velociraptor

aption \ap-shən\ caption
• adaption, contraption,
miscaption

aptive \ap-tiv\ captive • adaptive
• maladaptive, preadaptive

aptly \ap-lē\ aptly, haply, raptly
• inaptly, unaptly

aptor \ap-tər\ see APTER

apture \ap-chər\ rapture
• enrapture, recapture

apular \ap-yə-lər\ papular,
scapular

apus \ā-pəs\ see APIS

apy¹ \ā-pē\ see APEY

apy² \ap-ē\ see APPY

aq¹ \äk\ see OCK¹

aq² \ak\ see ACK²

aqi \äk-ē\ see OCKY

aque¹ \āk\ see AKE¹

aque² \ak\ see ACK²

aqui \äk-ē\ see OCKY

ar¹ \er\ see ARE⁴

ar² \ȯr\ see OR¹

ar³ \är\ ar, are, bar, barre, car,
carr, char, charr, czar, far, gar,
gnar, guar, jar, Lar, mar, moire,
noir, our, par, parr, Parr, R,
quare, Saar, scar, spar, SPAR,
star, tar, tahr, Thar, tsar, tzar,
yare • Adar, Adzhar, afar, ajar,
all-star, armoire, attar, bar car,
bazaar, Beauvoir, beaux arts,
bête noire, beurre noir, Bihar,
bizarre, boudoir, boxcar, boyar,
briard, Bronze Star, bulbar,
Bulgar, bursar, bus bar, canard,
cash bar, catarrh, Cathar, chair
car, chukar, cigar, clochard,
club car, coal tar, costar,
cougar, couloir, crossbar,
crowbar, Dakar, daystar, debar,
decare, devoir, dinar, disbar,
Dog Star, drawbar, Dunbar,
durbar, earthstar, Elgar, eschar,
eyebar, feldspar, fern bar, film
noir, five-star, fixed star, flatcar,
four-star, fulmar, gaydar, gazar,
guitar, Gunnar, Hagar, handcar,
Hoggar, horsecar, hussar,
Invar, Ishtar, Iyar, jaguar, Kádár,
Kolar, leaf scar, Lehár, lidar,
Lifar, Loire, lounge car, lumbar,
jack-tar, jowar, Khowar, lahar,
Lamar, lekvar, lodestar,
Magyar, malar, memoir, Mizar,
Mylar, NASCAR, Navarre,
nightjar, North Star, pace car,
paillard, peignoir, petard, pinch
bar, Pindar, pine tar, pissoir,
planar, plantar, polestar,
pourboire, prowl car, pulsar,

Qatar, qintar, quasar, radar, railcar, raw bar, rebar, red star, Renoir, roll bar, Safar, Samar, sandbar, scalar, scout car, Sennar, shikar, shofar, sidebar, sidecar, sirdar, sitar, slop jar, slot car, snack bar, sofar, solar, sonar, sports bar, sports car, stock car, streetcar, Svalbard, sway bar, tank car, T-bar, toolbar, town car, tramcar, trocar, unbar, volar, voussoir, Weimar • abattoir, acinar, Ahaggar, air guitar, Aligarh, aide-mémoire, arctic char, au revoir, avatar, blazing star, bolivar, Bolívar, brittle star, bumper car, cabin car, cable car, café noir, Castlebar, caviar, cinnabar, coffee bar, color bar, command car, commissar, communard, coplanar, Côte d'Ivoire, cultivar, deciare, deodar, dining car, double bar, double star, Dreyfusard, error bar, escolar, escritoire, evening star, exemplar, falling star, feather star, fluorspar, funny car, giant star, handlebar, Indy car, insofar, isobar, Issachar, jacamar, jaguar, jaunting car, Kandahar, kilobar, Krasnodar, Leyden jar, Malabar, mason jar, megabar, megastar, millibar, minibar, minicar, Miramar, montagnard, morning star, motorcar, Mudejar, multicar, muscle car, Myanmar, neutron star, Nicobar, objet d'art, open bar, parlor car, pinot noir, Qiqihar, registrar, rent-a-car, repertoire, reservoir, ricercar, rising star, salad bar, Salazar, samovar, scimitar, seminar, shooting star, Silver Star, simular, sleeping car, steak tartare, steel guitar, subahdar, superstar, tiki bar, torsion bar, touring car, tutelar, turbocar, Valdemar, VCR, Veadar, wrecking bar, wunderbar, X-ray star, Yourcenar, zamindar, Zanzibar • anti-roll bar, binary star, budgerigar, canopic jar, conservatoire, Doppler radar, goût de terroir, Gulf of Mannar, Hubli-Dharwar, juniper tar, kala-azar, Kathiawar, Madagascar, Mount Palomar, multiple star, proseminar, radio car, radio star, side-scan sonar, Viña del Mar • Hawaiian guitar, horizontal bar

ara[1] \är-ə\ Kara, Laura, Mara, Nara, para, vara • Asmara, Bambara, begorra, Bukhara, Camorra, Ferrara, Guevara, Gomorrah, kinara, saguaro, Samara, samsara, tantara, tiara • capybara, carbonara, Connemara, Demerara, deodara, Gemarara, Guanabara, sayonara, solfatara, tuatara • Guadalajara, Tarahumara, Timisoara

ara[2] \er-ə\ see ERA[1]

ara[3] \ar-ə\ see ARROW[1]

ara[4] \òr-ə\ see ORA

arab \ar-əb\ Arab, Carib, carob, scarab • pan-Arab • anti-Arab, Shatt al Arab

arable \ar-ə-bəl\ arable, bearable, parable, shareable, spareable, wearable

• declarable, nonarable, unbearable

aracen \ar-ə-sən\ see ARISON

aracin \ar-ə-sən\ see ARISON

arad \ar-əd\ see ARID

araday \ar-əd-ē\ faraday, parody • self-parody

arage \ar-ij\ see ARRIAGE

aragon \ar-ə-gən\ Aragon, paragon, tarragon

arah[1] \er-ə\ see ERA[1]

arah[2] \ar-ə\ see ARROW[1]

aral[1] \ar-əl\ see ARREL[2]

aral[2] \er-əl\ see ERRAL

aralee[2] \er-ə-lē\ see ARILY

aran[1] \er-ən\ see ARON[1]

aran[2] \ar-ən\ see ARON[2]

arant[1] \er-ənt\ see ARENT[1]

arant[2] \ar-ənt\ see ARENT[2]

araoh[1] \er-ō\ see ERO[2]

araoh[2] \ar-ō\ see ARROW[2]

araph \ar-əf\ see ARIFF

aras \är-əs\ see ORRIS[1]

arass \ar-əs\ see ARIS[2]

arat \ar-ət\ carat, caret, carrot, claret, garret, Garrett, karat, parrot • disparate

arate \ar-ət\ see ARAT

arative[1] \er-ət-iv\ declarative, imperative

arative[2] \ar-ət-iv\ narrative • comparative, declarative, preparative, reparative

arator \ar-ət-ər\ barrator • apparitor, comparator, preparator

arb \ärb\ arb, barb, carb, garb • bicarb, rhubarb

arbel \är-bəl\ see ARBLE[1]

arber \är-bər\ see ARBOR

arbered \är-bərd\ see ARBOARD

arbin \är-bən\ see ARBON

arble[1] \är-bəl\ barbel, garble, marble

arble[2] \òr-bəl\ see ORBEL

arboard \är-bərd\ barbered, larboard, starboard • astarboard, unbarbered

arbon \är-bən\ carbon, Harbin • hydrocarbon • radiocarbon

arbor \är-bər\ arbor, barber, harbor • Ann Arbor, Grays Harbor, Pearl Harbor

arc[1] \äk\ see OCK[1]

arc[2] \ärk\ see ARK[1]

arca \är-kə\ see ARKA[1]

arce[1] \ers\ scarce • Nez Percé

arce[2] \ärs\ see ARSE[1]

arcel \är-səl\ see ARSAL

arcener \ärs-nər\ larcener, parcener • coparcener

arch \ärch\ arch, larch, march, March, parch, starch • cornstarch, dead march, frogmarch, gill arch, grand march • countermarch, Gothic arch, horseshoe arch, lancet arch, on the march, Tudor arch, wedding march

archal \är-kəl\ darkle, sparkle • exarchal, monarchal, outsparkle • hierarchal, matriarchal, patriarchal

archate \är-kət\ see ARKET

arche \ärsh\ see ARSH

arched \ärcht\ arched, parched—*also* -ed *forms of verbs listed at* ARCH

archer \är-chər\ archer, marcher • departure

archic \är-kik\ anarchic, autarchic, autarkic, monarchic, tetrarchic • hierarchic, oligarchic

archical \är-ki-kəl\ autarchical, monarchical • oligarchical

archon \är-kən\ see ARKEN

archy \är-kē\ barky, larky, snarky • anarchy, autarchy, autarky, dyarchy, eparchy, exarchy, heptarchy, malarkey, men- arche, monarchy, pentarchy, squirearchy, tetrarchy, triarchy, trierarchy • hierarchy, matri- archy, patriarchy, oligarchy

arck \ärk\ see ARK[1]

arco \är-kō\ arco, narco

arct \ärkt\ see ARKED

arctic[1] \ärk-tik\ arctic, Arctic • antarctic, Antarctic, Holarctic, Nearctic, subarctic • Palearctic, subantarctic

arctic[2] \ärt-ik\ see ARTIC[1]

arcy \är-sē\ farcy, Farsi, Parsi

ard[1] \ärd\ bard, barred, card, chard, Dard, fard, guard, hard, lard, nard, pard, sard, shard, yard • Asgard, backyard, bankcard, Barnard, barnyard, Bernard, blackguard, blowhard, boatyard, bombard, boneyard, brassard, brickyard, canard, charge card, churchyard, cloth yard, coast guard, courtyard, dance card, deeryard, die-hard, diehard, discard, dockyard, dooryard, face card, farmyard, filmcard, fireguard, flash card, foreyard, foulard, Fugard, Gerard, graveyard, green card, Hansard, ill-starred, jacquard, junkyard, lifeguard, Lombard, main yard, mansard, mass card, Midgard, milliard, mudguard, noseguard, off guard, old guard, on guard, Oxnard, petard, phone card, Picard, placard, point guard, postcard, poularde, punch card, rear guard, rearguard, Red Guard, regard, retard, ritard, safeguard, scorecard, shipyard, smart card, sound card, spikenard, steelyard, stockyard, switchyard, tabard, tanyard, tiltyard, time card, unbarred, unguard, vanguard, vizard, wild card • Abelard, afterguard, avant-garde, Beauregard, bodyguard, boulevard, business card, calling card, cattle guard, Christmas card, color guard, compass card, credit card, debit card, disregard, drawing card, goliard, greeting card, Hildegard, honor guard, ID card, interlard, Kierkegaard, Langobard, leotard, Longobard, lumberyard, national guard, navy yard, no-holds-barred, playing card, postal card, provost guard, report card, Saint Bernard, Savoyard, Scotland Yard, self-regard, shooting guard, tourist card, undercard, union card, unitard • courtesy card, camelopard, expansion card, Peter Lombard, picture-postcard, video card, visiting card • affinity card, identity card —*also* -ed *forms of verbs listed at* AR[3]

ard² \är\ see AR[3]

ard³ \òrd\ see OARD

ardant \ärd-ᵊnt\ ardent, guardant • regardant, retardant • flame-retardant

arde \ärd\ see ARD[1]

arded¹ \ärd-əd\ guarded • mansarded, retarded, unguarded—*also* -ed *forms of verbs listed at* ARD[1]

arded² \òrd-əd\ corded, sordid, swarded, warded—*also* -ed *forms of verbs listed at* OARD

ardee \òrd-ē\ see ORDY[1]

arden¹ \ärd-ᵊn\ Arden, Dardan, garden, harden, pardon • bombardon, case-harden, Kincardine, knot garden, rock garden, roof garden, tea garden • Dolly Varden, kitchen garden, water garden

arden² \òrd-ᵊn\ cordon, Gordon, Jordan, warden • churchwarden

ardener \ärd-nər\ gardener, hardener, pardner, pardoner, partner • landscape gardener

ardent \ärd-ᵊnt\ see ARDANT

arder¹ \ärd-ər\ ardor, carder, guarder, larder, yarder • discarder, green-carder

arder² \òrd-ər\ see ORDER

ardi \ärd-ē\ see ARDY

ardian¹ \ärd-ē-ən\ guardian, Sardian • Edwardian, Lombardian • Kierkegaardian

ardian² \òrd-ē-ən\ see ORDION

ardic \ärd-ik\ bardic, Dardic • Lombardic, Sephardic • goliardic, Langobardic, Longobardic

ardine \ärd-ᵐ\ see ARDEN[1]

arding \òrd-iŋ\ see ORDING[1]

ardingly \òrd-iŋ-lē\ see ORDINGLY

ardom \ärd-əm\ czardom, stardom • megastardom, superstardom

ardon \ärd-ᵊn\ see ARDEN[1]

ardoner \ärd-nər\ see ARDENER

ardor \ärd-ər\ see ARDER[1]

ardy \ärd-ē\ hardy, Hardy, lardy, tardy • foolhardy, half-hardy, Lombardy, Sephardi

are¹ \er-ē\ see ARY[1]

are² \är\ see AR[3]

are³ \är-ē\ see ARI[1]

are⁴ \er\ air, Ayr, bare, bear, Blair, blare, care, chair, chare, Claire, dare, Dare, e'er, ere, err, eyre, fair, fare, flair, flare, glair, glare, hair, hare, Herr, heir, lair, mare, ne'er, pair, pare, pear, prayer, quare, rare, rear, scare, share, snare, spare, square, stair, stare, swear, tare, tear, their, there, they're, vair, ware, wear, weir, where, yare • affair, aglare, airfare, Ajmer, Altair, antbear, armchair, au pair, aware, bakeware, barware, Basseterre, bath chair, Baudelaire, beachwear, bergère, beware, bid fair, big hair, black bear, bricklayer, broodmare, brown bear, bugbear, caneware, carfare, Carrère, cave bear, chi-square, clayware, club chair, cochair, coheir, compare, compere, confrere, cookware, corsair, courseware, creamware, crosshair, cudbear, day-care, daymare, dead air, decare, deck chair, declare, delftware, despair, dishware, éclair, elsewhere, enclair, ensnare, eyewear, fanfare, fieldfare, firmware, flatware, Flaubert, footwear, forbear, forebear, forswear, foursquare, freeware, funfair, galère, giftware, glassware, Great Bear, groupware, Gruyère, guard hair, hardware, health care, hectare, high chair, horsehair, hot air, impair, infare, Khmer, Kildare, knitwear, Lake Eyre, life-care, light air, longhair, loungewear, Mayfair, menswear, meunière, midair, mohair, Molière, neckwear, nightmare, no fair, nonglare, outstare, out-there, outwear, Pierre, playwear, plein air, plowshare, Poor Clare, Port

Blair, portiere, premiere, prepare, pushchair, rainwear, redware, repair, root hair, Saint Pierre, Sancerre, sea hare, self-care, shank's mare, shareware, shorthair, side chair, Sinclair, skiwear, sleepwear, slipware, sloth bear, software, somewhere, spongeware, sportswear, stemware, stoneware, sun bear, swimwear, threadbare, tinware, torchère, trouvère, tuyere, unfair, unhair, unswear, Voltaire, warfare, welfare, wheelchair, wirehair, workfare • aftercare, agate ware, air-to-air, antiair, antiglare, anywhere, arctic hare, Asian pear, bayadere, bêche-de-mer, Belgian hare, billionaire, bill of fare, boutonniere, bring to bear, camel hair, Camembert, Canton ware, captain's chair, chinaware, compressed air, county fair, crackleware, Croix de Guerre, cultivar, debonair, deciare, de la Mare, Delaware, derriere, dinnerware, disrepair, doctrinaire, earthenware, easy chair, en plein air, étagère, everywhere, fighting chair, flying mare, fourragère, Frigidaire, germ warfare, get somewhere, graniteware, grizzly bear, here and there, hide or hair, hollowware, ice-cream chair, in one's hair, in the air, ironware, jasperware, kitchenware, La Bruyère, lacquerware, laissez-faire, Lake Saint Clair, Latin square, legionnaire, lion's share, Little Bear, love affair, luminaire, lusterware, magic square, maidenhair, mal de mer, managed care, market share, Medicare, metalware, millionaire, minaudière, miter square, Mon-Khmer, morris chair, Mousquetaire, nom de guerre, on the square, open-air, otherwhere, outerwear, overbear, overwear, perfect square, plasticware, polar bear, potty-chair, porte cochere, prickly pear, questionnaire, rivière, Robespierre, rocking chair, Santander, savoir faire, science fair, self-aware, self-despair, silverware, slipper chair, snowshoe hare, solar flare, solitaire, swivel chair, tableware, tear one's hair, teddy bear, then and there, thoroughfare, trench warfare, unaware, underwear, vaporware, Venushair, vivandière, wash-and-wear, water bear, wear and tear, willowware, Windsor chair, woodenware, world premiere, yellowware, zillionaire • breath of fresh air, butterfly chair, Cape Finisterre, chargé d'affaires, chemin de fer, commissionaire, concessionaire, couturiere, devil-may-care, director's chair, electric chair, enamelware, hyperaware, intensive care, Kodiak bear, lighter-than-air, memoriter, minimal pair, out of one's hair, Parian ware, pied-à-terre, primary care, ready-to-wear, social welfare, son et lumière, spectacled bear, surface-to-air, up in the air, vanity fair, vin ordinaire, vogue la galère

• Adirondack chair, castle in the air, cordon sanitaire, middle of nowhere

area \er-ē-ə\ see ARIA

areable¹ \er-ə-bəl\ see EARABLE¹

areable² \ar-ə-bəl\ see ARABLE

areal \er-ē-əl\ see ARIAL

arean¹ \er-ē-ən\ see ARIAN¹

arean² \ar-ē-ən\ see ARIAN²

ared \erd\ see AIRED

aredness \ar-ed-nəs\ see ARIDNESS

arel \ar-əl\ see ARREL²

arely¹ \er-lē\ see AIRLY

arely² \är-lē\ see ARLIE

arem \er-əm\ see ARUM²

arence¹ \er-əns\ Clarence, Terence • forbearance

arence² \ar-ən(ts)\ see ARENTS

arent¹ \er-ənt\ daren't, errant, parent • aberrant, afferent, apparent, declarant, deferent, efferent, godparent, grandparent, house parent, inerrant, knight-errant, nonparent, sederunt, stepparent, transparent • heir apparent

arent² \ar-ənt\ arrant, daren't, parent • apparent, declarant, godparent, grandparent, stepparent, transparent • heir apparent

aren't¹ \er-ənt\ see ARENT¹

aren't² \ar-ənt\ see ARENT²

arents \ar-ən(t)s\ Barents, Clarence—*also* -s, -'s, *and* -s' *forms of nouns listed at* ARENT[2]

arer \er-ər\ see EARER[1]

ares[1] \erz\ see AIRS

ares[2] \ar-ēz\ Ares, caries, nares • Antares • Buenos Aires • primus inter pares—*also* -s, -'s, *and* -s' *forms of nouns and* -s *forms of verbs listed at* ARRY[3]

ares[3] \är-əs\ see ORRIS[1]

aret \ar-ət\ see ARAT

areve \är-və\ see ARVA

arey[1] \ar-ē\ see ARRY[3]

arey[2] \er-ē\ see ARY[1]

arez \är-əs\ see ORRIS[1]

arf[1] \ärf\ barf, scarf

arf[2] \órf\ see ORPH

argain \är-gən\ bargain, jargon • outbargain, plea-bargain • in the bargain

arge \ärj\ barge, charge, large, marge, Marge, parge, sarge, sparge, targe • at-large, depth charge, discharge, enlarge, fixed charge, La Farge, litharge, recharge, surcharge, take-charge, uncharge, writ large • banzai charge, by and large, countercharge, cover charge, hypercharge, overcharge, service charge, supercharge, undercharge • carrying charge

argent \är-jənt\ argent, margent, Sargent, sergeant

arger \är-jər\ charger, sparger • discharger, enlarger, recharger • supercharger, turbocharger

arget \är-gət\ argot, target • nontarget, off target, on target

argle \är-gəl\ gargle • argle-bargle

argo \är-gō\ Argo, argot, cargo, Fargo, largo, Margot, embargo • Key Largo • supercargo

argon \är-gən\ see ARGAIN

argot[1] \är-gət\ see ARGET

argot[2] \är-gō\ see ARGO

arh \är\ see AR[3]

ari[1] \är-ē\ Bari, Chari, gharry, laari, quarry, sari, scarry, sorry, starry • Bihari, curare, Imari, Qatari, safari, Sassari, scalare, shikari, tamari, Vasari • calamari, certiorari, cheboksary, Kalahari, Lake Scudari, Stradivari, zamindari

ari[2] \er-ē\ see ARY[1]

ari[3] \ar-ē\ see ARRY[3]

aria \er-ē-ə\ area, Beria, feria, kerria, varia • Bavaria, Bulgaria, hysteria, Kaffraria, malaria, planaria, Samaria • adularia, Carpentaria, cineraria, fritillaria, Gulf of Paria, laminaria, luminaria, miliaria, militaria, sanguinaria • opera seria

arial \er-ē-əl\ aerial, areal, Ariel, burial, gharial • glossarial, malarial, notarial, subaerial, vicarial • actuarial, adversarial, estuarial, secretarial

arian[1] \er-ē-ən\ Arian, Aryan,
Carian, Marian, Marion, parian,
Parian • agrarian, Aquarian,
barbarian, Bavarian, Bulgarian,
Canarian, Cancerian, cesarean,
cnidarian, contrarian, frutarian,
grammarian, Hungarian,
Khymerian, librarian, Maid
Marian, ovarian, Pierian,
riparian, rosarian, Rotarian,
sectarian, Sumerian, Tartarean,
Tartarian, Tocharian, Tractarian,
Vulgarian, Wagnerian
• antiquarian, centenarian,
Indo-Aryan, libertarian,
millenarian, nonsectarian,
postlapsarian, prelapsarian,
Presbyterian, proletarian,
Rastafarian, Sabbatarian,
Sagittarian, seminarian,
trinitarian, Unitarian, vegetarian
• abecedarian, Austro-
Hungarian, authoritarian,
communitarian, disciplinarian,
documentarian, egalitarian,
humanitarian, majoritarian,
nonagenarian, octogenarian,
parliamentarian, post-
millenarian, premillenarian,
predestinarian, Sacramentarian,
sexagenarian, totalitarian,
utilitarian, veterinarian • estab-
lishmentarian, latitudinarian,
septuagenarian, valetudinarian

arian[2] \ar-ē-ən\ Arian, Aryan,
carrion, clarion, Marian, Marion,
parian, Parian • agrarian,
Aquarian, barbarian, Bavarian,
Bulgarian, cesarean, contrarian,
Hungarian, Megarian, ovarian,
rosarian, Tartarean, Tocharian,
vulgarian • Indo-Aryan,
Rastafarian • Austro-Hungarian

ariance \ar-ē-əns\ tarriance,
variance • at variance,
covariance, invariance,
vicariance

ariant \ar-ē-ənt\ variant
• vicariant

ariat[1] \er-ē-ət\ heriot, lariat,
variate • bivariate, covariate,
salariat, vicariate • commissariat, multivariate,
proletariat, secretariat

ariat[2] \är-ē-ət\ see AUREATE[1]

ariat[3] \ar-ē-ət\ chariot, lariat
• bivariate, salariat
• commissariat, proletariat
• Judas Iscariot

ariate \er-ē-ət\ see ARIAT[1]

arib \ar-əb\ see ARAB

aric \ar-ik\ barrack, carrack
• Amharic, barbaric, Dinaric,
Megaric, Pindaric • hyperbaric,
isobaric, Balearic

arice \ar-əs\ see ARIS[2]

aricide \ar-ə-sīd\ see ARRICIDE

arid \ar-əd\ arid, farad • semiarid

aridin \ar-ə-dᵉn\ see ARRIDAN

aridness \ar-əd-nəs\ aridness
• preparedness

aried[1] \er-ēd\ see ERRIED

aried[2] \ar-ēd\ see ARRIED

ariel \er-ē-əl\ see ARIAL

arier[1] \er-ē-ər\ see ERRIER

arier[2] \ar-ē-ər\ see ARRIER[2]

aries \ar-ēz\ see ARES[2]

ariff \ar-əf\ paraph, tariff

aril \ar-əl\ see ARREL[2]

arilee[1] \ar-ə-lē\ see ARALEE

arilee[2] \er-ə-lē\ see ARILY

arily \er-ə-lē\ charily, merrily, scarily, verily, warily • primarily, summarily • arbitrarily, customarily, honorarily, legendarily, literarily, militarily, momentarily, monetarily, necessarily, ordinarily, secondarily, temporarily, voluntarily • extraordinarily, hereditarily, involuntarily, preliminarily, uncustomarily, unnecessarily

arin \är-ən\ florin, foreign, Lauren, Orin, sarin, sporran, warren, Warren • Bukharin, Gagarin

arinate \ar-ə-nət\ see ARONET

arinet \ar-ə-nət\ see ARONET

aring[1] \er-iŋ\ airing, bearing, Bering, daring, fairing, flaring, glaring, herring, paring, raring, sparing, tearing, wearing • ball bearing, cheeseparing, child-bearing, seafaring, side bearing, talebearing, time-sharing, unerring, unsparing, wayfaring • overbearing, profit sharing—*also* -ing *forms of verbs listed at* ARE[4]

aring[2] \er-ən\ see ARON[1]

ario \er-ē-ō\ stereo, Ontario

arion[1] \ar-ē-ən\ see ARIAN[2]

arion[2] \er-ē-ən\ see ARIAN[1]

ariot \ar-ē-ət\ see ARIAT[3]

arious \er-ē-əs\ Arius, carious, Darius, scarious, various

• Aquarius, burglarious, calcareous, contrarious, denarius, gregarious, guarnerius, hilarious, malarious, nefarious, precarious, senarius, vagarious, vicarious
• multifarious, omnifarious, Stradivarius, Sagittarius, temerarious

aris[1] \är-əs\ see ORRIS[1]

aris[2] \ar-əs\ arras, arris, Clarice, harass, Harris, Paris, parous • coheiress, embarrass, Polaris • disembarrass • Lewis with Harris, plaster of paris

arish[1] \er-ish\ bearish, cherish, fairish, garish, perish, squarish • nightmarish

arish[2] \ar-ish\ garish, marish, parish • interparish, vinegarish

arison \ar-ə-sən\ characin, garrison, Garrison, Harrison, Saracen, warison • caparison, comparison

arist \er-əst\ Marist, querist • aquarist, pleinairist, scenarist • apiarist—*also* -est *forms of adjectives listed at* ARE[4]

aritan \er-ət-ᵊn\ see ERATIN

aritor \ar-ət-ər\ see ARATOR

arity[1] \er-ət-ē\ see ERITY

arity[2] \ar-ət-ē\ carroty, charity, clarity, parity, rarity • barbarity, disparity, hilarity, imparity, polarity, unclarity, vulgarity • angularity, bipolarity, circularity, familiarity, granularity, insularity, jocularity, linearity, muscularity, peculiarity, popularity, regularity, similarity, singularity, solidarity • complementarity, dissimilarity, irregularity, particularity, unfamiliarity, unpopularity

arium \er-ē-əm\ barium • aquarium, herbarium, puparium, sacrarium, samarium, solarium, terrarium, velarium, vivarium • cinerarium, honorarium, leprosarium, oceanarium, planetarium, sanitarium • armamentarium

arius \er-ē-əs\ see ARIOUS

ark¹ \ärk\ arc, ark, bark, Clark, Clarke, dark, hark, lark, marc, Marc, MARC, mark, Mark, marque, narc, nark, park, Park, quark, sark, shark, spark, stark • aardvark, airpark, anarch, autarch, ballpark, benchmark, birchbark, birthmark, Bismarck, blue shark, bookmark, check mark, chop mark, debark, demark, Denmark, D-mark, earmark, embark, endarch, exarch, footmark, futhark, Graustark, hallmark, hash mark, horned lark, ironbark, landmark, Lake Clark, Lamarck, monarch, ostmark, Ozark, Petrarch, pitch-dark, Plutarch, pockmark, postmark, pressmark, pugmark, reichsmark, remark, remarque, Remarque, ringbark, seamark, shagbark, sitzmark, skylark, soapbark, space mark, stress mark, tanbark, tetrarch, theme park, tidemark, titlark, touchmark, trademark, whale shark • accent mark, acritarch, antiquark, antishark, basking shark, cutty sark, deutsche mark, disembark, double-park, Estes Park, great white shark, hierarch, Joan of Arc, make one's mark, mako shark, matriarch, meadowlark, Menlo Park, metalmark, minipark, oligarch, paperbark, patriarch, Plimsoll mark, question mark, service mark, stringybark, telemark, thresher shark, tiger shark, toe the mark, trierarch, watermark, water park • amusement park, heresiarch, high-water mark, in the ballpark, shot in the dark, symposiarch, vest-pocket park, walk in the park • whistle in the dark

ark² \ȯrk\ see ORK²

ark³ \ərk\ see ORK¹

arka¹ \är-kə\ parka • anasarca • Hamilcar Barca

arka² \ər-kə\ see URKA¹

arke \ärk\ see ARK¹

arked \ärkt\ marked • chop-marked, infarct • ripple-marked, unremarked—*also* -ed *forms of verbs listed at* ARK¹

arken \är-kən\ darken, hearken

arker \är-kər\ barker, larker, marker, parker, Parker, sparker • bookmarker, debarker, Ozarker, skylarker • biomarker, Granville-Barker, Magic Marker, nosey parker • genetic marker—*also* -er *forms of adjectives listed at* ARK¹

arket \är-kət\ market • bear market, black market, bull market, down-market, flea market, free market, gray market, mass-market, meat market, newmarket, stock market, test-market, third market, upmarket • after-market, buyer's market, common market, hypermarket, in the market, matriarchate, money market, on the market, patriarchate, seller's market, supermarket

arkey \är-kē\ see ARCHY

arkian \är-kē-ən\ Graustarkian, Lamarckian, Monarchian, Ozarkian

arkic \är-kik\ see ARCHIC

arking \är-kiŋ\ barking, Barking, carking, marking, parking • loan-sharking, telemarking, valet parking—also -ing forms of verbs listed at ARK[1]

arkle \är-kəl\ see ARCHAL

arks \ärks\ Marx, Parks • Ozarks, stretch marks—also -s, -'s, and -s' forms of nouns and -s forms of verbs listed at ARK[1]

arky \är-kē\ see ARCHY

arl \ärl\ carl, Carl, farl, gnarl, jarl, Karl, marl, parle, quarrel, snarl • ensnarl, housecarl, unsnarl • Albemarle

arla \är-lə\ Carla, Darla, Karla, Marla

arlan \ä-lən\ see ARLINE

arlatan \är-lət-ᵉn\ charlatan, tarlatan

arlay \är-lē\ see ARLIE

arle \ärl\ see ARL

arlen \är-lən\ see ARLINE

arler \är-lər\ see ARLOR

arless \är-ləs\ Carlos, parlous, scarless, starless

arlet \är-lət\ charlotte, Charlotte, harlot, scarlet, starlet, varlet

arley \är-lē\ see ARLIE

arlic \är-lik\ garlic • pilgarlic

arlie \är-lē\ barley, charlie, Charlie, Farley, gnarly, Harley, marly, parlay, parley, snarly, yarely • bizarrely

arlin \är-lən\ see ARLINE

arline \är-lən\ Arlen, carline, Harlan, marlin, Marlin, marline, Marlyn • blue marlin, white marlin

arling \är-liŋ\ carling, darling, Darling, starling—also -ing forms of verbs listed at ARL

arlor \är-lər\ parlor, quarreler, snarler • massage parlor

arlos \är-ləs\ see ARLESS

arlot \är-lət\ see ARLET

arlotte \är-lət\ see ARLET

arlous \är-ləs\ see ARLESS

arlow \är-lō\ barlow, Barlow, Harlow

arly \är-lē\ see ARLIE

arlyn \ä-lən\ see ARLINE

arm[1] \ärm\ arm, barm, charm, farm, harm, smarm • alarm, disarm, dry farm, fat farm, firearm, fish farm, forearm, gendarme, gisarme, nonfarm, poor farm, rearm, schoolmarm, sidearm, stiff-arm, straight-arm, strong-arm, tonearm, tree farm, truck farm, unarm, wind farm, work farm, yardarm • arm in arm, buy the farm, false alarm, funny farm, overarm, rocker arm, still alarm, twist one's arm, underarm • collective farm, rollover arm, shot in the arm

arm² \äm\ see OM¹

arm³ \òrm\ see ORM²

arma¹ \är-mə\ dharma, karma, Parma

arma² \ər-mə\ see ERMA

arman \är-mən\ barman, Carmen, carmine

armed \ärmd\ armed, charmed • unarmed—*also* -ed *forms of verbs listed at* ARM¹

armen \är-mən\ see ARMAN

arment \är-mənt\ garment, varmint • debarment, disbarment • undergarment, overgarment

armer¹ \är-mər\ armor, charmer, farmer, harmer • dirt farmer, disarmer, dry farmer, snake charmer, truck farmer • tenant farmer • gentleman farmer

armer² \òr-mər\ see ORMER¹

armic \ər-mik\ see ERMIC

armine \är-mən\ see ARMAN

arming¹ \är-miŋ\ charming, farming • alarming, disarming, mixed farming, Prince

Charming—*also* -ing *forms of verbs listed at* ARM¹

arming² \òr-miŋ\ see ORMING

armint \är-mənt\ see ARMENT

armless \ärm-ləs\ armless, charmless, harmless

armoir \är-mər\ see ARMER¹

armon \är-mən\ see ARMAN

army \är-mē\ army, barmy, smarmy • standing army • Salvation Army

arn¹ \ärn\ Arne, barn, darn, Marne, tarn, yarn • carbarn, lucarne, spun yarn

arn² \òrn\ see ORN¹

arna \ər-nə\ see ERNA

arnal \ärn-ᵊl\ see ARNEL

arnate \är-nət\ Barnet, garnet • discarnate, incarnate

arne¹ \ärn\ see ARN¹

arne² \är-nē\ see ARNY

arnel \ärn-ᵊl\ carnal, charnel, darnel

arner¹ \är-nər\ darner, garner, yarner

arner² \òr-nər\ see ORNER

arness \är-nəs\ harness • bizarreness

arnet \är-nət\ see ARNATE

arney \är-nē\ see ARNY

arnhem \är-nəm\ see ARNUM

arning \òr-niŋ\ see ORNING

arnish \är-nish\ garnish, tarnish, varnish

arnum \är-nəm\ Arnhem, Barnum

arny \är-nē\ Barney, barny, blarney, carny, Kearney • Killarney • chili con carne

aro¹ \er-ō\ see ERO²

aro² \ar-ō\ see ARROW²

aro³ \är-ə\ see ARA¹

aro⁴ \är-ō\ see ORROW¹

arob \ar-əb\ see ARAB

arody \ar-əd-ē\ see ARADAY

aroe¹ \ar-ō\ see ARROW²

aroe² \er-ō\ see ERO²

arol \ar-əl\ see ARREL²

arold² \er-əld\ see ERALD

arole \ar-əl\ see ARREL²

arom \er-əm\ see ARUM²

aron¹ \er-ən\ Aaron, baron, Charon, Erin, garron, heron, perron, raring, Sharon • sierran • Plain of Sharon, robber baron, rose of Sharon, sub-Saharan

aron² \ar-ən\ Aaron, baron, barren, Charon, garron, Sharon • Plain of Sharon, robber baron, rose of Sharon, sub-Saharan

aronet \ar-ə-nət\ baronet, carinate, clarinet

arous¹ \er-əs\ see ERROUS

arous² \ar-əs\ see ARIS²

arp¹ \ärp\ Arp, carp, harp, scarp, sharp, tarp, Tharp • cardsharp, grass carp, Jew's harp, wind harp • Autoharp, endocarp, epicarp, exocarp, mesocarp, pericarp, Polycarp, supersharp, vibraharp • aeolian harp

arp² \orp\ see ORP

arpen \är-pən\ sharpen, tarpon

arper \är-pər\ carper, harper, scarper, sharper • cardsharper

arpie \är-pē\ see ARPY

arpon \är-pən\ see ARPEN

arpy \är-pē\ harpy, sharpie

arque \ärk\ see ARK¹

arquetry \är-kə-trē\ marquetry, parquetry

arqui \är-kē\ see ARCHY

arrable \ar-ə-bəl\ see ARABLE

arrack¹ \ar-ik\ see ARIC

arrack² \ar-ək\ arrack, barrack, carrack

arrage \är-ij\ see ¹ORAGE

arragon \ar-ə-gən\ see ARAGON

arral \ar-əl\ see ARREL²

arram \ar-əm\ see ARUM²

arrant¹ \ar-ənt\ see ARENT²

arrant² \or-ənt\ see ORRENT

arras \ar-əs\ see ARIS²

arrass \ar-əs\ see ARIS²

arrative \ar-ət-iv\ see ARATIVE²

arrator \ar-ət-ər\ see ARATOR

arre \är\ see AR³

arred \ärd\ see ARD¹

arrel¹ \orl\ see ORL²

arrel² \ar-əl\ Aral, aril, barrel, carol, Carol, Caryl, carrel,

Carroll, Darryl, Karol, parol, parral, parrel • apparel, cracker-barrel, double-barrel

arrel³ \òr-əl\ see ORAL¹

arreler \är-lər\ see ARLOR

arrell \ar-əl\ see ARREL²

arrely \är-lē\ see ARLIE

arren¹ \ar-ən\ see ARON²

arren² \òr-ən\ see ORIN¹

arren³ \är-ən\ see ARIN

arrener \òr-ə-nər\ see ORONER

arreness \är-nəs\ see ARNESS

arret \ar-ət\ see ARAT

arrett \ar-ət\ see ARAT

arrh \är\ see AR³

arriage \ar-ij\ carriage, marriage • disparage, miscarriage, mixed marriage • baby carriage, civil marriage, horseless carriage, intermarriage, open marriage, proxy marriage, shotgun marriage, undercarriage • common-law marriage

arriance \ar-ē-əns\ see ARIANCE

arricide \ar-ə-sīd\ parricide • acaricide

arrie \ar-ē\ see ARRY³

arried \ar-ēd\ harried, married, varied • unmarried

arrier¹ \òr-ē-ər\ see ARRIOR

arrier² \ar-ē-ər\ barrier, carrier, farrier, harrier, varier • ballcarrier, hod carrier, mail carrier, noncarrier, sound barrier, spear-carrier • aircraft carrier, blood-brain barrier,

common carrier, Jersey barrier, letter carrier, northern harrier, sonic barrier, vapor barrier

arrion \ar-ē-ən\ see ARIAN²

arrior \òr-ē-ər\ quarrier, sorrier, warrior • cold warrior, road warrior • weekend warrior

arris \ar-əs\ see ARIS²

arrison \ar-ə-sən\ see ARISON

arro \är-ō\ see ORROW¹

arroll \ar-əl\ see ARREL²

arron \ar-ən\ see ARON²

arrot \ar-ət\ see ARAT

arroty \ar-ət-ē\ see ARITY²

arrow¹ \ar-ə\ Clara, jarrah, Kara, Sarah, Tara • Bukhara, cascara, mascara, Sahara, samara, Tamara, tantara, tiara • capybara, caracara, marinara, Santa Clara

arrow² \ar-ō\ arrow, barrow, Darrow, Faeroe, faro, farrow, harrow, Harrow, marrow, narrow, pharaoh, sparrow, taro, tarot, yarrow • bone marrow, broad arrow, handbarrow, house sparrow, Point Barrow, song sparrow, straight-arrow, tree sparrow, wheelbarrow • straight and narrow • Kilimanjaro

arrowy \ar-ə-wē\ arrowy, marrowy

arry¹ \är-ē\ see ARI¹

arry² \òr-ē\ see ORY

arry³ \ar-ē\ Barrie, Barry, Carey, Carrie, carry, Cary, chary, Gary,

gharry, harry, Harry, Larry,
marry, nary, parry, Shari, tarry
• glengarry, miscarry, safari,
shikari • cash-and-carry, hari-
kari, intermarry, Stradivari
• Tom, Dick, and Harry

arryl \ar-əl\ see ARREL[2]

ars \ärz\ Kars, Lars, Mars, ours
• behind bars, Stars and
Bars— *also* -s, -'s, *and* -s'
forms of nouns and -s *forms
of verbs listed at* AR[3]

arsal \är-səl\ parcel, tarsal
• metatarsal, part and parcel

arse[1] \ärs\ arse, farce, parse,
sparse

arse[2] \ärz\ see ARS

arsh \ärsh\ harsh, marsh
• démarche, salt marsh

arshal \är-shəl\ see ARTIAL

arshall \är-shəl\ see ARTIAL

arshen \är-shən\ harshen,
martian

arsi \är-sē\ see ARCY

arsis \är-səs\ see ARSUS

arsle \äs-əl\ see OSSAL

arson \ärs-ᵊn\ arson, Carson,
parson

arsus \är-səs\ arsis, tarsus,
Tarsus • catharsis • metatarsus

art[1] \ärt\ art, Art, Bart, cart, chart,
Chartres, dart, fart, hart, Harte,
heart, kart, mart, part, Sartre,
scart, smart, start, tart • apart,
at heart, bar chart, blackheart,
bogart, Bogart, by heart, clip
art, compart, crash cart, depart,

Descartes, dispart, dogcart,
Earhart, eye chart, false start,
fine art, flowchart, folk art,
forepart, Froissart, go-cart, golf
cart, greenheart, handcart,
head start, Hobart, impart, in
part, jump-start, junk art, kick-
start, mouthpart, Mozart, op
art, outsmart, oxcart, oxheart,
pie chart, pop art, pushcart,
rampart, real part, redstart,
restart, street-smart, Stuttgart,
sweetheart, take heart, take
part, tea cart, time chart,
tipcart, tramp art, upstart, voice
part • à la carte, anti-art,
applecart, beauty part, bleeding
heart, Bonaparte, change of
heart, counterpart, egg and
dart, fall apart, flying start, for
one's part, heart-to-heart,
Liddell Hart, lose one's heart,
martial art, mini-mart, multipart,
on one's part, open-heart,
plastic art, poles apart,
purpleheart, Purple Heart,
running start, set apart, take
apart, term of art, underpart,
upperpart • conceptual art, for
the most part, kinetic art,
minimal art, optical art,
performance art, practical art,
state-of-the-art

art[2] \ȯrt\ see ORT[1]

arta \är-tə\ Marta, Sparta
• Jakarta • Magna Carta, Santa
Marta, Surakarta, yogyakarta

artable \ärt-ə-bəl\ see ARTIBLE

artan[1] \ärt-ᵊn\ see ARTEN

artan[2] \ȯrt-ᵊn\ see ORTEN

artar \ärt-ər\ see ARTER[1]

arte¹ \ärt-ē\ see ARTY¹

arte² \ärt\ see ART¹

arted¹ \ärt-əd\ see EARTED

arted² \ort-əd\ see ORTED

arten \ärt-ᵊn\ Barton, carton, hearten, marten, martin, Martin, smarten, Spartan, tartan • baum marten, dishearten, Dumbarton, freemartin, pine marten, Saint Martin • kindergarten, purple marten

arter¹ \ärt-ər\ barter, carter, Carter, charter, darter, garter, martyr, starter, tartar • kick-starter, nonstarter, self-starter, snail darter • protomartyr—*also* -er *forms of adjectives listed at* ART¹

arter² \ot-ər\ see ATER¹

arter³ \ort-ər\ see ORTER

artern \ot-ərn\ see AUTERNE

artery \ärt-ə-rē\ artery, martyry

artes \ärt\ see ART¹

artford \ärt-fərd\ Hartford, Hertford

arth \ärth\ garth, Garth, hearth • Hogarth • open-hearth

arti \ärt-ē\ see ARTY¹

artial \är-shəl\ marshal, Marshal, Marshall, martial, Martial, partial • court-martial, earl marshal, field marshal, grand marshal, impartial, sky marshal

artian \är-shən\ see ARSHEN

artible \ärt-ə-bəl\ partible, startable • impartible, restartable

artic¹ \ärt-ik\ arctic, Arctic • antarctic, Antarctic, cathartic, Nearctic • Palearctic

artic² \ort-ik\ quartic, aortic

article \ärt-i-kəl\ article, particle • alpha particle, beta particle, microparticle, nanoparticle

artile \ort-ᵊl\ see ORTAL

artily \ärt-ᵊl-ē\ artily, heartily

artin \ärt-ᵊn\ see ARTEN

arting \ärt-iŋ\ carting, charting, karting, parting, starting • flowcharting, self-starting —*also* -ing *forms of verbs listed at* ART¹

artisan \ärt-ə-zən\ artisan, bartizan, partisan • bipartisan, nonpartisan

artist \ärt-əst\ artist, chartist, Chartist • junk artist, op artist, pop artist • Bonapartist, escape artist, martial artist

artizan \ärt-ə-zən\ see ARTISAN

artless \ärt-ləs\ artless, heartless

artlet \ärt-lət\ martlet, partlet, tartlet

artly¹ \ärt-lē\ partly, smartly, tartly

artly² \ort-lē\ see ORTLY

artment \ärt-mənt\ apartment, compartment, department • fire department, glove compartment

artner \ärt-nər\ partner • general partner, kindergartner, secret partner, silent partner • domestic partner

arton[1] \òrt-ᵊn\ see ORTON

arton[2] \ärt-ᵊn\ see ARTEN

artre \ärt\ see ART[1]

artres \ärt\ see ART[1]

artridge \är-trij\ cartridge, partridge

arts[1] \är\ see AR[3]

arts[2] \ärts\ Hartz • street smarts • private parts • master of arts, principal parts—*also* -s, 's, *and* -s' *forms of nouns and* -s *forms of verbs listed at* ART[1]

arture \är-chər\ see ARCHER

arty[1] \ärt-ē\ arty, hearty, party, smarty, tarty • Astarte, block party, ex parte, Havarti, hen party, house party, tea party, third-party, two-party, war party • Buonaparte, cocktail party, major party, minor party, slumber party • commedia dell'arte

arty[2] \òrt-ē\ see ORTY

artyr \ärt-ər\ see ARTER[1]

artyry \ärt-ə-rē\ see ARTERY

artz[1] \òrts\ see ORTS

artz[2] \ärts\ see ARTS[2]

aru \ä-rü\ Barú • Bukaru • Pakanbaru

arum[1] \är-əm\ larum • alarum

arum[2] \er-əm\ arum, carom, harem, Sarum • Muharram, Old Sarum • harum-scarum • arbiter elegantiarum

arus \ar-əs\ see ARIS[2]

arva \är-və\ larva, pareve • Delmarva

arval \är-vəl\ see ARVEL

arve[1] \ärv\ carve, starve, varve

arve[2] \är-və\ see ARVA

arvel \är-vəl\ carvel, larval, marvel

arven \är-vən\ carven, Marvin • Caernarvon

arvin \är-vən\ see ARVEN

arvon \är-vən\ see ARVEN

ary[1] \er-ē\ aerie, airy, berry, bury, Carey, Cary, Cherie, cherry, Cherry, chary, clary, dairy, Derry, faerie, fairy, ferry, Gary, Gerry, glairy, glary, hairy, Jerry, kerry, Kerry, Mary, marry, merry, Merry, nary, perry, Perry, prairie, quaere, query, scary, serry, Shari, sherry, skerry, Sperry, terry, Terry, vary, very, wary, wherry • baneberry, barberry, bayberry, bearberry, bilberry, bing cherry, black-berry, black cherry, blaeberry, blueberry, Bradbury, bunch-berry, Burberry, canary, Canary, Carberry, chokeberry, chokecherry, cloudberry, contrary, costmary, cowberry, cranberry, crowberry, deer-berry, dewberry, equerry, gooseberry, ground-cherry, hackberry, Hail Mary, hegari, inkberry, Juneberry, knobkerrie, library, mulberry, nondairy, pokeberry, primary, raspberry, rosemary, Rosemary, scalare, shadberry, sheepberry, snow-berry, soapberry, strawberry, summary, sweet cherry, teaberry, tilbury, tooth fairy, twinberry, unwary, vagary, wheat berry, wolfberry, youngberry • actuary, adversary, airy-fairy, ancillary, antiquary, apiary, arbitrary, aviary, axillary, bacillary, beauty berry, beriberi, bestiary, biliary, black raspberry, Bloody Mary, boysenberry, breviary, budgetary, calamari, calamary, candleberry, Canterbury, capillary, carpellary, cassowary, catenary, cautionary, cavitary, cemetery, centenary, certiorari, checkerberry, chinaberry, cometary, commentary, commissary, condottiere, coralberry, corollary, coronary, culinary, customary, dictionary, dietary, dignitary, dingleberry, dromedary, dysentery, elderberry, emissary, estuary, farkleberry, February, formulary, fragmentary, fritillary, functionary, funerary, honorary, huckleberry, intermarry, janissary, January, lamasery, lapidary, lectionary, legendary, legionary, lingonberry, literary, loganberry, luminary, mammillary, mandatary, maxillary, medullary, mercenary, miliary, military, millenary, milliary, millinery, miserere, missionary, momentary, monastery, monetary, mortuary, necessary, ordinary, ossuary, partridgeberry, pensionary, pigmentary, planetary, Pondicherry, prebendary, presbytery, pulmonary, quaternary, red mulberry, reliquary, rowanberry,

salivary, salmonberry, salutary, sanctuary, sanguinary, sanitary, secondary, secretary, sedentary, seminary, serviceberry, silverberry, solitary, sour cherry, stationary, stationery, statuary, Stradivari, subcontrary, sublunary, sugarberry, sumptuary, syllabary, temporary, tertiary, thimbleberry, Tipperary, Tom and Jerry, topiary, tributary, tutelary, Typhoid Mary, unitary, urinary, vestiary, Virgin Mary, visionary, voluntary, vulnerary, Waterbury, whortleberry, winterberry • apothecary, bicentenary, confectionary, confectionery, consigliere, constabulary, contemporary, deflationary, disciplinary, discretionary, diversionary, epistolary, exclusionary, expansionary, extemporary, extraordinary, fiduciary, hereditary, illusionary, imaginary, incendiary, inflationary, insanitary, intercalary, interlibrary, involuntary, itinerary, judiciary, lending library, marionberry, nonmilitary, obituary, olallieberry, on the contrary, pecuniary, pituitary, precautionary, preliminary, presidiary, probationary, proprietary, provisionary, reactionary, subliterary, subsidiary, tercentenary, uncustomary, unnecessary, unsanitary, veterinary, vocabulary, voluptuary • antimilitary, beneficiary, devolutionary, eleemosynary, evidentiary, evolutionary, extraliterary, insurrectionary, intermediary, interplanetary, paramilitary, penitentiary, quatercentenary, revolutionary, semicentenary, sesquicentenary, supernumerary, valetudinary

ary² \ar-ē\ see ARRY³

ary³ \är-ē\ see ARI¹

aryan¹ \er-ē-ən\ see ARIAN¹

aryan² \ar-ē-ən\ see ARIAN²

aryl \ar-əl\ see ARREL²

as¹ \ash\ see ASH³

as² \as\ see ASS³

as³ \az\ see AZZ

as⁴ \ä\ see A¹

as⁵ \äsh\ see ASH¹

as⁶ \äz\ see OISE¹

as⁷ \əz\ see EUSE¹

as⁸ \äs\ see OS¹

as⁹ \ȯ\ see AW¹

asa¹ \äs-ə\ casa, fossa, glossa, Lhasa, masa, Ossa, Vaasa • Al-Hasa, kielbasa, Kinshasa, Landrace, Mombasa • Kalidasa • tabula rasa

asa² \äz-ə\ see AZA¹

asa³ \as-ə\ see ASSA

asable¹ \ā-zə-bəl\ grazeable • persuasible • paraphrasable

asable² \ā-sə-bəl\ see ACEABLE

asal¹ \ā-səl\ basal, Basil • staysail • forestaysail

asal² \ā-zəl\ basal, Basil, hazel, Hazel, nasal, phrasal • appraisal, Azazel, witch hazel

asally \āz-lē\ see AISLEY

asca \as-kə\ see ASKA

ascal \as-kəl\ paschal, rascal

ascan \as-kən\ see ASKIN

ascar \as-kər\ see ASKER

ascence¹ \ās-ᵊns\ nascence • complacence, complaisance, renascence

ascence² \as-ᵊns\ nascence • renascence

ascent¹ \as-ᵊnt\ nascent, passant • renascent

ascent² \ās-ᵊnt\ see ACENT

asch¹ \ask\ see ASK

asch² \äsh\ see ASH¹

asch³ \ȯsh\ see ASH²

aschal \as-kəl\ see ASCAL

ascia¹ \ā-shə\ see ACIA

ascia² \ash-ə\ see ASHA²

ascible \as-ə-bəl\ see ASSABLE

ascicle \as-i-kəl\ see ASSICAL

asco¹ \äs-kō\ see OSCOE

asco² \as-kō\ Belasco, fiasco, Tabasco

ascon \as-kən\ see ASKIN

ascot \as-kət\ see ASKET

ascus \as-kəs\ Damascus, Velázquez

ase¹ \ās\ see ACE¹

ase² \āz\ see AZE¹

ase³ \äz\ see OISE¹

asel \āz-əl\ see OZZLE

ased \āst\ see ACED

aseless \ā-sləs\ see ACELESS

aseman \ā-smən\ see ACEMAN

asement \ās-mənt\ basement, casement • abasement, debasement, encasement • bargain-basement, self-abasement

aser[1] \ā-sər\ see ACER[1]

aser[2] \ā-zər\ see AZER

asey \ā-sē\ see ACY

ash[1] \äsh\ Bosch, bosh, cosh, Foch, frosh, gosh, gouache, josh, mâche, mosh, nosh, posh, quash, slosh, squash, swash, tosh, wash • awash, backwash, blackwash, cohosh, czardas, Dias, downwash, eyewash, galosh, ganache, goulash, kibosh, Lammasch, midrash, mishmash, mouth-wash, musquash, Oskash, panache, rainwash, Siwash, whitewash, wish-wash • acorn squash, black cohosh, blue cohosh, hamantasch, hubbard squash, mackintosh, McIntosh, summer squash, winter squash

ash[2] \ȯsh\ Bosch, Foch, gosh, quash, slosh, squash, swash, wash • awash, backwash, Balkhash, blackwash, brain-wash, brioche, Bydgoszcz, car wash, downwash, eyewash, hogwash, mouthwash, out-wash, prewash, rainwash, Siwash, wet wash, whitewash, wish-wash • acorn squash, hamantasch, hubbard squash, summer squash, winter squash

ash[3] \ash\ Asch, ash, bash, brash, cache, cash, clash, crash, dash, fash, flash, gash, gnash, hash, lash, mash, Nash, pash, plash, rash, sash, slash, smash, splash, stash, thrash, thresh, trash • abash, backlash, backslash, backsplash, Balkhash, bone ash, calash, Chumash, cold cash, czardas, encash, eyelash, fly ash, gate-crash, goulash, green flash, heat rash, hot flash, Lagash, mishmash, moustache, mustache, panache, potash, rehash, slapdash, soutache, stramash, tongue-lash, unlash, Wabash, whiplash, white ash • balderdash, calabash, diaper rash, mountain ash, nettle rash, petty cash, prickly rash, soda ash, sour mash, succotash • red flannel hash, settle one's hash

asha[1] \äsh-ə\ kasha, pasha, quassia • dishdasha, Falasha

asha[2] \ash-ə\ cassia, fascia, pasha

ashan \ash-ən\ see ASSION

ashed[1] \ȯsht\ sloshed • stonewashed, unwashed • acid-washed—also -ed forms of verbs listed at ASH[2]

ashed[2] \asht\ dashed, Rasht, smashed • unabashed—also -ed forms of verbs listed at ASH[3]

ashen \ash-ən\ see ASSION

asher[1] \äsh-ər\ josher, mosher, nosher, squasher, swasher, washer • dishwasher

asher[2] \ȯsh-ər\ swasher, washer • brainwasher, dishwasher, whitewasher

asher[3] \ash-ər\ Asher, basher, clasher, crasher, dasher, flasher, lasher, masher, rasher, slasher, smasher, splasher, thrasher • backlasher, gate-crasher • atom-smasher, haberdasher

ashew \ash-ü\ cachou, cashew

ashi[1] \äsh-ē\ see ASHY[1]

ashi[2] \ash-ē\ see ASHY[2]

ashing \ash-iŋ\ crashing, dashing, flashing, mashing, slashing, smashing • tongue-lashing—also -ing forms of verbs listed at ASH[3]

ashion \ash-ən\ see ASSION

asht \asht\ see ASHED[2]

ashy[1] \äsh-ē\ dashi, Iasi, Kashi, Shashi, squashy, washy • Funabashi, Lubumbashi, Toyohashi, wishy-washy

ashy[2] \ash-ē\ ashy, flashy, Kashi, splashy, trashy

asi[1] \äs-ē\ see OSSY[1]

asi[2] \äz-ē\ see AZI[1]

asi[3] \äsh-ē\ see ASHY[1]

asia \ā-zhə\ Asia • aphasia, Aspasia, Austrasia, Caucasia, dysphasia, Eurasia, fantasia, Laurasia, Malaysia • anaplasia, Anastasia, Australasia, euthanasia, metaplasia, neoplasia • antonomasia, paronomasia

asian[1] \ā-shən\ see ATION[1]

asian[2] \ā-zhən\ see ASION

asible \ā-zə-bəl\ see ASABLE[1]

asic \ā-zik\ phasic • aphasic, biphasic, diphasic, dysphasic • euthanasic, multiphasic, polyphasic

asid \as-əd\ see ACID

asie \ā-sē\ see ACY

asil[1] \as-əl\ see ASSEL[2]

asil[2] \az-əl\ see AZZLE

asil[3] \ās-əl\ see ASAL[1]

asil[4] \āz-əl\ see ASAL[2]

asil[5] \āz-əl\ see OZZLE

asin \ās-ᵊn\ see ASON[1]

asing[1] \ā-siŋ\ see ACING

asing[2] \ā-ziŋ\ see AISING

asion \ā-zhən\ Asian, suasion • Abkhazian, abrasion, Caucasian, corrasion, dissuasion, equation, Eurasian, evasion, invasion, occasion, persuasion, pervasion, Verpasian, • Amerasian, anti-Asian, Athanasian, Australasian, dermabrasion, on occasion, Rabelaisian, Transcaucasian

asional \āzh-nəl\ equational, occasional

asis[1] \ā-səs\ basis, stasis • oasis • hemostasis • homeostasis

asis[2] \as-əs\ see ASSIS[2]

asium \ā-zē-əm\ dichasium, gymnasium

asive \ā-siv\ suasive • abrasive, assuasive, corrasive, dissuasive, embracive, evasive, invasive, persuasive, pervasive • noninvasive

ask \ask\ ask, bask, Basque, cask, casque, flask, mask, masque, Pasch, Rask, task • death mask, face mask, gas mask, ski mask, unmask • Florence flash, Monegasque, multitask, photomask, shadow mask, take to task, vacuum flask • oxygen mask

aska \as-kə\ Alaska, Itasca, Nebraska • Athabaska, Unalaska

askan \as-kən\ see ASKIN

asked \ast\ see AST²

asker \as-kər\ lascar, masker • Madagascar

asket \as-kət\ ascot, Ascot, basket, casket, gasket • breadbasket, handbasket, wastebasket, workbasket • blow a gasket, market basket

askin \as-kən\ Baskin, gascon, gaskin • Alaskan, Tarascan • Athabaskan

asking \as-kiŋ\ multitasking— *also* -ing *forms of verbs listed at* ASK

asm \az-əm\ chasm, plasm, spasm • chiasm, orgasm, phantasm, sarcasm • cataplasm, chiliasm, cytoplasm, ectoplasm, endoplasm, neoplasm, pleonasm, protoplasm, sarcoplasm • enthusiasm, iconoclasm

asma \az-mə\ asthma, plasma • chiasma, miasma, phantasma

asman \az-mən\ see ASMINE

asmine \az-mən\ jasmine, Tasman

asn't \əz-ᵊnt\ doesn't, wasn't

aso¹ \as-ō\ see ASSO¹

aso² \äs-ō\ see ASSO²

ason¹ \ās-ᵊn\ basin, caisson, chasten, hasten, Jason, mason, Mason • Foxe Basin, Freemason, Great Basin, stonemason, washbasin • diapason, Donets Basin

ason² \äz-ᵊn\ see AZON

asp \asp\ asp, clasp, gasp, grasp, hasp, rasp • enclasp, handclasp, last-gasp, unclasp

asper \as-pər\ clasper, grasper, jasper, Jasper, rasper

asperate \as-prət\ aspirate • exasperate

aspirate \as-prət\ see ASPERATE

asque \ask\ see ASK

asquer \as-kər\ see ASKER

ass¹ \ās\ see ACE¹

ass² \äs\ see OS¹

ass³ \as\ ass, bass, Bass, brass, class, crass, frass, gas, glass, grass, Grasse, has, lass, mass, pass, sass, strass, tace, tasse, trass, vas, wrasse • admass, air mass, alas, Alsace, amass, art glass, avgas, badass, bagasse, band-pass, beach grass, bear grass, bent grass, black bass, Black Mass, bluegrass, bromegrass, bunchgrass, bypass, cased glass, cheat-grass, cordgrass, crabgrass, crevasse, crown grass, cuirass, cut glass, cut-grass, declass, degas, Donbas, drop pass,

Drygas, eelgrass, en masse, eyeglass, first-class, flint glass, float glass, folk mass, ground glass, groundmass, hand glass, harass, hard-ass, haul ass, high-class, high mass, hourglass, impasse, jackass, jump pass, kelp bass, kick ass, kick-ass, knotgrass, Kuzbass, landmass, lead glass, low mass, Madras, milk glass, morass, nonclass, nut grass, oat grass, outclass, outgas, palliasse, Petras, pier glass, plate glass, quack grass, quartz glass, red mass, repass, rest mass, ribgrass, rock bass, rubasse, ryegrass, salt grass, sandglass, saw grass, screen pass, sea bass, sheet glass, shortgrass, smart-ass, South Pass, spot pass, spun glass, spyglass, stained glass, star grass, striped bass, subclass, sunglass, sung mass, surpass, sweetgrass, switchgrass, sword grass, tallgrass, teargas, third-class, trespass, Troas, turfgrass, wheatgrass, white bass, wineglass, wire grass, wiseass, witchgrass, word class, world-class, yard grass • biogas, biomass, bottled gas, Brenner Pass, cabin class, Cajon Pass, channel bass, cheval glass, cocktail glass, come to pass, demiglace, demitasse, Donner Pass, dressing glass, fiberglass, forward pass, gallowglass, gravitas, Hallowmas, hippocras, horse's ass, interclass, isinglass, Khyber Pass, Kiribati, largemouth bass, laughing gas, lemongrass, looking glass, Loveland Pass, lower-class, master class, middle-class, Montparnasse, opera glass, outlet pass, overclass, overpass, Plexiglas, Rogers Pass, ruby glass, safety glass, sassafras, second-class, shovel pass, Simplon Pass, smallmouth bass, solar mass, solemn mass, superclass, tourist class, underclass, underpass, upper-class, votive mass, water glass, weatherglass,working-class • atomic mass, critical mass, Depression glass, electron gas, laughing jackass, optical glass, play-action pass, snake in the grass, venetian glass, volcanic glass • Karakoram Pass

assa \as-ə\ massa, NASA • madrassa, Manasseh • Lake Nyasa

assable \as-ə-bəl\ chasuble, passable, passible • impassable, impassible, irascible, surpassable • unsurpassable

assail \äs-əl\ see OSSAL

assailer \äs-ə-lər\ see OSSULAR

assal \as-əl\ see ASSEL²

assant \as-ᵊnt\ see ASCENT¹

assar \as-ər\ see ASSER

asse¹ \as\ see ASS³

asse² \äs\ see OS¹

assed \ast\ see AST²

assee \as-ē\ see ASSY

asseh \as-ə\ see ASSA

assel¹ \äs-əl\ see OSSAL

assel² \as-əl\ acyl, Basil, castle, facile, gracile, hassle, Kassel, passel, tassel, vassal, wrestle • forecastle, Newcastle, Oldcastle

asser \as-ər\ crasser, gasser, Nasser, placer • amasser, harasser • antimacassar

asset \as-ət\ see ACET²

assia¹ \ash-ə\ see ASHA²

assia² \äsh-ə\ see ASHA¹

assian \ash-ən\ see ASSION

assible \as-ə-bəl\ see ASSABLE

assic \as-ik\ classic • Jurassic, Liassic, thalassic, Triassic • neoclassic, pseudoclassic, semiclassic

assical \as-i-kəl\ classical, fascicle • postclassical, unclassical • semiclassical

assid \as-əd\ see ACID

assie¹ \as-ē\ see ASSY

assie² \äs-ē\ see OSSY¹

assim¹ \äs-əm\ see OSSUM

assim² \as-əm\ passim • sargassum

assin \as-ᵊn\ see ASTEN²

assion \ash-ən\ ashen, fashion, passion, ration • Circassian, compassion, dispassion, high fashion, impassion, refashion, Wakashan • Bristol fashion • after a fashion

assional \ash-nəl\ see ATIONAL³

assis¹ \as-ē\ see ASSY

assis² \as-əs\ classis, Crassus, stasis • Parnassus • Halicarnassus

assist \ə-sist\ bassist, racist • contrabassist, double bassist

assive \as-iv\ massive, passive • impassive

assle \as-əl\ see ASSEL²

assless \as-ləs\ classless, glassless, grassless, massless

assment \as-mənt\ amassment, harassment

assness \as-nəs\ see ASTNESS

asso¹ \as-ō\ basso, lasso, Tasso • El Paso, Picasso, sargasso, Sargasso

asso² \äs-ō\ Picasso • Campo Basso • Burkina Faso

assock \as-ək\ cassock, hassock

assum \as-əm\ see ASSIM²

assus \as-əs\ see ASSIS

assy \as-ē\ brassy, chassis, classy, dassie, gassy, glacis, glassie, glassy, grassy, lassie, massy, sassy • morassy • Malagasy, Tallahassee • Haile Selassie

ast¹ \əst\ see UST¹

ast² \ast\ bast, blast, cast, caste, clast, fast, gast, ghast, hast, last, mast, Nast, past, vast • aghast, at last, avast, bedfast, Belfast, bombast, broadcast, bypast, contrast, dicast, dismast, downcast, dynast, fantast, flypast, forecast, foremast, forepassed, full blast, gymnast, half-caste, half-mast, handfast, holdfast, lightfast, mainmast, makefast, marchpast, miscast, newscast, oblast, offcast, outcast, outcaste, precast, recast, repast, roughcast, sandblast, sand-cast, shamefast, sportscast, steadfast, sunfast, topmast, trade-last, typecast, unasked, upcast, webcast, windblast • acid-fast, at long last, captain's mast, chiliast, cineast, colorcast, colorfast, counterblast, flabbergast, foretopmast, hard-and-fast, maintopmast, mizzenmast, narrowcast, opencast, overcast, pederast, phase-contrast, plaster cast, rebroadcast, scholiast, simulcast, telecast, weathercast • ecdysiast, encomiast, enthusiast, iconoclast, radiocast, symposiast *—also -ed forms of verbs listed at* ASS³

asta¹ \äs-tə\ *see* OSTA

asta² \as-tə\ Rasta • canasta, Jocasta, Mount Shasta

astable \at-ə-bəl\ *see* ATIBLE

astard \as-tərd\ bastard, dastard, plastered

aste¹ \āst\ *see* ACED

aste² \ast\ *see* AST²

asted \as-təd\ blasted, masted, plastid*—also -ed forms of verbs listed at* AST²

asteful \āst-fəl\ tasteful, wasteful • distasteful

asten¹ \ās-ᵉn\ *see* ASON¹

asten² \as-ᵉn\ fasten • assassin, unfasten

aster¹ \ā-stər\ baster, taster, waster • wine taster

aster² \as-tər\ aster, Astor, blaster, caster, castor, Castor, faster, gaster, master, pastor, plaster, raster • bandmaster, brewmaster, broadcaster, bushmaster, cadastre, choirmaster, court plaster, disaster, dockmaster, drillmaster, grand master, headmaster, jumpmaster, linecaster, loadmaster, newscaster, old master, past master, paymaster, piastre, pilaster, postmaster, quizmaster, remaster, ringmaster, sandblaster, schoolmaster, scoutmaster, shinplaster, shipmaster, sportscaster, spymaster, surf caster, taskmaster, three-master, toastmaster, truckmaster, webcaster, wharfmaster, whoremaster, yardmaster • alabaster, burgomaster, cellar master, China aster, concertmaster, criticaster, ghetto blaster, harbormaster, ironmaster, mustard plaster, oleaster, overmaster, poetaster, quartermaster, rallymaster, stationmaster, telecaster, wagon master, weathercaster, Zoroaster

astered \as-tərd\ *see* ASTARD

astering \as-tə-riŋ\ plastering • overmastering*—also -ing forms of verbs listed at* ASTER

astes \as-tēz\ Ecclesiastes—*also -s, -'s, and -s' forms of nouns listed at* ASTY²

asthma \az-mə\ see ASMA

astian \as-chən\ see ASTION

astic \as-tik\ drastic, mastic, nastic, plastic, spastic • bombastic, dynastic, elastic, fantastic, gymnastic, monastic, sarcastic, scholastic, stochastic • anelastic, chiliastic, chloroplastic, holophrastic, Hudibrastic, inelastic, metaplastic, onomastic, orgiastic, paraphrastic, pederastic, periphrastic, pleonastic, pyroclastic, superplastic, thermoplastic • ecclesiastic, encomiastic, enthusiastic, iconoclastic, interscholastic • trip the light fantastic

astics \as-tiks\ gymnastics, slimnastics

astid \as-təd\ see ASTED

astie \as-tē\ see ASTY²

astiness \ā-stē-nəs\ hastiness, pastiness, tastiness

asting¹ \ā-stiŋ\ basting, wasting—*also -ing forms of verbs listed at* ACED

asting² \as-tiŋ\ casting, lasting • fly casting, linecasting, sand casting, surf casting, typecasting • central casting, everlasting, narrowcasting, overcasting—*also -ing forms of verbs listed at* AST²

astion \as-chən\ bastion • Erastian

astle \as-əl\ see ASSEL²

astly \ast-lē\ ghastly, lastly, vastly • steadfastly

astment \as-mənt\ see ASSMENT

astness \as-nəs\ crassness, fastness, gastness, pastness • lightfastness, steadfastness • colorfastness

asto \as-tō\ impasto • antipasto

astor \as-tər\ see ASTER²

astoral \as-trəl\ see ASTRAL

astral \as-trəl\ astral, pastoral, plastral • cadastral

astre \as-tər\ see ASTER²

astric \as-trik\ gastric • digastric • epigastric, hypogastric, monogastric, nasogastric

astrophe \as-trə-fē\ anastrophe, catastrophe

asty¹ \ā-stē\ hasty, pasty, tasty

asty² \as-tē\ blastie, nasty, pasty, vasty • capacity, contrasty • Cornish pasty, pederasty, rhinoplasty • angioplasty, bepharoplasty, osteoplasty, overcapacity

asuble \as-ə-bəl\ see ASSABLE

asure¹ \ā-shər\ glacier, rasure • erasure

asure² \ā-zhər\ see AZIER

asy \as-ē\ see ASSY

at¹ \ä\ see A¹

at² \ät\ see OT¹

at³ \ət\ see UT¹

at⁴ \ȯt\ see OUGHT¹

at⁵ \at\ bat, batt, blat, brat, cat, Cat, catt, chat, chert, drat, fat, flat, frat, gat, gnat, hat, mat, Matt, matte, pat, Pat, phat, plait, plat, Pratt, rat, sat, scat, scatt, skat, slat, spat, splat, sprat, stat, tat, that, vat • all that, at bat, at that, backchat, bath mat, begat, brass hat, brickbat, brown fat, brown rat, bullbat, Cassatt, chitchat, cocked hat, combat, comsat, coon cat, cowpat, cravat, Croat, deep fat, defat, dingbat, doormat, expat, fat cat, fiat, firebrat, flat-hat, fly at, format, fruit bat, get at, go at, Hallstatt, hard hat, have at, hellcat, hepcat, high-hat, house cat, jurat, keep at, leaf fat, look at, Manx cat, MCAT, meerkat, milk fat, mole rat, mudflat, muscat, Muscat, muskrat, nonfat, old hat, pack rat, pick at, place mat, plug hat, polecat, pot hat, Rotblat, rug rat, Sadat, salt flat, savate, silk hat, slouch hat, sneeze at, snowcat, Sobat, stand pat, standpat, stonechat, strawhat, Surat, thereat, tin hat, tipcat, tomcat, top hat, trans fat, whereat, whinchat, white hat, wildcat, wombat, wool fat • acrobat, aerobat, aerostat, alley cat, apparat, Ararat, arrive at, assignat, autocrat, Automat, bell the cat, big brown bat, bureaucrat, butterfat, caveat, cervelat, Cheshire cat, chew the fat, civet cat, concordat, coolie hat, copycat, cowboy hat, democrat, diplomat, Dixiecrat, Eurocrat, fungo bat, habitat, hang one's hat, jungle cat, Kattegat, kleptocrat, Laundromat, leopard cat, marrowfat, mobocrat, monocrat, Montserrat, Norway rat, ochlocrat, off the bat, opera hat, pas de quatre, Persian cat, photostat, pit-a-pat, plutocrat, poke fun at, porkpie hat, pussycat, railroad flat, rat-a-tat, reformat, rheostat, scaredy-cat, semimatte, shovel hat, smell a rat, spoonbill cat, take aim at, technocrat, theocrat, thermostat, tiger cat, tit for tat, Uniate, vampire bat, water rat, welcome mat, where it's at, ziggurat • Angora cat, aristocrat, gerontocrat, go to the mat, heliostat, humidistat, Jehoshaphat, kangaroo rat, magnificat, meritocrat, Physiocrat, requiescat, Siamese cat, single combat, talk through one's hat, ten-gallon hat, thalassocrat, throw money at, under one's hat • proletariat, professoriat, secretariat

at⁶ \a\ see AH³

ata¹ \ät-e\ cotta, kata • balata, cantata, Carlotta, errata, fermata, frittata, La Plata, Maratha, Niigata, non grata, pinata, pro rata, reata, riata, regatta, ricotta, sonata, Sorata, toccata • caponata, Hirakata, Mar del Plata, serenata, terracotta, Uspallata, Yamagata • Basilicata, desiderata, inamorata, missa cantata, persona grata, res judicata • persona non grata, res adjudicata, Rio de la Plata

ata² \āt-ə\ beta, data, eta, strata, theta, zeta • muleta, peseta, potato, pro rata, substrata, tomato, viewdata

ata³ \at-ə\ data • errata, non grata, pro rata, reata, regatta, riata, viewdata • paramatta, Paramatta • persona grata • persona non grata

atable¹ \āt-ə-bəl\ datable, ratable, statable • debatable, dilatable, inflatable, locatable, relatable, rotatable, translatable • cultivatable, untranslatable

atable² \at-ə-bəl\ see ATIBLE

atal \āt-ᵊl\ fatal, natal, ratel, shtetl • hiatal, nonfatal, postnatal, prenatal • antenatal, neonatal, perinatal

atalie \at-ᵊl-ē\ see ATTILY

atally \āt-ᵊl-ē\ fatally, natally • postnatally, prenatally

atalyst \at-ᵊl-əst\ catalyst • philatelist

atan¹ \āt-ən\ see ATEN¹

atan² \at-ᵊn\ see ATIN²

atancy \āt-ᵊn-sē\ blatancy, latency • dilatancy

atant¹ \āt-ᵊnt\ blatant, latent, natant, patent • statant

atant² \at-ᵊnt\ patent • combatant • noncombatant

atar \āt-ər\ see OTTER

atary \āt-ə-rē\ see OTTERY

atch¹ \ech\ see ETCH

atch² \äch\ see OTCH

atch³ \öch\ see AUCH¹

atch⁴ \ach\ bach, batch, catch, cratch, hatch, klatch, latch, match, natch, patch, ratch, scratch, snatch, thatch • attach, book-match, bycatch, crosshatch, crosspatch, despatch, detach, dispatch, fair catch, from scratch, mismatch, night latch, nuthatch, oil patch, outmatch, potlatch, rematch, Sasquatch, slow match, test match, throatlatch, unlatch, Wasatch • booby hatch, circus catch, coffee klatch, escape hatch, kaffeeklatsch, over-match, safety match, shoestring catch, shoulder patch

atcher¹ \äch-ər\ botcher, watcher • bird-watcher, clock-watcher, debaucher, topnotcher

atcher² \ach-ər\ batcher, catcher, hatcher, matcher, satcher, scratcher, snatcher, stature, thatcher, Thatcher • cowcatcher, dispatcher, dogcatcher, dream catcher, eye-catcher, flycatcher, gnatcatcher, head-scratcher • body snatcher, oyster catcher, train dispatcher

atchet \ach-ət\ hatchet, latchet, ratchet • bury the hatchet

atchily \ach-ə-lē\ patchily, patchouli, scratchily

atching \ach-iŋ\ back-scratching, cross-hatching, eye-catching, head-scratching, nonmatching—*also* -ing *forms of verbs listed at* ATCH[4]

atchman \äch-mən\ see OTCHMAN

atchment \ach-mənt\
catchment, hatchment
• attachment, detachment

atchouli \ach-ə-lē\ see ATCHILY

atchy \ach-ē\ catchy, patchy, scratchy • Apache

ate[1] \āt\ ait, ate, bait, bate, blate, cate, Cate, crate, date, eight, fate, fete, freight, gait, gate, grate, great, haet, hate, Kate, late, mate, pate, plait, plate, prate, quoit, rate, sate, skate, slate, spate, state, straight, strait, teth, trait, wait, weight • abate, ablate, adnate, aerate, age-mate, agnate, airdate, airfreight, alate, arête, await, backdate, baldpate, bandmate, baseplate, Bass Strait, bedmate, bedplate, berate, birthrate, bistate, bite plate, blank slate, blind date, blue plate, bookplate, breastplate, casemate, castrate, caudate, cell plate, cerate, cheapskate, checkmate, chelate, chordate, citrate, classmate, clavate, cognate, collate, comate, conflate, connate, Cook Strait, cordate, create, cremate, crenate, curate, cut-rate, deadweight, death rate, debate, deflate, delate, dentate, derate, dictate, dilate, disrate, donate, doorplate, downstate, drawplate, elate, end plate, equate, estate, faceplate, falcate, fellate, filtrate, first-rate, fishplate, fixate, flatmate, floodgate, fluxgate, flyweight, folate, formate, Free State, frustrate, gelate, gestate, ground state, gyrate, hamate, hastate, headgate, Hell Gate, helpmate, home plate, hot plate, housemate, hydrate, iceskate, inflate, ingrate, inmate, innate, instate, irate, jailbait, jugate, khanate, Kuwait, lactate, lapse rate, legate, liftgate, ligate, lightweight, liquate, lobate, locate, lunate, lustrate, lych-gate, lyrate, magnate, makebate, makeweight, mandate, messmate, migrate, misstate, mutate, nameplate, narrate, negate, Newgate, nitrate, notate, nutate, oblate, of late, orate, ornate, outwait, ovate, palmate, palpate, peltate, phonate, pinnate, placate, playdate, playmate, plicate, portrait, postdate, predate, primate, prime rate, probate, prolate, pronate, prorate, prostate, prostrate, pulsate, punctate, pupate, quadrate, rain date, ramate, rebate, red-bait, relate, restate, roommate, rostrate, rotate, saccate, schoolmate, seatmate, sedate, sensate, septate, serrate, shipmate, short weight, slave state, soleplate, soul mate, spectate, spicate, squamate, stagnate, stalemate, stellate, striate, sublate, substrate, sulcate, summate, tailgate, teammate, Tebet, tenth-rate, ternate, terneplate, testate, third-rate, tinplate, to date, toeplate, tollgate, tractate, translate, tristate, truncate, unweight, update, uprate, upstate, V-8, vacate, vallate, valvate, vibrate, virgate, vulgate, whitebait, workmate, zonate • abdicate, abnegate, abrogate, absorbate, acclimate, acerbate, acetate, activate, actuate, acylate, adsorbate, advocate, adulate, adumbrate, aggravate, aggregate, agitate, allocate, altercate, alternate, ambulate, amputate, animate, annotate, annulate, antedate, antiquate, apartheid, apostate, approbate, arbitrate, arcuate, arrogate, aspirate, auscultate, automate, aviate, bantamweight, Bering Strait, bifurcate, billingsgate, bipinnate, boilerplate, bombinate, brachiate, buffer state, cabinmate, Cabot Strait, cachinnate, calculate, calibrate, caliphate, candidate, cannulate, cantillate, capitate, captivate, carbonate, carbon-date, carinate, carload rate, castigate, catenate, cavitate, celebrate, cerebrate, chief of state, chlorinate, circinate, circulate, city-state, client state, cocreate, cogitate, colligate, collimate, collocate, commentate, commutate, compensate, complicate, concentrate, condensate, confiscate, conglobate, conjugate, consecrate, constellate, consternate, constipate, consummate, contemplate, copperplate, copulate, coronate, correlate, corrugate, coruscate,

counterweight, crenulate, crepitate, criminate, cruciate, cucullate, culminate, cultivate, cumulate, cuneate, cupulate, cuspidate, cyclamate, Davis Strait, deaerate, decimate, decollate, decorate, decussate, dedicate, defalcate, defecate, deflagrate, dehydrate, delegate, demarcate, demonstrate, denigrate, Denmark Strait, depilate, deviate, deprecate, depredate, derivate, derogate, desecrate, desiccate, designate, desolate, desquamate, detonate, devastate, deviate, digitate, diplomate, discarnate, dislocate, dissertate, dissipate, distillate, divagate, dominate, double date, duplicate, edentate, educate, elevate, elongate, eluate, emanate, emigrate, emirate, emulate, enervate, ephorate, escalate, estimate, estivate, excavate, exchange rate, exculpate, execrate, expiate, explicate, expurgate, exsiccate, extirpate, extricate, exudate, fabricate, fascinate, fashion plate, featherweight, fecundate, federate, fenestrate, festinate, fibrillate, first estate, flabellate, flagellate, flocculate, fluctuate, fluoridate, foliate, formulate, fornicate, fourth estate, foviate, fractionate, fragmentate, fulminate, fumigate, fustigate, geminate, generate, germinate, glaciate, Golden Gate, graduate, granulate, gratulate, gravitate, heavyweight, hebetate, herniate, hesitate, hibernate,

Hudson Strait, hundredweight, hyphenate, ideate, illustrate, imamate, imbricate, imitate, immigrate, immolate, impetrate, implicate, imprecate, impregnate, incarnate, increate, incubate, inculcate, inculpate, incurvate, indagate, indicate, indurate, infiltrate, in-line skate, in-migrate, innervate, innovate, insensate, insolate, inspissate, instigate, insulate, interstate, intestate, intimate, intonate, intraplate, inundate, invocate, iodate, Iron Gate, irrigate, irritate, isolate, iterate, jubilate, juniorate, lacerate, laminate, Latinate, laureate, legislate, levigate, levitate, liberate, license plate, liquidate, litigate, littermate, lubricate, macerate, machinate, magistrate, marginate, margravate, marinate, masticate, masturbate, maturate, mediate, medicate, meditate, meliorate, menstruate, microstate, micturate, middleweight, militate, ministrate, miscreate, mithridate, mitigate, moderate, modulate, mortgage rate, motivate, multistate, mutilate, nation-state, nauseate, navigate, neonate, nictitate, niobate, nominate, numerate, obfuscate, objurgate, obligate, obovate, obviate, on a plate, operate, opiate, orchestrate, ordinate, oscillate, osculate, out-migrate, out-of-date, overstate, overweight, ovulate, paginate, palliate, palpitate, paperweight, patinate, peculate, penetrate, penny-

weight, percolate, perennate, perforate, permeate, perorate, perpetrate, personate, police state, pollinate, populate, postulate, potentate, predicate, procreate, profligate, promulgate, propagate, prorogate, pullulate, pulmonate, punctuate, quantitate, rabbinate, radiate, real estate, recreate, re-create, reclinate, regulate, reinstate, relegate, relocate, reluctate, remonstrate, renovate, replicate, reprobate, resonate, retardate, retranslate, roller-skate, roseate, rubricate, ruinate, ruminate, runagate, running mate, rusticate, sagittate, salivate, sanitate, satiate, saturate, scintillate, second-rate, segregate, self-portrait, separate, sequestrate, seriate, ship of state, sibilate, silver plate, simulate, sinuate, situate, solid state, speculate, spoliate, stablemate, starting gate, steady state, stimulate, stipulate, strangulate, stridulate, stylobate, subjugate, sublimate, subrogate, subulate, suffocate, sultanate, Sunda Strait, supplicate, surrogate, syncopate, syndicate, tablemate, tabulate, target date, Tatar Strait, terminate, tessellate, tête-à-tête, thirty-eight, titillate, titivate, tolerate, transmigrate, transudate, tribulate, tribunate, trifurcate, trilobate, tripinnate, triplicate, tunicate, turbinate, ulcerate, ululate, umbellate, uncinate, underrate, understate, underweight, undulate, ungulate, urinate, vaccinate, vacillate, validate, valuate, variate, vaticinate, vegetate, venerate, ventilate, vertebrate, vicarate, vindicate, violate, vitiate, water gate, Watergate, welfare state, welterweight • abbreviate, abominate, accelerate, accentuate, accommodate, acculturate, accumulate, adjudicate, adulterate, affiliate, agglomerate, alienate, alleviate, alliterate, amalgamate, ameliorate, amyl nitrate, annihilate, annunciate, anticipate, apostolate, appreciate, appropriate, approximate, arpeggiate, articulate, asphyxiate, assassinate, asseverate, assimilate, associate, at any rate, attenuate, authenticate, barbiturate, bicarbonate, calumniate, capacitate, capitulate, catholicate, certificate, coagulate, coelenterate, collaborate, commemorate, commiserate, communicate, compassionate, concatenate, conciliate, confabulate, confederate, conglomerate, congratulate, consolidate, contaminate, cooperate, coordinate, corroborate, deactivate, debilitate, decapitate, decelerate, decerebrate, deconcentrate, deconsecrate, decorticate, decrepitate, de-escalate, defibrinate, defoliate, defribrillate, degenerate, deliberate, delineate, de-modulate, denominate, depopulate, depreciate,

deracinate, deregulate, desegregate, desiderate, detoxicate, devaluate, diaconate, dilapidate, discriminate, disintegrate, disseminate, dissimulate, dissociate, domesticate, effectuate, ejaculate, elaborate, electroplate, eliminate, elucidate, emaciate, emancipate, emasculate, encapsulate, enumerate, enunciate, episcopate, equivocate, eradicate, etiolate, evacuate, evaluate, evaporate, eventuate, eviscerate, exacerbate, exaggerate, exasperate, excited state, excogitate, excoriate, exfoliate, exhilarate, exonerate, expatiate, expatriate, expec-torate, expostulate, expro-priate, extenuate, exterminate, extrapolate, facilitate, felicitate, fish or cut bait, garrison state, gesticulate, habilitate, habit-uate, hallucinate, humiliate, hydrogenate, hypothecate, illuminate, impersonate, inactivate, inaugurate, incarcer-ate, incinerate, incorporate, incriminate, indoctrinate, inebriate, infatuate, infuriate, ingratiate, ingurgitate, initiate, inoculate, inseminate, insinu-ate, instantiate, intercalate, interpolate, interrelate, interro-gate, intimidate, intoxicate, invalidate, investigate, in-vigorate, irradiate, Italianate, Korea Strait, lanceolate, legitimate, luxuriate, mandari-nate, manipulate, matriarchate, matriculate, Merthiolate, necessitate, negotiate, non-candidate, obliterate, officiate, Orange Free State, orientate, originate, oxygenate, participate, particulate, patriarchate, patriciate, perambulate, peregrinate, perpetuate, pontificate, precipitate, predestinate, predominate, prefabricate, premeditate, preponderate, prevaricate, procrastinate, prognosticate, proliferate, propitiate, proportionate, quadruplicate, quintuplicate, reciprocate, recriminate, recuperate, redecorate, reduplicate, reeducate, refrigerate, regenerate, regurgitate, reincarnate, reintegrate, reiterate, rejuvenate, remunerate, repatriate, repudiate, resuscitate, retaliate, reticulate, revaluate, reverberate, scholasticate, second estate, self-flagellate, self-immolate, self-pollinate, seventy-eight, sextuplicate, Singapore Strait, sophisticate, subordinate, substantiate, syllabicate, tergiversate, transliterate, triangulate, vanity plate, variegate, vituperate, vociferate • adjustable rate, circumambulate, circumnavigate, contraindicate, decontaminate, deteriorate, differentiate, disambiguate, disassociate, discombobulate, disorientate, disproportionate, excommunicate, expiration date, free-associate, hyperventilate, incapacitate, intermediate, interpenetrate, misappropriate, Moravian Gate,

multivariate, overcompensate, overeducate, overestimate, overmedicate, overpopulate, overstimulate, ratiocinate, recapitulate, rehabilitate, renegotiate, superannuate, supersaturate, transubstantiate, underestimate

ate² \at\ see AT⁵

ate³ \ät\ see OT¹

ate⁴ \ät-ē\ see ATI

ate⁵ \et\ see UT¹

ated \āt-əd\ dated, fated, gaited, gated, lated, pated, stated • belated, G-rated, ill-fated, outdated, related, striated, three-gaited, truncated, unbated, X-rated • addlepated, animated, antiquated, caffeinated, calculated, carbonated, castellated, complicated, corrugated, crenellated, dedicated, educated, elevated, hyphenated, integrated, laminated, liberated, mentholated, perforated, pileated, pixilated, saturated, simulated, syncopated, tessellated, unabated, uncreated, understated, variegated • affiliated, articulated, coordinated, decaffeinated, domesticated, encapsulated, incorporated, inebriated, interrelated, intoxicated, opinionated, premeditated, sophisticated, uncalculated, uncelebrated, uncomplicated, underinflated, unmediated, unmitigated, unsaturated, unsegregated

• superannuated, unadulterated, unanticipated, undereducated, under-populated, unsophisticated
• polyunsaturated, under-appreciated—*also* -ed *forms of verbs listed at* ATE[1]

ateful \āt-fəl\ fateful, grateful, hateful • ungrateful

atel[1] \et-əl\ see OTTLE

atel[2] \āt-əl\ see ATAL

ateless \āt-ləs\ dateless, stateless, weightless

atelist \at-əl-əst\ see ATALYST

ately[1] \āt-lē\ greatly, lately, stately, straightly, straitly, Whately • innately, irately, ornately, sedately • up-to-dately • Johnny-come-lately

ately[2] \at-əl-ē\ see ATTILY

atem \āt-əm\ see ATUM[1]

atement \āt-mənt\ statement
• abatement, debatement, misstatement, restatement
• overstatement, reinstatement, understatement

aten[1] \āt-ᵊn\ greaten, laten, Satan, straighten, straiten
• Keewatin

aten[2] \at-ᵊn\ see ATIN[2]

aten[3] \ät-ᵊn\ see OTTEN

atent[1] \āt-ᵊnt\ see ATANT[1]

atent[2] \at-ᵊnt\ see ATANT[2]

ater[1] \ȯt-ər\ daughter, slaughter, tauter, water • backwater, bathwater, bilgewater, black-water, blue-water, branch

water, breakwater, Clearwater, cold-water, cutwater, dewater, deepwater, dishwater, fire-water, first water, floodwater, forequarter, freshwater, goddaughter, Goldwater, granddaughter, gray water, groundwater, headwater, high-water, hindquarter, hold water, hot water, ice water, jerkwater, limewater, low water, make water, manslaughter, melt-water, rainwater, red water, rosewater, saltwater, seawater, self-slaughter, shearwater, springwater, stepdaughter, still water, tailwater, tap water, tidewater, tread water, waste-water, white-water • above water, Derwent Water, heavy water, holy water, in deep water, Javelle water, milk-and-water, mineral water, over-water, polywater, quinine water, running water, soda water, toilet water, underwater, Vichy water • dead in the water, fish out of water, hell or high water

ater[2] \āt-ər\ see ATOR

ateral \at-ə-rəl\ lateral • bilateral, collateral, trilateral • equilateral, multilateral, quadrilateral, unilateral

aterer \ȯt-ər-ər\ slaughterer, waterer • dewaterer

atering \ȯt-ə-riŋ\ mouthwatering—*also* -ing *forms of verbs listed at* ATER[1]

atery[1] \āt-ə-rē\ see OTTERY

atery[2] \ȯt-ə-rē\ cautery, watery

ates¹ \āts\ Bates, Yeats • Gulf
States • Levant States, Papal
States, Trucial States • Caspian
Gates, Cilician Gates, Indian
States, Persian Gulf States,
United States • house of
delegates—*also* -s, -'s, *and* -s'
forms of nouns and -s *forms of
verbs listed at* ATE¹

ates² \āt-ēz\ nates • Achates,
Euphrates, Penates—*also* -s,
-'s, *and* -s' *forms of nouns
listed at* ATY

atest \āt-əst\ latest, statist
• antistatist, at the latest—*also*
-est *forms of adjectives listed at*
ATE¹

atey \āt-ē\ *see* ATY

ath¹ \äth\ *see* OTH¹

ath² \o̊th\ *see* OTH²

ath³ \ath\ bath, hath, lath, math,
path, rathe, snath, strath, wrath
• base path, birdbath, blood-
bath, bypath, flight path,
footbath, footpath, glide path,
half bath, new math, sitz bath,
stop bath, sunbath, towpath,
warpath • aftermath, bridle
path, polymath, primrose path,
psychopath, shower bath, take
a bath, telepath, Turkish bath,
whirlpool bath • naturopath,
osteopath, sociopath

atha \ät-ə\ *see* ATA¹

athe¹ \āth\ swathe • enswathe,
unswathe

athe² \āth\ bathe, lathe, rathe,
saithe, scathe, spathe, swathe
• sunbathe, unswathe

athe³ \ath\ *see* ATH³

atheless \ath-ləs\ *see* AITHLESS

ather¹ \äth-ər\ bother, father,
pother, rather • forefather,
godfather, grandfather, house-
father, Our Father, stepfather
• city father, founding father,
Holy Father

ather² \əth-ər\ *see* OTHER¹

ather³ \ath-ər\ blather, Cather,
gather, lather, Mather, rather,
slather • forgather, ingather,
woolgather

athering \ath-riŋ\ ingathering,
woolgathering—*also* -ing *forms
of verbs listed at* ATHER³

athi \ät-ē\ *see* ATI

athic \ath-ik\ empathic
• allopathic, amphipathic,
hydropathic, neuropathic,
psychopathic, telepathic
• homeopathic, idiopathic,
naturopathic, osteopathic,
sociopathic

athlon \ath-lən\ biathlon,
decathlon, heptathlon,
pentathlon, triathlon

athy \ath-ē\ Cathy, wrathy
• Abernathy • allelopathy

ati¹ \ät-ē\ Ate, Dottie, dotty,
grotty, knotty, naughty, plotty,
potty, Scotty, snotty, spotty,
squatty • Amati, basmati,
chapati, coati, Dorati, flokati,
karate, Komati, Marathi,
metate, Scarlatti, Siswati,
Tol'yatti • digerati, glitterati,
Gujarati, Hakodate, literati,
manicotti • illuminati

ati² \atē\ see ATTY

ati³ \äts\ see OTS

ati⁴ \as\ see ASS³

atia \ā-shə\ see ACIA

atial \ā-shəl\ see ACIAL

atian \ā-shən\ see ATION¹

atians \ā-shənz\ see ATIONS

atible \at-ə-bəl\ compatible, getatable • incompatible, self-compatible • biocompatible, self-incompatible

atic¹ \ät-ik\ see OTIC¹

atic² \at-ik\ attic, Attic, batik, phatic, static, vatic • agnatic, aquatic, astatic, asthmatic, Carnatic, chromatic, climatic, comatic, dalmatic, dogmatic, dramatic, ecstatic, emphatic, erratic, eustatic, fanatic, hepatic, judgmatic, komatik, lymphatic, magmatic, neumatic, phlegmatic, plasmatic, pneumatic, pragmatic, prismatic, protatic, quadratic, rheumatic, schematic, schismatic, sciatic, sematic, Socratic, somatic, spermatic, stigmatic, sylvatic, thematic, traumatic, villatic • achromatic, acrobatic, Adriatic, aerobatic, anabatic, antistatic, aromatic, Asiatic, astigmatic, autocratic, automatic, bureaucratic, charismatic, cinematic, democratic, diplomatic, Eleatic, emblematic, enigmatic, enzymatic, Hanseatic, hieratic, Hippocratic, hydrostatic, kerygmatic, kleptocratic, melismatic, mobocratic,

monocratic, morganatic, nondramatic, nonemphatic, numismatic, operatic, phallocratic, photostatic, plutocratic, pre-Socratic, problematic, programmatic, symptomatic, systematic, technocratic, theocratic, thermostatic, undogmatic, undramatic • adiabatic, aristocratic, asymptomatic, axiomatic, diagrammatic, electrostatic, epigrammatic, gerontocratic, homeostatic, idiomatic, melodramatic, meritocratic, monochromatic, nonsystematic, overdramatic, overemphatic, paradigmatic, physiocratic, psychodramatic, psychosomatic, semiaquatic, soap-operatic, uncinematic, undemocratic, undiplomatic • antidemocratic, Austroasiatic, semiautomatic

atica \at-i-kə\ Attica • hepatica, sciatica, viatica

atical \at-i-kəl\ statical • fanatical, grammatical, piratical, sabbatical • enigmatical, mathematical, problematical, ungrammatical • epigrammatical

atics \at-iks\ statics • chromatics, dogmatics, dramatics, pneumatics, pragmatics • acrobatics, aerostatics, hydrostatics, informatics, mathematics, numismatics, systematics • melodramatics—*also* -s, -'s, *and* -s' *forms of nouns listed at* ATIC²

atie \āt-ē\ see ATY

atiens \ā-shənz\ see ATIONS

atient \ā-shənt\ patient
• impatient, inpatient,
outpatient • somnifacient
• abortifacient

atik \at-ik\ see ATIC[2]

atile \at-ᵊl-ē\ see ATTILY

atim \āt-əm\ see ATUM[2]

atin[1] \āt-ᵊn\ see OTTEN

atin[2] \at-ᵊn\ batten, fatten,
flatten, gratin, Grattan, Latin,
latten, matin, paten, patten,
Patton, platan, platen, ratton,
satin, statin • cisplatin,
manhattan, Manhattan,
Mountbatten, pig latin,
Powhatan • lovastatin

atin[3] \āt-ᵊn\ see ATEN[1]

atinate \at-ᵊn-ət\ concatenate,
Palatinate

ating \āt-iŋ\ bating, grating,
plaiting, plating, rating, skating,
slating • abating, bearbaiting,
bullbaiting, call-waiting,
frustrating, race-baiting, red-
baiting, self-hating, self-rating,
speed skating • aggravating,
calculating, carbon dating,
fascinating, figure skating, in-
line skating, maid-in-waiting,
nauseating, open dating,
operating, penetrating, self-
negating, suffocating, titillating
• accommodating, discrim-
inating, humiliating, lady-in-
waiting, self-deprecating, self-
educating, self-liquidating, self-
lubricating, self-mutilating, self-
operating, self-regulating, self-
replicating, subordinating,
uncalculating, undeviating,
unhesitating • self-
perpetuating—also -ing forms
of verbs listed at ATE[1]

atinous \at-nəs\ see ATNESS

ation[1] \ā-shən\ Asian, Haitian,
nation, Nation, ration, station,
Thracian • aeration, agnation,
Alsatian, carnation, castration,
causation, cessation, cetacean,
citation, Claymation, cognation,
collation, conflation, C ration,
creation, cremation, crenation,
Croatian, crustacean, dal-
matian, damnation, deflation,
delation, dictation, dilation,
donation, duration, earth
station, elation, equation,
Eurasian, filtration, fixation,
flirtation, flotation, formation,
foundation, frustration, gas
station, gestation, gradation,
gustation, guttation, gyration,
hydration, inflation, K ration,
lactation, legation, libation,
location, lunation, lustration,
luxation, migration, mutation,
narration, negation, notation,
oblation, oration, outstation,
ovation, palmation, palpation,
plantation, potation, predation,
privation, probation, pronation,
proration, prostration, pulsa-
tion, punctation, pupation,
purgation, quotation, relation,
rogation, rotation, salvation,
sedation, sensation, serration,
space station, stagflation,
stagnation, starvation, striation,
stylization, substation, sum-
mation, tarnation, taxation,

temptation, translation, truncation, vacation, vexation, vibration, vocation, way station, workstation • abdication, aberration, abjuration, abnegation, abrogation, acceptation, acclamation, accusation, activation, adaptation, adjuration, admiration, adoration, adulation, adumbration, affectation, affirmation, aggravation, aggregation, agitation, allegation, allocation, amputation, alteration, altercation, alternation, Amerasian, animation, annexation, annotation, Appalachian, appellation, application, approbation, arbitration, arrogation, aspiration, assignation, attestation, augmentation, automation, aviation, avocation, blaxploitation, botheration, calculation, calibration, cancellation, carbonation, castigation, celebration, cerebration, chlorination, circulation, cogitation, collocation, coloration, combination, comfort station, commendation, commutation, compensation, compilation, complication, computation, concentration, condemnation, condensation, confirmation, confiscation, conflagration, conformation, confrontation, congregation, conjugation, connotation, consecration, conservation, consolation, constellation, consternation, constipation, consultation, consummation, contemplation, conurbation, conversation, convocation,

copulation, coronation, corporation, correlation, corrugation, crenellation, crop rotation, culmination, cultivation, cumulation, cybernation, decimation, declamation, declaration, declination, decoration, dedication, defamation, defecation, deformation, degradation, dehydration, delectation, delegation, demarcation, demonstration, denigration, denotation, depilation, deportation, depravation, depredation, deprivation, deputation, derivation, derogation, desecration, designation, desolation, desperation, destination, detestation, detonation, devastation, deviation, dislocation, dispensation, disputation, dissertation, dissipation, distillation, divination, domination, duplication, education, elevation, elongation, emanation, embarkation, embrocation, emendation, emigration, emulation, enervation, escalation, estimation, evocation, exaltation, excavation, excitation, exclamation, exculpation, execration, exhalation, exhortation, exhumation, expectation, expiation, expiration, explanation, explication, exploitation, exploration, exportation, expurgation, extirpation, exultation, fabrication, fascination, federation, fenestration, fermentation, fibrillation, figuration, filling station, fire station, flagellation, fluoridation, fluctuation, forestation, formulation, fornication, fragmentation, fulmination, fumigation, gene mutation, generation, germination, glaciation, grade mutation, graduation, granulation, gravitation, habitation, heat prostration, hesitation, hibernation, hyphenation, ideation, illustration, imitation, immigration, immolation, implantation, implication, importation, imprecation, imputation, incantation, incarnation, inclination, incrustation, incubation, indentation, indication, indignation, infestation, infiltration, inflammation, information, inhalation, innovation, inspiration, installation, instigation, insulation, integration, intimation, intonation, inundation, invitation, invocation, irrigation, irritation, isolation, iteration, jubilation, laceration, lamentation, lamination, legislation, levitation, liberation, limitation, lineation, liquidation, litigation, lubrication, lucubration, maceration, machination, malformation, masturbation, maturation, mediation, medication, meditation, melioration, menstruation, ministration, misquotation, mistranslation, mitigation, moderation, modulation, molestation, motivation, multination,

mutilation, navigation, nomination, obfuscation, objurgation, obligation, observation, occupation, operation, orchestration, ordination, oscillation, osculation, ostentation, ovulation, oxidation, pagination, palpitation, penetration, percolation, perforation, permeation, permutation, peroration, perpetration, perspiration, perturbation, pigmentation, pixilation, police station, pollination, population, postulation, power station, predication, preparation, presentation, preservation, proclamation, procreation, profanation, prolongation, promulgation, propagation, prorogation, protestation, provocation, publication, punctuation, radiation, recantation, recitation, reclamation, recreation, recreation, reformation, refutation, registration, regulation, rehydration, relaxation, relocation, renovation, reparation, replication, reprobation, reputation, reservation, resignation, respiration, restoration, retardation, revelation, revocation, ruination, rumination, rustication, salutation, sanitation, saturation, segmentation, segregation, separation, sequestration, service station, sexploitation, simulation, situation, speciation, speculation, spoliation, stimulation, stipulation, strangulation, structuration, stylization, subjugation, sublimation, suffocation, syncopation, syndication, tabulation, termination, T formation, titillation, toleration, transfer station, transformation, translocation, transmigration, transmutation, transpiration, transplantation, transportation, trepidation, tribulation, ulceration, ululation, undulation, urination, usurpation, vaccination, vacillation, validation, valuation, variation, vegetation, veneration, ventilation, vindication, violation, visitation, weather station • abbreviation, abomination, acceleration, accentuation, accommodation, accreditation, acculturation, accumulation, actualization, adjudication, administration, adulteration, affiliation, agglomeration, alienation, alleviation, alliteration, amalgamation, amelioration, amortization, amplification, anglicization, annihilation, annunciation, anticipation, appreciation, appropriation, approximation, argumentation, articulation, asphyxiation, assassination, asseveration, assimilation, association, atomization, attenuation, authentication, authorization, autoxidation, balkanization, bastardization, beautification, bowdlerization, calcification, canonization, capitulation, centralization, certification, cicatrization, civilization, clarification, classification, coagulation, codification, coeducation, cogeneration, cohabitation,

collaboration, colonization, colorization, commemoration, commiseration, communication, concatenation, conciliation, confabulation, confederation, configuration, conglomeration, congratulation, consideration, consolidation, contamination, continuation, cooperation, coordination, corroboration, cross-pollination, crystallization, deactivation, debilitation, decapitation, deceleration, deconsecration, de-escalation, defenestration, defibrillation, deforestation, defragmentation, degeneration, deification, deliberation, delineation, demonization, denomination, denunciation, depopulation, depreciation, deracination, deregulation, desalination, desegregation, despoliation, determination, devaluation, digitization, disapprobation, discoloration, discrimination, disembarkation, disinclination, disinformation, disintegration, Disneyfication, dissemination, dissimulation, dissociation, documentation, domestication, dramatization, echolocation, edification, ejaculation, elaboration, elimination, elucidation, emaciation, emancipation, emasculation, enumeration, enunciation, equalization, equivocation, eradication, evacuation, evaluation, evaporation, evisceration, exaggeration, examination, exasperation, exhilaration, exoneration, expropriation, extenuation, extermination, extrapolation, facilitation, falsification, felicitation, feminization, fertilization, feudalization, finalization, Finlandization, formalization, fortification, fossilization, gasification, gentrification, gesticulation, globalization, glorification, gratification, habituation, hallucination, harmonization, humanization, humiliation, hyperinflation, idolization, illumination, imagination, immunization, impersonation, implementation, improvisation, inauguration, incarceration, incineration, incorporation, incrimination, indoctrination, inebriation, infatuation, initiation, inoculation, insemination, insinuation, instrumentation, internalization, interpretation, interrelation, interrogation, intimidation, intoxication, invagination, invalidation, investigation, invigoration, irradiation, itemization, justification, legalization, liberalization, magnetization, magnification, maladaptation, manifestation, manipulation, masculinization, matriculation, maximization, mechanization, memorization, misapplication, miscalculation, miscegenation, misinformation, mobilization, modernization, modification, monetization, monopolization, mortification, multiplication, mystification, nationalization, naturalization, negotiation, normalization, notification, novelization, nullification,

obliteration, organization, origination, orientation, ornamentation, ossification, overinflation, oxygenation, pacification, paralyzation, participation, pasteurization, perambulation, peregrination, perpetuation, personalization, petrification, polarization, pontification, postgraduation, post-Reformation, precipitation, predestination, prefabrication, prefiguration, premeditation, preoccupation, preordination, prepublication, preregistration, prettification, privatization, procrastination, prognostication, proliferation, pronunciation, propitiation, purification, qualification, ramification, randomization, ratification, ratiocination, reaffirmation, realization, reciprocation, recombination, recommendation, recrimination, recuperation, redecoration, rededication, reduplication, reforestation, reformulation, refrigeration, regeneration, regimentation, regurgitation, reification, reincarnation, reintegration, reiteration, rejuvenation, remuneration, renunciation, reoccupation, repatriation, representation, republication, repudiation, retaliation, reverberation, sanctification, scarification, sedimentation, sensitization, Serbo-Croatian, signification, simplification, socialization, solicitation, sophistication, specialization, specification, stabilization, standardization, sterilization, stratification, subordination, subpopulation, supplementation, synchronization, systemization, teleportation, tergiversation, transfiguration, transliteration, transvaluation, triangulation, uglification, unification, unionization, urbanization, verification, versification, victimization, vilification, vituperation, vocalization, vulgarization, westernization, x-radiation • characterization, circumnavigation, commercialization, Counter-Reformation, criminalization, cross-examination, de-Stalinization, decentralization, declassification, decontamination, dehumanization, demystification, deterioration, differentiation, disassociation, disorientation, disorganization, disqualification, diversification, electrification, excommunication, exemplification, experimentation, extemporization, externalization, generalization, homogenization, hospitalization, hyperventilation, idealization, identification, indemnification, indetermination, indiscrimination, individuation, institutionalization, insubordination, intensification, intermediation, italicization, megacorporation, militarization, miniaturization, misappropriation, miscommunication, misinterpretation, mispronunciation, misrepresentation, nonproliferation, overcompensation, overpopulation, personification, popularization, predetermination, ratiocination, rationalization, recapitulation, reconciliation, reconsideration, rehabilitation, reinterpretation, reorganization, revitalization, secularization, solidification, tintinnabulation, transubstantiation, underestimation, undervaluation, visualization

ation² \ā-zhən\ see ASION

ation³ \ash-ən\ see ASSION

ational¹ \ā-shnəl\ stational • citational, formational, gestational, gradational, migrational, narrational, notational, probational, relational, rotational, salvational, sensational, translational, vocational • aberrational, adaptational, avocational, computational, confrontational, congregational, conservational, conversational, educational, generational, gravitational, informational, innovational, inspirational, invitational, motivational, navigational, observational, operational, recreational, situational, transformational • coeducational, denominational, improvisational, organizational, representational

ational² \āzh-nəl\ see ASIONAL

ational³ \ash-nəl\ national, passional, rational • binational, cross-national, irrational, nonrational, subrational, transnational • international, multinational, supranational, suprarational, ultrarational

ationist \ā-shnəst\ salvationist, vacationist • annexationist, confrontationist, conservationist, educationist, integrationist, isolationist, liberationist, preservationist, segregationist, separationist • accomodationist, assimilationist, collaborationist, emancipationist

ations \ā-shənz\ Galatians, impatiens, relations • Lamentations, law of nations, League of Nations, Revelations • United Nations

atious \ā-shəs\ see ACIOUS

atis¹ \at-əs\ see ATUS³

atis² \ät-əs\ see OTTIS

atist \āt-əst\ see ATEST

atitude \at-ə-tüd\ see ATTITUDE

atium \ā-shē-əm\ cymatium, Latium • pancratium, solatium, spermatium

atius \ā-shəs\ see ACIOUS

ative \āt-iv\ dative, native, stative • ablative, constative, creative, dilative, mutative, nonnative, placative, rotative, summative, translative • aggregative, agitative, alterative, applicative, carminative, circulative, cogitative, combinative, commutative, connotative, consecrative, consultative, contemplative, copulative, corporative, cumulative, decorative, denotative, dissipative, duplicative, educative, explicative, facultative, federative, gener-

ative, germinative, gravitative, imitative, implicative, innovative, instigative, integrative, irritative, iterative, legislative, limitative, meditative, meliorative, motivative, nominative, nuncupative, operative, palliative, penetrative, procreative, propagative, qualitative, quantitative, recreative, regulative, replicative, separative, speculative, terminative, vegetative • accelerative, accumulative, administrative, alliterative, appreciative, assimilative, associative, authoritative, collaborative, commemorative, communicative, cooperative, corroborative, degenerative, deliberative, determinative, illuminative, interpretative, investigative, multiplicative, originative, postoperative, recuperative, regenerative, remunerative, vituperative • uncommunicative

atl \ät-ᵊl\ see OTTLE

atlas \at-ləs\ atlas, Atlas, fatless, hatless

atless \at-ləs\ see ATLAS

atli \ät-lē\ see OTLY

atling \at-liŋ\ fatling, flatling, rattling • saber rattling—also -ing forms of verbs listed at ATTLE

atly \at-lē\ fatly, flatly, rattly

atness \at-nəs\ fatness, flatness • gelatinous

ato¹ \ät-ō\ auto, blotto, grotto, lotto, motto, otto, Otto, potto,

Prato • Ambato, annatto, castrato, gelato, legato, marcato, mulatto, rabato, rebato, ridotto, rubato, sfumato, spiccato, staccato, vibrato, Waikato • agitato, animato, ben trovato, boniato, Guanajuato, Irapuato, moderato, obbligato, ostinato, pizzicato, Tupungato

ato² \ät-ō\ Cato, JATO, Plato • Orvieto, potato, tomato • couch potato, hot potato, new potato, plum tomato, seed potato, small potato, sweet potato • Barquisimeto, beefsteak tomato, cherry tomato

atomist \at-ə-məst\ atomist • anatomist

atomy \at-ə-mē\ atomy • anatomy • gross anatomy

aton \at-ᵉn\ see ATIN²

atony \at-ᵉn-ē\ see ATANY

ator \āt-ər\ baiter, cater, crater, Crater, dater, faitour, freighter, gaiter, gator, grater, hater, krater, later, mater, plaiter, plater, prater, rater, satyr, skater, slater, stater, stator, tater, traitor, waiter • aerator, castrator, collator, Chubb Crater, Bay Stater, creator, curator, debater, Decatur, deflator, dictator, dilator, donator, downstater, dumb-waiter, equator, first-rater, glossator, headwaiter, ice-skater, levator, locator, mandator, Mercator, migrator, narrator, pond skater, pronator,

pulsator, red-baiter, relater, rotator, spectator, speed skater, tailgater, testator, theater, third-rater, titrato., translator, upstater, vibratc • abdicator, abnegator, activator, actuator, adulator, advocator, agitator, alligator, allocator, alternator, animator, annotator, applicator, arbitrator, aspirator, aviator, brachiator, buccinator, calculator, cali-brator, captivator, carburetor, castigator, celebrator, circula-tor, cocreator, cocurator, commentator, commutator, compensator, compurgator, concentrator, confiscator, congregator, consecrator, consummator, contemplator, corporator, correlator, cultiva-tor, decorator, defalcator, delegator, demonstrator, denigrator, depredator, desecrater, desecrator, designator, detonator, deviator, dissipater, dominator, duplica-tor, dura mater, educator, elevator, emulator, escalator, estimator, excavator, explica-tor, expurgator, extirpator, fabricator, fascinator, figure skater, flocculator, formulator, fornicator, fractionator, fumiga-tor, generator, gladiator, hesitater, hibernator, illustrator, imitator, immolator, impregna-tor, incubator, indicator, infiltrator, in-line skater, innovator, inhalator, inspirator, instigator, insulator, integrator, lacrimator, liberator, liquidator, literator, lubricator, macerator, masticator, mediator, mitigator, moderator, modulator, motivator, mutilator, navigator, nomenclator, nominator, numerator, obturator, operator, orchestrator, oscillator, peculator, percolator, perforator, perpetrator, pia mater, pollinator, postulator, procreator, procurator, promulgator, propagator, punctuator, radiator, re-creator, regulator, remonstrator, renovator, resonator, respirator, revelator, roller skater, rubricator, rusticator, salivator, second-rater, selling-plater, separator, simulator, stimulator, subjugator, Sunset Crater, syncopator, syndicator, tabulator, terminator, vaccinator, vacillator, valuator, venerator, ventilator, vindicator, violator, vitiator • accelerator, accommodator, accumulator, administrator, adulterator, alienator, alleviator, annihilator, annunciator, anticipator, appreciator, appropriator, assassinator, attenuator, continuator, calumniator, collaborator, commemorator, communicator, conciliator, congratulator, consolidator, contaminator, cooperator, coordinator, corroborator, defibrillator, delineator, denominator, depreciator, determinator, discriminator, disseminator, dissimulator, ejaculator, eliminator, emancipator, enumerator, equivocator, eradicator, evaluator, evaporator, exterminator, extrapolator, facilitator, grain elevator,

impersonator, improvisator, incinerator, inseminator, interrogator, intimidator, investigator, negotiator, oxygenator, pacificator, perambulator, predestinator, procrastinator, purificator, redecorator, refrigerator, regenerator, resuscitator, sooner or later, subordinator, totalizator—*also* -er *forms of adjectives listed at* ATE[1]

atre[1] \ätr°\ coup de théâtre • pas de quatre

atre[2] \at\ see AT[5]

atric \a-trik\ Patrick • sympatric, theatric • allopatric, bariatric, geriatric, pediatric, podiatric, psychiatric

atrick \a-trik\ see ATRIC

atrics \a-triks\ theatrics • pediatrics

atrix \ā-triks\ matrix • Beatrix, cicatrix, dot matrix, square matrix, testatrix • active-matrix, aviatrix, dominatrix, generatrix, mediatrix, passive-matrix • administratrix

atron \ā-trən\ matron, natron, patron

ats[1] \äts\ see OTS

ats[2] \ats\ bats, rats • ersatz • Bonneville Salt Flats—*also* -s, -'s, *and* -s' *forms of nouns and* -s *forms of verbs listed at* AT[5]

atsa \ät-sə\ see ATZO[1]

atsch \ach\ see ATCH[4]

atsk \ätsk\ Bratsk • Okhotsk • Petrozavodsk

atsu \ät-sü\ Matsu • shiatsu • zaibatsu • Chikamatsu, Hamamatsu, Takamatsu

atsy \at-sē\ see AZI³

att¹ \at\ see AT⁵

att² \ät\ see OT¹

atta \ät-ə\ see ATA¹

attage \ät-ij\ see OTTAGE

attan \at-ᵊn\ see ATIN²

atte \at\ see AT⁵

atted \a-təd\ superfatted—*also* -ed *forms of verbs listed at* AT⁵

attel \at-ᵊl\ see ATTLE

atten \at-ᵊn\ see ATIN²

atter \at-ər\ attar, 'Attar, batter, blatter, chatter, clatter, fatter, flatter, hatter, latter, matter, natter, patter, plaiter, platter, ratter, satyr, scatter, shatter, smatter, spatter, splatter, tatter • back matter, backscatter, bespatter, dark matter, flat-hatter, front matter, gray matter, no matter, standpatter, the matter, white matter, wildcatter • antimatter, for that matter, pitter-patter, printed matter, subject matter

attering \at-ə-riŋ\ nattering, scattering, smattering • backscattering, earth-shattering, self-flattering, unflattering—*also* -ing *forms of verbs listed at* ATTER

attern \at-ərn\ pattern, Saturn, slattern • test pattern • holding pattern

attery \at-ə-rē\ battery, cattery, clattery, flattery, mattery • Cape Flattery, self-flattery

atti¹ \ät-ē\ see ATI¹

atti² \at-ē\ see ATTY

attic \at-ik\ see ATIC²

attica \at-i-kə\ see ATICA

attice¹ \at-əs\ see ATUS³

attice² \at-ish\ see ATTISH

attie \at-ē\ see ATTY

attily \at-ᵊl-ē\ cattily, chattily, Natalie, nattily, rattly • philately • sal volatile

atting \at-iŋ\ batting, matting, tatting—*also* -ing *forms of verbs listed at* AT⁵

attish \at-ish\ brattish, fattish, flattish

attitude \at-ə-tüd\ attitude, gratitude, latitude, platitude • beatitude, colatitude, ingratitude, midlatitude

attle \at-ᵊl\ battle, brattle, cattle, chattel, prattle, rattle, tattle • beef cattle, death rattle, embattle, pitched battle, Seattle • dairy cattle, tittle-tattle • order of battle

attler \at-lər\ battler, prattler, rattler, tattler

attling \at-liŋ\ see ATLING

attly¹ \at-ᵊl-ē\ see ATTILY

attly² \at-lē\ see ATLY

atto¹ \at-ə\ see ATA³

atto² \ät-ō\ see ATO¹

atton \at-ᵊn\ see ATIN²

atty \at-ē\ batty, bratty, catty, chatty, fatty, Hattie, natty, patty, Patty, platy, ratty, scatty, tattie, tatty • nonfatty • Cincinnati

atum¹ \ät-əm\ bottom, datum, satem • at bottom, bell-bottom, erratum, pomatum, rock-bottom, sense-datum • Foggy Bottom • desideratum

atum² \ät-əm\ datum • pomatum, sense-datum, substratum, verbatim • ageratum, literatim, seriatim, ultimatum • corpus allatum, corpus striatum, desideratum

atum³ \at-əm\ atom, datum • erratum, substratum • seriatim

atuous \ach-wəs\ fatuous • ignis fatuus

atur \ät-ər\ see ATOR

atural \ach-rəl\ natural • connatural, transnatural, unnatural • preternatural, seminatural, supernatural

ature¹ \ā-chər\ nature • denature, 4-H'er, renature • call of nature, force of nature, freak of nature, human nature, magistrature, Mother Nature, nomenclature, second nature, supernature

ature² \ach-ər\ see ATCHER²

aturn \at-ərn\ see ATTERN

atus¹ \āt-əs\ flatus, gratis, status, stratus • afflatus, hiatus, meatus • altostratus, apparatus, cirrostratus, nimbostratus • coitus reservatus

atus² \ät-əs\ see OTTIS

atus³ \at-əs\ brattice, gratis, lattice, status, stratus • clematis • altostratus, apparatus, cirrostratus, nimbostratus

atute \ach-ət\ see ATCHET

atuus \ach-wəs\ see ATUOUS

aty \āt-ē\ eighty, Haiti, Katie, Leyte, matey, platy, slaty, weighty, yeti • 1080 • Papeete

atyr \ät-ər\ see ATOR

atz¹ \ats\ see ATS²

atz² \äts\ see OTS

atzo¹ \ät-sə\ matzo, tazza • Hidatsa, piazza

atzo² \ät-sō\ see AZZO¹

atzu \ät-sü\ see ATSU

au¹ \ō\ see OW¹

au² \ü\ see EW¹

au³ \aů\ see OW²

au⁴ \ȯ\ see AW¹

aub \äb\ see OB¹

auba \ȯ-bə\ carnauba, Catawba

aube \ōb\ see OBE¹

auber \ȯb-ər\ dauber • Micawber, mud dauber

auble \äb-əl\ see ABBLE¹

auce \ȯs\ see OSS¹

aucer \ȯ-sər\ see OSSER

aucet \äs-ət\ see OSSET

auch[1] \óch\ nautch • debauch

auch[2] \äch\ see OTCH

auche \ōsh\ see OCHE[2]

auchely \ōsh-lē\ see OCIALLY

auckland \ók-lənd\ Auckland, Falkland

aucous \ó-kəs\ caucus, glaucous, raucous

aucus \ó-kəs\ see AUCOUS

aud[1] \ód\ awed, baud, bawd, broad, Claude, clawed, flawed, fraud, gaud, god, jawed, laud, Maude, yod • abroad, applaud, belaud, defraud, dewclawed, maraud, whipsawed • antifraud, eisteddfod, lanternjawed, quartersawed, wire fraud— also -ed forms of verbs listed at AW[1]

aud[2] \äd\ see OD[1]

audable \ód-ə-bəl\ audible, laudable • applaudable, illaudable, inaudible

audal \ód-ᵊl\ caudal, caudle, dawdle

audative \ód-ət-iv\ see AUDITIVE

aude[1] \aúd-ē\ see OWDY

aude[2] \ód-ē\ see AWDY

aude[3] \aúd-ə\ howdah • cum laude • magna cum laude, summa cum laude

aude[4] \ód\ see AUD[1]

audible \ód-ə-bəl\ see AUDABLE

auding \ód-iŋ\ auding • applauding, self-applauding

—also -ing forms of verbs listed at AUD[1]

audit \ód-ət\ audit, plaudit

audle \ód-ᵊl\ see AUDAL

audy[1] \äd-ē\ see ODY[1]

audy[2] \ód-ē\ see AWDY

auer \aúr\ see OWER[2]

auf \aúf\ see OWFF

auffeur \ō-fər\ see OFER

auga \ó-gə\ massasauga, Mississauga, Onondaga

auge \āj\ see AGE[3]

augeable \ā-jə-bəl\ see AGEABLE

auged \ājd\ see AGED

auger[1] \ó-gər\ see OGGER[2]

auger[2] \ā-jər\ see AGER[1]

augh[1] \af\ see APH

augh[2] \ä\ see A[1]

augh[3] \äk̠\ see ACH[1]

augh[4] \ó\ see AW[1]

aughable \af-ə-bəl\ see AFFABLE

augham \óm\ see AUM[1]

aughn[1] \än\ see ON[1]

aughn[2] \ón\ see ON[3]

aught[1] \ät\ see OT[1]

aught[2] \ót\ see OUGHT[1]

aughter[1] \af-tər\ see AFTER

aughter[2] \ót-ər\ see ATER[1]

aughterer \ót-ər-ər\ see ATERER

aughty[1] \ót-ē\ haughty, naughty, zloty • Buonarroti

aughty[2] \ät-ē\ see ATI

augre \óg-ər\ see OGGER[2]

augur \óg-ər\ see OGGER[2]

augury \ò-gə-rē\ see OGGERY[2]

aui \aú-ē\ see OWIE

auk \ók\ see ALK

aukee \ò-kē\ see ALKIE

aul \ól\ see ALL

aulay \ò-lē\ see AWLY

auld[1] \ól\ see ALL

auld[2] \ō\ see OW[1]

auldron \ól-drən\ see ALDRON

auled \óld\ see ALD

auler \ò-lər\ see ALLER[1]

aulin \ò-lən\ see ALLEN

auling \ò-lin\ see ALLING

aulish \ò-lish\ see ALLISH

aulk \ók\ see ALK

aulker \ò-kər\ see ALKER

aulking \ò-kin\ see ALKING

aulle \ól\ see ALL[1]

aulm \óm\ see AUM[1]

ault[1] \ólt\ see ALT

ault[2] \ō\ see OW[1]

aulter \ól-tər\ see ALTER

aulting \ól-tin\ see ALTING

aultless \ólt-ləs\ see ALTLESS

aulty \ól-tē\ see ALTY

aum[1] \óm\ gaum, haulm, Maugham, qualm, shawm • meerschaum, Radom

aum[2] \äm\ see OM[1]

aun[1] \än\ see ON[1]

aun[2] \ən\ see UN

aun[3] \ón\ see ON[3]

aun[4] \aún\ see OWN[2]

auna[1] \än-ə\ see ANA[1]

auna[2] \ón-ə\ see ONNA[1]

aunce \óns\ jaunce, launce

aunch[1] \änch\ conch, cranch, craunch, paunch, raunch, stanch • Romansh

aunch[2] \ónch\ craunch, haunch, launch, paunch, raunch, stanch, staunch • postlaunch, prelaunch

auncher \ón-chər\ launcher, stancher, stauncher

aunchy \ón-chē\ paunchy, raunchy

aund \ónd\ awned— *also* -ed *forms of verbs listed at* ON[3]

aunder[1] \ón-dər\ launder, maunder

aunder[2] \än-dər\ see ONDER[1]

aunish \än-ish\ see ONISH

aunt[1] \ónt\ daunt, flaunt, gaunt, haunt, jaunt, taunt, vaunt, want, wont • avant, avaunt, keeshond, romaunt • John of Gaunt

aunt[2] \ant\ see ANT[5]

aunt[3] \änt\ see ANT[2]

aunted \ónt-əd\ see ONTED

aunter[1] \änt-ər\ saunter, taunter • rencontre

aunter² \ȯnt-ər\ gaunter, haunter, saunter, taunter, vaunter

aunty¹ \ȯnt-ē\ flaunty, jaunty, vaunty

aunty² \änt-ē\ see ANTI¹

aunus \än-əs\ see ONUS¹

aup \ȯp\ gawp, scaup, whaup, yawp

aupe \ōp\ see OPE

auphin \ȯ-fən\ see OFFIN

aur¹ \au̇r\ see OWER²

aur² \ȯr\ see OR¹

aura¹ \ȯr-ə\ see ORA

aura² \är-ə\ see ARA¹

aural \ȯr-əl\ see ORAL¹

aure \ȯr\ see OR¹

aurea \ȯr-ē-ə\ see ORIA

aurean \ȯr-ē-ən\ see ORIAN

aureate¹ \är-ē-ət\ baccalaureate • commissariat

aureate² \ȯr-ē-ət\ aureate, laureate • baccalaureate, poet laureate, professoriat

aurel \ȯr-əl\ see ORAL¹

auren¹ \är-ən\ see ARIN

auren² \ȯr-ən\ see ORIN¹

aurence \ȯr-ən(t)s\ see AWRENCE

aureus \ȯr-ē-əs\ see ORIOUS

auri \au̇r-ē\ see OWERY

aurian \ȯr-ē-ən\ see ORIAN

auric \ȯr-ik\ see ORIC

aurice¹ \är-əs\ see ORRIS¹

aurice² \ȯr-əs\ see AURUS

auricle \ȯr-i-kəl\ see ORICAL

aurie¹ \ȯr-ē\ see ORY

aurie² \är-ē\ see ARI

aurous \ȯr-əs\ see AURUS

aurus \ȯr-əs\ Boris, chorus, Doris, Flores, Horace, Horus, Ioris, Maurice, morris, Morris, Norris, orris, porous, sorus, Taurus, Torres, torus • canorous, Centaurus, clitoris, decorous, Dolores, pelorus, phosphorous, sonorous, thesaurus • allosaurus, brontosaurus, Epidaurus, stegosaurus • ankylosaurus, apatosaurus, tyrannosaurus

aury \ȯr-ē\ see ORY

aus¹ \ā-əs\ see AIS¹

aus² \au̇s\ see OUSE²

aus³ \ȯz\ see AUSE¹

ausal \ȯ-zəl\ causal, clausal • menopausal, multicausal • postmenopausal

ause¹ \ȯz\ cause, 'cause, clause, gauze, hawse, pause, tawse, yaws • applause, because, first cause, kolkhoz, sovkhoz • aeropause, diapause, grasp at straws, menopause, mesopause, reserve clause, Santa Claus, self-applause, tropopause • grandfather clause, make common cause, male menopause, probable cause— *also* -s, -'s, *and* -s' *forms of nouns and* -s *forms of verbs listed at* AW¹

ause² \əz\ see EUSE¹

auseous \ȯ-shəs\ see AUTIOUS

auser \ȯ-zər\ causer, hawser

ausey \ȯ-zē\ causey, gauzy

auss \aús\ see OUSE[1]

aussie[1] \äs-ē\ see OSSY[1]

aussie[2] \ȯ-sē\ see OSSY[2]

aust[1] \aúst\ see OUST

aust[2] \ȯst\ see OST[3]

austen \ȯs-tən\ see OSTON

austin \ȯs-tən\ see OSTON

austless \ȯst-ləs\ costless
• exhaustless

austral[1] \äs-trəl\ see OSTREL

austral[2] \ȯs-trəl\ see OSTRAL[1]

aut[1] \ō\ see OW[1]

aut[2] \aút\ see OUT[3]

aut[3] \ät\ see OT[1]

aut[4] \ȯt\ see OUGHT[1]

autch \ȯch\ see AUCH[1]

aute \ōt\ see OAT

auten \ȯt-ᵊn\ boughten, tauten

auterne \ȯt-ərn\ quartern,
sauterne, sauternes

auternes \ȯt-ərn\ see AUTERNE

autery \ȯt-ə-rē\ see ATERY

autic \ȯt-ik\ orthotic
• aeronautic, astronautic

autical \ȯt-i-kəl\ nautical
• aeronautical, astronautical

autics \ät-iks\ see OTICS

aution \ȯ-shən\ caution,
groschen • incaution,
precaution

autious \ȯ-shəs\ cautious,
nauseous • incautious
• overcautious

auto[1] \ȯt-ō\ auto, Giotto • risotto

auto[2] \ät-ō\ see ATO[1]

auve \ōv\ see OVE[2]

auze \ȯz\ see AUSE[1]

auzer \aú-zər\ see OUSER

auzy \ȯ-zē\ see AUSEY

av[1] \äv\ see OLVE[2]

av[2] \av\ see ALVE[2]

ava[1] \äv-ə\ brava, Drava, fava,
guava, java, Java, kava, lava,
Sava • baklava, cassava,
ottava, Poltava, Warszawa
• balaclava, Bratislava, Costa
Brava, lavalava, piassava
• Dufferin and Ava

ava[2] \av-ə\ java • Ungava
• balaclava

avage \av-ij\ ravage, savage

avan \ā-vən\ see AVEN[1]

avant \av-ənt\ haven't, savant

avarice \av-rəs\ see AVEROUS

ave[1] \äv-ā\ ave, clave, grave,
Jahveh, soave

ave[2] \āv\ brave, cave, clave,
crave, Dave, fave, gave, glaive,
grave, knave, lave, nave, pave,
rave, save, shave, slave, stave,
they've, trave, waive, wave,
Wave • airwave, behave, brain
wave, close shave, cold wave,
concave, conclave, Cosgrave,
deprave, dissave, drawshave,
enclave, engrave, enslave,
exclave, forgave, Great Slave,

ground wave, heat wave, margrave, new wave, octave, outbrave, Palgrave, p-wave, palsgrave, repave, shock wave, shortwave, sine wave, sky wave, sound wave, spoke-shave, S wave, wage slave, white slave, Wind Cave • after-shave, alpha wave, architrave, autoclave, beta wave, bicon-cave, delta wave, Fingal's Cave, finger wave, Mammoth Cave, microwave, misbehave, pressure wave, standing wave, tidal wave, transverse wave • gravity wave, permanent wave, photoengrave, plano-concave, radio wave

ave³ \av\ see ALVE³

ave⁴ \äv\ see OLVE²

aved \āvd\ waved • depraved, unsaved—*also* -ed *forms of verbs listed at* AVE²

avel \av-əl\ cavil, gavel, gravel, ravel, travel • unravel • gavel-to-gavel

aveless \āv-ləs\ graveless, waveless

aveling \av-liŋ\ raveling, traveling • fellow-traveling—*also* -ing *forms of verbs listed at* AVEL

avement \āv-mənt\ pavement • depravement, enslavement

aven¹ \ā-vən\ Avon, Cavan, craven, graven, haven, maven, raven, shaven • New Haven, night raven • riboflavin, Winter Haven • Stratford-upon-Avon

aven² \av-ən\ see AVIN

aven't \av-ənt\ see AVANT

aver¹ \äv-ər\ slaver • palaver, windhover • Peter Claver

aver² \ā-vər\ caver, claver, favor, flavor, graver, haver, laver, quaver, raver, saver, savor, shaver, slaver, waiver, waver • disfavor, engraver, enslaver, face-saver, flag-waver, lifesaver, new waver, screen saver, time-saver, white slaver • semiquaver • demisemi-quaver • hemidemisemi-quaver—*also* -er *forms of adjectives listed at* AVE²

aver³ \av-ər\ slaver • cadaver, palaver

avern \av-ərn\ cavern, klavern, tavern

averous \av-rəs\ avarice • cadaverous

avery \āv-rē\ Avery, bravery, knavery, Lavery, quavery, savory, slavery, wavery • unsavory, white slavery • antislavery, summer savory

avey \ā-vē\ see AVY

avia \ā-vē-ə\ Belgravia, Moldavia, Moravia • Scandinavia

avial \ā-vē-əl\ gavial • margravial

avian \ā-vē-ən\ avian, Shavian • Moravian, subclavian • Scandinavian

avid \av-əd\ avid, gravid

avie \ā-vē\ see AVY

avil \av-əl\ see AVEL

avin \av-ən\ Avon, raven, ravin, savin, spavin

aving \ā-viŋ\ caving, craving, paving, raving, saving, shaving • engraving, face-saving, flag-waving, lifesaving, point-shaving, time-saving • labor-saving, line engraving, steel engraving, wood engraving • photoengraving—*also* -ing *forms of verbs listed at* AVE[2]

avis \ā-vəs\ Davis, favus, mavis, Mavis • rara avis

avish[1] \ā-vish\ knavish, slavish

avish[2] \av-ish\ lavish, ravish

avist \äv-əst\ Slavist • Pan-Slavist

avity \av-ət-ē\ cavity, gravity • concavity, depravity • antigravity, biconcavity, body cavity, microgravity, super-gravity, zero gravity • center of gravity, specific gravity, total depravity

avl \äv-əl\ see OVEL[1]

avo[1] \äv-ō\ bravo, Bravo, Savo • centavo, octavo • Rio Bravo

avo[2] \ā-vō\ octavo, relievo • mezzo relievo

avon[1] \ā-vən\ see AVEN[1]

avon[2] \a-vən\ see AVIN

avor \ā-vər\ see AVER[2]

avored \ā-vərd\ favored, flavored • ill-favored, well-favored—*also* -ed *forms of verbs listed at* AVER[2]

avory \āv-rē\ see AVERY

avus \ā-vəs\ see AVIS

avvy \av-ē\ navvy, savvy

avy \ā-vē\ cavy, Davy, gravy, navy, shavie, slavey, wavy

aw[1] \o\ aw, awe, blaw, braw, ca, caw, chaw, claw, craw, daw, draw, faugh, flaw, gnaw, haugh, haw, jaw, la, law, maw, pa, paw, pshaw, Ra, rah, raw, saw, shah, shaw, Shaw, slaw, spa, squaw, straw, tau, taw, thaw, yaw • backsaw, band saw, bashaw, bear claw, bedstraw, blue law, bow saw, Boyle's law, bucksaw, buzz saw, bylaw, case law, catclaw, cat's-paw, chain saw, Choc-taw, coleslaw, Corn Law, crenshaw, cumshaw, cushaw, Danelaw, declaw, dewclaw, Esau, forepaw, fretsaw, geegaw, glass jaw, grandma, grandpa, Grimm's law, guffaw, hacksaw, handsaw, hawkshaw, hee-haw, Hooke's law, hurrah, in-law, jackdaw, jackstraw, jigsaw, kickshaw, last straw, leash law, lockjaw, lynch law, macaw, Moore's law, Moose Jaw, Nassau, Ohm's law, old-squaw, outdraw, outlaw, pasha, pawpaw, pit saw, pooh-bah, poor law, rickshaw, ringtaw, ripsaw, scofflaw, scrimshaw, scroll saw, seesaw, shield law, southpaw, The Skaw, Skiddaw, tack claw, trishaw, tussah, undraw, Utah, vizsla, Warsaw, whipsaw, windflaw, wiredraw, withdraw • Arkansas, blue-sky law, canon law, Chickasaw, Chippewa, civil law, clapperclaw, common-law, coping saw, Coulomb's Law, court of law, crosscut saw, decree-law, devil's claw, foofaraw, Gresham's law, higher law, homestead law, in the raw, jinrikisha, keyhole saw, Kiowa, lantern jaw, lemon law, lumpy jaw, Mackinac, mackinaw, Mendel's law, Morgenthau, Murphy's Law, Omaha, Ottawa, overawe, overdraw, oversaw, overslaugh, padishah, panama, private law, public law, roman law, saber saw, Saginaw, Salic law, son-in-law, tragic flaw, usquebaugh, Verner's law, Wichita, williwaw, windlestraw, Yakima • brother-in-law, circular saw, counselor-at-law, criminal law, daughter-in-law, father-in-law, mother-in-law, musical saw, Parkinson's law, pipsissewa, positive law, serjeant-at-law, sister-in-law, stick in one's craw, unwritten law • attorney-at-law, dietary law, fundamental law, periodic law, red in tooth and claw, Straits of Mackinac

aw² \äv\ see OLVE²

aw³ \óf\ see OFF²

aw⁴ \äf\ see OFF¹

awa¹ \ä-wə\ Chihuahua, Kagawa, Sumbawa, Tarawa, Urawa, Yukawa • Fujisawa, Ichikawa, Kanazawa, Okinawa, Shirakawa, Tokugawa, Tonegawa • Ahashikawa

awa² \ä-və\ see AVA¹

awain \aú-ən\ see OWAN²

awan \aú-ən\ see OWAN²

awar \aúr\ see OWER²

awba \ó-bə\ see AUBA

awber¹ \äb-ər\ see OBBER

awber² \ób-ər\ see AUBER

awd \ód\ see AUD¹

awddle \äd-°l\ see ODDLE

awdle \ód-°l\ see AUDAL

awdry \ó-drē\ Audrey, bawdry, tawdry

awdust \ód-əst\ see ADIST¹

awdy \ód-ē\ bawdy, gaudy • summa cum laude

awe \ó\ see AW¹

awed \ód\ see AUD¹

aweless \ó-ləs\ see AWLESS

awer \ór\ see OR¹

awers \órz\ see OORS

awful \ó-fəl\ awful, coffle, lawful, offal • god-awful, unlawful

awfully \óf-ə-lē\ awfully, lawfully, Offaly • unlawfully

awing \óiŋ\ cloying, drawing • line drawing, wash drawing • wappenschawing—*also* -ing *forms of verbs listed at* AW¹

awk \ók\ see ALK

awker \ó-kər\ see ALKER

awkes \óks\ Fawkes—*also* -s, -'s, *and* -s' *forms of nouns and* -s *forms of verbs listed at* ALK

awkish \ó-kish\ gawkish, hawkish, mawkish

awky \ó-kē\ see ALKIE

awl \ȯl\ see ALL

awler \ȯ-lər\ see ALLER[1]

awless \ȯ-ləs\ aweless, flawless, lawless

awling \ȯ-liŋ\ see ALLING

awly \ȯ-lē\ brawly, crawly, dolly, drawly, Raleigh, rawly, scrawly, squally • Bengali, Macaulay

awm \ȯm\ see AUM[1]

awn[1] \än\ see ON[1]

awn[2] \ȯn\ see ON[3]

awned \ȯnd\ see AUND

awner[1] \ȯn-ər\ fawner, goner, pawner, prawner, spawner, yawner

awner[2] \än-ər\ see ONOR[1]

awney \ȯ-nē\ see AWNY[1]

awning \än-iŋ\ see ONING[1]

awnly \än-lē\ see ANLY[1]

awny[1] \ȯ-nē\ brawny, fawny, lawny, scrawny, Taney, tawny • mulligatawny

awny[2] \än-ē\ see ANI[1]

awp \ȯp\ see AUP

awrence \ȯr-ən(t)s\ Florence, Lawrence • abhorrence, Saint Lawrence—*also* -s, -'s, *and* -s' *forms of nouns and* -s *forms of verbs listed at* ORRENT

awry \ȯr-ē\ see ORY

aws \ȯz\ see AUSE[1]

awse \ȯz\ see AUSE[1]

awser \ȯ-zər\ see AUSER

awsi \au̇-sē\ see OUSY[2]

awy \ȯi\ see OY

awyer \ȯ-yər\ lawyer, sawyer • sea lawyer • canon lawyer, jailhouse lawyer, trial lawyer • criminal lawyer • Philadelphia lawyer

ax[1] \äks\ see OX

ax[2] \aks\ ax, fax, flax, lax, max, Max, pax, rax, sax, Sfax, tax, wax • addax, Ajax, anthrax, banjax, beeswax, borax, broadax, climax, coax, Colfax, death tax, earwax, Fairfax, flat tax, galax, gravlax, hyrax, ice axe, Lomax, lost wax, meat-ax, panchax, pickax, poleax, poll tax, pretax, relax, sales tax, sin tax, smilax, stamp tax, storax, styrax, surtax, syntax, thorax, toadflax • aftertax, ball of wax, battle-ax, direct tax, disclimax, estate tax, Halifax, hidden tax, income tax, Japan wax, mineral wax, minimax, montan wax, nuisance tax, overtax, parallax, prothorax, sealing wax, single tax, supertax, telefax, to the max • anticlimax, Astyanax, bikini wax, carnauba wax, hydrothorax, Levant storax, mesothorax, metathorax, property tax, selling climax, vegetable wax, withholding tax—*also* -s, -'s, *and* -s' *forms of nouns and* -s *forms of verbs listed at* ACK[2]

axant \ak-sənt\ see ACCENT

axen \ak-sən\ see AXON

axi \ak-sē\ see AXY

axic \ak-sik\ ataxic • stereotaxic

axis \ak-səs\ axis, Naxos, praxis
• }x-axis, y-axis, z-axis
• parataxis, phototaxis, prophylaxis

axman \ak-smən\ axman, cracksman, Flaxman

axon \ak-sən\ axon, flaxen, Jackson, Klaxon, Saxon, waxen
• Old Saxon, Port Jackson, West Saxon • Anglo-Saxon

axos \ak-səs\ see AXIS

axy \ak-sē\ flaxy, maxi, taxi, waxy • air taxi • water taxi

ay[1] \ā\ a, ae, bay, bey, blae, brae, bray, chez, clay, Clay, Cray, day, dey, dray, eh, fay, Faye, fey, flay, fley, frae, fray, Frey, gay, Gay, gey, gley, gray, Gray, Grey, hae, hay, he, hey, Hue, j, jay, Jay, Jaye, k, kay, Kay, Kaye, lay, lei, may, May, nay, né, née, neigh, Ney, pay, pe, play, pray, prey, qua, quai, quay, Rae, ray, Ray, re, say, sei, shay, slay, sleigh, spae, spay, Spey, splay, spray, stay, stray, sway, Tay, they, tray, trey, way, weigh, whey, yea
• abbé, affray, agley, airplay, airway, aisleway, all-day, allay, allée, Angers, Anhui, Anhwei, archway, array, ashtray, assay, astray, Augier, away, aweigh, backstay, ballet, base pay, bat ray, beignet, belay, beltway, benday, Benet, beret, betray, bewray, bidet, bikeway, birthday, Biscay, Bizet, blasé, bobstay, Bombay, bombe, Bossuet, bouchée, bouclé, boule, bouquet, Bourget,

bourrée, breezeway, Bouvet, Broadway, buffet, byplay, byway, cachet, café, cahier, Cambay, Cape May, Cartier, Cathay, causeway, chaîné, chalet, chambray, chassé, child's play, ciré, cliché, cloqué, congé, convey, Coos Bay, co-pay, Corday, corvée, coudé, coupé, crawlway, crochet, croquet, crossway, cube, curé, cy pres, DA, daresay, Daudet, D-day, death ray, decay, deejay, defray, delay, dengue, dismay, display, distrait, DJ, donnée, doomsday, doorway, dossier, downplay, dragée, driveway, duvet, Earl Grey, embay, entrée, épée, essay, estray, Ewe, fair play, fairway, False Bay, Feuillet, field day, filé, filet, fillet, fireclay, fishway, Flag Day, flambé, flight pay, floodway, flyway, folkway, footway, foray, force play, forebay, foreplay, forestay, formée, forte, fouetté, foul play, Fouquet, four-way, fourchée, foyer, franglais, frappé, freeway, Friday, frieze, frisé, fumet, gainsay, Galway, gamay, gangway, Gaspé, gateway, gelée, Genet, give way, glacé, godet, gourmet, Green Bay, greenway, guideway, gunplay, hair spray, halfway, hallway, Hannay, harm's way, hatchway, headway, hearsay, Hebei, Hefei, heyday, highway, hold sway, homestay, hooray, horseplay, Hubei, in play, in re, inlay, inveigh, Islay, issei, jackstay, James Bay, jennet, jeté, Jetway, Jolliet, keyway,

Kobe, koine, kouprey, lamé, laneway, lay day, leeway, lifeway, Lomé, long day, Lord's day, Lough Neagh, lwei, lycée, M-day, maguey, mainstay, make hay, Malay, malgré, man-day, Mande, Manet, manqué, margay, Marseilles, massé, match play, maté, May Day, Mayday, Medway, melee, metier, meze, midday, midway, Midway, Millay, Millet, mislay, misplay, moiré, Monday, Monet, moray, Mornay, name day, nevé, Niamey, nisei, noonday, Norway, nosegay, no way, obey, OK, olé, ombré, one-way, osprey, Otway, outlay, outplay, outré, outstay, outweigh, oyez, PA, parfait, parkway, parlay, parquet, partway, passé, pâté, pathway, pavé, payday, pearl gray, per se, pince-nez, pipe clay, piqué, piquet, pith ray, PK, plié, plissé, pommée, Pompeii, portray, prepay, projet, pulque, puree, purvey, quale, Quesnay, raceway, Rahway, railway, rappee, red bay, relay, Rene, Renee, repay, replay, risqué, roadway, Roget, role-play, ropeway, rosé, rosebay, Roubaix, roué, routeway, runway, sachet, saint's day, Salé, sansei, sashay, sauté, screenplay, scrub jay, seaway, semé, Shark Bay, shar-pei, shipway, short-day, sick bay, sick day, sick pay, sideway, Skopje, skyway, slideway, slipway, sluiceway, soigné, soiree, someday, someway, soothsay, soufflé, speedway,

spillway, squeeze play, stair-way, sternway, stingray, straightway, strathspey, stroke play, subway, Sunday, survey, sweet bay, swordplay, Taipei, tea tray, tempeh, thoughtway, three-way, thruway, Thursday, tideway, Tigré, today, Tokay, tollway, Torbay, touché, toupee, trackway, tramway, Tuesday, Twelfth Day, two-way, unlay, unsay, valet, V-day, veejay, vide, visé, Vouvray, walkway, waylay, Wednesday, weekday, white way, windway, wireway, wood ray, wordplay, workday, X ray, Yaoundé
• Adige, Advent Bay, Agnus Dei, A-OK, alleyway, All Fools' Day, All Saints' Day, All Souls' Day, all the way, antigay, anyway, appliqué, Arbor Day, arrivé, atelier, attaché, back away, Baffin Bay, ballonet, bang away, Bantry Bay, Bastille Day, Beaujolais, beta ray, beurre manié, BHA, bird of prey, Biscayne Bay, blow away, botonée, Boxing Day, braciole, breakaway, break away, Bristol Bay, bustier, Buzzards Bay, by the way, cabaret, cableway, Camagüey, Cam Ranh Bay, canapé, cap-a-pie, Cape Cod Bay, caraway, carriageway, Cartier, cassoulet, castaway, cathode ray, champlevé, chansonnier, chardonnay, Charolais, chevalier, china clay, Chippewa, Cleveland bay, cloisonné, cog railway, color-way, Condorcet, consommé, coryphée, cosmic ray, croupier, crudités, cutaway, day-to-day,

debauchee, déclassé, dégagé, degree-day, delta ray, démodé, devotee, Dingle Bay, disarray, disobey, distingué, divorcé, divorcée, DNA, dollar day, double play, draw away, dress-down day, du Bellay, eagle ray, eightfold way, ember day, émigré, Empire Day, engagé, entranceway, entremets, entryway, espalier, étouffée, everyday, exposé, expressway, fadeaway, fallaway, fall away, faraday, Faraday, faraway, Fathers Day, feet of clay, fiancé, fiancée, fill away, fire away, flageolet, flyaway, foldaway, gal Friday, Galloway, gamma ray, garde-manger, Georgian Bay, getaway, girl Friday, giveaway, give away, Glacier Bay, gratiné, gratinée, Greenaway, Groundhog Day, Guy Fawkes Day, guillemet, Harare, haulageway, hell to pay, Hemingway, hereaway, hideaway, hit the hay, HLA, holiday, holy day, Hornaday, Hudson Bay, Hugh Capet, Humboldt Bay, in a way, inter se, interplay, intraday, IPA, IRA, Ise Bay, Jervis Bay, Joliet, judgment day, keep-away, Kootenay, Kutenai, kyrie, Labor Day, lackaday, latter-day, layaway, lay away, lingerie, Loch Achray, macramé, Mandalay, manta ray, Massenet, matinee, medal play, meet halfway, MIA, Milky Way, Monterrey, Moreton Bay, Mother's Day, motorway, multiday, muscadet, mystery play, negligee, New Year's Day, New York Bay, Nicolet, night and day, Nottaway, off Broadway, Ojibwa, on the way, out of play, overlay, overpay, overplay, overstay, overweigh, Paraguay, passageway, pass away, passion play, patissier, pepper spray, Petare, photo-play, pikake, piolet, pis aller, play-by-play, plug-and-play, Ponape, popinjay, potter's clay, pourparler, pousse-café, power play, present-day, protégé, protégée, Prudhoe Bay, pull away, put away, Put-in-Bay, Rabelais, rack railway, rainy-day, rambouillet, ratiné, recamier, rechauffé, recherché, reconvey, repartee, repoussé, résumé, retroussé, ricochet, right away, right-of-way, rockaway, roentgen ray, rondelet, roundelay, RNA, runaway, run away, Saguenay, salt away, San Jose, Santa Fe, São Tomé, Saturday, satyr play, semplice, Seventh-Day, severance pay, shadow play, sleepaway, sobriquet, sock away, sommelier, square away, steerageway, standaway, Steller's jay, stowaway, straightaway, street railway, Table Bay, taboret, take-away, tarsier, taxiway, tearaway, tear away, teleplay, Tenebrae, thataway, throwaway, throw away, Thunder Bay, triple play, turn away, Turtle Bay, Udine, underlay, underpay, underplay, underway, Uruguay, velouté, Venite, vérité, vertebra, virelay, walkaway, Walvis Bay, Wang Ching-wei, waterway, wellaway, Whitsunday, workaday, working day, Yenisey, Zuider Zee • African gray, Appian Way, April Fool's Day, Aransas Bay, areaway, Armistice Day, Ascension Day, Australia Day, auto-da-fé, bank holiday, Bay of Biscay, beta decay, bichon frisé, bioassay, Botany Bay, boulevardier, cabriolet, café au lait, cantabile, Cardigan Bay, carry away, cDNA, Chesapeake Bay, Chincteague Bay, chronicle play, Columbus Day, communiqué, companionway, corps de ballet, costumier, couturier, décolleté, Delaware Bay, devil to pay, diamanté, Dies Irae, Discovery Day, Dominion Day, eglomisé, Election Day, electric ray, far and away, felo-de-se, fiddle away, Fiesole, Frobisher Bay, Giant's Causeway, habitué, High Holiday, instant replay, Jamaica Bay, Jubilate, Korea Bay, laissez-passer, Lavoisier, marrons glacé, medley relay, mezzo forte, microarray, Midsummer Day, miracle play, Montego Bay, Morgan le Fay, objet trouvé, off-off-Broadway, out-of-the-way, papier collé, papier-mâché, pas de bourrée, Patriots' Day, photo-essay, Port Philip Bay, postholiday, Pouilly-Fuissé, Pouilly-Fumé, preholiday, prêt-à-porter, Presidents' Day, roche moutonnée, Rogation Day, roman à clef, roturier, Saginaw Bay, Saint Patrick's Day, sine die, sub judice, superhighway, Suruga Bay, Thanksgiving Day,

Tillamook Bay, ukiyo-e, Ulan-Ude, Valentine's Day, Veterans Day, yerba maté • Alto Adige, arrière-pensée, Guanabara Bay, Independence Day, lettre de cachet, Memorial Day, morality play • catalogue raisonné, cinema verité, vers de société, video verité

ay² \ē\ see EE¹

ay³ \ī\ see Y¹

aya¹ \ä-yə\ maya, taille

aya² \ī-ə\ see IAH¹

aya³ \ä-ə\ see AIA¹

ayable \ā-ə-bəl\ payable, playable, sayable • defrayable, displayable, unplayable, unsayable

ayah \ī-ə\ see IAH¹

ayal \āl\ see AIL

ayan¹ \ā-ən\ crayon • Chilean, Malayan, ouabain, papain, Pompeian • Galilean, Himalayan

ayan² \ī-ən\ see ION¹

aybe¹ \ā-bē\ see ABY

aybe² \eb-ē\ see EBBY

ayday \ā-dā\ Ede, Mayday, May Day

aye¹ \ā\ see AY¹

aye² \ī\ see Y¹

ayed \ād\ see ADE¹

ayer \ā-ər\ Ayer, brayer, layer, mayor, payer, player, prayer, preyer, sayer, slayer, sprayer, stayer, strayer, swayer, Thayer • arrayer, assayer, ballplayer, belayer, betrayer, bilayer, bricklayer, cardplayer, conveyor, crocheter, decayer, delayer, D layer, doomsayer, doomsdayer, E layer, essayer, F layer, forayer, gainsayer, horseplayer, inlayer, inveigher, manslayer, minelayer, naysayer, obeyer, portrayer, purveyor, ratepayer, soothsayer, swordplayer, surveyor, taxpayer, tracklayer, yea-sayer • disobeyer, holidayer— *also* -er *forms of adjectives listed at* AY¹

ayered \erd\ see AIRED

ayest \ā-əst\ mayest, sayest • épéeist, essayist, fideist, Hebraist, Mithraist—*also* -est *forms of adjectives listed at* AY¹

ayin¹ \ī-ən\ see ION¹

ayin² \īn\ see INE¹

ayin³ \ä-yən\ see AIIAN

aying \ā-iŋ\ fraying, gleying, maying, playing, saying • bricklaying, doomsaying, long-playing, nay-saying, soothsaying, surveying, taxpaying, tracklaying—*also* -ing *forms of verbs listed at* AY¹

ayish \ā-ish\ clayish, grayish

ayist \ā-əst\ see AYEST

ayle \āl\ see AIL

ayless \ā-ləs\ rayless, talus, wayless • Morelos • aurora australis, Corona Australis

ayling \ā-liŋ\ see AILING

aylor \ā-lər\ see AILER

ayly \ā-lē\ see AILY

ayman \ā-mən\ see AMEN¹

ayment \ā-mənt\ ament, claimant, clamant, payment, raiment • co-payment, down payment, embayment, nonpayment, prepayment, stop payment • underlayment, underpayment

ayne \ān\ see ANE¹

ayness \ā-nəs\ anus, feyness, gayness, grayness, heinous, Janus, manus • awayness, pandanus, Sejanus, uranous, Uranus • everydayness

aynim \ā-nəm\ see ANUM¹

ayn't \ā-ənt\ see EYANT

ayo¹ \ā-ō\ see EO¹

ayo² \ī-ō\ see IO¹

ayon \ā-ən\ see AYAN¹

ayor \ā-ər\ see AYER¹

ayou¹ \ī-ə\ see IAH¹

ayou² \ī-ō\ see IO¹

ayr \er\ see ARE⁴

ays¹ \ez\ fez, Fez, Geez, prez, says • Boulez, Chávez, Cortez, gainsays, Hafez, Herez, Inez, López, Suez, unsays • à l'anglaise, Alvarez, crème anglaise, Louis Seize, Louis Treize, Martínez, Mayagüez • à la française, Isthmus of Suez, Vincente López

ays² \āz\ see AZE¹

aysia \ā-zhə\ see ASIA

ay-so \ā-sō\ see ESO¹

ayyid¹ \ī-əd\ see YAD

ayyid² \ēd-ē\ see EEDY

az¹ \az\ see AZZ

az² \äz\ see OISE¹

az³ \äts\ see OTS

aza¹ \äz-ə\ Gaza, plaza
• Pastaza, piazza • calabaza
• tabula rasa

aza² \az-ə\ plaza, piazza

azar¹ \äz-ər\ see OZZER

azar² \az-ər\ lazar • alcazar,
Belshazzar

azard \az-ərd\ hazard, mazzard
• at hazard, haphazard
• biohazard, moral hazard

aze¹ \āz\ baize, blaze, braise,
braze, chaise, craze, days,
daze, Draize, faze, feaze, fraise,
gaze, glaze, graze, Hays, haze,
lase, laze, maize, maze, phase,
phrase, praise, raise, raze,
smaze, vase, ways • ablaze,
agaze, amaze, appraise,
breadthways, catchphrase,
crossways, deglaze, dispraise,
dog days, edgeways, emblaze,
endways, flatways, foodways,
gainsays, in phase, Lachaise,
leastways, lengthways, liaise,
malaise, mores, noun phrase,
pj's, post chaise, rephrase,
sideways, slantways, stargaze,
The Naze, ukase, upraise,
weekdays • anyways,
chrysoprase, color phase,
cornerways, crème anglaise,
hereaways, holidays,
hollandaise, Louis Seize, Louis
Treize, lyonnaise, mayonnaise,

metaphrase, multiphase,
nowadays, out of phase,
overglaze, overgraze, over-
praise, paraphrase, photo-
phase, polonaise, polyphase,
single-phase, underglaze
• parting of the ways—*also* -s,
-'s, *and* -s' *forms of nouns and*
-s *forms of verbs listed at* AY¹

aze² \az\ see OISE¹

aze³ \äz-ē\ see AZI¹

azeable \ā-zə-bəl\ see ASABLE¹

azed \āzd\ unfazed—*also* -ed
forms of verbs listed at AZE¹

azel \ā-zəl\ see ASAL²

azement \āz-mənt\ amazement,
appraisement

azen \āz-ᵊn\ see AZON

azer \ā-zər\ blazer, brazer,
Fraser, Frazer, gazer, Glaser,
glazer, grazer, hazer, laser,
maser, mazer, praiser, razer,
razor, Taser • appraiser, fund-
raiser, hair-raiser, hell-raiser,
stargazer, trailblazer • crystal-
gazer, curtain-raiser,
paraphraser

azi¹ \äz-ē\ quasi, Swazi
• Benghazi, Anasazi,
Ashkenazi, kamikaze

azi² \az-ē\ see AZZY

azi³ \at-sē\ Nazi, patsy, Patsy
• neo-Nazi

azi⁴ \ät-sē\ Nazi • neo-Nazi

azier \ā-zhər\ brazier, Frasier,
glazier, grazier, leisure,
measure, pleasure, rasure,

treasure • admeasure, embrasure, erasure

azing \ā-ziŋ\ see AISING

azo \az-ō\ diazo, terrazzo

azon \az-ᵊn\ blazon, brazen, raisin • emblazon, Marquesan • diapason

azor \ā-zər\ see AZER

azquez \as-kəs\ see ASCUS

azy \ā-zē\ crazy, daisy, Daisy, hazy, lazy, mazy • like crazy, stir-crazy • Shasta daisy • witch of Agnesi

azz \az\ as, has, jazz, razz • free jazz, Hejaz, La Paz, pizzazz, topaz, whenas, whereas • razzmatazz

azza[1] \az-ə\ see AZA[2]

azza[2] \äz-ə\ see AZA[1]

azza[3] \ät-sə\ see ATZO[1]

azzar \az-ər\ see AZAR[2]

azzard \az-ərd\ see AZARD

azzle \az-əl\ basil, Basil, dazzle, frazzle • bedazzle, sweet basil • razzle-dazzle

azzo[1] \ät-sō\ matzo • Milazzo, palazzo, terrazzo • paparazzo

azzo[2] \az-ō\ see AZO

azzy \az-ē\ jazzy, snazzy • pizzazzy • Ashkenazi

e

e¹ \ā\ see AY¹

e² \ē\ see EE¹

e³ \ə\ see U³

é \ā\ see AY¹

ea¹ \ā\ see AY¹

ea² \ā-ə\ see AIA¹

ea³ \ē\ see EE¹

ea⁴ \ē-ə\ see IA¹

eabee \ē-bē\ see EBE¹

eace \ēs\ see IECE

eaceable \ē-sə-bəl\ see EASABLE¹

each \ēch\ beach, beech, bleach, breach, breech, each, fleech, leach, leech, peach, pleach, preach, reach, screech, speech, teach • beseech, forereach, free beach, free speech, impeach, Long Beach, outreach, Palm Beach, unteach • copper beech, Myrtle Beach, Newport Beach, overreach, part of speech, practice-teach • Daytona Beach, figure of speech, Huntington Beach, Miami Beach, Omaha Beah, Redondo Beach, Virginia Beach, visible speech

eachable \ē-chə-bəl\ bleachable, leachable, reachable, teachable

• impeachable, unreachable, unteachable • unimpeachable

eacher \ē-chər\ bleacher, creature, feature, leacher, preacher, reacher, screecher, teacher • disfeature, school-teacher • double feature, overreacher, practice teacher, student teacher

eacherous \ech-rəs\ see ECHEROUS

eachery \ech-rē\ see ECHERY

eaching \ē-chiŋ\ see EECHING

eachment \ēch-mənt\ preachment • impeachment

eachy \ē-chē\ beachy, chichi, Nietzsche, peachy, preachy, screechy • caliche, Campeche

eacle \ē-kəl\ see ECAL¹

eacly \ē-klē\ see EEKLY

eacon \ē-kən\ beacon, deacon, sleeken, weaken • archdeacon, Mohican, subdeacon • Nuyorican, radar beacon • radio beacon

ead¹ \ed\ bed, bled, bread, bred, dead, dread, ed, Ed, fed, fled, Fred, head, Jed, lead, led, med, Ned, ped, pled, read, red, Red, redd, said, shed, shred, sled,

130

sped, spread, stead, ted, Ted, thread, tread, wed, zed • abed, ahead, airhead, baldhead, beachhead, bedspread, bedstead, beebread, behead, bestead, bighead, biped, blackhead, blockhead, blood-red, bloodshed, bobsled, bonehead, brain-dead, break bread, bridgehead, brown bread, bulkhead, bullhead, catch dead, cathead, childbed, clubhead, coed, cokehead, corn bread, corn-fed, cowshed, crackhead, crispbread, crisphead, crossbred, cross-head, daybed, deadhead, death's-head, deathbed, dispread, dogsled, dopehead, drop-dead, drophead, drum-head, dumbhead, egghead, embed, far-red, farmstead, fathead, flatbed, Flathead, forehead, foresaid, French bread, fry bread, gainsaid, Gateshead, gearhead, god-head, greenhead, half-bred, hardhead, highbred, hogshead, homebred, homestead, hophead, hotbed, hothead, ill-bred, inbred, instead, jarhead, juicehead, knock dead, lamed, light bread, longhead, lowbred, lunkhead, make head, mast-head, meathead, misled, misread, moped, naled, nonsked, outsped, outspread, packthread, phys ed, pinhead, pithead, point spread, pothead, premed, printhead, purebred, quick bread, railhead, redhead, red lead, re-tread, retread, roadbed, roadstead, Round-head, saphead, scarehead,

screw thread, seabed, seedbed, sheep ked, sheeps-head, sheetfed, shewbread, shortbread, sickbed, skinhead, snowshed, softhead, sorehead, spearhead, spoon bread, springhead, steelhead, straight-bred, streambed, subhead, sweetbread, swellhead, thickhead, toolhead, toolshed, towhead, trailhead, Turk's head, unbred, undead, unread, unsaid, unthread, untread, Volstead, warhead, webfed, well-bred, wellhead, well-read, white-bread, whitehead, Whitehead, white lead, widespread, wingspread, woodshed, woolshed • acid-head, aforesaid, arrowhead, barrelhead, Birkenhead, bubblehead, bufflehead, butterhead, chowderhead, chucklehead, colorbred, copperhead, Diamond Head, dragonhead, dunderhead, Dunnet Head, featherbed, featherhead, fiddlehead, figurehead, fountainhead, get ahead, gingerbread, go-ahead, hammerhead, head-to-head, Holinshed, infrared, interbred, Java Head, knucklehead, letterhead, Lizard Head, loggerhead, lowlihead, maidenhead, Malin Head, Marblehead, metalhead, newlywed, overhead, over-spread, pinniped, pointy-head, poppyhead, quadruped, riverbed, running head, saddlebred, Saint John's bread, Samoyed, scratch one's head, showerhead, sleepyhead, slugabed, soda bread, standardbred, straight-ahead, talking head, thoroughbred, thunderhead, timberhead, turn one's head, turtlehead, underbred, underfed, watershed, woodenhead • cylinder head, far-infrared, fire-engine red, Flamborough Head, go to one's head, near-infrared, over one's head, Tintagel Head, West Quoddy Head

ead² \ēd\ see EED

ead³ \ed\ see UD¹

eadable¹ \ēd-ə-bəl\ kneadable, pleadable, readable • unreadable • machine-readable

eadable² \ed-ə-bəl\ see EDIBLE

eaded¹ \ed-əd\ bedded, headed • airheaded, bareheaded, bigheaded, bullheaded, clearheaded, coolheaded, eggheaded, embedded, fatheaded, hardheaded, hotheaded, light-headed, longheaded, lunkheaded, pigheaded, pinheaded, redheaded, roundheaded, sapheaded, softheaded, soreheaded, swelled-headed, swellheaded, thickheaded, towheaded, unleaded, whiteheaded, wrongheaded • bubbleheaded, chowderheaded, chuckleheaded, dunderheaded, empty-headed, featherheaded, gingerbreaded, hydra-headed, knuckleheaded, levelheaded, muddleheaded, pointy-headed, puzzleheaded, woodenheaded, woolly-headed

eaded² \ē-dəd\ see EEDED

eaden \ed-ᵊn\ deaden, leaden, redden, steading • Armageddon

eader¹ \ēd-ər\ beader, bleeder, breeder, cedar, ceder, feeder, kneader, leader, pleader, reader, seeder, speeder, weeder • bandleader, cheerleader, conceder, floor leader, impeder, lay reader, lip-reader, loss leader, mind reader, misleader, mouth breeder, newsreader, nonreader, proofreader, repleader, ringleader, seceder, self-feeder, sight reader, stampeder, stockbreeder, succeeder • bottom feeder, copyreader, filter feeder, interpleader

eader² \ed-ər\ bedder, cheddar, chedar, header, shedder, shredder, sledder, spreader, tedder, threader, treader, wedder • homesteader • doubleheader, triple-header

eadily \ed-ᵊl-ē\ headily, readily, steadily • unsteadily

eading¹ \ed-in\ bedding, heading, Reading, Redding, sledding, wedding • bobsledding, farmsteading, subheading, wide-spreading • featherbedding—also -ing forms of verbs listed at EAD¹

eading² \ed-ᵊn\ see EADEN

eading³ \ēd-ᵊn\ see EDON

eading⁴ \ēd-in\ see EEDING¹

eadle¹ \ed-ᵊl\ see EDAL¹

eadle² \ēd-ᵊl\ see EEDLE

eadly \ed-lē\ see EDLEY

eadsman[1] \edz-mən\ headsman, leadsman

eadsman[2] \ēdz-mən\ see EEDSMAN

eady[1] \ed-ē\ bready, Eddie, eddy, Freddie, heady, leady, ready, steady, teddy, Teddy, thready • already, go steady, makeready, unsteady • at the ready, gingerbready, rough-and-ready

eady[2] \ēd-ē\ see EEDY

eaf[1] \ef\ see EF[1]

eaf[2] \ēf\ see IEF[1]

eafy \ē-fē\ see EEFY

eag \ēg\ see IGUE

eagan \ā-gən\ see AGIN

eager \ē-gər\ eager, leaguer, meager • beleaguer, big leaguer, bush leaguer, intriguer • Ivy Leaguer, Junior Leaguer, Little Leaguer, major leaguer, overeager, Texas leaguer, Xinjiang Uygur

eagh \ā\ see AY[1]

eagle \ē-gəl\ see EGAL

eague \ēg\ see IGUE

eaguer \ē-gər\ see EAGER

eah \ē-ə\ see IA[1]

eak[1] \ēk\ beak, bleak, cheek, chic, cleek, clique, creak, creek, Creek, eke, flic, freak, geek, gleek, Greek, keek, leak, leek, meek, peak, peek, peke, pic, pique, reek, screak, seek, sheikh, shriek, sic, Sikh, sleek, sneak, speak, squeak, steek, streak, streek, teak, tweak, weak, week, wreak • antique, apeak, batik, Belgique, Belleek, bespeak, bezique, blue streak, boutique, cacique, caique, Cloud Peak, critique, debeak, forepeak, forespeak, Grays Peak, grosbeak, hairstreak, halfbeak, houseleek, Late Greek, Longs Peak, midweek, misspeak, muzhik, mystique, newspeak, nonpeak, oblique, off-peak, outspeak, perique, physique, Pikes Peak, pip-squeak, pratique, relique, technic, technique, Tajik, unique, unspeak, workweek • Battle Creek, biunique, Blanca Peak, Bolshevik, Boundary Peak, Chesapeake, control freak, dominique, doublespeak, ecofreak, fenugreek, Granite Peak, hide-and-seek, Holy Week, Lassen Peak, Lenin Peak, Martinique, Menshevik, Middle Greek, Modern Greek, Mozambique, Passion Week, tongue-in-cheek, up the creek, verd antique, Veronique, Wheeler Peak, widow's peak • bubble-and-squeak, electroweak, microtechnique, quarterback sneak, semi-antique • Communism Peak, opéra comique, realpolitik, turn the other cheek

eak[2] \āk\ see AKE[1]

eak[3] \ek\ see ECK

eakable \ā-kə-bəl\ see AKABLE

eake \ēk\ see EAK[1]

eaked[1] \ē-kəd\ peaked, streaked

eaked² \ēkt\ beaked, freaked, peaked, streaked • apple-cheeked—*also* -ed *forms of verbs listed at* EAK¹

eaked³ \ik-əd\ see ICKED¹

eaken \ē-kən\ see EACON

eaker¹ \ē-kər\ beaker, leaker, phreaker, reeker, seeker, sneaker, speaker, squeaker • loudspeaker, self-seeker, sunseeker • doublespeaker, keynote speaker—*also* -er *forms of adjectives listed at* EAK¹

eaker² \ā-kər\ see AKER¹

eaking¹ \ē-kiŋ\ freaking, phreaking, sneaking, speaking, streaking • heat-seeking, self-seeking • public speaking —*also* -ing *forms of verbs listed at* EAK¹

eaking² \ā-kiŋ\ see AKING¹

eakish \ē-kish\ cliquish, freakish, weakish

eakly \ē-klē\ see EEKLY

eaky \ē-kē\ beaky, cheeky, cliquey, creaky, freaky, geeky, leaky, piki, reeky, sneaky, screaky, squeaky, streaky, tiki • boutique, dashiki • cock-a-leekie, Kurashiki, Manihiki

eal¹ \ē-əl\ paleal, tineal • empyreal, epigeal, gonorrheal, hymeneal, laryngeal, marmoreal, phalangeal, pharyngeal

eal² \ēl\ ceil, chiel, creel, deal, deil, eel, feel, heal, heel, he'll, keel, Kiel, kneel, leal, meal, Neil, peal, peel, real, reel, seal, seel, she'll, shiel, speel, spiel, squeal, steal, steel, Steele, streel, teal, tuille, veal, weal, we'll, wheal, wheel, zeal • aiguille, allheal, all-wheel, anneal, appeal, Arbil, bastille, Bastille, big deal, big wheel, bilge keel, bonemeal, bonspiel, Camille, cam wheel, Castile, cartwheel, Cecile, chainwheel, chenille, cogwheel, conceal, congeal, cornmeal, done deal, eared seal, enwheel, Erbil, fifth wheel, fish meal, flywheel, forefeel, for real, four-wheel, freewheel, fur seal, genteel, get real, good deal, great seal, handwheel, harp seal, ideal, inchmeal, Irbil, irreal, Kuril, Lucille, mild steel, mill wheel, misdeal, mobile, Mobile, monk seal, mouthfeel, New Deal, newsreel, nosewheel, oatmeal, O'Neill, ordeal, pastille, piecemeal, pinwheel, prayer wheel, raw deal, repeal, reveal, schlemiel, self-heal, side-wheel, singspiel, somedeal, spike heel, stabile, surreal, tahsil, Tar Heel, thumbwheel, unreal, unreel, unseal, worm wheel • acetyl, airmobile, Ardabil, bearded seal, beau ideal, bidonville, blastocoel, bloodmobile, Bogomil, bookmobile, buffing wheel, campanile, carbon steel, Catherine wheel, chamomile, cochineal, cockatiel, color wheel, commonweal, conger eel, Cuban heel, curb appeal, cut a deal, daisy wheel, difficile, dishabille, down-at-heel, Ferris wheel, glockenspiel, golden-seal, Guayaquil, harbor seal, idler wheel, lamprey eel, leopard seal, manchineel, megadeal, mercantile, moray eel, orange peel, package deal, paddle wheel, pedal steel, pimpmobile, planet wheel, potter's wheel, reel-to-reel, sex appeal, skimobile, snob appeal, snowmobile, spinning reel, stainless steel, thunderpeal, tracing wheel, under heel, waterwheel • automobile, chemical peel, crucible steel, cylinder seal, Damascus steel, ego ideal, electric eel, elephant seal, Solomon's seal, stiletto heel, structural steel, Virginia reel, varicocele

eal[3] \āl\ see AIL

eal[4] \il\ see ILL

ealable \ē-lə-bəl\ peelable, reelable, stealable • appealable, concealable, repealable, resealable, revealable • irrepealable, unappealable

ealand \ē-lənd\ see ELAND

eald \ēld\ see IELD

ealed \ēld\ see IELD

ealer \ē-lər\ dealer, feeler, healer, heeler, kneeler, peeler, reeler, sealer, Sheeler, spieler, squealer, stealer, stelar, vealer, velar, wheeler • appealer, cartwheeler, concealer, faith healer, four-wheeler, free-wheeler, New Dealer, news-dealer, repealer, revealer, scene-stealer, side-wheeler, stern-wheeler, three-wheeler, two-wheeler, ward heeler • double-dealer, eighteen-wheeler, 18-wheeler, paddle wheeler, snowmobiler, wheeler-dealer

ealie \ē-lē\ see EELY

ealing \ē-liŋ\ see EELING

eally[1] \ē-ə-lē\ leally • ideally, surreally • hymeneally

eally[2] \il-ē\ see ILLY[1]

eally[3] \ē-lē\ see EELY

ealm \elm\ see ELM

ealment \ēl-mənt\ concealment, congealment, revealment

ealot \el-ət\ see ELLATE

ealotry \el-ə-trē\ see ELOTRY

ealous \el-əs\ Ellis, Hellas, jealous, trellis, zealous • cancellous, Marcellus, nucellus, ocellus

ealousy \el-ə-sē\ see ELACY

ealth \elth\ health, stealth, wealth • bill of health, commonwealth, public health

ealthy \el-thē\ healthy, stealthy, wealthy • heart-healthy, unhealthy

ealty \ēl-tē\ fealty, realty

eam[1] \ēm\ beam, bream, cream, deem, deme, dream, gleam, meme, neem, Nîmes, ream, scheme, scream, seam, seem, seme, steam, stream, team, teem, theme • abeam, agleam, airstream, berseem, beseem, bireme, blaspheme, blood-stream, centime, coal seam, cold cream, crossbeam, daydream, downstream, dream team, drill team, egg cream, esteem, extreme, French seam, grapheme, Gulf Stream, hakim, headstream, high beam, hornbeam, I beam, ice cream, inseam, jet stream, kilim, lexeme, live steam, low beam, mainstream, midstream, millime, millstream, moonbeam, morpheme, onstream, outscheme, phoneme, pipe dream, redeem, regime, rhyme scheme, sealed-beam, sememe, sidestream, slipstream, sour cream, sunbeam, supreme, tag team, Tarim, taxeme, third-stream, toneme, trireme, unseam, upstream, warp beam, wet dream • academe, balance beam, blow off steam, buttercream, clotted cream, disesteem, double-team, enthymeme, head of steam, heavy cream, misesteem, monotreme, on the beam, Ponzi scheme, selfesteem, treponeme • ancien régime, Devonshire cream, in the extreme, pyramid scheme, succès d'estime, vanishing cream • American dream, Bavarian cream, groves of academe

eam² \im\ see IM¹

eaman \ē-mən\ see EMON¹

eamed¹ \emt\ see EMPT

eamed² \emd\ steamed—*also* -ed forms of verbs listed at EAM¹

eamer \ē-mər\ creamer, dreamer, femur, lemur, reamer, schemer, screamer, seamer, steamer, streamer • blasphemer, daydreamer, redeemer—*also* -er forms of adjectives listed at EAM¹

eaming \ē-miŋ\ see EEMING

eamish \ē-mish\ beamish, squeamish

eamless \ēm-ləs\ dreamless, seamless

eamon \ē-mən\ see EMON¹

eamster \ēm-stər\ seamster, teamster

eamy \ē-mē\ beamy, creamy, dreamy, gleamy, preemie, seamy, steamy • polysemy

ean¹ \ē-ən\ aeon, eon, Ian, Leon, paean, peon, paeon, zein • Achaean, Actaeon, Aegean, Antaean, Archean, Augean, Chaldean, Chilean, Crimean, Cumaean, Fijian, Judaean, Korean, Kuchean, Linnaean, Mandaean, Matthean, Nicaean, plebeian, pygmaean, Tupian • Aeschylean, Anacreon, apogean, Aramaean, Atlantean, Caribbean, Cerberean, cyclopean, Clytherean, Damoclean, empyrean, epigean, European, Galilean, Hasmonaean, Herculean, Idumaean, Ituraean, Jacobean, kallikrein, Maccabean, Manichaean, Mycenaean, nemertean, nepenthean, Odyssean, panacean, perigean, Sadducean, Sisyphean, Tacitean, Tennessean, Typhoean • antipodean, epicurean, Laodicean, Ponce de Leon, proboscidean,

Pythagorean, terpsichorean, Thucydidean, un-European • epithalamion, Indo-European, Tupi-Guaranian

ean² \ēn\ see INE³

ean³ \ȯn\ see ON³

ean⁴ \ā-ən\ see AYAN¹

eane \ēn\ see INE³

eaner \ē-nər\ cleaner, gleaner, meaner, preener, screener, teener, tweener, weaner, wiener • congener, convener, demeanor, dry cleaner, fourteener, pipe cleaner • carabiner, contravener, intervenor, misdemeanor, submariner, trampoliner, vacuum cleaner

eanery \ēn-rē\ beanery, deanery, greenery, scenery • machinery

eanid \ē-ə-nəd\ Leonid • Oceanid

eanie \ē-nē\ see INI¹

eaning \ē-niŋ\ greening, leaning, meaning, screening • dry cleaning, housecleaning, spring-cleaning, sunscreening, unmeaning, well-meaning • overweening—*also* -ing *forms of verbs listed at* INE³

eanist¹ \ē-nəst\ see INIST²

eanist² \ē-ə-nist\ see IANIST

eanliness \en-lē-nəs\ see ENDLINESS

eanling \ēn-liŋ\ greenling, weanling, yeanling

eanly¹ \ēn-lē\ cleanly, greenly, keenly, leanly, meanly, queenly

• pristinely, routinely, uncleanly • serpentinely

eanly² \en-lē\ see ENDLY

eanne \ēn\ see INE³

eanness \ēn-nəs\ cleanness, greenness, keenness, meanness • betweenness, uncleanness

eannie \ē-nē\ see INI¹

eano \ē-nō\ see INO²

eanor \ē-nər\ see EANER

eanse \enz\ see ENS¹

eant \ent\ see ENT¹

eany \ē-nē\ see INI¹

eap \ēp\ see EEP

eapen \ē-pən\ see EEPEN

eaper \ē-pər\ see EEPER

eapie \ē-pē\ see EEPY

eapish \ē-pish\ see EEPISH

eapo \ē-pō\ see EPOT

ear¹ \er\ see ARE⁴

ear² \ir\ see EER²

earable¹ \er-ə-bəl\ bearable, shareable, spareable, tearable, terrible, wearable • unbearable, unwearable

earable² \ar-ə-bəl\ see ARABLE

earage \ir-ij\ see EERAGE

earance¹ \ir-əns\ see ERENCE¹

earance² \er-əns\ see ARENCE

earch \ərch\ see URCH

earchist \ər-chəst\ see URCHLESS

eard¹ \ird\ beard, eared, tiered, weird • afeard, bat-eared, bluebeard, crop-eared, dog-eared, graybeard, jug-eared, lop-eared, misleared, spade beard, whitebeard • chandeliered, engineered, multitiered, old-man's beard • pre-engineered—*also -ed forms of verbs listed at* EER²

eard² \erd\ see IRD

eare \ir\ see EER²

earean \ir-ē-ən\ see ERIAN¹

eared¹ \erd\ see AIRED

eared² \ird\ see EARD¹

earer¹ \er-ər\ airer, bearer, carer, error, sharer, starer, swearer, terror, wearer • casebearer, crossbearer, cupbearer, declarer, despairer, forbearer, forebearer, furbearer, impairer, live-bearer, pallbearer, repairer, seafarer, talebearer, torchbearer, trainbearer, wayfarer • color-bearer, standard-bearer, stretcher-bearer, Water Bearer—*also -er forms of adjectives listed at* ARE⁴

earer² \ir-ər\ cheerer, fearer, hearer, mirror, shearer, smearer, spearer • coherer, sheepshearer, veneerer • rearview mirror • electioneerer—*also -er forms of adjectives listed at* EER²

earful \ir-fəl\ cheerful, earful, fearful, tearful

earies \ir-ēz\ see ERIES

earing¹ \ir-iŋ\ clearing, earing, earring, gearing, searing • God-fearing, sheepshearing • engineering, fictioneering, hard-of-hearing, mountaineering, power steering • orienteering • bioengineering, reverse engineering, social engineering—*also -ing forms of verbs listed at* EER²

earing² \er-iŋ\ see ARING¹

earish \er-ish\ see ARISH¹

earl \erl\ see IRL¹

earle \irl\ see IRL¹

earler \er-lər\ see IRLER

earless \ir-ləs\ cheerless, fearless, gearless, peerless, tearless

earling¹ \ir-liŋ\ shearling, yearling

earling² \er-lən\ see ERLIN

early¹ \ir-lē\ cheerly, clearly, dearly, merely, nearly, queerly, sheerly, yearly • austerely, biyearly, severely, sincerely • cavalierly, insincerely, semiyearly

early² \er-lē\ see URLY

earn \ərn\ see URN

earned \ərnd\ see URNED

earner \ər-nər\ see URNER

earnist \ər-nəst\ see ERNIST

earnt \ərnt\ burnt, learnt, weren't

earring \ir-iŋ\ see EARING¹

earsal \ər-səl\ see ERSAL¹

earse \ərs\ see ERSE

earser \ər-sər\ see URSOR

earst \ərst\ see URST

eart \ärt\ see ART[1]

earted \ärt-əd\ hearted, parted
• bighearted, coldhearted,
departed, downhearted,
fainthearted, freehearted,
good-hearted, greathearted,
halfhearted, hard-hearted,
kindhearted, largehearted,
lighthearted, proudhearted,
softhearted, stouthearted,
truehearted, uncharted,
warmhearted, weakhearted,
wholehearted • brokenhearted,
chickenhearted, heavyhearted,
ironhearted, lionhearted,
openhearted, single-hearted,
stonyhearted, tenderhearted
—*also* -ed *forms of verbs listed
at* ART[1]

earth[1] \ärth\ see ARTH

earth[2] \ərth\ see IRTH

eartha \ər-thə\ see ERTHA

earthen \ər-thən\ see URTHEN

earthy \ər-thē\ see ORTHY

eartily \ärt-əl-ē\ see ARTILY

eartless \ärt-ləs\ see ARTLESS

earty \ärt-ē\ see ARTY[1]

eary \ir-ē\ aerie, beery, bleary,
cheery, dreary, eerie, Erie,
leery, Peary, peri, quaere,
query, smeary, sphery, teary,
veery, weary • aweary, Fort
Erie, Kashmiri, Lake Erie,
Valkyrie, world-weary • al-
Hariri, hara-kiri, miserere,
overweary, whigmaleerie

eas \ē-əs\ see EUS[1]

easable[1] \ē-sə-bəl\ leasable,
peaceable • increasable,
releasable

easable[2] \ē-zə-bəl\ see EASIBLE

easand[1] \iz-ən\ see ISON[2]

easand[2] \ēz-ənd\ see EASONED

ease[1] \ēs\ see IECE

ease[2] \ēz\ see EZE

eased[1] \ēzd\ diseased, self-
pleased—*also* -ed *forms of
verbs listed at* EZE

eased[2] \ēst\ see EAST[1]

easel \ē-zəl\ bezel, deasil, diesel,
easel, measle, teasel, weasel

easeless \ē-sləs\ ceaseless,
creaseless, greaseless

easelly \ē-zlē\ see EASLY

easement \ēz-mənt\ easement
• appeasement

easer[1] \ē-sər\ creaser, greaser,
piecer • degreaser, increaser,
one-piecer, releaser, two-
piecer

easer[2] \ē-zər\ Caesar, freezer,
geezer, greaser, pleaser, seizer,
sneezer, squeezer, teaser,
tweezer • appeaser,
brainteaser, crowd-pleaser,
degreaser, misfeasor,
stripteaser

eash \ēsh\ see ICHE[2]

easible \ē-zə-bəl\ feasible,
squeezable • appeasable,
defeasible, infeasible
• inappeasable, indefeasible,
unappeasable

easil \ē-zəl\ see EASEL

easily \ēz-lē\ see EASLY

easing¹ \ē-siŋ\ leasing
• unceasing—*also* -ing *forms of verbs listed at* IECE

easing² \ē-ziŋ\ pleasing
• subfreezing—*also* -ing *forms of verbs listed at* EZE

easingly \ē-siŋ-lē\ decreasingly, increasingly, unceasingly

easle \ē-zəl\ see EASEL

easly \ēz-ə-lē\ easily, measly, weaselly

eason \ēz-ᵉn\ reason, season, seisin, treason • disseisin, high treason, in reason, in season, off-season, postseason, preseason, unreason, with reason • age of reason, diocesan, open season, out of season, rhyme or reason, silly season, within reason

easonable \ēz-nə-bəl\ reasonable, seasonable, treasonable • unreasonable, unseasonable

easoned \ēz-ᵉnd\ weasand
• unreasoned—*also* -ed *forms of verbs listed at* EASON

easoning \ēz-niŋ\ reasoning, seasoning • unreasoning

easonless \ēz-ᵉn-ləs\ reasonless, seasonless

easor \ē-zər\ see EASER²

east¹ \ēst\ beast, east, East, feast, fleeced, least, piste, priest, reest, triste, yeast
• archpriest, artiste, at least, batiste, black beast, deceased, down east, Far East, love feast, modiste, Near East, northeast, simpliste, southeast, tachiste
• arriviste, baker's yeast, dirigiste, harteebeest, Middle East, north-northeast, pointillist, wildebeest • à l'improviste —*also* -ed *forms of verbs listed at* IECE

east² \est\ see EST

easted \es-təd\ see ESTED

easter \ē-stər\ Dniester, Easter, feaster, keister, leister, quaestor • down-easter, northeaster, southeaster

eastie \ē-stē\ see EASTY

eastly \ēst-lē\ beastly, Priestley, priestly

easty \ē-stē\ beastie, yeasty

easurable \ezh-rə-bəl\ pleasurable, treasurable • immeasurable

easure¹ \ezh-ər\ leisure, measure, pleasure, treasure
• admeasure, displeasure, dry measure, square measure, tape measure • common measure, countermeasure, cubic measure, for good measure, gold of pleasure, liquid measure, made-to-measure

easure² \ā-zhər\ see AZIER

easurer \ezh-ər-ər\ measurer, treasurer

easy¹ \ē-zē\ breezy, cheesy, easy, greasy, queasy, sleazy, sneezy, wheezy • breathe easy, go easy, pachisi, Parcheesi, speakeasy, uneasy, Zambezi
• free and easy, over easy

easy² \ē-sē\ see EECY

eat¹ \ēt\ beat, beet, bleat, cheat, cleat, Crete, deet, eat, feat, fleet, Geat, gleet, greet, heat, keet, lied, meat, meet, mete, neat, peat, Pete, pleat, seat, sheet, skeet, sleet, street, suite, sweet, teat, treat, tweet, weet, wheat • accrete, aesthete, afreet, athlete, backbeat, backseat, backstreet, bed-sheet, bench seat, big beat, bolete, box pleat, box seat, Bradstreet, break beat, broadsheet, browbeat, buck-wheat, bystreet, call sheet, car seat, cheat sheet, clipsheet, cloud street, cold feet, compete, compleat, complete, conceit, concrete, crabmeat, crib sheet, deadbeat, dead heat, dead meat, deceit, defeat, delete, deplete, discreet, discrete, disseat, downbeat, drop seat, drumbeat, dutch treat, effete, elite, en suite, entreat, escheat, esthete, excrete, facete, Fleet Street, fly sheet, forcemeat, foresheet, four-peat, gamete, ground-sheet, Grub Street, hard wheat, heartbeat, heat-treat, helpmeet, hoofbeat, hot seat, house seat, ice sheet, ill-treat, jump seat, kick pleat, love seat, mainsheet, Main Street, maltreat, mesquite, mincemeat, mistreat, offbeat, Ossete, petite, pink sheet, preheat, rap sheet, receipt, recheat, red heat, red meat, red wheat, regreet, reheat, repeat, replete, retreat, scratch sheet, secrete, side street, slip-sheet, soft wheat, spreadsheet, stand treat, swap meet, sweetmeat, tear sheet, terete, three-peat, through street, time sheet, unmeet, unseat, upbeat, vegete, volkslied, Wall Street, white heat • aquavit, at one's feet, balance sheet, biathlete, bittersweet, booster seat, bucket seat, catbird seat, cellulite, cookie sheet, corps d'elite, countryseat, county seat, crystal pleat, decathlete, drag one's feet, driver's seat, durum wheat, easy street, exegete, incomplete, indiscreet, indiscrete, latent heat, letter sheet, lorikeet, make ends meet, marguerite, Marguerite, Masorete, meadowsweet, meet and greet, miss a beat, Nayarit, nonathlete, obsolete, off one's feet, on one's feet, on the street, overeat, overheat, Paraclete, parakeet, pentath-lete, prickly heat, rumble seat, saddle seat, scandal sheet, self-conceit, semisweet, shredded wheat, sliding seat, spirochete, superheat, to one's feet, triathlete, trick or treat, two-way street, undertreat, up one's street, winding-sheet, window seat • animal heat, banana seat, beat a retreat, ejection seat, ferroconcrete, man in the street, radiant heat, sensible heat, souvenir sheet, take a back seat, vote with one's feet

eat² \āt\ see ATE¹

eat³ \et\ see ET¹

eat⁴ \it\ see IT¹

eatable \ēt-ə-bəl\ beatable, eatable, heatable, treatable • defeatable, depletable, escheatable, repeatable, unbeatable

eated¹ \ēt-əd\ heated, pleated • conceited, deep-seated, repeated • overheated, superheated—*also* -ed *forms of verbs listed at* EAT¹

eated² \et-əd\ see ETID

eated³ \it-əd\ see ITTED

eaten¹ \ēt-ᵊn\ eaten, beaten, Cretan, cretin, Eaton, Eton, neaten, Seton, sweeten, wheaten • browbeaten, Grand Teton, moth-eaten, secretin, unbeaten, worm-eaten • overeaten, weather-beaten

eaten² \āt-ᵊn\ see ATEN¹

eater¹ \ēt-ər\ beater, bleater, cheater, eater, fetor, greeter, heater, liter, meeter, meter, peter, Peter, pleater, praetor, rhetor, seater, sheeter, skeeter, teeter, treater, tweeter • ammeter, anteater, bee-eater, beefeater, blue peter, Demeter, depleter, drumbeater, eggbeater, excreter, fire-eater, flowmeter, heat treater, light meter, long meter, Main Streeter, maltreater, man-eater, ohmmeter, preheater, propraetor, quartz heater, ratemeter, repeater, retreater, saltpeter, secretor, seedeater, space heater, toadeater, voltmeter, Wall Streeter, wattmeter, windcheater, world-beater • altimeter, centiliter, centimeter, deciliter, decimeter, dekaliter, dekameter, hectoliter, honeyeater, lotus-eater, microliter, milliliter, millimeter, nanometer, overeater, parking meter, postage meter, superheater, taximeter, trick-or-treater, water heater, water meter—*also* -er *forms of adjectives listed at* EAT¹

eater² \et-ər\ see ETTER

eatery \ēt-ə-rē\ see ETORY

eath¹ \ēth\ eath, heath, Keith, Meath, neath, sheath, wreath • beneath, bequeath, hadith, monteith • bridal wreath, underneath

eath² \ēth\ see EATHE

eathe \ēth\ breathe, Meath, seethe, sheathe, teethe, wreathe • bequeath, ensheathe, enwreathe, inbreathe, unsheathe, unwreathe, Westmeath

eathean \ē-thē-ən\ lethean • Promethean

eather¹ \eth-ər\ see ETHER¹

eather² \ē-thər\ see EITHER

eathern \eth-ərn\ see ETHERN

eathery \eth-rē\ feathery, heathery, leathery

eathing \ē-thiŋ\ breathing, sheathing, teething • airbreathing, fire-breathing, rough breathing, smooth breathing —*also* -ing *forms of verbs listed at* EATHE

eathless \eth-ləs\ breathless, deathless

eathy \ē-thē\ heathy, lethe, wreathy

eating \ēt-iŋ\ beating, eating, fleeting, greeting, Keating, meeting, seating, sheeting, sweeting • breast-beating, camp meeting, drumbeating, fire-eating, man-eating, prayer meeting, space heating, town meeting, unweeting • Monthly Meeting, Yearly Meeting • induction heating • Sunday-go-to-meeting—*also* -ing *forms of verbs listed at* EAT¹

eatise \ēt-əs\ see ETUS

eatly¹ \āt-lē\ see ATELY¹

eatly² \ēt-lē\ see EETLY

eaton \ēt-ᵊn\ see EATEN¹

eats¹ \ēts\ Keats—*also* -s, -'s, *and* -s' *forms of nouns and* -s *forms of verbs listed at* EAT¹

eats² \āts\ see ATES¹

eature \ē-chər\ see EACHER

eaty \ēt-ē\ meaty, peaty, sleety, sweetie, treaty, ziti • entreaty, graffiti, Tahiti • Dolomiti, spermaceti

eau \ō\ see OW¹

eaucracy \äk-rə-sē\ see OCRACY

eauteous \üt-ē-əs\ see UTEOUS

eautiful \üt-i-fəl\ see UTIFUL

eauty \üt-ē\ see OOTY¹

eaux \ō\ see OW¹

eavable \ē-və-bəl\ see EIVABLE

eaval \ē-vəl\ see IEVAL

eave¹ \ēv\ breve, cleave, eave, eve, Eve, greave, grieve, heave, leave, lief, peeve, reave, reeve, reive, scrieve, sheave, sleeve, steeve, Steve, thieve, weave, we've • Abib, achieve, aggrieve, believe, bereave, cap sleeve, conceive, deceive, French leave, frost heave, Hoccleve, inweave, khedive, Maldive, motive, naive, perceive, pet peeve, plain weave, qui vive, receive, relieve, reprieve, retrieve, shirtsleeve, shore leave, sick leave, unreeve, unweave, upheave • apperceive, basket weave, by-your-leave, disbelieve, dolman sleeve, family leave, flutter sleeve, Genevieve, interleave, interweave, Laccadive, make-believe, misbelieve, mis-conceive, on one's sleeve, preconceive, raglan sleeve, satin weave, semibreve, Tel Aviv, undeceive, up one's sleeve • adam-and-eve, overachieve, recitative, Saint Agnes' Eve, terminal leave, ticket-of-leave, underachieve • absent without leave

eave² \iv\ see IVE²

eaved \ēvd\ leaved, sleeved • aggrieved, bereaved, broad-leaved, relieved—*also* -ed *forms of verbs listed at* EAVE¹

eavement \ēv-mənt\ see EVEMENT

eaven \ev-ən\ Bevin, devon, Devon, Evan, heaven, Kevin, leaven, levin, seven, sweven

• eleven, hog heaven, replevin, South Devon • seventh heaven, tree of heaven

eaver \ē-vər\ *see* IEVER

eavers \ē-vərz\ cleavers, vivers

eaves \ēvz\ eaves • shirtsleeves • in one's shirtsleeves

eavey \ē-vē\ peavey, divi-divi • Paasikivi

eaward \ē-wərd\ *see* EEWARD

eaze¹ \ēz\ *see* EZE

eaze² \āz\ *see* AZE¹

eazo \ē-zō\ *see* IZO¹

eazy \ē-zē\ *see* EASY¹

eb \eb\ bleb, deb, ebb, neb, pleb, reb, Reb, web • ardeb, celeb, cobweb, cubeb, Deneb, food web, Horeb, orb web, subdeb, Zagreb, zineb • cause célèbre, Johnny Reb, spider-web, World Wide Web

eba \ē-bə\ Chiba, Reba, Sheba • amoeba, Beersheba, Bourguiba, zareba • Curitiba, entamoeba

ebate \ab-ət\ *see* ABIT

ebb \eb\ *see* EB

ebbie \eb-ē\ *see* EBBY

ebble \eb-əl\ pebble, Preble, rebel, treble

ebbuck \eb-ək\ kebbuck, rebec

ebby \eb-ē\ blebby, Debbie, webby • cobwebby

ebe¹ \ē-bē\ BB, Beebe, freebie, Hebe, phoebe, Phoebe, Seabee • caribe

ebe² \ēb\ glebe, grebe, plebe • ephebe, sahib, sun-grebe

ebec \eb-ək\ *see* EBBUCK

ebel \eb-əl\ *see* EBBLE

eber \ā-bər\ *see* ABOR

ebes \ēbz\ Thebes—*also* -s, -'s, *and* -s' *forms of nouns listed at* EBE²

eble \eb-əl\ *see* EBBLE

ebo \ē-bō\ *see* IBO

ebral \ē-brəl\ cerebral, palpebral, vertebral

ebrity \eb-rət-ē\ celebrity • muliebrity

ebs¹ \eps\ *see* EPS

ebs² \ebz\ Debs—*also* -s, -'s, *and* -s' *forms of nouns and* -s *forms of verbs listed at* EB

ebt \et\ *see* ET¹

ebted \et-əd\ *see* ETID

ebtor \et-ər\ *see* ETTER

ebus \ē-bəs\ Phoebus, rebus • ephebus

ec¹ \ek\ *see* ECK

ec² \ets\ *see* ETS

eca \ē-kə\ *see* IKA¹

ecal \ē-kəl\ cecal, fecal, meikle, thecal, treacle • intrathecal, oothecal • bibliothecal

ecan \ek-ən\ *see* ECKON

ecant \ē-kənt\ piquant, secant

ecas \ä-kəs\ Turks and Caicos, Zacatecas

ecca \ek-ə\ Decca, mecca, Mecca, weka • Rebecca, Rijeka

eccable \ek-ə-bəl\ see ECKABLE

eccan \ek-ən\ see ECKON

ecce \ek-ē\ see ECKY

ecco \ek-ō\ see ECHO

ecency \ēs-ᵊn-sē\ decency, recency • indecency

ecent \ēs-ᵊnt\ decent, recent • indecent, obeisant

eces \ē-sēz\ see ECIES

ech¹ \ek\ see ECK

ech² \ək\ see UCK

ech³ \esh\ see ESH¹

eche¹ \āsh\ crèche, flèche, Laoighis, resh, seiche • bobeche • Andhra Pradesh, Madhya Pradesh, Uttar Pradesh

eche² \esh\ see ESH¹

eche³ \ē-chē\ see EACHY

êche \esh\ see ESH¹

èche \esh\ see ESH¹

eched \echt\ see ETCHED

echerous \ech-rəs\ lecherous, treacherous

echery \ech-rē\ lechery, treachery

echie \ek-ē\ see ECKY

echin \ek-ən\ see ECKON

echo \ek-ō\ deco, echo, gecko, secco • art deco, El Greco, reecho • Torre del Greco

echt \ekt\ see ECT

ecia \ē-shə\ see ESIA¹

ecially \esh-lē\ see ESHLY

ecian \ē-shən\ see ETION¹

ecibel \es-ə-bəl\ see ESSIBLE

ecie¹ \ē-sē\ see EECY

ecie² \ē-shē\ see ISHI

ecies \ē-sēz\ feces, species, theses • prostheses, subspecies • exegeses

ecil¹ \ē-səl\ Cecil, diesel

ecil² \es-əl\ see ESTLE¹

ecile \es-əl\ see ESTLE¹

ecily \es-ə-lē\ see ESSALY

ecimal \es-ə-məl\ see ESIMAL

eciman \es-mən\ see ESSMAN

ecious \ē-shəs\ specious • capricious, facetious, Lucretius

ecium \ē-shē-əm\ aecium • lutecium, technetium, zooecium • paramecium

eck \ek\ beck, Cech, check, cheque, Czech, deck, dreck, Eck, fleck, heck, Lech, lek, neck, pec, peck, reck, sec, sneck, spec, speck, trek, wreak, wreck • Alsec, Atrek, Aztec, Baalbek, backcheck, bed check, bedeck, Birkbeck, Bishkek, blank check, boatneck, breakneck, bull neck, Capek, cowl-neck, crew neck, cromlech, crookneck, cross-check, cusec, ewe-neck, exec, fact-check, flight deck, flyspeck, forecheck, foredeck, gooseneck, gut check, haček, hatcheck, henpeck, high tech, hook check, in check, Kazbek, kopeck, limbeck, longneck, low-tech, Lubeck, Mixtec, on deck, OPEC, parsec, paycheck, pinchbeck, poop deck, Quebec, rain check, rebec, ringneck, roll-neck, roughneck, samekh, shipwreck, spell-check, spot-check, Steinbeck, sundeck, tape deck, tenrec, Toltec, Uzbek, V-neck, vo-tech, Waldeck, Warbeck, well deck, wryneck, xebec • afterdeck, à la grecque, Aquidneck, biotech, bodycheck, bottleneck, cashier's check, Chiang Kai-shek, countercheck, demi-sec, discotheque, double-check, double-deck, hunt-and-peck, Janácek, leatherneck, little-neck, nanotech, neck and neck, New Quebec, orlop deck, Pont l'Évêque, quarterdeck, rubber check, rubberneck, shepherd's check, triple sec, turtleneck, weather deck, Yucatec, Zapotec • breathe down one's neck, cinematheque, Isle of Purbeck, kiloparsec, mega-parsec, Melchizedek, mock turtleneck, promenade deck, Toulouse-Lautrec, traveler's check, winter crookneck • perpetual check, play with a full deck, reality check

eckable \ek-ə-bəl\ checkable • impeccable

ecked \ekt\ see ECT

ecker \ek-ər\ Becker, checker, decker, Necker, pecker, trekker, wrecker • back-checker, exchequer, fact-checker, forechecker, oxpecker, Quebecer, spell-checker, three-decker, woodpecker • dominicker, double-decker, rubbernecker, triple-decker

ecking \ek-iŋ\ decking, necking—*also* -ing *forms of verbs listed at* ECK

ecklace \ek-ləs\ see ECKLESS

eckle \ek-əl\ deckle, freckle, heckle, shekel, speckle • kenspeckle

eckless \ek-ləs\ feckless, checkless, necklace, reckless • affectless

ecko \ek-ō\ see ECHO

eckon \ek-ən\ beckon, Brecon, Deccan, reckon, zechin • Aztecan, dead reckon, misreckon, Toltecan • Yucatecan

ecks, eks see EX

ecky \ek-ē\ Becky, recce, techie

econ \ek-ən\ see ECKON

econd¹ \ek-ənd\ see ECUND

econd² \ek-ənt\ see ECCANT

ecque \ek\ see ECK

ecs \eks\ see EX

ect \ekt\ Brecht, necked, sect, specked • abject, advect, affect, aspect, bisect, bull-necked, cathect, collect, confect, connect, convect, correct, cowl-necked, defect, deflect, deject, detect, direct, dissect, Dordrecht, effect,

eject, elect, erect, ewe-necked,
expect, goosenecked, infect,
inflect, inject, insect, inspect,
neglect, object, pandect,
perfect, porrect, prefect,
prelect, project, prospect,
protect, refect, reflect, reject,
resect, respect, ring-necked,
roll-necked, select, stiff-
necked, subject, suspect,
traject, transect, trisect,
Utrecht, V-necked • acrolect,
architect, birth defect, circum-
spect, deselect, dialect,
disaffect, disconnect, disinfect,
disrespect, double-decked,
edge effect, genuflect, grapho-
lect, incorrect, indirect, in
effect, intellect, interject,
intersect, introject, introspect,
lake effect, misdirect, preselect,
re-collect, recollect, reconnect,
redirect, reelect, resurrect,
retrospect, self-respect, side
effect, turtlenecked, vivisect
• aftereffect, benign neglect,
bioprospect, Doppler effect,
halo effect, hypercorrect,
idiolect, interconnect, mega-
project, ripple effect, semierect
• domino effect, landscape
architect, placebo effect, semi-
indirect • politically correct
—also -ed forms of verbs listed
at ECK

ecta \ek-tə\ dejecta, ejecta,
perfecta, trifecta

ectable \ek-tə-bəl\ affectable,
collectible, connectable,
correctable, deflectable,
delectable, detectable,
ejectable, electable, erectable,
expectable, inflectable,

injectable, perfectible, project-
able, protectable, resectable,
respectable, selectable
• disrespectable, indefectible,
undetectable

ectacle \ek-ti-kəl\ see ECTICAL

ectal \ek-təl\ see ECTILE

ectance \ek-təns\ expectance,
reflectance

ectant \ek-tənt\ expectant,
humectant, injectant,
protectant • disinfectant

ectar \ek-tər\ see ECTOR

ectarous \ek-trəs\ see ECTRESS

ectary \ek-tə-rē\ nectary, sectary
• insectary

ected \ek-təd\ affected,
collected, complected,
connected, dejected, directed,
dissected • disaffected,
disconnected, fuel-injected,
recollected, self-affected, self-
collected, self-elected, self-
selected, unaffected,
undirected, unexpected,
unprotected, unselected
• inner-directed, inter-
connected, other-directed
—also -ed forms of verbs listed
at ECT

ecten \ek-tən\ lectin, nekton,
pecten, pectin

ecter \ek-tər\ see ECTOR

ectible \ek-tə-bəl\ see ECTABLE

ectic \ek-tik\ hectic, pectic
• cachectic, cathectic, eclectic,
synectic • anorectic,
apoplectic, catalectic, dialectic

ectical \ek-ti-kəl\ spectacle
• dialectical

ectile \ek-tᵊl\ rectal, sectile, tectal • erectile, insectile, projectile • colorectal, dialectal

ectin \ek-tən\ see ECTEN

ecting \ek-tiŋ\ affecting, respecting • self-correcting, self-respecting—*also* -ing *forms of verbs listed at* ECT

ection \ek-shən\ flexion, lection, section • abjection, advection, affection, bisection, collection, complexion, confection, connection, convection, correction, cross section, C-section, defection, deflection, dejection, detection, ejection, direction, dissection, ejection, election, erection, evection, infection, inflection, injection, inspection, midsection, objection, perfection, prelection, projection, protection, refection, reflection, rejection, resection, selection, subjection, subsection, trajection, transection, trisection • by-election, circumspection, conic section, disaffection, disconnection, disinfection, fuel injection, genuflection, golden section, imperfection, indirection, insurrection, intellection, interjection, intersection, introjection, introspection, kin selection, misdirection, predilection, preselection, recollection, reconnection, redirection, reelection, reinfection, resurrection, retroflexion, retrospection, self-direction,

self-protection, self-reflection, self-selection, stage direction, vivisection, yeast infection • antirejection, equal protection, general election, house of correction, hypercorrection, interconnection, microdissection, microinjection • cesarean section

ectional \ek-shnəl\ sectional • affectional, bisectional, complexional, connectional, convectional, correctional, cross-sectional, directional, inflectional, projectional, reflectional • bidirectional, introspectional, interjectional, intersectional, resurrectional, vivisectional • omnidirectional, unidirectional

ectionist \ek-shə-nəst\ perfectionist, projectionist, protectionist, selectionist • insurrectionist, introspectionist, resurrectionist, vivisectionist

ective \ek-tiv\ advective, affective, bijective, collective, connective, convective, corrective, defective, deflective, detective, directive, effective, elective, ejective, infective, inflective, injective, invective, objective, perfective, perspective, projective, prospective, protective, reflective, respective, selective, subjective • cost-effective, house detective, imperfective, ineffective, intellective, introspective, nondirective, nonobjective, retrospective,

self-reflective, unselective
• intersubjective, private
detective

ectless \ek-ləs\ see ECKLESS

ectly \ekt-lē\ abjectly, correctly,
directly, erectly
• circumspectly, incorrectly,
indirectly

ectness \ekt-nəs\ abjectness,
correctness, directness,
erectness, selectness
• incorrectness, indirectness
• hypercorrectness

ecto \ek-tō\ recto • perfecto

ectomy \ek-tə-mē\ gastrectomy,
lobectomy, lumpectomy,
mastectomy, vasectomy
• appendectomy, gonad-
ectomy, hysterectomy,
laryngectomy, tonsillectomy
• clitoridectomy

ector \ek-tər\ hector, Hector,
lector, nectar, rector, sector,
specter, vector • bisector,
collector, connector, convector,
corrector, defector, deflector,
detector, director, dissector,
effector, ejector, elector,
erector, infector, injector,
inspector, neglecter, objector,
perfecter, projector, prosector,
prospector, protector, reflector,
selector, subsector, trisector
• lie detector, smoke detector,
stage director, vivisector
• casting director, caveat
lector, funeral director, program
director, solar collector

ectoral \ek-trəl\ pectoral,
spectral, sectoral • electoral,
protectoral • multispectral

ectorate \ek-tə-rət\ rectorate
• directorate, electorate,
inspectorate, protectorate

ectory \ek-tə-rē\ rectory
• directory, protectory,
refectory, trajectory

ectral \ek-trəl\ see ECTORAL

ectress \ek-trəs\ nectarous
• directress, electress,
protectress

ectrix \ek-triks\ rectrix • directrix

ectrum \ek-trəm\ plectrum,
spectrum • broad-spectrum,
electrum, mass spectrum

ectual[1] \ek-chə-wəl\ effectual
• ineffectual, intellectual • anti-
intellectual

ectual[2] \eksh-wəl\ see EXUAL

ectually \ek-chə-lē\ effectually
• ineffectually, intellectually

ectural[1] \ek-chə-rəl\ conjectural,
prefectural • architectural

ectural[2] \ek-shrəl\ flexural
• conjectural • architectural

ecture \ek-chər\ lecture
• conjecture, prefecture
• architecture, curtain lecture

ectus \ek-təs\ rectus
• conspectus, prospectus

ecular \ek-yə-lər\ secular,
specular • molecular

ecum \ē-kəm\ cecum • vade
mecum

ecund \ek-ənd\ fecund, second
• leap second, split-second
• femtosecond, microsecond,
millisecond, nanosecond,

picosecond, yoctosecond, zeptosecond—*also* -ed *forms of verbs listed at* ECKON

ecutive \ek-ət-iv\ consecutive, executive • chief executive, inconsecutive, nonconsecutive

ed \ed\ see EAD[1]

e'd \ēd\ see EED

eda[1] \ēd-ə\ Blida, Frieda, Leda, Vida • alameda, Alameda • olla podrida

eda[2] \äd-ə\ see ADA[3]

edal[1] \ed-əl\ heddle, medal, meddle, pedal, peddle, treadle • Air Medal, backpedal, bipedal, soft-pedal • inter-meddle, service medal, soldier's medal

edal[2] \ēd-əl\ see EEDLE

edance \ēd-əns\ see EDENCE

edar[1] \ed-ər\ see EADER[2]

edar[2] \ēd-ər\ see EADER[1]

edator \ed-ət-ər\ see EDITOR

edd \ed\ see EAD[1]

edda \ed-ə\ Jedda, Vedda

eddar \ed-ər\ see EADER[2]

edded \ed-əd\ see EADED

edden \ed-ən\ see EADEN

edder \ed-ər\ see EADER[2]

eddie \ed-ē\ see EADY[1]

edding \ed-iŋ\ see EADING[1]

eddle \ed-əl\ see EDAL[1]

eddler \ed-lər\ meddler, medlar, peddler • intermeddler

eddon \ed-ən\ see EADEN

eddy \ed-ē\ see EADY[1]

ede[1] \ād\ see ADE[1]

ede[2] \ēd\ see EED

ede[3] \ā-dā\ see AYDAY

edeas \ēd-ē-əs\ see EDIOUS[1]

eded \ē-dəd\ see EEDED

edel \äd-əl\ see ADLE

eden \ēd-ən\ Eden, Sweden • Dunedin, New Sweden • Garden of Eden

edence \ēd-əns\ credence • exceedance, impedance, precedence • antecedence

edent \ed-ənt\ credent, needn't • decedent, precedent, succedent • antecedent

eder[1] \äd-ər\ see ADER

eder[2] \ēd-ər\ see EADER[1]

edes \ē-dēz\ Archimedes, Diomedes

edge \ej\ dredge, edge, fledge, hedge, kedge, ledge, pledge, sedge, sledge, veg, wedge • allege, frankpledge, gilt-edge, hard-edge, knife-edge, nutsedge, old sledge, on edge, straightedge • cutting edge, deckle edge, featheredge, flying wedge, leading edge, sortilege, trailing edge

edged \ejd\ edged, wedged • alleged, full-fledged, gilt-edged, hard-edged, rough-edged, unfledged • deckle-edged, double-edged—*also* -ed *forms of verbs listed at* EDGE

edger \ej-ər\ dredger, edger, hedger, ledger, leger, pledger

edgie \ej-ē\ see EDGY

edgy \ej-ē\ edgy, ledgy, Reggie, sedgy, veggie, wedgie, wedgy

edi \ād-ē\ see ADY

edia \ēd-ē-ə\ media, Media • acedia, mixed media • cyclopedia, hypermedia, multimedia, via media • encyclopedia

edial \ēd-ē-əl\ medial, predial • remedial, stapedial

edian \ēd-ē-ən\ median • comedian, tragedian

ediant \ēd-ē-ənt\ see EDIENT

edible \ed-ə-bəl\ credible, edible, spreadable • incredible, inedible

edic¹ \ēd-ik\ comedic • cyclopedic, logaoedic, orthopedic • encyclopedic

edic² \ed-ik\ Eddic, medic • paramedic, samoyedic

edic³ \ād-ik\ see ADIC¹

edicable \ed-i-kə-bəl\ medicable, predicable • immedicable

edical \ed-i-kəl\ medical, pedicle • premedical • biomedical, major-medical, paramedical

edicate \ed-i-kət\ dedicate, predicate

edicle \ed-i-kəl\ see EDICAL

edience \ēd-ē-əns\ expedience, obedience • disobedience, inexpedience

edient \ēd-ē-ənt\ mediant • expedient, ingredient, obedient, submediant • disobedient, inexpedient

ediment \ed-ə-mənt\ pediment, sediment • impediment

edin \ēd-ⁿn\ see EDEN

eding \ēd-iŋ\ see EEDING¹

edious¹ \ēd-ē-əs\ tedious • supersedeas

edious² \ē-jəs\ see EGIS

edist \ēd-əst\ orthopedist • encyclopedist

edit \ed-ət\ credit, edit • accredit, coedit, discredit, noncredit, reedit, subedit • copyedit, line of credit, reaccredit

editor \ed-ət-ər\ creditor, editor, predator • chief editor, coeditor, subeditor • city editor, copy editor

edium \ēd-ē-əm\ medium, tedium • mass medium

edlar \ed-lər\ see EDDLER

edley \ed-lē\ deadly, medley, redly • chance-medley

edly \ed-lē\ see EDLEY

edo¹ \ēd-ō\ credo, lido, Lido, speedo • aikido, albedo, amido, libido, Perdido, Toledo, torpedo, tuxedo

edo² \äd-ō\ see ADO²

edo³ \ēd-ə\ see EDA¹

edo⁴ \e-dō\ Edo, meadow, Yedo

edom \ēd-əm\ see EDUM

edon \ēd-ᵊn\ Eden • Sarpedon
• cotyledon

edouin \ed-wən\ see EDWIN

edra \ē-drə\ Phaedra • cathedra
• ex cathedra

edral \ē-drəl\ cathedral, dihedral, trihedral • hemihedral, holohedral, octahedral, pentahedral, polyhedral, procathedral, rhombohedral, tetrahedral • dodecahedral, icosahedral

edulous \ej-ə-ləs\ credulous, sedulous • incredulous

edum \ēd-əm\ Edam, Edom, freedom, sedum • Medal of Freedom

edure \ē-jər\ besieger, procedure • supersedure

edwin \ed-wən\ Edwin • bedouin

ee¹ \ē\ b, be, bee, Brie, c, cay, cee, Cree, d, dee, Dee, dree, e, fee, flea, flee, free, g, gee, ghee, gie, glee, gree, he, key, Key, knee, lea, lee, Lee, Leigh, me, mi, p, pea, pee, plea, pree, quay, re, Rhee, scree, sea, see, she, si, ski, spree, sri, t, tea, tee, the, thee, three, ti, tree, Tshi, twee, Twi, v, vee, we, wee, whee, ye, z, zee • ackee, Agee, agley, aiguille, agree, Albee, alee, ani, at sea, Attlee, Bacchae, bailee, Bangui, banshee, bargee, bawbee, bee tree, Belgae, big tree, Black Sea, bohea, bootee, bo tree, bougie, break free, buckshee, bungee, burgee, Bt, callee, Capri, carefree, CB, CD,

Chablis, Chaldee, chickpea, chili, church key, Coetzee, confit, cowpea, croquis, curie, Curie, Dead Sea, dead-tree, debris, decree, deep-sea, degree, Denis, donee, DP, draftee, drawee, Dundee, emcee, ennui, esprit, etui, farci, feoffee, flame tree, foresee, for free, fringe tree, fusee, GB, germfree, glacis, goatee, grandee, grand prix, grantee, greens fee, green tea, GT, heart-free, he/she, high sea, high tea, home-free, Horae, hot key, Humvee, IC, in fee, IV, Jaycee, jaygee, jayvee, Jiangxi, knock-knee, KP, latchkey, lessee, listee, look-see, low-key, LP, lychee, mamey, maquis, Marie, marquee, MC, mentee, métis, Midi, mille-feuille, ming tree, muggee, must-see, Nancy, ngwee, North Sea, OD, off-key, ogee, Osee, Parcae, pardie, Parsi, passkey, Pawnee, payee, PC, Pee Dee, peewee, pewee, PG, pledgee, pollee, pongee, post-free, précis, puree, puttee, qt, raki, rani, razee, Red Sea, rooftree, Ross Sea, rupee, rushee, RV, sati, scot-free, settee, Shaanxi, shade tree, Shanxi, Shawnee, s/he, shift key, shoe tree, sightsee, signee, silk tree, sirree, smoke tree, snap pea, snow pea, spadille, spahi, spondee, squeegee, standee, state tree, strophe, suttee, sweat bee, sycee, TB, tepee, testee, 3-D, titi, to-be, toll-free, topee, to sea, towhee, townee, trainee, Tralee, trochee, trustee,

Tupi, turfski, turnkey, tutee, Tutsi, tutti, TV, unbe, vendee, vestee, Volsci, vouchee, whangee, White Sea, whoopee, wind tee, would-be, Yangtze, yen-shee • abatis, ABC, ABD, abductee, absentee, acquiree, addressee, adoptee, advisee, alienee, allottee, ambergris, amputee, apogee, appellee, appointee, appraisee, après-ski, Aral Sea, arrestee, assignee, attendee, auditee, awardee, axletree, BVD, Baha'i, bain-marie, barley-bree, batterie, Beaufort Sea, Bering Sea, billi-bi, boiserie, bonhomie, booboisie, bourgeoisie, brasserie, brusquerie, bumble-bee, camphor tree, camporee, cap-a-pie, causerie, CCD, Chamonix, Cherokee, chick-adee, chickaree, chimpanzee, China Sea, Christmas tree, chroma-key, coati, Coligny, conferee, consignee, cop a plea, Coral Sea, counselee, context-free, counterplea, cruelty-free, Danaë, DDT, debauchee, Debussy, departee, deportee, dernier cri, deshabille, designee, detainee, devisee, devotee, diploe, disagree, dischargee, dishabille, divorcé, divorcée, DME, dungaree, duty-free, eau-de-vie, employee, endorsee, enlistee, enrollee, enshrinee, epopee, escadrille, escapee, ESP, evictee, expellee, family tree, fancy-free, fantasy, fedayee, fever tree, filigree, fleur-de-lis, formulae, franchisee, fricassee, function key, galilee, Galilee, garnishee,

gaucherie, Gemini, Greenland Sea, guarani, guarantee, Hawaii, HIV, Holy See, honeybee, honoree, house-maid's knee, humble-bee, inductee, Inland Sea, internee, invitee, Irish Sea, IUD, jacquerie, jamboree, Java Sea, Joshua tree, jubilee, Judas tree, jumper's knee, jus soli, Kayseri, kedgeree, kidnappee, killer bee, LCD, LED, legatee, libelee, licensee, LSD, maître d', Malay Sea, manatee, master key, Medici, Mormon tea, mort-gagee, Mount Tyree, murderee, nominee, obligee, oversea, oversee, Park Chung Hee, parolee, parti pris, pass degree, patentee, pedigree, peppertree, perigee, permittee, pharisee, picotee, piroshki, planer tree, point d'appui, potpourri, praecipe, presentee, promisee, public-key, rapparee, referee, refugee, rejectee, renminbi, repartee, retiree, returnee, Rosemarie, RPV, rubber tree, saddletree, Sadducee, Salton Sea, San Luis, sangaree, Savaii, selectee, Semele, shivaree, slotting fee, snicker-snee, spelling bee, spindle tree, SST, STD, Tappan Zee, Tenebrae, Tennessee, third degree, thirty-three, TNT, to a tee, toile de Jouy, torii, transferee, tulip tree, undersea, Urümqi, user fee, vaccinee, value-free, varnish tree, verdigris, VIP, vis-à-vis, wannabe, warrantee, Wounded Knee • Adar Sheni, advanced degree, Aegean Sea, Agri Dagi, alienee, Amundsen Sea, biographee, bouquet garni, carpenter bee, Caspian Sea, casus belli, Celebes Sea, charcuterie, charivari, chincherinchee, chinoiserie, consent decree, covenantee, cucumber tree, decision tree, dedicatee, delegatee, distributee, East China Sea, ESOP, evacuee, examinee, exuviae, facetiae, fait accompli, felo-de-se, fortunately, Galilei, HTLV, interrogee, interviewee, jaborandi, Labrador Sea, millidegree, minutiae, New Jersey tea, omega-3, Oswego tea, Pasiphaë, patisserie, persecutee, poète maudit, prima facie, reliquiae, relocatee, Sargasso Sea, Sault Sainte Marie, Simon Legree, skeleton key, South China Sea, Southend on Sea, to a degree, umbrella tree, wayfaring tree • Adriatic Sea, Africanized bee, angelica tree, Arabian Sea, bark up the wrong tree, Caribbean Sea, communicatee, contingency fee, external degree, Ionian Sea, japonaiserie, Sea of Galilee, taedium vitae, Tupi-Guarani, water on the knee • Tweedledum and Tweedledee

ee² \ā\ see AY¹

ée \ā\ see AY¹

eeable \ē-ə-bəl\ seeable, skiable • agreeable, foreseeable • disagreeable, unforeseeable

eebie \ē-bē\ see EBE¹

eece \ēs\ see IECE

eeced \ēst\ see EAST¹

eech \ēch\ see EACH

eecher \ē-chər\ see EACHER

eeches \ich-əz\ see ITCHES

eeching \ē-chiŋ\ breeching, screeching, teaching • far-reaching • practice teaching, student teaching—*also* -ing *forms of verbs listed at* EACH

eechy \ē-chē\ see EACHY

eecy \ē-sē\ fleecy, greasy, specie • Tbilisi, AC/DC

eed \ēd\ bead, Bede, bleed, brede, breed, cede, creed, deed, feed, Gide, gleed, greed, he'd, heed, keyed, knead, kneed, lead, mead, Mead, Mede, meed, need, plead, read, rede, reed, Reed, Reid, screed, seed, she'd, Snead, speed, steed, swede, Swede, treed, tweed, Tweed, we'd, weed • accede, airspeed, bindweed, birdseed, blueweed, bourride, breast-feed, bugseed, bur reed, burweed, cheerlead, chickweed, concede, crossbreed, cudweed, debride, degreed, duckweed, exceed, fairlead, fern seed, fireweed, flaxseed, force-feed, free reed, Godspeed, ground speed, gulfweed, half-breed, hand-feed, hawkweed, hayseed, high-speed, horseweed, impede, implead, inbreed, indeed, ironweed, Jamshid, jetbead, knapweed, knotweed, Lake Mead, linseed, lip-read, milkweed, misdeed, mislead, misread, moonseed, nosebleed, off-speed, oilseed, pigweed, pinweed, pokeweed, pondweed, precede, proceed, proofread, ragweed, rapeseed, recede, reseed, rockweed, seaweed, secede, self-feed, Siegfried, sight-read, silkweed, smartweed, snakeweed, sneezeweed, speed-read, spoon-feed, stall-feed, stampede, stickseed, stickweed, stinkweed, succeed, tenspeed, tickseed, warp speed, weak-kneed, witchweed, wormseed • aniseed, antecede, beating reed, beggarweed, bitterweed, bottle-feed, bugleweed, butterweed, carpetweed, centipede, chicken feed, copyread, cottonseed, cottonweed, crazyweed, double reed, Ganymede, giant reed, go to seed, interbreed, intercede, interplead, jewelweed, jimsonweed, Klamath weed, locoweed, millipede, Nicene Creed, overfeed, pedigreed, pickerelweed, poppy seed, Port Said, pumpkinseed, quitclaim deed, retrocede, riverweed, rosinweed, Runnymede, silverweed, supersede, thimbleweed, title deed, tumbleweed, underfeed, up to speed, waterweed • Apostles' Creed, canary seed, caraway seed, velocipede, warranty deed—*also* -ed *forms of verbs listed at* EE

eedal \ēd-ᵊl\ see EEDLE

eeder \ēd-ər\ see EADER¹

eedful \ēd-fəl\ heedful, needful

eeding¹ \ēd-iŋ\ bleeding, breeding, leading, reading, reeding • inbreeding, linebreeding, lipreading, outbreeding, preceding, proceeding, speed-reading • bottomfeeding, care and feeding—*also* -ing *forms of verbs listed at* EED

eeding² \ēd-ᵊn\ see EDON

eedle \ēd-ᵊl\ aedile, beadle, credal, creedal, daedal, needle, wheedle • darning needle

eedless \ēd-ləs\ deedless, heedless, leadless, needless, seedless

eedn't \ēd-ᵊnt\ see EDENT

eedo \ēd-ō\ see EDO¹

eedom \ēd-əm\ see EDUM

eeds \ēdz\ Leeds, needs • Beskids, love beads, prayer beads, proceeds • special needs, worry beads—*also* -s, -'s, *and* -s' *forms of nouns and* -s *forms of verbs listed at* EED

eedsman \ēdz-mən\ beadsman, seedsman

eedy \ēd-ē\ beady, deedy, greedy, needy, reedy, seedy, speedy, tweedy, weedy

eef \ēf\ see IEF¹

eefe \ēf\ see IEF¹

eefy \ē-fē\ beefy, leafy, reefy

eegee \ē-jē\ see IJI

eeing \ē-iŋ\ being, seeing, skiing • farseeing, ill-being, sightseeing, turfskiing, well-being • heli-skiing, waterskiing—*also* -ing *forms of verbs listed at* EE¹

eek[1] \ik\ see ICK

eek[2] \ēk\ see EAK[1]

eeked \ēkt\ see EAKED[2]

eeken \ē-kən\ see EACON

eeker \ē-kər\ see EAKER[1]

eekie \ē-kē\ see EAKY

eeking \ē-kiŋ\ see EAKING[1]

eekly \ē-klē\ bleakly, chicly, meekly, sleekly, weakly, weekly, treacly • biweekly, midweekly, newsweekly, triweekly • semiweekly

eeks \ēks\ see IXE[1]

eeky \ē-kē\ see EAKY

eel \ēl\ see EAL[2]

eelable \ē-lə-bəl\ see EALABLE

eele \ēl\ see EAL[2]

eeled \ēld\ see IELD

eeler \ē-lər\ see EALER

eeley \ē-lē\ see EELY

eelie \ē-lē\ see EELY

eelin \ē-lən\ see ELIN

eeling \ē-liŋ\ ceiling, dealing, Ealing, feeling, peeling, shieling, wheeling • appealing, Darjeeling, faith healing, freewheeling, glass ceiling, revealing, self-dealing, self-feeling, self-sealing, unfeeling • double-dealing, fellow feeling, hit the ceiling, self-revealing, snowmobiling, unappealing —also -ing forms of verbs listed at EAL[2]

eelson \el-sən\ see ELSON

eely \ē-lē\ dele, eely, Ely, freely, Greeley, mealy, really, seely, steelie, steely, stele, vealy, wheelie • scungilli, surreally, Swahili • campanile, contumely, Isle of Ely, monostele, touchy-feely

eem \ēm\ see EAM[1]

eeman \ē-mən\ see EMON[1]

eemer \ē-mər\ see EAMER

eemie \ē-mē\ see EAMY

eeming \ē-miŋ\ scheming, screaming, seeming, streaming • redeeming • unbeseeming —also -ing forms of verbs listed at EAM[1]

eemly \ēm-lē\ seemly • extremely, supremely, unseemly

een[1] \in\ see IN[1]

een[2] \ēn\ see INE[3]

e'en \ēn\ see INE[3]

eena \ē-nə\ see INA[2]

eene \ēn\ see INE[3]

eener \ē-nər\ see EANER

eenery \ēn-rē\ see EANERY

eening \ē-niŋ\ see EANING

eenling \ēn-liŋ\ see EANLING

eenly \ēn-lē\ see EANLY[1]

eenness \ēn-nəs\ see EANNESS

eens \ēnz\ Queens, teens • by all means, by no means, Grenadines, New Orleans, Philippines, refried beans, smithereens, ways and means

eenwich \in-ich\ see INACH

eeny \ē-nē\ see INI¹

eep \ēp\ beep, bleep, cheap, cheep, creep, deep, heap, jeep, Jeep, keep, leap, neap, neep, peep, reap, seep, sheep, sleep, steep, sweep, threap, veep, weep • asleep, barkeep, black sheep, bopeep, dirt cheap, dustheap, housekeep, knee-deep, scrap heap, skin-deep, upkeep, upsweep • bighorn sheep, bracket creep, chimney sweep, Lakshadweep, mountain sheep, on the cheap, overleap, oversleep, quantum leap • Louis Philippe

eepage \ē-pij\ creepage, seepage

eepen \ē-pən\ cheapen, deepen, steepen

eepence \ēp-əns\ see UPPANCE

eepenny \ēp-nē\ see OPENNY

eeper \ē-pər\ beeper, creeper, Dnieper, keeper, leaper, peeper, reaper, sleeper, sweeper, weeper • barkeeper, beekeeper, bookkeeper, crowkeeper, doorkeeper, gamekeeper, gatekeeper, goalkeeper, greenkeeper, grim reaper, groundskeeper, housekeeper, innkeeper, lockkeeper, minesweeper, peacekeeper, scorekeeper, shopkeeper, spring peeper, stockkeeper, storekeeper, timekeeper, zookeeper • chimney sweeper, honey-creeper • Virginia creeper—*also* -er *forms of adjectives listed at* EEP

eepie \ē-pē\ see EEPY

eeping \ē-piŋ\ creeping, keeping, weeping • beekeeping, bookkeeping, gatekeeping, housekeeping, minesweeping, peacekeeping, safekeeping, timekeeping—*also* -ing *forms of verbs listed at* EEP

eepish \ē-pish\ cheapish, sheepish

eeple \ē-pəl\ see EOPLE

eepy \ē-pē\ cheapie, creepy, seepy, sleepy, sweepy, tepee, weepie, weepy

eer¹ \ē-ər\ seer, skier, we're • CBer, decreer, foreseer, sightseer • couturiere, overseer, water-skier

eer² \ir\ beer, bier, blear, cere, cheer, clear, dear, deer, Deere, drear, ear, fear, fere, fleer, gear, hear, here, jeer, Lear, leer, mere, mir, near, peer, pier, Pierre, queer, rear, schmear, sear, seer, sere, shear, sheer, skirr, smear, sneer, spear, speer, sphere, steer, tear, tier, Trier, Tyr, veer, weir, we're, year • adhere, Aesir, Ajmer, all clear, ambeer, ampere, appear, arrear, Asir, austere, Ayrshire, Berkshire, besmear, brassiere, Bronx cheer, by ear, Cape Fear, career, cashier, cashmere, Cheshire, chimere, clavier, cohere, compeer, destrier, dog-ear, Ellesmere, emir, Empire, endear, ensphere, eyrir, Fafnir, Fifeshire, Flintshire, footgear, frontier, gambier, Goodyear,

Hampshire, headgear, inhere, Izmir, Kashmir, kefir, killdeer, Landseer, laveer, leap year, life peer, light-year, man-year, menhir, midyear, mishear, monsieur, mouse-ear, mule deer, musk deer, nadir, Nairnshire, near beer, New Year, off year, out-year, Pamir, Pap smear, Perthshire, pickeer, portiere, premier, premiere, red deer, redear, rehear, reindeer, revere, Revere, revers, Robespierre, roe deer, root beer, Saint Pierre, santir, severe, Shakespeare, Shropshire, sincere, slick-ear, small beer, spruce beer, steer clear, Tangier, tapir, tin ear, uprear, Vanir, veneer, Vermeer, vizier, voir dire, wheatear, Wiltshire, wind shear, wood ear, worm gear, Ymir, Yorkshire, zaire, Zaire • Agadir, Alamgir, atmosphere, auctioneer, balladeer, bandolier, bathysphere, bayadere, Bedfordshire, Bedivere, belvedere, bend one's ear, biosphere, black-tailed deer, bombardier, boutonniere, brigadier, buccaneer, budgeteer, Cambridgeshire, cameleer, cannoneer, canyoneer, cassimere, cavalier, chandelier, chanticleer, chevalier, chiffonier, chocolatier, chromosphere, commandeer, corsetiere, crystal clear, cuirassier, Denbighshire, Derbyshire, diapir, disappear, domineer, Dumfriesshire, ecosphere, Elzevir, engineer, exosphere, fallow deer, fictioneer, financier,

fiscal year, fourdrinier, fusilier, gadgeteer, gasolier, gazetteer, ginger beer, Gloucestershire, gondolier, grenadier, Guinevere, halberdier, hemisphere, Herefordshire, Hertfordshire, Holy Year, IJsselmere, inner ear, insincere, interfere, in the clear, jardiniere, junketeer, kerseymere, Lanarkshire, Lancashire, landing gear, lavaliere, leafleteer, marketeer, Meyerbeer, middle ear, missileer, Monmouthshire, Morayshire, mountaineer, Mount Rainier, muleteer, multiyear, musketeer, mutineer, on one's ear, outer ear, overhear, overseer, oversteer, Oxfordshire, pamphleteer, Pembrokeshire, persevere, photosphere, pioneer, pistoleer, pontonier, privateer, profiteer, puppeteer, racketeer, Radnorshire, rocketeer, running gear, Rutlandshire, scrutineer, Selkirkshire, sloganeer, sonneteer, souvenir, Staffordshire, steering gear, stratosphere, summiteer, swimmer's ear, thermosphere, troposphere, Tyne and Wear, understeer, vintage year, Vladimir, volunteer, Warwickshire, white-tailed deer, Windermere, Worcestershire, yesteryear • acyclovir, animalier, black marketeer, boulevardier, Buckinghamshire, Clackmannanshire, carabineer, Caernarvonshire, Cardiganshire, Carmarthenshire, celestial sphere, charioteer, conventioneer, dollar-a-year, Dunbartonshire, electioneer, elephant's ear, Eskisehir, free marketeer, Glamorganshire, harquebusier, heliosphere, Huntingdonshire, Invernessshire, ionosphere, Kincardineshire, Montgomeryshire, Northamptonshire, Nottinghamshire, orienteer • academic year, bioengineer, cauliflower ear, civil engineer, Jammu and Kashmir, Merionethshire, sabbatical year, sidereal year, social engineer

e'er \er\ see ARE[4]

eerage \ir-ij\ peerage, steerage • arrearage

eered \ird\ see EARD[1]

eerer \ir-ər\ see EARER[2]

eeress \ir-əs\ see EROUS

eerful \ir-fəl\ see EARFUL

eerie[1] \ir-ē\ see EARY

eerie[2] \ē-rē\ see EIRIE

eering \ir-iŋ\ see EARING[1]

eerist \ir-əst\ see ERIST[1]

eerless \ir-ləs\ see EARLESS

eerly \ir-lē\ see EARLY[1]

eersman \irz-mən\ steersman • frontiersman

eerut \ir-ət\ see IRIT

eery \ir-ē\ see EARY

ees \ēz\ see EZE

eese \ēz\ see EZE

eesh \ēsh\ see ICHE[2]

eesi \ē-zē\ see EASY[1]

eesia \ē-zhə\ see ESIA[2]

eesome \ē-səm\ gleesome, threesome

eest[1] \āst\ see ACED

eest[2] \ēst\ see EAST[1]

eesy \ē-zē\ see EASY[1]

eet \ēt\ see EAT[1]

eetah \ēt-ə\ see ITA[2]

eete \āt-ē\ see ATY

eeten \ēt-ᵊn\ see EATEN[1]

eeter \ēt-ər\ see EATER[1]

eethe \ēth\ see EATHE

eether \ē-thər\ see EITHER

eething \ē-thiŋ\ see EATHING

eetie \ēt-ē\ see EATY

eeting \ēt-iŋ\ see EATING

eetle \ēt-ᵊl\ see ETAL

eetly \ēt-lē\ featly, fleetly, meetly, neatly, sweetly • completely, concretely, discreetly, discretely, effetely • bittersweetly, incompletely, indiscreetly

eety \ēt-ē\ see EATY

ee-um \ē-əm\ see EUM[1]

eeve \ēv\ see EAVE[1]

eeved \ēvd\ see EAVED

eeves \ēvz\ see EAVES

eevil \ē-vəl\ see IEVAL

eevish \ē-vish\ peevish, thievish

eeward \ē-wərd\ leeward, Leeward, seaward

eewee \ē-wē\ kiwi, peewee, pewee

eewit \ü-ət\ see UET

eez \ēz\ see EZE

eezable \ē-zə-bəl\ see EASIBLE

eeze \ēz\ see EZE

eezer \ē-zər\ see EASER²

eezing \ē-ziŋ\ see EASING²

eezy \ē-zē\ see EASY¹

ef¹ \ef\ chef, clef, deaf, ef, f, kef, lev, ref, teff • aleph, bass clef, Brezhnev, C clef, enfeoff, HF, Kiev, Narew, stone-deaf, tone-deaf • emf, Gorbachev, Kishinev, treble clef, UNICEF • Diaghilev, Prokofiev

ef² \ā\ see AY¹

ef³ \ēf\ see IEF¹

efanie \ef-ə-nē\ see EPHONY

efany \ef-ə-nē\ see EPHONY

efe \ef-ē\ see EFFIE

eferable \ef-rə-bəl\ preferable, referable

eference \ef-rəns\ deference, preference, reference • cross-reference • frame of reference

eferent \ef-rənt\ deferent, referent

eff \ef\ see EF¹

effer \ef-ər\ see EPHOR

efic \ef-ik\ Efik • benefic, malefic

eficence \ef-ə-səns\ beneficence, maleficence

efik \e-fik\ see EFIC

eft \eft\ cleft, deft, eft, heft, klepht, left, theft, weft • bereft, grand theft, New Left, stage left • ultraleft • identity theft

efty \ef-tē\ hefty, lefty

eg¹ \āg\ Craig, Haig, plague, vague • stravage, The Hague • Ailsa Craig • Bethmann-Hollweg, bubonic plague

eg² \eg\ beg, Craig, dreg, egg, gleg, Greg, keg, leg, peg, reg, skeg, yegg • blackleg, bootleg, bowleg, dogleg, foreleg, jackleg, jake leg, JPEG, milk leg, MPEG, muskeg, nutmeg, peg leg, redleg, renege, roughleg, Tuareg, unpeg • break a leg, powder keg, pull one's leg, Winnipeg • mumblety-peg

eg³ \ej\ see EDGE

ega¹ \eg-ə\ mega • omega • Lake Onega, rutabaga

ega² \ā-gə\ see AGA²

ega³ \ē-gə\ see IGA¹

egal \ē-gəl\ beagle, eagle, legal, regal, Segal • bald eagle, half eagle, illegal, porbeagle, sea eagle, spread-eagle, viceregal • double eagle, extralegal, golden eagle, harpy eagle, legal eagle, paralegal

egan \ē-gən\ Megan, vegan • Mohegan, Monhegan, Waukegan

egas \ā-gəs\ see AGUS

ege¹ \ezh\ cortege, Liège, manège, solfège

ege² \eg\ see EG²

ege³ \ej\ see EDGE

ege⁴ \ēg\ see IGUE

ege⁵ \ig\ see IG

eged \ejd\ see EDGED

egel \āgəl\ see AGEL

egent \ē-jənt\ regent, sejant • allegiant, vice-regent

eger \ej-ər\ see EDGER

egg \eg\ see EG²

eggar \eg-ər\ see EGGER

eggary \eg-ə-rē\ beggary, Gregory

egger \eg-ər\ beggar, kegger • bootlegger, Heidegger • thousand-legger, Winnipegger

eggie \ej-ē\ see EDGY

eggio \ej-ē-ō\ Reggio • arpeggio, Correggio, solfeggio, Taleggio

eggs \egz\ see EGS

eggy \eg-ē\ dreggy, eggy, leggy, Peggy, plaguey • Carnegie

egia \ē-jə\ Ouija • diplegia • aqua regia, aquilegia, hemiplegia, paraplegia, quadriplegia

egian \ē-jən\ see EGION

egiant \ē-jənt\ see EGENT

egiate \ē-jət\ collegiate, elegit • intercollegiate

egic \ē-jik\ strategic • hemiplegic, paraplegic, quadriplegic • geostrategic

egie \eg-ē\ see EGGY

egion \ē-jən\ legion, region • collegian, Glaswegian, Norwegian, subregion • bioregion

egious \ē-jəs\ see EGIS

egis \ē-jəs\ aegis, egis, Regis, tedious • egregious

egit \ē-jət\ see EGIATE

egm \em\ see EM¹

egn \ān\ see ANE¹

egnant \eg-nənt\ pregnant, regnant • impregnant, queen regnant, unpregnant • pseudopregnant

egnly \ān-lē\ see AINLY

egno \ān-yō\ see ENO¹

ego¹ \ē-gō\ chigoe, ego, Vigo • amigo • alter ego, impetigo, superego

ego² \ā-gō\ see AGO²

egory \eg-ə-rē\ see EGGARY

egs \egz\ sheerlegs • yellowlegs • butter-and-eggs, daddy longlegs—*also* -s, -'s, *and* -s' *forms of nouns and* -s *forms of verbs listed at* EG²

egular \eg-lər\ see EGLER

eh¹ \ā\ see AY¹

eh² \a\ see AH³

ehen \ān\ see ANE¹

ehner \ā-nər\ see AINER

ei¹ \ēk\ dreich, skeigh

ei² \ā\ see AY¹

ei³ \ī\ see Y¹

eia¹ \ē-ə\ see IA¹

eia² \ī-ə\ see IAH¹

eial \ē-əl\ see EAL¹

eian¹ \ē-ən\ see EAN¹

eian² \ā-ən\ see AYAN¹

eic \ē-ik\ apneic, choreic, dyspneic, oleic • diarrheic, epigeic, logorrheic, mythopoeic • onomatopoeic

eich \ēk\ see EI¹

eiche \āsh\ see ECHE¹

eickel \ī-kəl\ see YCLE

eid¹ \āt\ see ATE¹

eid² \īt\ see ITE¹

eid³ \ēd\ see EED

eidel¹ \ād-əl\ see ADLE

eidel² \īd-ᵊl\ see IDAL

eidi \īd-ē\ see IDAY

eidon \īd-ᵊn\ see IDEN

eier \īr\ see IRE¹

eifer \ef-ər\ see EPHOR

eige \āzh\ beige, greige • Mount Neige

eiger \ī-gər\ see IGER

eigh¹ \ā\ see AY¹

eigh² \ē\ see EE¹

eighbor \ā-bər\ see ABOR

eight¹ \āt\ see ATE¹

eight² \īt\ see ITE¹

eighter \āt-ər\ see ATOR

eightless \āt-ləs\ see ATELESS

eights \īts\ see IGHTS

eighty \āt-ē\ see ATY

eign \ān\ see ANE¹

eigner \ā-nər\ see AINER

eii \ā\ see AY¹

eiian \ā-ən\ see AYAN¹

eiji \ā-jē\ see AGY

eik \ēk\ see EAK¹

eikh \ēk\ see EAK¹

eikle \ē-kəl\ see ECAL

eil¹ \āl\ see AIL

eil² \el\ see EL¹

eil³ \ēl\ see EAL²

eil⁴ \īl\ see ILE¹

eila \ē-lə\ see ELA¹

eiled \āld\ see AILED

eiler \ī-lər\ see ILAR

eiling¹ \ā-liŋ\ see AILING

eiling² \ē-liŋ\ see EELING

eill \ēl\ see EAL²

eillance \ā-ləns\ see ALENCE

eillant \ā-lənt\ see ALANT

eilles¹ \ā\ see AY¹

eilles² \ālz\ see ALES

eilly \ā-lē\ see AILY

eim¹ \ām\ see AME¹

eim² \īm\ see IME¹

eimer \ī-mər\ see IMER¹

eims¹ \äⁿs\ see ANCE¹

eims² \ēmz\ Rheims, Weems —also -s, -'s, and -s' forms of nouns and -s forms of verbs listed at EAM¹

ein¹ \ān\ see ANE¹

ein² \ē-ən\ see EAN¹

ein³ \ēn\ see INE³

ein⁴ \īn\ see INE¹

eine¹ \ān\ see ANE¹

eine² \ēn\ see INE³

eine³ \ī-nə\ see INA¹

eine⁴ \en\ see EN¹

eined \ānd\ see AINED

einer¹ \ā-nər\ see AINER

einer² \ē-nər\ see EANER

eing \ē-iŋ\ see EEING

einie \ī-nē\ see INY¹

eining \ā-niŋ\ see AINING

einous \ā-nəs\ see AYNESS

eins \ānz\ see AINS

einsman \ānz-mən\ see AINSMAN

eint \ānt\ see AINT

einte \ant\ see ANT⁵

einture \an-chər\ see ANCHER²

einy \ā-nē\ see AINY

eipt \ēt\ see EAT¹

eir \er\ see ARE⁴

eira \ir-ə\ see ERA²

eird \ird\ see EARD¹

eiress \ar-əs\ see ARIS²

eiric \ī-rik\ see YRIC

eiro \er-ō\ see ERO²

eirs \erz\ see AIRS

eis¹ \ās\ see ACE¹

eis² \ē-əs\ see EUS¹

eis³ \īs\ see ICE¹

eisant \ēs-ᵊnt\ see ECENT

eise \ēz\ see EZE

eisel \ī-zəl\ see ISAL²

eisen \īz-ᵊn\ see IZEN¹

eiser¹ \ī-sər\ see ICER

eiser² \ī-zər\ see IZER

eisha¹ \ā-shə\ see ACIA

eisha² \ē-shə\ see ESIA¹

eisin \ēz-ᵊn\ see EASON

eiss \īs\ see ICE¹

eissen \īs-ᵊn\ see ISON¹

eist¹ \ā-əst\ see AYEST

eist² \īst\ see IST¹

eister¹ \ī-stər\ keister, meister, shyster, tryster • spinmeister • concertmeister, kapellmeister

eister² \ē-stər\ see EASTER

eisure \ē-zhər\ see EIZURE

eit¹ \ē-ət\ fiat • albeit, howbeit

eit² \it\ see IT¹

eit³ \ēt\ see EAT¹

eit⁴ \īt\ see ITE¹

eited \ēt-əd\ see EATED¹

eiter¹ \it-ər\ see ITTER

eiter² \ī-tər\ see ITER¹

eith \ēth\ see EATH¹

either \ē-thər\ breather, either, neither, sheather, teether • fire-breather

eitus \īt-əs\ see ITIS

eity \ē-ət-ē\ deity • velleity • corporeity, spontaneity, synchroneity • homogeneity, instantaneity, simultaneity

eivable \ē-və-bəl\ cleavable • achievable, believable, conceivable, deceivable, perceivable, receivable, relievable, retrievable • imperceivable, inconceivable, irretrievable, unbelievable, unconceivable

eive \ēv\ see EAVE[1]

eiver \ē-vər\ see IEVER

eix \āsh\ see ECHE[1]

eize[1] \āz\ see AZE[1]

eize[2] \ēz\ see EZE

eizure \ē-zhər\ leisure, seizure

ejant \ē-jənt\ see EGENT

eji \ej-ē\ see EDGY

ejo \ā-ō\ see EO[1]

ek \ek\ see ECK

eka[1] \ek-ə\ see ECCA

eka[2] \ē-kə\ see IKA[1]

ekah \ek-ə\ see ECCA

eke \ēk\ see EAK[1]

ekel \ek-əl\ see ECKLE

ekh \ek\ see ECK

eki \ek-ē\ see ECKY

ekker \ek-ər\ see ECKER

ekoe \ē-kō\ see ICOT

ekton \ek-tən\ see ECTEN

el[1] \el\ bel, bell, Bell, belle, cel, cell, dell, dwell, el, ell, fell, gel, Hel, hell, jell, knell, l, mell, quell, sell, shell, smell, snell, spell, swell, tell, they'll, well, yell • Adele, band shell, barbell, Becquerel, befell, Blackwell, bluebell, bombshell, Boswell, bridewell, cadelle, cartel, chandelle, Chanel, clamshell, compel, cormel, cornel, Cornell, corral, cowbell, Cromwell, cupel, Danielle, diel, dispel, doorbell, dry cell, dry well, dumbbell, duxelles, ear shell, eggshell, Estelle, excel, expel, farewell, fat cell, foretell, fuel cell, gazelle, germ cell, Giselle, Glaspell, gromwell, groundswell, half shell, handbell, hard sell, hard-shell, harebell, hotel, impel, indwell, inkwell, Jarrell, jurel, Kandel, lampshell, lapel, Mandel, marcel, maxwell, Maxwell, micelle, Michelle, misspell, morel, Moselle, motel, nacelle, nerve cell, Nobel, noel, nouvelle, nutshell, oat-cell, oil well, Orel, Orwell, outsell, pall-mall, Parnell, pastel, pell-mell, pixel, pointelle, Ponselle, presell, propel, quenelle, rakehell, rappel, Ravel, rebel, refel, repel, respell, retell, riel, Rochelle, rondel, Roswell, saurel, scalpel, seashell, sequel, Seychelles, sleigh bell, soft sell, soft-shell, solgel, speedwell, spinel, stairwell, star shell, stem cell, tooth shell, unsell, unwell, upwell, Weddell, wind-bell • Annabelle, APL, Appenzell, aquarelle, asphodel, Azazel, bagatelle, barbicel, béchamel, brocatelle, Camberwell, Cape Farewell, caramel, caravel, carousel, cascabel, chanterelle, chaparral, Charles Martel, citadel, clientele, cockleshell, Cozumel, damozel, decibel, demoiselle, diving bell, fare-thee-well, fontanel, immortelle, Isabel, Jezebel, killer cell, kiss-and-tell, lenticel, mangonel, muscatel, ne'er-dowell, Neuchâtel, Neufchâtel, New Rochelle, nonpareil, organelle, oversell, parallel, pedicel, pennoncel, personnel, petronel, Philomel, pimpernel, Raphael, rebel yell, red blood cell, Sanctus bell, San Rafael, São Miguel, show-and-tell, sickle cell, silver bell, solar cell, tortoiseshell, undersell, villanelle, white blood cell, William Tell, zinfandel • Aix-la-Chapelle, artesian well, au naturel, crème caramel, mademoiselle, maître d'hôtel, matériel, Mont-Saint-Michel, spirituel • antiparallel, anti-personnel, AWOL

el[2] \āl\ see AIL

ela[1] \ē-lə\ chela, Gila, Leila, selah, sheila, Sheila, stela, Vila • Braila, candela, Kabila, tequila, weigela • Coahuila, Philomela, sinsemilla

ela[2] \ā-lə\ see ALA[3]

ela[3] \el-ə\ see ELLA

elable \el-ə-bəl\ see ELLABLE

elacy \el-ə-sē\ jealousy, prelacy

elagh \ā-lē\ see AILY

elah \ē-lə\ see ELA[1]

eland \ē-lənd\ eland, Leland, Zeeland • New Zealand

elanie \el-ə-nē\ see ELONY

elar \ē-lər\ see EALER

elate \el-ət\ see ELLATE

elatin \el-ət-ᵊn\ see ELETON

elative \el-ət-iv\ relative • appellative, correlative, irrelative

elba \el-bə\ Elba, Elbe, Melba

elbe \el-bə\ see ELBA

elbert \el-bərt\ Delbert, Elbert • Mount Elbert

elch \elch\ belch, squelch, welch

eld[1] \eld\ eld, geld, held, meld, shelled, weld • beheld, butt weld, danegeld, handheld, hard-shelled, Rumsfeld, upheld, withheld • closely held, jet-propelled, self-propelled • unparalleled—*also* -ed *forms of verbs listed at* EL[1]

eld[2] \elt\ see ELT

eldam \el-dəm\ see ELDOM

elder \el-dər\ elder, welder

eldom \el-dəm\ beldam, seldom • hoteldom

eldon \el-dən\ Eldon, Sheldon, Weldon

eldt \elt\ see ELT

ele[1] \ā-lē\ see AILY

ele[2] \el\ see EL[1]

ele[3] \el-ē\ see ELLY

ele[4] \ē-lē\ see EELY

eled[1] \eld\ see ELD[1]

eled[2] \ēld\ see IELD

elen \el-ən\ see ELON

elena \el-ə-nə\ Elena, Helena

elens \el-ənz\ Saint Helens • Mount Saint Helens—*also* -s, -'s, *and* -s' *forms of nouns listed at* ELON

eleon \ēl-yən\ see ELIAN[2]

eletal \el-ət-ᵊl\ pelletal, skeletal
• endoskeletal, exoskeletal

eleton \el-ət-ᵊn\ gelatin, skeleton

eleus \ē-lē-əs\ see ELIOUS

elf \elf\ elf, Guelf, pelf, self, shelf
• bookshelf, herself, himself,
itself, myself, nonself, oneself,
ourself, top-shelf, thyself,
yourself • mantelshelf, off-the-
shelf, Ross Ice Shelf • do-it-
yourself, thing-in-itself
• continental shelf

elfish \el-fish\ elfish, selfish
• unselfish

elhi \el-ē\ see ELLY

eli \el-ē\ see ELLY

elia¹ \ēl-yə\ Delia, Lelia, Sheila
• abelia, Amelia, camellia,
Camellia, Cecilia, Cornelia,
Karelia, lobelia, obelia, Ophelia,
Rumelia, sedilia, stapelia
• psychedelia, seguidilla

elia² \il-ē-ə\ see ILIA¹

elian¹ \ē-lē-ən\ Caelian, Delian,
Melian, Pelion • abelian,
Handelian, Karelian, Mendelian

elian² \ēl-yən\ anthelion,
aphelion, Aurelian, carnelian,
chameleon, cornelian,
Mendelian, parhelion
• perihelion • Aristotelian,
Mephistophelian

elian³ \el-ē-ən\ see ELLIAN

elible \el-ə-bəl\ see ELLABLE

elic¹ \ē-lik\ parhelic • autotelic

elic² \el-ik\ melic, relic, telic
• angelic, Goidelic, smart aleck

• archangelic, autotelic,
philatelic, psychedelic

elical \el-i-kəl\ helical, pellicle
• angelical • double-helical,
evangelical

elier \el-yer\ see ELURE

elin \ē-lən\ shieling, theelin

elion¹ \el-ē-ən\ see ELLIAN

elion² \ēl-yən\ see ELIAN²

elion³ \ēl-ē-ən\ see ELIAN¹

elios \ē-lē-əs\ see ELIOUS

elious \ē-lē-əs\ Delius, Helios,
Peleus • Berzelius, Cornelius
• contumelious

elish \el-ish\ see ELLISH

elist \el-əst\ cellist, trellised
• Nobelist, pastelist

elius¹ \ā-lē-əs\ see ALIUS

elius² \ē-lē-əs\ see ELIOUS

elix \ē-liks\ Felix, helix • double
helix

elk¹ \elk\ elk, whelk

elk² \ilk\ see ILK

ell \el\ see EL¹

e'll \ēl\ see EAL²

ella \el-ə\ Celle, Della, Ella, fella,
fellah, Pella, stella, Stella
• candela, Capella, chlorella,
Estella, favela, Gisela, glabella,
lamella, Luella, Marcella,
Mandela, nigella, novella,
paella, patella, predella,
prunella, quiniela, rubella,
sequela, umbrella, vanilla • a
cappella, Cinderella, citronella,
columella, fraxinella, Isabella,

mortadella, mozzarella, panatela, salmonella, sarsaparilla, subumbrella, tarantella, villanella • valpolicella

ellable \el-ə-bəl\ fellable, gelable, sellable • compellable, expellable, indelible

ellah \el-ə\ see ELLA

ellan \el-ən\ see ELON

ellant \el-ənt\ gellant • appellant, flagellant, propellant, repellent • water-repellent

ellar \el-ər\ see ELLER

ellas \el-əs\ see EALOUS

ellate \el-ət\ helot, pellet, prelate, zealot • appellate, flagellate, lamellate, scutellate

ellative \el-ət-iv\ see ELATIVE

elle[1] \el\ see EL[1]

elle[2] \el-ə\ see ELLA

ellean \el-ē-ən\ see ELLIAN

elled \eld\ see ELD[1]

ellen \el-ən\ see ELON

ellent \el-ənt\ see ELLANT

eller \el-ər\ cellar, dweller, feller, heller, Heller, Keller, Kneller, seller, sheller, smeller, speller, stellar, teller, yeller • best seller, bookseller, flagellar, foreteller, glabellar, impeller, indweller, lamellar, ocellar, patellar, propeller, rathskeller, repeller, rostellar, saltcellar, tale-teller • cerebellar, circumstellar, columellar, fortune-teller,

interstellar, Rockefeller, storyteller

elles[1] \el\ see EL[1]

elles[2] \elz\ see ELLS

ellet \el-ət\ see ELLATE

elletal \el-ət-ᵊl\ see ELETAL

elley \el-ē\ see ELLY

elli \el-ē\ see ELLY

ellia \el-yə\ see ELIA

ellian \el-ē-ən\ Chellean, Elion • Boswellian, Cromwellian, Maxwellian, Orwellian, Rockwellian, Sabellian, triskelion • Pirandellian • Machiavellian, Pantagruelian

ellicle \el-i-kəl\ see ELICAL

ellie \el-ē\ see ELLY

elline \el-ən\ see ELON

elling \el-iŋ\ dwelling, selling, spelling, swelling, telling • best-selling, clear-felling, book-selling, cliff-dwelling, com-pelling, indwelling, lake dwelling, misspelling, tale-telling, tax selling, upwelling • finger spelling, fortune-telling, self-propelling, storytelling —also -ing forms of verbs listed at EL[1]

ellington \el-iŋ-tən\ Ellington, Wellington • beef Wellington

ellion \el-yən\ hellion • rebellion

ellis \el-əs\ see EALOUS

ellised \el-əst\ see ELIST

ellish \el-ish\ hellish, relish • disrelish, embellish

ellist \el-əst\ see ELIST

ello \el-ō\ bellow, Bellow, cello, fellow, Jell-O, mellow, yellow • Bandello, bargello, bedfellow, bordello, duello, hail-fellow, Longfellow, marshmallow, morello, niello, Odd Fellow, Othello, playfellow, school-fellow, Sordello, Torcello, Uccello, yokefellow • Pirandello, punchinello, ritornello, saltarello • Robin Goodfellow, violoncello

ell-o \el-ō\ see ELLO

ellous \el-əs\ see EALOUS

ellow¹ \el-ə\ see ELLA

ellow² \el-ō\ see ELLO

ells \elz\ Welles • Seychelles • Dardanelles—*also* -s, -'s, *and* -s' *forms of nouns and* -s *forms of verbs listed at* EL¹

ellum \el-əm\ blellum, skellum, vellum • clitellum, flagellum, haustellum, labellum, postbellum, rostellum, scutellum • antebellum, cerebellum

ellus \el-əs\ see EALOUS

elly \el-ē\ belly, Delhi, deli, felly, jelly, Kelly, Nellie, Pelly, shelly, Shelley, smelly, tele, telly, wellie • Corelli, New Delhi, nice-nelly, O'Kelly, pork belly, potbelly, rakehelly, scoundrelly, sowbelly • Botticelli, casus belli, Delhi belly, Gabrieli, nervous Nellie, Ponchielli, royal jelly, Schiaparelli, underbelly, vermicelli • Machiavelli

ellyn \el-ən\ see ELON

elm \elm\ elm, helm, realm, whelm • Anselm • overwhelm, underwhelm

elma \el-mə\ Selma, Velma

elmar \el-mər\ see ELMER

elmer \el-mər\ Delmar, Elmer

elmet \el-mət\ helmet, Helmut, pelmet • crash helmet, pith helmet

elmut \el-mət\ see ELMET

elo \ē-lō\ see ILO²

elon \el-ən\ Ellen, felon, Helen, melon • avellan, Magellan, McClellan, muskmelon, vitelline • watermelon • Strait of Magellan

elony \el-ə-nē\ felony, Melanie

elop \el-əp\ develop, envelop • redevelop • overdevelop

elos \ā-ləs\ see AYLESS

elot \el-ət\ see ELLATE

elotry \el-ə-trē\ helotry, zealotry

elp \elp\ help, kelp, whelp, yelp • self-help

elsea \el-sē\ see ELSIE

elsie \el-sē\ Chelsea, Elsie

elson \el-sən\ keelson, nelson, Nelson • Fort Nelson, full nelson, half nelson

elt \elt\ belt, celt, Celt, dealt, delt, dwelt, felt, gelt, melt, pelt, Scheldt, smelt, spelt, svelte, veld, welt • black belt, Dehmelt, flybelt, forefelt, Frostbelt, greenbelt, heartfelt, hot-melt, jacksmelt, Krefeld, lap belt, rust belt, seat belt, self-belt, snowbelt, snowmelt, Sunbelt, web belt • Bible Belt, Bielefeld, cartridge belt, Roosevelt, safety belt, Sam Browne belt, shelterbelt, shoulder belt • asteroid belt, below the belt, chastity belt, Van Allen belt

elte \elt\ see ELT

elted \el-təd\ belted • self-belted—*also* -ed *forms of verbs listed at* ELT

elter \el-tər\ belter, melter, pelter, shelter, skelter, smelter, spelter, swelter, welter • tax shelter • helter-skelter

eltered \el-tərd\ earth-sheltered, tax-sheltered—*also* -ed *forms of verbs listed at* ELTER

elting \el-tiŋ\ belting, felting, melting, pelting—*also* -ing *forms of verbs listed at* ELT

elure \el-yər\ velure • hotelier, Saint Helier

elve \elv\ delve, helve, shelve, twelve

elves \elvz\ elves • ourselves, themselves, yourselves—*also* -s, -'s, *and* -s' *forms of nouns and* -s *forms of verbs listed at* ELVE

elvin \el-vən\ Elvin, Kelvin, Melvin

elvyn \el-vən\ see ELVIN

ely \ē-lē\ see EELY

em¹ \em\ Clem, crème, em, femme, gem, hem, LEM, m, mem, phlegm, REM, Shem, stem, them • ad rem, ahem,

AM, Arnhem, Belém, bluestem, brain stem, condemn, contemn, FM, found poem, idem, in rem, item, main stem, mayhem, Menem, millieme, modem, poem, problem, pro tem, proem, Shechem • ABM, anadem, Angoulême, apothegm, apothem, Bethlehem, diadem, exanthem, fax modem, ibidem, line-item, meristem, OEM, prose poem, SAM, stratagem, tone poem • ad hominem, alter idem, cable modem, carpe diem, cave canem, crème de la crème, ICBM, semper idem • collector's item, heroic poem, post meridiem, star-of-Bethlehem, symphonic poem, terminus ad quem • ante meridiem

em² \əm\ see UM¹

ema \ē-mə\ bema, Lima, Pima, schema • Colima, eczema, edema, Kohima, Kolyma • diastema, emphysema, Hiroshima, Iwo Jima, Kagoshima, Matsushima, terza rima, Tokushima • ottava rima

emacist \em-ə-səst\ see EMICIST

eman¹ \em-ən\ see EMON²

eman² \ē-mən\ see EMON¹

emane \em-ə-nē\ see EMONY

emanence \em-ə-nəns\ see EMINENCE

emanent \em-ə-nənt\ see EMINENT

ematis \em-ət-əs\ see EMITUS

ematist \em-ət-əst\ see EMITIST

ematous \em-ət-əs\ see EMITUS

ember \em-bər\ ember, member • December, dismember, nonmember, November, remember, September, web member • charter member, disremember

emble¹ \äm-bəl\ wamble • ensemble

emble² \em-bəl\ Kemble, tremble • assemble, atremble, dissemble, resemble • disassemble

embler \em-blər\ temblor, trembler • assembler, dissembler

emblor \em-blər\ see EMBLER

embly \em-blē\ trembly • assembly • disassembly, self-assembly, subassembly

eme¹ \em\ see EM¹

eme² \ēm\ see EAM¹

emel \ā-məl\ see EMILE

emely \ēm-lē\ see EEMLY

emen¹ \ē-mən\ see EMON¹

emen² \em-ən\ see EMON²

emen³ \ā-mən\ see AMEN¹

emer \ē-mər\ see EAMER

emeral \em-rəl\ femoral • ephemeral

emery \em-rē\ emery, Emory, memory • flash memory, screen memory • bubble memory

emesis \em-ə-səs\ emesis, nemesis

emi \em-ē\ see EMMY

emia \ē-mē-ə\ anemia, bohemia, Bohemia, leukemia, toxemia, uremia • academia, hyperemia, septicemia, thalassemia

emian \ē-mē-ən\ anthemion, Bohemian

emic¹ \ē-mik\ emic, hemic • anemic, glycemic, graphemic, morphemic, lexemic, phonemic, taxemic, tonemic, uremic • emphysemic, epistemic • hyperglycemic, hypoglycemic

emic² \em-ik\ chemic • alchemic, anthemic, endemic, pandemic, polemic, sachemic, systemic, totemic • academic, epidemic, epistemic

emical \em-i-kəl\ chemical • alchemical, polemical • academical, biochemical, epidemical, petrochemical, photochemical

emicist \em-ə-səst\ polemicist, supremacist • white supremacist

emics \ē-miks\ graphemics, morphemics, phonemics, proxemics

eminal \em-ən-ᵊl\ geminal, seminal

eminate \em-ə-nət\ geminate • effeminate

eminence \em-ə-nəns\ eminence, remanence • gray eminence, preeminence

eminent \em-ə-nənt\ eminent, remanent • preeminent

eming \em-iŋ\ Fleming, Heminge, lemming—*also* -ing *forms of verbs listed at* EM[1]

eminge \em-iŋ\ see EMING

emini \em-ə-nē\ see EMONY

eminy \em-ə-nē\ see EMONY

emion \ē-mē-ən\ see EMIAN

emis \ē-məs\ see EMUS

emish \em-ish\ blemish, Flemish

emist \em-əst\ chemist • polemist • biochemist, geochemist

emitist \em-ət-əst\ Semitist • systematist

emitus \em-ət-əs\ clematis, fremitus • eczematous, edematous

emlin \em-lən\ gremlin, kremlin, Kremlin

emma \em-ə\ Emma, gemma, lemma, stemma • dilemma

emme \em\ see EM[1]

emmer \em-ər\ emmer, hemmer, stemmer, tremor • condemner, contemner

emming \em-iŋ\ see EMING

emmy \em-ē\ Emmy, gemmy, jemmy, phlegmy, semi, stemmy

emn \em\ see EM[1]

emner \em-ər\ see EMMER

emnity \em-nət-ē\ indemnity, solemnity

emo \em-ō\ demo, memo

emon[1] \ē-mən\ demon, freeman, Freeman, gleeman, Piman, seaman, semen • Lake Leman, pentstemon, Philemon • cacodemon, Lacedaemon

emon[2] \em-ən\ Bremen, leman, lemon, Yemen

emone \em-ə-nē\ see EMONY

emony \em-ə-nē\ Gemini, lemony • anemone, bigeminy, Gethsemane, hegemony

emor \em-ər\ see EMMER

emoral \em-rəl\ see EMERAL

emory \em-rē\ see EMERY

emous \ē-məs\ see EMUS

emp \emp\ hemp, kemp, temp

emperer \em-pər-ər\ emperor, Klemperer, temperer

emperor \em-pər-ər\ see EMPERER

emplar \em-plər\ Templar • exemplar, Knight Templar

emps \äⁿ\ see ANT[1]

empt \emt\ dreamt, kempt, tempt • attempt, contempt, exempt, preempt, undreamed, unkempt • nonexempt, tax-exempt

emptable \em-tə-bəl\ temptable • attemptable, contemptible

emptible \em-tə-bəl\ see EMPTABLE

emption \em-shən\ exemption, preemption, redemption

emptive \em-tiv\ preemptive, redemptive

emptor \em-tər\ tempter • preemptor • caveat emptor

emptory \em-trē\ peremptory, redemptory

emulous \em-yə-ləs\ emulous, tremulous

emur \ē-mər\ see EAMER

emus \ē-məs\ Remus • in extremis, Polyphemus, polysemous

emy \ē-mē\ see EAMY

en¹ \en\ ben, Ben, den, en, fen, Fenn, gen, glen, Glen, Gwen, hen, ken, Ken, Len, men, n, pen, Penn, Rennes, Seine, sen, Sten, ten, then, wen, when, wren, Wren, yen, Zen • again, amen, Ardennes, Big Ben, bull pen, Cayenne, Cevennes, Cheyenne, Chosen, Dairen, domaine, doyen, doyenne, Duchenne, Estienne, fen-phen, game hen, hang ten, hapten, hymen, Karen, La Tène, light pen, marsh hen, moorhen, peahen, pigpen, Phnom Penh, playpen, RN, Sheyenne, somewhen, Touraine, Turenne, Tynmen • Adrienne, born-again, cactus wren, Debrecen, five-and-ten, fountain pen, guinea hen, hazel hen, julienne, Kerguelen, La Fontaine, lion's den, LPN, madrilene, mise-en-scène, mother hen, poison pen, Saint-Etienne, samisen, Sun Yat-sen, water hen • carcinogen, comedienne, equestrienne, tamoxifen, time and again, tragedienne, Valenciennes • again and again

en² \ēn\ see INE³

en³ \aⁿ\ see IN⁴

en⁴ \ən\ see UN

en⁵ \äⁿ\ see ANT¹

ena¹ \ā-nä\ see AENA¹

ena² \ā-nə\ see ANA²

ena³ \än-yə\ see ANIA³

ena⁴ \ē-nə\ see INA²

enable \en-ə-bəl\ tenable • amenable, untenable

enace \en-əs\ see ENIS¹

enacle \en-i-kəl\ see ENICAL

enae \e-nē\ see INI¹

enal \ēn-ᵊl\ penal, renal, venal • adrenal, dentinal, vaccinal • duodenal

enancy \en-ən-sē\ tenancy • lieutenancy, subtenancy

enant \en-ənt\ pennant, tenant • lieutenant, se tenant, subtenant • sublieutenant, undertenant

enary \en-ə-rē\ hennery, plenary, senary, venery • centenary, millenary • bicentenary, bimillenary, quincentenary, tercentenary

enas \ē-nəs\ see ENUS¹

enate \en-ət\ see ENNET

enator \en-ət-ər\ see ENITOR

ençal \en-səl\ see ENCIL

ence¹ \ens\ see ENSE

ence² \äⁿs\ see ANCE¹

ence³ \äns\ see ANCE²

encel \en-səl\ see ENCIL

enceless \en-sləs\ see ENSELESS

encer \en-sər\ see ENSOR

ench \ench\ bench, blench, clench, drench, french, French, Hench, mensch, quench, stench, tench, trench, wench, wrench • backbench, entrench, front bench, King's Bench, luftmensch, Old French, pipe wrench, Queen's Bench, retrench, slit trench, unclench, workbench • Allen wrench, Anglo-French, deacon's bench, Middle French, monkey wrench, Norman-French, socket wrench • optical bench • Mariana Trench

enchant \en-chənt\ see ENTIENT

enched \encht\ trenched • unblenched—*also* -ed *forms of verbs listed at* ENCH

encher \en-chər\ see ENTURE

enchman \ench-mən\ Frenchman, henchman

encia \en-chə\ see ENTIA

encil \en-səl\ mensal, pencel, pencil, stencil, tensile • blue-pencil, commensal, extensile, grease pencil, lead pencil, Provençal, prehensile, red-pencil, utensil • eyebrow pencil, intercensal, styptic pencil

ençon \en-sən\ see ENSIGN

ency \en-sē\ Montmorency, residency • nonresidency

end \end\ bend, blend, blende, end, fend, friend, lend, mend, rend, scend, send, shend, spend, tend, trend, vend, wend, Wend • addend, amend, append, ascend, attend, bartend, befriend, Big Bend, bookend, boyfriend, closed-end, commend, compend, contend, dead end, dead-end, defend, depend, descend, distend, downtrend, emend, expend, extend, fag end, forfend, front-end, girlfriend, godsend, Gravesend, headend, high-end, hornblende, impend, intend, Land's End, loose end, low-end, missend, misspend, next friend, no end, offend, on end, Ostend, outspend, perpend, pitchblende, portend, pretend, propend, protend, rear-end, resend, sheet bend, South Bend, split end, stipend, subtend, suspend, tag end, tail end, tight end, top-end, transcend, unbend, unkenned, upend, uptrend, weekend, year-end • apprehend, bitter end, business end, carrick bend, comprehend, condescend, Damavend, discommend, dividend, in the end, minuend, on the mend, open-end, overspend, recommend, repetend, reprehend, subtrahend, vilipend • around the bend, at one's wit's end, fisherman's bend, hyperextend, misapprehend, overextend, peace dividend, receiving end, stock dividend, superintend • go off the deep end—*also* -ed *forms of verbs listed at* EN[1]

enda \en-də\ Brenda, Glenda, Venda • addenda, agenda, pudenda • corrigenda,

hacienda, referenda
• definienda, hidden agenda

endable \en-də-bəl\ lendable, mendable, spendable, vendible • amendable, ascendable, commendable, defendable, dependable, descendible, emendable, expendable, extendable, unbendable • comprehendable, recommendable, undependable

endal \en-dᵊl\ Grendel, Kendall, Mendel, Wendell • prebendal, pudendal

endall \en-dᵊl\ see ENDAL

endance \en-dəns\ see ENDENCE

endancy \en-dən-sē\ see ENDENCY

endant \en-dənt\ see ENDENT

ende¹ \end\ see END

ende² \en-dē\ see ENDI

ended \en-dəd\ ended, splendid • extended, intended, pretended, unfriended • doubleended, open-ended, undescended—also -ed forms of verbs listed at END

endel \en-dᵊl\ see ENDAL

endell \en-dᵊl\ see ENDAL

endence \en-dəns\ tendance • ascendance, attendance, dependence, intendance, resplendence, transcendence • condescendence, dance attendance, independence, Independence • superintendence

endency \en-dən-sē\ pendency, tendency • ascendancy, dependency, resplendency, transcendency • codependency, independency

endent \en-dənt\ pendant, pendent, splendent • appendant, ascendant, attendant, defendant, dependent, descendant, impendent, intendant, respendent, transcendent • codependent, independent • overdependent, superintendent

ender \en-dər\ bender, blender, fender, gender, lender, mender, render, sender, slender, spender, splendor, tender, vendor • amender, ascender, attender, auslander, bartender, commender, contender, defender, descender, emender, engender, expender, extender, fork-tender, goaltender, hellbender, intender, offender, pretender, surrender, suspender, tailender, transgender, weekender • double-ender, moneylender, over-spender, self-surrender

endi \en-dē\ bendy, Mende, trendy, Wendy • effendi • furor loquendi, furor scribendi, modus vivendi

endible \en-də-bəl\ see ENDABLE

endid \en-dəd\ see ENDED

ending \en-diŋ\ ending, pending, sending • ascending, attending, fence-mending, goaltending, heartrending, mind-bending, nerve ending, unbending, unending • condescending, gender-bending, unpretending

• deficit spending, un-comprehending—*also* -ing *forms of verbs listed at* END

endium \en-dē-əm\ compendium • antependium

endless \end-ləs\ endless, friendless

endliness \en-lē-nəs\ cleanliness, friendliness • uncleanliness, unfriendliness

endly \en-lē\ cleanly, friendly • uncleanly, unfriendly • user-friendly

endment \en-mənt\ amendment, intendment

endo \en-dō\ kendo • crescendo, stringendo • decrescendo, innuendo • diminuendo, se defendendo

endor \en-dər\ see ENDER

endous \en-dəs\ horrendous, stupendous, tremendous

endron \en-drən\ philodendron, rhododendron

ends \enz\ see ENS[1]

endum \en-dəm\ addendum, agendum, pudendum • corrigendum, referendum • definiendum

endy \en-dē\ see ENDI

ene[1] \ā-nā\ nene, sene

ene[2] \en\ see EN[1]

ene[3] \en-ē\ see ENNY

ene[4] \ē-nē\ see INI[1]

ene[5] \ēn\ see INE[3]

ene[6] \ān\ see ANE[1]

enel \en-ᵊl\ see ENNEL

eneous \ē-nē-əs\ genius, splenious • Arrhenius, Comenius • homogeneous • heterogeneous

ener \ē-nər\ see EANER

enerable \en-rə-bəl\ generable, venerable • regenerable

eneracy \en-rə-sē\ degeneracy, regeneracy

enerate \en-rət\ degenerate, regenerate • unregenerate

enerative \en-rət-iv\ generative • degenerative, regenerative

eneris \en-ə-rəs\ mons veneris • sui generis

enery[1] \en-ə-rē\ see ENARY[2]

enery[2] \ēn-rē\ see EANERY

enet[1] \en-ət\ see ENNET

enet[2] \ē-nət\ see EANUT

eng[1] \aŋ\ see ANG[2]

eng[2] \əŋ\ see UNG[1]

enge \enj\ venge • avenge, revenge, Stonehenge

english \iŋ-glish\ English, Yinglish

engo \eŋ-gō\ marengo • camerlengo

ength[1] \eŋth\ length, strength • arm's-length, at length, floor length, full-length, half-length, wavelength • cable length, focal length, tensile strength, understrength • from strength to strength • industrial-strength

ength[2] \enth\ see ENTH

engthen \eŋ-thən\ lengthen, strengthen

engue \eŋ-gē\ see ENGI

enh \en\ see EN[1]

enia[1] \ē-nē-ə\ taenia • Armenia, asthenia, Messenia, Mutenia, Slovenia • neurasthenia, sarracenia, schizophrenia

enia[2] \ē-nyə\ Armenia, Encaenia, Eugenia, gardenia, Ruthenia, Tigrinya

enial \ē-nē-əl\ genial, menial, venial • congenial • catamenial

enian \ē-nē-ən\ Fenian • Armenian, Athenian, Cyrenian, Essenian, Icenian, Ruthenian, sirenian, Slovenian, Turkmenian, Tyrrhenian, Veblenian • Achaemenian, Magdalenian

enic[1] \ēn-ik\ genic, scenic • Essenic, hygienic, Icenic, irenic

enic[2] \en-ik\ fennec, pfennig, phrenic, splenic • arsenic, asthenic, Edenic, Essenic, eugenic, Hellenic, hygienic, irenic, transgenic • allergenic, androgenic, autogenic, biogenic, calisthenic, chromogenic, cryogenic, cryptogenic, hygienic, mutagenic, Panhellenic, pathogenic, photogenic, Saracenic, schizophrenic, telegenic • carcinogenic, cariogenic • hallucinogenic, hypoallergenic

enical \en-i-kəl\ cenacle • arsenical, galenical • ecumenical

enice \en-əs\ see ENIS[1]

enicist \en-ə-səst\ eugenicist • ecumenicist

enics \en-iks\ eugenics, euphenics, euthenics, hygienics • calisthenics, cryogenics, ecumenics—*also* -s, -'s, *and* -s' *forms of nouns listed at* ENIC[2]

enie[1] \en-ē\ see ENNY

enie[2] \ē-nē\ see INI[1]

enience \ē-nyəns\ lenience • convenience, provenience • inconvenience

enient \ēn-yənt\ lenient • convenient, prevenient • inconvenient

enim \en-əm\ see ENOM

enin \en-ən\ see ENNON

enior \ē-nyər\ senior • monsignor

enis[1] \en-əs\ Dennis, genus, menace, tenace, tennis, Venice • lawn tennis, Saint Denis • summum genus, table tennis

enis[2] \ē-nəs\ see ENUS[1]

enison[1] \en-ə-sən\ benison, Tennyson, venison

enison[2] \en-ə-zən\ benison, denizen, venison

enist \en-əst\ tennist • euthenist

enitive \en-ət-iv\ genitive, lenitive • philoprogenitive • polyphiloprogenitive

enitor \en-ət-ər\ senator • progenitor • primogenitor

enity \en-ət-ē\ see ENTITY

enium \ē-nē-əm\ rhenium
• hymenium, proscenium, ruthenium, selenium

enius \ē-nē-əs\ see ENEOUS

enizen \en-ə-zən\ see ENISON²

enn \en\ see EN¹

enna \en-ə\ Glenna, henna, senna • antenna, duenna, Gehenna, McKenna, sienna, Vienna • Avicenna, whip antenna

ennae \en-ē\ see ENNY

ennant \en-ənt\ see ENANT

enne¹ \en\ see EN¹

enne² \en-ē\ see ENNY

enne³ \an\ see AN⁵

ennec \en-ik\ see ENIC²

enned \end\ see END

ennel \en-ᵊl\ crenel, fennel, kennel • dog fennel, unkennel

enner \en-ər\ see ENOR¹

ennery \en-ə-rē\ see ENARY²

ennes \en\ see EN¹

ennet \en-ət\ Bennett, genet, jennet, rennet, senate, sennet, sennit, tenet

ennett \en-ət\ see ENNET

enney \en-ē\ see ENNY

enni \en-ē\ see ENNY

ennial \en-ē-əl\ biennial, centennial, decennial, millennial, perennial, quadrennial, quinquennial, septennial, triennial, vicennial
• bicentennial, bimillennial,

postmillennial, premillennial, quincentennial, tercentennial

ennies \en-ēz\ tennies—*also* -s, -'s, *and* -s' *forms of nouns listed at* ENNY

ennig \en-ik\ see ENIC²

ennin \en-ən\ see ENNON

ennis \en-əs\ see ENIS¹

ennist \en-əst\ see ENIST

ennit \en-ət\ see ENNET

ennium \en-ē-əm\ biennium, decennium, millennium, quadrennium, quinquennium, triennium

ennon \en-ən\ guenon, Lenin, Lennon, pennon, rennin, tenon • tusk tenon • antivenin

enny \en-ē\ any, benne, benny, Benny, blenny, Dene, Denny, fenny, genie, jenny, Jenny, Kenny, many, penni, penny, Penny • antennae, catchpenny, halfpenny, Kilkenny, Na-Dene, pinchpenny, sixpenny, so many, tenpenny, threepenny, truepenny, twopenny
• lilangeni, nota bene, spinning jenny

ennyson \en-ə-sən\ see ENISON¹

eño¹ \ān-yō\ segno • dal segno
• jalapeño, Madrileño

eno² \en-ō\ steno • ripieno

eno³ \ā-nō\ see ANO²

enoch \ē-nik\ see INIC¹

enom \en-əm\ denim, plenum, venom • envenom

enon \en-ən\ see ENNON

enor¹ \en-ər\ Brenner, Jenner, tenner, tenor • countertenor, heldentenor

enor² \ē-nər\ see EANER

enour \en-ər\ see ENOR¹

enous \ē-nəs\ see ENUS¹

ens¹ \enz\ cleanse, gens, lens • amends, beam-ends, field lens, hand lens, weekends, zoom lens • Fresnel lens, odds and ends, sapiens • definiens, locum tenens, vas deferens • Homo sapiens—*also* -s, -'s, *and* -s' *forms of nouns and* -s *forms of verbs listed at* EN¹

ens² \ens\ see ENSE

ensable \en-sə-bəl\ see ENSIBLE

ensal \en-səl\ see ENCIL

ensary \ens-rē\ see ENSORY

ensch \ench\ see ENCH

ense \ens\ cense, dense, fence, flense, gens, hence, mense, pence, sense, spence, tense, thence, whence • commence, condense, defense, dispense, expense, horse sense, immense, incense, intense, missense, nonsense, offense, past tense, prepense, pretense, propense, sequence, sixpence, sixth sense, suspense, twopence • accidence, antisense, commonsense, common sense, confidence, consequence, diffidence, evidence, frankincense, multisense, nondefense, no-nonsense, present tense, providence, Providence, recompense, residence, self-defense, subsequence, zone defense • coincidence, ego-defense, inconsequence, New Providence, nonresidence, self-confidence, self-evidence

enseful \ens-fəl\ senseful • suspenseful

enseless \en-sləs\ fenceless, senseless • defenseless, offenseless

ensem \en-səm\ see ENSUM

enser \en-sər\ see ENSOR

ensian \en-chən\ see ENSION

ensible \en-sə-bəl\ sensible • compensable, condensable, defensible, dispensable, distensible, extensible, insensible, ostensible • apprehensible, commonsensible, comprehensible, incondensable, indefensible, indispensable, reprehensible, supersensible • incomprehensible

ensign \en-sən\ ensign • alençon

ensil \en-səl\ see ENCIL

ensile \en-səl\ see ENCIL

ension \en-shən\ gentian, mention, pension, tension • abstention, ascension, attention, contention, convention, declension, descension, detention, dimension, dissension, distension, extension, high-tension, indention, intension, intention, invention, Laurentian, low-tension, posttension, prehension, pretension, prevention,

recension, retention, subvention,
suspension, sustention,
Vincentian, Waldensian
• Albigensian, apprehension,
circumvention, comprehension,
condescension, contravention,
fourth dimension, hypertension,
hypotension, inattention,
reinvention, reprehension,
salientian, surface tension, third
dimension • hyperextension,
incomprehension, misap-
prehension, nonintervention,
overextension • Geneva
convention, honorable mention

ensional \ench-nəl\ tensional
• ascensional, attentional,
conventional, declensional,
dimensional, extensional,
intensional, intentional • four-
dimensional, one-dimensional,
three-dimensional, tridimen-
sional, two-dimensional,
unconventional, unintentional

ensioner \ench-nər\ see ENTIONER

ensis \en-səs\ see ENSUS

ensitive \en-sət-iv\ sensitive
• insensitive • hypersensitive,
oversensitive, photosensitive,
supersensitive

ensity \en-sət-ē\ density, tensity
• extensity, immensity,
intensity, propensity

ensive \en-siv\ pensive, tensive
• ascensive, defensive,
expensive, extensive, intensive,
offensive, ostensive, protensive,
suspensive • apprehensive,
coextensive, comprehensive,
hypertensive, hypotensive,
inexpensive, inoffensive,

reprehensive, self-defensive
• counteroffensive, labor-
intensive

ensor \en-sər\ censer, censor,
fencer, sensor, spencer,
Spencer, Spenser, tensor
• commencer, condenser,
dispenser, extensor, precensor,
sequencer, suspensor
• biosensor, microsensor
• intelligencer—*also* -er *forms
of adjectives listed at* ENSE

ensory \ens-rē\ sensory
• dispensary, suspensory
• extrasensory, multisensory,
supersensory

ensual[1] \en-chəl\ see ENTIAL

ensual[2] \ench-wəl\ see ENTUAL[1]

ensum \en-səm\ sensum • per
mensem

ensurable \ens-rə-bəl\
censurable, mensurable
• commensurable, immensurable
• incommensurable

ensure \en-chər\ see ENTURE

ensus \en-səs\ census
• consensus, dissensus
• amanuensis

ent[1] \ent\ bent, Brent, cent, dent,
gent, Ghent, Gwent, hent, Kent,
leant, lent, Lent, meant, pent,
rent, scent, sent, spent, sprent,
stent, tent, Trent, vent, went
• absent, accent, Advent,
anent, ascent, assent, augment,
besprent, cement, comment,
consent, content, convent,
descent, detent, dissent,
docent, event, extent, ferment,
foment, forewent, fragment,

frequent, hell-bent, indent,
intent, invent, lament, loment,
low-rent, mordent, outspent,
outwent, percent, pigment,
portent, present, prevent, pup
tent, quitrent, rack-rent, relent,
repent, resent, segment,
Shymkent, Tashkent, torment,
unbent, well-meant, wisent
• accident, aliment, argument,
Blaenau Gwent, circumvent,
compartment, complement,
compliment, confident,
devilment, diffident, discontent,
document, evident, heaven-
sent, implement, incident,
instrument, Jack-a-Lent,
malcontent, nonevent, Occident,
ornament, orient, president,
provident, regiment, reinvent,
represent, re-present, resident,
Saint-Laurent, sediment, self-
content, Stoke on Trent,
subsequent, supplement,
underwent • age of consent,
coincident, disorient, experiment, ferro-cement, glove
compartment, inconsequent,
informed consent, misrepre-
sent, nonresident, oxygen tent,
portland cement, privatdozent,
rubber cement, self-confident,
self-evident, sentence fragment,
vice president • in any event,
letter of intent, media event

ent² \änt\ see ANT²

ent³ \äⁿ\ see ANT¹

enta \ent-ə\ menta, yenta
• magenta, momenta, placenta,
polenta, Polenta, tegmenta,
tomenta • irredenta
• impedimenta

entable \ent-ə-bəl\ rentable
• fermentable, lamentable,
presentable, preventable
• documentable, representable,
sedimentable

entacle \ent-i-kəl\ see ENTICAL

entage \ent-ij\ tentage, ventage
• percentage

ental \ent-ᵊl\ cental, dental,
dentil, gentle, lentil, mental,
rental • cliental, fragmental,
judgmental, parental, placental,
segmental, vestmental
• accidental, adjustmental,
apartmental, biparental,
compartmental, complemental,
condimental, continental,
departmental, detrimental,
documental, excremental,
elemental, firmamental,
fundamental, governmental,
grandparental, incidental,
incremental, instrumental,
managemental, monumental,
nonjudgmental, occidental,
oriental, ornamental, regimental,
rudimental, sacramental,
sentimental, supplemental,
temperamental, transcendental,
vestamental • coincidental,
developmental, environmental,
experimental, subcontinental,
transcontinental, uniparental
• intercontinental, inter-
departmental

entalist \ent-ᵊl-əst\ mentalist
• documentalist, funda-
mentalist, governmentalist,
incrementalist, instrumentalist,
orientalist, sacramentalist,
sentimentalist, transcenden-

talist • environmentalist, experimentalist

entalness \ent-ᵊl-nəs\ see ENTLENESS

entance \ent-ᵊns\ see ENTENCE

entary \en-trē\ entry, gentry, sentry • passementerie, reentry, subentry • alimentary, complementary, complimentary, documentary, double entry, elementary, filamentary, mockumentary, parliamentary, port of entry, rudimentary, sedimentary, single entry, supplementary, tenementary, testamentary • uncomplimentary

entative \ent-ət-iv\ tentative • augmentative, fermentative, frequentative, presentative, preventative • argumentative, representative

ente¹ \en-tā\ al dente • lentamente

ente² \ent-ē\ see ENTY

ente³ \änt\ see ANT²

ented \ent-əd\ tented • augmented, contented, demented, lamented, segmented, untented • battlemented, discontented, malcontented, oriented, selfcontented, unfrequented • unprecedented • objectoriented, overrepresented, underrepresented—*also* -ed *forms of verbs listed at* ENT¹

enten \ent-ᵊn\ Benton, dentin, Denton, Kenton, Lenten, Quentin, Trenton • SaintQuentin

entence \ent-ᵊns\ sentence • death sentence, loose sentence, repentance

enter \ent-ər\ center, enter, mentor, renter, stentor, tenter, venter • assenter, augmentor, cementer, concenter, consenter, dissenter, fermenter, fomenter, frequenter, incenter, indenter, inventor, nerve center, precentor, presenter, preventer, rack-renter, reenter, repenter, subcenter, tormentor • documenter, epicenter, front and center, hypocenter, metacenter, multicenter, profit center, representer, shopping center, supplementer, trauma center • experimenter, hundredpercenter

entered \en-tərd\ centered • face-centered, self-centered • body-centered, multicentered —*also* -ed *forms of verbs listed at* ENTER

enterie \en-trē\ see ENTARY

entful \ent-fəl\ eventful, resentful • uneventful

enth \enth\ nth, strength, tenth • crème de menthe, tensile strength • industrial-strength

enthe \enth\ see ENTH

enthesis \en-thə-səs\ epenthesis, parenthesis

enti \ent-ē\ see ENTY

entia \en-shə\ dementia, sententia, Valencia • differentia, in absentia

ential \en-shəl\ cadential, consensual, credential, demential, essential, eventual, potential, prudential, sciential, sentential, sequential, tangential, torrential • componential, conferential, confidential, consequential, deferential, differential, evidential, existential, expediential, exponential, inessential, inferential, influential, nonessential, penitential, pestilential, preferential, presidential, providential, quintessential, referential, residential, reverential, transferential, unessential • circumferential, equipotential, experiential, inconsequential, intelligential, interferential, jurisprudential, multipotential, vice presidential

entialist \en-shə-ləst\ essentialist • existentialist

entian \en-shən\ see ENSION

entiary \ensh-rē\ century • penitentiary • plenipotentiary

entic \ent-ik\ lentic • authentic, crescentic, identic • inauthentic

entical \ent-i-kəl\ denticle, pentacle, tentacle • conventicle, identical • nonidentical, self-identical

entice \ent-əs\ see ENTOUS

enticle \ent-i-kəl\ see ENTICAL

entient \en-chənt\ penchant, sentient, trenchant • dissentient, insentient, presentient

entil \ent-ºl\ see ENTAL

entin \ent-ºn\ see ENTEN

enting \ent-iŋ\ dissenting • unrelenting—*also* -ing *forms of verbs listed at* ENT[1]

ention \en-shən\ see ENSION

entionable \ensh-nə-bəl\ mentionable, pensionable • unmentionable

entional \ensh-nəl\ see ENSIONAL

entioned \en-shənd\ aforementioned, well-intentioned—*also* -ed *forms of verbs listed at* ENSION

entioner \ensh-nər\ mentioner, pensioner, tensioner

entious \en-chəs\ abstentious, contentious, dissentious, licentious, pretentious, sententious, tendentious • conscientious, unpretentious

entis \ent-əs\ see ENTOUS

entist \ent-əst\ dentist • cinquecentist, irredentist

entity \en-ət-ē\ entity, lenity • amenity, identity, nonentity, obscenity, serenity • self-identity

entium \ent-ē-əm\ Pentium • jus gentium • unnilpentium

entive \ent-iv\ adventive, attentive, incentive, inventive, pendentive, preventive, retentive • argumentive, disincentive, inattentive • anal-retentive

entle \ent-ºl\ see ENTAL

entleness \ent-ºl-nəs\ gentleness • accidentalness

entment \ent-mənt\
contentment, presentment,
resentment • discontentment,
self-contentment

ento \en-tō\ cento, lento, Trento
• memento, pimento, pimiento,
seicento, Sorrento, trecento
• Agrigento, cinquecento,
Papiamento, pentimento,
portamento, quattrocento,
Sacramento • aggiornamento,
divertimento, risorgimento
• pronunciamento

enton \ent-ᵊn\ see ENTEN

entor \ent-ər\ see ENTER

entous \ent-əs\ prentice
• apprentice, argentous,
momentous, portentous
• compos mentis, filamentous,
ligamentous, non compos
mentis, in loco parentis

entral \en-trəl\ central, ventral
• subcentral • dorsiventral,
hypocentral

entress \en-trəs\ gentrice
• inventress

entric \en-trik\ centric • acentric,
concentric, dicentric, eccentric
• acrocentric, Afrocentric,
androcentric, Anglocentric,
biocentric, Christocentric,
egocentric, ethnocentric,
Eurocentric, geocentric,
gynocentric, phallocentric,
polycentric, theocentric,
topocentric • anthropocentric,
areocentric, Europocentric,
heliocentric, selenocentric

entrice \en-trəs\ see ENTRESS

entry \en-trē\ see ENTARY

ents \ents\ gents • two cents • at
all events, dollars-and-cents
—also -s, -'s, and -s' forms of
nouns and -s forms of verbs
listed at ENT¹

entual¹ \ən-shə-wəl\ sensual
• accentual, consensual,
conventual, eventual

entual² \en-chəl\ see ENTIAL

entum \ent-əm\ centum,
mentum • cementum,
momentum, omentum, per
centum, tegmentum, tomentum
• Agrigentum, argumentum

enture \en-chər\ bencher,
censure, denture, drencher,
quencher, trencher, venture,
wencher • adventure,
backbencher, debenture, front-
bencher, indenture • at a
venture, misadventure,
peradventure

enturer \ench-rər\ venturer
• adventurer

enturess \ench-rəs\ see
ENTUROUS

entury \ench-rē\ see ENTIARY

enty \ent-ē\ plenty, sente, senti,
tenty, twenty • aplenty, licente
• Bay of Plenty, cognoscente,
horn of plenty, twenty-twenty
• Deo volente • dolce far niente

enuis \en-yə-wəs\ see ENUOUS

enum \en-əm\ see ENOM

enuous \en-yə-wəs\ strenuous,
tenuis, tenuous • ingenuous
• disingenuous

enus¹ \ē-nəs\ genus, lenis, penis, venous, Venus • Campinas, Delphinus, Maecenas, Quirinus, silenus, subgenus • Gallienus, intravenous

enus² \en-əs\ see ENIS¹

eny \ā-nē\ see AINY

enys \en-əs\ see ENIS¹

enza¹ \en-zə\ Penza • cadenza, credenza • influenza

enza² \en-sə\ Vicenza • Piacenza

eo¹ \ā-ō\ kayo, mayo, Mayo • Bermejo, cacao, laus Deo, paseo, rodeo, Vallejo • aparejo, Bulawayo, cicisbeo, Galileo, San Mateo, zapateo • Bartolommeo, Mission Viejo, Montevideo

eo² \ē-ō\ see IO²

eoff¹ \ef\ see EF¹

eoff² \ēf\ see IEF¹

eoffor \ef-ər\ see EPHOR

eolate \ē-ə-lət\ triolet • alveolate, areolate, urceolate

eoman \ō-mən\ see OMAN

eon¹ \ē-ən\ see EAN¹

eon² \ē-än\ eon, Freon, neon, paeon, prion

eonid \ē-ə-nəd\ see EANID

eopard \ep-ərd\ jeopard, leopard, peppered, Shepard, shepherd • snow leopard • English shepherd, German shepherd

eopardess \ep-ərd-əs\ leopardess, shepherdess

eople \ē-pəl\ people, pipal, steeple • boat people, craftspeople, dispeople, laypeople, newspeople, Plain People, salespeople, spokespeople, townspeople, tradespeople, tribespeople, unpeople, workpeople • anchorpeople, businesspeople, congresspeople, little people • beautiful people

eopled \ē-pəld\ unpeopled—also -ed forms of verbs listed at EOPLE

eordie \órd-ē\ see ORDY¹

eorem \ir-əm\ see ERUM

eorge \órj\ see ORGE

eorgian \ór-jən\ see ORGIAN

eorist \ir-əst\ see ERIST¹

eoul \ōl\ see OLE¹

eous \ē-əs\ see EUS¹

ep \ep\ hep, pep, prep, rep, schlepp, skep, step, steppe, strep, yep • Alep, crowstep, doorstep, footstep, goose-step, half step, instep, in step, keep step, lockstep, misstep, one-step, quickstep, route step, salep, sidestep, twelve-step, two-step, unstep, whole step • corbiestep, demirep, in lockstep, out of step, overstep, step-by-step, stutter step • Gaziantep

eparable \ep-rə-bəl\ reparable, separable • inseparable, irreparable

epard \ep-ərd\ see EOPARD

epe \āp\ see APE[1]

epee \ē-pē\ see EEPY

eper \ep-ər\ see EPPER

eperous \ep-rəs\ leprous
• obstreperous

epey \ā-pē\ see APEY

eph \ef\ see EF[1]

ephen \ē-vən\ see EVEN

epherd \ep-ərd\ see EOPARD

epherdess \ep-ərd-əs\ see
EOPARDESS

ephone \ef-ə-nē\ see EPHONY

ephony \ef-ə-nē\ Stephanie
• Persephone, telephony

ephor \ef-ər\ ephor, feoffor,
heifer, zephyr • hasenpfeffer

epht \eft\ see EFT

ephyr \ef-ər\ see EPHOR

epi \ā-pē\ see APEY

epid \ep-əd\ tepid, trepid
• intrepid

epo \ēp-ō\ see EPOT

epot \ēp-ō\ depot, pepo • el
cheapo

epp \ep\ see EP

eppe \ep\ see EP

epped \ept\ see EPT

epper \ep-ər\ leper, pepper,
stepper • bell pepper,
Colepeper, Culpeper, green
pepper, hot pepper, red
pepper, sidestepper, sweet
pepper • chili pepper

eppy \ep-ē\ peppy, preppy
• orthoepy

eprous \ep-rəs\ see EPEROUS

eps \eps\ biceps, forceps,
triceps • quadriceps—*also* -s,
-'s, *and* -s' *forms of nouns and*
-s *forms of verbs listed at* EP

epsis \ep-səs\ sepsis, skepsis
• asepsis, prolepsis, syllepsis
• antisepsis • omphaloskepsis

epsy \ep-sē\ catalepsy, epilepsy,
narcolepsy, nympholepsy

ept \ept\ crept, kept, sept, slept,
stepped, swept, wept • accept,
adept, backswept, concept,
except, incept, inept, percept,
precept, transept, upswept,
windswept, yclept • high-
concept, intercept,
nympholept, overslept, self-
concept—*also* -ed *forms of*
verbs listed at EP

eptable \ep-tə-bəl\ see EPTIBLE

eptacle \ep-ti-kəl\ skeptical
• conceptacle, receptacle

epter \ep-tər\ see EPTOR

eptible \ep-tə-bəl\ acceptable,
perceptible, susceptible
• imperceptible, insusceptible,
unacceptable

eptic \ep-tik\ peptic, septic,
skeptic • aseptic, dyspeptic,
eupeptic, proleptic, sylleptic
• analeptic, antiseptic,
cataleptic, epileptic,
narcoleptic, nympholeptic

eptical \ep-ti-kəl\ see EPTACLE

eptile \ep-t^əl\ see EPTAL

eption \ep-shən\ conception, deception, exception, inception, perception, reception, subreption
• apperception, contraception, depth perception, interception, misconception, preconception, self-conception, self-perception, take exception

eptional \ep-shnəl\ conceptional, deceptional, exceptional
• unexceptional

eptive \ep-tiv\ acceptive, conceptive, deceptive, exceptive, inceptive, perceptive, preceptive, receptive, susceptive
• apperceptive, contraceptive, imperceptive

eptor \ep-tər\ scepter
• accepter, acceptor, inceptor, preceptor, receptor
• intercepter, interceptor

eptual \ep-chəl\ conceptual, perceptual

epy \ep-ē\ see EPPY

epys \ēps\ Pepys • for keeps
—also -s, -'s, and -s' forms of nouns and -s forms of verbs listed at EEP

equal \ē-kwəl\ equal, prequel, sequel • coequal, unequal

eque \ek\ see ECK

equel \ē-kwəl\ see EQUAL

equence \ē-kwəns\ frequence, sequence • infrequence, subsequence

equency \ē-kwən-sē\ frequency, sequency • high frequency, infrequency, low frequency

equent \ē-kwənt\ frequent, sequent • infrequent

equer \ek-ər\ see ECKER

er¹ \ā\ see AY¹

er² \er\ see ARE⁴

er³ \ər\ see EUR¹

er⁴ \ir\ see EER²

era¹ \er-ə\ era, Gera, Hera, Sarah, sclera, terra • caldera, Herrera, mascara, Ribera, Rivera, Sahara, sierra, tiara
• aloe vera, ciguatera, Common Era, cordillera, de Valera, Ginastera, guayabera, habanera, Halmahera, primavera, riviera, Riviera, Santa Clara • Islamic Era, Spanish Sahara, Western Sahara

era² \ir-ə\ era, gerah, Hera, lira, Pyrrha, sera, sirrah, Vera, wirra
• chimaera, chimera, hetaera, lempira, Madeira, mbira
• Altamira, Common Era
• Islamic Era

erable \ər-ə-bəl\ thurible
• conferrable, deferrable, deterrable, inferable, referable, transferable

erah \ir-ə\ see ERA²

eral¹ \ir-əl\ Cyril, feral, seral, spheral, virile

eral² \er-əl\ see ERIL

eral³ \ər-əl\ see ERRAL

erald \er-əld\ Gerald, Harold, herald

eraph \er-əf\ see ERIF

eratin \er-ət-°n\ keratin, Sheraton • Samaritan

erative \er-ət-iv\ see ARATIVE¹

eraton \er-ət-°n\ see ERATIN

erb \ərb\ blurb, curb, herb, kerb, Serb, verb • acerb, adverb, disturb, exurb, perturb, potherb, pro-verb, proverb, reverb, suburb, superb

erbal \ər-bəl\ burble, gerbil, herbal, verbal • deverbal, nonverbal, preverbal

erbalist \ər-bə-ləst\ herbalist, verbalist • hyperbolist

erbally \ər-bə-lē\ verbally • hyperbole, nonverbally

erber \ər-bər\ see URBER

erberis \ər-bər-əs\ berberis, Cerberus

erberus \ər-bər-əs\ see ERBERIS

erbet \ər-bət\ see URBIT

erbia \ər-bē-ə\ see URBIA

erbial \ər-bē-əl\ adverbial, proverbial

erbid \ər-bəd\ see URBID

erbil \ər-bəl\ see ERBAL

erbium \ər-bē-əm\ erbium, terbium • ytterbium

erbole \ər-bə-lē\ see ERBALLY

erbolist \ər-bə-ləst\ see ERBALIST

erby \ər-bē\ derby, Derby, herby, Kirby • Roller Derby • demolition derby

ercal \ər-kəl\ see IRCLE

erce \ərs\ see ERSE

ercé \ərs\ see ARCE¹

ercel \ər-səl\ see ERSAL¹

ercement \ər-smənt\ amercement, disbursement • reimbursement

ercer \ər-sər\ see URSOR

ercery \ərs-rē\ see URSARY

erch \ərch\ see URCH

ercia \ər-shə\ see ERTIA

ercial \ər-shəl\ Herschel • commercial, inertial • controversial, infomercial, uncommercial

ercian \ər-shən\ see ERTIAN

ercible \ər-sə-bəl\ see ERSIBLE

ercion \ər-zhən\ see ERSION¹

ercis \ər-səs\ see ERSUS

ercive \ər-siv\ see ERSIVE

ercular \ər-kyə-lər\ see IRCULAR

ercy \ər-sē\ Circe, mercy, Percy, pursy • gramercy • controversy

erd \ərd\ see IRD

erde¹ \ərd\ see AIRED

erde² \ərd\ see IRD

erde³ \ərd-ē\ see URDY

erder \ərd-ər\ birder, girder, herder, murder • blackbirder, self-murder, sheepherder • bloody murder, lattice girder

erderer \ərd-ər-ər\ see URDERER

erdi¹ \ər-dē\ see URDY

erdi² \er-dē\ Verdi • Monteverdi

erdin \ərd-°n\ see URDEN

erding \ərd-iŋ\ wording
• sheepherding—*also* -ing
forms of verbs listed at IRD

erdu \ər-dü\ perdu, perdue, Urdu

erdue \ər-dü\ see ERDU

erdure \ər-jər\ see ERGER

ere¹ \er\ see ARE⁴

ere² \er-ē\ see ARY¹

ere³ \ir\ see EER²

ere⁴ \ir-ē\ see EARY

ere⁵ \ər\ see EUR¹

e're \ē-ər\ see EER¹

ère \er\ see ARE⁴

ereal \ir-ē-əl\ see ERIAL

ereid \ir-ē-əd\ see ERIOD

erek \irik\ see ERIC¹

erely \ir-lē\ see EARLY¹

erement \er-ə-mənt\ see ERIMENT

erence¹ \ir-əns\ clearance
• adherence, appearance,
coherence, inherence
• disappearance, incoherence,
interference, perseverance
• run interference

erence² \ər-əns\ see URRENCE

erence³ \er-əns\ see ARENCE

erency¹ \ir-ən-sē\ coherency,
vicegerency

erency² \er-ən-sē\ see ERRANCY

erent¹ \ir-ənt\ gerent • adherent,
coherent, inherent, sederunt,
vicegerent • incoherent

erent² \er-ənt\ see ARENT¹

eren't¹ \ərnt\ see EARNT

eren't² \er-ənt\ see URRENT

ereo \er-ē-ō\ see ARIO

ereous \ir-ē-əs\ see ERIOUS

erer \ir-ər\ see EARER²

eres¹ \erz\ see AIRS

eres² \ir-ēz\ see ERIES

eres³ \ərs\ see ERS

eresy \er-ə-sē\ clerisy, heresy

ereth \er-ət\ see ERIT

ereus \ir-ē-əs\ see ERIOUS

erf \ərf\ see URF

erg \ərg\ berg, Berg, burg, erg
• Arlberg, Augsburg, Boksburg,
Coburg, exergue, Flensburg,
Freyberg, Galesburg, Ginsberg,
Ginsburg, Goldberg, hamburg,
Hamburg, Hapsburg, Herzberg,
homburg, iceberg, Lemberg,
Limburg, Lindbergh, Lynchburg,
Marburg, Newburg, Pittsburgh,
Romberg, Salzburg, Sandburg,
Schoenberg, Spielberg,
Stahlberg, Sternberg, Stras-
bourg, Strindberg, svedberg,
Tilburg, Vicksburg, Warburg,
Weinberg, Wolfsburg,
Würzburg • Brandenburg,
Drakensberg, Duisburg,
Fredericksburg, Gaithersburg,
Gettysburg, Godesberg,
Gutenberg, Hardenberg,
Harrisburg, Hattiesburg,
Heidelberg, Heisenberg,
Hindenburg, inselberg,
Königsberg, Lederberg,
Ludwigsburg, Luxembourg,
Magdeburg, Mecklenburg,
Mühlenberg, Münsterberg,
Nuremberg, Oldenburg,

Orenburg, Regensburg, Rosenberg, Rube Goldberg, Spartanburg, Starhemberg, Toggenburg, Vandenberg, Venusberg, Vorarlberg, Wallenberg, Williamsburg, Württemberg • Johannesburg, St. Petersburg • Baden-Württemberg, Yekaterinburg, tip of the iceberg

ergative \ər-gə-tiv\ ergative, purgative

erge \ərj\ see URGE

ergeant \är-jənt\ see ARGENT

ergence \ər-jəns\ mergence • convergence, divergence, emergence, insurgence, resurgence, submergence

ergency \ər-jən-sē\ urgency • convergency, detergency, divergency, emergency, insurgency • counterinsurgency

ergent \ər-jənt\ see URGENT

ergeon \ər-jin\ see URGEON

erger \ər-jər\ merger, perjure, purger, scourger, urger, verdure, verger • deterger

ergh \ərg\ see ERG

ergic \ər-jik\ allergic, synergic, theurgic • demiurgic, dramaturgic, thaumaturgic

ergid \ər-jid\ see URGID

ergne[1] \ərn\ see URN

ergne[2] \ərn\ see ERN[1]

ergo \ər-gō\ ergo, Virgo

ergue \ərg\ see ERG

ergy \ər-jē\ see URGY

eri[1] \er-ē\ see ARY[1]

eri[2] \ir-ē\ see EARY

eria[1] \ir-ē-ə\ feria, Styria, Syria • Algeria, Assyria, asteria, bacteria, collyria, criteria, diphtheria, Egeria, Elyria, franseria, Iberia, Illyria, Liberia, Nigeria, plumeria, porphyria, Siberia, wisteria • cafeteria, cryptomeria, sansevieria, washateria, opera seria

eria[2] \er-ē-ə\ see ARIA

erial \ir-ē-əl\ aerial, cereal, ferial, serial • arterial, bacterial, diphtherial, empyreal, ethereal, funereal, imperial, material, sidereal, venereal, vizierial • immaterial, magisterial, managerial, ministerial, presbyterial, raw material • antibacterial, biomaterial

erian[1] \ir-ē-ən\ therian • Adlerian, Algerian, Assyrian, Aterian, Cancerian, Chaucerian, Cimmerian, criterion, Faulknerian, Forsterian, Hesperian, Hitlerian, Hutterian, Hyperion, Iberian, Illyrian, Keplerian, Liberian, Mahlerian, Mousterian, Mullerian, Nigerian, Pierian, Shakespearean, Siberian, Skinnerian, Spencerian, Spenserian, Spenglerian, Sumerian, valerian, Valerian, Wagnerian, Weberian, Whistlerian • Hanoverian, Presbyterian

erian[2] \er-ē-ən\ see ARIAN[1]

eric[1] \er-ik\ Berwick, cleric, Derek, derrick, Eric, ferric, Herrick, steric, xeric • aspheric, chimeric, choleric, enteric, entheric, generic, Homeric, mesmeric, numeric • atmospheric, biospheric, cholesteric, climacteric, congeneric, dysenteric, esoteric, exoteric, hemispheric, stratospheric • alphanumeric, elastomeric, ionospheric

eric² \ir-ik\ lyric, pyrrhic, Pyrrhic, spheric, xeric • aspheric, chimeric, empiric, Illyric, satiric, satyric, vampiric • atmospheric, hemispheric, panegyric, stratospheric

erica \er-i-kə\ erica, Erica • America • esoterica, North America, South America • British America, Central America, Latin America, Mesoamerica, Middle America, Spanish America

erical¹ \er-i-kəl\ clerical, spherical • chimerical, hysterical, numerical • anticlerical

erical² \ir-i-kəl\ lyrical, miracle, spherical, spiracle • empirical • hemispherical

erich \erik\ see ERIC¹

erics \er-iks\ sferics • hysterics—*also* -s, -'s, *and* -s' *forms of nouns listed at* ERIC¹

eried \ir-ē-əd\ see ERIOD

eries \ir-ēz\ Ceres, series • dundrearies, in series, time series, World Series • miniseries —*also* -s, -'s, *and* -s' *forms of nouns and* -s *forms of verbs listed at* EARY

erif \er-əf\ seraph, serif, sheriff, teraph • sans serif

eriff \er-əf\ see ERIF

erik \erik\ see ERIC¹

erika \er-i-kə\ see ERICA

eril \er-əl\ beryl, Beryl, Cheryl, Errol, feral, ferrule, ferule, Merrill, peril, Sheryl, sterile • imperil • chrysoberyl, yellow peril

erilant \er-ə-lənt\ see ERULENT

erile \er-əl\ see ERIL

erilous \er-ə-ləs\ perilous, querulous • glomerulus

eriment \er-ə-mənt\ cerement • experiment

erin \er-ən\ see ARON¹

ering \ar-iŋ\ see ARING¹

eriod \ir-ē-əd\ myriad, nereid, Nereid, period • grace period

erion \ir-ē-ən\ see ERIAN¹

erior \ir-ē-ər\ querier • anterior, exterior, inferior, interior, posterior, superior, ulterior, Lake Superior—*also* -er *forms of adjectives listed at* EARY

eriot \er-ē-ət\ see ARIAT¹

erious \ir-ē-əs\ cereus, Nereus, serious, Sirius • cinereous, delirious, Guarnerius, imperious, mysterious, Tiberius • deleterious

eris¹ \ir-əs\ see EROUS

eris² \er-əs\ see ERROUS

erist¹ \ir-əst\ querist, theorist, verist • careerist • panegyrist

—also -est *forms of adjectives listed at* EER[2]

erist[2] \er-əst\ *see* ARIST

erisy \er-ə-sē\ *see* ERESY

erit \er-ət\ ferret, merit, terret • demerit, inherit • disinherit

eritable \er-ət-ə-bəl\ heritable, veritable • inheritable

eritor \er-ət-ər\ ferreter, heritor • inheritor

erity \er-ət-ē\ ferity, ferrety, rarity, verity • alterity, asperity, austerity, celerity, dexterity, legerity, posterity, prosperity, severity, sincerity, temerity • insincerity

erium \ir-ē-əm\ Miriam • bacterium, collyrium, criterium, delirium, deuterium, imperium, psalterium • magisterium

erius[1] \er-ē-əs\ *see* ARIOUS

erius[2] \ir-ē-əs\ *see* ERIOUS

erjure \ər-jər\ *see* ERGER

erjury \ərj-rē\ perjury, surgery • tree surgery • microsurgery, neurosurgery, plastic surgery, psychosurgery

erk \ərk\ *see* ORK[1]

erker \ər-kər\ *see* ORKER[1]

erkin \ər-kən\ *see* IRKIN

erking \ər-kiŋ\ *see* ORKING

erkly \ər-klē\ clerkly • berserkly

erky \ər-kē\ birkie, jerky, murky, perky, smirky, turkey, Turkey • cold turkey, talk turkey

• Albuquerque, herky-jerky, water turkey

erle \ərl\ *see* IRL[1]

erlie \ər-lē\ *see* AIRLY

erlin \ər-lən\ merlin, Merlin, merlon, purlin, yearling

erling \ər-liŋ\ *see* URLING

erlon \ər-lən\ *see* ERLIN

erlyn \ər-lən\ *see* ERLIN

erm \ərm\ *see* ORM[1]

erma \ər-mə\ dharma, herma, Irma • scleroderma, terra firma

ermal \ər-məl\ dermal, thermal • nonthermal, subdermal, transdermal • ectodermal, endodermal, epidermal, exothermal, hydrothermal, hypodermal, hypothermal, isothermal

erman \ər-mən\ ermine, german, German, germen, Herman, merman, sermon, Sherman, Thurman, vermin • determine, extermine, Mount Hermon • cousin-german, predetermine

ermanent \ərm-nənt\ permanent • determinant, impermanent • semipermanent

ermann \ər-mən\ *see* ERMAN

ermary \ərm-rē\ *see* IRMARY

erment \ər-mənt\ averment, conferment, deferment, determent, interment, preferment • disinterment

ermer \ər-mər\ *see* URMUR

ermes \ər-mēz\ Hermes, kermes

ermi \ər-mē\ see ERMY

ermic \ər-mik\ dharmic, karmic, thermic • geothermic, hypodermic, taxidermic

ermin \ər-mən\ see ERMAN

erminable \ərm-nə-bəl\ terminable • determinable, interminable • indeterminable

erminal \ərm-nəl\ germinal, terminal • preterminal, subterminal

erminant \ərm-nənt\ see ERMANENT

ermine \ər-mən\ see ERMAN

ermined \ər-mənd\ ermined • determined • self-determined • overdetermined

erminous \ər-mə-nəs\ terminus, verminous • conterminous, coterminous

erminus \ər-mə-nəs\ see ERMINOUS

ermis \ər-məs\ dermis, kermis, thermos • endodermis, epidermis, exodermis, hypodermis

ermit \ər-mət\ hermit, Kermit, Thermit

ermon \ər-mən\ see ERMAN

ermos \ər-məs\ see ERMIS

ermy \ər-mē\ fermi, germy, squirmy, wormy • diathermy, endothermy, taxidermy

ern¹ \ern\ bairn, Bern, cairn, Nairn • Auvergne, moderne, Pitcairn, Sauternes, Ygerne • art moderne

ern² \ərn\ see URN

erna \ər-nə\ dharna, Myrna, sterna, Verna • cisterna

ernal \ərn-əl\ colonel, journal, kernel, sternal, vernal • diurnal, eternal, external, fraternal, hibernal, infernal, internal, maternal, nocturnal, paternal, supernal • coeternal, sempiternal

ernary \ər-nə-rē\ fernery, ternary, turnery • quaternary

erne¹ \ern\ see ERN¹

erne² \ərn\ see URN

erned \ərnd\ see URNED

ernel \ərn-əl\ see ERNAL

erner \ər-nər\ see URNER

ernes¹ \ern\ see ERN¹

ernes² \ərn\ see URN

ernest \ər-nəst\ see ERNIST

ernia \ər-ne-ə\ hernia • Hibernia

ernian \ər-nē-ən\ Hibernian, Melbournian, quaternion, Saturnian

ernible \ər-nə-bəl\ see URNABLE

ernie \ər-nē\ see OURNEY¹

ernier \ər-nē-ər\ see OURNEYER

ernion \ər-nē-ən\ see ERNIAN

ernist \ər-nəst\ earnest, Ernest • internist

ernity \ər-nət-ē\ eternity, fraternity, maternity, modernity, paternity, quaternity • confraternity, sempiternity

ernment \ern-mənt\
adjournment, attornment,
concernment, discernment,
internment

ernum \ər-nəm\ see URNUM

erny \ər-nē\ see OURNEY[1]

ero[1] \ē-rō\ giro, gyro, hero, Hero,
Nero, zero • ground zero,
subzero • antihero, superhero,
zero-zero

ero[2] \er-ō\ aero, cero, Faeroe,
faro, pharaoh, taro, tarot
• bolero, bracero, cruzeiro,
Guerrero, Herero, Madero,
montero, pampero, Pinero,
primero, ranchero, sombrero,
torero, vaquero • burladero,
caballero, Mescalero, pistolero
• banderillero, carabinero,
embarcadero • Rio de Janeiro

ero[3] \ir-ō\ giro, guiro, gyro, hero,
zero • ground zero, nonzero,
Pinero, primero, subzero
• zero-zero • absolute zero

erod \er-əd\ Herod • out-Herod,
viverrid

erold \er-əld\ see ERALD

eron \er-ən\ see ARON[1]

erous \ir-əs\ cerous, cirrus, Eris,
peeress, Pyrrhus, scirrhous,
seeress, serous

erp \ərp\ see URP

erpe \ər-pē\ see IRPY

erque \ər-kē\ see ERKY

err[1] \er\ see ARE[4]

err[2] \ər\ see EUR[1]

erra \er-ə\ see ERA[1]

errable \ər-ə-bəl\ see ERABLE

errace \er-əs\ see ERROUS

erral \ər-əl\ bharal, scurrile,
squirrel • conferral, deferral,
demurral, referral, transferal

errance \er-əns\ see ARENCE

errancy \er-ən-sē\ errancy
• aberrancy, coherency,
inerrancy

errand \er-ənd\ errand, gerund

errant \er-ənt\ see ARENT[1]

erre \er\ see ARE[4]

errell \er-əl\ see ERIL

errence[1] \ər-əns\ see URRENCE

errence[2] \er-əns\ see ARENCE

errent \ər-ənt\ see URRENT

errer \ər-ər\ burrer, stirrer
• conferrer, deferrer, demurrer,
deterrer, inferrer, preferrer,
referrer, transferrer

erret \er-ət\ see ERIT

erreter \er-ət-ər\ see ERITOR

erria \er-ē-ə\ see ARIA

errible \er-ə-bəl\ see EARABLE[1]

erric \er-ik\ see ERIC[1]

errick \er-ik\ see ERIC[1]

errid \er-əd\ see EROD

errie \er-ē\ see ARY[1]

erried \er-ēd\ berried, serried,
varied—*also* -ed *forms of verbs
listed at* ARY[1]

errier \er-ē-ər\ burier, terrier,
varier • bull terrier, fox terrier,
toy terrier, Welsh terrier—*also*

-er *forms of adjectives listed at* ARY[1]

errill \er-əl\ *see* ERIL

errily \er-ə-lē\ *see* ARILY

erring[1] \ar-iŋ\ *see* ARING[1]

erring[2] \ər-iŋ\ *see* URRING

erris \er-əs\ *see* ERROUS

errol \er-əl\ *see* ERIL

errold \er-əld\ *see* ERALD

erron \er-ən\ *see* ARON[1]

error \er-ər\ *see* EARER[1]

errous \er-əs\ derris, Eris, ferrous, parous, Perris, terrace • nonferrous • millionairess

errule \er-əl\ *see* ERIL

erry \er-ē\ *see* ARY[1]

ers[1] \ərz\ furze, hers • somewheres • Voyageurs —*also* -s, -'s, *and* -s' *forms of nouns and* -s *forms of verbs listed at* EUR[1]

ers[2] \ā\ *see* AY[1]

ersa \ər-sə\ bursa, Bursa • vice versa

ersable \ər-sə-bəl\ *see* ERSIBLE

ersal[1] \ər-səl\ bursal, tercel, versal • dispersal, rehearsal, reversal, transversal, traversal • dress rehearsal, time reversal, universal

ersal[2] \är-səl\ *see* ARSAL

ersary \ərs-rē\ *see* URSARY

erse \ərs\ birse, burse, curse, Erse, hearse, nurse, perse, purse, terce, terse, verse, worse • adverse, amerce, asperse, averse, coerce, commerce, converse, cutpurse, disburse, disperse, diverse, dry nurse, free verse, immerse, inverse, Nez Percé, obverse, perverse, rehearse, reverse, scrub nurse, sesterce, submerse, transverse, traverse, wet nurse • e-commerce, in reverse, intersperse, nonsense verse, privy purse, reimburse, shepherd's purse, universe • biodiverse, chapter and verse, heroic verse, practical nurse, registered nurse, visiting nurse • chamber of commerce, island universe

ersed \ərst\ *see* URST

erser \ər-sər\ *see* URSOR

ersey \ər-zē\ furzy, jersey, Jersey, kersey, Mersey • New Jersey

erschel \ər-shəl\ *see* ERCIAL

ershel \ər-shəl\ *see* ERCIAL

ersial \ər-shəl\ *see* ERCIAL

ersian \ər-zhən\ *see* ERSION[1]

ersible \ər-sə-bəl\ coercible, conversable, dispersible, eversible, immersible, reversible, submersible, traversable • incoercible, irreversible

ersion[1] \ər-zhən\ Persian, version • aspersion, aversion, coercion, conversion, dispersion, diversion, emersion, eversion, excursion, immersion, incursion, inversion, perversion, recursion, reversion, sub-

mersion, subversion • ambi-
version, Douay Version,
extroversion, gene conversion,
interspersion, introversion, King
James Version, reconversion,
retroversion • animadversion,
Authorized Version, bio-
conversion, seroconversion

ersion² \ər-shən\ see ERTIAN

ersional \ərzh-nəl\ versional
• conversional, reversional

ersity¹ \ər-sət-ē\ adversity,
diversity, perversity • multi-
versity, university

ersity² \ər-stē\ see IRSTY

ersive \ər-siv\ cursive
• ambersive, aversive, coercive,
detersive, discursive, dis-
persive, excursive, inversive,
perversive, recursive, sub-
versive • introversive

erson \ərs-ᵊn\ person, worsen
• chairperson, craftsperson,
draftsperson, first person,
houseperson, in person,
layperson, MacPherson,
newsperson, nonperson,
salesperson, spokesperson,
third person, unperson
• anchorperson, business-
person, gentleperson, second
person, weatherperson

erst \ərst\ see URST

ersted \ər-stəd\ oersted,
worsted

ersus \ər-səs\ cercis, thyrsus,
versus • excursus

ersy \ər-sē\ see ERCY

ert¹ \ərt\ Bert, blurt, chert, curt,
Curt, dirt, flirt, girt, hurt, pert,
quirt, shirt, skirt, spurt, squirt,
sturt, vert, wert, wort • advert,
alert, assert, avert, bellwort,
birthwort, Blackshirt, brown-
shirt, bush shirt, camp shirt,
colewort, concert, convert,
covert, desert, dessert, dissert,
divert, dress shirt, evert, exert,
expert, exsert, figwort, fleawort,
frankfurt, glasswort, hair shirt,
Hastert, hoopskirt, hornwort,
inert, insert, invert, lousewort,
lungwort, madwort, milkwort,
mugwort, nightshirt, outskirt,
overt, pay dirt, pervert,
pilewort, ragwort, redshirt,
revert, ribwort, saltwort,
sandwort, Schubert, seagirt,
sea squirt, soapwort, spearwort, spleenwort, stitchwort,
stonewort, stuffed shirt,
subvert, sweatshirt, toothwort,
T-shirt, ungirt • ambivert,
bladderwort, bloody shirt, body
shirt, butterwort, controvert,
disconcert, extrovert, feverwort,
hobble skirt, in concert,
inexpert, introvert, liverwort,
malapert, miniskirt, mitrewort,
moneywort, overshirt, overskirt,
pennywort, pettiskirt, polo shirt,
preconcert, reconvert, red alert,
Saint-John's-wort, spiderwort,
swallowwort, tail covert,
thoroughwort, undershirt,
underskirt, wing covert • aloha
shirt, animadvert, Hawaiian
shirt, interconvert

ert² \er\ see ARE⁴

ert³ \at\ see AT⁵

erta \ərt-ə\ Gerta • Alberta, Roberta

ertain \ərt-ᵊn\ Burton, certain, curtain, Merton • for certain, uncertain

ertant \ərt-ᵊnt\ see ERTENT

erted \ərt-əd\ skirted • concerted, perverted, T-shirted • extroverted, miniskirted, undershirted—*also* -ed *forms of verbs listed at* ERT¹

ertedly \ərt-əd-lē\ assertedly, concertedly, pervertedly

erter \ərt-ər\ blurter, flirter, Herter, hurter, skirter, squirter, stertor • converter, deserter, frankfurter, Frankfurter, inserter, inverter, perverter, reverter, subverter • controverter, torque converter—*also* -er *forms of adjectives listed at* ERT¹

ertes¹ \ərt-ēz\ certes • Laertes

ertes² \ərts\ see ERTS

ertford \ärt-fərd\ see ARTFORD

erth \ərth\ see IRTH

ertha \ər-thə\ bertha, Bertha, Eartha

ertia \ər-shə\ Mercia, Murcia • inertia

ertial \ər-shəl\ see ERCIAL

ertian \ər-shən\ Mercian, tertian • assertion, Cistercian, desertion, exertion, insertion • self-assertion

ertible \ərt-ə-bəl\ convertible, invertible, revertible • controvertible, inconvertible • incontrovertible

ertile \ərt-ᵊl\ fertile, hurtle, kirtle, myrtle, Myrtle, spurtle, turtle • crape myrtle, cross-fertile, infertile, sand myrtle, sea turtle, self-fertile, turn turtle, wax myrtle • interfertile, snapping turtle

ertinence \ərt-ᵊn-əns\ pertinence, purtenance • appurtenance, impertinence

ertinent¹ \ərt-ᵊn-ənt\ pertinent • appurtenant, impertinent

ertinent² \ərt-nənt\ see IRTINENT

erting \ərt-iŋ\ shirting, skirting • disconcerting, self-asserting—*also* -ing *forms of verbs listed at* ERT¹

ertion \ər-shən\ see ERTIAN

ertisement \ərt-əs-mənt\ advertisement, divertissement

ertium \ər-shəm\ see URTIUM

ertive \ərt-iv\ furtive • assertive • self-assertive, unassertive

erton \ərt-n\ see ERTAIN

ertor \ərt-ər\ see ERTER

erts \ərts\ certes, hertz, Hertz, nerts • gigahertz, kilohertz, megahertz—*also* -s, -'s, *and* -s' *forms of nouns and* -s *forms of verbs listed at* ERT¹

erty \ər-tē\ see IRTY

ertz \ərts\ see ERTS

erule \er-əl\ see ERIL

erulent \er-ə-lənt\ sterilant • puberulent, pulverulent

erulous \er-ə-ləs\ see ERILOUS

erum \ir-əm\ theorem, serum
 • blood serum, truth serum
 • Gödel's theorem • Fourier's theorem

erund \er-ənd\ see ERRAND

erunt \er-ənt\ see ARENT[1]

erval \ər-vəl\ see ERVIL

ervancy \ər-vən-sē\ see ERVENCY

ervant \ər-vənt\ fervent, servant
 • bond servant, maidservant, manservant, observant • civil servant, fellow servant, inobservant, public servant

ervative \ər-vət-iv\ conservative, preservative • archconservative
 • neoconservative, ultra-conservative

ervator \ər-vət-ər\ see ERVITOR

erve \ərv\ curve, MIRV, nerve, serve, slurve, swerve, verve
 • bell curve, conserve, deserve, disserve, french curve, hors d'oeuvre, incurve, observe, preserve, recurve, reserve, self-serve, sine curve, skew curve, subserve, unnerve • facial nerve, in reserve, learning curve, normal curve, optic nerve, spinal nerve, unreserve, vagus nerve • cranial nerve, legal reserve, sciatic nerve, Western Reserve

erved \ərvd\ nerved • decurved, deserved, recurved, reserved
 • underserved, unreserved
 —also -ed forms of verbs listed at ERVE

ervency \ər-vən-sē\ fervency
 • conservancy

ervent \ər-vənt\ see ERVANT

erver \ər-vər\ fervor, server
 • conserver, deserver, observer, preserver, timeserver
 • altar server, life preserver

ervice \ər-vəs\ nervous, service
 • curb service, debt service, disservice, full-service, in-service, lip service, room service, self-service, wire service • civil service, divine service, fee-for-service, foreign service, interservice, point-of-service, public service, secret service, silent service, social service

ervil \ər-vəl\ chervil, serval, servile

ervile \ər-vəl\ see ERVIL

erviness \ər-vē-nəs\ nerviness, scurviness • topsy-turviness

erving \ər-viŋ\ Irving, serving
 • deserving, self-serving, timeserving, unswerving
 —also -ing forms of verbs listed at ERVE

ervitor \ər-vət-ər\ servitor
 • conservator

ervor \ər-vər\ see ERVER

ervous \ər-vəs\ see ERVICE

ervy \ər-vē\ see URVY

erwick \er-ik\ see ERIC[1]

erwin \ər-wən\ Irwin, Sherwin

ery[1] \er-ē\ see ARY[1]

ery[2] \ir-ē\ see EARY

eryl \er-əl\ see ERIL

erz \erts\ see ERTZ[1]

es¹ \ā\ see AY¹

es² \ās\ see ACE¹

es³ \āz\ see AZE¹

es⁴ \es\ see ESS

es⁵ \ēz\ see EZE

e's \ēz\ see EZE

esa¹ \ā-sə\ mesa, Mesa, presa
• omasa, Theresa • Costa
Mesa

esa² \ā-zə\ presa, Stresa
• impresa, marchesa, Theresa
• Bel Paese

esage \es-ij\ see ESSAGE

esan¹ \āz-ᵊn\ see AZON

esan² \ēz-ᵊn\ see EASON

esant \ez-ᵊnt\ Besant, bezant,
peasant, pheasant, pleasant,
present • at present,
unpleasant, omnipresent

esas \ā-zəs\ Marquesas—*also*
-s, -'s, *and* -s' *forms of nouns
listed at* ESA²

esce \es\ see ESS

escence \es-ᵊns\ essence
• candescence, concrescence,
excrescence, florescence,
fluorescence, pearlescence,
pubescence, putrescence,
quiescence, quintessence,
senescence, tumescence,
turgescence, virescence
• acquiescence, adolescence,
arborescence, coalescence,
convalescence, decalescence,
defervescence, deliquescence,
detumescence, effervescence,
efflorescence, evanescence,
incandescence, inflorescence,

iridescence, juvenescence,
luminescence, obsolescence,
opalescence, phosphorescence,
prepubescence, recrudescence

escency \es-ᵊn-sē\ excrescency,
incessancy

escent \es-ᵊnt\ crescent,
Crescent, candescent,
canescent, concrescent,
decrescent, depressant,
excrescent, fluorescent,
incessant, increscent,
liquescent, pearlescent,
pubescent, putrescent,
quiescent, rufescent,
senescent, suppressant,
tumescent, turgescent,
virescent • acquiescent,
adolescent, arborescent,
coalescent, convalescent,
detumescent, effervescent,
efflorescent, evanescent, Fertile
Crescent, incandescent,
inflorescent, intumescent,
iridescent, juvenescent,
luminescent, obsolescent,
opalescent, phosphorescent,
prepubescent, recrudescent,
viridescent • antidepressant,
preadolescent

escible \es-ə-bəl\ see ESSIBLE

escience \ēsh-əns\ nescience,
prescience

escive \es-iv\ see ESSIVE

esco \es-kō\ fresco • alfresco,
UNESCO • Ionesco

escue \es-kyü\ fescue, rescue

ese¹ \ēs\ see IECE

ese² \ēz\ see EZE

ese³ \ā-sē\ see ACY

esence \ez-ᵊns\ pleasance, presence • real presence • omnipresence

eseus \ē-sē-əs\ Theseus • Tiresias

esh¹ \esh\ crèche, flèche, flesh, fresh, mesh, thresh • afresh, bobeche, calèche, crème fraîche, enmesh, gooseflesh, horseflesh, immesh, parfleche, refresh, tête-bêche • Bangladesh, Gilgamesh, intermesh, in the flesh, Marrakech, pound of flesh, press the flesh • Andhra Pradesh, Madhya Pradesh, Uttar Pradesh

esh² \āsh\ see ECHE¹

esh³ \ash\ see ASH³

eshed \esht\ fleshed, meshed —also -ed forms of verbs listed at ESH¹

eshen \esh-ən\ see ESSION

eshener \esh-nər\ see ESSIONER

esher \esh-ər\ see ESSURE

eshly \esh-lē\ fleshly, freshly, specially • especially

eshment \esh-mənt\ fleshment • enmeshment, refreshment

esi¹ \ā-zē\ see AZY

esi² \ā-sē\ see ACY

esia¹ \ē-shə\ Moesia • Letitia, Lucretia, Magnesia, Phoenicia • alopecia

esia² \ē-zhə\ freesia • amnesia, atresia, esthesia, frambesia, magnesia, rafflesia, Rhodesia, Silesia, Tunisia • analgesia, anesthesia, Austronesia, Indonesia, kinesthesia, Melanesia, Micronesia, paramnesia, Polynesia, synesthesia • milk of magnesia

esial \ē-zē-əl\ mesial • ecclesial

esian¹ \ē-zhən\ Frisian, lesion • adhesion, Arlesian, Cartesian, cohesion, Ephesian, Etesian, Gaspesian, magnesian, Rhodesian, Salesian, Silesian • Austronesian, Celebesian, Holstein-Friesian, Indonesian, manganesian, Melanesian, Micronesian, Polynesian • Peloponnesian

esian² \ē-shən\ see ETION¹

esias \ē-sē-əs\ see ESEUS

esicant \es-i-kənt\ see ESICCANT

esiccant \es-i-kənt\ desiccant, vesicant

esidency \ez-əd-ən-sē\ presidency, residency • nonresidency, vice presidency

esident \ez-əd-ənt\ president, resident • nonresident, vice president

esimal \es-ə-məl\ centesimal, millesimal, vigesimal • duodecimal, hexadecimal, planetesimal, sexagesimal • infinitesimal

esin \ez-ᵊn\ resin • muezzin

esion \ē-zhən\ see ESIAN¹

esis \ē-səs\ Croesus, thesis, tmesis • ascesis, askesis, esthesis, kinesis, mimesis, paresis, prosthesis • anamnesis, apheresis, catachresis, catechesis, Dionysus, exegesis, kinesthesis • hyperkinesis, Peloponnesus, photokinesis, psychokinesis, telekinesis • amniocentesis

esium \ē-zē-əm\ see EZIUM

esive \ē-siv\ adhesive, cohesive • self-adhesive

esk \esk\ see ESQUE

esley \es-lē\ see ESSLY

eslie \es-lē\ see ESSLY

esne \ēn\ see INE[3]

eso[1] \ā-sō\ peso, say-so

eso[2] \es-ō\ see ESSO

espass \es-pəs\ Thespis, trespass

espis \es-pəs\ see ESPASS

espite \es-pət\ see ESPOT

espot \es-pət\ despot, respite

esque \esk\ desk • burlesque, Dantesque, grotesque, moresque • arabesque, Bunyanesque, copydesk, gigantesque, humoresque, Junoesque, Kafkaesque, picaresque, picturesque, plateresque, Romanesque, Rubenesque, Runyonesque, sculpturesque, statuesque, Whitmanesque • churrigueresque

ess \es\ bless, cess, chess, cress, dress, ess, fess, guess, Hess, Hesse, jess, less, loess, mess, ness, press, s, stress, tress, yes • abscess, access, address, aggress, assess, bench-press, caress, clothes-press, coatdress, cold-press, compress, confess, cross-dress, CS, depress, de-stress, digress, distress, drill press, duress, egress, excess, express, finesse, fluoresce, French press, full-dress, handpress, headdress, housedress, idlesse, impress, ingress, largess, Loch Ness, Meknes, much less, nightdress, noblesse, no less, obsess, oppress, outguess, pantdress, possess, precess, prestress, princess, process, profess, progress, recess, redress, regress, re-press, repress, shirtdress, side-dress, SS, success, sundress, suppress, tendresse, top-dress, trans-gress, undress, unless, web press, winepress, word stress • ABS, acquiesce, baroness, bitter cress, coalesce, conva-lesce, crown princess, DES, decompress, deliquesce, derepress, dispossess, due process, effervesce, effloresce, evanesce, fancy press, full-court press, gentilesse, granny dress, IHS, incandesce, in-process, intumesce, inverness, Inverness, less and less, letterpress, luminesce, Lyonnesse, minidress, more or less, nonetheless, obsolesce, otherguess, overdress, pennycress, phosphoresce, politesse, prepossess, preprocess, recrudesce, repossess, reprocess, retrogress, second-guess, SOS, sweaterdress, underdress, unsuccess, watercress, window-dress, word process • ancienne noblesse, another-guess, keynote address, nevertheless, random-access • Bessemer process, limited-access

essa \es-ə\ see ESSE[3]

essable \es-ə-bəl\ see ESSIBLE

essage \es-ij\ message, presage • expressage

essaly \es-ə-lē\ Cecily, Thessaly

essamine \es-mən\ see ESSMAN

essan \es-ᵊn\ see ESSEN

essancy \es-ᵊn-sē\ see ESCENCY

essant \es-ᵊnt\ see ESCENT

esse[1] \es\ see ESS

esse[2] \es-ē\ see ESSY

esse[3] \es-ə\ Hesse • Odessa, Vanessa

essed \est\ see EST

essedly \es-əd-lē\ blessedly • compressedly, confessedly, professedly, possessedly • self-confessedly, self-possessedly

essel \es-əl\ see ESTLE[1]

essen \es-ᵊn\ Essen, lessen, lesson, messan • object lesson • delicatessen

essence \es-ᵊns\ see ESCENCE

esser \es-ər\ see ESSOR

essex \es-iks\ Essex, Wessex

essful \es-fəl\ stressful • distressful, successful • unsuccessful

essian \esh-ən\ see ESSION

essible \es-ə-bəl\ decibel, guessable • accessible, addressable, assessable, compressible, confessable, depressible, expressible, impressible, processable, putrescible, repressible, suppressible • inaccessible, incompressible, inexpressible, insuppressible, irrepressible

essie \es-ē\ see ESSY

essile \es-əl\ see ESTLE[1]

ession \esh-ən\ cession, freshen, hessian, session • accession, aggression, bull session, compression, concession, confession, depression, digression, discretion, egression, expression, impression, ingression, jam session, obsession, oppression, possession, precession, procession, profession, progression, recession, refreshen, regression, repression, secession, succession, suppression, transgression • deaccession, decompression, dispossession, indiscretion, intercession, intersession, introgression, misimpression, nonaggression, poster session, preposFsession, reimpression, repossession, retrogression, self-confession, self-expression, self-possession, skull session, supersession

essional \esh-nəl\ sessional
• accessional, concessional,
congressional, diagressional,
expressional, obsessional,
possessional, precessional,
processional, professional,
progressional, recessional,
successional • intercessional,
nonprofessional, preprofes-
sional, subprofessional,
unprofessional

essioner \esh-nər\ freshener
• concessioner

essionist \esh-nəst\
expressionist, impressionist,
repressionist, secessionist

essity \es-tē\ see ESTY

essive \es-iv\ crescive
• aggressive, caressive,
compressive, concessive,
degressive, depressive,
digressive, excessive,
expressive, impressive,
ingressive, obsessive,
oppressive, possessive,
progressive, recessive,
regressive, successive,
suppressive, transgressive
• inexpressive, retrogressive,
self-expressive, unexpressive
• manic-depressive, passive-
aggressive

essly \es-lē\ Leslie, Wesley
• expressly

essman \es-mən\ chessman,
pressman • expressman,
jessamine, specimen

essment \es-mənt\ see ESTMENT

esso \es-ō\ gesso • espresso

esson \es-ən\ see ESSEN

essor \es-ər\ dresser, guesser,
lesser, presser, pressor,
stressor • addresser, aggres-
sor, assessor, caresser,
compressor, confessor, cross-
dresser, depressor, expressor,
food processor, hairdresser,
oppressor, processor, profes-
sor, regressor, repressor,
successor, suppressor,
transgressor, vinedresser
• antecessor, dispossessor,
intercessor, predecessor,
repossessor, second-guesser,
window dresser, word processor

essory \es-ə-rē\ pessary
• accessory, possessory
• intercessory

essure \esh-ər\ pressure • blood
pressure, high-pressure,
impressure, low-pressure,
refresher, root pressure, sound
pressure • acupressure,
overpressure—also -er forms of
adjectives listed at ESH

essy \es-ē\ Bessie, dressy,
Jesse, Jessie, messy

est \est\ best, breast, Brest,
chest, crest, gest, geste, guest,
hest, jessed, jest, lest, nest,
pest, quest, rest, test, tressed,
vest, west, West, wrest, zest
• abreast, abscessed,
appressed, armrest, arrest, at
best, at rest, attest, backrest,
beau geste, bed rest, behest,
bequest, bird's-nest, blood
test, celeste, Celeste, compressed, congest, conquest,
contest, crow's nest, depressed,
detest, devest, Dick test,
digest, distressed, divest,

egest, eighth rest, field-test, flight-test, footrest, gabfest, half rest, hard-pressed, headrest, high-test, hillcrest, hope chest, houseguest, imprest, incest, infest, ingest, inquest, interest, invest, Key West, lovefest, love nest, low-test, Mae West, mare's nest, means test, Midwest, molest, northwest, patch test, posttest, pretest, professed, protest, redbreast, repressed, request, retest, revest, road test, Schick test, scratch test, screen test, sea chest, skin test, slop chest, slugfest, southwest, spot test, steam chest, stress test, suggest, trapnest, Trieste, t-test, unblessed, undressed, unrest, unstressed, war chest, whole rest, Wild West • acid test, almagest, anapest, beta test, blanket chest, Bucharest, Budapest, decongest, disinfest, disinvest, empty-nest, false arrest, galley-west, Hammerfest, hornet's nest, house arrest, inkblot test, manifest, north-northwest, palimpsest, placement test, predigest, quarter rest, reinvest, rinderpest, Rorschach test, Sackville-West, second-best, self-addressed, self-confessed, self-interest, self-possessed, sweatervest, true-false test, uninterest, unprofessed, vision quest • aptitude test, auto-suggest, beauty contest, chanson de geste, close to the vest, compound interest, disinterest, feather one's nest, robin redbreast, simple interest, special interest, supraprotest, under arrest, underinvest, vested interest • citizen's arrest, paternity test, Stanford-Binet test, thirty-second rest —*also* -ed *forms of verbs listed at* ESS

esta \es-tə\ cesta, cuesta, testa, vesta, Vesta • Avesta, celesta, egesta, fiesta, ingesta, siesta • Zend-Avesta

estable \es-tə-bəl\ *see* ESTIBLE

estae \es-tē\ *see* ESTY

estal \es-tᵊl\ crestal, pestle, vestal

estan \es-tən\ *see* ESTINE

estant \es-tənt\ arrestant, contestant, infestant, protestant, Protestant • decongestant, disinfestant, manifestant

este \est\ *see* EST

ested \es-təd\ crested, tested, vested • means-tested, time-tested • barrel-chested, double-breasted, hairy-chested, indigested, single-breasted—*also* -ed *forms of verbs listed at* EST

ester \es-tər\ Chester, ester, Esther, fester, Hester, jester, Leicester, Lester, nester, Nestor, pester, quaestor, quester, tester, wester, yester, zester • ancestor, arrester, attester, contester, detester, digester, infester, investor, Manchester, molester, northwester, requester, Rochester, semester, sequester, southwester, sou'wester, suggester,

Sylvester, trimester, Winchester • beta tester, empty nester, monoester, polyester

esti \es-tē\ *see* ESTY

estial \es-tē-əl\ celestial, forestial

estible \es-tə-bəl\ testable • comestible, detestable, digestible, harvestable, ingestible, investable, suggestible • incontestable, indigestible

estic \es-tik\ gestic • domestic, majestic • alkahestic, anamnestic, anapestic, catachrestic

estical \es-ti-kəl\ *see* ESTICLE

esticle \es-ti-kəl\ testicle • catachrestical

estimate \es-tə-mət\ estimate, guesstimate • underestimate

estinate \es-tə-nət\ festinate • predestinate

estine \es-tən\ Creston, destine, Preston • Avestan, clandestine, intestine, predestine • large intestine, small intestine

esting \es-tiŋ\ cresting, resting, vesting, westing • arresting • interesting—*also* -ing *forms of verbs listed at* EST

estion \es-chən\ question • congestion, cross-question, digestion, egestion, ingestion, self-question, suggestion, tag question • beg the question, call in question, decongestion, essay question, indigestion, pop the question, self-suggestion • autosuggestion

estis \es-təs\ cestus, Festus, Sestos, testis • Alcestis, asbestos, Hephaestus

estival \es-tə-vəl\ estival, festival

estive \es-tiv\ festive, restive • congestive, digestive, egestive, ingestive, suggestive • decongestive

estle¹ \es-əl\ Cecil, decile, nestle, pestle, sessile, trestle, vessel, wrestle • blood vessel • Indian-wrestle

estle² \as-əl\ *see* ASSEL²

estle³ \əs-əl\ *see* USTLE

estless \est-ləs\ crestless, restless, zestless

estment \es-mənt\ vestment • arrestment, assessment, divestment, impressment, investment • disinvestment, reinvestment

esto \es-tō\ pesto, presto • Modesto • manifesto

eston \es-tən\ *see* ESTINE

estor \es-tər\ *see* ESTER

estos \es-təs\ *see* ESTIS

estra \es-trə\ fenestra, olestra, orchestra, palaestra • Clytemnestra

estral \es-trəl\ estral, kestrel • ancestral, campestral, fenestral, orchestral, semestral

estrel \es-trəl\ *see* ESTRAL

estress \es-trəs\ *see* ESTRUS

estrial \es-trē-əl\ semestrial, terrestrial • extraterrestrial

estrian \es-trē-ən\ equestrian, pedestrian

estrous \es-trəs\ see ESTRUS

estrus \es-trəs\ estrous, estrus, ancestress

estry \es-trē\ vestry • ancestry

estuous \es-chə-wəs\ incestuous, tempestuous

esture \es-chər\ gesture, vesture

estus \es-təs\ see ESTIS

esty \es-tē\ chesty, pesty, testae, testy, zesty • necessity, res gestae, Tibesti

esus \ē-səs\ see ESIS

et¹ \et\ bet, Bret, Chet, debt, et, fête, fret, get, het, jet, let, Lett, met, net, pet, ret, set, stet, sweat, Tet, threat, vet, wet, whet, yet • abet, aigrette, all wet, Annette, asset, Babette, backset, baguette, banquette, barbette, barquette, barrette, beget, beset, blanquette, boneset, brevet, briquette, brochette, brunet, burette, burnet, cadet, cassette, cermet, Claudette, Colette, coquet, coquette, cornet, corselet, corvette, coset, courgette, croquette, curette, curvet, cuvette, daleth, dinette, dip net, diskette, dragnet, duet, egret, fan-jet, fishnet, flechette, fly net, forget, gazette, georgette, Georgette, Gillette, gillnet, gill net, godet, grisette, handset, hard-set, headset, ink-jet, inlet, inset, Jeanette, jet set, Juliet, jump net, kismet, layette, life net, lorgnette, lunette, Lynette, maquette, Marquette, mind-set, mist net, moonset, moquette, motet, musette, Nanette, nerve net, noisette, nonet, nymphet, octet, offset, onset, outlet, outset, paillette, pallette, palmette, pipette, piquet, planchette, pound net, poussette, preset, quartet, quickset, quintet, raclette, ramet, ramjet, regret, reset, revet, rocket, roomette, rosette, roulette, saw set, saw-whet, septet, sestet, sextet, sharp-set, soubrette, spinet, stage set, stylet, sublet, subset, sunset, syrette, tacet, tea set, thickset, Tibet, toilette, tonette, trijet, twinset, typeset, Undset, unset, upset, vedette, vignette, well-set, Yvette • aiguillette, alphabet, anchoret, andouillette, anisette, Antoinette, avocet, banneret, basinet, bassinet, bayonet, Bernadette, bobbinet, bouncing bet, briolette, burgonet, calumet, canzonet, castanet, cellarette, chemisette, cigarette, clarinet, consolette, Cook Inlet, coronet, corselet, crepe suzette, dragonet, dresser set, electret, en brochette, epaulet, epithet, Ethernet, etiquette, falconet, farmerette, featurette, flageolet, flannelette, great egret, guillemet, heavyset, jaconet, Joliet, Juliet, kitchenette, Lafayette, landaulet, lanneret, launderette, leatherette, luncheonette, maisonette, majorette, marmoset, marquisette, martinet, mignonette, minaret, minuet, miquelet, netiquette, novelette, Olivet, oubliette, parapet, paupiette, photoset, pirouette, plasma jet, quodlibet, rondelet, safety net, satinet, scilicet, sermonette, serviette, silhouette, sobriquet, solleret, somerset, Somerset, soviet, space cadet, spinneret, statuette, stockinette, suffragette, superjet, swimmeret, taboret, teacher's pet, thermoset, towelette, trebuchet, tricolette, triple threat, underlet, usherette, vinaigrette, wagonette, web-offset • analphabet, bachelorette, drum majorette, electrojet, Hospitalet, marionette, microcassette, micropipette, mosquito net, musique concrète, photo-offset, Russian roulette, snowy egret, solution set, videlicet, working asset • audiocassette, caulifloweret, hail-fellow-well-met, Marie Antoinette, videocassette

et² \ā\ see AY¹

et³ \āt\ see ATE¹

et⁴ \es\ see ESS

eta¹ \ät-ə\ see ATA²

eta² \et-ə\ see ETTA

eta³ \ēt-ə\ see ITA²

etable¹ \et-ə-bəl\ see ETTABLE

etable² \ēt-ə-bəl\ see EATABLE

etal¹ \ēt-ᵊl\ beetle, betel, chaetal, fetal • decretal, excretal

etal² \et-ᵊl\ see ETTLE

etan¹ \et-ᵊn\ Breton, threaten • Cape Breton, Tibetan

etan² \ēt-ᵊn\ see EATEN¹

etch \ech\ catch, etch, fetch, fletch, ketch, kvetch, lech, letch, retch, sketch, stretch, vetch, wretch • backstretch, crown vetch, homestretch, outstretch

etched \echt\ teched • far-fetched—also -ed forms of verbs listed at ETCH

etcher \ech-ər\ etcher, catcher, fetcher, fletcher, Fletcher, kvetcher, lecher, sketcher, stretcher • cowcatcher, dogcatcher, dream catcher, eye-catcher, flycatcher, gnatcatcher • oystercatcher

etching \ech-iŋ\ etching, fetching, fletching—also -ing forms of verbs listed at ETCH

etchy \ech-ē\ kvetchy, sketchy, stretchy, tetchy

ete¹ \āt\ see ATE¹

ete² \et\ see ET¹

ete³ \ēt\ see EAT¹

ete⁴ \āt-ē\ see ATY

ête \āt\ see ATE¹

eted \ād\ see ADE¹

etel \ēt-ᵊl\ see ETAL¹

etely \ēt-lē\ see EETLY

eteor \ēt-ē-ər\ meteor • confiteor—also -er forms of adjectives listed at EATY

eter \ēt-ər\ see EATER¹

etera \e-trə\ see ETRA

eterate \et-ə-rət\ see ETERIT

eterit \et-ə-rət\ preterit
• inveterate

etes \ēt-əs\ see ETUS

eth¹ \eth\ Beth, breath, breadth, death, heth, meth, saith, Seth, snath • black death, brain death, crib death, daleth, handbreadth, hairbreadth, Lambeth, Macbeth • Ashtoreth, baby's breath, crystal meth, hold one's breath, in one breath, isopleth, kiss of death, life-and-death, living death, megadeath, morning breath, out of breath, shibboleth, sudden death, waste one's breath, wrongful death
• Elizabeth, under one's breath

eth² \ās\ see ACE¹

eth³ \āt\ see ATE¹

eth⁴ \et\ see ET¹

etha \ē-thə\ Aretha, Ibiza

ethane \e-thān\ ethane, methane

ethe \ē-thē\ see EATHY

ether¹ \eth-ər\ blether, feather, heather, Heather, leather, nether, tether, weather, wether, whether • aweather, bellwether, buff leather, fair-weather, glove leather, kid leather, pinfeather, shoe-leather, together, untether, white feather
• altogether, get-together, hang together, hell-for-leather, knock together, patent leather, prince's feather, pull together, put together, Russia leather, saddle leather, tar and feather, throw together • under the weather

ether² \eth-ər\ see OTHER¹

ethyl \eth-əl\ bethel, Bethel, Ethel, ethyl, methyl

eti¹ \ēt-ē\ see EATY

eti² \āt-ē\ see ATY

etia \ē-shə\ see ESIA¹

etian \ē-shən\ see ETION¹

etic¹ \ēt-ik\ thetic • acetic, docetic, gametic

etic² \et-ik\ etic, thetic
• aesthetic, ascetic, athletic, balletic, bathetic, cosmetic, docetic, eidetic, emetic, frenetic, gametic, genetic, hermetic, kinetic, limnetic, magnetic, mimetic, noetic, Ossetic, paretic, pathetic, phenetic, phonetic, phrenetic, phyletic, poetic, prophetic, prosthetic, pyretic, splenetic, syncretic, syndetic, synthetic, tonetic, Venetic • alphabetic, analgetic, anesthetic, antithetic, apathetic, asyndetic, copacetic, cybernetic, diabetic, diarrhetic, diathetic, dietetic, digenetic, diphyletic, diuretic, empathetic, energetic, epithetic, geodetic, homiletic, Masoretic, nomo-thetic, parenthetic, sympathetic, synergetic, synesthetic • antimagnetic, antipathetic, antipoetic, antipyretic, apologetic, geomagnetic, hydromagnetic, hyperkinetic, paramagnetic, pathogenetic, peripatetic,

psychokinetic, telekinetic, unsympathetic • electro-magnetic, general anesthetic, unapologetic • onomatopoetic

etical \et-i-kəl\ metical, reticle • aesthetical, genetical, heretical, pathetical, phonetical, poetical • antithetical, arithmetical, catechetical, cybernetical, epithetical, exegetical, geodetical, hypothetical, parenthetical, theoretical

eticist \et-ə-səst\ geneticist, kineticist, pheneticist • cyberneticist

etics \et-iks\ aesthetics, athletics, genetics, kinetics, phonetics, poetics, prosthetics, tonetics • cybernetics, dietetics, homiletics, apologetics, cytogenetics—*also* -s, -'s, *and* -s' *forms of nouns listed at* ETIC

etid \et-əd\ fetid, fretted, sweated • indebted • parapeted—*also* -ed *forms of verbs listed at* ET[1]

etin \et-ᵊn\ *see* EATEN[1]

etion[1] \ē-shən\ Grecian, Raetian • accretion, Capetian, completion, concretion, deletion, depletion, excretion, Helvetian, Lucretian, Ossetian, Phoenician, repletion, secretion, suppletion, Tahitian, Venetian • Austronesian, Diocletian, Epictetian, Melanesian, Polynesian

etion[2] \esh-ən\ *see* ESSION

etious \ē-shəs\ *see* ECIOUS

etis[1] \ēt-əs\ *see* ETUS

etis[2] \et-əs\ *see* ETTUCE

etist \et-əst\ cornetist, librettist, vignettist • clarinetist, exegetist, operettist—*also* -est *forms of adjectives listed at* ET[1]

etitive \et-ət-iv\ competitive, repetitive • noncompetitive, uncompetitive

etium \ē-shē-əm\ *see* ECIUM

etius \ē-shəs\ *see* ECIOUS

etive \ēt-iv\ accretive, completive, decretive, depletive, secretive, suppletive

etl[1] \ät-ᵊl\ *see* ATAL

etl[2] \et-ᵊl\ *see* ETTLE

etland \et-lənd\ Shetland, wetland

etment \et-mənt\ abetment, besetment, curettement, revetment

eto[1] \āt-ō\ *see* ATO[2]

eto[2] \ēt-ō\ *see* ITO[1]

eton \et-ᵊn\ *see* EATEN[1]

etor[1] \et-ər\ *see* ETTER

etor[2] \ēt-ər\ *see* EATER[1]

etory \ēt-ə-rē\ eatery • decretory, secretory, suppletory

etous \ēt-əs\ *see* ETUS

etra[1] \e-trə\ Petra, tetra • etcetera, osetra

etra[2] \ē-trə\ Petra • Kenitra

etral[2] \e-trəl\ *see* ETREL[1]

être \etr°\ fête champêtre, raison d'être

etrel² \ē-trəl\ see ETRAL¹

etric \e-trik\ metric • obstetric, symmetric • astrometric, asymmetric, barometric, biometric, chromometric, decametric, dekametric, diametric, dissymmetric, geometric, hypermetric, hypsometric, isometric, optometric, parametric, photometric, psychometric, telemetric, volumetric

etrical \e-tri-kəl\ metrical • obstetrical, symmetrical • asymmetrical, barometrical, diametrical, geometrical, unsymmetrical

etrics \e-triks\ obstetrics • biometrics, cliometrics, geometrics, isometrics, psychometrics, sabermetrics

etrist \e-trəst\ metrist • belletrist

etrol \e-trəl\ see ETREL¹

ets \ets\ let's, Metz, Retz • Donets, rillettes, Steinmetz • pantalets, Sosnowiec—*also -s, -'s, and -s' forms of nouns and -s forms of verbs listed at* ET¹

etsk \etsk\ Donetsk, Kuznetsk, Lipetsk • Novokuznetsk

ett \et\ see ET¹

etta \et-ə\ betta, Etta, feta, geta, Greta, Quetta • Barletta, biretta, bruschetta, cabretta, galleta, Gambetta, Loretta, mozzetta, pancetta, poinsettia, Rosetta, Valletta, vendetta • anchoveta, arietta, cabaletta, Henrietta, Marietta, operetta, sinfonietta

ettable \et-ə-bəl\ wettable • forgettable, regrettable, resettable • unforgettable

ette \et\ see ET¹

etter \et-ər\ better, bettor, debtor, fetter, getter, letter, netter, petter, rhetor, setter, sweater, tetter, whetter • abettor, air letter, bed wetter, begetter, black letter, block letter, bonesetter, chain letter, day letter, dead letter, enfetter, fan letter, forgetter, four-letter, gillnetter, go-getter, jet-setter, Ledbetter, newsletter, night letter, pacesetter, pinsetter, red-letter, regretter, trendsetter, typesetter, unfetter, upsetter, vignetter • carburettor, English setter, go one better, Gordon setter, Irish setter, open letter, scarlet letter—*also -er forms of adjectives listed at* ET¹

ettered \et-ərd\ lettered • unfettered, unlettered

ettes \ets\ see ETS

ettia \et-ə\ see ETTA

ettie \et-ē\ see ETTY¹

ettier \it-ē-ər\ see ITTIER

ettiness \it-ē-nəs\ see ITTINESS

etting \et-iŋ\ netting, setting • bed-wetting, besetting, bloodletting, filmsetting, go-getting, jet-setting, pacesetting, place setting, trendsetting,

typesetting, wire netting
• thermosetting—*also* -ing
forms of verbs listed at ET[1]

ettish \et-ish\ fetish, Lettish,
pettish, wettish • coquettish
• novelettish

ettle \et-əl\ fettle, kettle, metal,
mettle, nettle, petal, settle,
shtetl • bimetal, gunmetal,
nonmetal, teakettle, unsettle
• grasp the nettle • Citlaltépetl
• Popocatépetl

ettlesome \et-əl-səm\
mettlesome, nettlesome

ettling \et-lin\ fettling, settling
• unsettling—*also* -ing *forms of
verbs listed at* ETTLE

etto \et-ō\ ghetto, stretto
• cavetto, falsetto, in petto,
larghetto, libretto, palmetto,
stiletto, zucchetto • allegretto,
amaretto, amoretto, Canaletto,
fianchetto, Kazan Retto,
lazaretto, saw palmetto,
Tintoretto, vaporetto

ettor \et-ər\ see ETTER

ettuce \et-əs\ lettuce • Hymettus
• Lycabettus

ettus \et-əs\ see ETTUCE

etty[1] \et-ē\ Betty, Getty, jetty,
Nettie, netty, petit, petty,
sweaty, yeti • brown Betty,
Canetti, cavetti, confetti, libretti,
machete, Rossetti, spaghetti
• amoretti, cappelletti,
cavalletti, Donizetti, Giacometti,
Marinetti, Serengeti, spermaceti,
vaporetti • Irish confetti

etty[2] \it-ē\ see ITTY

etum \ēt-əm\ pinetum
• arboretum, equisetum

etus \ēt-əs\ Cetus, fetus, Thetis,
treatise • acetous, Admetus,
boletus, coitus, Miletus,
quietus, Servetus • diabetes,
Epictetus

etzsche \ē-chē\ see EACHY

euben \ü-bən\ Cuban, Reuben,
Steuben

euce \üs\ see USE[1]

euced \ü-səd\ see UCID

eucey \ü-sē\ see UICY

euch \ük\ see UKE

euchre \ü-kər\ see UCRE

eucid \ü-səd\ see UCID

eud[1] \üd\ see UDE

eud[2] \öid\ see OID[1]

eudal \üd-əl\ see OODLE

eudist \üd-əst\ see UDIST[1]

eudo \üd-ō\ see UDO

eue \ü\ see EW[1]

euer \ü-ər\ see EWER[1]

euil \āl\ see AIL

euille \ē\ see EE[1]

euk \ük\ see UKE

eukin \ü-kən\ see UCAN

eul[1] \əl\ see ULL[1]

eul[2] \ərl\ see IRL[1]

eulah \ü-lə\ see ULA

eulean \ü-lē-ən\ see ULEAN

eum[1] \ē-əm\ geum • lyceum,
museum, no-see-um, odeum,

per diem, Te Deum
• athenaeum, coliseum, colosseum, hypogeum, mausoleum, wax museum

eum² \ā-əm\ see AHUM

eum³ \üm\ see OOM¹

euma \ü-mə\ see UMA

eume \üm\ see OOM¹

eumon \ü-mən\ see UMAN

eumy \ü-mē\ see OOMY

eunice \ü-nəs\ see EWNESS

eunt \únt\ see UNT¹

eunuch \ü-nik\ see UNIC

eur¹ \ər\ birr, blur, burr, Burr, chirr, churr, cur, curr, err, fir, for, fur, her, knur, murre, myrrh, per, purr, shirr, sir, skirr, slur, spur, stir, thir, 'twere, were, whir, your, you're • as per, astir, auteur, aver, bestir, Big Sur, Bonheur, chasseur, chauffeur, claqueur, coiffeur, concur, confer, Crèvecoeur, danseur, defer, demur, deter, douceur, du jour, farceur, flaneur, frondeur, hauteur, him/her, his/her, incur, infer, inter, jongleur, larkspur, liqueur, longspur, masseur, millefleur, occur, Pasteur, poseur, prefer, recur, refer, sandbur, sandspur, seigneur, transfer, voyeur, white fir • accoucheur, amateur, balsam fir, cocklebur, colporteur, connoisseur, cri de coeur, cross-refer, curvature, de rigueur, disinter, Douglas fir, force majeure, franc-tireur, Fraser fir, monseigneur,

nonconcur, pasticheur, prosateur, raconteur, rapporteur, regisseur, saboteur, secateur, underfur, voyageur
• arbitrageur, carillonneur, entrepreneur, litterateur, provocateur, restaurateur
• conglomerateur • agent provocateur

eur² \ur\ see URE¹

eure \ər\ see EUR¹

eurial \ur-ē-əl\ see URIAL¹

eurish \ər-ish\ see OURISH

eurs \ərz\ see ERS¹

eury \ur-ē\ see URY¹

eus¹ \ē-əs\ Aeneas, Aggeus, Alcaeus, Alpheus, Arius, Chryseis, Linnaeus, Micheas, Piraeus, uraeus • coryphaeus, epigeous, scarabaeus • Judas Maccabaeus

eus² \üs\ see USE¹

euse¹ \əz\ buzz, 'cause, coz, does, fuzz, 'twas, was • abuzz, because, outdoes, undoes
• overdoes

euse² \üs\ see USE¹

euse³ \üz\ see USE²

eusel¹ \ü-səl\ see USAL¹

eusel² \ü-zəl\ see USAL²

eut \üt\ see UTE

euter \üt-ər\ see UTER

euth \üth\ see OOTH²

eutian \ü-shən\ see UTION

eutic \üt-ik\ see UTIC

eutical \üt-i-kəl\ see UTICAL

eutics \üt-iks\ toreutics
• hermeneutics, therapeutics

eutist \üt-əst\ see UTIST

euton \üt-ᵊn\ see UTAN

eutonist \üt-ᵊn-əst\ see UTENIST

euve \əv\ see OVE¹

euver \ü-vər\ see OVER³

eux \ü\ see EW¹

ev¹ \ef\ see EF¹

ev² \ȯf\ see OFF²

eva \ē-və\ see IVA²

eval \ē-vəl\ see IEVAL

evalent \ev-ə-lənt\ see EVOLENT

evan¹ \ē-vən\ see EVEN

evan² \ev-ən\ see EAVEN

eve¹ \ev\ breve, rev, Sèvres
• Kiev, Negev • alla breve

eve² \ēv\ see EAVE¹

evel \ev-əl\ bevel, devil, level,
Neville, revel • A level,
baselevel, bedevil, bi-level,
daredevil, dishevel, dust devil,
go-devil, high-level, low-level,
O level, S level, sea level, split-
level • entry-level, on the level,
water level

eveler \ev-lər\ leveler, reveler

evelly \ev-ə-lē\ heavily, levelly,
reveille

evement \ēv-mənt\ achievement,
aggrievement, bereavement
• underachievement

even \ē-vən\ even, Stephen
• break even, Genevan, get
even, uneven

eventh \ev-ənth\ seventh
• eleventh

ever¹ \ev-ər\ clever, ever, lever,
never, sever, Trevor • dissever,
endeavor, forever, however,
soever, whatever, whenever,
wherever, whichever, whoever,
whomever • cantilever,
howsoever, live-forever,
whatsoever, whencesoever,
whensoever, wheresoever,
whichsoever, whomsoever,
whosesoever, whosoever

ever² \ē-vər\ see IEVER

everage \ev-rij\ beverage,
leverage

everence \ev-rəns\ reverence,
severance • disseverance,
irreverence

every \ev-rē\ every, reverie

eves \ēvz\ see EAVES

eviate \ē-vē-ət\ deviate, qiviut

evice \ev-əs\ clevis, crevice
• Ben Nevis

evil \ē-vəl\ see IEVAL

eville \ev-əl\ see EVEL

evilry \ev-əl-rē\ devilry, revelry
• daredevilry

evin \ev-ən\ see EAVEN

evious \ē-vē-əs\ devious,
previous

evis¹ \ev-əs\ see EVICE

evis² \ē-vəs\ see EVUS

evity \ev-ət-ē\ brevity, levity
• longevity

evo \ē-vō\ in vivo, relievo • ring-a-lievo • alto-relievo, basso-relievo, mezzo-relievo, recitativo • Antananarivo

evocable \ev-ə-kə-bəl\ evocable, revocable • irrevocable

evolence \ev-ə-ləns\ prevalence • benevolence, malevolence

evolent \ev-ə-lənt\ prevalent • benevolent, malevolent

evor \ev-ər\ see EVER¹

evous \ē-vəs\ grievous, Nevis, nevus • longevous • redivivus, Saint Kitts-Nevis

evsk \efsk\ see EFSK

evus \ē-vəs\ see EVOUS

evy \ev-ē\ bevy, heavy, levee, levy • replevy, top-heavy

ew¹ \ü\ blue, boo, brew, chew, clew, clue, coo, coup, crew, cue, dew, do, doux, Drew, due, ewe, few, flew, flu, flue, fou, glue, gnu, goo, hew, hue, Hugh, Jew, knew, Koo, lieu, loo, Lou, mew, moo, moue, mu, new, nu, ooh, pew, phew, piu, pooh, q, queue, roux, rue, screw, shoe, shoo, shrew, Sioux, skew, slew, slough, slue, smew, sou, sous, spew, sprue, stew, strew, sue, Sue, thew, threw, through, to, too, true, two, u, view, whew, who, woo, Wu, xu, yew, you, zoo • accrue, achoo, adieu, ado, Agnew, aircrew, airscrew, anew, Anjou, askew, au jus, babu, Baku, bamboo, battu, battue, bayou, bedew, beshrew, bestrew, bijou, boo-boo, boubou, brand-new, breakthrough, burgoo, cachou, can-do, canoe, caoutchouc, Carew, Cebu, Chonju, construe, Corfu, corkscrew, coypu, CQ, cuckoo, curfew, debut, Depew, doo-doo, ecu, endue, ensue, eschew, floor-through, fondue, fordo, foreknew, Gansu, Gentoo, Gifu, goo-goo, ground crew, gumshoe, guru, hairdo, hereto, Hindu, home brew, Honshu, horseshoe, how-to, HQ, Hutu, igloo, imbrue, imbue, IQ, jackscrew, K2, Kansu, karoo, Karoo, kazoo, Khufu, kung fu, Kwangju, leadscrew, lean-to, long view, make-do, Matthew, me-too, mildew, milieu, miscue, misdo, misknew, muumuu, Nehru, non-U, old-shoe, one-two, on view, outdo, outgrew, perdu, Peru, poilu, prau, preview, pursue, purview, ragout, redo, renew, Renfrew, review, revue, rough-hew, run-through, sandshoe, Sardou, see-through, set-to, setscrew, shampoo, Shih Tzu, sinew, skiddoo, snafu, snowshoe, soft-shoe, span-new, subdue, surtout, taboo, Taegu, tattoo, thank-you, thereto, thumb-screw, to-do, too-too, tree shrew, undo, undue, unglue, unscrew, untrue, vatu, vendue, venue, vertu, virtu, voodoo, wahoo, walk-through, where-through, whereto, who's who, withdrew, worldview, yahoo, yoo-hoo • aperçu, avenue, babassu, baby blue, ballyhoo, barbecue, barley-broo, billet-doux, bird's-eye view, black-and-blue, Brunswick stew, buckaroo, bugaboo, callaloo, caribou, catechu, clerihew, cobalt blue, cockapoo, cockatoo, Cotonou, counterview, curlicue, déjà vu, derring-do, detinue, feverfew, follow-through, gardyloo, hitherto, honeydew, Iguaçu, ingenue, interview, IOU, Irish stew, jabiru, Jiangsu, kangaroo, Kathmandu, kinkajou, loup-garou, Makalu, manitou, marabou, McAdoo, microbrew, midnight blue, Montague, Montesquieu, Mountain View, ormolu, overdo, overdue, overflew, overgrew, overshoe, overstrew, overthrew, overview, parvenu, parvenue, pas de deux, passe-partout, pay-per-view, PDQ, peacock blue, peekaboo, peer review, petting zoo, point of view, Pompidou, Port Salut, rendezvous, residue, retinue, revenue, Richelieu, Roh Tae Woo, Ryukyu, seppuku, Shikoku, sneak preview, succès fou, switcheroo, talking-to, teleview, Telugu, thereunto, thirty-two, thitherto, Timbuktu, tinamou, twenty-two, view halloo, vindaloo, w, wallaroo, waterloo, well-to-do, what have you, whoop-de-do, witches' brew, Xanadu • Aracaju, bolt from the blue, Brian Boru, cardinal virtue, cornflower blue, didgeridoo, downy mildew, easy virtue, hullabaloo, in deep doo-doo, Kalamazoo, merry-andrew, mulligan stew,

Ouagadougou, out of the blue, Papandreou, pirarucu, Port du Salut, tu-whit tu-whoo, Vanuatu, Wandering Jew • Nova Iguaçu

ew² \ō\ see OW¹

ewable¹ \ō-ə-bəl\ see OWABLE¹

ewable² \ü-ə-bəl\ see UABLE

ewage \ü-ij\ brewage, sewage

ewal \ü-əl\ see UEL¹

ewar \ü-ər\ see EWER¹

eward¹ \u̇rd\ see URED¹

eward² \ü-ərd\ Seward, steward • shop steward

ewd \üd\ see UDE

ewdness \üd-nəs\ see UDINOUS

ewe¹ \ō\ see OW¹

ewe² \ü\ see EW¹

ewed \üd\ see UDE

ewee \ē-wē\ see EEWEE

ewel \ü-əl\ see UEL¹

eweled \üld\ see OOLED

ewell \ü-əl\ see UEL¹

ewer¹ \ü-ər\ brewer, chewer, dewar, Dewar, doer, ewer, fewer, hewer, queuer, screwer, sewer, skewer, spewer, suer, viewer, wooer, you're • horseshoer, me-tooer, misdoer, previewer, renewer, reviewer, shampooer, snowshoer, undoer, wrongdoer • barbecuer, evildoer, interviewer, microbrewer, revenuer, televiewer—*also* -er *forms of adjectives listed at* EW¹

ewer² \ùr\ see URE¹

ewer³ \ō-ər\ see OER⁴

ewerage \ùr-ij\ see OORAGE¹

ewery \ùr-ē\ see URY¹

ewey \ü-ē\ see EWY

ewie \ü-ē\ see EWY

ewing¹ \ō-iŋ\ see OING¹

ewing² \ü-iŋ\ see OING²

ewis \ü-əs\ see OUIS²

ewish \ü-ish\ bluish, Hewish, Jewish, newish, shrewish • aguish

ewl \ül\ see OOL¹

ewless \ü-ləs\ clueless, crewless, dewless, shoeless, viewless

ewly \ü-lē\ see ULY

ewman \ü-mən\ see UMAN

ewment \ü-mənt\ strewment • accruement

ewn \ün\ see OON¹

ewness \ü-nəs\ blueness, dueness, Eunice, fewness, newness, skewness, Tunis • askewness

ewpie \ü-pē\ see OOPY

ewry \ùr-ē\ see URY¹

ews \üz\ see USE²

ewsman \üz-mən\ bluesman, newsman

ewsy \ü-zē\ see OOZY

ewt \üt\ see UTE

ewter \üt-ər\ see UTER

ewterer \üt-ər-ər\ see UITERER

ewton \üt-ᵉn\ see UTAN

ewy \ü-ē\ bluey, buoy, chewy, Dewey, dewy, flooey, gluey, gooey, hooey, Louie, Louis, newie, phooey, rouille, screwy, sloughy, viewy • andouille, bell buoy, chop suey, life buoy, mildewy, Port Louis • breeches buoy, ratatouille

ex \eks\ dex, ex, flex, hex, lex, rex, Rex, sex, specs, vex, x • annex, apex, codex, complex, convex, cortex, culex, desex, duplex, DX, fourplex, funplex, ibex, ilex, index, Kleenex, latex, mirex, murex, MX, narthex, perplex, Perspex, phone sex, pollex, Pyrex, reflex, Rx, safe sex, scolex, silex, silvex, simplex, spandex, telex, Tex-Mex, triplex, unsex, vertex, vortex • analects, belowdecks, biconvex, circumflex, Cornish rex, cross-index, Devon rex, gentle sex, googolplex, haruspex, intersex, Malcolm X, megaplex, Middlesex, multiplex, oral sex, PBX, pontifex, price index, retroflex, spinifex, subindex, thumb index, unisex • compound-complex, facial index, herpes simplex, videotex • body mass index, cerebral cortex, Electra complex, misery index, Oedipus complex—*also* -s; -'s, *and* -s' *forms of nouns and* -s *forms of verbs listed at* ECK

exas \ek-səs\ see EXUS

exed \ekst\ see EXT

exedly \ek-səd-lē\ vexedly
• perplexedly

exer \ek-sər\ flexor, hexer
• duplexer, indexer
• multiplexer

exia \ek-sē-ə\ alexia, cachexia,
dyslexia, pyrexia • anorexia

exic \ek-sik\ dyslexic, pyrexic
• anorexic

exical \ek-si-kəl\ lexical
• indexical, nonlexical

exion \ek-shən\ see ECTION

exis \ek-səs\ see EXUS

exity \ek-sət-ē\ complexity,
convexity, perplexity

exor \ek-sər\ see EXER

ext \ekst\ next, sexed, sext, text,
vexed • context, deflexed,
inflexed, perplexed, plaintext,
pretext, reflexed, subtext,
urtext, ciphertext • hypertext,
oversexed, teletext,
undersexed—*also* -ed *forms of
verbs listed at* EX

extant \ek-stənt\ extant, sextant

exterous \ek-strəs\ dexterous
• ambidextrous

extrous \ek-strəs\ see EXTEROUS

exual \eksh-wəl\ sexual
• asexual, bisexual, effectual,
pansexual, transsexual
• ambisexual, homosexual,
hypersexual, intersexual,
parasexual, psychosexual,
unisexual • heterosexual

exural \ek-shrəl\ see ECTURAL[2]

exus \ek-səs\ lexis, nexus,
plexus, texas, Texas • Alexis,
amplexus • solar plexus

exy \ek-sē\ prexy, sexy
• apoplexy, cataplexy

ey[1] \ā\ see AY[1]

ey[2] \ē\ see EE[1]

ey[3] \ī\ see Y[1]

eya[1] \ā-ə\ see AIA[1]

eya[2] \ē-ə\ see IA[1]

eyance \ā-əns\ abeyance,
conveyance, purveyance,
surveillance • reconveyance

eyant \ā-ənt\ mayn't • abeyant,
surveillant

eyas \ī-əs\ see IAS

ey'd \ād\ see ADE[1]

eye \ī\ see Y[1]

eyed[1] \ēd\ see EED

eyed[2] \īd\ see IDE[1]

eyedness \īd-nəs\ eyedness,
snideness, wideness
• cockeyedness

eyeless \ī-ləs\ see ILUS

eyelet \ī-lət\ see ILOT

eyen \īn\ see INE[1]

eyer[1] \ā-ər\ see AYER[1]

eyer[2] \īr\ see IRE[1]

eyes \īz\ see IZE

eying \ā-iŋ\ see AYING

ey'll[1] \āl\ see AIL

ey'll[2] \el\ see EL[1]

eyn \in\ see IN[1]

eynes \ānz\ see AINS

eyness \ā-nəs\ see AYNESS

eyor \ā-ər\ see AYER[1]

eyre \er\ see ARE[4]

ey're \er\ see ARE[4]

eyrie \ir-ē\ see IRY[1]

eys \ēz\ see EZE

eyser \ī-zər\ see IZER

eyte \ā-tē\ see ATY

ey've \āv\ see AVE[2]

ez[1] \ez\ see AYS[1]

ez[2] \ā\ see AY[1]

ez[3] \ās\ see ACE[1]

eza \ē-zə\ Giza, Lisa, Pisa, visa • Ibiza, mestiza • lespedeza

eze \ēz\ breeze, cheese, ease, feeze, freeze, frieze, he's, jeez, lees, please, res, seize, she's, sleaze, sneeze, squeeze, tease, tweeze, wheeze • Andes, appease, Aries, at ease, bee's knees, Belize, Bernese, betise, big cheese, blue cheese, brain freeze, Burmese, camise, Castries, cerise, chemise, Chinese, deep-freeze, degrease, Denise, disease, displease, disseise, d.t.'s, Elise, en prise, fasces, fauces, Ganges, headcheese, heartsease, Hermes, jack cheese, Kirghiz, Louise, Maltese, marquise, menses, nates, Pisces, quick-freeze, Ramses, reprise, sea breeze, soubise, striptease, strong breeze, Swiss cheese, Tabriz, Thales, trapeze, unease, unfreeze, Xerxes • Ambonese, Androcles, Annamese, antifreeze, Assamese, Balinese, Bengalese, Bhutanese, Bolognese, Brooklynese, Cantonese, Cervantes, Ceylonese, cheddar cheese, Chersonese, Congolese, cottage cheese, Cyclades. Damocles, diocese, Eloise, Erinyes, expertise, Faeroese, federalese, fifth disease, Genovese, gourmandise, Hebrides, Heracles, Hercules, Hunanese, Hyades, ill at ease, in a breeze, Japanese, Javanese, Johnsonese, journalese, Kanarese, Lake Louise, legalese, litotes, manganese, Milanese, Nepalese, Nipponese, overseas, Pekingese, Pericles, Pleiades, Portuguese, Pyrenees, shoot the breeze, Siamese, Sienese, Silures, Sinhalese, Socrates, Sophocles, Sporades, to one's knees • Abdülaziz, Albigenses, antipodes, Aragonese, archdiocese, Averroës, Barcelonese, bona fides, bureaucratese, cheval-de-frise, computerese, Diogenes, Dodecanese, Dutch elm disease, Egas Moniz, eminence grise, Eumenides, Euripides, Florida Keys, Gaucher's disease, governmentese, Great Pyrenees, Hesperides, Hippocrates, Hippomenes, Hodgkin's disease, Indo-Chinese, kissing disease, mad cow disease, Marie-Louise, nephritides, officialese, pentagonese, Philoctetes, Sammarinese, social disease, suicide squeeze, superficies, telegraphese, Themistocles, Thucydides, Vietnamese • Alcibiades, Aristophanes, educationese, ferromanganese, foot-and-mouth disease, Legionnaires' disease, Lou Gehrig's disease, Mephistopheles, Parkinson's disease, sociologese, sword of Damocles • Pillars of Hercules—*also* -s, -'s, *and* -s' *forms of nouns and* -s *forms of verbs listed at* EE[1]

ezel \ē-zəl\ see EASEL

ezi \ē-zē\ see EASY[1]

ezium \ē-zē-əm\ cesium • magnesium, trapezium

ezzle \ez-əl\ bezel • embezzle

i

i¹ \ē\ see EE¹

i² \ī\ see Y¹

i³ \ā\ see AY¹

ia¹ \ē-ə\ Gaea, kea, Leah, Mia, rhea, Rhea, rya, via • Achaea, Apia, Bahia, buddleia, cabrilla, cattleya, Chaldea, Crimea, Euboea, Hygeia, idea, Judaea, kaffiyeh, Korea, mantilla, Maria, Medea, mens rea, Morea, Nicaea, ohia, Omiya, Oriya, ouguiya, rupiah, sangria, Sofia, Sophia, spirea, tortilla • Barranquilla, barathea, bougainvillea, camarilla, Caesarea, cascarilla, Cytherea, diarrhea, dulcinea, Eritrea, fantasia, Galatea, gonorrhea, granadilla, hamartia, Hialeah, Idumaea, Ikaria, Ituraea, Jicarilla, Kampuchea, latakia, Latakia, logorrhea, Manzanilla, mausolea, mythopoeia, Nabatea, Nicosia, panacea, Parousia, pizzeria, pyorrhea, ratafia, sabadilla, Santeria, sapodilla, seborrhea, seguidilla, sinfonia, Tanzania, trattoria • amenorrhea, Andalusia, Arimathea, Ave Maria, Cassiopeia, echeveria, Ismailia, Laodicea, peripeteia, pharmacopoeia, prosopopoeia,

Sacagawea • Diego Garcia • onomatopoeia

ia² \ī-ə\ see IAH¹

ia³ \ä\ see A¹

iable¹ \ī-ə-bəl\ dryable, dyeable, flyable, friable, liable, pliable, triable, viable • deniable, inviable, reliable • certifiable, classifiable, falsifiable, justifiable, liquefiable, notifiable, pacifiable, qualifiable, quantifiable, rectifiable, satisfiable, specifiable, undeniable, unifiable, verifiable • emulsifiable, identifiable, unfalsifiable

iable² \ē-ə-bəl\ see EEABLE

iacal \ī-ə-kəl\ dandiacal, heliacal, maniacal, theriacal, zodiacal • ammoniacal, elegiacal, simoniacal • dipsomaniacal, egomaniacal, hypochondriacal, monomaniacal, nymphomaniacal, pyromaniacal, paradisiacal • bibliomaniacal, megalomaniacal

iad \ī-əd\ see YAD

iah¹ \ī-ə\ ayah, maya, Maya, playa, Praia, stria, via • Aglaia, Mariah, messiah, papaya, pariah, Thalia • Hezekiah, jambalaya, Jeremiah, Nehemiah, Obadiah, Surabaya, Zechariah,

219

Zephaniah • Atchafalaya, Iphigenia, peripeteia

iah² \ē-ə\ see IA¹

ial¹ \ī-əl\ dial, diel, pial • redial

ial² \īl\ see ILE¹

ialer \ī-lər\ see ILAR

ially \ē-ə-lē\ see EALLY¹

iam \ī-əm\ Priam • per diem • carpe diem

ian¹ \ē-ən\ see EAN¹

ian² \ī-ən\ see ION¹

iance \ī-əns\ science • affiance, alliance, appliance, compliance, defiance, nonscience, reliance • mesalliance, misalliance, noncompliance, self-reliance

iant \ī-ənt\ Bryant, client, giant, pliant, riant • affiant, compliant, defiant, reliant • incompliant, self-reliant, sleeping giant, supergiant

iao \aú\ see OW²

iaour \aúr\ see OWER²

iaper \ī-pər\ see IPER

iar \īr\ see IRE¹

iary¹ \ī-ə-rē\ briary, diary, fiery, friary, priory

iary² \īr-ē\ see IRY¹

ias¹ \ī-əs\ Aias, bias, dais, eyas, Laius, Lias, pious, Pius • Abdias, Elias, Messias, Tobias • Ananias, Jeremias, Malachias, Nehemias, on the bias, Roncesvalles, Sophonias, Zacharias • Mount Saint Elias

ias² \ē-əs\ see EUS¹

ias³ \äsh\ see ASH¹

iasis \ī-ə-səs\ diesis, diocese • archdiocese, lithiasis, psoriasis, trichiasis • acariasis, amebiasis, ascariasis, bilharziasis, candidiasis, helminthiasis, leishmaniasis, satyriasis • elephantiasis, hypochondriasis, schistosomiasis

iat¹ \ē-ət\ see EIT¹

iat² \ī-ət\ see IET

iate \ī-ət\ see IET

iath¹ \ī-əth\ Wyeth • Goliath

iath² \ē-ə\ see IA¹

iatry \ī-ə-trē\ podiatry, psychiatry

iaus \aús\ see OUSE²

ib¹ \ib\ bib, bibb, crib, drib, fib, gib, glib, Hib, jib, lib, nib, rib, sib, squib • ad-lib, corncrib, false rib, midrib, sahib, true rib • floating rib, flying rib, memsahib • cut of one's jib

ib² \ēb\ see EBE²

ib³ \ēv\ see EAVE¹

iba \ē-bə\ see EBA

ibable \ī-bə-bəl\ bribable • ascribable, describable • indescribable

ibal \ī-bəl\ bible, Bible, libel, scribal, tribal • Bishops' Bible, family Bible

ibb \ib\ see IB¹

ibband \ib-ən\ see IBBON

ibbed \ibd\ bibbed • rock-ribbed
—*also* -ed *forms of verbs listed at* IB¹

ibber \ib-ər\ bibber, cribber, dibber, fibber, gibber, glibber, jibber, ribber

ibbet \ib-ət\ gibbet • exhibit, inhibit, prohibit • flibbertigibbet

ibbing \ib-iŋ\ cribbing, ribbing
—*also* -ing *forms of verbs listed at* IB¹

ibble \ib-əl\ dibble, dribble, fribble, gribble, kibble, nibble, quibble, scribble, sibyl, Sibyl • double dribble

ibbler \ib-lər\ dribbler, nibbler, quibbler, scribbler

ibbly \ib-lē\ dribbly, glibly

ibbon \ib-ən\ gibbon, Gibbon, ribbon • blue ribbon, inhibin, red ribbon

ibby \ib-ē\ Libby, ribby

ibe¹ \īb\ bribe, gibe, gybe, jibe, kibe, scribe, tribe, vibe • ascribe, conscribe, describe, imbibe, inscribe, prescribe, proscribe, subscribe, transcribe • circumscribe, diatribe, redescribe, superscribe • oversubscribe

ibe² \ē-bē\ *see* EBE¹

ibel \ī-bəl\ *see* IBAL

iber \ī-bər\ briber, fiber, giber, Khyber, scriber, Tiber • describer, inscriber, prescriber, proscriber, subscriber, transcriber

ibi \ē-bē\ *see* EBE¹

ibia \i-bē-ə\ Libya, tibia • Namibia

ibin \ib-ən\ *see* IBBON

ibit \ib-ət\ *see* IBBET

ibitive \ib-ət-iv\ exhibitive, inhibitive, prohibitive

ibitor \ib-ət-ər\ exhibitor, inhibitor

ible \ī-bəl\ *see* IBAL

iblet \ib-lət\ driblet, giblet, riblet

ibli \ib-lē\ *see* IBBLY

ibly \ib-lē\ *see* IBBLY

ibo \ē-bō\ Ibo, Kibo • gazebo, placebo • Arecibo, Essequibo

iboly \i-ə-lē\ *see* YBELE

ibs \ibz\ dibs, nibs • short ribs, spareribs—*also* -s, -'s, *and* -s' *forms of nouns and* -s *forms of verbs listed at* IB¹

ibular \ib-yə-lər\ fibular • mandibular, vestibular • infundibular

ibute¹ \ib-yət\ tribute • attribute, contribute, distribute • redistribute

ibute² \ib-ət\ *see* IBBET

ibutive \ib-yət-iv\ attributive, contributive, distributive, retributive • redistributive

ibutor \ib-ət-ər\ *see* IBITOR

ibyl \ib-əl\ *see* IBBLE

ic¹ \ik\ *see* ICK

ic² \ēk\ *see* EAK¹

ica¹ \ī-kə\ mica, Micah, pica, pika, plica, spica, Spica • Formica, lorica • balalaika

ica² \ē-kə\ see IKA¹

icable \ik-ə-bəl\ despicable, explicable, extricable
• inexplicable, inextricable

icah \ī-kə\ see ICA¹

ical \ik-əl\ see ICKLE

icament \ik-ə-mənt\ medicament, predicament

ican \ē-kən\ see EACON

icar \ik-ər\ see ICKER¹

icative \ik-ət-iv\ fricative, siccative • affricative, applicative, explicative, indicative, vindicative
• multiplicative

iccative \ik-ət-iv\ see ICATIVE

iccio \ē-chō\ capriccio, pasticcio

ice¹ \īs\ Bryce, dice, gneiss, ice, lice, lyse, mice, nice, pice, price, rice, slice, spice, splice, syce, thrice, trice, twice, vice, vise • advice, allspice, black ice, Brandeis, bride-price, brown rice, concise, cut ice, cut-price, deice, device, dry ice, entice, excise, fried rice, list price, make nice, no dice, off-price, on ice, pack ice, precise, shelf ice, strike price, suffice, white rice, wild rice • asking price, beggars-lice, break the ice, cockatrice, comma splice, dirty rice, edelweiss, hammer price, imprecise, market price, merchandise, on thin ice, overprice, paradise, point-device, reserve price, roll the dice, sacrifice, Spanish rice, sticker price, underprice, upset price, water ice, wellhead price
• basmati rice, glutinous rice, imparadise, self-sacrifice

ice² \ē-chā\ see ICHE¹

ice³ \ēs\ see IECE

ice⁴ \ī-sē\ see ICY

ice⁵ \īz\ see IZE

ice⁶ \ēt-zə\ see ITZA¹

iceless \ī-sləs\ iceless, priceless, spiceless

icely \īs-lē\ see ISTLY

iceous \ish-əs\ see ICIOUS¹

icer \ī-sər\ dicer, Dreiser, pricer, ricer, slicer, splicer • deicer, sufficer • sacrificer • self-sacrificer

ices \ī-sēz\ Pisces • Anchises • Polynices • Coma Berenices

icety \ī-stē\ see EISTY

icey \ī-sē\ see ICY

ich¹ \ich\ see ITCH

ich² \ik\ see ICK

ichael \ī-kəl\ see YCLE¹

iche¹ \ē-chā\ seviche • Beatrice, cantatrice

iche² \ēsh\ fiche, leash, niche, quiche, sheesh • baksheesh, corniche, hashish, maxixe, pastiche, postiche, schottische, unleash • microfiche, nouveau riche

iche³ \ish\ see ISH¹

iche⁴ \ich\ see ITCH

iche⁵ \ē-chē\ see EACHY

ichen¹ \ī-kən\ lichen, liken, Steichen

ichen² \ich-ən\ see ITCHEN

ichener \ich-nər\ see ITCHENER

icher \ich-ər\ see ITCHER

iches \ich-əz\ see ITCHES

ichi¹ \ē-chē\ see EACHY

ichi² \ē-shē\ see ISHI

ichment \ich-mənt\ see ITCHMENT

ichore \ik-rē\ see ICKERY

ichu \ish-ü\ see ISSUE¹

icia¹ \ish-ə\ see ITIA

icia² \ēsh-ə\ see ESIA¹

icial \ish-əl\ altricial, comitial, initial, judicial, official, simplicial, solstitial, surficial • artificial, beneficial, cicatricial, interstitial, prejudicial, sacrificial, superficial, unofficial

ician \ē-shən\ see ETION¹

iciency \ish-ən-sē\ deficiency, efficiency, proficiency, sufficiency • inefficiency, insufficiency, self-sufficiency

icient \ish-ənt\ deficient, efficient, omniscient, proficient, sufficient • coefficient, cost-efficient, inefficient, insufficient, self-sufficient

icinable \is-nə-bəl\ see ISTENABLE

icinal \is-ᵊn-əl\ vicinal • medicinal, officinal, vaticinal

icing¹ \ī-siŋ\ icing, splicing • gene-splicing • self-sacrificing, self-sufficing—*also* -ing *forms of verbs listed at* ICE¹

icing² \ī-ziŋ\ see IZING

icious¹ \ish-əs\ vicious • ambitious, auspicious, capricious, delicious, factitious, fictitious, flagitious, judicious, lubricious, malicious, Mauritius, nutritious, officious, pernicious, propitious, pumiceous, seditious, sericeous, suspicious • adscititious, adventitious, avaricious, cementitious, expeditious, inauspicious, injudicious, meretricious, prejudicious, Red Delicious, repetitious, subreptitious, superstitious, supposititious, surreptitious • excrementitious, supposititious

icious² \ē-shəs\ see ECIOUS

icipal \is-ə-bəl\ see ISSIBLE

icipant \is-ə-pənt\ anticipant, participant

icit \is-ət\ licit • complicit, elicit, explicit, illicit, implicit, solicit • inexplicit

icitor¹ \is-ət-ər\ elicitor, solicitor

icitor² \is-tər\ see ISTER

icitous \is-ət-əs\ complicitous, duplicitous, felicitous, solicitous • infelicitous

icity¹ \is-ət-ē\ basicity, causticity, centricity, chronicity, clonicity, complicity, conicity, cyclicity, duplicity, ethnicity, facticity, felicity, lubricity, mendicity, plasticity, publicity, rhythmicity, seismicity, simplicity, spasticity, sphericity, tonicity, toxicity, triplicity • authenticity, catholicity, domesticity, eccentricity, elasticity, electricity, historicity, infelicity, multiplicity, specificity, synchronicity • egocentricity, ethnocentricity, inauthenticity, inelasticity, periodicity

icity² \is-tē\ christie, Christie, misty, twisty, wristy • Corpus Christi, sacahuiste

ick \ik\ brick, chick, click, crick, creek, Dick, flick, Frick, hick, kick, KWIC, lick, mick, nick, Nick, pic, pick, prick, quick, rick, Schick, shtick, sic, sick, slick, snick, stick, strick, thick, tic, tick, trick, wick • airsick, big stick, bluetick, bootlick, boychick, brainsick, broomstick, carsick, Chadwick, chick flick, chopstick, cowlick, crabstick, dabchick, deadstick, deer tick, detick, dik-dik, dipstick, dog tick, drop-kick, drumstick, ear pick, firebrick, fish stick, flagstick, Fosdick, free kick, frog kick, goal kick, goldbrick, greensick, handpick, hat trick, hayrick, heartsick, homesick, ice pick, joss stick, joystick, lipstick, lovesick, matchstick, muzhik, nightstick, nitpick, nonstick, nutpick, odd trick, oil slick, Old Nick, outslick, peacenik, pigstick, pinprick, placekick, Prestwick, quick kick, redbrick, Renwick, rubric, salt lick, seasick, selfstick, shashlik, sidekick, slapstick, slipstick, squib kick, Tajik, toothpick, topkick, unpick, unstick, uptick, wood tick, yardstick • bailiwick, biopic, Bolshevik, bone to pick,

call in sick, candlestick, candlewick, cattle tick, cherry-pick, corner kick, Dominic, do the trick, double-quick, EBCDIC, fiddlestick, fingerpick, flutter kick, hemistich, heretic, lunatic, Menshevik, meterstick, needlestick, onside kick, overtrick, pogo stick, point-and-click, politic, politick, polyptych, Reykjavik, rhythm stick, scissors kick, shooting stick, singlestick, swagger stick, swizzle stick, taperstick, turn the trick, undertrick, walking stick, Watson-Crick • arithmetic, carrot-and-stick, composing stick, computernik, impolitic, kinnikinnick, penalty kick • body politic

icka \ē-kə\ see IKA¹

icked¹ \ik-əd\ picked, wicked

icked² \ikt\ see ICT¹

ickel \ik-əl\ see ICKLE

icken \ik-ən\ chicken, quicken, sicken, stricken, thicken • awestricken, spring chicken • panic-stricken, planet-stricken, prairie chicken, rubber-chicken • poverty-stricken

ickens \ik-ənz\ dickens, Dickens, pickings • hen and chickens —also -s, -'s, and -s' forms of nouns and -s forms of verbs listed at ICKEN

icker¹ \ik-ər\ bicker, clicker, dicker, flicker, icker, kicker, liquor, nicker, picker, pricker, sicker, slicker, snicker, sticker, ticker, tricker, vicar, whicker, wicker • billsticker, bootlicker, brain-picker, deticker, drop-kicker, flea-flicker, nitpicker, pigsticker, placekicker, pot likker, pot sticker, ragpicker • bumper sticker, cherry picker, city slicker, dominicker, politicker—*also* -er *forms of adjectives listed at* ICK

icker² \ek-ər\ *see* ECKER

ickery \ik-rē\ chicory, flickery, hickory, snickery, trickery • Terpsichore

icket \ik-ət\ cricket, picket, Pickett, pricket, spigot, stickit, thicket, ticket, wicket • Big Thicket, big-ticket, high-ticket, hot ticket, house cricket, meal ticket, mole cricket, split ticket • season ticket, sticky wicket • write one's own ticket

ickett \ik-ət\ *see* ICKET

ickety \ik-ət-ē\ rickety, thickety • pernickety, persnickety

ickey \ik-ē\ *see* ICKY

icki \ik-ē\ *see* ICKY

ickie \ik-ē\ *see* ICKY

icking \ik-iŋ\ ticking, wicking • brain-picking, flat-picking, high-sticking, nit-picking, rollicking • cotton-picking, fingerpicking—*also* -ing *forms of verbs listed at* ICK

ickings \ik-ənz\ *see* ICKENS

ickish \ik-ish\ hickish, sickish, thickish, trickish

ickit \ik-ət\ *see* ICKET

ickle \ik-əl\ brickle, chicle, fickle, mickle, nickel, pickle, prickle, sickle, stickle, tical, tickle, trickle • bicycle, dill pickle, icicle, obstacle, Popsicle, tricycle • pumpernickel • hammer and sickle

ickler \ik-lər\ stickler, tickler • bicycler, particular

ickly \ik-lē\ fickly, prickly, quickly, sickly, slickly, thickly • brainsickly • impoliticly

ickness \ik-nəs\ lychnis, quickness, sickness, slickness, thickness • airsickness, car sickness, heartsickness, homesickness, lovesickness, milk sickness, seasickness • morning sickness, motion sickness, mountain sickness, sleeping sickness

icksy \ik-sē\ *see* IXIE

icky \ik-ē\ dickey, hickey, icky, kicky, Mickey, picky, quickie, rickey, shticky, sickie, sticky, tricky, Vicky • doohickey, slapsticky

icle \ik-əl\ *see* ICKLE

icly¹ \ik-lē\ *see* ICKLY

icly² \ē-klē\ *see* EEKLY

ico \ē-kō\ *see* ICOT

icory \ik-rē\ *see* ICKERY

icot \ē-kō\ fico, pekoe, picot, RICO, tricot, Vico • Tampico • Puerto Rico

ics \iks\ *see* IX¹

ict¹ \ikt\ picked, Pict, strict, ticked • addict, afflict, conflict, constrict, convict, delict, depict, district, edict, evict, inflict, lipsticked, predict, restrict, unlicked, verdict • benedict, Benedict, contradict, derelict, interdict, Lake District, maledict, retrodict, Scotch verdict • eggs Benedict —*also* -ed *forms of verbs listed at* ICK

ict² \īt\ *see* ITE¹

ictable \īt-ə-bəl\ *see* ITABLE¹

ictal \ik-təl\ fictile, rictal • edictal

icted \ik-təd\ conflicted, restricted—*also* -ed *forms of verbs listed at* ICT

icter \ik-tər\ *see* ICTOR

ictic \ik-tik\ panmictic • apodictic

ictile \ik-təl\ *see* ICTAL

ictim \ik-təm\ *see* ICTUM

iction \ik-shən\ diction, fiction, friction, stiction • addiction, affliction, confliction, constriction, conviction, depiction, eviction, indiction, infliction, nonfiction, prediction, reliction, restriction, transfixion • benediction, contradiction, crucifixion, dereliction, interdiction, jurisdiction, malediction, metafiction, science fiction, valediction • self-contradiction

ictional \ik-shnəl\ dictional, fictional, frictional • nonfictional • jurisdictional, metafictional, science-fictional

ictionist \ik-shnəst\ fictionist • restrictionist • metafictionist

ictive \ik-tiv\ fictive • addictive, afflictive, conflictive, constrictive, inflictive, predictive, restrictive, vindictive • interdictive, nonrestrictive

ictment \īt-mənt\ *see* ITEMENT

ictor \ik-tər\ lictor, victor • constrictor, depicter, evictor, inflicter • contradictor • boa constrictor, vasoconstrictor

ictory \ik-tə-rē\ victory • benedictory, contradictory, interdictory, maledictory, valedictory

ictual \it-əl\ *see* ITTLE

ictualler \it-əl-ər\ *see* ITALER

ictum \ik-təm\ dictum, victim • obiter dictum

icture \ik-chər\ picture, stricture • big picture • motion picture

ictus \ik-təs\ ictus, rictus • Benedictus

icula \ik-yə-lə\ auricula, corbicula

iculant \ik-yə-lənt\ gesticulant, matriculant

icular¹ \ik-yə-lər\ spicular • acicular, articular, auricular, canicular, clavicular, curricular, cuticular, fascicular, follicular, funicular, lenticular, navicular, orbicular, ossicular, particular, radicular, reticular, testicular, vehicular, ventricular, vermicular, versicular, vesicular • appendicular, in particular, perpendicular • extracurricular, extravehicular

icular² \ik-lər\ *see* ICKLER

iculate \ik-yə-lət\ apiculate, articulate, auriculate, denticulate, geniculate, particulate, reticulate, vermiculate
• inarticulate

iculous \ik-yə-ləs\ meticulous, pediculous, ridiculous

iculum \ik-yə-ləm\ curriculum, Janiculum, reticulum
• diverticulum

icuous \ik-yə-wəs\ conspicuous, perspicuous, transpicuous
• inconspicuous

icy \ī-sē\ dicey, icy, pricey, spicy

id¹ \id\ bid, chid, Cid, did, fid, gid, grid, hid, id, kid, Kidd, lid, mid, quid, rid, skid, slid, squid, SQUID, whid • amid, backslid, bifid, El Cid, equid, eyelid, forbid, grandkid, Madrid, nonskid, outdid, resid, schoolkid, trifid, undid • arachnid, camelid, giant squid, katydid, ootid, overbid, overdid, pyramid, underbid • tertium quid, Valladolid

id² \ēd\ see EED

I'd \īd\ see IDE¹

ida¹ \ēd-ə\ see EDA¹

ida² \ī-də\ Haida, Ida • Oneida

idable¹ \īd-ə-bəl\ guidable, rideable • decidable, dividable
• subdividable

idable² \id-ə-bəl\ see IDDABLE

idal \īd-ᵊl\ bridal, bridle, idle, idol, idyll, seidel, sidle, tidal
• cotidal, unbridle • Barmecidal, biocidal, ecocidal, fratricidal,

fungicidal, genocidal, germicidal, herbicidal, homicidal, intertidal, larvicidal, lunitidal, matricidal, ovicidal, parricidal, patricidal, pesticidal, regicidal, septicidal, spermicidal, suicidal, viricidal, virucidal

idance \īd-ᵊns\ guidance, stridence • abidance, misguidance

idas \īd-əs\ Cnidus, Midas, nidus

iday \īd-ē\ Friday, Heidi, tidy, vide • alcaide, girl Friday, Good Friday, man Friday, untidy
• bona fide, mala fide

idays \īd-ēz\ see IDES¹

idd \id\ see ID¹

iddable \id-ə-bəl\ biddable
• formidable

iddance \id-ᵊns\ riddance
• forbiddance

idden \id-ᵊn\ bidden, chidden, hidden, midden, ridden, stridden, swidden • bedridden, bestridden, forbidden, outbidden, unbidden • kitchen midden, overridden

idder \id-ər\ bidder, gridder, kidder, siddur, skidder
• consider, forbidder
• reconsider, underbidder

iddie \id-ē\ see IDDY

iddish \id-ish\ kiddish, Yiddish

iddity \id-ət-ē\ see IDITY

iddle \id-ᵊl\ Biddle, diddle, fiddle, griddle, middle, piddle, riddle, twiddle • bass fiddle, bull fiddle, unriddle • paradiddle, second fiddle, taradiddle • play second fiddle

iddler \id-lər\ diddler, fiddler, middler, riddler, tiddler • bull fiddler

iddling \id-liŋ\ fiddling, middling, piddling, riddling

iddly \id-lē\ diddly, piddly, ridley, Ridley, tiddly

iddock \id-ik\ see IDIC

iddur \id-ər\ see IDDER

iddy \id-ē\ biddy, giddy, kiddie, middy, midi, MIDI, skiddy, widdy

ide¹ \īd\ bide, bride, chide, Clyde, eyed, fried, glide, guide, hide, I'd, pied, plied, pride, ride, side, slide, snide, stride, thighed, tide, tried, wide • abide, allied, applied, aside, astride, backside, backslide, bankside, beachside, bedside, beside, bestride, betide, bleareyed, blindside, blow-dried, blue-eyed, broadside, bromide, bug-eyed, Burnside, cleareyed, cockeyed, cold-eyed, collide, confide, courtside, cowhide, cross-eyed, curbside, dayside, decide, deride, divide, dockside, doe-eyed, downside, downslide, dry-eyed, ebb tide, elide, field guide, fireside, flip side, flood tide, fluoride, foreside, four-eyed, free ride, freeze-dried, Girl Guide, glasseyed, graveside, green-eyed, hagride, hang glide, hard-eyed, hawkeyed, hayride, high tide, hillside, horsehide, inside, in stride, ironside, joyride, kingside, lakeside, landslide, low tide, lynx-eyed, misguide, moon-eyed, neap tide, nearside, nightside, noontide, offside, onside, outride, outside, pie-eyed, poolside, pop-eyed, preside, prompt side, provide, quayside, queenside, rawhide, red tide, reside, ringside, riptide, roadside, seaside, self-pride, sharp-eyed, shipside, shoreside, Shrovetide, sloe-eyed, snowslide, springtide, squinteyed, stateside, statewide, storewide, Strathclyde, streamside, strong side, subside, tailslide, tongue-tied, topside, trackside, trailside, untried, upside, vat-dyed, walleyed, war bride, waveguide, wayside, wide-eyed, wild-eyed, worldwide, yuletide • Akenside, algicide, alkoxide, almond-eyed, alongside, Argus-eyed, Barmecide, blearyeyed, bona fide, chicken-fried, Christmastide, citified, citywide, classified, coincide, corporatewide, countrified, countryside, countrywide, cut-and-dried, cyanide, deicide, demand-side, dewy-eyed, dignified, dioxide, double-wide, eagle-eyed, Eastertide, ecocide, eventide, far and wide, feticide, formamide, fratricide, freedom ride, fungicide, genocide, germicide, gimlet-eyed, glassyeyed, goggle-eyed, googlyeyed, gospel side, great divide, harborside, herbicide, homicide, honeyguide, humified, matricide, Merseyside, misty-eyed, miticide, monoxide, mountain-side, nationwide, Naugahyde, Oceanside, on the side, open-eyed, override, overstride, parricide, Passiontide, patricide, pesticide, planetwide, qualified, rarefied, raticide, regicide, riverside, Riverside, set-aside, side by side, silverside, sissified, slickenside, spermi-cide, starry-eyed, subdivide, suicide, supply-side, trisulfide, underside, verbicide, vermicide, viricide, waterside, Whitsuntide, wintertide • by the wayside, dissatisfied, fit to be tied, formaldehyde, infanticide, initial side, insecticide, interallied, Jekyll and Hyde, preoccupied, rodenticide, self-satisfied, terminal side, thalidomide, Trinitytide, tyrannicide, uxoricide • carbon dioxide, carbon monoxide, overqualified *—also -ed forms of verbs listed at* Y[1]

ide[2] \ēd\ *see* EED

idean \id-ē-ən\ *see* IDIAN

ided \īd-əd\ sided • divided, lopsided, misguided, one-sided, slab-sided, two-sided • many-sided, sobersided *—also -ed forms of verbs listed at* IDE[1]

ideless \īd-les\ idlesse, tideless

iden \īd-ᵊn\ guidon, Haydn, Leiden, Sidon, widen • Poseidon

idence \īd-ᵊns\ *see* IDANCE

ideness \īd-nes\ *see* EYEDNESS

ident \īd-ᵊnt\ strident, trident

ideon \id-ē-ən\ *see* IDIAN

ideous \id-ē-əs\ *see* IDIOUS

ider[1] \īd-ər\ bider, cider, eider, glider, guider, hider, rider, slider, spider, strider, stridor • abider, backslider, collider, confider, decider, derider, divider, free rider, hang glider, hard cider, insider, joyrider, lowrider, misguider, night rider, outrider, outsider, presider, provider, resider, rough rider, sea spider, Top-Sider, wolf spider • circuit rider, freedom rider, paraglider, subdivider, supply-sider, water-strider • supercollider *—also -er forms of adjectives listed at* IDE[1]

ider[2] \id-ər\ *see* IDDER

ides[1] \īd-ēz\ Fridays • Aristides *—also -s, -'s, and -s' forms of nouns and -s forms of verbs listed at* IDAY

ides[2] \īdz\ ides • besides, burnsides • silversides, sobersides *—also -s, -'s, and -s' forms of nouns and -s forms of verbs listed at* IDE[1]

idge \ij\ bridge, fidge, fridge, midge, ridge • abridge, Banbridge, Blue Ridge, browridge, drawbridge, footbridge, gall midge, Lethbridge, Oak Ridge, Oxbridge, Stourbridge, teethridge, truss bridge • Adam's Bridge, auction bridge, biting midge, Brecken-ridge, contract bridge, covered bridge, flying bridge, Mug-

geridge, rubber bridge • mid-
ocean ridge, suspension bridge

idged \ijd\ ridged • unabridged
—also -ed *forms of verbs listed
at* IDGE

idgen \ij-ən\ see YGIAN

idget \ij-ət\ Brigitte, digit, fidget,
midget, widget • double-digit

idgin \ij-ən\ see YGIAN

idi \id-ē\ see IDDY

idia \i-dē-ə\ Lydia • basidia,
chlamydia, clostridia, coccidia,
conidia, glochidia, nephridia,
Numidia, oidia, peridia, Pisidia,
presidia, pycnidia, pygidia
• antheridia, enchiridia,
hesperidia, miricidia, ommatidia

idian \id-ē-ən\ Gideon, Lydian,
Midian • ascidian, Chalcidian,
Dravidian, euclidean, Floridian,
meridian, obsidian, ophidian,
Ovidian, Pisidian, quotidian,
viridian • enchiridion, non-
euclidean, prime meridian

idic \id-ik\ piddock • acidic,
bromidic, Davidic, druidic,
fatidic, fluidic, Hasidic, iridic,
lipidic, nuclidic

idical \id-i-kəl\ druidical, fatidical,
juridical, veridical • pyramidical

idice \id-ə-sē\ Chalcidice,
Eurydice

idiem \id-ē-əm\ idiom • iridium,
perideum, presidium, rubidium
• post meridiem • ante
meridiem

iding \īd-iŋ\ riding, Riding,
siding, tiding • abiding,

confiding, deciding, East
Riding, hang gliding, joyriding,
West Riding • law-abiding,
nondividing, paragliding—*also*
-ing *forms of verbs listed at* IDE[1]

idiom \id-ē-əm\ see IDIEM

idious \id-ē-əs\ hideous
• fastidious, insidious,
invidious, perfidious

idity \id-ət-ē\ quiddity • acidity,
aridity, avidity, cupidity,
flaccidity, floridity, fluidity,
frigidity, gelidity, gravity,
humidity, hybridity, limpidity,
liquidity, lividity, lucidity,
morbidity, placidity, rabidity,
rancidity, rapidity, rigidity,
sapidity, solidity, stupidity,
tepidity, timidity, torridity,
turbidity, turgidity, validity,
vapidity, viridity, viscidity
• illiquidity, insipidity,
intrepidity, invalidity

idium \id-ē-əm\ see IDIEM

idle \īd-əl\ see IDAL

idlesse \īd-ləs\ see IDELESS

idley \id-lē\ see IDDLY

idney \id-nē\ kidney, Sidney,
Sydney

ido[1] \īd-ō\ dido, Dido, fido
• Hokkaido

ido[2] \ēd-ō\ see EDO[1]

idol \īd-əl\ see IDAL

ids[1] \idz\ Beskids, rapids
• Grand Rapids—*also* -s, -'s,
and -s' *forms of nouns and* -s
forms of verbs listed at ID[1]

ids[2] \ēdz\ see EEDS

---

idst \idst\ didst, midst • amidst

idual¹ \ij-wəl\ residual • individual

idual² \ij-əl\ see IGIL

idulent \ij-ə-lənt\ see IGILANT

idulous \ij-ə-ləs\ stridulous • acidulous

idus \īd-əs\ see IDAS

iduum \ij-ə-wəm\ triduum • residuum

idy \īd-ē\ see IDAY

idyll \īd-ᵊl\ see IDAL

ie¹ \ā\ see AY¹

ie² \ē\ see EE¹

ie³ \ī\ see Y¹

iece \ēs\ cease, crease, fleece, grease, Greece, kris, lease, Nice, niece, peace, piece • apiece, at peace, Bernice, Burmese, camise, caprice, cassis, cerise, chemise, Chinese, Clarice, Cochise, codpiece, coulisse, crosspiece, decease, decrease, degrease, Denise, Dumfries, earpiece, Elise, eyepiece, Felice, field-piece, Ghanese, grandniece, hairpiece, headpiece, heel-piece, increase, lend-lease, Maltese, Matisse, Maurice, mouthpiece, nosepiece, obese, one-piece, pastis, pelisse, police, re-lease, release, seapiece, set piece, shank-piece, showpiece, sidepiece, stringpiece, sublease, surcease, tailpiece, Therese, think piece, timepiece, toepiece, three-piece, two-piece, valise, wool grease, workpiece • afterpiece, altarpiece, Amboinese, Annamese, Assamese, Balinese, Bengalese, Beninese, Bhutanese, Bolognese, Brooklynese, Cantonese, centerpiece, Ceylonese, Chersonese, chimneypiece, Congolese, Cremonese, diocese, directrice, ex libris, expertise, Faeroese, fowling piece, frontispiece, Gabonese, Genovese, Golden Fleece, Guyanese, hold one's peace, Japanese, Javanese, John-sonese, journalese, kiss of peace, Lebanese, legalese, manganese, mantelpiece, masterpiece, Nepalese, Nipponese, of a piece, Pekingese, piece by piece, Portuguese, predecease, Siamese, Sikkimese, Sinhalese, timed-release, Timorese, Tirolese, verdigris, Viennese • Aragonese, archdiocese, Barcelonese, bureaucratese, companion piece, computerese, crème de cassis, Dodecanese, Indo-Chinese, museum piece, officialese, Peloponnese, Pentagonese, period piece, secret police, sustained-release, telegraphese, Vietnamese • conversation piece, educationese, justice of the peace

iecer \ē-sər\ see EASER¹

ied¹ \ēd\ see EED

ied² \ēt\ see EAT¹

ied³ \īd\ see IDE¹

ieda \ēd-ə\ see EDA[1]

ief[1] \ēf\ beef, brief, chief, fief, grief, kef, leaf, lief, reef, sheaf, thief • bay leaf, belief, chipped beef, crew chief, debrief, drop leaf, endleaf, enfeoff, fig leaf, fire chief, flyleaf, gold leaf, in brief, in chief, kerchief, loose-leaf, massif, motif, naïf, O'Keeffe, red leaf, relief, sharif, shinleaf, sneak thief, Tallchief • bas-relief, cloverleaf, come to grief, disbelief, handkerchief, high relief, leatherleaf, leitmotiv, misbelief, neckerchief, overleaf, Tenerife, unbelief, waterleaf • aperitif, barrier reef, Calvados Reef, Capitol Reef, comic relief, Vinson Massif, Great Barrier Reef • commander in chief, editor in chief

ief[2] \ēv\ see EAVE[1]

iefly \ē-flē\ briefly, chiefly

ieg[1] \ēg\ see IGUE

ieg[2] \ig\ see IG

iege[1] \ēj\ liege, siege • besiege, prestige

iege[2] \ēzh\ see IGE[1]

ieger \ē-jər\ see EDURE

iek \ēk\ see EAK[1]

iel[1] \əl\ see EAL[2]

iel[2] \ī-əl\ see IAL[1]

iela \el-ə\ see ELLA

ield \ēld\ bield, field, keeled, shield, weald, wheeled, wield, yield • afield, airfield, backfield, Bloomfield, brickfield, brown-field, Burchfield, coalfield, cornfield, downfield, dress shield, Enfield, Fairfield, force field, four-wheeled, Garfield, goldfield, grainfield, greenfield, Hadfield, heat shield, Houns-field, ice field, infield, left field, Mansfield, Masefield, midfield, minefield, oil field, outfield, playfield, right field, Schofield, Sheffield, snowfield, Spring-field, subfield, unsealed, upfield, Wakefield, well-heeled, windshield, Winfield • Bakers-field, battlefield, broken-field, center field, chesterfield, Chesterfield, color-field, depth of field, Huddersfield, killing field, landing field, Mount Mansfield, Merrifield, playing field, play the field, potter's field, reverse field, sustained yield, track-and-field, unaneled, water shield—*also* -ed *forms of verbs listed at* EAL[2]

ielder \ēl-dər\ fielder, shielder, wielder, yielder • infielder, left fielder, midfielder, outfielder, right fielder • center fielder

ields \ēldz\ South Shields • elysian fields—*also* -s, -'s, *and* -s' *forms of nouns and* -s *forms of verbs listed at* IELD

ieler \ē-lər\ see EALER

ieless \ī-ləs\ see ILUS

ieling[1] \ē-lən\ see ELIN

ieling[2] \ē-liŋ\ see EELING

iem[1] \ē-əm\ see EUM[1]

iem[2] \ī-əm\ see IAM

ien \ēn\ see INE[3]

ience \ī-əns\ see IANCE

iend \end\ see END

iendless \en-ləs\ see ENDLESS

iendliness \en-lē-nəs\ see ENDLINESS

iendly \en-lē\ see ENDLY

iene \ēn\ see INE³

iener¹ \ē-nər\ see EANER

iener² \ē-nē\ see INI¹

ienic \en-ik\ see ENIC²

ienics \en-iks\ see ENICS

ienie \ē-nē\ see INI¹

ienist \ē-nəst\ see INIST²

iennes \en\ see EN¹

ient \ī-ənt\ see IANT

ieper \ē-pər\ see EEPER

ier¹ \ir\ see EER²

ier² \ē-ər\ see EER¹

ier³ \īr\ see IRE¹

ierate \ir-ət\ see IRIT

ierce \irs\ Bierce, birse, fierce, pierce, Pierce, tierce
• transpierce

iere¹ \er\ see ARE⁴

iere² \ir\ see EER²

iered \ird\ see EARD¹

ieria \ir-ē-ə\ see ERIA¹

ierial \ir-ē-əl\ see ERIAL

ierian \ir-ē-ən\ see ERIAN¹

ierly \ir-lē\ see EARLY¹

ierre¹ \ir\ see EER²

ierre² \er\ see ARE⁴

iers \irz\ Algiers, Pamirs—*also -s, -'s, and -s'* forms of nouns and *-s* forms of verbs listed at EER²

iersman \irz-mən\ see EERSMAN

iery \ī-ə-rē\ see IARY¹

ies¹ \ēz\ see EZE

ies² \ē\ see EE¹

ies³ \ēs\ see IECE

iesel¹ \ē-zəl\ see EASEL

iesel² \ē-səl\ see ECIL¹

ieseling \ēz-liŋ\ see ESLING

iesian \ē-zhən\ see ESIAN¹

iesis \ī-ə-səs\ see IASIS

iesling \ēz-liŋ\ see ESLING

iest \ēst\ see EAST¹

iester \ē-stər\ see EASTER

iestley \ēst-lē\ see EASTLY

iestly \ēst-lē\ see EASTLY

iet \ī-ət\ Byatt, diet, fiat, Hyatt, quiet, riot, striate, Wyatt
• disquiet, race riot, run riot, unquiet

ietal \ī-ət-ᵊl\ parietal, societal, varietal

ieter \ī-ət-ər\ dieter, quieter, rioter • proprietor

ietor \ī-ət-ər\ see IETER

iety \ī-ət-ē\ piety • anxiety, dubiety, impiety, nimiety, propriety, satiety, sobriety, society, Society, variety
• contrariety, impropriety, inebriety, insobriety, notoriety
• café society, garden variety, honor society, secret society

ietzsche \ē-chē\ see EACHY

ieu \ü\ see EW¹

ieur \ir\ see EER²

iev \ef\ see EF¹

ievable \ē-və-bəl\ see EIVABLE

ieval \ē-vəl\ evil, shrieval, weevil
• boll weevil, coeval, khedival, king's evil, medieval, primeval, reprieval, retrieval, upheaval

ieve¹ \iv\ see IVE²

ieve² \ēv\ see EAVE¹

ieved \ēvd\ see EAVED

ievement \ēv-mənt\ see EVEMENT

iever \ē-vər\ beaver, cleaver, fever, griever, heaver, leaver, reaver, reiver, weaver
• achiever, believer, conceiver, deceiver, enfever, orb weaver, perceiver, receiver, reliever, retriever, school-leaver, transceiver, upheaver
• cantilever, disbeliever, eager beaver, misbeliever, misconceiver, true believer, unbeliever, wide receiver
• golden retriever, overachiever, underachiever

ievish \ē-vish\ see EEVISH

ievo \ē-vō\ see EVO

ievous \ē-vəs\ see EVOUS

ieze \ēz\ see EZE

if¹ \if\ see IFF

if² \ēf\ see IEF¹

ife¹ \īf\ fife, Fife, knife, life, rife, strife, wife • alewife, case knife, clasp knife, drawknife,

farmwife, fishwife, flick-knife, folklife, good life, goodwife, half-life, highlife, housewife, jackknife, loosestrife, lowlife, midlife, midwife, nightlife, oldwife, penknife, pro-life, real-life, shelf life, steak knife, still life, true-life, wakerife, whole-life, wildlife • afterlife, antilife, bowie knife, Duncan Phyfe, fact of life, get a life, nurse-midwife, palette knife, paper knife, paring knife, pocketknife, putty knife, right-to-life, slice-of-life, staff of life, tree of life, Yellowknife • larger-than-life, purple loosestrife • utility knife

ife² \ēf\ see IEF¹

ifeless \ī-fləs\ lifeless, strifeless, wifeless

ifer \ī-fər\ see IPHER

iferous \if-ər-əs\ aquiferous, auriferous, coniferous, floriferous, lactiferous, luciferous, pestiferous, somniferous, splendiferous, vociferous • carboniferous, odoriferous

iff \if\ biff, cliff, diff, glyph, if, iff, jiff, kif, miff, quiff, riff, skiff, sniff, spiff, spliff, stiff, syph, tiff, whiff
• Er Rif, midriff, Plovdiv, triglyph, what-if, Wycliffe
• anaglyph, bindle stiff, hieroglyph, hippogriff, logograph, petroglyph

iffany \if-ə-nē\ see IPHONY

iffe \if\ see IFF

iffed \ift\ see IFT

iffen \if-ən\ see IFFIN

iffey \if-ē\ see IFFY

iffian \if-ē-ən\ Pecksniffian, Wycliffian

iffin \if-ən\ griffin, Griffin, stiffen, tiffin

iffish \if-ish\ sniffish, stiffish

iffle \if-əl\ piffle, riffle, skiffle, sniffle, whiffle, Wiffle

iffler \if-lər\ riffler, sniffler, whiffler

iffness \if-nəs\ stiffness, swiftness

iffy \if-ē\ iffy, cliffy, jiffy, Liffey, sniffy, spiffy

ific \if-ik\ glyphic • calcific, febrific, horrific, magnific, pacific, Pacific, prolific, salvific, specific, terrific, vivific • anaglyphic, beatific, calorific, colorific, felicific, frigorific, hieroglyphic, honorific, scientific, soporific, South Pacific, sudorific, tenebrific • prescientific

ifical \if-i-kəl\ magnifical, pontifical

ificate \if-i-kət\ certificate, pontificate • birth certificate, gift certificate, stock certificate

ificent \if-ə-sənt\ magnificent, munificent, omnificent

ifle \ī-fəl\ rifle, stifle, trifle • air rifle, a trifle • assault rifle, Enfield rifle, M1 rifle, Springfield rifle, squirrel rifle

ifling \ī-fliŋ\ rifling, stifling, trifling

ift \ift\ drift, gift, grift, lift, rift, shift, shrift, sift, squiffed, swift, Swift, thrift • adrift, airlift, blueshift, chairlift, dead lift, downshift, face-lift, festschrift, forklift, frameshift, gearshift, Great Rift, makeshift, redshift, sealift, shape-shift, shoplift, short shrift, ski lift, snowdrift, spendthrift, spindrift, split shift, spoondrift, stick shift, swing shift, unshift, uplift, upshift • chimney swift, graveyard shift, J-bar lift, lobster shift, Vandegrift • consonant shift, functional shift, genetic drift, great vowel shift • continental drift—also -ed forms of verbs listed at IFF

ifter \if-tər\ drifter, grifter, lifter, shifter, sifter, snifter, swifter • sceneshifter, shape-shifter, shoplifter, uplifter, weight lifter

ifth \ith\ see ITH[2]

iftness \if-nəs\ see IFFNESS

ifty \if-tē\ drifty, fifty, nifty, shifty, thrifty, wifty • fifty-fifty, LD$_{50}$

ig \ig\ big, brig, cig, dig, fig, gig, Grieg, grig, jig, pig, prig, rig, sprig, swig, trig, twig, vig, Whig, wig, zig • bagwig, bigwig, bushpig, cat rig, Danzig, earwig, fright wig, Gehrig, hedgepig, Leipzig, lime-twig, pfennig, renege, Schleswig, shindig, square rig, unrig, zaftig • caprifig, guinea pig, hit it big, infra dig, jury-rig, periwig, strangler fig, thimblerig, weeping fig, whirligig, WYSIWYG, Zagazig • fore-and-aft rig, Marconi rig, potbellied pig, thingamajig

iga¹ \ē-gə\ Riga, Vega, viga
• Antigua, omega, quadriga

iga² \ī-gə\ see AIGA

igamous \ig-ə-məs\ bigamous
• polygamous

igamy \ig-ə-mē\ bigamy, digamy
• polygamy

igan² \ig-ən\ see IGGIN

igand \ig-ənd\ brigand, ligand

igas \ī-gəs\ see YGOUS

igate \ig-ət\ see IGOT¹

ige¹ \ēzh\ siege • prestige
• noblesse oblige

ige² \ēj\ see IEGE¹

igel \ij-əl\ see IGIL

igenous \ij-ə-nəs\ see IGINOUS

igeon \ij-ən\ see YGIAN

iger \ī-gər\ Eiger, tiger • blind
tiger, braunschweiger • Bengal
tiger, paper tiger • saber-
toothed tiger, Siberian tiger,
Tasmanian tiger

igerent \ij-rənt\ belligerent,
refrigerant • cobelligerent

iggan \ig-ən\ see IGGIN

iggard \ig-ərd\ niggard,
triggered—*also* -ed *forms of
verbs listed at* IGGER

igged \igd\ twigged, wigged
• bewigged, cat-rigged,
square-rigged • jerry-rigged,
periwigged, schooner-rigged
—*also* -ed *forms of verbs listed
at* IG

igger \ig-ər\ chigger, digger,
jigger, rigger, rigor, snigger,
swigger, trigger, vigor
• ditchdigger, gold digger, hair
trigger, outrigger, rejigger,
reneger, square-rigger • pull
the trigger, thimblerigger

iggered \ig-ərd\ see IGGARD

iggery \ig-ə-rē\ piggery, priggery,
Whiggery

iggie \ig-ē\ see IGGY

iggin \ig-ən\ biggin, piggin,
wigan, Wiggin • balbriggan

iggish \ig-ish\ biggish, piggish,
priggish, Whiggish

iggle \ig-əl\ giggle, higgle, jiggle,
niggle, sniggle, squiggle,
wiggle, wriggle

iggler \ig-lər\ giggler, higgler,
niggler, wiggler, wriggler

iggy \ig-ē\ biggie, piggy, twiggy

igh \ī\ see Y¹

ighed \īd\ see IDE¹

ighland \ī-lənd\ highland,
Highland, island, Thailand
• Long Island, North Island,
Rhode Island, Wake Island
• Baffin Island, Christmas
Island, Coney Island, Devil's
Island, Easter Island, Ellesmere
Island, Ellis Island, floating
island, Parris Island, Pitcairn
Island, Saint John Island,
Staten Island • Aquidneck
Island, Cape Breton Island,
Sanibel Island, Prince Edward
Island, Vancouver Island

ighlander \ī-lən-dər\ highlander,
islander

ighlands \ī-lənz\ Highlands • Sea Islands • Aran Islands, Cayman Islands, Channel Islands, Falkland Islands, Gilbert Islands, Leeward Islands, Marshall Islands, Phoenix Islands, Thousand Islands, Virgin Islands, Windward Islands • Aegean Islands, Aleutian Islands, Canary Islands, Hawaiian Islands, Philippine Islands

ighly \ī-lē\ see YLY

ighness \ī-nəs\ see INUS[1]

ight \īt\ see ITE[1]

ightable \īt-ə-bəl\ see ITABLE[1]

ighted \īt-əd\ blighted, sighted, whited • attrited, benighted, clear-sighted, farsighted, foresighted, long-sighted, nearsighted, sharp-sighted, shortsighted, skylighted, united • self-excited, unrequited—*also* -ed *forms of verbs listed at* ITE[1]

ighten \īt-ᵊn\ brighten, Brighton, chitin, chiton, frighten, heighten, lighten, tighten, titan, Titan, triton, Triton, whiten • enlighten

ightener \īt-nər\ brightener, lightener, tightener, whitener

ightening \īt-niŋ\ see IGHTNING

ighter \īt-ər\ see ITER[1]

ightful \īt-fəl\ frightful, rightful, spiteful, sprightful • delightful, despiteful, foresightful, insightful

ightie \īt-ē\ see ITE[2]

ightily \īt-ᵊl-ē\ flightily, mightily

ightiness \īt-ē-nəs\ flightiness, mightiness • almightiness

ighting \īt-iŋ\ see ITING

ightless \īt-ləs\ flightless, lightless, nightless, sightless

ightly \īt-lē\ brightly, knightly, lightly, nightly, rightly, sightly, slightly, sprightly, tightly, tritely, whitely • contritely, down-rightly, finitely, forthrightly, fortnightly, midnightly, out-rightly, politely, unsightly, uprightly • eruditely, impolitely, reconditely

ightment \īt-mənt\ see ITEMENT

ightning \īt-niŋ\ lightning, tightening • ball lightning, belt-tightening, heat lightning, sheet lightning, white lightning—*also* -ing *forms of verbs listed at* IGHTEN

ightn't \īt-ᵊnt\ see ITANT

ighton \īt-ən\ see IGHTEN

ights \īts\ lights, nights, tights • by rights, footlights, houselights, last rites, states' rights, weeknights • bill of rights, bragging rights, civil rights, dead to rights, Dolomites, Golan Heights, human rights, northern lights, Shaker Heights, southern lights • animal rights—*also* -s, -'s, *and* -s' *forms of nouns and* -s *forms of verbs listed at* ITE[1]

ightsome \īt-səm\ lightsome • delightsome

ighty \īt-ē\ see ITE[2]

igian \ij-ən\ see YGIAN

igid \ij-əd\ Brigid, frigid, rigid

igil \ij-əl\ Rigel, sigil, strigil, vigil
• residual

igilant \ij-ə-lənt\ vigilant
• acidulent

igine \ij-ə-nē\ polygyny
• aborigine

iginous \ij-ə-nəs\ caliginous,
fuliginous, indigenous,
polygynous, serpiginous,
terrigenous, vertiginous

igion \ij-ən\ see YGIAN

igious \ij-əs\ litigious,
prestigious, prodigious,
religious • irreligious

igit \ij-ət\ see IDGET

igitte \ij-ət\ see IDGET

iglet \ig-lət\ piglet, wiglet

igm[1] \im\ see IM[1]

igm[2] \īm\ see IME[1]

igma \ig-mə\ sigma, stigma
• enigma, kerygma

igment \ig-mənt\ figment,
pigment

ign \īn\ see INE[1]

ignable \ī-nə-bəl\ see INABLE

ignancy \ig-nən-sē\ benignancy,
malignancy

ignant \ig-nənt\ benignant,
indignant, malignant

igned \īnd\ see IND[1]

igneous \ig-nē-əs\ igneous,
ligneous

igner \ī-nər\ see INER[1]

igness \ig-nəs\ bigness, Cygnus

ignet \ig-nət\ see YGNET

igning \ī-niŋ\ see INING

ignity \ig-nət-ē\ dignity
• benignity, indignity, malignity

ignly \īn-lē\ see INELY[1]

ignment \īn-mənt\ alignment,
assignment, confinement,
consignment, enshrinement,
refinement • nonalignment, on
consignment, realignment

ignon \in-yən\ see INION

ignor \ē-nyər\ see ENIOR

igo[1] \ī-gō\ Sligo • prurigo
• impetigo, vitiligo

igo[2] \ē-gō\ see EGO

igoe \ē-gō\ see EGO

igor \ig-ər\ see IGGER

igorous \ig-rəs\ rigorous,
vigorous

igot[1] \ig-ət\ bigot, frigate, gigot,
spigot

igot[2] \ik-ət\ see ICKET

igour \ig-ər\ see IGGER

igrapher \ig-rə-fər\ calligrapher,
epigrapher, polygrapher,
serigrapher

igraphist \ig-rə-fəst\
calligraphist, epigraphist,
polygraphist

igraphy \ig-rə-fē\ calligraphy,
epigraphy, serigraphy,
stratigraphy • pseudepigraphy

igua \ē-gə\ see IGA[1]

igue \ēg\ gigue, Grieg, league • big-league, blitzkrieg, bush-league, colleague, fatigue, garigue, intrigue, squeteague • Ivy League, Little League, major-league, minor-league, wampumpeag • battle fatigue, combat fatigue

iguer \ē-gər\ see EAGER

iguous \ig-yə-wəs\ ambiguous, contiguous, exiguous • unambiguous

igured \ig-ərd\ see IGGARD

ii \ī\ see Y[1]

iing \ē-iŋ\ see EEING

ija \ē-jə\ see EGIA

ijah \ī-jə\ Elijah • steatopygia

iji \ē-jē\ Fiji, squeegee

ijl \īl\ see ILE[1]

ijn \īn\ see INE[1]

ijssel \ī-səl\ see ISAL

ik¹ \ik\ see ICK

ik² \ēk\ see EAK[1]

ika¹ \ē-kə\ pika, sika, theca • areca, eureka, paprika, Topeka • Costa Rica, Dominica, Frederica, oiticica, ootheca, Tanganyika • bibliotheca

ika² \ī-kə\ see ICA[1]

ike¹ \ī-kē\ crikey, Nike, Psyche, spiky

ike² \īk\ bike, caique, dike, fyke, haik, hike, like, mike, Mike, pike, psych, shrike, sike, spike, strike, trike, tyke • alike, apelike, armlike, barnlike, bearlike, belike, birdlike, bladelike, boatlike, boxlike, called strike, catlike, childlike, Christlike, clawlike, claylike, clocklike, dirgelike, dirt bike, dislike, doglike, dreamlike, feel like, first strike, fishlike, flu-like, fly-strike, garpike, godlike, grasslike, handspike, hitchhike, homelike, horselike, hymnlike, jazzlike, Klondike, lifelike, mislike, moonlike, nunlike, parklike, pealike, prooflike, push-bike, rampike, ratlike, rent strike, restrike, ringlike, rocklike, rootlike, ropelike, scalelike, sharklike, sheaflike, shrimplike, shunpike, snakelike, sphinxlike, springlike, suchlike, tanklike, ten-strike, Thorndike, trail bike, trancelike, turnpike, unlike, Updike, Vandyke, Van Dyck, vicelike, warlike, wave-like, whalelike, wifelike, wing-like, wraithlike • adultlike, and the like, berrylike, businesslike, cartoonlike, craftsmanlike, desertlike, down the pike, fatherlike, fingerlike, humanlike, hunger strike, ladylike, leather-like, lemminglike, lionlike, look-alike, machinelike, marlinespike, marlinspike, minibike, mirrorlike, motorbike, mountain bike, northern pike, nothing like, open mike, ostrichlike, phantomlike, powderlike, puppetlike, rubberlike, saucerlike, Scafell Pike, seamanlike, soundalike, spiderlike, sportsmanlike, statesmanlike, take a hike, thunderstrike, womanlike, workmanlike, zombielike • animallike, anything like, exercise bike, sympathy strike, unsportsmanlike

iked¹ \īkt\ piked, spiked
• vandyked—*also* -ed *forms of verbs listed at* IKE²

iked² \ī-kəd\ see YCAD

iken \ī-kən\ see ICHEN¹

iker \ī-kər\ biker, diker, duiker, hiker, piker, spiker, striker
• disliker, hitchhiker, shunpiker
• dolphin striker, hunger striker, minibiker, mountain biker

ikes \īks\ yikes—*also* -s, -'s, *and* -s' *forms of nouns and* -s *forms of verbs listed at* IKE²

ikey \ī-kē\ see IKE¹

ikh \ēk\ see EAK¹

iki¹ \ik-ē\ see ICKY

iki² \ē-kē\ see EAKY

iking \ī-kiŋ\ liking, striking, Viking
• shunpiking—*also* -ing *forms of verbs listed at* IKE²

ikker \ik-ər\ see ICKER¹

iky \ī-kē\ see IKE¹

il¹ \il\ see ILL

il² \ēl\ see EAL²

ila¹ \il-ə\ see ILLA²

ila² \ē-lə\ see ELA¹

ilae \ī-lē\ see YLY

ilage \ī-lij\ mileage, silage

ilah \ī-lə\ see ILA³

ilament \il-ə-mənt\ filament
• habiliment

ilar \ī-lər\ dialer, filar, filer, hilar, miler, Schuyler, smiler, stylar,

styler, tiler, Tyler • beguiler, bifilar, compiler, defiler, freestyler, profiler, rottweiler, stockpiler

ilary \il-ə-rē\ see ILLARY

ilate \ī-lət\ see ILOT

ilbe \il-be\ see ILBY

ilbert \il-bərt\ filbert, gilbert, Gilbert, Hilbert

ilby \il-bē\ bilby, Kilby, trilby
• astilbe

ilch¹ \ilk\ see ILK

ilch² \ilch\ filch, milch, zilch

ild¹ \īld\ child, Child, Childe, mild, piled, wild, Wilde
• brainchild, Fairchild, godchild, grandchild, hog-wild, love child, man-child, pantiled, Rothschild, schoolchild, self-styled, stepchild, with child • deuces wild, flower child, latchkey child, poster child, self-exiled
—*also* -ed *forms of verbs listed at* ILE¹

ild² \il\ see ILL

ild³ \ilt\ see ILT

ild⁴ \īld\ see ILLED

ilda \il-də\ Hilda, tilde, Wilda

ilde¹ \il-də\ see ILDA

ilde² \īld\ see ILD¹

ilder¹ \il-dər\ builder, gilder, guilder • bewilder, boatbuilder, Mound Builder, shipbuilder, upbuilder • bodybuilder, jerry-builder

ilder² \īl-dər\ Wilder—*also* -er *forms of adjectives listed at* ILD

ilding \il-diŋ\ building, gilding, hilding • abuilding, boatbuilding, outbuilding, shipbuilding • bodybuilding —also -ing forms of verbs listed at ILLED

ildish \īl-dish\ childish, wildish

ildly \īld-lē\ childly, mildly, wildly

ile¹ \īl\ aisle, bile, Crile, dial, faille, file, guile, I'll, isle, Kyle, lisle, Lyle, mile, Nile, phial, pile, Pyle, rile, roil, Ryle, smile, spile, stile, style, tile, trial, vial, vile, viol, while, wile • abseil, aedile, agile, air mile, anile, argyle, Argyll, audile, awhile, axile, bass viol, beguile, black bile, Blue Nile, Carlisle, Carlyle, compile, condyle, cross-file, de Stijl, decile, defile, denial, docile, ductile, enisle, ensile, erewhile, erstwhile, espial, exile, Fair Isle, febrile, fictile, field trial, fissile, flexile, fragile, freestyle, futile, genial, gentile, gracile, grisaille, habile, hairstyle, high style, hostile, Kabyle, labile, lifestyle, meanwhile, mistrial, mobile, motile, nail file, New Style, nubile, old style, Old Style, on file, pantile, penile, pensile, pretrial, profile, puerile, quartile, quintile, redial, reptile, resile, retrial, revile, rocaille, sandpile, scissile, sectile, senile, servile, sessile, show trial, stabile, stockpile, sundial, tactile, tensile, textile, time trial, turnstile, typestyle, unpile, utile, vagile, virile, woodpile, worthwhile • afebrile, airmobile, Anglophile, chamomile, cinephile, contractile, country mile, crocodile, cyclostyle, discophile, domicile, endostyle, epistyle, erectile, extensile, family style, Francophile, Gallophile, halophile, homophile, hypostyle, in denial, infantile, insectile, interfile, juvenile, low-profile, mercantile, oenophile, otherwhile, pedophile, percentile, peristyle, prehensile, projectile, protractile, pulsatile, rat-tail file, rank and file, reconcile, refractile, retractile, self-denial, single file, Slavophile, spermophile, statute mile, technophile, thermopile, turophile, urostyle, versatile, vibratile, xenophile • ailurophile, amphiprostyle, archaic smile, audiophile, bibliophile, circular file, Devils Postpile, electrophile, fluviatile, Germanophile, heterophile, Indian file, in the woodpile, Italophile, nucleophile, once in a while, vertical file, videophile • cafeteria-style, International Style

ile² \il\ see ILL

ile³ \ē-lē\ see EELY

ile⁴ \əl\ see EAL²

ile⁵ \il-ē\ see ILLY¹

ilead \il-ē-əd\ see ILIAD

ileage \ī-lij\ see ILAGE

ileal \il-ē-əl\ see ILIAL¹

ileless \īl-ləs\ guileless, pileless, smileless

iler¹ \ē-lər\ see EALER

iler² \ī-lər\ see ILAR

iles \īlz\ Giles, Miles, Niles
• Wade-Giles • British Isles,
Western Isles

ileum \il-ē-əm\ see ILIUM

iley \ī-lē\ see YLY

ilford \il-fərd\ Milford, Wilford

ili¹ \il-ē\ see ILLY¹

ili² \ē-lē\ see EELY

ilia¹ \il-ē-ə\ Celia, cilia • Cecilia,
Massilia • Anglophilia,
basophilia, biophilia,
coprophilia, Francophilia,
hemophilia, juvenilia,
necrophilia, neophilia,
paraphilia, pedophilia,
sensibilia, technophilia
• memorabilia

ilia² \il-yə\ Brasília, sedilia
• bougainvillea, sensibilia
• memorabilia

ilia³ \ēl-yə\ see ELIA

iliad \il-ē-əd\ chiliad, Gilead, Iliad
• balm of Gilead

ilial \il-ē-əl\ filial, ileal • familial,
unfilial

ilian¹ \il-ē-ən\ Gillian, Ilian, Lillian
• Basilian, caecilian, reptilian,
Virgilian • Abbevillian,
crocodilian, preexilian,
vespertilian

ilian² \il-yən\ see ILLION

ilias \il-ē-əs\ see ILIOUS¹

iliate \il-ē-ət\ ciliate • affiliate

ilic \il-ik\ killick • acrylic, allylic,
Cyrillic, dactylic, exilic, idyllic,
sibylic • amphiphilic, Anglo-

philic, cryophilic, hemophilic,
hydrophilic, necrophilic,
pedophilic, postexilic,
thermophilic, zoophilic
• bibliophilic

ilica \il-i-kə\ silica • basilica

ilience \il-yəns\ see ILLIANCE

iliency \il-yən-sē\ see ILLIANCY

ilient \il-yənt\ brilliant • resilient

iliment \il-ə-mənt\ see ILAMENT

iling¹ \ī-liŋ\ filing, piling, spiling,
styling, tiling • hairstyling

iling² \ē-liŋ\ see EELING

ilion¹ \il-yən\ see ILLION

ilion² \il-ē-ən\ see ILIAN¹

ilious¹ \il-ē-əs\ punctilious
• supercilious • materfamilias,
paterfamilias

ilious² \il-yəs\ bilious
• atrabilious, supercilious

ilitant \il-ə-tənt\ militant
• rehabilitant

ility \il-ət-ē\ ability, agility, anility,
civility, debility, docility,
ductility, facility, fertility,
fragility, futility, gentility,
gracility, hostility, humility,
lability, mobility, motility,
nobility, nubility, scurrility,
sectility, senility, servility,
stability, sterility, suability,
tactility, tranquility, utility,
vagility, virility • actability,
affability, arability, audibility,
bankability, bearability,
biddability, breathability,
brushability, capability,
changeability, clubbability,

coilability, contractility,
countability, credibility,
crossability, culpability,
curability, cutability, disability,
disutility, drapability, drillability,
drinkability, drivability, durability,
dyeability, edibility, equability,
erectility, fallibility, feasibility,
fishability, flammability,
flexibility, forgeability, form-
ability, frangibility, friability,
fungibility, fusibility, gullibility,
hatchability, ignobility,
imbecility, immobility, inability,
incivility, indocility, infantility,
infertility, instability, inutility,
juvenility, laudability, leach-
ability, legibility, liability,
likability, livability, lovability,
mailability, meltability, miscibility,
movability, mutability, notability,
packability, placability,
plausibility, playability, pliability,
portability, possibility, potability,
pregnability, prehensility,
printability, probability, puerility,
quotability, readability,
rentability, risibility, roadability,
salability, sensibility, sewability,
shareability, sociability,
solubility, solvability, spread-
ability, squeezability, stainability,
stretchability, suitability,
tenability, testability, trace-
ability, trainability, treatability,
tunability, usability, vendibility,
versatility, viability, visibility,
volatility, washability, wear-
ability, wettability, workability
• acceptability, accessibility,
accountability, adaptability,
adjustability, advisability,
affordability, agreeability,
applicability, attainability,

availability, believability,
compatibility, deniability,
dependability, desirability,
electability, eligibility, excitability,
expendability, illegibility,
immutability, implausibility,
impossibility, improbability,
incapability, infallibility,
inflexibility, invisibility,
manageability, marketability,
measurability, navigability,
permissibility, practicability,
predictability, profitability,
public utility, reliability,
respectability, responsibility,
reusability, reversability,
separability, strict liability,
survivability, susceptibility,
sustainability, upward mobility,
variability, vulnerability

ilium \il-ē-əm\ cilium, ileum,
ilium, Ilium, milium, psyllium,
trillium • beryllium • painted
trillium, penicillium

ilk \ilk\ bilk, ilk, milch, milk, silk
• corn silk, ice milk, skim milk,
tie silk, top milk • buttermilk,
condensed milk, liebfraumilch,
malted milk • cry over spilled
milk

ilker \il-kər\ bilker, milker

ilky \il-kē\ milky, silky

ill \il\ bill, Bill, brill, chill, dill, drill,
fill, frill, gill, grill, grille, hill, ill,
Jill, kill, krill, mil, mill, mille, nil,
nill, Phil, pill, prill, quill, rill, shill,
shrill, sild, sill, skill, spill, squill,
still, swill, thill, thrill, til, till, trill,
twill, vill, will, Will • anthill, at
will, backfill, ball mill, bluegill,
Brazil, breast drill, Catskill,

Churchill, cranesbill, crossbill, de Mille, dentil, de-skill, distill, doorsill, downhill, duckbill, dullsville, dunghill, fire drill, foothill, freewill, free will, fulfill, gin mill, goodwill, Granville, gristmill, handbill, hawksbill, hornbill, Huntsville, ill will, instill, Knoxville, lambkill, landfill, limekiln, manille, McGill, Melville, mixed grill, molehill, mudsill, Nashville, no-till, pep pill, per mill, playbill, pot still, pug mill, quadrille, red squill, refill, roadkill, sawmill, Schuylkill, self-will, Seville, sheathbill, shoebill, show bill, sidehill, sigil, spadille, spoonbill, stabile, stamp mill, standstill, stock-still, storksbill, T-bill, treadmill, true bill, twin bill, twist drill, unreal, until, uphill, vaudeville, waxbill, waybill, windchill, windmill, Zangwill • back and fill, Brazzaville, Bunker Hill, Chapel Hill, chlorophyll, coffee mill, daffodil, de Tocqueville, dishabille, double bill, escadrille, espadrille, Evansville, fiberfill, fill the bill, fit to kill, foreign bill, Francophil, general will, hammer mill, Hooverville, if you will, Jacksonville, Libreville, living will, Louisville, microphyll, minimill, overfill, overkill, overspill, pepper mill, poison pill, puppy mill, razorbill, rolling mill, rototill, San Juan Hill, sleeping pill, Smoky Hill, sugar pill, tormentil, verticil, water mill, water pill, windowsill, whip-poor-will, winter-kill, Yggdrasil • Buffalo Bill, Capitol Hill, ivorybill, over-the-hill, run-of-the-mill

I'll \ī\ see ILE[1]

illa[1] \ē-yə\ barilla, cabrilla, cuadrilla, mantilla, tortilla • banderilla, Bobadilla, camarilla, cascarilla, granadilla, Manzanilla, quesadilla, sapodilla, seguidilla, sinsemilla, sopaipilla

illa[2] \il-ə\ scilla, Scylla, squilla, villa, Willa • ancilla, Anguilla, Aquila, Attila, axilla, cabrilla, Camilla, cedilla, chinchilla, Comilla, flotilla, gorilla, guerrilla, hydrilla, manila, Manila, maxilla, megillah, papilla, perilla, Priscilla, scintilla, vanilla • camarilla, cascarilla, granadilla, Manzanilla, plain-vanilla, potentilla, premaxilla, sabadilla, sapodilla, sarsaparilla

illa[3] \ē-ə\ see IA[1]

illa[4] \əl-yə\ see ELIA

illa[5] \ē-lə\ see ELA[1]

illable \il-ə-bəl\ billable, drillable, fillable, spillable, syllable, tillable • disyllable, refillable, trisyllable • decasyllable, monosyllable, octosyllable, open syllable, polysyllable

illage \il-ij\ grillage, millage, pillage, spillage, tillage, village • no-tillage, permillage • global village, Greenwich Village, intertillage • Potemkin village

illah \il-ə\ see ILLA[2]

illain \il-ən\ see ILLON

illar \il-ər\ see ILLER

illary \il-ə-rē\ Hillary, phyllary
• codicillary

illate \il-ət\ see ILLET

ille¹ \il\ see ILL

ille² \ē\ see EE¹

ille³ \ēl\ see EAL²

illea \il-yə\ see ILIA²

illed \ild\ build, dilled, gild, gilled,
guild, skilled, twilled, willed
• Brynhild, engild, gold-filled,
goodwilled, rebuild, road-killed,
self-willed, spoonbilled,
tendriled, unbuild, unskilled,
upbuild, wergild • jerry-build,
overbuild, semiskilled—also -ed
forms of verbs listed at ILL

illedness \il-nəs\ see ILLNESS

illein \il-ən\ see ILLON

iller \il-ər\ biller, chiller, driller,
filler, giller, griller, hiller, killer,
miller, Miller, pillar, schiller,
Schiller, spiller, swiller, thriller,
tiller, triller • axillar, distiller,
fulfiller, instiller, painkiller,
pralltriller, time killer • caterpillar,
dusty miller, lady-killer,
microvillar, Rototiller, techno-
thriller—also -er forms of
adjectives listed at ILL

illery \il-rē\ pillory • artillery,
distillery • field artillery

illes \il-ēz\ see ILLIES

illet \il-ət\ billet, fillet, millet, rillet,
skillet, willet • distillate, pearl
millet

illful \il-fəl\ skillful, willful
• unskillful

illi¹ \il-ē\ see ILLY¹

illi² \ē-lē\ see EELY

illian¹ \il-ē-ən\ see ILIAN¹

illian² \il-yən\ see ILLION

illiance \il-yəns\ brilliance
• consilience, resilience

illiancy \il-yən-sē\ brilliancy
• resiliency

illiant \il-yənt\ see ILIENT

illick \il-ik\ see ILIC

illie \il-ē\ see ILLY¹

illies \il-ēz\ willies • Achilles,
Antilles • Greater Antilles,
Lesser Antilles—also -s, -'s,
and -s' forms of nouns listed at
ILLY¹

illikan \il-i-kən\ see ILICON

illikin \il-i-kən\ see ILICON

illin¹ \il-ən\ see ILLUM

illin² \il-ən\ see ILLON

illing \il-iŋ\ billing, drilling, filling,
killing, milling, schilling, shilling,
skilling, twilling, willing • bone-
chilling, fulfilling, painkilling,
spine-chilling, top billing,
unwilling • mercy killing, self-
fulfilling—also -ing forms of
verbs listed at ILL

illion \il-yən\ billion, jillion, Lillian,
million, pillion, trillion, zillion
• Brazilian, caecilian, Castilian,
centillion, civilian, cotillion,
decillion, gazillion, kazillion,
modillion, nonillion, octillion,
pavilion, postilion, quadrillion,
Quintilian, quintillion, reptilian,
septillion, sextillion, Sicilian,
tourbillion, vaudevillian,
vermilion • crocodilian,

Maximilian, preexilian, quinde-
cillion, sexdecillion, tredecillion,
undecillion, vespertilian,
vigintillion • duodecillion,
novemdecillion, octodecillion,
septendecillion

illis \il-əs\ see ILLUS

illium \il-ē-əm\ see ILIUM

illness \il-nəs\ chillness, illness,
shrillness, stillness

illo¹ \il-ō\ billow, pillow, willow
• Murillo, Negrillo, tornillo,
Utrillo • Amarillo, armadillo,
cigarillo, coyotillo, Manzanillo,
peccadillo, tamarillo

illo² \ē-ō\ see IO²

illon \il-ən\ billon, Dylan, Uilleann,
villain, villein • tefillin • penicillin
• amoxicillin

illory \il-rē\ see ILLERY

illous \il-əs\ see ILLUS

illow¹ \il-ə\ see ILLA²

illow² \il-ō\ see ILLO¹

illowy \il-ə-wē\ billowy, pillowy,
willowy

ills \ilz\ Black Hills, no-frills
• Alban Hills, Berkshire Hills,
Chiltern Hills, Cotswold Hills,
Malvern Hills, Naga Hills
• Beverly Hills, Cheviot Hills,
Grampian Hills • green around
the gills—*also* -s, -'s, *and* -s'
forms of nouns and -s *forms of
verbs listed at* ILL

illum \il-əm\ chillum • spirillum,
vexillum

illus \il-əs\ Phyllis, villous, Willis
• bacillus, lapillus • amaryllis,
microvillus • toga virilis

illy¹ \il-ē\ Billie, billy, Chile, chili,
chilly, dilly, filly, frilly, gillie, hilly,
illy, Lillie, lily, Lily, Millie, really,
Scilly, shrilly, silly, stilly, Tilly,
Willie • bacilli, Caerphilly,
daylily, fusilli, guidwillie, hillbilly
• piccalilli, rockabilly, willy-nilly

illy² \il-lē\ shrilly, stilly

iln¹ \il\ see ILL

iln² \iln\ kiln, Milne • limekiln

ilne \iln\ see ILN²

ilo¹ \ī-lō\ milo, Milo, phyllo, silo

ilo² \ē-lō\ helo, kilo, phyllo • Iloilo

ilom \ī-ləm\ see ILUM

iloquence \il-ə-kwens\
grandiloquence,
magniloquence

iloquent \il-ə-kwənt\
grandiloquent, magniloquent

iloquist \il-ə-kwəst\ soliloquist,
ventriloquist

iloquy \il-ə-kwē\ soliloquy,
ventriloquy

ilot \ī-lət\ eyelet, islet, Pilate,
pilot, stylet • bush pilot, copilot,
sky pilot, test pilot • autopilot,
Pontius Pilate • automatic pilot

ils \ils\ fils, grilse

ilse \ils\ see ILS

ilt \ilt\ built, gilt, guilt, hilt, jilt, kilt,
lilt, milt, quilt, silt, stilt, tilt, wilt
• atilt, bloodguilt, Brunhild, full
tilt, homebuilt, inbuilt, oak wilt,
rebuilt, unbuilt, uptilt • basket
hilt, carvel-built, clinker-built,
crazy-quilt, custom-built, jerry-

built, patchwork quilt, purpose-built, to the hilt, Vanderbilt

ilter \il-tər\ filter, jilter, kilter, milter, philter, quilter, tilter
• off-kilter • band-pass filter, color filter

ilth \ilth\ filth, spilth, tilth

iltie \il-tē\ see ILTY

ilton \ilt-ᵊn\ Hilton, Milton, Stilton, Wilton

ilty \il-tē\ guilty, kiltie, silty
• bloodguilty

ilum \ī-ləm\ hilum, phylum, whilom, xylem • asylum, subphylum

ilus \ī-ləs\ eyeless, pilus, stylus, tieless

ily¹ \ī-lē\ see YLY

ily² \il-ē\ see ILLY¹

im¹ \im\ bream, brim, dim, glim, grim, Grimm, gym, him, hymn, Jim, Kim, limb, limn, mim, nim, prim, rim, scrim, shim, skim, slim, swim, Tim, trim, vim, whim
• bedim, dislimn, forelimb, McKim, Mirim, passim, Perim, prelim, Purim, Sikkim, slim-jim, snap-brim • acronym, anonym, antonym, cryptonym, eponym, homonym, metonym, paronym, pseudonym, retronym, seraphim, synonym, tautonym, toponym, underbrim • ad interim, heteronym, Pacific Rim

im² \ēm\ see EAM¹

I'm \īm\ see IME¹

ima \ē-mə\ see EMA

imable \ī-mə-bəl\ climbable
• sublimable, unclimbable

imace \im-əs\ grimace, tzimmes

image \im-ij\ image, scrimmage
• real image, self-image
• afterimage, father image, graven image, microimage, mirror image, spitting image, line of scrimmage

iman \ē-mən\ see EMON¹

imate \ī-mət\ climate, primate
• acclimate

imb¹ \im\ see IM¹

imb² \īm\ see IME¹

imba \im-bə\ limba • marimba

imbable \ī-mə-bəl\ see IMABLE

imbal \im-bəl\ see IMBLE

imbale \im-bəl\ see IMBLE

imbed \imd\ brimmed, limbed, rimmed • clean-limbed—*also* -ed *forms of verbs listed at* IM¹

imber¹ \im-bər\ limber, timber
• half-timber, sawtimber, unlimber

imber² \ī-mər\ see IMER¹

imble \im-bəl\ cymbal, gimbal, nimble, symbol, thimble, timbal, timbale, Trimble, tymbal, wimble • peace symbol, sex symbol

imbo \im-bō\ bimbo, limbo
• akimbo • gumbo-limbo

imbral \am-brəl\ see AMBREL

imbre \am-bər\ see AMBAR²

imbrel \im-brəl\ timbrel, whimbrel

imbus \im-bes\ limbus, nimbus
• cumulonimbus

ime¹ \īm\ chime, climb, clime, crime, cyme, dime, disme, grime, I'm, lime, mime, prime, rhyme, rime, slime, stime, thyme, time • airtime, all-time, bedtime, begrime, big time, big-time, birdlime, buy time, call time, crunch time, cut time, daytime, downtime, dreamtime, drive time, end-time, enzyme, eye rhyme, face time, flextime, foretime, free-climb, full-time, half dime, halftime, hang time, hate crime, hill climb, in time, key lime, lead time, lifetime, longtime, lunchtime, make time, Mannheim, mark time, Maytime, mealtime, meantime, Mülheim, nighttime, noontime, old-time, onetime, on time, part-time, pastime, peacetime, Pforzheim, playtime, post time, prime time, quicklime, quick time, ragtime, real time, rock climb, schooltime, seedtime, showtime, sight rhyme, small-time, sometime, Sondheim, space-time, springtime, sublime, teatime, two-time, uptime, Waldheim, war crime, wartime, wind chime • access time, aftertime, Anaheim, anytime, beforetime, Bettelheim, borrowed time, central time, Christmastime, common time, dinnertime, double prime, double-time, drop a dime, eastern time, elapsed time, Father Time, harvesttime, Hildesheim, in jig time, Jotunheim, just-in-time, Kaffir lime, lemon thyme, local time, lysozyme, Mannerheim, maritime, monorhyme, mountain time, nursery rhyme, on a dime, overtime, pantomime, Pappenheim, paradigm, question time, released time, running time, soda lime, standard time, summertime, take one's time, vowel rhyme, wintertime • Alaska time, apparent time, Atlantic time, at the same time, corrected time, from time to time, Greenwich mean time, initial rhyme, internal rhyme, Pacific time, nickel-and-dime, residence time • daylight saving time, geologic time, military time, Universal time

ime² \ēm\ see EAM¹

imel \im-əl\ gimel, gimmal, kümmel

imeless \īm-ləs\ crimeless, rhymeless, timeless

imely \īm-lē\ primely, timely • sublimely, untimely

imen \ī-mən\ Cimon, flyman, hymen, Hymen, limen, Lyman, Simon

imeon \im-ē-ən\ see IMIAN

imeous \ī-məs\ see IMIS

imer¹ \ī-mər\ chimer, climber, dimer, mimer, primer, rhymer, timer, trimer • big-timer, egg timer, full-timer, old-timer, part-timer, small-timer, sublimer, two-timer • Oppenheimer, wisenheimer

imer² \im-ər\ see IMMER

imerick \im-rik\ see YMRIC

imes[1] \īmz\ times • at times, betimes, daytimes, sometimes • betweentimes, oftentimes —*also* -s, -'s, *and* -s' *forms of nouns and* -s *forms of verbs listed at* IME[1]

imes[2] \ēm\ see EAM[1]

imeter \im-ət-ər\ dimeter, limiter, scimitar, trimeter • altimeter, delimiter, perimeter

imetry \im-ə-trē\ symmetry • altimetry, gravimetry

imian \im-ē-ən\ Simeon, simian • Endymion, prosimian

imic \im-ik\ see YMIC[2]

imical \im-i-kəl\ inimical • metonymical, synonymical, toponymical

imicry \im-i-krē\ gimmickry, mimicry

imile \im-ə-lē\ simile, swimmily • facsimile

iminal[1] \im-ən-ᵊl\ criminal, liminal, Viminal • subliminal, war criminal

iminal[2] \im-nəl\ see YMNAL

iminy \im-ə-nē\ see IMONY

imis \ī-məs\ primus, thymus, timeous • imprimis, untimeous

imitable \im-ət-ə-bəl\ imitable, limitable • illimitable, inimitable

imitar \im-ət-ər\ see IMETER

imiter \im-ət-ər\ see IMETER

imits \im-its\ Nimitz • off-limits

imity \im-ət-ē\ dimity • proximity, sublimity • anonymity, equanimity, longanimity, magnanimity, pseudonymity, synonymity, unanimity • pusillanimity

imitz \im-its\ see IMITS

imm \im\ see IM[1]

immable \im-ə-bəl\ dimmable, swimmable

immage \im-ij\ see IMAGE

immal \im-əl\ see IMEL

imme \i-mē\ see IMMY

immed \imd\ see IMBED

immer \im-ər\ brimmer, dimmer, glimmer, limmer, limner, primer, shimmer, simmer, skimmer, slimmer, swimmer, trimmer • backswimmer—*also* -er *forms of adjectives listed at* IM[1]

immes \im-əs\ see IMACE

immick \im-ik\ see YMIC[2]

immickry \im-i-krē\ see IMICRY

immily \im-ə-lē\ see IMILE

immy \im-ē\ gimme, jimmy, limby, shimmy, swimmy

imn \im\ see IM[1]

imner \im-ər\ see IMMER

imo \ē-mō\ primo • sentimo

imon \ī-mən\ see IMEN

imony \im-ə-nē\ simony • niminy-piminy

imothy \im-ə-thē\ timothy, Timothy • polymathy

imp \imp\ blimp, chimp, crimp, gimp, guimpe, imp, limp, pimp, primp, scrimp, shrimp, simp, skimp, wimp • brine shrimp, rock shrimp • Colonel Blimp, fairy shrimp, tiger shrimp

impe \imp\ see IMP

imper \im-pər\ crimper, limper, shrimper, simper, whimper

imping \im-pən\ see YMPAN

impish \im-pish\ blimpish, impish, wimpish

imple \im-pəl\ dimple, pimple, simple, wimple • fee simple • oversimple

imply \im-plē\ dimply, limply, pimply, simply • oversimply

impy \im-pē\ crimpy, gimpy, scrimpy, shrimpy, skimpy, wimpy

imsy \im-zē\ flimsy, slimsy, whimsy

imulus \im-yə-ləs\ limulus, stimulus

imus \ī-məs\ see IMIS

imy \ī-mē\ grimy, limey, limy, rimy, slimy, stymie, thymy • old-timey

in¹ \in\ been, bin, blin, chin, din, fin, Finn, Fyn, gin, grin, Gwyn, hin, in, inn, kin, linn, Lynn, pin, shin, Shin, sin, skin, spin, thin, tin, twin, whin, win, wynn, yin, zin • add-in, again, agin, akin, all-in, backspin, bearskin, begin, Benin, Berlin, blow in, Boleyn, bowfin, break-in, bring in, buckskin, build in, built-in, burn-in, butt in, calfskin, call in, call-in, capeskin, cash in, cave-in, chagrin, check in, check-in, chime in, chip in, close in, clothespin, come in, coonskin, Corinne, crankpin, cut in, deerskin, dig in, doeskin, do in, draw in, drive-in, drop in, duckpin, dustbin, edge in, fade-in, fall in, fill in, fill-in, foreskin, Fuxin, get in, give in, goatskin, go in, Guilin, hairpin, hand in, hang in, Harbin, has-been, headpin, herein, horn in, Jilin, kick in, kidskin, kingpin, lambskin, lay in, lead-in, lie-in, linchpin, live-in, lived-in, lobe-fin, locked-in, log in, look-in, love-in, moleskin, move in, munchkin, Nankin, ninepin, no-win, oilskin, phone-in, pigskin, pinyin, pitch in, plug-in, plugged-in, pull in, punch in, pushpin, put in, rub in, ruin, run in, run-in, saimin, scarfpin, scarfskin, sealskin, send in, set in, sharkskin, shear pin, sheepskin, shoo-in, shut-in, sidespin, sign in, sit-in, sleep in, sleep-in, sloe gin, snakeskin, sock in, stand in, stand-in, step in, stickpin, suck in, swanskin, swear in, swim fin, tail fin, tailspin, take in, tap-in, teach-in, tenpin, therein, tholepin, threadfin, throw in, tie-in, tiepin, tip-in, toe-in, Tonkin, topspin, trade in, trade-in, tune in, tuned-in, Turin, turn in, unpin, walk-in, wear thin, weigh in, wherein, whip in, wineskin, win-win, within, woolskin, work in, wrist pin, write-in, Yeltsin • bathtub gin, bobby pin, born-

again, candlepin, catechin,
Chinquapin, come again, cotter
pin, cotton gin, deadly sin,
figure in, firing pin, Ho Chi
Minh, listen in, listener-in,
Lohengrin, loony bin, lying-in,
mandolin, maximin, Mickey
Finn, mortal sin, motor inn, next
of kin, ob-gyn, onionskin,
palanquin, paper-thin, pelvic
fin, rejoice in, rolling pin,
rooming-in, safety pin, set foot
in, thick and thin, Tianjin,
underpin, underspin, Vietminh,
violin, whipper-in • Bight of
Benin, Gulf of Tonkin, Jiang
Zemin, keep one's hand in,
original sin, pectoral fin, rub
one's nose in, Siamese twin,
under one's skin, under the
skin, venial sin • again and
again, take it on the chin • on-
again off-again

in² \ēn\ see INE³

in³ \an\ see AN⁵

in⁴ \aⁿ\ Baudouin, boudin,
Chardin, Chopin, Coquelin,
dauphin, doyen, Gauguin,
Guesclin, Louvain, moulin,
Perrin, Petain, Poussin, Rodin,
serin • Claude Lorrain, coq au
vin, coup de main, fleur de
coin, Gobelin, Limousin,
Maritain, Mazarin, Saint-
Germain • Brillat-Savarin,
Teilhard de Chardin

in⁵ \ən\ see UN¹

ina¹ \ī-nə\ china, China, Dinah,
Heine, Ina, mina, mynah
• Aegina, angina, bone china,
Carina, Lucina, nandina,
piscina, Regina, salina,
shechinah, stone china, vagina
• Agrippina, Cochin China,
Carolina, Indochina, kamaaina,
Poland China • North Carolina,
South Carolina

ina² \ē-nə\ Deena, kina, Lena,
Nina, Shina, Skeena, Tina,
vena, vina • arena, Athena,
Bernina, cantina, catena,
Christina, coquina, corbina,
corvina, czarina, dracaena,
Edwina, euglena, farina, Farina,
fontina, galena, Georgina,
hyena, kachina, Kristina,
marina, Marina, medina,
Medina, Messina, Molina,
nandina, novena, patina,
piscina, platina, Regina, retsina,
Rowena, Salina, sestina,
Shechinah, subpoena, verbena
• Agrippina, amberina,
Angelina, Argentina, ballerina,
casuarina, Carolina, Catalina,
catilena, cavatina, Chianina,
concertina, Filipina, javelina,
Katerina, ocarina, Palestrina,
Pasadena, Saint Helena, sand
verbena, semolina, signorina,
sonatina, Taormina, Teresina,
Wilhelmina • Herzegovina,
Pallas Athena, Strait of Messina

inable \ī-nə-bəl\ minable
• combinable, consignable,
declinable, definable, inclinable
• indeclinable, indefinable

inach \in-ich\ Greenwich,
spinach

inah¹ \ē-nə\ see INA²

inah² \ī-nə\ see INA¹

inal¹ \īn-ᵊl\ clinal, final, rhinal, spinal, trinal, vinyl • anginal, doctrinal, synclinal • matutinal, officinal, quarterfinal, semifinal, serotinal

inal² \ēn-ᵊl\ see ENAL

inally \īn-ᵊl-ē\ clinally, finally, spinally • matutinally

inary \ī-nə-rē\ binary, trinary

inas¹ \ī-nəs\ see INUS¹

inas² \ē-nəs\ see ENUS¹

inative \in-ət-iv\ see INITIVE

inc \iŋk\ see INK

inca \iŋ-kə\ Dinka, finca, Glinka, Inca, vinca • Mandinka, Soyinka, stotinka

incal \iŋ-kəl\ see INKLE

incan \iŋ-kən\ Incan, Lincoln

ince¹ \ins\ blintz, chintz, mince, prince, quince, rinse, since, wince • convince, crown prince, evince, long since, shin splints • Port-au-Prince

ince² \äns\ see ANCE³

incely \in-slē\ princely, tinselly

incer \in-chər\ see INCHER

inch \inch\ chinch, cinch, clinch, finch, flinch, grinch, inch, lynch, Minch, pinch, squinch, winch • Bulfinch, bullfinch, chaffinch, goldfinch, greenfinch, hawfinch, unclinch • acre-inch, every inch, inch by inch, purple finch

incher \in-chər\ clincher, flincher, lyncher, pincer, pincher, wincher • affenpinscher, penny-pincher • Doberman pinscher

inching \in-chiŋ\ unflinching • penny-pinching—*also* -ing *forms of verbs listed at* INCH

incible \in-sə-bəl\ principal, principle, vincible • evincible, invincible • inconvincible, Peter Principle, pleasure principle

incing \in-siŋ\ ginseng, mincing • convincing • unconvincing —*also* -ing *forms of verbs listed at* INCE¹

incipal \in-sə-bəl\ see INCIBLE

inciple \in-sə-bəl\ see INCIBLE

inck \iŋk\ see INK

incky \iŋ-kē\ see INKY

incoln \iŋ-kən\ see INCAN

inct \iŋt\ linked, kinked, tinct • distinct, extinct, instinct, precinct, succinct, unlinked • death instinct, indistinct • killer instinct

inction \iŋ-shən\ distinction, extinction, intinction • contradistinction

incture \iŋ-chər\ cincture, tincture

ind¹ \īnd\ bind, blind, find, grind, hind, kind, mind, rind, signed, spined, tined, wind, wynd • affined, behind, confined, fly blind, inclined, in-kind, mankind, month's mind, night-blind, purblind, refined, remind, rewind, sand-blind, snow-blind, spellbind, stone-blind, streamlined, unbind, unkind, unwind • ax to grind, bear in mind, blow one's mind, bring to mind, color-blind, double bind, double-blind, drop behind, fall behind, frame of mind, gavelkind, gravel-blind, hoodman-blind, humankind, in a bind, mastermind, mortal mind, never mind, nonaligned, put in mind, single-blind, unaligned, undersigned, well-defined, womankind • back of one's mind, four of a kind, piece of one's mind, presence of mind, three of a kind, time out of mind, venetian blind —*also* -ed *forms of verbs listed at* INE¹

ind² \ind\ finned, Sind, skinned, wind • break wind, buckskinned, crosswind, downwind, exscind, headwind, prescind, rescind, tailwind, thick-skinned, thin-skinned, upwind, whirlwind, woodwind • Amerind, in the wind, near the wind, off the wind, on the wind, second wind, solar wind, spiny-finned, stellar wind, tamarind • capful of wind, close to the wind, straw in the wind, twist in the wind, under the wind • three sheets in the wind—*also* -ed *forms of verbs listed at* IN¹

ind³ \int\ see INT

inda \in-də\ Linda • Lucinda, Melinda • Samarinda

indar \in-dər\ see INDER²

inded¹ \īn-dəd\ minded, rinded • air-minded, broad-minded, fair-minded, high-minded, large-minded, like-minded, low-minded, right-minded, small-minded, snow-blinded, strong-minded, tough-minded, weak-minded • absentminded, bloody-minded, civic-minded, evil-minded, feebleminded, narrow-minded, open-minded, simpleminded, single-minded, social-minded, tender-minded, worldly-minded • serious-minded—*also* -ed *forms of verbs listed at* IND¹

inded² \in-ded\ brinded • long-winded, short-winded • broken-winded—*also* -ed *forms of verbs listed at* IND²

inder¹ \īn-dər\ binder, blinder, finder, grinder, hinder, minder, winder • bookbinder, fact finder, faultfinder, highbinder, netminder, pathfinder, range finder, reminder, ring binder, self-binder, sidewinder, spellbinder, stem-winder, viewfinder, organ-grinder • direction finder—*also* -er *forms of adjectives listed at* IND¹

inder² \in-dər\ cinder, hinder, Pindar, tinder

indful \īn-fəl\ mindful • remindful, unmindful

indhi \in-dē\ see INDY

indi \in-dē\ see INDY

indic \in-dik\ Indic, syndic

indie \in-dē\ see INDY

inding \īn-diŋ\ binding, finding, winding • bookbinding, fact-finding, faultfinding, field winding, half binding, pathfinding, self-winding, spell-binding, stem-winding—*also* -ing *forms of verbs listed at* IND[1]

indlass \in-ləs\ see INLESS

indle \in-dᵊl\ bindle, brindle, dwindle, kindle, spindle, swindle • enkindle

indless \īn-ləs\ kindless, mindless, spineless

indling[2] \ind-liŋ\ dwindling, kindling, spindling—*also* -ing *forms of verbs listed at* INDLE[1]

indly[1] \in-lē\ see INLY

indly[2] \īn-lē\ see INELY[1]

indness \īn-nəs\ blindness, fineness, kindness • moonblindness, night blindness, purblindness, snow blindness, unkindness • color blindness, loving-kindness, river blindness

indowed \in-dəd\ see INDED[2]

indus \in-dəs\ Indus, Pindus

indy \in-dē\ Cindy, Hindi, indie, lindy, shindy, Sindhi, windy • red sindhi • Rawalpindi

ine[1] \īn\ bine, brine, chine, cline, dine, dyne, eyen, fine, Jain, kine, line, Line, Main, mine, nine, pine, Quine, Rhine, rind, shine, shrine, sign, spine, spline, stein, Stein, swine, syne, thine, tine, trine, twine, vine, whine, wine • A-line, affine, airline, align, alkyne, alpine, assign, at sign, balkline, baseline, beeline, benign, Bernstein, bloodline, blue line, blush wine, bovine, bowline, branchline, breadline, bright-line, buntline, bustline, byline, call sign, canine, caprine, carbine, carmine, cervine, chow line, clothesline, cloud nine, coastline, combine, compline, condign, confine, consign, corvine, cosign, cutline, dateline, deadline, decline, define, design, divine, dragline, driveline, earthshine, Einstein, eiswein, end line, enshrine, ensign, entwine, equine, ethyne, fall line, fault line, feline, ferine, first-line, flatline, flight line, foul line, fräulein, frontline, front line, gantline, goal line, gold mine, grapevine, guideline, hairline, hard-line, hard pine, headline, hemline, high sign, hipline, Holbein, Holstein, hotline, ice wine, incline, indign, in fine, in-line, Irvine, jawline, jug wine, landline, land mine, lang syne, lead line, lifeline, load line, longline, lupine, mainline, main line, malign, midline, moline, moonshine, neckline, off-line, old-line, online, opine, outline, outshine, ovine, Pauline, peace sign, Pennine, Petrine, pipeline, piscine, pitch pine, plotline, plumb line, plus sign, pontine, Pontine, porcine, potline, pound sign, propine, punch line, quinine, rapine, recline, redline, red pine, refine, reline, repine, resign, Rhine wine, ridgeline, roofline, Sabine, saline, Scotch pine, scrub pine, setline, shoreline, short line, sideline, sight line, skyline, snow line, soft-line, spring line, straight-line, strandline, straw wine, streamline, strip mine, strychnine, subline, sunshine, supine, syncline, taurine, tie-line, time-line, times sign, topline, touchline, towline, tramline, trapline, tree line, trephine, trotline, truckline, trunk line, tumpline, turbine, untwine, ursine, vespine, V sign, vulpine, waistline, white line, white pine, white wine, woodbine, yard line, zayin, zebrine, Z line • aerodyne, agate line, alkaline, androgyne, Angeline, anodyne, anticline, Apennine, aquiline, argentine, asinine, auld lang syne, Aventine, Ballantyne, balloon vine, battle line, borderline, bottom-line, Byzantine, calamine, calcimine, Caroline, catarrhine, Catiline, celandine, centerline, cisalpine, Cisalpine, claymore mine, clementine, colubrine, columbine, Colum-bine, concubine, conga line, Constantine, contour line, Coppermine, coralline, countermine, countersign, credit line, crystalline, cytokine, dessert wine, disincline, dollar sign, down-the-line, draw the line, eglantine, endocrine, equal sign, Esquiline, exocrine, falconine, fescennine, finish line, firing line, Florentine, Frankenstein, gas turbine, genuine, gregarine, infantine, interline, intertwine, iodine, Johannine, knotty pine, ledger line, leonine, Levantine, Liechtenstein, limber pine, lodgepole pine, longleaf pine,

lubber line, minus sign, monkeyshine, morning line, mugho pine, muscadine, on deadline, on the line, opaline, palatine, Palatine, Palestine, party line, passerine, picket line, porcupine, psittacine, realign, redefine, redesign, riverine, Rubenstein, sac-charine, sapphirine, saturnine, second-line, serpentine, service line, shortleaf pine, sibylline, Siegfried line, sixty-nine, sounding line, subalpine, sparkling wine, static line, steam turbine, story line, table wine, Theatine, three-point line, timberline, toe the line, transalpine, Tridentine, turnverein, turpentine, under-line, undermine, Ursuline, uterine, valentine, vespertine, viperine, vulturine, waterline, wind turbine, worry line • accipitrine, adamantine, adulterine, alexandrine, amaranthine, assembly line, attention line, Australian pine, Austrian pine, Capitoline, count palatine, die on the vine, elephantine, Evangeline, fall into line, fortified wine, Frankfurt am Main, graphic design, heterodyne, labyrinthine, lateral line, loblolly pine, Maginot Line, Monterey pine, poverty line, production line, receiving line, Rembrandt van Rijn, Schleswig-Holstein, ship of the line, sweetheart neckline, top-of-the-line • Mason-Dixon line

ine² \ē-nā\ fine • wahine

ine³ \ən\ bean, clean, dean, Dean, Deane, dene, e'en, gene, Gene, glean, green, Green, Greene, jean, Jean, Jeanne, keen, lean, lien, mean, mesne, mien, peen, preen, quean, queen, scene, screen, seen, sheen, shin, sin, skean, skene, spean, spleen, teen, tween, wean, ween, wheen, Wien, yean • Aileen, Andine, arene, Arlene, baleen, beguine, Beguine, Benin, benzene, benzine, Bernstein, between, black bean, boreen, bovine, broad bean, buckbean, caffeine, canteen, carbine, careen, Carlene, Cathleen, Charlene, chlorine, chopine, chorine, Christine, citrine, Claudine, codeine, colleen, Colleen, convene, Coreen, cotquean, cuisine, Darlene, dasheen, dauphine, demean, demesne, dentine, Doreen, dry-clean, dudeen, eighteen, Eileen, Essene, Eugene, e-zine, fanzine, fascine, fifteen, flavine, fluorine, fourteen, Francine, gamine, gangrene, glassine, gyrene, Helene, Hellene, Hermine, hoatzin, Holstein, horsebean, houseclean, hygiene, Ilene, Irene, Jacqueline, Jeannine, Jolene, Justine, Kathleen, khamsin, Kristine, Ladin, lateen, latrine, Lorene, Lublin, machine, malines, marine, Marlene, Maureen, Maxine, moline, moreen, morphine, mung bean, Nadine, nankeen, naphthene, Nicene, nineteen, nongreen, Noreen, obscene, offscreen, on-screen, patine, Pauline, piscine, Pontine, poteen, praline, preteen, pristine, propine, protein, Rabin, Racine, ratteen, ravine, red bean, routine, saline, saltine, Salween, sardine, sateen, scalene, serene, shagreen, Sharlene, shebeen, siren, Sistine, sixteen, Slovene, snap bean, soybean, spalpeen, string bean, strychnine, subteen, sunscreen, Szczecin, tacrine, takin, taurine, terrene, terrine, thirteen, Tolkien, tontine, tureen, umpteen, unclean, undine, unseen, vaccine, vitrine, wax bean, white bean, windscreen, yestreen, Yibin, zechin • Aberdeen, almandine, amandine, Angeline, argentine, Argentine, atropine, Augustine, Balanchine, barkentine, bengaline, Benzadrine, Bernadine, blanc de chine, bombazine, Borodin, brigandine, brigantine, brilliantine, Byzantine, carotene, carrageen, celandine, clandestine, clozapine, columbine, Constantine, contravene, crepe de chine, crystalline, damascene, Dexedrine, dopamine, Dramamine, drum machine, duvetyn, eglantine, endocrine, Eocene, epicene, Ernestine, estuarine, evergreen, fava bean, fescennine, figurine, Florentine, gabardine, gaberdine, gadarene, galantine, gasoline, Geraldine, Ghibelline, go-between, golden mean, grenadine, Gretna Green, guillotine, Halloween, haute cuisine, Hippocrene, histamine, Holocene, Imogene, in-between, indigene, intervene, jelly bean, Josephine, jumping bean, kerosene, kidney bean, langoustine, legatine, lethal gene, Levantine, libertine, lima bean, limousine, lycopene, M16, magazine, make the scene, mangosteen, margravine, Medellín, melamine, messaline, Methedrine, mezzanine, Miocene, mousseline, navy bean, Nazarene, nectarine, nicotine, overseen, opaline, organzine, palanquin, pelerine, percaline, peregrine, philhellene, Philistine, pinto bean, plasticene, Pleistocene, Pliocene, riverine, quarantine, reserpine, saccharine, Sakhalin, Saladin, San Joaquin, San Martín, sapphirine, schizophrene, serpentine, seventeen, sibylline, silkaline, slot machine, submarine, subroutine, supervene, tambourine, tangerine, Theatine, time machine, tonka bean, tourmaline, trampoline, transmarine, travertine, Tridentine, Ursuline, Vaseline, velveteen, wintergreen, wolverine, yard-long bean, zibeline • acetylene, adamantine, alexandrine, amphetamine, aquamarine, Benedictine, carbon 13, elephantine, Evangeline, flying machine, Forest of Dean, garbanzo bean, Grau St. Martín, heart-lung machine, internecine, labyrinthine, merchant marine, milling machine, mujahideen, nano-machine, nouvelle cuisine, Oligocene, Paleocene, Paracutín, pentamedine, pinball machine, rowing machine, simple machine, talking machine, threshing machine, ultramarine, vanilla bean, vending machine, voting machine, washing machine • answering machine, antihistamine, arithmetic mean, infernal machine, Mary Magdalene, NC-17 • General San Martín, oleomargarine

ine⁴ \in-ē\ see INNY

ine⁵ \ē-nē\ see INI¹

ine⁶ \ən\ see UN

inea \in-ē\ see INNY

ineal \in-ē-əl\ finial, lineal, tineal • matrilineal, patrilineal, unilineal

ined \īnd\ see IND¹

inee \ī-nē\ see INY¹

ineless \īn-ləs\ see INDLESS

inely¹ \īn-lē\ blindly, finely, kindly • affinely, bovinely, condignly, divinely, equinely, felinely, purblindly, supinely, unkindly • asininely

inely² \ēn-lē\ see EANLY¹

inement \īn-mənt\ see IGNMENT

ineness \īn-nəs\ see INDNESS

ineous \in-ē-əs\ gramineous, sanguineous • consan-guineous, ignominious

iner¹ \ī-nər\ briner, diner, liner, miner, minor, Reiner, shiner,

Shriner, signer, twiner, whiner • airliner, aligner, assigner, baseliner, blueliner, byliner, combiner, confiner, cosigner, decliner, definer, designer, diviner, eyeliner, flatliner, hardliner, headliner, incliner, jetliner, Landsteiner, leaf miner, longliner, moonshiner, one-liner, recliner, refiner, repiner, resigner, sideliner, soft-liner, streamliner, strip miner • Asia Minor, bottom-liner, Canis Minor, Döbereiner, forty-niner, golden shiner, party-liner, superliner, Ursa Minor • graphic designer

iner² \ē-nər\ see EANER

inery¹ \īn-rē\ finery, pinery, vinery, winery • refinery

inery² \ēn-rē\ see EANERY

ines¹ \ēn\ see INE³

ines² \ēnz\ see EENS

ines³ \īnz\ Mainz • skew lines • Apennines, to the nines • between the lines—*also* -s, -'s, *and* -s' *forms of nouns and* -s *forms of verbs listed at* INE¹

inest \ī-nəst\ see INIST¹

inet \in-ət\ see INNET

inew \in-yü\ see INUE

infield \in-fēld\ infield, Winfield

ing \iŋ\ bring, Ching, cling, ding, fling, king, King, ling, Ming, ping, ring, sing, sling, spring, sting, string, swing, thing, wing, wring, zing • Anqing, backswing, Baoding, Beijing, bi-swing,

bitewing, bowstring, bullring, Chongqing, clearwing, downswing, drawstring, D ring, earring, first-string, forewing, G-string, greenwing, growth ring, hairspring, hamstring, handspring, headspring, heartstring, hind wing, hot spring, Kunming, lacewing, lapwing, latchstring, left-wing, mainspring, Nanjing, Nankin, Nan Ling, Nanning, O-ring, offspring, plaything, redwing, right-wing, seal ring, shoestring, showring, slip ring, sure thing, unsling, unstring, upspring, upswing, waxwing, wellspring, whitewing, wingding, Xining • à la king, anything, apron string, buck-and-wing, cosmic string, delta wing, ding-a-ling, double-ring, everything, fairy ring, Highland fling, innerspring, Liaoning, new jack swing, on the string, on the wing, pigeonwing, pull the string, second-string, signet ring, single wing, superstring, teething ring, underwing, western swing, wing and wing • buffalo wing, cedar waxwing, if anything, under one's wing

inga \iŋ-gə\ anhinga, syringa

inge \inj\ binge, cringe, dinge, fringe, hinge, singe, springe, swinge, tinge, twinge, whinge • butt hinge, impinge, infringe, syringe, unhinge • lunatic fringe, piano hinge

inged \ind\ ringed, stringed, winged • net-winged—*also* -ed *forms of verbs listed at* ING

ingement \inj-mənt\
impingement, infringement

ingency \in-jən-sē\ stringency
• astringency, contingency

ingent \in-jənt\ stringent
• astringent, constringent,
contingent

inger[1] \iŋ-ər\ bringer, clinger,
dinger, flinger, pinger, ringer,
Schwinger, singer, slinger,
springer, stinger, stringer,
swinger, winger, wringer, zinger
• Beijinger, first-stringer,
folksinger, gunslinger, hand-
wringer, humdinger, left-winger,
mudslinger, right-winger, torch
singer • mastersinger, Meister-
singer, minnesinger

inger[2] \iŋ-gər\ finger, linger
• five-finger, forefinger,
malinger, ring finger • index
finger, ladyfinger, little finger,
middle finger

inger[3] \in-jər\ binger, ginger,
Ginger, injure, singer, swinger
• infringer, wild ginger

ingery \inj-rē\ gingery, injury

inghy \iŋ-ē\ see INGY[1]

ingian \in-jən\ Thuringian
• Carlovingian, Carolingian,
Merovingian

inging \iŋ-iŋ\ ringing, springing,
stringing, swinging • change
ringing, folksinging, free-
swinging, gunslinging, hand-
wringing, mudslinging,
upbringing—*also* -ing *forms of
verbs listed at* ING

ingit \iŋ-kət\ see INKET

ingle \iŋ-gəl\ cringle, dingle,
jingle, mingle, shingle, single,
tingle • atingle, commingle,
immingle, Kriss Kringle,
surcingle • intermingle

ingler \iŋ-glər\ jingler, shingler

inglet \iŋ-lət\ kinglet, ringlet,
winglet

ingletree \iŋ-gəl-trē\ singletree,
swingletree

ingli \iŋ-glē\ see INGLY

inglish \iŋ-glish\ see ENGLISH

ingly \iŋ-glē\ jingly, shingly,
singly, tingly, Zwingli

ingo \iŋ-gō\ bingo, dingo, gringo,
jingo, lingo, pingo • flamingo,
Mandingo • Santo Domingo

ings \iŋz\ Kings, springs
• eyestrings, Hot Springs, Palm
Springs, pull strings, purse
strings, see things • Coral
Springs, in the wings
• Colorado Springs, Saratoga
Springs—*also* -s, -'s, *and* -s'
forms of nouns and -s *forms of
verbs listed at* ING

ingue \aŋ\ see ANG[2]

inguish \iŋ-wish\ distinguish,
extinguish

ingy[1] \iŋ-ē\ clingy, dinghy,
springy, stringy, swingy, wingy,
zingy

ingy[2] \in-jē\ dingy, mingy, stingy

inh \in\ see IN[1]

ini[1] \ē-nē\ beanie, genie, greeny,
Jeannie, meanie, jinni, Meany,
sheeny, spleeny, teeny, weanie,
weeny, wienie • Alcmene,

Athene, Bellini, Bernini, bikini, Bikini, Cabrini, Cellini, cremini, crostini, Cyrene, Eugenie, Houdini, linguine, Mancini, Marini, martini, Mazzini, Mbini, Messene, Mycenae, Panini, Pannini, porcini, Puccini, rapini, Rossini, Selene, tahini, tankini, wahine, zucchini • Boccherini, capellini, Cherubini, Contarini, fantoccini, fettuccine, Hippocrene, kundalini, malihini, Mistassini, Mussolini, Mytilene, nota bene, Paganini, Sabatini, scaloppine, spaghettini, string bikini, teeny-weeny, tetrazzini, tortellini, Toscanini • vodka martini

ini² \in-ē\ see INNY

inia \in-ē-ə\ zinnia • Bithynia, Gdynia, gloxinia, Lavinia, Mordvinia, Sardinia, vaccinia, Virginia • Abyssinia, West Virginia

inial \in-ē-əl\ see INEAL

inian¹ \in-ē-ən\ actinian, Arminian, Darwinian, Godwinian, Latinian, Sardinian, Socinian, Virginian • Abyssinian, Apollinian, Argentinian, Augustinian, Carolinian, Carthaginian, Palestinian

inian² \in-yən\ see INION

inic¹ \ē-nik\ Enoch • nicotinic

inic² \in-ik\ clinic, cynic, Finnic • platinic, rabbinic • Jacobinic, mandarinic, misogynic, muscarinic, nicotinic, paraffinic

inical \in-i-kəl\ binnacle, clinical, cynical, finical, pinnacle • dominical • Jacobinical

inican \in-i-kən\ see INIKIN

inikin \in-i-kən\ minikin • Dominican

inim \in-əm\ minim • Houyhnhnm

ining \ī-niŋ\ lining, mining, shining • declining, designing, inclining, long-lining • interlining, silver lining, undesigning —also -ing forms of verbs listed at ¹INE

inion \in-yən\ minion, minyan, pinion, piñon • champignon, dominion, Justinian, opinion, Sardinian • Abyssinian, self-opinion

inis¹ \in-əs\ finis, pinnace • Erinys

inis² \ī-nəs\ see INUS¹

inish \in-ish\ finish, Finnish, thinnish • diminish, refinish • photo finish

inist¹ \ī-nəst\ dynast, finest

inist² \ē-nəst\ hygienist, machinist • magazinist, trampolinist • dental hygienist

initive \in-ət-iv\ carminative, definitive, infinitive • split infinitive

inity \in-ət-ē\ trinity, Trinity • affinity, bovinity, concinnity, divinity, felinity, feminity, infinity, latinity, salinity, sanguinity, vicinity, virginity • alkalinity, aquilinity, clandestinity, consanguinity, crystallinity, femininity, inconcinnity, masculinity, saccharinity

inium \in-ē-əm\ delphinium, triclinium • condominium

injure \in-jər\ see INGER³

injury \inj-rē\ see INGERY

ink \iŋk\ blink, brink, chink, clink, dink, drink, fink, gink, ink, jink, kink, link, mink, pink, plink, prink, rink, shrink, sink, skink, slink, stink, swink, sync, think, wink, zinc • bethink, chewink, cross-link, cuff link, downlink, dry sink, eyeblink, eyewink, groupthink, heat sink, hoodwink, hot link, iceblink, lipsynch, misthink, mixed drink, moss pink, outthink, preshrink, rat fink, red ink, rethink, rose pink, sea pink, shell pink, snowblink, soft drink, strong drink, unkink, uplink, wild pink • bobolink, countersink, distelfink, doublethink, hyperlink, interlink, in the pink, kitchen-sink, Maeterlinck, missing link, on the blink, rinky-dink, salmon pink, shocking pink

inka \iŋ-kə\ see INCA

inkable \iŋ-kə-bəl\ drinkable, shrinkable, sinkable, thinkable • undrinkable, unsinkable, unthinkable

inkage \iŋ-kij\ linkage, shrinkage, sinkage • cross-linkage, sex-linkage

inke \iŋ-kē\ see INKY

inked \iŋt\ see INCT

inker \iŋ-kər\ blinker, clinker, drinker, linker, pinker, prinker, shrinker, sinker, skinker, stinker, thinker, tinker, winker • freethinker, headshrinker, hoodwinker, nondrinker • hook line and sinker

inket \iŋ-kət\ Tlingit, trinket

inkey \iŋ-kē\ see INKY

inkgo \iŋ-kō\ see INKO

inki \iŋ-kē\ see INKY

inkie \iŋ-kē\ see INKY

inking \iŋ-kiŋ\ freethinking, unblinking, unthinking • wishful thinking—*also* -ing *forms of verbs listed at* INK

inkle \iŋ-kəl\ crinkle, inkle, sprinkle, tinkle, twinkle, winkle, wrinkle • besprinkle • periwinkle, Rip van Winkle

inkling \iŋ-kliŋ\ inkling, sprinkling, twinkling—*also* -ing *forms of verbs listed at* INKLE

inkly \iŋ-klē\ crinkly, pinkly, tinkly, twinkly, wrinkly

inko \iŋ-kō\ ginkgo, pinko

inks \iŋs\ see INX

inky \iŋ-kē\ dinkey, dinky, hinky, inky, kinky, pinkie, pinky, slinky, stinky, zincky • Helsinki, Malinke

inland \in-lənd\ Finland, inland, Vinland

inless \in-ləs\ chinless, sinless, skinless, spinless, windlass

inley \in-lē\ see INLY

inly \in-lē\ inly, spindly, thinly • McKinley • Mount McKinley

inn \in\ see IN¹

innace \in-əs\ see INIS[1]

innacle \in-i-kəl\ see INICAL

inned \ind\ see IND[2]

inner \in-ər\ dinner, ginner, grinner, inner, pinner, sinner, skinner, spinner, spinor, thinner, tinner, winner • beginner, blood thinner, breadwinner, prizewinner, shore dinner, web spinner • money-spinner, TV dinner

innet \in-ət\ linnet, minute, spinet

inney \in-ē\ see INNY

inni \ē-nē\ see INI[1]

innia \in-ē-ə\ see INIA

innic \in-ik\ see INIC[2]

innie \in-ē\ see INNY

inning \in-iŋ\ ginning, inning, spinning, winning • beginning, blood-thinning, breadwinning, prizewinning • underpinning —also -ing forms of verbs listed at IN[1]

innish \in-ish\ see INISH

innity \in-ət-ē\ see INITY

innow \in-ō\ minnow, winnow • topminnow

inny \in-ē\ cine, finny, ginny, guinea, Guinea, hinny, mini, Minnie, ninny, pinny, Pliny, shinny, skinny, spinney, squinny, tinny, whinny, Winnie • New Guinea • ignominy, micromini • Papua New Guinea

ino[1] \ī-nō\ dino, lino, rhino, Taino, wino • albino

ino[2] \ē-nō\ beano, chino, fino, keno, leno, Pinot, vino, Zeno • Aquino, bambino, casino, cioppino, ladino, Latino, merino, neutrino, pepino, Quirino, sordino, Ticino, zecchino • andantino, Angeleno, Aretino, Bardolino, campesino, cappuccino, clams casino, concertino, Filipino, langostino, maraschino, palomino, Perugino, San Marino, pecorino, sopranino • Cape Mendocino, Parmigianino, San Bernardino

ino[3] \ē-nə\ see INA[2]

iñon \in-yən\ see INION

inor[1] \in-ər\ see INNER

inor[2] \ī-nər\ see INER[1]

inos \ī-nəs\ see INNS

inot \ē-nō\ see INO[2]

inous \ī-nəs\ see INUS[1]

inscher \in-chər\ see INCHER

inse \ins\ see INCE

inselly \in-slē\ see INCELY

inseng \in-siŋ\ see INCING

insk \insk\ Minsk, Pinsk • Dzerzhinsk • Semipalatinsk

insky \in-skē\ buttinsky, Kandinsky, kolinsky, Nijinsky, Stravinsky, Vyshinsky

inster \in-stər\ minster, spinster • Axminster, Westminster • Kidderminster

int \int\ bint, Clint, dint, flint, Flint, glint, hint, lint, mint, print, quint, skint, splint, sprint, squint, stint, suint, tint • blueprint, catmint, footprint, forint, gunflint, handprint, hoofprint, horsemint, imprint, in-print, large-print, newsprint, offprint, preprint, remint, reprint, skinflint, **spearmint**, thumbprint, voiceprint, **wind sprint**, work print • **aquatint**, calamint, contact print, cuckoopint, fingerprint, mezzotint, monotint, overprint, peppermint, photoprint, wunderkind • Septuagint

intage \int-ij\ mintage, vintage • nonvintage

intager \int-i-jər\ see INTEGER

intain \int-ᵊn\ see INTON

intal¹ \int-ᵊl\ lintel, pintle, quintal • Septuagintal

intal² \ant-ᵊl\ see ANTLE

integer \int-i-jər\ integer, vintager

intel \int-ᵊl\ see INTAL¹

inter \int-ər\ hinter, linter, minter, Pinter, printer, sinter, splinter, sprinter, squinter, tinter, winter • imprinter, line printer, midwinter, reprinter • aquatinter, impact printer, laser printer, overwinter, teleprinter • nuclear winter

intery \int-ə-rē\ printery, splintery

inth \inth\ plinth, synth • absinthe, helminth, hyacinth • colocynth, labyrinth, terebinth

inthia \in-thē-ə\ Cynthia • Carinthia

inthine \in-thən\ hyacinthine, labyrinthine

inting \int-iŋ\ printing • imprinting, unstinting—*also* -ing *forms of verbs listed at* INT

intle \int-ᵊl\ see INTAL¹

into¹ \in-tō\ pinto, Shinto, spinto

into² \in-tü\ back into, break into, build into, bump into, buy into, check into, come into, get into, go into, lay into, light into, look into, pitch into, plug into, rip into, run into, sail into, tap into, tear into, thereinto, tie into, whereinto • enter into, marry into

inton \int-ᵊn\ Clinton, Minton, quintain, Winton • badminton

ints \ins\ see INCE

inty \int-ē\ flinty, linty, minty, squinty • pepperminty

intz \ins\ see INCE

inue \in-yü\ sinew • continue • discontinue

inuous \in-yə-wəs\ sinuous • continuous • discontinuous

inus¹ \ī-nəs\ dryness, finis, highness, Minas, Minos, minus, shyness, sinus, slyness, spinous, spryness, vinous, wryness • Aquinas, Delphinus, echinus, Ictinus, Longinus, Plotinus, Quirinus • Antoninus, plus or minus • Pontus Euxinus

inus² \ē-nəs\ see ENUS¹

inute \in-ət\ see INNET

inx \iŋs\ jinx, links, lynx, minx, sphinx • hijinks, methinks • tiddledywinks

iny¹ \ī-nē\ briny, heinie, liny, piny, shiny, spiny, tiny, twiny, viny, whiny, winy • enshrinee, sunshiny

iny² \in-ē\ see INNY

inya \ē-nyə\ see ENIA²

inyan \in-yən\ see INION

inyl \īn-ᵊl\ see INAL¹

inys \in-əs\ see INIS¹

io¹ \ī-ō\ bayou, bio, Clio, Io • Chiclayo, Lucayo, Ohio • Cinco de Mayo

io² \ē-ō\ brio, Cleo, Clio, guyot, Krio, Leo, Rio, trio • caudillo, con brio, Negrillo, tornillo, Trujillo • Bío-Bío, cigarillo, Hermosillo, Manzanillo, ocotillo

iocese \ī-ə-səs\ see IASIS

iolate \ī-ə-lət\ see IOLET¹

iolet¹ \ī-ə-lət\ triolet, violate, violet, Violet • inviolate • dogtooth violet, shrinking violet, ultraviolet • African violet, near-ultraviolet

iolet² \ē-ə-lət\ see EOLATE

ion¹ \ī-ən\ ayin, Brian, Bryan, cyan, ion, lion, Lyon, Mayan, Ryan, scion, Zion • Amphion, anion, Biscayan, Ixion, Orion, Visayan • counterion, dandelion, Paraguayan, Uruguayan, zwitterion

ion² \ē-ən\ see EAN¹

ion³ \ē-än\ see EON²

ior \īr\ see IRE¹

iory \ī-ə-rē\ see IARY¹

iot \ī-ət\ see IET

ioter \ī-ət-ər\ see IETER

iouan \ü-ən\ see UAN

ious \ī-əs\ see IAS

ioux \ü\ see EW¹

ip \ip\ blip, chip, clip, dip, drip, flip, grip, grippe, gyp, hip, kip, lip, nip, pip, quip, rip, scrip, ship, sip, skip, slip, snip, strip, tip, trip, whip, yip, zip • airship, airstrip, atrip, backflip, blue-chip, bullwhip, call slip, catnip, chiefship, cleft lip, clerkship, corn chip, courtship, cowslip, deanship, death grip, drag strip, dress ship, ear clip, equip, felt-tip, fieldstrip, field trip, filmstrip, fireship, flagship, foul tip, friendship, frostnip, guildship, guilt-trip, gunship, half-slip, handgrip, hardship, harelip, headship, horsewhip, inclip, judgeship, jump ship, key grip, kingship, kinship, landslip, let rip, lightship, longship, lordship, Mendip, nonslip, outstrip, oxlip, palship, pink slip, pip-pip, princeship, Q-ship, queenship, reship, roach clip, road trip, rose hip, round-trip, saintship, sales slip, sea whip, sheep-dip, sideslip, spaceship, starship, steamship, storeship, strike-slip, take ship, tall ship, thaneship, township, transship, troopship, unship, unzip, V-chip, wardship, warship, white chip, wing tip • airmanship, athwartship, authorship, battleship, biochip, brinkmanship, censorship, chairmanship, chieftainship, churchmanship, comic strip, consulship, coverslip, crack the whip, dealership, draftsmanship, ego trip, ego-trip, externship, fellowship, filter tip, fingertip, gamesmanship, Gaza Strip, grantsmanship, helmsmanship, horsemanship, internship, ladyship, landing strip, leadership, lectureship, listenership, marksmanship, membership, mentorship, microchip, mother ship, motor ship, oarsmanship, overslip, ownership, paper clip, partnership, penmanship, pistol grip, pistol-whip, pogonip, power strip, praetorship, premiership, readership, ridership, rocket ship, rulership, rumble strip, salesmanship, scholarship, seamanship, showmanship, skinny-dip, speakership, sponsorship, sportsmanship, statesmanship, stewardship, studentship, swordsmanship, trusteeship, underlip, upmanship, viewership, weather ship, weather strip, workmanship • accountantship, acquaintanceship, apostleship, apprenticeship, artisanship, assistantship, attorneyship, championship, chancellorship, citizenship, commandership, companionship, containership, cross-ownership, dictatorship, directorship, discipleship, editorship, factory ship, Freudian slip, good-fellowship, governorship, guardianship, headmastership, instructorship, landownership, laureateship,

managership, median strip, Möbius strip, musicianship, ombudsmanship, one-upmanship, outdoorsmanship, overlordship, partisanship, postnasal drip, potato chip, professorship, protectorship, receivership, rejection slip, relationship, run a tight ship, shoot from the hip, stiff upper lip, survivorship, treasurership • alligator clip, ambassadorship, associateship, bipartisanship, entrepreneurship, free alongside ship, librarianship, nonpartisanship, pocket battleship, proprietorship, secretaryship, solicitorship

ipal \ē-pəl\ see EOPLE

ipari \ip-rē\ see IPPERY

ipatus \ip-ət-əs\ see IPITOUS

ipe \īp\ Cuyp, gripe, hype, pipe, ripe, slype, snipe, stipe, stripe, swipe, tripe, type, wipe • bagpipe, blood type, blowpipe, cold type, downpipe, drainpipe, flue pipe, half-pipe, hornpipe, hosepipe, lead-pipe, light pipe, n-type, pitch pipe, p-type, panpipe, pinstripe, rareripe, reed pipe, rock tripe, sideswipe, soil pipe, standpipe, stovepipe, tailpipe, tintype, touch-type, unripe, waist pipe, wild type, windpipe • allotype, ambrotype, archetype, calotype, collotype, corncob pipe, Dutchman's-pipe, ecotype, ferrotype, genotype, guttersnipe, haplotype, holotype, Linotype, liripipe, logotype, monotype, neotype, overripe, prototype, serotype, stenotype, Teletype, tuning pipe • daguerreotype, electrotype, Indian pipe, somatotype, stereotype

iped¹ \ī-pəd\ biped
• parallelepiped

iped² \īpt\ stiped, striped • pinstriped—*also* -ed *forms of verbs listed at* IPE

ipend \ī-pənd\ ripend, stipend

iper \ī-pər\ diaper, griper, hyper, piper, sniper, striper, viper, wiper • bagpiper, pied piper, pit viper, sandpiper • candy striper, pay the piper • stereotyper

iperous \ī-prəs\ see YPRESS

ipety \ip-ət-ē\ snippety
• peripety • serendipity

iph \if\ see IFF

iphany \if-ə-nē\ see IPHONY

ipher \ī-fər\ cipher, lifer
• decipher, encipher, pro-lifer
• right-to-lifer

iphery \if-rē\ see IFERY

iphon \ī-fən\ see YPHEN

iphony \if-ə-nē\ tiffany, Tiffany
• antiphony, epiphany, polyphony

ipi \ē-pē\ see EEPY

ipid \ip-əd\ lipid • insipid

iping \ī-piŋ\ piping, striping
• blood-typing—*also* -ing *forms of verbs listed at* IPE

ipit \ip-ət\ see IPPET

ipital \ip-ət-əl\ see IPETAL

ipitance \ip-ət-əns\ see IPOTENCE

ipitant \ip-ət-ənt\ see IPOTENT

ipitous \ip-ət-əs\ peripatus, precipitous • serendipitous

ipity \ip-ət-ē\ see IPETY

iple¹ \ip-əl\ see IPPLE

iple² \ī-pəl\ see YPAL

ipless \ip-ləs\ dripless, lipless, zipless

ipling \ip-liŋ\ Kipling, stripling
—*also* -ing *forms of verbs listed at* IPPLE

ipment \ip-mənt\ shipment
• equipment, transshipment

ipo \ēp-ō\ see EPOT

ipoli \ip-ə-lē\ see IPPILY

ipotence \ip-ət-əns\ omnipotence, precipitance

ipotent \ip-ət-ənt\ omnipotent, plenipotent, pluripotent, precipitant

ippe¹ \ip\ see IP

ippe² \ip-ē\ see IPPY

ippe³ \ēp\ see EEP

ipped \ipt\ see IPT

ippee \ip-ē\ see IPPY

ippen \ip-ən\ lippen, pippin

ipper \ip-ər\ chipper, clipper, dipper, dripper, flipper, gripper, kipper, quipper, nipper, ripper, shipper, sipper, skipper, slipper, snipper, stripper, tipper, tripper, whipper, zipper
• Big Dipper, blue-chipper, day-tripper, horsewhipper, mudskipper, Yom-Kippur
• bodice-ripper, double-dipper,

ego-tripper, gallinipper, lady's slipper, Little Dipper, skinny-dipper

ippery \ip-rē\ frippery, Lipari, slippery

ippet \ip-ət\ pipit, sippet, snippet, tippet, whippet • incipit

ippety \ip-ət-ē\ see IPETY

ippi \ip-ē\ see IPPY

ippie \ip-ē\ see IPPY

ippily \ip-ə-lē\ nippily, snippily, tripoli, Tripoli • Gallipoli

ippin \ip-ən\ see IPPEN

ipping \ip-iŋ\ clipping, dripping, lipping, nipping, ripping, shipping, whipping • double-dipping, skinny-dipping—*also* -ing *forms of verbs listed at* IP

ippingly \ip-iŋ-lē\ grippingly, nippingly, trippingly

ipple \ip-əl\ cripple, nipple, ripple, stipple, tipple, triple, Whipple • participle

ippur \ip-ər\ see IPPER

ippy \ip-ē\ chippy, dippy, drippy, flippy, hippie, hippy, Lippi, lippy, nippy, quippy, slippy, snippy, tippy, trippy, whippy, yippee, yippie, zippy • Xanthippe • Mississippi

ips \ips\ snips, thrips, yips • eclipse, ellipse, midships • amidships, athwartships, fish-and-chips, tidytips • apocalypse, lunar eclipse, solar eclipse, total eclipse
—*also* -s, -'s, *and* -s' *forms of*

nouns and -s *forms of verbs listed at* IP

ipse \ips\ see IPS

ipso \ip-sō\ dipso • calypso, Calypso

ipster \ip-stər\ hipster, quipster, tipster

ipsy \ip-sē\ see YPSY

ipt \ipt\ crypt, hipped, lipped, ripped, script • conscript, decrypt, encrypt, harelipped, postscript, prescript, rescript, subscript, tight-lipped, transcript, typescript • eucalypt, filter-tipped, manuscript, nondescript, shooting script, superscript, swivel-hipped
—*also* -ed *forms of verbs listed at* IP

ipter \ip-tər\ scripter • lithotripter

iptic \ip-tik\ see YPTIC

iption \ip-shən\ ascription, conniption, conscription, decryption, description, Egyptian, encryption, inscription, prescription, proscription, subscription, transcription • circumscription, nonprescription

iptive \ip-tiv\ ascriptive, descriptive, inscriptive, prescriptive, proscriptive

iptych \ip-tik\ see YPTIC

ipular \ip-yə-lər\ stipular • manipular

ipy \ī-pē\ stripy, typey • stenotypy • daguerrotypy, stereotypy

iquant \ē-kənt\ see ECANT

ique \ēk\ see EAK[1]

iquey \ē-kē\ see EAKY

iquish \ē-kish\ see EAKISH

iquitous \ik-wət-əs\ iniquitous, ubiquitous

iquity \ik-wət-ē\ antiquity, iniquity, obliquity, ubiquity

iquor \ik-ər\ see ICKER[1]

ir[1] \ir\ see EER[2]

ir[2] \ər\ see EUR[1]

ira[1] \ir-ə\ see ERA[2]

ira[2] \ī-rə\ see YRA

irable \ī-rə-bəl\ wirable
• acquirable, desirable, respirable • undesirable

iracle \ir-i-kəl\ see ERICAL[2]

irae \īr-ē\ see IRY[1]

iral \ī-rəl\ chiral, gyral, spiral, viral

irant \ī-rənt\ spirant, tyrant
• aspirant

irate \ir-ət\ see IRIT

irby \ər-bē\ see ERBY

irca \ər-kə\ see URKA[1]

irce \ər-sē\ see ERCY

irch \ərch\ see URCH

irchen[1] \ər-chən\ see URCHIN

irchen[2] \ər-kən\ see IRKIN

ircher \ər-chər\ Bircher, nurture

irchist \ər-chəst\ Birchist
• researchist

ircon \ər-kən\ see IRKIN

ircuit \ər-kət\ circuit • borscht circuit, closed-circuit, ride circuit, short-circuit, trifurcate
• microcircuit, printed circuit

ircular \ər-kyə-lər\ circular
• opercular, tubercular
• semicircular

ird \ərd\ bird, burred, curd, furred, gird, heard, Heard, herd, nerd, spurred, surd, third, urd, word • absurd, bean curd, begird, bellbird, blackbird, bluebird, boobird, buzzword, byword, Cape Verde, catbird, catchword, cowbird, cowherd, crossword, cussword, engird, game bird, ghost word, guide word, headword, jailbird, jaybird, key word, kingbird, last word, loanword, lovebird, lyrebird, my word, oilbird, password, potsherd, railbird, rainbird, redbird, reword, ricebird, seabird, Sigurd, shorebird, snakebird, snowbird, songbird, state bird, sunbird, surfbird, swearword, swineherd, textured, ungird, unheard, watchword, yardbird
• afterword, bowerbird, butcher-bird, cedarbird, dickey bird, dirty word, dolly bird, early bird, fighting word, frigate bird, gallows bird, hummingbird, in a word, ladybird, lemon curd, mockingbird, ovenbird, overheard, riflebird, tailorbird, thunderbird, undergird, wading bird, wattlebird, weasel word, weaverbird, whirlybird, word for word—also -ed forms of verbs listed at EUR[1]

irder \ərd-ər\ see ERDER

irdie \ərd-ē\ see URDY

irdle \ərd-ᵉl\ see URDLE

irdum \ərd-əm\ dirdum
• reductio ad absurdum

ire¹ \īr\ briar, byre, choir, crier, dire, drier, fire, flier, friar, fryer, gyre, hire, ire, liar, lyre, mire, prier, prior, pyre, quire, shire, sire, Speyer, spier, spire, squire, tier, tire, trier, tyer, Tyre, wire, zaire • acquire, admire, afire, Altair, aspire, attire, backfire, balefire, barbed wire, barbwire, bemire, Blantyre, blow-dryer, bonfire, brushfire, bushfire, campfire, catbrier, catch fire, cease-fire, complier, conspire, cross fire, defier, denier, desire, drumfire, empire, Empire, entire, esquire, expire, flytier, for hire, fox fire, grandsire, Greek fire, greenbrier, grey friar, gunfire, hang fire, haywire, hellfire, highflier, high-wire, hot-wire, inquire, inspire, live wire, misfire, on fire, outlier, perspire, pismire, prior, quagmire, replier, require, respire, retire, rimfire, saltire, samphire, sapphire, satire, sea fire, Shropshire, snow tire, spitfire, surefire, suspire, sweetbriar, tightwire, town crier, transpire, trip wire, umpire, vampire, watch fire, white friar, wildfire • amplifier, ball of fire, balloon tire, beautifier, Biedermeier, butterflyer, certifier, chicken wire, classifier, fly-by-wire, fortifier, gasifier, glorifier, lammergeier, like wildfire, magnifier, modifier, multiplier, nitrifier, nullifier, pacifier, play with fire, purifier, qualifier, quantifier, rapid-fire, ratifier, razor wire, rectifier, retrofire, Ring of Fire, sanctifier, signifier, simplifier, specifier, star sapphire, testifier, under fire, versifier, vilifier • baptism of fire, British Empire, down-to-the-wire, identifier, Inland Empire, intensifier, Saint Elmo's fire, Second Empire, under the wire, water saffire • concertina wire, iron in the fire • Holy Roman Empire—*also -er forms of adjectives listed at* Y¹

ire² \ir\ see EER²

ire³ \īr-ē\ see IRY¹

ire⁴ \ər\ see EUR

ired \īrd\ fired, spired, tired, wired • all-fired, hardwired, inspired, retired—*also -ed forms of verbs listed at* IRE¹

ireless \īr-ləs\ fireless, tireless, wireless

ireman \īr-mən\ fireman, wireman

irement \īr-mənt\ acquirement, environment, requirement, retirement • semiretirement

iren \ī-rən\ Byron, Myron, siren
• environ • ribavirin

irge \ərj\ see URGE

irgin \ər-jən\ see URGEON

irgo \ər-gō\ see ERGO

iri \ir-ē\ see EARY

iriam \ir-ē-əm\ see ERIUM

iric \ir-ik\ see ERIC[2]

irile \ir-əl\ see ERAL[1]

irin \ī-rən\ see IREN

irine \ī-rən\ see IREN

iring \īr-iŋ\ firing, wiring
• inspiring, retiring—*also* -ing
forms of verbs listed at [1]IRE

irious \ir-ē-əs\ see ERIOUS

iris \ī-rəs\ see IRUS

irish \īr-ish\ Irish, squirish
• vampirish

irit \ir-ət\ Meerut, spirit • dispirit,
emirate, free spirit, inspirit,
proof spirit, vizierate • Holy
Spirit • familiar spirit

irium \ir-ē-əm\ see ERIUM

irius \ir-ē-əs\ see ERIOUS

irk[1] \irk\ birk, kirk

irk[2] \ərk\ see ORK[1]

irker \ər-kər\ see ORKER[1]

irkie \ər-kē\ see ERKY

irkin \ər-kən\ firkin, gherkin,
jerkin, Serkin, zircon
• Gelsenkirchen

irky \ər-kē\ see ERKY

irl[1] \ərl\ birl, burl, churl, curl, dirl,
earl, furl, girl, hurl, knurl,
merle, Merle, pearl, Pearl, purl,
skirl, squirrel, swirl, thirl, thurl,
tirl, twirl, virl, whirl, whorl
• aswirl, awhirl, ball girl, bat girl,
B-girl, call girl, cowgirl, home
girl, impearl, pas seul, pin curl,
playgirl, salesgirl, schoolgirl,
shopgirl, showgirl, spit curl,
uncurl, unfurl • Camp Fire girl,
chorus girl, cover girl, flower
girl, Gibson girl, pinup girl,
poster girl, sweater girl, Valley
girl • mother-of-pearl

irl[2] \irl\ dirl, skirl

irler \ər-lər\ birler, curler, pearler,
twirler, whirler

irley \ər-lē\ see URLY

irlie \ər-lē\ see URLY

irling \ər-liŋ\ see URLING

irlish \ər-lish\ see URLISH

irly \ər-lē\ see URLY

irm \ərm\ see ORM[1]

irma \ər-mə\ see ERMA

irmary \ərm-rē\ spermary
• infirmary

irmess \ər-məs\ see ERMIS

irmity \ər-mət-ē\ furmity
• infirmity

irmy \ər-mē\ see ERMY

irn[1] \irn\ firn, girn, pirn

irn[2] \ərn\ see URN

iro[1] \ir-ō\ see ERO[3]

iro[2] \ē-rō\ see ERO[1]

iro[3] \ī-rō\ see YRO[1]

iron[1] \īrn\ iron • andiron, cast-
iron, environ, flatiron, gridiron,
pig iron, pump iron, sadiron,
steam iron, wrought iron
• angle iron, climbing iron,
curling iron, shooting iron,
waffle iron • soldering iron

iron[2] \ī-rən\ see IREN

ironment \īr-mənt\ see IREMENT

irp \ərp\ see URP

irps \ərps\ stirps, turps—*also* -s, -'s, *and* -s' *forms of nouns and* -s *forms of verbs listed at* URP

irpy \ər-pē\ chirpy • Euterpe

irque \ərk\ see ORK[1]

irr[1] \ir\ see EER[2]

irr[2] \ər\ see EUR[1]

irra \ir-ə\ see ERA[2]

irrah \ir-ə\ see ERA[2]

irrel[1] \ərl\ see IRL[1]

irrel[2] \ər-əl\ see ERRAL

irrely \ər-lē\ see URLY

irrer \ər-ər\ see ERRER

irrhous \ir-əs\ see EROUS

irring \ər-iŋ\ see URRING

irror \ir-ər\ see EARER[2]

irrup \ər-əp\ chirrup, stirrup, syrup • corn syrup, cough syrup • maple syrup

irrupy \ər-ə-pē\ chirrupy, syrupy

irrus \ir-əs\ see EROUS

irry \ər-ē\ see URRY

irs \irz\ see IERS

irse[1] \irs\ see IERCE

irse[2] \ərs\ see ERSE

irst \ərst\ see URST

irt \ərt\ see ERT[1]

irted \ərt-əd\ see ERTED

irter \ərt-ər\ see ERTER

irth \ərth\ berth, birth, dearth, earth, firth, girth, mirth, Perth, worth • Ainsworth, brown earth, childbirth, Cudworth, Edgeworth, Ellsworth, Farnsworth, Fort Worth, give birth, Harmsworth, Hepworth, on earth, rare earth, rebirth, scorched-earth, self-worth, stillbirth, Tamworth, unearth, Wandsworth, Wentworth, Woolworth, Wordsworth • afterbirth, down-to-earth, fuller's earth, Moray Firth, pennyworth, Solway Firth, two cents' worth, virgin birth, wrongful birth

irthful \ərth-fəl\ mirthful, worthful

irthless \ərth-ləs\ mirthless, worthless

irtinent \ərt-nənt\ pertinent • appurtenant, impertinent

irting \ərt-iŋ\ see ERTING

irtle \ərt-ᵊl\ see ERTILE

irtually \ərch-lē\ see URCHLY

irtue \ər-chə\ see ERCHA

irty \ərt-ē\ dirty, flirty, QWERTY, shirty, thirty • down and dirty, thirty-thirty

irus \ī-rəs\ Cyrus, gyrus, iris, Iris, Skyros, virus • AIDS virus, desirous, Epirus, Osiris, papyrus, slow virus • arbovirus, bearded iris, echovirus, hantavirus, herpesvirus, lentivirus, Marburg virus, parvovirus, rhinovirus, rotavirus, West Nile virus

irv \ərv\ see ERVE

irving \ər-viŋ\ see ERVING

irwin \ər-wən\ see ERWIN

iry \ī-rē\ diary, eyrie, friary, miry, spiry, wiry • expiry, inquiry, venire • praemunire • anno hegirae, court of inquiry

is¹ \is\ see ISS¹

is² \iz\ see IZ¹

is³ \ē\ see EE¹

is⁴ \ēs\ see IECE

is⁵ \ish\ see ISH¹

i's \īz\ see IZE

isa¹ \ē-zə\ see EZA

isabeth \iz-ə-beth\ see IZABETH

isable \ī-zə-bəl\ see IZABLE

isal¹ \ī-səl\ Faisal, IJssel, sisal, skysail, trysail • paradisal

isal² \ī-zəl\ Geisel, sisal • incisal, reprisal, revisal, surprisal • paradisal

isan \is-ᵊn\ see ISTEN

isbane \iz-bən\ see ISBON

isbe \iz-bē\ Frisbee, Thisbe

isbee \iz-bē\ see ISBE

isbon \iz-bən\ Brisbane, Lisbon

isc \isk\ see ISK

iscable \is-kə-bəl\ confiscable, episcopal

iscan \is-kən\ see ISKIN

iscate \is-kət\ see ISKET

isce \is\ see ISS¹

iscean¹ \ī-sē-ən\ Piscean • Dionysian

iscean² \is-kē-ən\ Piscean • saurischian • ornithischian

iscean³ \is-ē-ən\ see YSIAN¹

iscence \is-ᵊns\ puissance • dehiscence, impuissance • indehiscence, reminiscence, reviviscence

iscent \is-ᵊnt\ puissant • dehiscent, impuissant • indehiscent, reminiscent, reviviscent

isces \ī-sēz\ see ICES

ische \ēsh\ see ICHE²

ischian \is-kē-ən\ see ISCEAN²

iscia \ish-ə\ see ITIA

iscible \is-ə-bəl\ see ISSIBLE

iscience \ish-əns\ see ICIENCE

iscient \ish-ənt\ see ICIENT

isco \is-kō\ cisco, disco • Francisco, Jalisco, Morisco • San Francisco

iscopal \is-kə-bəl\ see ISCABLE

iscous \is-kəs\ see ISCUS

iscuit \is-kət\ see ISKET

iscus \is-kəs\ discus, viscous, viscus • hibiscus, meniscus

ise¹ \ēs\ see IECE

ise² \ēz\ see EZE

ise³ \īs\ see ICE¹

ise⁴ \īz\ see IZE

ised¹ \īst\ see IST¹

ised² \īzd\ see IZED

isel \iz-əl\ see IZZLE

iseled \iz-əld\ see IZZLED

iseler \iz-lər\ see IZZLER

isement \īz-mənt\ advisement, chastisement, despisement, disguisement • advertisement, disfranchisement, enfranchisement • disenfranchisement

iser \ī-zər\ see IZER

ises \ī-sēz\ see ICES

ish¹ \ish\ dish, fiche, fish, flysch, Gish, Nis, pish, squish, swish, whish, wish • batfish, billfish, blackfish, blindfish, blowfish, bluefish, bonefish, catfish, clownfish, codfish, cold fish, cowfish, crawfish, crayfish, death wish, deep-dish, dogfish, filefish, finfish, flatfish, fly-fish, game fish, garfish, globefish, goatfish, goldfish, goosefish, hagfish, hogfish, Irtysh, jewfish, kingfish, knish, lungfish, lumpfish, milkfish, monkfish, moonfish, oarfish, panfish, pigfish, pinfish, pipefish, ratfish, redfish, rockfish, rough fish, sailfish, sawfish, shellfish, side dish, spearfish, sport fish, starfish, stonefish, sunfish, swordfish, tilefish, toadfish, trash fish, trunkfish, unwish, weakfish, whitefish • angelfish, anglerfish, archerfish, bony fish, butterfish, candlefish, Cavendish, chafing dish, cuttlefish, damselfish, devilfish, flying fish, guitarfish, jawless fish, jellyfish, John Bullish, ladyfish, lantern fish, lionfish, microfiche, muttonfish, needlefish, overfish, paddlefish, parrot fish, petri dish, pilot fish, puffer fish, rainbow fish, ribbonfish, silverfish, surgeonfish, trigger-fish, zebra fish • butterfly fish, channel catfish, gefilte fish, kettle of fish, mosquito fish, porcupine fish, satellite dish, scorpion fish, tropical fish, walking catfish

ish² \ēsh\ see ICHE²

isha \ish-ə\ see ITIA

ishable \ish-ə-bəl\ fishable • justiciable

ished \isht\ dished, whisht—*also* -ed *forms of verbs listed at* ISH¹

isher \ish-ər\ fisher, fissure, swisher • ill-wisher, kingfisher, well-wisher

ishery \ish-rē\ fishery, Tishri • shellfishery

ishi \ē-shē\ chichi, specie • maharishi

ishing \ish-iŋ\ bonefishing, fly-fishing, sportfishing, well-wishing—*also* -ing *forms of verbs listed at* ISH¹

ishioner \ish-nər\ see ITIONER

ishna \ish-nə\ Krishna, Mishnah

ishnah \ish-nə\ see ISHNA

isht \isht\ see ISHED

ishu \ish-ü\ see ISSUE¹

ishy \ish-ē\ dishy, fishy, squishy, swishy

isi¹ \ē-zē\ see EASY¹

isi² \ē-sē\ see EECY

isia¹ \izh-ə\ baptisia, Tunisia • artemisia, Dionysia

isia² \ē-zhə\ see ESIA²

isian¹ \izh-ən\ see ISION

isian² \ē-zhən\ see ESIAN¹

isible \iz-ə-bəl\ risible, visible
• divisible, invisible • indivisible

isin \i-zən\ see ISON²

ising \ī-ziŋ\ see IZING

ision \izh-ən\ fission, Frisian, scission, vision • abscission, collision, concision, decision, derision, division, dream vision, elision, elysian, envision, excision, incision, Leavisian, misprision, Nevisian, North Frisian, Parisian, precisian, precision, prevision, provision, recision, rescission, revision, Tunisian • cell division, circumcision, Dionysian, double vision, field of vision, imprecision, indecision, long division, short division, split decision, subdivision, supervision, television, tunnel vision

isional \izh-nəl\ visional
• collisional, decisional, divisional, excisional, previsional, provisional

isis \ī-səs\ crisis, Isis, lysis, nisus
• Dionysus, midlife crisis
• stare decisis

isit \iz-ət\ visit • exquisite, revisit

isite \iz-ət\ see ISIT

isitive \iz-ət-iv\ acquisitive, inquisitive

isitor \iz-ət-ər\ visitor
• acquisitor, inquisitor

isive¹ \ī-siv\ decisive, derisive, divisive, incisive • indecisive

isk \isk\ bisque, brisk, disk, fisc, frisk, risk, whisk • fly whisk,

hard disk, lutefisk, slipped disk, sun disk • assigned risk, asterisk, basilisk, blastodisc, compact disc, floppy disk, laser disc, obelisk, odalisque, optic disk, tamarisk • optical disk, videodisc

isker \is-kər\ frisker, risker, whisker

isket \is-kət\ biscuit, brisket, frisket

iskey \is-kē\ see ISKY

iskie \is-kē\ see ISKY

isky \is-kē\ frisky, pliskie, risky, whiskey

island \ī-lənd\ see IGHLAND

islander \ī-lən-dər\ see
IGHLANDER

islands \ī-lənz\ see IGHLANDS

isle \īl\ see ILE¹

isles \īlz\ see ILES

islet \ī-lət\ see ILOT

isling \iz-liŋ\ brisling, quisling

isly \iz-lē\ see IZZLY

ism \iz-əm\ chrism, chrisom, ism, prism, schism • abysm, ageism, autism, baalism, baptism, Birchism, bossism, bruxism, Buddhism, casteism, centrism, charism, Chartism, chemism, classism, cubism, cultism, czarism, deism, dwarfism, faddism, fascism, fauvism, Gaullism, Grecism, Hobbism, holism, Jainism, Klanism, leftism, lyrism, Mahdism, Maoism, Marxism,

monism, mutism, Nazism,
nudism, Orphism, priggism,
purism, racism, Ramism,
rightism, sadism, Saivism,
sapphism, Scotism, sexism,
Shaktism, Shiism, Sikhism,
simplism, snobbism, sophism,
statism, Sufism, tachism,
Tantrism, Taoism, theism,
Thomism, tourism, tropism,
truism, Turkism, verism,
Whiggism, Yahwism • absurd-
ism, activism, Adventism,
alarmism, albinism, alpinism,
altruism, amorphism, anarchism,
aneurysm, anglicism, animism,
aphorism, Arabism, archaism,
asterism, atavism, atheism,
atomism, atticism, Bahaism,
barbarism, Benthamism,
biblicism, blackguardism,
bolshevism, boosterism,
botulism, bourbonism,
Brahmanism, Briticism,
Byronism, cabalism, Caesarism,
Calvinism, can-do-ism,
careerism, Castroism,
cataclysm, catechism,
Catharism, centralism,
chauvinism, chimerism,
classicism, colorism,
communism, concretism,
conformism, cretinism,
criticism, cronyism, cynicism,
dadaism, dandyism,
Darwinism, defeatism, de
Gaullism, despotism, die-
hardism, dimorphism,
dirigisme, Docetism, do-
goodism, dogmatism,
Donatism, Don Juanism,
druidism, dualism, dynamism,
egoism, egotism, elitism,
embolism, endemism, erethism,

ergotism, erotism, escapism,
Essenism, etatism, eunuchism,
euphemism, euphuism,
exorcism, expertism,
extremism, fairyism, familism,
fatalism, feminism, feudalism,
fideism, Fidelism, fogyism,
foreignism, formalism, futurism,
Galenism, gallicism, galvanism,
gangsterism, genteelism,
Germanism, giantism,
gigantism, globalism,
gnosticism, Gongorism,
Gothicism, gourmandism,
gradualism, grangerism,
greenbackism, Hasidism,
heathenism, Hebraism,
hedonism, Hellenism, helotism,
herbalism, hermetism,
hermitism, heroism,
highbrowism, Hinduism,
hipsterism, hirsutism,
hispanism, Hitlerism,
hoodlumism, hoodooism,
hucksterism, humanism,
Hussitism, hybridism,
hypnotism, Ibsenism, idealism,
imagism, Irishism, Islamism,
Jansenism, jim crowism,
jingoism, journalism, John
Bullism, Judaism, Junkerism,
kabbalism, kaiserism,
Krishnaism, Ku Kluxism,
laconism, laicism, Lamaism,
Lamarckism, landlordism,
Latinism, legalism, Leninism,
lobbyism, localism, locoism,
Lollardism, luminism, lyricism,
magnetism, mammonism,
mannerism, Marcionism,
masochism, mechanism,
melanism, meliorism, Men-
shevism, Mendelism, mental-
ism, mesmerism, methodism,

me-tooism, modernism, Mohockism, monachism, monadism, monarchism, mongolism, Montanism, moralism, Mormonism, morphinism, mullahism, mysticism, narcissism, nationalism, nativism, nepotism, neutralism, new dealism, nihilism, NIMBYism, nomadism, occultism, onanism, optimism, oralism, Orangeism, organism, ostracism, pacifism, paganism, Pan-Slavism, pantheism, paroxysm, Parsiism, passivism, pauperism, pessimism, phallicism, pianism, pietism, plagiarism, Platonism, pleinairism, Plotinism, pluralism, pointillism, populism, pragmatism, presentism, privatism, prosaism, Prussianism, puerilism, pugilism, Puseyism, Pyrrhonism, Quakerism, quietism, rabbinism, racialism, rationalism, realism, reformism, rheumatism, rigorism, robotism, Romanism, Rousseauism, rowdyism, royalism, satanism, saturnism, savagism, scapegoatism, schematism, scientism, sciolism, Scotticism, Semitism, Shakerism, Shamanism, Shintoism, skepticism, socialism, solecism, solipsism, Southernism, specialism, speciesism, Spartanism, Spinozism, spiritism, spoonerism, Stalinism, standpattism, stoicism, syllogism, symbolism, synchronism, syncretism, synergism, talmudism, tarantism, tectonism, tenebrism, terrorism, Teutonism, titanism, Titoism, toadyism, tokenism, Toryism, totalism, totemism, transvestism, traumatism, tribalism, tritheism, Trotskyism, ultraism, unionism, urbanism, utopism, Vaishnavism, vampirism, vandalism, vanguardism, Vedantism, veganism, verbalism, virilism, vitalism, vocalism, volcanism, voodooism, vorticism, voyeurism, vulcanism, vulgarism, Wahhabism, warlordism, welfarism, Wellerism, witticism, womanism, yahooism, Yankeeism, Yiddishism, Zionism, zombiism • absenteeism, absolutism, abstractionism, adventurism, aestheticism, Africanism, Afrocentrism, agnosticism, alcoholism, amateurism, anabaptism, anachronism, Anglicanism, animalism, antagonism, Arianism, astigmatism, athleticism, automatism, behaviorism, Big Brotherism, bilingualism, Bonapartism, cannibalism, capitalism, Cartesianism, Catholicism, charlatanism, collectivism, commercialism, communalism, Confucianism, conservatism, constructivism, consumerism, corporatism, creationism, determinism, do-nothingism, eclecticism, ecotourism, ecumenism, egocentrism, empiricism, epicurism, eroticism, essentialism, ethnocentrism, evangelism, exoticism, expansionism, expressionism, Fabianism, factionalism, fanaticism, favoritism, federalism, Fenianism, feuilletonism, Fourierism, fraternalism, Freudianism, funambulism, functionalism, hermeticism, Hispanicism, historicism, hooliganism, illiberalism, illusionism, impressionism, infantilism, inflationism, initialism, insularism, irredentism, Jacobinism, Keynesianism, know-nothingism, lesbianism, liberalism, libertinism, literalism, Lutheranism, Lysenkoism, magic realism, malapropism, McCarthyism, mercantilism, messianism, metabolism, metamorphism, militarism, minimalism, monasticism, monetarism, monotheism, mutualism, naturalism, Naziritism, negativism, neologism, neo-Nazism, neorealism, nominalism, nonconformism, objectivism, obscurantism, obstructionism, opportunism, pacificism, Pantagruelism, parallelism, pastoralism, paternalism, patriotism, Peeping Tomism, perfectionism, photo-realism, plebeianism, polytheism, positivism, postmodernism, primitivism, progressivism, protectionism, Protestantism, provincialism, puritanism, radicalism, rationalism, recidivism, reductionism, regionalism, relativism, revisionism, revivalism, ritualism, romanticism, salvationism, sansculottism,

scholasticism, sectionalism, secularism, separatism, serialism, Slavophilism, somnambulism, Stakhanovism, structuralism, subjectivism, surrealism, teetotalism, theocentrism, triumphalism, Uncle Tomism, ventriloquism, vigilantism, Wesleyanism, workaholism • abolitionism, academicism, agrarianism, anthropomorphism, anti-Semitism, bicameralism, colloquialism, colonialism, constitutionalism, cosmo-politism, ecumenicism, exceptionalism, exhibitionism, existentialism, fundamentalism, Hegelianism, hermaphroditism, hyperrealism, imperialism, industrialism, instrumentalism, interventionism, irrationalism, isolationism, Malthusianism, Manichaeanism, materialism, millennialism, Monophysitism, multilingualism, neoclassicism, Neoplatonism, neorealism, Nestorianism, Occidentalism, orientalism, parochialism, particularism, Pelagianism, phenomenalism, photo-journalism, pictorialism, Postimpressionism, profes-sionalism, pseudoclassicism, reconstructionism, repub-licanism, Rosicrucianism, sacerdotalism, self-determinism, sadomasochism, sectarianism, sensationalism, sentimentalism, spiritualism, Tractarianism, traditionalism, transcendental-ism, trilateralism, ultra-montanism, universalism, utopianism, vocationalism

isma \iz-mə\ charisma, melisma

ismal \iz-məl\ see YSMAL

isme[1] \īm\ see IME[1]

isme[2] \iz°m\ see ISM

ismo \ēz-mō\ machismo, verismo • caudillismo

iso \ē-sō\ miso, piso

isom \iz-əm\ see ISM

ison[1] \īs-°n\ bison, hyson, Meissen • streptomycin

ison[2] \iz-°n\ dizen, mizzen, prison, risen, weasand, wizen • arisen, imprison, Tok Pisin, uprisen

isor \ī-zər\ see IZER

isored \ī-zərd\ guisard, visored

isory \īz-rē\ advisory, provisory, revisory • supervisory

isp \isp\ crisp, lisp, LISP, wisp • will-o-the-wisp

isper \is-pər\ crisper, lisper, whisper • stage whisper

ispy \is-pē\ crispy, wispy

isque \isk\ see ISK

iss \is\ bis, bliss, bris, cis, Chris, cuisse, dis, Dis, hiss, kiss, miss, sis, Swiss, this, vis, wis • abyss, amiss, Brown Swiss, can't miss, coulisse, dehisce, dismiss, French kiss, iwis, koumiss, near miss, remiss, submiss • ambergris, dotted swiss, hit-and-miss, hit-or-miss, junior miss, reminisce, verdigris

issa \is-ə\ abscissa, Larissa, mantissa, Melissa, Orissa, vibrissa • Masinissa

issable \is-ə-bəl\ see ISSIBLE

issal \is-əl\ see ISTLE

issance \is-°ns\ see ISCENCE

issant \is-°nt\ see ISCENT

isse[1] \is\ see ISS

isse[2] \ēs\ see IECE

issed \ist\ see IST[2]

issel \is-əl\ see ISTLE

isser \is-ər\ hisser, kisser

issible \is-ə-bəl\ kissable, miscible • admissible, immiscible, municipal, omissible, permissible, remissible, transmissible • impermissible, inadmissible

issile \is-əl\ see ISTLE

ission[1] \ish-ən\ see ITION

ission[2] \izh-ən\ see ISION

issionable \ish-nə-bəl\ fissionable • conditionable

issioner \ish-nər\ see ITIONER

issive \is-iv\ missive • admissive, derisive, dismissive, emissive, permissive, submissive, transmissive

issome \is-əm\ lissome • alyssum

issor \iz-ər\ scissor, whizzer

issue[1] \ish-ü\ fichu, issue, tissue • at issue, nonissue, reissue, scar tissue, take issue, wedge issue • Mogadishu, overissue, standard issue

issue[2] \ish-ə\ see ITIA

issure \ish-ər\ see ISHER

issus \is-əs\ byssus, Issus, missus, Mrs. • narcissus, Narcissus

issy \is-ē\ hissy, missy, prissy, sissy

ist[1] \īst\ Christ, feist, heist, hist, Kleist, tryst • zeitgeist • Antichrist, black-a-vised, poltergeist—also -ed forms of verbs listed at ICE[1]

ist[2] \ist\ cist, cyst, fist, gist, grist, kist, list, Liszt, mist, schist, tryst, twist, whist, wist, wrist • A-list, assist, backlist, blacklist, B-list, checklist, consist, dean's list, delist, desist, encyst, enlist, entwist, exist, handlist, hit list, insist, life list, mailed fist, persist, playlist, protist, Rehnquist, resist, short list, short-list, subsist, untwist, wait-list, white list, wish list • catechist, coexist, dadaist, exorcist, intertwist, preexist • love-in-a-mist—also -ed forms of verbs listed at ISS

ist[3] \ēst\ see EAST[1]

ista[1] \ē-stə\ barista, turista • camorrista, fashionista, Fidelista, Sandinista • hasta la vista

ista[2] \is-tə\ crista, vista • arista, ballista • Chula Vista, sacahuiste

istaed \is-təd\ see ISTED

istal \is-təl\ Bristol, crystal, Crystal, distal, listel, pistil, pistol • liquid crystal, microcrystal, nanocrystal, polycrystal

istan \is-tən\ see ISTON

istance \is-təns\ see ISTENCE

istant \is-tənt\ see ISTENT

iste[1] \is-tē\ see ICITY[2]

iste[2] \ēst\ see EAST[1]

iste[3] \is-tə\ see ISTA[2]

isted \is-təd\ twisted, vistaed • closefisted, enlisted, hamfisted, hardfisted, limp-wristed, tightfisted, two-fisted, unlisted, untwisted, white-listed • ironfisted, unassisted—also -ed forms of verbs listed at IST[2]

istel \is-təl\ see IST[2]

isten \is-ən\ christen, glisten, listen, Nisan

istenable \is-nə-bəl\ listenable • medicinable

istence \is-təns\ distance • assistance, consistence, existence, insistence, longdistance, mean distance, outdistance, persistence, resistance, subsistence • coexistence, go the distance, inconsistence, inexistence, keep one's distance, nonexistence, nonresistance, preexistence, shouting distance, striking distance • aesthetic distance, passive resistance, public assistance

istency \is-tən-sē\ consistency, insistency, persistency • inconsistency, selfconsistency

istent \is-tənt\ distant • assistant, consistent,

existent, insistent, persistent, resistant, subsistent • coexistent, equidistant, inconsistent, inexistent, nonexistent, nonpersistent, nonresistant, preexistent, self-consistent, self-subsistent

ister \is-tər\ bister, blister, clyster, glister, klister, lister, Lister, mister, sister, tryster, twister • half sister, persister, resister, resistor, sob sister, solicitor, stepsister, tongue twister, transistor, weak sister • water blister

istery \is-trē\ see ISTORY

istful \ist-fəl\ tristful, wistful

isthmus \is-məs\ see ISTMAS

isti \is-tē\ see ICITY²

istic \is-tik\ cystic, distich, fistic, mystic • artistic, autistic, ballistic, Buddhistic, cladistic, cubistic, deistic, ekistic, eristic, fascistic, faunistic, floristic, heuristic, holistic, hubristic, juristic, linguistic, logistic, meristic, monistic, patristic, phlogistic, puristic, sadistic, simplistic, sophistic, statistic, stylistic, Taoistic, theistic, Thomistic, touristic, tropistic, truistic, veristic, wholistic, Yahwistic • activistic, agonistic, albinistic, alchemistic, altruistic, amoristic, anarchistic, animistic, annalistic, aphoristic, archaistic, atavistic, atheistic, atomistic, belletristic, cabalistic, Calvinistic, casuistic, catechistic, Catharistic, centralistic, chauvinistic, classicistic,

coloristic, columnistic, communistic, crosslinguistic, dadaistic, diaristic, dualistic, dyslogistic, egoistic, egotistic, essayistic, eucharistic, eulogistic, euphemistic, euphuistic, exorcistic, fabulistic, familistic, fatalistic, feministic, fetishistic, feudalistic, fideistic, folkloristic, formalistic, futuristic, gongoristic, haggadistic, Hebraistic, hedonistic, Hellenistic, humanistic, humoristic, idealistic, imagistic, inartistic, Jansenistic, jargonistic, jingoistic, journalistic, Judaistic, kabbalistic, Lamaistic, legalistic, manneristic, masochistic, mechanistic, melanistic, mentalistic, methodistic, modernistic, moralistic, narcissistic, nationalistic, nativistic, nepotistic, nihilistic, novelistic, onanistic, optimistic, pantheistic, parodistic, pessimistic, pianistic, pietistic, plagiaristic, Platonistic, pluralistic, pointillistic, populistic, pragmatistic, pugilistic, quietistic, realistic, Romanistic, sciolistic, shamanistic, shintoistic, socialistic, solecistic, solipsistic, specialistic, surrealistic, syllogistic, symbolistic, synchronistic, syncretistic, synergistic, terroristic, totalistic, totemistic, ultraistic, unrealistic, urbanistic, utopistic, vandalistic, verbalistic, vitalistic, voodooistic, voyeuristic, Zionistic • anachronistic, antagonistic, behavioristic, cannibalistic, capitalistic, characteristic, collectivistic, deterministic, expressionistic, extralinguistic, impressionistic, militaristic, metalinguistic, monopolistic, monotheistic, naturalistic, neologistic, opportunistic, paternalistic, polytheistic, propagandistic, psycholinguistic, reductionistic, relativistic, secularistic, socio-linguistic • imperialistic, materialistic, sadomasochistic, sociolinguistic

istical \is-ti-kəl\ mystical • deistical, eristical, linguistical, logistical, monistical, patristical, sophistical, statistical, theistical • alchemistical, atheistical, casuistical, egoistical, egotistical, exorcistical, pantheistical • biostatistical, hypocoristical, monotheistical, polytheistical

istich \is-tik\ see ISTIC

istics \is-tiks\ ballistics, ekistics, linguistics, logistics, patristics, statistics, stylistics • futuristics • biostatistics, criminalistics, psycholinguistics, vital statistics—*also* -s, -'s, *and* -s' *forms of nouns listed at* ISTIC

istie \is-tē\ see ICITY[2]

istil \is-təl\ see ISTAL

istin \is-tən\ see ISTON

istine \is-tən\ see ISTON

istle \is-əl\ bristle, fissile, gristle, missal, missile, scissile, thistle, whistle • abyssal, bull thistle, cruise missile, dickcissel, dismissal, epistle, globe thistle, musk thistle, star thistle, wolf whistle • blow the whistle, guided missile, wet one's whistle, pennywhistle • ballistic missile

istler \is-lər\ whistler, Whistler • epistler

istless \ist-ləs\ listless • resistless

istly \is-lē\ bristly, gristly, thistly • sweet cicely

istmas \is-məs\ Christmas, isthmus • Kiritimati

isto \is-tō\ Christo • aristo, Callisto

istol \is-təl\ see ISTAL

iston \is-tən\ Kristin, piston, Tristan • Philistine, phlogiston • amethystine

istor \is-tər\ see ISTER

istory \is-trē\ blistery, history, mystery • case history, consistory, life history, prehistory • ancient history, ethnohistory, natural history, oral history, psychohistory

istral \is-trəl\ mistral • magistral, sinistral

istress \is-trəs\ mistress • headmistress, postmistress, schoolmistress, sinistrous, taskmistress, toastmistress

istrophe \is-trə-fē\ antistrophe, epistrophe

istrous \is-trəs\ see ISTRESS

isty \is-tē\ see ICITY[2]

isus \ī-səs\ see ISIS

iszt \ist\ see IST[2]

it¹ \it\ bit, bitt, brit, Brit, chit, dit, fit, flit, frit, git, grit, hit, it, kit, knit, lit, mitt, nit, pit, Pitt, quit, sit, skit, slit, snit, spit, split, Split, sprit, teat, tit, twit, whit, wit, writ, zit • a bit, acquit, admit, armpit, backbit, backfit, base hit, befit, bowsprit, Brigitte, bushtit, catch it, cesspit, close-knit, cockpit, commit, cool it, culprit, cut it, demit, Dewitt, dimwit, dog it, do it, emit, firelit, fleapit, gaslit, get it, gill slit, godwit, hack it, half-wit, hard-hit, henbit, house-sit, legit, lit crit, make it, mess kit, misfit, mishit, moonlit, mosh pit, nitwit, no-hit, obit, omit, outfit, outwit, owe it, peewit, permit, pinch-hit, Prakrit, press kit, pulpit, refit, remit, rough it, sandpit, Sanskrit, scratch hit, snakebit, snake pit, starlit, stock split, submit, sunlit, switch-hit, tar pit, tidbit, tight-knit, tomtit, to wit, transmit, turnspit, twilit, two-bit, unfit, unknit, warp knit, watch it, weft knit, well-knit, with-it • babysit, benefit, bit-by-bit, borrow pit, cable-knit, candlelit, come off it, counterfeit, cuckoo spit, double knit, get with it, hissy fit, holy writ, hypocrite, infield hit, intermit, intromit, manumit, megahit, mother wit, out of it, put to it, recommit, retrofit, step on it • banana split, bully pulpit, cost-benefit, death benefit, extra-base hit, fringe benefit, goodness of fit, lickety-split, nothing for it, overcommit, sacrifice hit • jack-in-the-pulpit

it² \ē\ see EE¹

it³ \ət\ see EAT¹

ita¹ \īt-ə\ vita • amanita

ita² \ēt-ə\ cheetah, eta, Nita, pita, Rita, theta, vita, zeta • Akita, Anita, Bonita, bonito, casita, excreta, fajita, gordita, Granita, Juanita, Lolita, partita • amanita, arboreta, incognita, manzanita, margarita, senhorita, señorita • Bhagavad Gita

itable¹ \īt-ə-bəl\ citable, writable • excitable, ignitable, indictable • copyrightable, extraditable

itable² \it-ə-bəl\ see ITTABLE

itae \īt-ē\ see ITE²

itain \it-n\ see ITTEN

ital¹ \īt-əl\ title, vital • detrital, entitle, half title, nontitle, recital, requital, subtitle • disentitle, intravital, running title, supravital • courtesy title

ital² \it-əl\ see ITTLE

italer \it-əl-ər\ whittler, victualler • belittler, Hospitaler

italist \īt-əl-əst\ titlist, vitalist • recitalist

itan \īt-ən\ see IGHTEN

itant \īt-ənt\ mightn't • excitant, incitant, renitent

itany \it-ən-ē\ Brittany, dittany, litany

itch \ich\ bitch, ditch, fitch, flitch, glitch, hitch, itch, kitsch, niche, pitch, quitch, rich, snitch, stitch, such, switch, twitch, which, witch • backstitch,

bewitch, Bowditch, chain
stitch, clove hitch, cross-stitch,
enrich, fast-pitch, fast-twitch,
flame stitch, half hitch,
hemstitch, jock itch, lockstitch,
knit stitch, last-ditch, purl
stitch, slow-pitch, slow-twitch,
tent stitch, topstitch, unhitch,
whipstitch, wild pitch • bait and
switch, Blackwall hitch, blanket
stitch, concert pitch, czare-
vitch, featherstitch, fever pitch,
microswitch, perfect pitch,
rolling hitch, running stitch,
satin stitch, swimmer's itch,
timber hitch, toggle switch,
water witch • absolute pitch

itchen \ich-ən\ kitchen, richen
• soup kitchen • summer
kitchen

itchener \ich-nər\ Kitchener,
Michener

itcher \ich-ər\ hitcher, pitcher,
richer, snitcher, stitcher,
switcher • enricher, hemstitcher
• Lubavitcher, water witcher

itchery \ich-e-rē\ bitchery,
stitchery, witchery
• bewitchery, obituary

itches \ich-əz\ britches, riches
• in stitches • Dutchman's-
breeches—also -s, -'s, and -s'
forms of nouns and -s forms of
verbs listed at ITCH

itchman \ich-mən\ pitchman,
switchman

itchment \ich-mənt\
bewitchment, enrichment
• self-enrichment

itchy \ich-ē\ bitchy, glitchy, itchy,
kitschy, pitchy, twitchy, witchy

it'd \it-əd\ see ITTED

ite¹ \īt\ bight, bite, blight, bright,
byte, cite, dight, dite, Dwight,
fight, flight, fright, height, hight,
kite, knight, krait, kyte, light,
lite, might, mite, night, plight,
quite, right, rite, sight, site,
sleight, slight, smite, spite,
sprite, tight, trite, white, White,
wight, Wight, wite, wright,
Wright, write • affright, air right,
airtight, albite, Albright, alight,
all right, all-night, a mite, aright,
backbite, backlight, bauxite,
bedight, Birchite, birthright,
black light, bleed white, bob-
white, bombsight, box kite,
bullfight, calcite, campsite,
catfight, cockfight, contrite,
cordite, Cushite, daylight,
deadlight, delight, dendrite,
despite, dogfight, downlight,
downright, droplight, dust mite,
earthlight, excite, eyebright,
eyesight, fanlight, felsite, ferrite,
finite, fire blight, firefight,
firelight, first night, fistfight,
flashlight, fleabite, floodlight,
foresight, forthright, fortnight,
freewrite, frostbite, Gadite, gall
mite, gaslight, gastight,
ghostwrite, goethite, graphite,
green light, gummite, gunfight,
Gunite, half-light, halite,
Hamite, handwrite, headlight,
highlight, hindsight, Hittite,
homesite, hoplite, Hussite,
ignite, illite, infight, in-flight,
incite, indict, indite, insight, in
sight, invite, jacklight, jadeite,
key light, klieg light, lamplight,
late blight, leucite, Levite,
lighttight, lignite, limelight,

lintwhite, lowlight, Lucite, Luddite, lyddite, marmite, Melchite, Memphite, midnight, millwright, miswrite, moonlight, New Right, night-light, nitrite, off-site, off-white, on sight, on-site, outright, outsight, partite, peep sight, penlight, perlite, playwright, polite, preflight, prizefight, pyrite, quartzite, ratite, recite, red light, red-light, requite, respite, rewrite, rushlight, rust mite, safelight, samite, searchlight, Semite, Servite, Shemite, Shiite, shipwright, sidelight, sit tight, skintight, skylight, skywrite, slant height, smectite, snakebite, snow-white, sound bite, spaceflight, spotlight, stage fright, starlight, sternite, sticktight, stoplight, streetlight, stylite, sulfite, sunlight, Sunnite, taillight, termite, thermite, tonight, top-flight, torchlight, trothplight, Twelfth Night, twilight, twi-night, typewrite, unite, unsight, upright, uptight, wainwright, watch night, wax light, Web site, weeknight, wheelwright, white flight, white knight, x-height, York rite, zinc white • acolyte, aconite, aerolite, Ammonite, Amorite, amosite, anchorite, andesite, anthracite, antiwhite, apartheid, appetite, arsenite, azurite, Bakelite, bedlamite, Bengal light, Benthamite, biotite, bipartite, black-and-white, blatherskite, bleacherite, bring to light, Brooklynite, bryophyte, calamite, Canaanite, candle-light, Carmelite, Castroite,

catamite, cellulite, cenobite, chalcocite, Chester White, chestnut blight, Chinese white, columbite, coprolite, copyright, cryolite, crystallite, disinvite, disunite, divine right, dolerite, dolomite, dynamite, ebonite, epiphyte, eremite, erudite, expedite, extradite, Fahrenheit, featherlight, fight-or-flight, fly-by-night, gelignite, geophyte, gesundheit, gigabyte, Gilsonite, Hashemite, hematite, hemocyte, Hepplewhite, hessonite, Himyarite, Hitlerite, Houstonite, hug-me-tight, Hutterite, hyalite, Ibsenite, impolite, inner light, Ishmaelite, Isle of Wight, Israelite, Jacobite, Jerseyite, Josephite, kilobyte, kimberlite, laborite, lazulite, leading light, Leavisite, Leninite, leukocyte, Lewisite, lily-white, line of sight, localite, lympho-cyte, macrophyte, magnetite, malachite, manganite, Marcionite, Masonite, megabyte, Mennonite, Minorite, Moabite, Mr. Right, muscovite, Muscovite, Nazirite, neophyte, oocyte, open sight, out-of-sight, overbite, overflight, overnight, oversight, overwrite, parasite, patent right, perovskite, phagocyte, pilot light, plebiscite, proselyte, Puseyite, pyrrhotite, recondite, reunite, rhyolite, running light, Saint Paulite, saprolite, satellite, Scottish rite, second sight, see the light, self-ignite, serve one right, shergottite, socialite, sodalite, sodomite, speed of light, spider mite, Stagirite, stalactite, stalagmite, Sybarite, Sydneyite, taconite, tanzanite, terabyte, time-of-flight, traffic light, transfinite, transvestite, tripartite, troglodyte, Trotskyite, Ulsterite, ultralight, underwrite, urbanite, Very light, vigil light, Wahhabite, water right, water sprite, watertight, writ of right, Wycliffite, xerophyte, yesternight, zoophyte • adipocyte, alexandrite, amazonite, amoebocyte, amyl nitrite, anthophyllite, anti-Semite, butyl nitrite, cosmopolite, dermatophyte, electrolyte, embryophyte, exurbanite, gemütlichkeit, Gibeonite, Gileadite, go fly a kite, hermaphrodite, idiot light, Indo-Hittite, McCarthyite, meteorite, Michiganite, Midianite, multipartite, New Hampshirite, New Jerseyite, potato blight, property right, quadripartite, Rhode Island White, spermatocyte, substantive right, suburbanite, sweetness and light, theodolite, Turkish delight, Wyomingite • Areopagite, Great Australian Bight, Pre-Raphaelite, riparian right, titanium white, zodiacal light

ite² \īt-ē\ flighty, mighty, nightie, righty, whity • almighty, Almighty, Venite • Aphrodite, aqua vitae, arborvitae, high and mighty, lignum vitae, taedium vitae

ite³ \it\ see IT¹

ite⁴ \ēt\ see EAT¹

ited \īt-əd\ see IGHTED

iteful \īt-fəl\ see IGHTFUL

itely \īt-lē\ see IGHTLY

item \īt-əm\ item • line-item • ad infinitum, collector's item

itement \īt-mənt\ alightment, excitement, incitement, indictment • bill of indictment

iten \īt-ᵊn\ see IGHTEN

itener \īt-nər\ see IGHTENER

itent \īt-ᵊnt\ see ITANT

iteor \ēt-ē-ər\ see ETEOR

iter¹ \īt-ər\ biter, blighter, fighter, kiter, lighter, miter, niter, plighter, smiter, titer, writer • all-nighter, backbiter, braillewriter, bullfighter, dogfighter, exciter, firefighter, first-nighter, gauleiter, ghostwriter, gunfighter, highlighter, igniter, inciter, inditer, infighter, inviter, lamplighter, moonlighter, nail-biter, one-nighter, prizefighter, reciter, requiter, rewriter, screenwriter, scriptwriter, skywriter, songwriter, speechwriter, sportswriter, states' righter, street fighter, typewriter • candlelighter, copywriter, expediter, fly-by-nighter, freedom fighter, underwriter, und so weiter • teletypewriter —also -er forms of adjectives listed at ITE¹

iter² \it-ər\ see ITTER

iter³ \ēt-ər\ see EATER¹

iteral \it-ə-rəl\ clitoral, literal, littoral • sublittoral, triliteral

iterally \it-ər-lē\ see ITTERLY

iterate \it-ə-rət\ literate
• aliterate, illiterate, nonliterate, postliterate, preliterate, presbyterate, subliterate
• semiliterate

ites[1] \īt-ēz\ barytes, sorites, Thersites—*also* -s, -'s, *and* -s' *forms of nouns listed at* ITE[2]

ites[2] \īts\ see IGHTS

itey \īt-ē\ see ITE[2]

ith \ith\ fifth, frith, grith, kith, myth, pith, sith, smith, Smith, swith, with, withe • bear with, blacksmith, do with, forthwith, goldsmith, Goldsmith, go with, gunsmith, herewith, hold with, live with, locksmith, run with, songsmith, therewith, tinsmith, tunesmith, wherewith, whitesmith, wordsmith • batholith, be friends with, come out with, come up with, complete with, coppersmith, dispense with, eolith, fall in with, gastrolith, Granny Smith, Hammersmith, have done with, Hindemith, laccolith, make off with, megalith, metalsmith, microlith, monolith, neolith, put up with, reckon with, run off with, silversmith, take up with, walk off with, xenolith • come to grips with, do away with, get away with, get even with, go to bed with, have to do with, make away with, paleolith, run away with, wipe the floor with

ith[3] \ēt\ see EAT[1]

ith[4] \ēth\ see EATH[1]

ithe[1] \īth\ blithe, kithe, lithe, scythe, tithe, withe, writhe

ithe[2] \ith\ see ITH[2]

ithe[3] \ith\ see ITH[1]

ithee[1] \ith-ē\ see ITHY[2]

ithee[2] \ith-ē\ see ITHY[1]

ither \ith-ər\ blither, cither, dither, hither, slither, swither, thither, whither, wither, zither • come-hither, nowhither, somewhither

itherward \ith-ər-wərd\ hitherward, thitherward, whitherward

ithesome \īth-səm\ blithesome, lithesome

ithia \ith-ē-ə\ see YTHIA

ithic \ith-ik\ lithic • ornithic • batholithic, endolithic, Eolithic, granolithic, laccolithic, megalithic, Mesolithic, monolithic, neolithic, xenolithic • Paleolithic

ithing \ī-thiŋ\ tithing, trithing —*also* -ing *forms of verbs listed at* [1]ITHE

ithmic \ith-mik\ see YTHMIC

ithy[1] \ith-ē\ prithee, withy

ithy[2] \ith-ē\ mythy, pithy, prithee, smithy, withy

iti \ēt-ē\ see EATY

itia[1] \ish-ə\ Lycia, Mysia, wisha • Alicia, Cilicia, comitia, episcia, Galicia, indicia, Letitia, militia, Patricia, Phoenicia • Dionysia

itia[2] \ē-shə\ see ESIA[1]

itial \ish-əl\ see ICIAL

itian[1] \ish-ən\ see ITION

itian[2] \ē-shen\ see ETION[1]

itiate \ish-ət\ initiate, novitiate
 • uninitiate

itic \it-ik\ clitic, critic • arthritic, bauxitic, bronchitic, calcitic, chloritic, Cushitic, dendritic, enclitic, form critic, granitic, graphitic, Hamitic, jaditic, lignitic, mephitic, nephritic, New Critic, pleuritic, proclitic, pruritic, pyritic, rachitic, Sanskritic, Semitic, Shemitic, Sinitic, stylitic, sulfitic • ammonitic, anaclitic, analytic, anchoritic, anthracitic, catalytic, cenobitic, coprolitic, crystallitic, diacritic, dialytic, doleritic, dolomitic, dynamitic, eremitic, granulitic, higher critic, hypercritic, jesuitic, laryngitic, paralytic, parasitic, sodomitic, stalactitic, stalagmitic, sybaritic, syphilitic, thallophytic, thrombolytic, troglodytic, Ugaritic • anti-Semitic, cryptanalytic, electrolytic, hermaphroditic, meteoritic, Monophysitic, textual critic • psychoanalytic

itical \it-i-kəl\ critical • form-critical, Levitical, New Critical, political, uncritical • analytical, apolitical, cenobitical, diacritical, eremitical, hypercritical, hypocritical, impolitical, Jacobitical, jesuitical, parasitical, sodomitical, supercritical • geopolitical, meteoritical

itics \it-iks\ Semitics • analytics • meteoritics—*also* -s, -'s, *and* -s' *forms of nouns listed at* ITIC

itid \it-əd\ see ITTED

itimati \is-məs\ see ISTMAS

itin \īt-ᵉn\ see IGHTEN

iting \īt-iŋ\ biting, flyting, lighting, whiting, writing • backbiting, bullfighting, cockfighting, daylighting, exciting, freewriting, frostbiting, handwriting, infighting, inviting, nail-biting, newswriting, playwriting, prewriting, prizefighting, skywriting, songwriting, sportswriting, typewriting • picture writing, spirit writing • automatic writing—*also* -ing *forms of verbs listed at* [1]ITE

ition \ish-ən\ fission, hycian, mission, titian, Titian • addition, admission, ambition, attrition, audition, beautician, clinician, cognition, coition, commission, condition, contrition, demission, dentition, dismission, Domitian, edition, emission, ethician, fruition, ignition, Kittitian, lenition, logician, magician, Mauritian, monition, mortician, munition, musician, Mysian, nutrition, omission, optician, partition, patrician, perdition, permission, petition, Phoenician, physician, Politian, position, punition, remission, rendition, sedition, submission, suspicion, tactician, technician, tradition, transition, transmission, tuition, volition • abolition, acoustician, acquisition, admonition, aesthetician, air-condition, ammunition, apparition, apposition, coalition, coedition, competition, composition, cosmetician, decommission, decondition, definition, demolition, deposition, dietitian, Dionysian, disposition, disquisition, electrician, erudition, exhibition, expedition, exposition, extradition, first edition, imposition, in addition, inanition, in commission, inhibition, inquisition, intermission, intromission, intuition, linguistician, logistician, malnutrition, malposition, manumission, mathematician, mechanician, micturition, obstetrician, on commission, opposition, Ordovician, parturition, phonetician, politician, precognition, precondition, premonition, preposition, prohibition, proposition, recognition, recondition, repetition, requisition, rescue mission, rhetorician, self-ignition, statistician, submunition, superstition, supposition, text edition, trade edition, transposition • academician, arithmetician, biometrician, decomposition, dental technician, diagnostician, dialectician, disinhibition, family physician, fetal position, general admission, geometrician, geriatrician, high-definition, indisposition, interposition, juxtaposition, lotus position, metaphysician, onomastician, open admission, out of commission, pediatrician, pocket edition, presupposition, pyrotechnician, redefinition,

self-definition, self-recognition, semiotician, theoretician • fishing expedition, limited edition, superimposition

itionable \ish-nə-bəl\ see ISSIONABLE

itional \ish-nəl\ additional, attritional, cognitional, coitional, conditional, nutritional, positional, traditional, transitional, tuitional, volitional • acquisitional, apparitional, appositional, compositional, definitional, depositional, dispositional, expositional, inquisitional, intuitional, oppositional, prepositional, propositional, repetitional, suppositional, transpositional, unconditional

itioner \i-shə-nər\ missioner • commissioner, conditioner, parishioner, partitioner, petitioner, practitioner • air conditioner, exhibitioner, malpractitioner, nurse-practitioner • family practitioner, general practitioner

itionist \i-shə-nəst\ nutritionist, partitionist • abolitionist, coalitionist, demolitionist, exhibitionist, intuitionist, oppositionist, prohibitionist

itious \ish-əs\ see ICIOUS[1]

itis \īt-əs\ situs, Titus • arthritis, botrytis, bronchitis, bursitis, colitis, cystitis, detritus, gastritis, iritis, mastitis, nephritis, neuritis, phlebitis, rhinitis, tinnitus • adenitis, arteritis, cellulitis, dermatitis, enteritis, gingivitis, hepatitis, Heracleitus, ileitis, keratitis, laryngitis, meningitis, myelitis, pharyngitis, pneumonitis, Polyclitus, prostatitis, retinitis, sinusitis, tonsillitis, spondylitis, tendinitis, urethritis, vaginitis • appendicitis, conjunctivitis, encephalitis, endocarditis, endometritis, folliculitis, Hermaphroditus, pericarditis, peritonitis • diverticulitis, gastroenteritis, poliomyelitis

itish \it-ish\ British, skittish

itius \ish-əs\ see ICIOUS

itle \īt-ᵊl\ see ITAL¹

it'll \it-ᵊl\ see ITTLE

itment \it-mənt\ fitment • commitment, remitment • recommitment • overcommitment

itness \it-nəs\ fitness, witness • earwitness, eyewitness, unfitness • character witness, Jehovah's Witness

itney \it-nē\ jitney, Whitney • Mount Whitney

ito¹ \ēt-ō\ Ito, keto, Quito, Tito, veto • bandito, bonito, burrito, graffito, Lobito, magneto, Miskito, mosquito, Negrito, Spoleto • Akihito, Hirohito, incognito, pocket veto, sanbenito • line-item veto

ito² \ēt-ə\ see ITA²

iton¹ \it-ᵊn\ see ITTEN

iton² \īt-ᵊn\ see IGHTEN

itoral \it-ə-rəl\ see ITERAL

itra \ē-trə\ see ETRA²

itral \ī-trəl\ mitral, nitrile

itrile \ī-trəl\ see ITRAL

its \its\ blitz, ditz, fritz, Fritz, glitz, grits, its, it's, quits, Ritz, spitz, spritz • Auschwitz, Chemnitz, kibitz, Kollwitz, Saint Kitts, Stieglitz, Stiglitz • Clausewitz, Horowitz, Leibovitz, Markowitz, Saint Moritz, slivovitz • hominy grits—*also* -s, -'s, *and* -s' *forms of nouns and* -s *forms of verbs listed at* IT¹

it's \its\ see ITS

itsail \it-səl\ see ITZEL

itsch \ich\ see ITCH

itschy \ich-ē\ see ITCHY

itsy \it-sē\ see ITZY

itt \it\ see IT¹

itta \it-ə\ shittah, vitta

ittable \it-ə-bəl\ committable, habitable, hospitable, remittable, transmittable • inhospitable

ittah \it-ə\ see ITTA

ittal \it-ᵊl\ see ITTLE

ittance \it-ᵊns\ pittance, quittance • acquittance, admittance, emittance, immittance, remittance, transmittance • intermittence

ittany \it-ᵊn-ē\ see ITANY

itte \it\ see IT¹

itted \it-əd\ fitted, it'd, nitid, pitted, teated, witted • committed, dim-witted, fat-witted, half-witted, quick-witted, sharp-witted, slow-witted, thick-witted, unbitted, unfitted • uncommitted—*also* -ed *forms of verbs listed at* IT[1]

ittee \it-ē\ see ITTY

itten \it-ᵊn\ bitten, Britain, Briton, Britten, kitten, litten, Lytton, mitten, smitten, witting, written • backbitten, flea-bitten, Great Britain, hard-bitten, New Britain, rewritten, sex kitten, snakebitten, unwritten

ittence \it-ᵊns\ see ITTANCE

ittent \it-ᵊnt\ remittent • intermittent, intromittent

itter \it-ər\ bitter, chitter, critter, fitter, flitter, fritter, glitter, hitter, jitter, knitter, litter, quitter, quittor, sitter, skitter, slitter, spitter, titter, twitter • acquitter, aglitter, atwitter, beam splitter, bed-sitter, embitter, emitter, fence-sitter, gas fitter, hair-splitter, house sitter, no-hitter, outfitter, permitter, pinch hitter, pipe fitter, rail-splitter, remitter, Salzgitter, shipfitter, steamfitter, switch-hitter, transmitter • babysitter, benefiter, contact hitter, counterfeiter, heavy hitter, intermitter, intromitter • neurotransmitter

itterer \it-ər-ər\ fritterer, litterer

itterly \it-ər-lē\ bitterly, literally

ittern \it-ərn\ bittern, cittern, gittern

ittery \it-ə-rē\ glittery, jittery, littery, skittery, twittery

ittie \it-ē\ see ITTY

ittier \it-ē-ər\ Whittier—*also* -er *forms of verbs listed at* ITTY

ittiness \it-ē-nəs\ grittiness, prettiness, wittiness

itting[1] \it-iŋ\ fitting, knitting, pitting, sitting, splitting, witting • befitting, earsplitting, fee splitting, fence-sitting, form-fitting, hairsplitting, hard-hitting, house-sitting, pipe fitting, resitting, sidesplitting, steam fitting, unfitting, unwitting • unremitting—*also* -ing *forms of verbs listed at* IT[1]

itting[2] \it-ᵊn\ see ITTEN

ittish \it-ish\ see ITISH

ittle \it-ᵊl\ brittle, it'll, kittle, little, skittle, spital, spittle, tittle, victual, whittle, wittol • acquittal, a little, belittle, committal, Doolittle, hospital, in little, lickspittle, remittal, transmittal • Chicken Little, noncommittal, • little by little

ittler \it-ᵊl-ər\ see ITALER

ittol \it-ᵊl\ see ITTLE

ittor \it-ər\ see ITTER

ittoral \it-ə-rəl\ see ITERAL

itts \its\ see ITS

itty \it-ē\ bitty, city, ditty, gritty, kitty, Kitty, pity, pretty, tittie, witty • committee, Dodge City, edge city, self-pity, Sioux City • Carson City, central city, garden city, holy city, itty-bitty, Kansas City, little bitty, mega-city, New York City, nitty-gritty, open city, Quezon City, Rapid City, Salt Lake City, subcommittee, supercity, Walter Mitty • Atlantic City, Ho Chi Minh City, Long Island City, Mexico City, Panama City, Vatican City

itual \ich-ə-wəl\ ritual • habitual

ituary \ich-ə-rē\ see ITCHERY[1]

itum \īt-əm\ see ITEM

itus \īt-əs\ see ITIS

ity[1] \it-ē\ see ITTY

ity[2] \īt-ē\ see ITE[2]

itz \its\ see ITS

itza \ēt-sə\ pizza • Chichén Itzá, Katowice

itzel \it-səl\ schnitzel, spritsail • Wiener schnitzel

itzi \it-sē\ see ITZY

itzy \it-sē\ bitsy, ditzy, glitzy, Mitzi, ritzy, schizy

iu \ü\ see EW[1]

ius[1] \ē-əs\ see EUS[1]

ius[2] \ī-əs\ see IAS[1]

iv[1] \iv\ see IVE[2]

iv[2] \ēf\ see IEF[1]

iv[3] \if\ see IFF

iv[4] \ēv\ see EAVE

iva[1] \ī-və\ Saiva • gingiva, Godiva, saliva

iva[2] \ē-və\ diva, Eva, kiva, Neva, Shiva, viva • geneva, Geneva, yeshiva

ivable[1] \ī-və-bəl\ drivable • derivable, revivable, survivable

ivable[2] \iv-ə-bəl\ livable • forgivable

ival \ī-vəl\ rival • archival, archrival, arrival, ogival, revival, survival • adjectival, conjunctival, genitival, Greek Revival, substantival • Gothic Revival, infinitival

ivalent \iv-ə-lənt\ ambivalent, equivalent • unambivalent

ivan \iv-ən\ see IVEN

ivance \ī-vəns\ connivance, contrivance, survivance

ivative \iv-ət-iv\ privative • derivative

ive[1] \īv\ chive, Clive, dive, drive, five, gyve, hive, I've, jive, live, rive, shrive, skive, strive, thrive, wive • alive, archive, Argive, arrive, back dive, beehive, connive, contrive, crash-dive, deprive, derive, disk drive, endive, front drive, hard drive, high five, high-five, line drive, nosedive, ogive, revive, self-drive, skin-dive, skydive, survive, swan dive, take five, test-drive • eat alive, forty-five, four-wheel drive, friction drive, garlic chive, hyperdrive, overdrive, power-dive, scuba dive • Belgian endive, curly endive

ive[2] \iv\ give, live, sheave, shiv, sieve, spiv • forgive, misgive, outlive, relive, unlive • underactive

ive[3] \ēv\ see EAVE[1]

ivel \iv-əl\ civil, drivel, frivol, shrivel, snivel, swivel • uncivil

iven \iv-ən\ driven, given, riven, Sivan, striven, thriven • forgiven, self-given • menu-driven

iver¹ \ī-vər\ diver, driver, fiver, skiver, stiver, striver, thriver • arriver, cabdriver, conniver, contriver, deriver, free diver, mass driver, pile driver, reviver, screwdriver, skin diver, skydiver, slave driver, survivor

iver² \iv-ər\ flivver, giver, liver, quiver, river, shiver, sliver • almsgiver, aquiver, caregiver, chopped liver, deliver, downriver, East River, Fall River, fatty liver, forgiver, lawgiver, upriver, • Guadalquivir, up the river • Indian River, sell down the river

ivers¹ \ī-vərz\ divers, vivers —*also* -s, -'s, *and* -s' *forms of nouns listed at* IVER¹

ivers² \ē-vərz\ see EAVERS

ivery \iv-rē\ livery, shivery • delivery • breech delivery • general delivery, special delivery

ives \īvz\ fives, hives, Ives—*also* -s, -'s, *and* -s' *forms of nouns and* -s *forms of verbs listed at* IVE¹

ivet \iv-ət\ civet, divot, pivot, privet, rivet, swivet, trivet

ivi¹ \iv-ē\ see IVVY

ivi² \ē-vē\ see EAVEY

ivia \iv-ē-ə\ clivia, Bolivia, Olivia, trivia

ivial \iv-ē-əl\ trivial • convivial, quadrivial

ivid \iv-əd\ livid, vivid

ivil \iv-əl\ see IVEL

ivilly \iv-ə-lē\ civilly, privily • uncivilly

ivily \iv-ə-lē\ see IVILLY

iving \īv-iŋ\ giving, living • almsgiving, caregiving, forgiving, free-living, life-giving, misgiving, thanksgiving • cost of living, unforgiving • assisted living, standard of living—*also* -ing *forms of verbs listed at* ²IVE

ivion \iv-ē-ən\ Vivian • Bolivian, Maldivian, oblivion

ivious \iv-ē-əs\ lascivious, oblivious

ivir \iv-ər\ see IVER²

ivity \iv-ət-ē\ privity • acclivity, activity, captivity, declivity, festivity, motivity, nativity, passivity, proclivity • absorptivity, adaptivity, additivity, affectivity, aggressivity, coercivity, cognitivity, collectivity, compulsivity, conductivity, connectivity, creativity, destructivity, diffusivity, directivity, effectivity, emissivity, emotivity, exclusivity, exhaustivity, expansivity, expressivity, impassivity, impulsivity, inactivity, inclusivity, infectivity, negativity, objectivity, perceptivity, perfectivity, permittivity, positivity, primitivity, productivity,

progressivity, reactivity,
receptivity, reflexivity, relativity,
resistivity, retentivity,
selectivity, self-activity,
sensitivity, subjectivity,
transitivity • hyperactivity,
insensitivity, overactivity
• hypersensitivity, radioactivity

ivium \iv-ē-əm\ trivium
• quadrivium

iviut \ē-vē-ət\ see EVIATE

ivo \ē-vō\ see EVO

ivocal \iv-ə-kəl\ equivocal,
univocal • unequivocal

ivol \iv-əl\ see IVEL

ivor \ī-vər\ see IVER¹

ivorous \iv-rəs\ carnivorous,
granivorous, herbivorous,
omnivorous • insectivorous

ivot \iv-ət\ see IVET

ivus \ē-vəs\ see EVOUS

ivver \iv-ər\ see IVER²

ivvy \iv-ē\ chivy, civvy, divvy,
Livy, privy, skivvy • tantivy
• divi-divi

ivy \iv-ē\ see IVVY

iwi \ē-wē\ see EEWEE

ix¹ \iks\ Brix, Dix, fix, mix, nix,
pyx, six, Styx • admix, affix,
blanc fixe, commix, deep-six,
immix, infix, postfix, prefix,
premix, prix fixe, prolix, quick
fix, subfix, suffix, trail mix,
transfix, unfix • antefix, cicatrix,
crucifix, eighty-six, intermix,
politics, six-o-six, superfix
• geopolitics • RU 486—*also
-s, -'s, and -s' forms of nouns*

*and -s forms of verbs listed
at* ICK

ix² \ē\ see EE¹

ixal \ik-səl\ pixel • affixal,
prefixal, suffixal • megapixel

ixe¹ \ēks\ breeks • prix fixe, idée
fixe • Macgillicuddy's Reeks
—*also -s, -'s, and -s' forms of
nouns and -s forms of verbs
listed at* EAK¹

ixe² \iks\ see IX¹

ixe³ \ēsh\ see ICHE²

ixed \ikst\ fixed, mixed, twixt
• betwixt, well-fixed—*also -ed
forms of verbs listed at* IX¹

ixel \ik-səl\ see IXAL

ixen \ik-sən\ Dixon, Nixon, vixen
• Mason-Dixon

ixer \ik-sər\ fixer, mixer • elixir

ixia \ik-sē-ə\ asphyxia, panmixia

ixie \ik-sē\ Dixie, nixie, pixie,
pyxie, tricksy

ixion \ik-shən\ see ICTION

ixir \ik-sər\ see IXER

ixit \ik-sət\ quixote • ipse dixit

ixon \ik-sən\ see IXEN

ixote \ik-sət\ see IXIT

ixt \ikst\ see IXED

ixture \iks-chər\ fixture, mixture
• admixture, commixture,
immixture • bordeaux mixture,
intermixture

iya \ē-ə\ see IA¹

iyeh \ē-ə\ see IA¹

iz¹ \iz\ biz, fizz, frizz, his, is, Ms.,
phiz, quiz, 'tis, whiz, wiz

• Cádiz, gee-whiz, pop quiz, show biz

iz² \ēz\ see EZE

iza¹ \ē-zə\ see EZA

iza² \ē-thə\ see ETHA

izable \ī-zə-bəl\ sizable
• advisable, cognizable, devisable, excisable
• amortizable, analyzable, criticizable, customizable, dramatizable, exercisable, fertilizable, hypnotizable, inadvisable, localizable, magnetizable, mechanizable, memorizable, organizable, pulverizable, rationalizable, realizable, recognizable, satirizable, vaporizable

izar \ī-zər\ see IZER

izard \iz-ərd\ blizzard, gizzard, izzard, lizard, vizard, wizard
• horned lizard, lounge lizard
• thunder lizard

ize¹ \īz\ guise, prise, prize, rise, size, wise • abscise, advise, apprise, apprize, arise, assize, baptize, bite-size, breadthwise, capsize, chastise, clockwise, coastwise, cognize, comprise, crabwise, crack wise, crosswise, demise, despise, devise, disguise, disprize, door prize, downsize, earthrise, edgewise, emprise, endwise, excise, fanwise, franchise, full-size, grecize, high-rise, incise, king-size, leastwise, lengthwise, Levi's, life-size, likewise, low-rise, man-size, mid-rise, midsize, misprize, moonrise, nowise, outsize, piecewise,

pint-size, premise, quantize, queen-size, remise, reprise, revise, rightsize, slantwise, streetwise, stylize, suffice, sunrise, surmise, surprise, trim size, twin-size, unwise, uprise
• advertise, aggrandize, agonize, alchemize, amortize, analyze, anglicize, anodize, anywise, aphorize, arabize, arborize, atomize, authorize, autolyze, balkanize, barbarize, bastardize, bestialize, bolshevize, booby prize, botanize, bowdlerize, brutalize, burglarize, canalize, canonize, capsulize, caramelize, carbonize, cartelize, catalyze, catechize, cauterize, centralize, channelize, Christianize, cicatrize, circumcise, civilize, classicize, colonize, colorize, communize, compromise, concertize, concretize, creolize, criticize, crystalize, customize, demonize, deputize, dialyze, digitize, disfranchise, dogmatize, dramatize, elegize, empathize, emphasize, energize, enfranchise, enterprise, equalize, erotize, eternize, etherize, eulogize, euphemize, exercise, exorcise, factorize, fantasize, feminize, fertilize, feudalize, fictionize, finalize, focalize, formalize, formulize, fossilize, fragmentize, fraternize, gallicize, galvanize, germanize, ghettoize, glamorize, globalize, gormandize, gothicize, gourmandize, grecianize, harmonize, heathenize, hebraize, hellenize, heroize, hierarchize, humanize, hybridize,

hypnotize, idolize, immunize, improvise, iodize, ionize, ironize, Islamize, itemize, jeopardize, journalize, Judaize, laicize, latinize, legalize, lionize, liquidize, localize, magnetize, marbleize, martyrize, maximize, mechanize, melanize, melodize, memorize, merchandise, merchandize, mesmerize, methodize, metricize, minimize, mobilize, modernize, moisturize, monetize, mongrelize, moralize, motorize, mythicize, narcotize, nasalize, nebulize, neutralize, Nobel Prize, normalize, notarize, novelize, obelize, odorize, optimize, organize, ostracize, otherwise, oversize, oxidize, paganize, palletize, paradise, paralyze, pasteurize, patronize, pauperize, penalize, penny-wise, personalize, pidginize, plagiarize, plasticize, Platonize, pluralize, pocket-size, poetize, polarize, polemize, pressurize, privatize, profitwise, prussianize, publicize, pulverize, racialize, randomize, rationalize, realize, recognize, rhapsodize, robotize, romanize, rubberize, sanitize, satirize, scandalize, schematize, schismatize, scrutinize, sensitize, sermonize, signalize, simonize, sinicize, slenderize, sloganize, socialize, sodomize, solarize, solemnize, sonnetize, specialize, stabilize, Stalinize, standardize, sterilize, stigmatize, strategize, subsidize, summarize, supervise, syllogize, symbolize, sympathize, synchronize,

syncretize, synopsize, synthesize, systemize, tantalize, televise, temporize, tenderize, terrorize, tetanize, teutonize, texturize, theorize, thermalize, totalize, tranquilize, traumatize, tyrannize, unionize, unitize, urbanize, utilize, valorize, vandalize, vaporize, verbalize, vernalize, victimize, vitalize, vocalize, vulcanize, vulgarize, weather-wise, weatherize, westernize, winterize, womanize, worldly-wise • accessorize, acclimatize, actualize, aerobicize, aestheticize, Africanize, allegorize, alphabetize, analogize, anatomize, anesthetize, animalize, annualize, antagonize, anthologize, anticlockwise, apologize, apostatize, apostrophize, arabicize, aromatize, automatize, baby blue-eyes, bureaucratize, cannibalize, capitalize, categorize, catheterize, catholicize, characterize, collectivize, commercialize, commoditize, communalize, computerize, conservatize, containerize, contrariwise, conveyorize, cosmeticize, counterclockwise, criminalize, cross-fertilize, cryptanalize, cut down to size, decentralize, decolonize, de-emphasize, de-energize, defeminize, deformalize, deglamorize, dehumanize, deionize, demagnetize, demobilize, democratize, demoralize, denationalize, deodorize, depersonalize, depolarize, depressurize, desalinize, desensitize, destabilize, destigmatize, detribalize, devitalize, diabolize, digitalize, disenfranchise, disorganize, economize, emblematize, emotionalize, epitomize, epoxidize, eroticize, eternalize, euthanatize, evangelize, extemporize, externalize, familiarize, fanaticize, federalize, fictionalize, floor exercise, fool's paradise, formularize, free enterprise, gelatinize, generalize, geologize, Hispanicize, historicize, homogenize, hospitalize, hypothesize, idealize, illegalize, immobilize, immortalize, impersonalize, Indianize, indigenize, infantilize, initialize, internalize, italicize, legitimize, liberalize, literalize, lobotomize, lysogenize, macadamize, marginalize, metabolize, metastasize, militarize, mineralize, monop-olize, mythologize, nationalize, naturalize, parenthesize, philosophize, poeticize, politicize, popularize, prioritize, proselytize, Pulitzer prize, radicalize, regularize, re-organize, revitalize, ritualize, romanticize, secularize, self-fertilize, sensualize, sexualize, sovietize, subjectivize, suburbanize, subvocalize, systematize, temporalize, theologize, traditionalize, transistorize, trivialize, ventriloquize, visualize • Americanize, apotheosize, colonialize, compartmentalize, conceptualize, consolation

prize, contextualize, de-criminalize, delegitimize, demilitarize, denaturalize, departmentalize, depoliticize, desexualize, epigrammatize, etymologize, Europeanize, exteriorize, ideologize, immaterialize, individualize, industrialize, internationalize, legitimatize, materialize, memorialize, miniaturize, particularize, politicalize, private enterprise, pro-fessionalize, psychoanalyze, revolutionize, self-actualize, sensationalize, sentimentalize, spiritualize, underutilize, universalize • constitutionalize, dematerialize, editorialize, intellectualize—*also* -s, -'s, *and* -s' *forms of nouns and* -s *forms of verbs listed at* Y[1]

ize[2] \ēz\ *see* EZE

ized \īzd\ sized • advised, outsized • ergotized, ill-advised, king-sized, organized, pearlized, queen-sized, Sanforized, unadvised, undersized, varisized, well-advised • elasticized, modularized, unexercised • immunocompromised, ultra-pasteurized—*also* -ed *forms of verbs listed at* IZE[1]

izen[1] \īz-ᵊn\ bison, dizen, greisen • bedizen, horizon • spiegeleisen • event horizon

izen[2] \iz-ᵊn\ *see* ISON[2]

izer \ī-zər\ Dreiser, geyser, kaiser, miser, prizer, riser, sizar, visor, wiser • adviser, baptiser, chastiser, despiser, deviser, disguiser, divisor, franchiser, incisor, upriser • advertiser, appetizer, atomizer, authorizer, bowdlerizer, catechizer, circumciser, civilizer, compromiser, criticizer, customizer, digitizer, dogmatizer, empathizer, energizer, enterpriser, equalizer, eulogizer, exerciser, fantasizer, fertilizer, formalizer, fraternizer, galvanizer, generalizer, glamorizer, Goldenweiser, harmonizer, humanizer, idealizer, idolizer, improviser, lionizer, maximizer, memorizer, mesmerizer, minimizer, modernizer, moisturizer, moralizer, nationalizer, nebulizer, neutralizer, normalizer, organizer, oxidizer, plagiarizer, poetizer, pollenizer, pressurizer, pulverizer, randomizer, rationalizer, scrutinizer, sermonizer, socializer, stabilizer, sterilizer, subsidizer, summarizer, supervisor, sympathizer, synchronizer, synthesizer, tantalizer, temporizer, tenderizer, theorizer, totalizer, tranquilizer, tyrannizer, utilizer, vaporizer, verbalizer, victimizer, visualizer, vocalizer, vulcanizer, westernizer, womanizer • alphabetizer, free enterpriser, popularizer, proselytizer, systematizer

izing \ī-ziŋ\ rising, sizing • uprising • advertising, agonizing, appetizing, enterprising, merchandising, self-sufficing, unsurprising • self-sacrificing, unappetizing, uncompromising—*also* -ing *forms of verbs listed at* IZE[1]

izo[1] \ē-zō\ sleazo • chorizo, mestizo

izo[2] \ē-sō\ see ISO

izon \īz-ᵊn\ see IZEN[1]

izy \it-sē\ see ITZY

izz \iz\ see IZ[1]

izza \ēt-sə\ see ITZA[1]

izzard \iz-ərd\ see IZARD

izzen \iz-ᵊn\ see ISON[2]

izzer \iz-ər\ see ISSOR

izzical \iz-i-kəl\ see YSICAL

izzie \i-zē\ see IZZY

izzle \iz-əl\ chisel, drizzle, fizzle, frizzle, grizzle, mizzle, pizzle, sizzle, swizzle • cold chisel

izzled \iz-əld\ chiseled, grizzled—*also* -ed *forms of verbs listed at* IZZLE

izzler \iz-lər\ chiseler, sizzler, swizzler

izzly \iz-lē\ drizzly, grisly, grizzly, mizzly

izzy \iz-ē\ busy, dizzy, fizzy, frizzy, tizzy • tin lizzie

O

o¹ \ü\ see EW¹

o² \ō\ see OW¹

oa¹ \ō-ə\ boa, Goa, koa, moa, Noah, proa, Shoah, stoa • aloha, balboa, Balboa, feijoa, jerboa, Samoa • Figueroa, Krakatoa, Mauna Loa, Mount Gilboa, Shenandoah, Sinaloa • Guanabacoa, João Pessoa

oa² \ō\ see OW¹

oable \ü-ə-bəl\ see UABLE

oach \ōch\ broach, brooch, coach, loach, poach, roach • abroach, approach, caroche, cockroach, encroach, reproach, stagecoach • hackney coach

oachable \ō-chə-bəl\ coachable • approachable • inapproachable, irreproachable, unapproachable

oacher \ō-chər\ broacher, coacher, cloture, poacher • encroacher, reproacher

oad¹ \ōd\ see ODE

oad² \od\ see AUD¹

oader \ōd-ər\ see ODER

oadie \ōd-ē\ see ODY²

oady \ōd-ē\ see ODY²

oaf \ōf\ loaf, oaf, qoph • meat loaf, witloof • autotroph, sugarloaf

oafer \ō-fər\ see OFER

oagie \ō-gē\ see OGIE

oah \ō-ə\ see OA¹

oak \ōk\ see OKE

oaken \ō-kən\ see OKEN

oaker \ō-kər\ see OKER

oakum \ō-kəm\ see OKUM

oaky \ō-kē\ see OKY

oal \ōl\ see OLE¹

oalie \ō-lē\ see OLY¹

oam¹ \ō-əm\ see OEM¹

oam² \ōm\ see OME¹

oamer \ō-mər\ see OMER¹

oaming \ō-miŋ\ coaming, gloaming • Wyoming—also -ing forms of verbs listed at OME¹

oamy \ō-mē\ foamy, homey, loamy, show-me • Dahomey, Naomi, Salome

oan¹ \ō-ən\ Goan, Owen, roan, rowan • Lisboan, Minoan, Samoan, Tanoan, waygoing • Eskimoan, Idahoan, protozoan • strawberry roan, spermatozoan

298

oan² \ōn\ see ONE¹

oaner \ō-nər\ see ONER¹

oaning \ō-niη\ see ONING²

oap \ōp\ see OPE

oaper \ō-pər\ see OPER

oapy \ō-pē\ see OPI

oar \òr\ see OR¹

oard \òrd\ board, bored, chord, cord, cored, floored, ford, Ford, gourd, hoard, horde, lord, Lord, oared, pored, sward, sword, toward, ward, Ward • aboard, accord, afford, award, backboard, backsword, bargeboard, baseboard, billboard, blackboard, boxboard, breadboard, broadsword, buckboard, cardboard, chalkboard, chessboard, chipboard, clapboard, clipboard, concord, corkboard, dart board, dashboard, discord, draft board, duckboard, face cord, fjord, flashboard, floorboard, footboard, freeboard, Gaylord, greensward, hardboard, headboard, inboard, keyboard, kickboard, landlord, lapboard, leeboard, longsword, matchboard, moldboard, nerve cord, onboard, on board, outboard, packboard, pasteboard, patchboard, patch cord, PegBoard, pressboard, punchboard, rearward, record, reward, sailboard, scoreboard, seaboard, shipboard, sideboard, signboard, skateboard, slumlord, smallsword, snowboard, soundboard, splashboard, springboard, surfboard, switchboard, tack board, tailboard, tote board, untoward, wakeboard, wallboard, warlord, washboard, whiteboard, whipcord, word-hoard • aboveboard, astarboard, beaverboard, Bedford cord, bottle gourd, bristol board, bungee cord, centerboard, checkerboard, circuit board, clavichord, College Board, cutting board, daggerboard, disaccord, diving board, drawing board, emery board, fiberboard, fingerboard, free on board, gold record, harpsichord, leaderboard, mortarboard, motherboard, of record, overboard, overlord, paddleboard, paperboard, pinafored, plasterboard, pompadoured, room and board, running board, sandwich board, shoulder board, shuffleboard, silver cord, smorgasbord, sounding board, spinal cord, storyboard, sweep the board, tape-record, teeterboard, tetrachord, untoward, weatherboard • across-the-board, bulletin board, court of record, extension cord, go by the board, ironing board, misericord, off-the-record, on-the-record, out of one's gourd, particleboard • platinum record • Federal Reserve Board—*also* -ed *forms of verbs listed at* OR¹

oarder \òrd-ər\ see ORDER

oarding \òrd-iη\ see ORDING¹

oared \òrd\ see OARD

oarer \òr-ər\ see ORER

oaring \ȯr-iŋ\ see ORING

oarious \ȯr-ē-əs\ see ORIOUS

oarish \ȯr-ish\ see ORISH¹

oarse \ȯrs\ see ORSE¹

oarsen \ȯrs-ᵊn\ coarsen, hoarsen, whoreson

oarsman \ȯrz-mən\ oarsman • outdoorsman

oart \ȯrt\ see ORT¹

oary \ȯr-ē\ see ORY

oast \ōst\ see OST²

oastal \ōs-tᵊl\ see OSTAL¹

oaster \ō-stər\ boaster, coaster, poster, roaster, throwster, toaster • four-poster • roller-coaster, roller coaster • Ivory Coaster

oasty \ō-stē\ see OSTY

oat \ōt\ bloat, boat, coat, cote, dote, float, gloat, goat, groat, haute, moat, mote, note, oat, quote, rote, shoat, smote, stoat, throat, tote, vote, wrote • afloat, airboat, banknote, bareboat, bluecoat, blue note, box coat, bumboat, capote, car coat, catboat, C-note, compote, connote, coyote, cutthroat, deep throat, demote, denote, devote, dovecote, dreamboat, eighth note, emote, endnote, fireboat, fistnote, flatboat, foldboat, footnote, frock coat, gemot, grace note, greatcoat, gunboat, half note, headnote, Hohhot, houseboat, housecoat, iceboat, johnboat, keelboat, keynote, lab coat, lifeboat, longboat, mash note, one-note, peacoat, pigboat, promote, Q-boat, raincoat, Rajkot, redcoat, remote, rewrote, rowboat, sack coat, sailboat, sauceboat, scapegoat, seed coat, shape note, sheepcote, showboat, sore throat, speedboat, steamboat, stoneboat, straw vote, strep throat, Sukkoth, surcoat, surfboat, swan boat, tailcoat, topcoat, towboat, trench coat, tugboat, turncoat, U-boat, unquote, wainscot, whaleboat, whitethroat, whole note, woodnote, workboat • anecdote, antidote, assault boat, asymptote, billy goat, Capriote, cashmere goat, casting vote, Corfiote, creosote, dead man's float, demand vote, duffle coat, entrecôte, ferryboat, flying boat, get one's goat, Huhehot, jolly boat, locomote, matelote, miss the boat, morning coat, motorboat, mountain goat, nanny goat, overcoat, paddleboat, papillote, passing note, pedal-note, petticoat, picketboat, polo coat, powerboat, PT boat, quarter note, redingote, riverboat, rock the boat, rubythroat, Shabuoth, Sialkot, sixteenth note, sticky note, sugarcoat, symbiote, table d'hôte, Terre Haute, undercoat, yellowthroat • Angora goat, in the same boat, lump in one's throat, torpedo boat, treasury note • promissory note, thirty-second note

oate \ō-ət\ see OET¹

oated \ōt-əd\ bloated, coated, moated, noted, throated • devoted, hard-coated, tailcoated, waistcoated • petticoated, self-devoted —*also* -ed *forms of verbs listed at* OAT

oaten \ōt-ᵊn\ see OTON

oater \ōt-ər\ bloater, boater, coater, doter, floater, gloater, motor, noter, oater, quoter, rotor, scoter, toter, voter • emoter, houseboater, iceboater, keynoter, promoter, pulmotor, sailboater, showboater, tilt-rotor, trimotor • dynamotor, locomotor, motorboater, outboard motor, powerboater, servomotor

oath \ōth\ see OWTH

oathe \ōth\ see OTHE

oathing \ō-thiŋ\ see OTHING

oating \ōt-iŋ\ coating, floating • free-floating, iceboating, sailboating, speedboating, wainscoting • motorboating, powerboating, undercoating —*also* -ing *forms of verbs listed at* OAT

oatswain \ōs-ᵊn\ see OSIN

oaty \ōt-ē\ see OTE¹

oax \ōks\ coax, hoax—*also* -s, -'s, *and* -s' *forms of nouns and* -s *forms of verbs listed at* OKE

ob¹ \äb\ Ab, blob, bob, Bob, cob, daub, fob, glob, gob, hob, job, knob, lob, mob, nob, rob, slob, snob, sob, squab, stob, swab, throb, yob • bedaub, corncob, day job, demob, doorknob, heartthrob, hobnob, kebab, macabre, McJob, memsahib, nabob, nawab, plumb bob, Punjab, snow job, stop knob, Welsh cob • shish kebab • thingamabob

ob² \ōb\ see OBE¹

oba \ō-bə\ soba • arroba, jojoba • algaroba, Manitoba • ginkgo biloba, Lake Manitoba

obably \äb-lē\ see OBBLY

obal \ō-bəl\ see OBLE

obally \ō-bə-lē\ globally • primum mobile

obar \ō-bər\ see OBER

obber \äb-ər\ bobber, caber, clobber, cobber, jobber, robber, slobber, swabber, throbber • hobnobber, Micawber, stockjobber

obbery \äb-rē\ bobbery, jobbery, robbery, slobbery, snobbery • corroboree • highway robbery

obbes \äbz\ Hobbes—*also* -s, -'s, *and* -s' *forms of nouns and* -s *forms of verbs listed at* OB¹

obbet \äb-ət\ gobbet, probit

obbie \äb-ē\ see OBBY

obbin \äb-ən\ see OBIN

obbish \äb-ish\ mobbish, slobbish, snobbish

obble \äb-əl\ see ABBLE¹

obbler \äb-lər\ cobbler, gobbler, hobbler, nobbler, squabbler, wobbler

obbly \äb-lē\ knobbly, probably, wobbly, Wobbly

obby \äb-ē\ Bobbie, bobby, Bobby, cobby, dobby, globby, hobby, knobby, lobby, nobby, Sabi, slobby, snobby, swabbie • kohlrabi, Mesabi, Punjabi, Wahhabi • Abu Dhabi, Hammurabi

obe[1] \ōb\ daube, Dobe, globe, Job, lobe, probe, robe, strobe • aerobe, bathrobe, conglobe, disrobe, earlobe, enrobe, garderobe, lap robe, microbe, wardrobe • acrophobe, aerophobe, agoraphobe, Anglophobe, chifferobe, chromophobe, claustrophobe, cryophobe, Francophobe, frontal lobe, homophobe, microphobe, negrophobe, optic lobe, technophobe, xenophobe • ailurophobe, arachnophobe, celestial globe, computerphobe, election probe, temporal lobe • occipital lobe, olfactory lobe, parietal lobe

obe[2] \ō-bē\ see OBY

obeah \ō-bē-ə\ see OBIA

obee \ō-bē\ see OBY

obelus \äb-ə-ləs\ see ABILIS

ober \ō-bər\ lobar, prober, sober • October

obi \ō-bē\ see OBY

obia \ō-bē-ə\ cobia, obeah, phobia • Zenobia • acrophobia, aerophobia, algophobia, Anglophobia, claustrophobia, Frankophobia, homophobia, hydrophobia, negrophobia, photophobia, technophobia, xenophobia • agoraphobia, arachnophobia, computerphobia

obic \ō-bik\ phobic • aerobic • acrophobic, aerophobic, anaerobic, Anglophobic, claustrophobic, homophobic, hydrophobic, photophobic, technophobic, xenophobic • agoraphobic, arachnophobic, computerphobic

obile[1] \ō-bə-lē\ see OBALLY

obile[2] \ō-bəl\ see OBLE

obin \äb-ən\ bobbin, dobbin, graben, robin, Robin • round-robin, sea robin, wake-robin • ragged robin

obit[1] \ō-bət\ obit, Tobit

obit[2] \äb-ət\ see OBBET

oble \ō-bəl\ coble, global, mobile, noble • airmobile, ennoble, Grenoble, ignoble, immobile • San Cristóbal • upwardly mobile

obo \ō-bō\ gobo, hobo, kobo, lobo, oboe • adobo, bonobo

oboe \ō-bō\ see OBO

obol \äb-əl\ see ABBLE[1]

oboree \äb-ə-rē\ see OBBERY

obot \ō-bət\ see OBIT[1]

obra \ō-brə\ cobra, dobra • king cobra • spitting cobra

obster \äb-stər\ lobster, mobster • spiny lobster

obular \äb-yə-lər\ globular, lobular

obule \äb-yül\ globule, lobule

oby \ō-bē\ Gobi, goby, Kobe, obi, Obie, Toby • adobe, Nairobi • Okeechobee

obyn \äb-ən\ see OBIN

oc¹ \ōk\ see OKE

oc² \äk\ see OCK¹

oc³ \ok\ see ALK

oca \ō-kə\ coca, mocha, oca, soca • Asoka, carioca, Fukuoka, mandioca, Shizuoka, tapioca

ocable \ō-kə-bəl\ smokable, vocable • evocable

ocage \äk-ij\ see OCKAGE

ocal \ō-kəl\ focal, local, socle, vocal, yokel • bifocal, confocal, parfocal, subvocal, trifocal, unvocal

ocally \ō-kə-lē\ locally, vocally • confocally, subvocally

ocative \äk-ət-iv\ locative, vocative • evocative, provocative

occa \äk-ə\ see AKA¹

occer \äk-ər\ see OCKER

occie \äch-ē\ see OTCHY

occhi \ó-kē\ see ALKIE

occo \äk-ō\ socko, taco • cheechako, guanaco, morocco, Morocco, sirocco

occule \äk-yül\ floccule, locule

occulent \äk-yə-lənt\ flocculent • inoculant

occulus \äk-yə-ləs\ flocculus, loculus, oculus

oce \ō-chē\ see OCHE¹

ocean \ō-shən\ see OTION

ocent \ōs-ᵊnt\ docent, nocent • privatdozent

ocess \äs-əs\ Knossos, process • colossus, due process, in-process, proboscis, word process

och¹ \äk\ see OCK¹

och² \ósh\ see ASH²

och³ \ok\ see ALK

ocha \ō-kə\ see OCA

ochal \äk-əl\ see OCKLE

ochan \ä-ḵən\ see ACHEN

oche¹ \ō-chē\ Kochi, Sochi • veloce • mezza voce, sotto voce

oche² \ōsh\ cloche, gauche, skosh • brioche, caroche, guilloche

oche³ \ō-kē\ see OKY

oche⁴ \ōch\ see OACH

oche⁵ \ósh\ see ASH²

ochee \ō-kē\ see OKY

ocher \ō-kər\ see OKER

ochi \ō-chē\ see OCHE¹

ochle \ek-əl\ see UCKLE

ochs \äks\ see OX

ochum \ō-kəm\ see OKUM

ocia \ō-shə\ see OTIA¹

ociable \ō-shə-bəl\ sociable • dissociable, insociable, negotiable, unsociable • indissociable, renegotiable

ocial \ō-shəl\ social • asocial, box social, dissocial, precocial, unsocial • antisocial, biosocial, homosocial, psychosocial

ocile \äs-əl\ see OSSAL

ocious \ō-shəs\ atrocious, ferocious, precocious • Theodosius

ock¹ \äk\ Bach, bloc, block, bock, brock, chock, clock, cock, croc, crock, doc, dock, floc, flock, frock, grok, hock, Jacque, Jacques, jock, knock, lakh, loch, lock, Locke, lough, Mach, moc, mock, nock, pock, roc, rock, schlock, shock, smock, sock, Spock, stock, wok, yock • acock, ad hoc, air lock, alt-rock, amok, Arak, armlock, art-rock, Ayers Rock, backblock, ball cock, Balzac, bangkok, Bangkok, baroque, Bartók, bawcock, bedrock, bemock, bitstock, blackcock, blesbok, bloodstock, bois d'arc, bow shock, breechblock, burdock, buttstock, caprock, coldcock, Comstock, crew sock, deadlock, debacle, defrock, dreadlock, dry dock, duroc, Dvořák, earlock, elflock, en bloc, epoch, fatstock, feedstock, fetlock, firelock, flintlock, forelock, foreshock, gamecock, gemsbok, gridlock, gunlock, half cock, Hancock, hard rock, havelock, haycock, headlock, headstock, heart block, hemlock, in stock, Iraq, jazz-rock, Kanak, Kazak, Kazakh, kapok, kneesock, Ladakh, Laubach, livestock, lovelock, matchlock, Médoc, Mohock, Moloch, nostoc, o'clock, oarlock, padlock, peacock, penstock, petcock, pibroch, picklock, pinchcock, post doc, post hoc, punk rock, rhebok, rimrock, roadblock, rootstock, Rorschach, Rostock, rowlock, scalp lock, Schirach, seed stock, shamrock, Sheetrock, shell shock, sherlock, Ship Rock, shock jock, shot clock, shylock, Sirach, slickrock, Slovak, smock frock, snatch block, soft rock, springbok, steenbok, stopcock, sunblock, swage block, ticktock, time clock, time lock, traprock, unblock, uncock, undock, van Gogh, wall rock, warlock, wedlock, wheel lock, whipstock, windsock, woodblock, woodcock, wristlock, zwieback • acid rock, aftershock, alarm clock, alpenstock, Anahuac, antiknock, antilock, Antioch, Arawak, Ayers Rock, banjo clock, billycock, building block, butcher-block, chockablock, chopping block, cinder block, clean one's clock, common stock, country rock, cuckoo clock, culture shock, floating dock, four-o'clock, future shock, glitter rock, hammerlock, hollyhock, Holy Loch, interlock, in the dock, John Hancock, kill the clock, lady's-smock, Languedoc, laughingstock, Little Rock, manioc, mantlerock, monadnock, Mount Greylock, Offenbach, on the block, out of stock, penny stock, phosphate rock, pillow block, Plymouth Rock, poppycock, preferred stock, Ragnarok, rolling stock, Sarawak, septic shock, starting block, shuttlecock, spatterdock, sticker shock, stumbling block, summer stock, superblock, tracking stock, treasury stock, turkey-cock, vapor lock, water clock, weathercock, writer's block • against the clock, around-the-clock, atomic clock, Bialystok, capital stock, Czechoslovak, electroshock, grandfather clock, insulin shock, Inupiaq, Mount Monadnock, out of wedlock, poison hemlock, Pontianak, run out the clock, turn back the clock, Vladivostok • chip off the old block

ock² \ók\ see ALK

ockage \äk-ij\ blockage, brockage, dockage, socage

ocke \äk\ see OCK¹

ocked \äkt\ blocked, crocked • concoct, decoct, dreadlocked, entr'acte, half-cocked, landlocked, shell-shocked • entoproct—*also* -ed *forms of verbs listed at* OCK¹

ocker \äk-ər\ blocker, clocker, cocker, docker, hocker, knocker, locker, makar, mocker, rocker, shocker, soccer, stocker • alt-rocker, art-rocker, footlocker, punk rocker • apple-knocker, beta-blocker, Boston rocker, knickerbocker, platform rocker • Davy Jones's locker

ockery \äk-rē\ crockery, mockery, rockery

ocket \äk-ət\ brocket, crocket, Crockett, docket, locket, pocket, rocket, socket, sprocket • air pocket, dame's rocket, deep pocket, patch pocket, pickpocket, skyrocket, slash pocket, vest-pocket, wall rocket, watch pocket • cargo pocket, in one's pocket, out-of-pocket, retro-rocket, sounding rocket

ockett \äk-ət\ see OCKET

ockey \äk-ē\ see OCKY

ockian \äk-ē-ən\ Comstockian, Hitchcockian, Slovakian • Czechoslovakian

ockiness \äk-ē-nəs\ cockiness, rockiness, stockiness

ocking \äk-iŋ\ flocking, shocking, smocking, stocking • bluestocking, self-cocking, silk-stocking • beta-blocking, body stocking—*also* -ing *forms of verbs listed at* OCK¹

ockish \äk-ish\ blockish, stockish • peacockish

ockle \äk-əl\ coccal, cockle, socle • corn cockle, debacle, epochal • cryptococcal, streptococcal

ockney \äk-nē\ cockney, Hockney, Procne

ocko \äk-ō\ see OCCO

ocks \äks\ see OX

ocky \äk-ē\ blocky, cocky, hockey, jockey, pocky, rocky, Rocky, sake, schlocky, stocky, Yaqui • bench jockey, chop-socky, desk jockey, disc jockey, field hockey, ice hockey, Iraqi, peacocky, street hockey • jabberwocky, Kawasaki, Miyazaki, Nagasaki, Okazaki, sukiyaki, teriyaki

ocle \ō-kəl\ see OCAL

ocne \äk-nē\ see OCKNEY

oco \ō-kō\ coco, cocoa, loco, poco • Bioko, iroko, rococo • crème de cacao, Locofoco, Orinoco, suo loco • poco a poco

ocoa \ō-kō\ see OCO

ocracy \äk-rə-sē\ autocracy, bureaucracy, democracy, Eurocracy, hypocrisy, kleptoc-racy, mobocracy, plantocracy, plutocracy, slavocracy, technocracy, theocracy • aristocracy, gerontocracy, gynecocracy, meritocracy, punditocracy, pure democracy, thalassocracy

ocre \ō-kər\ see OKER

ocrisy \äk-rə-sē\ see OCRACY

ocsin \äk-sən\ see OXIN

oct \äkt\ see OCKED

oction \äk-shən\ concoction, decoction

octor \äk-tər\ doctor, proctor • concocter, spin doctor, witch doctor • family doctor, Juris Doctor

oculant \äk-yə-lənt\ see OCCULENT

ocular \äk-yə-lər\ jocular, locular, ocular • binocular, monocular • intraocular

ocule \äk-yül\ see OCCULE

oculus \äk-yə-ləs\ see OCCULUS

ocum \ō-kəm\ see OKUM

ocus \ō-kəs\ crocus, focus, hocus, locus • deep focus, in focus, prefocus, refocus, soft-focus • autumn crocus, hocus-pocus

ocused \ō-kəst\ see OCUST

ocust \ō-kəst\ locust • black locust, unfocused • desert locust, honey locust

ocutor \äk-yət-ər\ prolocutor • interlocutor

od[1] \äd\ bod, clod, cod, fade, Fahd, gaud, god, hod, mod, nod, od, odd, plod, pod, prod, quad, quod, rod, scrod, shod, sod, squad, tod, trod, wad • Akkad, Arad, Ashdod, aubade, ballade, Belgrade, bipod, black cod, Black Rod, Cape Cod, couvade, croustade, death squad, de Sade, dry-shod, ephod, facade, fantod, fly rod, glissade, hot-rod, jihad, lingcod, Nimrod, oeillade, peasecod, pomade, push rod, ramrod, Riyadh, roughshod, roulade, saccade, scalade, seedpod, slipshod, sun god, synod, tie-rod, tightwad, tomcod, torsade, tripod, unshod, vice squad • accolade, act of God, amphipod, arthropod, Ashkhabad, Beograd, bigarade, carbonnade, cattle prod, chiffonade, decapod, defilade, demigod, diplopod, dowsing rod, enfilade, escalade, esplanade, firing squad, flying squad, fusillade, gallopade, gastropod, goldenrod, hexapod, isopod, lightning rod, lycopod, man of God, monkeypod, monopod, Novgorod, Novi Sad, octopod, piston rod, promenade, pseudopod, rémoulade, rhizopod, son of God, spinning rod, tapenade, tetrapod, theropod, traverse rod • Ahmadabad, Allahabad, brachiopod, branchiopod, cephalopod, connecting rod, Cuisenaire rod, dégringolade, divining rod, Faisalabad, fanfaronade, Holy Synod, Islamabad, leveling rod, ornithopod, prosauropod, rodomontade, Scheherazade, Upanishad • Nizhniy Novgorod

od² \ō\ see OW¹

od³ \ōd\ see ODE

od⁴ \ùd\ see OOD¹

od⁵ \òd\ see AUD¹

o'd \ùd\ see UDE

oda \ōd-ə\ coda, Rhoda, Skoda, soda • Baroda, club soda, cream soda, pagoda • baking soda

odal \ōd-ᵊl\ modal, nodal, yodel • bimodal, cathodal • intermodal, internodal

odden \äd-ᵊn\ Flodden, sodden, trodden • downtrodden, Ibadan, untrodden

odder \äd-ər\ dodder, fodder, khaddar, Modder, nodder, plodder, prodder, solder, wadder • Cape Codder, flyrodder, glissader, hot-rodder • cannon fodder, Leningrader, promenader—*also* -er *forms of adjectives listed at* OD¹

oddery \äd-rē\ see AWDRY

oddess \äd-əs\ bodice, goddess • bitch goddess, sun goddess • demigoddess

oddish \äd-ish\ cloddish, kaddish

oddle \äd-ᵊl\ coddle, model, noddle, swaddle, toddle, twaddle, waddle • remodel, role model, spokesmodel • mollycoddle, supermodel

oddler \äd-lər\ coddler, modeler, toddler, twaddler, waddler • mollycoddler

oddly \äd-lē\ see ODLY

oddy \äd-ē\ see ODY¹

ode \ōd\ bode, bowed, code, goad, load, lode, mode, node, ode, road, rode, Spode, strode, toad, toed, woad • abode, anode, bar code, bestrode, boatload, busload, byroad, carload, cartload, caseload, cathode, church mode, commode, corrode, crossroad, dead load, decode, diode, displode, download, dress code, dynode, embowed, encode, epode, erode, explode, forebode, freeload, front-load, geode, high road, horned toad, implode, inroad, live load, lymph node, Morse code, no-load, off-load, outmode, payload, planeload, postcode, post road, railroad, rhapsode, sarod, shipload, side road, Silk Road, skid road, source code, spring-load, square-toed, tetrode, threnode, trainload, triode, truckload, two-toed, unload, upload, zip code • à la mode, antipode, carbo-load, Comstock Lode, discommode, down the road, eigenmode, electrode, episode, frontage road, front-end load, hit the road, impastoed, incommode, internode, Kozhikode, microcode, mother lode, Nesselrode, object code, overrode, palinode, penal code, pigeon-toed, service road, sinus node, spadefoot toad, trematode, wagonload • area code, genetic code, genetic load, rule of the road, tobacco road, Wilderness Road • middle-of-the- road, Underground Railroad—also -ed forms of verbs listed at OW[1]

odeine \ōd-ē-ən\ see ODIAN

odel \ōd-ᵊl\ see ODAL

odeler \äd-lər\ see ODDLER

oden \ōd-ᵊn\ loden, Odin

odeon \ōd-ē-ən\ see ODIAN

oder \ōd-ər\ coder, loader, Oder, odor • breechloader, decoder, encoder, exploder, foreboder, freeloader, malodor, off-roader, railroader, self-loader, unloader, vocoder • autoloader, front-end loader • middle-of-the-roader

oderate \äd-rət\ moderate, quadrate • immoderate

odes \ōdz\ Rhodes—also -s, -'s, and -s' forms of nouns and -s forms of verbs listed at ODE

odest \äd-əst\ Mahdist, modest • haggadist, immodest—also -est forms of adjectives listed at OD[1]

odesy \äd-ə-sē\ odyssey • geodesy, theodicy

odeum \ōd-ē-əm\ see ODIUM

odge \äj\ see AGE[1]

odger \äj-ər\ codger, dodger, lodger, roger, Roger • Jolly Roger

odgy \äj-ē\ dodgy, podgy, stodgy • demagogy, mystagogy

odian \ōd-ē-ən\ Rhodian • Cambodian, custodian, melodeon • nickelodeon

odic \äd-ik\ zaddik • anodic, cathodic, dipodic, ergodic, haggadik, melodic, methodic, monodic, parodic, prosodic, rhapsodic, saccadic, spasmodic, synodic, threnodic • episodic, periodic • antispasmodic, aperiodic, upanishadic

odical \äd-i-kəl\ methodical, monodical, prosodical, synodical • episodical, immethodical, periodical

odice \äd-əs\ see ODDESS

odicy \äd-ə-sē\ see ODESY

odie \ō-dē\ see ODY²

odin \ōd-ᵊn\ see ODEN

odious \ōd-ē-əs\ odious
• commodious, melodious
• incommodious

odity \äd-ət-ē\ oddity
• commodity • incommodity

odium \ōd-ē-əm\ odeum, odium, podium, rhodium, sodium

odius \ō-dē-əs\ see ODIOUS

odless \äd-ləs\ godless, rodless

odling \äd-liŋ\ codling, godling
—*also* -ing *forms of verbs listed at* ODDLE

odly \äd-lē\ godly, oddly
• ungodly

odo \ōd-ō\ dodo • Komodo
• grosso modo, Quasimodo

odom \äd-əm\ shahdom, Sodom

odor \ōd-ər\ see ODER

odsk \ätsk\ see ATSK

odular \äj-ə-lər\ modular, nodular

odule \äj-ül\ module, nodule
• command module, lunar module, service module

ody¹ \äd-ē\ body, cloddy, gaudy, Mahdi, noddy, sadhe, shoddy, toddy, waddy, wadi • Barr body, blackbody, cell body, dogsbody, embody, homebody, nobody, somebody, stake body, wide-body • antibody, anybody, busybody, disem-
body, everybody, Irrawaddy, out-of-body, student body, underbody

ody² \ōd-ē\ Cody, Jodie, roadie, toady • polypody

odyssey \äd-ə-sē\ see ODESY

odz \üj\ see UGE¹

oe¹ \ō\ see OW¹

oe² \ō-ē\ see OWY

oe³ \ē\ see EE¹

oea¹ \òi-ə\ see OIA

oea² \ē-ə\ see IA¹

oeba \ē-bə\ see EBA

oebe \ē-bē\ see EBE¹

oebel \ā-bəl\ see ABLE

oebus \ē-bəs\ see EBUS

oed \ōd\ see ODE

oehn \ən\ see UN

oeia \ē-ə\ see IA¹

oeic \ē-ik\ see EIC

oek \ùk\ see OOK¹

oel \ō-əl\ Joel, Lowell, Noel
• bestowal • Baden-Powell, metazoal, protozoal

oeless¹ \ō-ləs\ see OLUS

oeless² \ü-ləs\ see EWLESS

oem¹ \ō-əm\ phloem, poem, proem • found poem, prose poem, tone poem • jeroboam
• heroic poem, symphonic poem

oem² \ōm\ see OME¹

oeman \ō-mən\ see OMAN

oena \ē-nə\ see INA[2]

oentgen[1] \en-chən\ see ENSION

oentgen[2] \ən-chən\ see UNCHEON

oepha \ē-fə\ see EPHA

oer[1] \òr\ see OR[1]

oer[2] \ü-ər\ see EWER[1]

oer[3] \ùr\ see URE[1]

oer[4] \ō-ər\ blower, grower, hoer, knower, lower, mower, rower, sewer, shower, sower, thrower • beachgoer, churchgoer, fairgoer, flamethrower, filmgoer, foregoer, forgoer, glassblower, lawn mower, mindblower, playgoer, snowblower, snowthrower, spear-thrower, vetoer, winegrower • concertgoer, moviegoer, partygoer, whistle-blower • cinemagoer, operagoer, theatergoer

o'er \òr\ see OR[1]

oes[1] \əz\ see EUSE[1]

oes[2] \ōz\ see OSE[2]

oes[3] \üz\ see USE[2]

oesia \ē-shə\ see ESIA[1]

oesn't \əz-ᵊnt\ see ASN'T

oest \ü-əst\ see OOIST

oesus \ē-səs\ see ESIS

oet \ō-ət\ poet • inchoate, introit, prose poet, tone poet

oetess \ō-ət-əs\ coitus, poetess

oeuf \əf\ see UFF

oeur \ər\ see EUR[1]

oeuvre \ərv\ see ERVE

oey \ō-ē\ see OWY

of[1] \äv\ see OLVE[2]

of[2] \əv\ see OVE[1]

of[3] \òf\ see OFF[2]

ofar \ō-fər\ see OFER

ofer \ō-fər\ chauffeur, gofer, gopher, loafer, Ophir, shofar • penny loafer

off[1] \äf\ boff, coif, doff, kaph, prof, quaff, scoff, shroff, taw, toff • carafe, cook-off, pilaf, Wroclaw • Romanov

off[2] \òf\ cough, doff, off, scoff, taw, trough • Azov, back off, beg off, bind off, blastoff, blow off, break off, bring off, brush-off, bug off, bump off, burn off, buy off, call off, cast-off, castoff, change off, charge off, checkoff, check off, Chekhov, choke off, come off, cook-off, cry off, cutoff, cut off, die-off, die off, draw off, drop-off, drop off, dust off, face-off, face off, falloff, far-off, fire off, first off, flip off, fob off, get off, give off, go off, goof-off, handoff, hand off, hands-off, haul off, head off, hold off, jump-off, Khartov, kickoff, kick off, kill off, Kirov, kiss-off, kiss off, knockoff, knock off, Khrushchev, laugh off, layoff, lay off, leadoff, lead off, leave off, lie off, liftoff, make off, nod off, one-off, palm off, pass off, Pavlov, pawn off, payoff, pay off, peel off, pick off, pickoff, play-off, pop off, pull off, push off, put off, rake-off, reel off, rip-off, rip off, roll-off, Rostov, rub off, runoff,

Sarnoff, sawed-off, seal off, sell off, sell-off, send-off, setoff, set off, show-off, show off, shrug off, shutoff, shut off, sign off, sign-off, sound off, spin-off, spin off, square off, squeeze off, standoff, stand off, stave off, straight off, strike off, swear off, takeoff, take off, Tambov, tap-off, teed off, tee off, tell off, throw off, tick off, tip-off, touch off, trade-off, turnoff, turn off, well-off, Wolof, work off, write-off, write off • better-off, carry off, cooling-off, damping-off, Gorbachev, hit it off, level off, Molotov, Nabokov, philosophe, polish off, Pribilof, sugar off, taper off • beat the pants off, beef Stroganoff, knock one's socks off, power take-off, Rachmaninoff, sugaring off • Mexican standoff, Rimsky-Korsakov

offal¹ \äf-əl\ see AFEL

offal² \ȯ-fəl\ see AWFUL

offaly \ȯf-ə-lē\ see AWFULLY

offee \ȯ-fē\ coffee, toffee • Irish coffee, Turkish coffee

offer¹ \äf-ər\ coffer, goffer, offer, proffer, quaffer, scoffer, troffer • reoffer • counteroffer, tender offer

offer² \ȯf-ər\ coffer, goffer, offer, scoffer, troffer • reoffer • counteroffer, tender offer

offin \ȯ-fən\ coffin, dauphin, often, soften • uncoffin • every so often

offit \äf-ət\ see OFIT

offle \ȯ-fəl\ see AWFUL

ofit \äf-ət\ profit, prophet, soffit • for-profit, nonprofit • not-for-profit, paper profit

ofle \ü-fəl\ see UEFUL

oft¹ \ȯft\ croft, loft, oft, soft, toft • aloft, Ashcroft, Bancroft, choir loft, cockloft, hayloft • semisoft, undercroft—*also* -ed *forms of verbs listed at* OFF²

oft² \äft\ see AFT¹

often \ȯ-fən\ see OFFIN

ofty \ȯf-tē\ lofty, softy • toplofty

og¹ \äg\ blog, bog, clog, cog, flog, fog, frog, grog, hog, jog, log, nog, Prague, prog, quag, shog, slog, smog, tog • agog, backlog, befog, bullfrog, defog, eclogue, eggnog, footslog, gas log, groundhog, gulag, hedge-hog, ice fog, leapfrog, photog, prologue, putlog, quahog, road hog, Rolvaag, sandhog, saw log, stalag, tree frog, unclog, warthog, Weblog, whole hog, wood frog, Yule log • analog, analogue, antilog, apologue, catalog, decalogue, dem-agogue, dialogue, epilogue, golliwog, homologue, leopard frog, monologue, mummichog, mystagogue, nouvelle vague, pedagogue, pollywog, semilog, sinologue, synagogue, Tagan-rog, theologue, travelogue, waterlog • card catalogue • Lake Memphremagog

og² \ȯg\ blog, bog, clog, dog, fog, frog, hog, jog, log, smog • backlog, bandog, befog, bird dog, bird-dog, bulldog, bullfrog, corn dog, coydog, defog, eclogue, feed dog, firedog, foo dog, gas log, groundhog, guide dog, gundog, hangdog, hedgehog, hotdog, ice fog, lapdog, leapfrog, prologue, putlog, pye-dog, quahog, red dog, road hog, sandhog, saw log, sea dog, sheepdog, sled dog, sun dog, top dog, tree frog, warthog, watchdog, Weblog, whole-hog, wild dog, wolf dog, wood frog, Yule log • analog, analogue, apologue, attack dog, catalog, chili dog, decalogue, dialogue, dog-eat-dog, duologue, epilogue, hearing dog, homologue, leopard frog, monologue, Mount Pulog, mummichog, overdog, pettifog, police dog, pollywog, prairie dog, running dog, shaggy-dog, sinologue, theologue, Tagalog, travelogue, underdog, water dog, waterlog, working dog, yellow-dog • card catalog, Eskimo dog, ideologue, Shetland sheepdog

og³ \ōg\ see OGUE¹

oga \ō-gə\ toga, yoga • Kyoga • Conestoga, Cuyahoga, hatha yoga

ogamous \äg-ə-məs\ endogamous, exogamous, monogamous • heterogamous

ogamy \äg-ə-mē\ endogamy, exogamy, homogamy, misogamy, monogamy • heterogamy

ogan \ō-gən\ brogan, shogun, slogan • Mount Logan

ogany \äg-ə-nē\ see OGONY

ogative \äg-ət-iv\ derogative, prerogative • interrogative

oge¹ \ōj\ doge • gamboge • horologe

oge² \ōzh\ loge • Limoges

oge³ \ō-jē\ see OJI

oge⁴ \üzh\ see UGE²

ogel \ō-gəl\ see OGLE¹

ogenous \äj-ə-nəs\ androgynous, autogenous, endogenous, erogenous, exogenous, homogenous, hydrogenous, monogynous, nitrogenous • heterogenous

ogeny \äj-ə-nē\ progeny • androgyny, autogeny, homogeny, misogyny, monogyny, ontogeny, orogeny, phylogeny • heterogeny

oger¹ \äj-ər\ see ODGER

oger² \óg-ər\ see OGGER²

oges \ōzh\ see OGE²

ogey¹ \ō-gē\ see OGIE

ogey² \ùg-ē\ see OOGIE

oggan \äg-ən\ see OGGIN

oggar \äg-ər\ see OGGER¹

ogger¹ \äg-ər\ agar, blogger, clogger, flogger, Hoggar, jogger, laager, lager, logger, slogger • Ahaggar • defogger, footslogger • agar-agar, cataloger, pettifogger

ogger² \ȯg-ər\ auger, augur, clogger, jogger, logger, maugre, sauger • defogger, hotdogger • cataloger, pettifogger

oggery¹ \äg-rē\ toggery • demagoguery

oggery² \ȯ-gə-rē\ augury, doggery

oggin \äg-ən\ noggin • Remagen, toboggan • Androscoggin, Copenhagen

oggle \äg-əl\ boggle, goggle, joggle, toggle • boondoggle, hornswoggle • synagogal

oggy¹ \äg-ē\ boggy, foggy, groggy, moggy, quaggy, ragi, smoggy, soggy, yagi • demagogy

oggy² \ȯg-ē\ doggy, foggy, soggy

ogh¹ \ōg\ see OGUE¹

ogh² \ōk\ see OKE

ogh³ \äk\ see OCK¹

ogh⁴ \ō\ see OW

ogi \ō-gē\ see OGIE

ogian \ō-jən\ see OJAN

ogic \äj-ik\ logic • choplogic, chop logic, illogic • anagogic, analogic, biologic, chronologic, cryptologic, cytologic, demagogic, dendrologic, dialogic, ecologic, ethnologic, fuzzy logic, geologic, histologic, horologic, hydrologic, mythologic, neurologic, nosologic, oncologic, pathologic, pedagogic, pedologic, petrologic,

phonologic, proctologic, psychologic, serologic, technologic, theologic, virologic, zoologic • dermatologic, etiologic, gerontologic, gynecologic, hagiologic, hematologic, ideologic, immunologic, ophthalmologic, ornithologic, pharmacologic, physiologic, roentgenologic, sociologic, symbolic logic, teleologic, teratologic, toxicologic, volcanologic

ogical \äj-i-kəl\ logical • alogical, illogical • anagogical, astrological, biological, Christological, chronological, cosmological, cryptological, dendrological, ecological, ethnological, extralogical, gemological, geological, graphological, horological, hydrological, morphological, mycological, mythological, neurological, oncological, pathological, pedagogical, philological, phrenological, psychological, scatological, seismological, tautological, technological, theological, topological, typological, zoological • anthropological, archaeological, climatological, criminological, dermatological, entomological, eschatological, etiological, etymological, genealogical, gerontological, gynecological, iconological, ideological, immunological, mineralogical, musicological, numerological, ornithological, physiological, radiological, sociological, terminological

• bacteriological, epistemo-
logical, phenomenological

ogie \ō-gē\ bogey, bogie, dogie,
fogy, hoagie, logy, pogy,
stogie, vogie, yogi • pierogi

ogle[1] \ō-gəl\ Gogol, ogle

ogle[2] \äg-əl\ see OGGLE

oglio \ōl-yō\ see OLLO[1]

ogna[1] \ō-nə\ see ONA

ogna[2] \ō-nē\ see ONY[1]

ogna[3] \ōn-yə\ see ONIA[2]

ogne \ōn\ see ONE[1]

ogned \ōnd\ see ONED[1]

ogo \ō-gō\ go-go, logo, Logo,
Togo • a-go-go

ogony \äg-ə-nē\ cosmogony,
mahogany, theogony

ographer \äg-rə-fər\ biographer,
cartographer, chorographer,
cosmographer, cryptographer,
demographer, discographer,
ethnographer, geographer,
lithographer, mythographer,
phonographer, photographer,
pornographer, stenographer,
typographer • bibliographer,
choreographer, chromatog-
rapher, hagiographer, heli-
ographer, iconographer,
lexicographer, oceanographer,
paleographer, videographer
• cinematographer,
historiographer

ography \äg-rə-fē\ aerography,
autography, biography,
cacography, cartography,
chorography, chronography,
cosmography, cryptography,

demography, discography,
ethnography, filmography,
geography, holography,
hydrography, hypsography,
lithography, lymphography,
mammography, mythography,
nomography, orthography,
phonography, photography,
pictography, planography,
pornography, reprography,
sonography, stenography,
thermography, tomography,
topography, typography,
venography, xerography,
xylography • bibliography,
choreography, hagiography,
iconography, lexicography,
oceanography • autobiography,
cinematography

ogress \ō-grəs\ ogress, progress

ogrom \äg-rəm\ grogram,
pogrom

ogue[1] \ōg\ brogue, drogue,
rogue, togue, vogue, yogh
• collogue, pirogue, prorogue
• disembogue

ogue[2] \äg\ see OG[1]

ogue[3] \óg\ see OG[2]

oguery \äg-rē\ see OGGERY[1]

oguish \ō-gish\ roguish, voguish

ogun \ō-gən\ see OGAN

ogynous \äj-ə-nəs\ see OGENOUS

ogyny \äj-ə-nē\ see OGENY

oh \ō\ see OW[1]

oha \ō-ə\ see OA[1]

ohl \ōl\ see OLE[1]

ohm \ōm\ see OME[1]

ohn \än\ see ON[1]

ohns \änz\ see ONZE

ohn's \onz\ see ONZE

ohnson \än-sən\ Johnson, Jonson, sponson • Wisconsin

ohr \ór\ see OR[1]

oi[1] \ä\ see A[1]

oi[2] \ói\ see OY

oia \ói-ə\ cholla, Goya, hoya, olla, toea • Nagoya, sequoia, Sequoya • atemoya, cherimoya, paranoia • giant sequoia, metasequoia

oian \ói-ən\ see OYEN

oic \ō-ik\ stoic • azoic, echoic, heroic • anechoic, Cenozoic, Mesozoic, mock-heroic • antiheroic, Paleozoic

oice \óis\ choice, Joyce, Royce, voice • devoice, DuBois, invoice, of choice, pro-choice, rejoice, Rolls-Royce, unvoice • fielder's choice, Hobson's choice, sailor's-choice, with one voice • multiple-choice

oiced \óist\ see OIST

oicer \ói-sər\ choicer, voicer • pro-choicer, rejoicer

oid[1] \óid\ Boyd, Floyd, Freud, void • android, avoid, chancroid, colloid, conoid, crinoid, cuboid, cycloid, deltoid, dendroid, devoid, discoid, factoid, fibroid, fungoid, ganoid, globoid, hydroid, hypnoid, keloid, mastoid, mucoid, Negroid, ovoid, percoid, prismoid, pygmoid, rhizoid, rhomboid, schizoid, scombroid, sigmoid, spheroid, steroid, styloid, tabloid, thalloid, thyroid, toroid, toxoid, trochoid, typhoid, Veddoid, viroid • adenoid, alkaloid, amoeboid, aneroid, anthropoid, arachnoid, asteroid, Australoid, carcinoid, Caucasoid, celluloid, crystalloid, echinoid, ellipsoid, embryoid, eunuchoid, flavonoid, helicoid, hemorrhoid, hominoid, humanoid, hysteroid, metalloid, Mongoloid, myeloid, nautiloid, nucleoid, null and void, obovoid, opioid, osteoid, overjoyed, paranoid, planetoid, Polaroid, retinoid, rheumatoid, solenoid, Stalinoid, trapezoid, unalloyed, unemployed • cannabinoid, carotenoid, meteoroid, philanthropoid, tuberculoid, underemployed • bioflavonoid, Neanderthaloid —*also* -ed *forms of verbs listed at* OY

oid[2] \ä\ see A[1]

oidal \óid-ᵊl\ chancroidal, choroidal, colloidal, conchoidal, cuboidal, cycloidal, discoidal, keloidal, prismoidal, spheroidal, toroidal • adenoidal, alkaloidal, asteroidal, ellipsoidal, emulsoidal, hemorrhoidal, metalloidal, planetoidal, saccharoidal, trapezoidal

oider \óid-ər\ broider, voider • avoider, embroider

oie \ä\ see A[1]

oif \äf\ see OFF[1]

oign \óin\ see OIN[1]

oil \òil\ boil, Boyle, broil, coil, Doyle, foil, hoyle, Hoyle, moil, loyal, noil, oil, roil, royal, soil, spoil, toil, voile • aboil, airfoil, assoil, charbroil, cinquefoil, coal oil, corn oil, despoil, disloyal, embroil, entoil, fish oil, fixed oil, free-soil, fuel oil, garboil, gargoyle, gas oil, gumboil, hard-boil, Isle Royal, langue d'oïl, milfoil, night soil, non-oil, palm oil, parboil, potboil, recoil, red soil, rhyme royal, rose oil, shale oil, snake oil, sperm oil, subsoil, surroyal, tall oil, tinfoil, topsoil, train oil, trefoil, tung oil, turmoil, white oil • baby oil, castor oil, counterfoil, desert soil, drying oil, holy oil, hydrofoil, linseed oil, London broil, mineral oil, neat's-foot oil, olive oil, peanut oil, prairie soil, quatrefoil, pennyroyal, rapeseed oil, safflower oil, salad oil, soybean oil, supercoil, tick trefoil • canola oil, coconut oil, cod-liver oil, cottonseed oil, essential oil, induction coil, neroli oil, nondrying oil, residual oil, sandalwood oil, sesame oil, tropical oil, vegetable oil, volatile oil, water milfoil • burn the midnight oil

oilage \òi-lij\ soilage, spoilage

oile¹ \äl\ see AL¹

oile² \òil\ see OIL

oiled \òild\ foiled, oiled • hard-boiled, soft-boiled, uncoiled, well-oiled—*also* -ed *forms of verbs listed at* OIL

oiler \òi-lər\ boiler, broiler, moiler, oiler, spoiler, toiler • charbroiler, despoiler, Free-Soiler, potboiler, steam boiler, subsoiler • double boiler

oiling \òi-liŋ\ boiling, broiling, moiling—*also* -ing *forms of verbs listed at* OIL

oilless \òil-ləs\ soilless • recoilless

oilsman \òilz-mən\ foilsman, spoilsman

oilus \òi-ləs\ see OYLESS

oily \òi-lē\ doily, oily, roily

oin¹ \òin\ coin, foin, groin, groyne, join, loin, quoin • adjoin, Alboin, benzoin, Burgoyne, conjoin, Des Moines, disjoin, eloign, enjoin, essoin, purloin, recoin, rejoin, sainfoin, short loin, sirloin, subjoin • sandwich coin, tenderloin • Assiniboin

oin² \aⁿ\ see IN⁴

oine \än\ see ON¹

oined \òind\ conjoined, uncoined—*also* -ed *forms of verbs listed at* OIN¹

oiner \òi-nər\ coiner, joiner • purloiner

oines \òin\ see OIN¹

oing¹ \ō-iŋ\ bowing, going, knowing, rowing, sewing, showing • churchgoing, deep-going, foregoing, free-flowing, glassblowing, ingrowing, mind-blowing, ongoing, outgoing, seagoing, self-knowing, waygoing • concertgoing, easygoing, moviegoing, oceangoing, operagoing, theatergoing, thoroughgoing, whistle-blowing • to-ing and fro-ing—*also* -ing *forms of verbs listed at* ow¹

oing² \ü-iŋ\ bluing, doing, Ewing • misdoing, undoing, wrongdoing • evildoing, nothing doing—*also* -ing *forms of verbs listed at* EW¹

oing³ \ō-ən\ see OAN¹

o-ing \ō-iŋ\ see OING¹

oings \ō-iŋz\ outgoings—*also* -s, -'s, *and* -s' *forms of nouns and* -s *forms of verbs listed at* OING¹

oint¹ \óint\ joint, point • adjoint, anoint, appoint, aroint, ballpoint, bluepoint, blue point, break point, butt joint, checkpoint, choke point, clip joint, conjoint, dew point, disjoint, drypoint, end point, fixed-popint, flash point, game point, grade point, gunpoint, High Point, hinge joint, hip joint, ice point, juke joint, knifepoint, lap joint, match point, midpoint, near point, nonpoint, outpoint, pen point, pinpoint, pourpoint, price point, seal point, set point, standpoint, strongpoint, tuckpoint, viewpoint, waypoint • at gunpoint, at knifepoint, Barbers Point, basis point, boiling point, breaking point, brownie point, cardinal point, case in point, counterpoint, Curie point, disappoint, extra point, floating-point, focal point,

freezing point, growing point, ideal point, knuckle joint, melting point, miter joint, Montauk Point, needlepoint, out of joint, pedal point, petit point, point-to-point, pressure point, rabbet joint, selling point, silverpoint, sticking point, strain a point, stretch a point, talking point, to the point, trigger point, triple point, try for point, turning point, vantage point, vowel point • beside the point, decimal point, inflection point, percentage point, vanishing point

oint² \ant\ see ANT⁵

ointe \ant\ see ANT⁵

ointed \óint-əd\ jointed, pointed • disjointed, lap-jointed, loose-jointed • disappointed, double-jointed, self-appointed, well-appointed—*also* -ed *forms of verbs listed at* OINT¹

ointer \óint-ər\ jointer, pointer • anointer, hip pointer, three-pointer

ointing \óin-tiŋ\ disappointing, finger-pointing—*also* -ing *forms of verbs listed at* OINT¹

ointment \óint-mənt\ ointment • anointment, appointment • disappointment • fly in the ointment

oir¹ \īr\ see IRE¹

oir² \är\ see AR³

oir³ \óir\ see OYER

oir⁴ \ór\ see OR¹

oire¹ \är\ see AR³

oire² \óir\ see OYER

oire³ \ór\ see OR¹

ois¹ \ä\ see A¹

ois² \ói\ see OY

ois³ \ō-əs\ Lois, Powys

ois⁴ \óis\ see OICE

oise¹ \äz\ poise, 'twas, vase, was
• Ahwaz, bourgeoise, framboise, genoise, Lamaze, Shiraz, vichyssoise • Afars and the Issas—also -s, -'s, and -s' forms of nouns and -s forms of verbs listed at A¹

oise² \óiz\ hoise, noise, Noyes, poise • pink noise, self-poise, turquoise, white noise • counterpoise, equipoise • avoirdupois—also -s, -'s, and -s' forms of nouns and -s forms of verbs listed at OY

oise³ \ói-zē\ see OISY

oison \óiz-ᵉn\ foison, poison • empoison

oist \óist\ foist, hoist, joist, moist, voiced • unvoiced—also -ed forms of verbs listed at OICE

oister \ói-stər\ cloister, hoister, moister, oyster, roister • seed oyster

oisterous \ói-strəs\ see OISTRESS

oistral \ói-strəl\ cloistral, coistrel

oistrel \ói-strəl\ see OISTRAL

oistress \ói-strəs\ boisterous, cloistress, roisterous

oisy \ói-zē\ Boise, Doisy, noisy

oit¹ \óit\ doit, droit, quoit • adroit, Detroit, exploit, introit • maladroit, Massasoit

oit² \āt\ see ATE¹

oit³ \ō-ət\ see OET¹

oit⁴ \ä\ see A¹

oite \āt\ see OT¹

olter \óit-ər\ goiter, loiter • Detroiter, exploiter • reconnoiter

oitus \ō-ət-əs\ see OETESS

oivre \äv\ see OLVE¹

oix¹ \ä\ see A¹

oix² \ói\ see OY

oiz \óis\ see OISE²

ojan \ō-jən\ Trojan • theologian

oje \ō-jē\ see OJI

oji \ō-jē\ Moji, shoji • anagoge, Hachioji

ok¹ \äk\ see OCK¹

ok² \ək\ see UCK

ok³ \ók\ see ALK

oka \ō-kə\ see OCA

okable \ō-kə-bəl\ see OCABLE

oke¹ \ōk\ bloke, broke, choke, cloak, coke, Coke, croak, folk, hoke, joke, moke, oak, oke, poke, Polk, roque, smoke, soak, soke, spoke, stoke, stroke, toke, toque, woke, yogh, yoke, yolk • ad hoc, awoke, backstroke, baroque, bespoke, blow smoke, breast-stroke, brushstroke, bur oak, chain-smoke, convoke, cork oak, cowpoke, downstroke, evoke, ground stroke, heat-stroke, holm oak, housebroke, in-joke, invoke, keystroke, kinfolk, kinsfolk, live oak, menfolk, outspoke, pin oak, post oak, presoak, provoke, red oak, revoke, scrub oak, she-oak, sidestroke, silk oak, slowpoke, sunchoke, sunstroke, tan oak, townsfolk, uncloak, unyoke, upstroke, white oak, workfolk • artichoke, at a stroke, Bolingbroke, chestnut oak, durmast oak, equivoque, fisherfolk, gentlefolk, go for broke, herrenvolk, hub-and-spoke, masterstroke, ministroke, monocoque, mourning cloak, okeydoke, poison oak, Roanoke, thunderstroke, trudgeon stroke, turkey oak, water oak, womenfolk

oke² \ō-kē\ see OKY

oke³ \ō\ see OW¹

oke⁴ \uk\ see OOK¹

oked \ōkt\ stoked, yolked

okee \ō-kē\ see OKY

okel \ō-kəl\ see OCAL

oken \ō-kən\ broken, oaken, spoken, token, woken • awoken, bespoken, betoken, fair-spoken, foretoken, free-spoken, heartbroken, housebroken, outspoken, plainspoken, short-spoken, soft-spoken, unbroken, well-spoken, wind-broken • hard-times token • by the same token

oker \ō-kər\ broker, choker, croaker, joker, ocher, poker, soaker, smoker, stoker, stroker • backstroker, black smoker, breaststroker, chain-smoker, draw poker, invoker, pawn-broker, provoker, red ocher, revoker, stockbroker, straight poker, strip poker, stud poker • honest broker, mediocre, power broker, red-hot poker, yellow ocher

okey \ō-kē\ see OKY

oki \ō-kē\ see OKY

oking \ō-kiŋ\ broking, choking —*also* -ing forms of verbs listed at OKE¹

oko \ō-kō\ see OCO

okum \ō-kəm\ Bochum, hokum, locum, oakum

oky \ō-kē\ choky, croaky, folkie, hokey, jokey, Loki, poky, smoky, troche, trochee, yolky • enoki, Great Smoky • hokeypokey, karaoke • Okefenokee

ol¹ \ōl\ see OLE¹

ol² \äl\ see AL¹

ol³ \ol\ see ALL

ola \ō-lə\ bola, cola, Kola, Lola, tola, Zola • Angola, boffola, canola, crapola, Ebola, gondola, granola, mandola, payola, pergola, plugola, scagliola, Tortola, Victrola, Vignola, viola, Viola • acerola, ayatollah, braciola, Española, Fabiola, gladiola, Gorgonzola, hemiola, Hispaniola, moviola,

Osceola, Pensacola, roseola, rubeola, variola • Savonarola

olable \ō-lə-bəl\ see OLLABLE

olace \äl-əs\ see OLIS

olan \ō-lən\ see OLON

oland \ō-lənd\ see OWLAND

olar¹ \ō-lər\ see OLLER

olar² \äl-ər\ see OLLAR

olas \ō-ləs\ see OLUS

olater \äl-ət-ər\ bardolater, idolater • bibliolater, Mariolater

olatrous \äl-ə-trəs\ idolatrous • bibliolatrous, heliolatrous

olatry \äl-ə-trē\ bardolatry, idolatry, zoolatry • bibliolatry, heliolatry, iconolatry, Mariolatry

old¹ \ōld\ bold, bowled, cold, fold, gold, hold, mold, mould, old, polled, scold, sold, soled, souled, told, wold • acold, age-old, ahold, all told, behold, bifold, billfold, black gold, blindfold, blue mold, bread mold, choke hold, controlled, Cotswold, cuckold, eightfold, enfold, fanfold, fivefold, fool's gold, foothold, foretold, fourfold, freehold, gatefold, go gold, green mold, handhold, head cold, household, ice-cold, infold, knock cold, kobold, leaf mold, leasehold, make bold, ninefold, old gold, onefold, on hold, pinfold, potholed, roothold, scaffold, sheepfold, sixfold, slime mold, stokehold, stone-cold, stronghold, take hold, tenfold, threefold, threshold, toehold, twice-told, twofold, unfold, unmold, untold, uphold, white gold, whole-souled, withhold • centerfold, common cold, copyhold, fingerhold, hundredfold, manifold, manyfold, marigold, multifold, oversold, petioled, scissors hold, sevenfold, severalfold, sooty mold, stranglehold, thousandfold, throttlehold, water mold • as good as gold, basket-of-gold, blow hot and cold, lo and behold, marsh marigold, out in the cold—*also* -ed *forms of verbs listed at* OLE¹

old² \òld\ see ALD

oldan \ōl-dən\ see OLDEN

olden \ōl-dən\ golden, holden, olden, soldan • beholden, embolden

older¹ \ōl-dər\ boulder, folder, holder, molder, polder, scolder, shoulder, smolder • beholder, bondholder, cardholder, freeholder, gasholder, hand-holder, householder, jobholder, landholder, leaseholder, penholder, pewholder, placeholder, pot holder, shareholder, slaveholder, stadtholder, stakeholder, stallholder, stockholder, toolholder, officeholder, titleholder, upholder, withholder • policyholder—*also* -er *forms of adjectives listed at* OLD¹

older² \äd-ər\ see ODDER

oldi \òl-dē\ see ALDI

oldie \ōl-dē\ see OLDY

olding \ōl-diŋ\ folding, holding, molding, scolding • bed molding, crown molding, hand-holding, inholding, landholding, scaffolding, shareholding, slaveholding, stakeholding —*also* -ing *forms of verbs listed at* OLD[1]

oldster \ōl-stər\ see OLSTER

oldt \ōlt\ see OLT[1]

oldy \ōl-dē\ moldy, oldie • golden oldie

ole[1] \ōl\ bole, boll, bowl, coal, cole, Cole, dhole, dole, droll, foal, goal, hole, knoll, kohl, Kohl, mole, ole, pole, Pole, poll, prole, role, roll, scroll, Seoul, shoal, skoal, sol, sole, soul, stole, stroll, thole, tole, toll, troll, vole, whole • airhole, armhole, atoll, bankroll, beadroll, beanpole, bedroll, black hole, blackpoll, blowhole, bolthole, borehole, bunghole, cajole, catchpole, charcoal, chuckhole, clodpole, condole, console, control, creole, Creole, dipole, drumroll, dry hole, Dutch roll, egg roll, enroll, ensoul, extol, eyehole, field goal, fishbowl, flagpole, foxhole, frijol, funk hole, hard coal, half sole, heart-whole, hellhole, Huichol, inscroll, insole, in whole, keyhole, kneehole, knothole, leaf roll, logroll, loophole, manhole, maypole, midsole, Mongol, Nicolle, North Pole, outsole, parole, patrol, payroll, peephole, pesthole, pie hole, pinhole, pistole, pitchpole, porthole, posthole, pothole, redpoll, resole, ridgepole, Sheol, shot hole, sinkhole, ski pole, slipsole, snap roll, sotol, sound hole, South Pole, spring roll, stokehole, tadpole, taphole, thumbhole, top-hole, touchhole, turnsole, unroll, Walpole, washbowl, weep hole, white hole, wormhole • aureole, banderole, bannerol, barcarole, barrel roll, buttonhole, cabriole, camisole, capriole, caracole, carmagnole, casserole, coffee roll, croquignole, cubbyhole, decontrol, Demerol, Dover sole, escarole, exit poll, farandole, finger hole, fumarole, girandole, girasole, Grand Guignol, honor roll, innersole, in the hole, Jackson Hole, jelly roll, kaiser roll, lemon sole, meadow vole, methanol, micromole, millimole, monopole, muster roll, on a roll, on the whole, oriole, ostiole, oversoul, ozone hole, petiole, pick-and-roll, pigeonhole, protocol, rabbit hole, rigmarole, rock and roll, Seminole, star-nosed mole, totem pole, tracheole, vacuole, water hole • ace in the hole, animal pole, arteriole, bibliopole, celestial pole, cholesterol, Costa del Sol, Haitian Creole, Kure Atoll, Lake Seminole, liberty pole, magnetic pole

ole[2] \ō-lē\ see OLY[1]

ole[3] \ȯl\ see ALL

olean \ō-lē-ən\ see OLIAN[1]

oled \ōld\ see OLD[1]

oleful \ōl-fəl\ doleful, soulful

olely \ō-lē\ see OLY¹

olem¹ \ō-ləm\ golem, solum

olem² \ä-ləm\ see ALAAM

olemn \äl-əm\ see OLUMN

oleon¹ \ō-lē-ən\ see OLIAN¹

oleon² \ōl-yən\ see OLIAN²

oler¹ \ō-lər\ see OLLER

oler² \äl-ər\ see OLLAR

olery \ōl-rē\ see OLLERY

olesome \ōl-səm\ dolesome,
Folsom, wholesome
• unwholesome

oless \ō-ləs\ see OLUS

oleum \ō-lē-əm\ see OLIUM

oleus \ō-lē-əs\ coleus, soleus

oley \ō-lē\ see OLY¹

olf¹ \älf\ golf, Rolf • Adolph,
Randolph, Rudolph, Lake
Rudolf • miniature golf

olf² \əlf\ see ULF

olfing \òf-iŋ\ see OFFING

olga \äl-gə\ Olga, Volga

oli \ō-lē\ see OLY¹

olia \ō-lē-ə\ Aetolia, Mongolia,
pignolia, Podolia • Anatolia,
melancholia • Inner Mongolia,
Outer Mongolia

olian \ō-lē-ən\ aeolian, Aeolian,
Bristolian, eolian, Mongolian,
napoleon, Napoleon, simoleon,
Tyrolean, Walpolian • Anatolian
• Louis-Napoléon

olic¹ \äl-ik\ colic, frolic, Gaelic,
rollick • Aeolic, Argolic, bucolic,
carbolic, embolic, Mongolic,
symbolic, systolic • alcoholic,
anabolic, apostolic, catabolic,
chocoholic, diabolic, diastolic,
hyperbolic, hypergolic, melan-
cholic, metabolic, painter's
colic, parabolic, shopaholic,
vitriolic, workaholic

olic² \ō-lik\ colic • fumarolic

olicking \ä-lik-iŋ\ frolicking,
rollicking

olicy \äl-ə-sē\ policy, Wallasey
• foreign policy

olid \äl-əd\ solid, squalid, stolid
• biosolid, semisolid

olin¹ \äl-ən\ see OLLEN⁵

olin² \ō-lən\ see OLON

olis \äl-əs\ braless, polis, solace,
tallith, Wallace, Wallis
• Cornwallis • Manizales,
torticollis

olish \äl-ish\ polish • abolish,
demolish • apple-polish, spit-
and-polish

olitan \äl-ət-ᵊn\ cosmopolitan,
megapolitan, metropolitan,
Neapolitan

olity \äl-ət-ē\ see ALITY¹

olium \ō-lē-əm\ oleum
• scholium • linoleum,
petroleum, trifolium

olivar \äl-ə-vər\ see OLIVER

olk¹ \elk\ see ELK¹

olk² \ōk\ see OKE

olk³ \əlk\ see ULK

olk⁴ \òk\ see ALK

olked \ōkt\ see OKED

olkie \ō-kē\ see OKY

olky \ō-kē\ see OKY

oll[1] \ōl\ see OLE[1]

oll[2] \äl\ see AL[1]

oll[3] \ȯl\ see ALL

olla[1] \äl-ə\ see ALA[2]

olla[2] \ȯi-ə\ see OIA

ollable \ō-lə-bəl\ controllable
• inconsolable, uncontrollable

ollack \äl-ək\ see OLOCH

ollah[1] \ō-lə\ see OLA

ollah[2] \äl-ə\ see ALA[2]

ollah[3] \əl-ə\ see ULLAH[1]

ollands \äl-ənz\ see OLLINS

ollar \äl-ər\ choler, collar, dollar, haler, holler, loller, Mahler, scholar, squalor, taler • blue-collar, dog collar, flea collar, half-dollar, pink-collar, sand dollar, shawl collar, Straits dollar, top dollar, trade dollar, white-collar • Emmentaler, Eton collar, Eurodollar, petrodollar, Roman collar, sailor collar • clerical collar, mandarin collar, Peter Pan collar, radio collar

ollard \äl-ərd\ bollard, collard, collared, hollered, Lollard, pollard

olled \ōld\ see OLD[1]

ollee \ō-lē\ see OLY[1]

ollege \äl-ij\ see OWLEDGE

ollen[1] \ō-lən\ see OLON

ollen[2] \əl-ə\ see ULLAH[1]

ollen[3] \əl-ən\ see ULLEN

ollen[4] \ȯ-lən\ see ALLEN

ollen[5] \äl-ən\ Colin, pollen
• Nordrhein-Westfalen

oller \ō-lər\ bowler, choler, dolor, droller, molar, polar, poler, poller, roller, solar, stroller, troller • bankroller, cajoler, comptroller, controller, extoller, high roller, leaf roller, logroller, patroller, premolar, road roller, steamroller, stone roller • antisolar, buttonholer, Maryknoller, pigeonholer, rock and roller

ollery \ōl-rē\ drollery • cajolery

ollet \äl-ət\ collet, Smollett, tallith, wallet • whatchamacallit

ollett \äl-ət\ see OLLET

olley \äl-ē\ see OLLY[1]

ollick \äl-ik\ see OLIC[1]

ollicking \ä-lik-iŋ\ see OLICKING

ollie \äl-ē\ see OLLY[1]

ollin \äl-ən\ see OLLEN[5]

olling \ō-liŋ\ bowling • high-rolling, logrolling • exit polling
—*also* -ing *forms of verbs listed at* OLE[1]

ollins \äl-ənz\ collins, Collins, Hollands • Tom Collins

ollis \äl-əs\ see OLIS

ollity \äl-ət-ē\ see ALITY[1]

ollo[1] \ōl-yō\ Badaglio, imbroglio
• arroz con pollo

ollo[2] \ō-yō\ yo-yo • criollo

ollo[3] \äl-ō\ see OLLOW[1]

ollop \äl-əp\ collop, dollop, lollop, polyp, scallop, trollop, wallop • bay scallop, codswallop, sea scallop

ollow[1] \äl-ō\ follow, hollo, hollow, swallow, wallow • Apollo, barn swallow, cliff swallow, robalo, tree swallow • Leoncavallo

ollow[2] \äl-ə\ see ALA[2]

ollower \äl-ə-wər\ follower, swallower, wallower • camp follower

ollster \ōl-stər\ see OLSTER

olly[1] \äl-ē\ Bali, brolly, Cali, collie, colly, Dalí, dolly, folly, golly, Halle, holly, Holly, jolly, lolly, Mali, molly, Molly, Ollie, Pali, poly, Polly, quale, Raleigh, trolley, volley • Denali, finale, Kigali, loblolly, Nepali, petrale, sea holly, Somali, Svengali, tamale • Boutros-Ghali, English holly, melancholy, Mexicali, teocalli

olly[2] \ȯ-lē\ see AWLY

olm \ōm\ see OME[1]

olman \ōl-mən\ dolman, dolmen • patrolman

olmen \ōl-mən\ see OLMAN

olmes \ōmz\ Holmes—*also* -s, -'s, *and* -s' *forms of nouns and* -s *forms of verbs listed at* OME[1]

olo \ō-lō\ bolo, kolo, nolo, polo, solo • Barolo • Marco Polo, water polo

oloch \äl-ək\ Moloch, pollack, rowlock

ologer \äl-ə-jər\ astrologer, chronologer, mythologer

ologist \äl-ə-jəst\ anthologist, apologist, biologist, cetologist, chronologist, conchologist, cosmologist, cryptologist, cytologist, dendrologist, ecologist, enologist, ethnologist, ethologist, fetologist, garbologist, gemologist, geologist, graphologist, histologist, horologist, hydrologist, Indologist, limnologist, mixologist, morphologist, mycologist, mythologist, necrologist, nephrologist, neurologist, oncologist, ontologist, oologist, pathologist, pedologist, penologist, petrologist, philologist, phonologist, phrenologist, phycologist, psychologist, seismologist, serologist, sexologist, sinologist, technologist, topologist, typologist, ufologist, urologist, virologist, zoologist • anthropologist, archaeologist, audiologist, cardiologist, climatologist, cosmetologist, criminologist, dermatologist, Egyptologist, embryologist, entomologist, enzymologist, escapologist, etymologist, futurologist, genealogist, gerontologist, gynecologist, hematologist, herpetologist, ichthyologist, ideologist, immunologist, kremlinologist, lexicologist, martyrologist, methodologist, mineralogist, musicologist, nematalogist, numerologist, oceanologist, ophthalmologist, ornithologist, osteologist, papyrologist, pharmacologist, phraseologist, physiologist, planetologist, primatologist, rheumatologist, roentgenologist, semiologist, sociologist, speleologist, teleologist, teratologist, thanatologist, toxicologist, urbanologist, volcanologist • endocrinologist, paleontologist, phenomenologist • anesthesiologist, epidemiologist, gastroenterologist, otolaryngologist

ologous \äl-ə-gəs\ autologous, homologous, tautologous • heterologous

ology \äl-ə-jē\ andrology, anthology, apology, astrology, biology, bryology, cetology, Christology, chronology, conchology, cosmology, cryptology, cytology, dendrology, doxology, ecology, enology, ethnology, ethology, fetology, garbology, gemology, geology, graphology, haplology, histology, homology, horology, hydrology, hymnology, Indology, limnology, lithology, mixology, morphology, mycology, myology, mythology, necrology, nephrology, neurology, nosology, oncology, ontology, oology, pathology, pedology, penology, petrology, philology, phlebology, phonology, phrenology, phycology, proctology, psychology, scatology, seismology, serology, sexology, sinology, symbology, tautology, technology, tetralogy, theology, topology, trichology, typology, ufology, urology, virology, zoology • anthropology, archaeology, cardiology, climatology, cosmetology, criminology, dermatology, Egyptology, entomology, eschatology, etiology, etymology, futurology, genealogy, gerontology, glaciology, gynecology, hematology, herpetology, ideology, immunology, kremlinology, laryngology, lexicology, Mariology, martyrology, methodology, mineralogy, musicology, numerology, oceanology, ophthalmology, ornithology, pharmacology, phraseology, physiology, primatology, radiology, reflexology, rheumatology, semiology, sociology, terminology, thanatology, toxicology, urbanology, volcanology, vulcanology • bacteriology, endocrinology, epistemology, Gestalt psychology, kinesiology, metapsychology, microbiology, nanotechnology, neurobiology, neuropsychology, paleontology, parasitology, phenomenology • anesthesiology, epidemiology, ethnomusicology, gastroenterology, otolaryngology

olon \ō-lən\ bowline, Colin, colon, Nolan, solon, stolen, stollen, stolon, swollen • eidolon • semicolon

olonel \ərn-ᵊl\ see ERNAL

olonist \äl-ə-nəst\ colonist, Stalinist

olor[1] \əl-ər\ color, cruller, culler, huller, muller, sculler • bicolor, discolor, false color, off-color, oil color, three-color, tricolor, turn color • local color, Technicolor, watercolor

olor[2] \ō-lər\ see OLLER

olor[3] \äl-ər\ see OLLAR

olored \əl-ərd\ colored, dullard • bicolored, off-colored, rose-colored, tricolored • varicolored

olp \ōp\ see OPE

olpen \ō-pən\ see OPEN

olph \älf\ see OLF

ols \älz\ Hals, hols • Casals

olsom \ōl-səm\ see OLESOME

olster \ōl-stər\ bolster, holster, oldster, pollster • upholster

olt[1] \ōlt\ bolt, colt, dolt, Holt, jolt, molt, poult, smolt, volt • dead bolt, eyebolt, Humboldt, kingbolt, revolt, ringbolt, spring bolt, unbolt • shoot one's bolt, thunderbolt, toggle bolt

olt[2] \ólt\ see ALT

olta \äl-tə\ see ALTA

olter \ōl-tər\ bolter, coulter, jolter, molter • revolter

oltish \ōl-tish\ coltish, doltish

oluble \äl-yə-bəl\ soluble, voluble • dissoluble, insoluble, resoluble • indissoluble, irresoluble

olum \ō-ləm\ see OLEM

olumn \äl-əm\ column, slalom, solemn • fifth column • giant slalom, lally column, Malayalam, spinal column, steering column

olus \ō-ləs\ bolas, bolus, solus, snowless, toeless • Pactolus • Coriolis, electroless, gladiolus, holus-bolus

olvable \äl-və-bəl\ solvable • dissolvable, evolvable, insolvable, resolvable, revolvable • irresolvable

olve[1] \älv\ salve, solve • absolve, au poivre, convolve, devolve, dissolve, evolve, involve, resolve, revolve • coevolve

olve[2] \äv\ grave, of, salve, Slav, suave, taw, waw • Gustav, moshav, thereof, whereof, Zouave • Stanislav, Tishah-b'Ab, unheard-of, well-thought-of, Yugoslav

olvement \älv-mənt\ evolvement, involvement • noninvolvement, self-involvement

olvent \äl-vənt\ solvent • dissolvent, insolvent, resolvent

olver \äl-vər\ solver • absolver, dissolver, involver, resolver, revolver

oly[1] \ō-lē\ goalie, holey, holy, lowly, mole, moly, pollee, slowly, solely • aioli, amole, anole, cannoli, frijole, jus soli, pignoli, pinole, unholy • guacamole, ravioli, roly-poly

oly[2] \äl-ē\ see OLLY[1]

olyp \äl-əp\ see OLLOP

om[1] \äm\ balm, Baum, bomb, bombe, calm, from, gaum, Guam, glom, mom, palm, Pom, pram, prom, psalm, qualm, rhomb, ROM, tom • A-bomb, aplomb, ashram, becalm, bee balm, buzz bomb, car bomb, Ceram, cheongsam, coulomb, Coulomb, dive-bomb, dot-com, embalm, EPROM, firebomb, grande dame, H-bomb, imam, Islam, Long Tom, napalm, nizam, noncom, oil palm, phenom, pogrom, pom-pom, réclame, rhabdom, salaam, seram, sitcom, skip bomb, Songnam, stink bomb, tam-tam, therefrom, time bomb, tom-tom, wax palm, wherefrom, wigwam • atom bomb, cardamom, carpet bomb, CD-ROM, cherry bomb, cluster bomb, diatom, intercom, lemon balm, letter bomb, logic bomb, neutron bomb, Peeping Tom, royal palm, sago palm, soccer mom, supermom, telecom, Uncle Tom, Vietnam • atomic bomb, coconut palm, Dar es Salaam, hydrogen bomb, in personam, Omar Khayyám • fragmentation bomb

om[2] \ōm\ see OME[1]

om[3] \üm\ see OOM[1]

om[4] \əm\ see UM[1]

om[5] \u̇m\ see UM[2]

om[6] \ȯm\ see AUM[1]

oma \ō-mə\ chroma, coma, noma, Roma, soma, stoma, stroma • aroma, diploma, fibroma, glaucoma, lymphoma, sarcoma, Tacoma • adenoma, carcinoma, granuloma, hematoma, melanoma, Mount Tacoma, myeloma, Oklahoma, papilloma, teratoma, tokonoma

omac \ō-mik\ see OMIC[2]

omace[1] \äm-əs\ see OMISE

omace[2] \əm-əs\ see UMMOUS

omach \əm-ək\ see UMMOCK

omache \äm-ə-kē\ see OMACHY

omachy \äm-ə-kē\ Andromache, logomachy

omal \ō-məl\ domal, stomal • prodromal • autosomal, chromosomal, liposomal, microsomal

omaly \äm-ə-lē\ balmily, homily • anomaly

oman \ō-mən\ bowman, foeman, gnomon, nomen, omen, Roman, showman, snowman, soman, yeoman • agnomen, cognomen, crossbowman, Dahoman, longbowman, praenomen, Sertoman

omany \äm-ə-nē\ see OMINY

omas \äm-əs\ see OMISE

omathy \äm-ə-thē\ chrestomathy, stichomythy

omb[1] \ōm\ see OME[1]

omb[2] \üm\ see OOM[1]

omb[3] \äm\ see OM[1]

omb[4] \əm\ see UM[1]

omba \äm-bə\ see AMBA

ombe[1] \ōm\ see OME[1]

ombe[2] \üm\ see OOM[1]

ombe³ \äm\ see OM¹

ombed \ümd\ see OOMED

omber¹ \äm-ər\ bomber, calmer, palmar, palmer, Palmer • dive-bomber, embalmer • fighter-bomber

omber² \äm-bər\ ombre, sambar, somber

omber³ \ō-mər\ see OMER¹

ombic \ō-mik\ see OMIC²

ombical \ō-mi-kəl\ see OMICAL²

ombie \äm-bē\ zombie • Abercrombie

ombing \ō-miŋ\ see OAMING

ombo¹ \äm-bō\ combo, mambo, sambo • Ovambo

ombo² \əm-bō\ see UMBO

ombre¹ \äm-brē\ hombre, ombre

ombre² \äm-bər\ see OMBER²

ombre³ \əm-brē\ see UMBERY

ombus \äm-bəs\ rhombus, thrombus

ome¹ \ōm\ brougham, chrome, comb, combe, dome, foam, gloam, gnome, holm, home, loam, mome, nome, ogham, ohm, om, poem, pome, roam, Rom, Rome, tome • airdrome, at-home, beachcomb, Beer-bohm, bichrome, Bornholm, bring home, Cape Nome, clay loam, cockscomb, coulomb, coxcomb, defoam, down-home, fall home, genome, group home, hot comb, Jerome, megohm, Nichrome, prodome, radome, rest home, rhizome, salt dome, seadrome, shalom, sheet home, Stock-holm, syndrome, Vendôme • aerodrome, astrodome, catacomb, chromosome, Clingmans Dome, close to home, currycomb, double-dome, Down syndrome, fine-tooth comb, foster home, funeral home, gastronome, harvest home, hecatomb, hippodrome, honeycomb, loxodrome, meadowfoam, metronome, mobile home, monochrome, motor home, nursing home, onion dome, palindrome, plastic foam, pleasure dome, polychrome, Reye's syndrome, ribosome, semidome, soldiers' home, stay-at-home, Styrofoam, velodrome • China Syndrome, detention home, Gulf War syndrome, Marfan syndrome, Mercurochrome, Stockholm syndrome, X chromosome, Y chromosome

ome² \ō-mē\ see OAMY

ome³ \əm\ see UM¹

omedy \äm-əd-ē\ comedy, psalmody • high comedy, low comedy • tragicomedy

omely \əm-lē\ see UMBLY²

omen \ō-mən\ see OMAN

omenal \äm-ən-el\ see OMINAL

omene \äm-ə-nē\ see OMINY

omer¹ \ō-mər\ comber, foamer, homer, Homer, omer, roamer, vomer • beachcomber, Lag b'Omer, misnomer

omer² \əm-ər\ see UMMER

omery \əm-ə-rē\ see UMMERY

omet \äm-ət\ comet, grommet, vomit

ometer \äm-ət-ər\ barometer, ceilometer, chronometer, cyclometer, ergometer, Fathometer, gasometer, geometer, hydrometer, hygrometer, kilometer, manometer, micrometer, odometer, pedometer, photometer, pulsometer, pyrometer, rheometer, seismometer, spectrometer, speedometer, tachometer, thermometer, viscometer • anemometer, audiometer, diffractometer, dynamometer, electrometer, galvanometer, magnetometer, mass spectrometer

ometry \äm-ə-trē\ astrometry, barometry, chronometry, cytometry, geometry, isometry, micrometry, optometry, photometry, psychometry, seismometry, spirometry, thermometry • craniometry, mass spectrometry, plane geometry, sociometry, trigonometry

omey \ō-mē\ see OAMY

omi \ō-mē\ see OAMY

omia \ō-mē-ä\ peperomia, Utsunomiya

omic¹ \äm-ik\ comic • anomic, atomic, coelomic, Islamic, oghamic, tsunamic • agronomic, anatomic, antinomic, autonomic, diatomic, economic, ergonomic, gastronomic, metronomic, subatomic, taxonomic, tragicomic • Deuteronomic, heroicomic, physiognomic, polyatomic, seriocomic • macroeconomic, microeconomic

omic² \ō-mik\ gnomic • Potomac, rhizomic • catacombic, hypochromic, monochromic, palindromic

omical¹ \äm-i-kəl\ comical, domical • anatomical, astronomical, economical

omical² \ō-mi-kəl\ domical • coxcombical

omics \äm-iks\ comics • Islamics • bionomics, economics, ergonomics • home economics, proteomics • macroeconomics, microeconomics—also -s, -'s, and -s' forms of nouns listed at OMIC¹

omily \äm-ə-lē\ see OMALY

ominal \äm-ən-əl\ nominal • abdominal, cognominal, phenomenal • epiphenomenal

ominance \äm-nəns\ dominance, prominence • predominance

ominant \äm-nənt\ dominant, prominent • predominant, subdominant

omine \äm-ə-nē\ see OMINY

ominence \äm-nəns\ see OMINANCE

ominent \äm-nənt\ see OMINANT

oming[1] \əm-iŋ\ coming, numbing, plumbing • becoming, forthcoming, have coming, homecoming, incoming, mind-numbing, oncoming, short-coming, upcoming • Second Coming, unbecoming, up-and-coming—*also* -ing *forms of verbs listed at* UM[1]

oming[2] \ō-miŋ\ see OAMING

omini \äm-ə-nē\ see OMINY

ominous \äm-ə-nəs\ ominous • prolegomenous

ominy \äm-ə-nē\ hominy, Romany • ignominy, Melpomene • anno Domini, eo nomine

omise \äm-əs\ pomace, promise, shammes, shamus, Thomas • Saint Thomas • breach of promise, doubting Thomas • lick and a promise

omit \äm-ət\ see OMET

omium \ō-mē-əm\ chromium, holmium • encomium, prostomium

omma[1] \äm-ə\ see AMA[2]

omma[2] \əm-ə\ see UMMA

ommel[1] \äm-əl\ pommel, Jamil, Rommel, trommel

ommel[2] \əm-əl\ pommel, pummel • Beau Brummell

ommet \äm-ət\ see OMET

ommie \äm-ē\ see AMI[1]

ommon \äm-ən\ Ammon, Brahman, common, shaman, yamen • in common, Roscommon • Tutankhamen

ommoner \äm-ə-nər\ almoner, commoner • gewürztraminer

ommy[1] \äm-ē\ see AMI[1]

ommy[2] \əm-ē\ see UMMY

omo \ō-mō\ bromo, Como, homo, Pomo, promo • Oromo • majordomo

omon \ō-mən\ see OMAN

omp[1] \ämp\ champ, chomp, clomp, comp, pomp, romp, stamp, stomp, swamp, tramp, tromp, whomp • workers' comp

omp[2] \əmp\ see UMP

ompass \əm-pəs\ compass, rumpus • encompass • gyro-compass

omper \äm-pər\ romper, stamper, stomper, swamper • wafflestomper

ompers \äm-pərz\ Gompers—*also* -s, -'s, *and* -s' *forms of nouns listed at* OMPER

ompey \äm-pē\ see OMPY

ompo \äm-pō\ campo, compo

ompous \äm-pəs\ see OMPASS[1]

ompson \äm-sən\ see AMSUN

ompt \aunt\ see OUNT[2]

ompy \äm-pē\ Pompey, swampy

omythy \äm-ə-thē\ see OMATHY

on[1] \än\ ban, Bonn, chon, con, conn, dawn, don, Don, drawn, faun, fawn, gone, guan, Han, John, Jon, khan, Mann, maun, mon, on, pan, pawn, prawn, Ron, Shan, spawn, swan, wan, yawn, yon, yuan • aeon, add-on, agon, agone, Akan, alençon, Ambon, Amman, anon, Anshan, Anton, archon, argon, Argonne, Aswan, atman, Avon, axon, bank on, barchan, baton, big on, Bion, blouson, bon ton, bonbon, boron, boson, bouillon, bring on, Brython, build on, bygone, caisson, Calgon, call on, canton, capon, cast on, catch on, Ceylon, chaconne, Charon, chew on, chiffon, chignon, chiton, chrismon, Cimon, cistron, clip-on, codon, come-on, cordon, coupon, crampon, crayon, crepon, cretonne, crouton, Dacron, dead-on, Dear John, doggone, doggoned, Dogon, Don Juan, eon, exon, fall on, far-gone, flacon, foregone, form on, Freon, fronton, futon, Garonne, get on, Gibran, gluon, gnomon, Golan, go on, guidon, hadron, Hainan, hand on, hands-on, hang on, have on, hazan, head-on, Henan, hereon, high on, hit on, hogan, hold on, Huainan, Hunan, icon, Inchon, intron, ion, Ivan, jargon, Jinan, jomon, kanban, kaon, Kashan, Kazan, keen on, Khoisan, Kirman, koan, krypton, kurgan, Kurgan, lauan, Leon, lepton, let on, lock on, log on, look on, Luzon, macron, Masan, Medan, Memnon, meson, micron, Milan, mod con, moron, mouton, Multan, muon, natron, nekton, neon, nephron, neuron, neutron, ninon, Nippon, nylon, odds-on, Oman, Oran, Orlon,

outgone, paeon, parton, Pathan, pavane, pecan, peon, Phaëthon, photon, phyton, pick on, pion, pinon, piton, plankton, pluton, pompon, prion, proton, Pusan, push on, put-on, pylon, python, Qur'an, racon, radon, rag on, rayon, recon, rhyton, right-on, run-on, run on, Saint John, Saipan, salon, San Juan, Schliemann, Schumann, Shaban, shaman, shaitan, Shingon, Sichuan, sign on, Simplon, sit on, Sjaelland, slip-on, snap-on, solon, Solon, soupçon, soutane, spot on, stand on, Stefan, stolon, stuck on, Suwon, sweet on, Szechwan, Tainan, Taiwan, taipan, take on, tampon, taxon, Teflon, Tehran, teston, Tétouan, Tetuán, thereon, Tian Shan, tisane, torchon, toucan, toyon, trade on, trigon, Tristan, triton, trogon, try on, Tucson, turned-on, turn on, Typhon, tzigane, uhlan, Ulsan, upon, wait on, walk-on, witan, whereon, Wonsan, wonton, work on, Wuhan, xenon, Xi'an, yaupon, Yukon, Yunnan, Yvonne, zircon • Abadan, Abijan, Acheron, Ahriman, aileron, Alençon, amazon, Amazon, amnion, and so on, antiphon, Aragon, autobahn, Avalon, Babylon, Bakhtaran, Balaton, balmacaan, Bantustan, Barbizon, baryon, Basilan, bear down on, beat up on, betatron, biathlon, cabochon, call upon, calutron, carillon, carry-on, carry on, celadon, check up on, chorion, colophon, come upon,

Culiacán, cyclotron, decagon, decathlon, demijohn, deuteron, dine out on, dipteron, early on, echelon, electron, elevon, enteron, epsilon, ethephon, etymon, fall back on, fall upon, fermion, follow-on, Fuji-san, Genghis Khan, get it on, go back on, going on, goings-on, gonfalon, Grand Teton, graviton, hanger-on, harijan, helicon, heptagon, hereupon, hexagon, hold out on, hopping John, Huascarán, hyperon, Isfahan, isochron, Kazakhstan, Kublai Khan, Kyrgyzstan, Lake Huron, lay eyes on, Lebanon, leprechaun, lexicon, liaison, Lipizzan, load up on, logion, looker-on, macédoine, make good on, marathon, Marathon, marzipan, mastodon, Mazatlán, Mellotron, Miquelon, miss out on, morion, move in on, myrmidon, nonagon, noumenon, nucleon, Oberon, octagon, off and on, omicron, Oregon, organon, ostracon, Pakistan, Palawan, pantheon, paragon, Parmesan, parmigiana, Parthenon, peloton, pentagon, pentathlon, Percheron, Phaethon, Phlegethon, Phocion, pick up on, polygon, positron, Procyon, put-upon, Rajasthan, Ramadan, ride herd on, Rubicon, run low on, run out on, run upon, set eyes on, set foot on, set store on, set upon, silicon, sneak up on, Süleyman, tachyon, Taiyuan, talkathon, Teheran, telamon, telethon, thereupon, tie one on, triathlon, Tucumán, undergone,

upsilon, virion, walkathon, walk out on, whereupon, woebe-gone, work upon, Yerevan, Xiangtan, Zahedan • abutilon, Agamemnon, anticodon, antiproton, archenteron, arrière-ban, asyndeton, automaton, Azerbaijan, Bellerophon, bildungsroman, carrying-on, diazinon, dodecagon, emoticon, encephalon, ephemeron, get a move on, himation, interferon, kakiemon, keep an eye on, Lake Balaton, Laocoön, mesenteron, Michoacán, millimicron, oxymoron, phenomenon, protozoon, pteranodon, put the arm on, put the bite on, put the make on, rear echelon, Rostov-on-Don, Saskatchewan, septentrion, set one's heart on, set one's sights on, sine qua non, steal a march on, t'ai chi ch'uan, take it out on, Taklimakan, turn one's back on, Vientiane, West Irian, wipe one's boots on, zero coupon, zooplankton • a leg to stand on, Anti-Lebanon, ever and anon, prolegomenon, prothalamion, put one's finger on, put the finger on, throw cold water on, ultramarathon • epiphenomenon • kyrie eleison

on² \ōⁿ\ fond, ton • ballon, baton, belon, bouillon, Danton, Dijon, flacon, frisson, Gabon, garçon, lorgnon, Lyon, macon, marron, mouflon, Redon, salon, soupçon, Toulon, Villon • Aubusson, bourguignon, feuilleton, Ganelon, gueridon, limaçon, papillon, Simenon • filet mignon • Saint Emilion

on³ \ȯn\ awn, Bonn, bonne, brawn, dawn, Dawn, drawn, faun, fawn, gone, lawn, maun, on, pawn, prawn, Sean, spawn, Vaughn, won, yawn • add-on, agon, agone, Ambon, Argonne, begone, bygone, chaconne, clip-on, come-on, dead-on, doggone, far-gone, foregone, hands-on, head-on, Heilbronn, hereon, impawn, indrawn, jeon, Kherson, odds-on, outgone, put-on, Quezon, run-on, sign-on, slip-on, snap-on, thereon, turned-on, turn-on, turn on, upon, walk-on, whereon, wiredrawn, withdrawn • Ben-Gurion, bourguignonne, carry-on, follow-on, goings-on, hanger-on, hereupon, lep-rechaun, looker-on, put-upon, thereupon, undergone, where-upon, woebegone • carrying-on

on⁴ \ōn\ see ONE¹

on⁵ \ən\ see UN

ona¹ \ō-nə\ dona, Jonah, krona, krone, Mona, Nona, Rhona, Rona, Shona, trona • Ancona, Bellona, bologna, Bologna, Carmona, cinchona, corona, kimono, Leona, madrona, madrone, Pamplona, persona, Pomona, Ramona, Verona • Arizona, Barcelona, Desdemona

ona² \än-ə\ see ANA¹

oña \ōn-yə\ see ONIA³

onachal \än-i-kəl\ see ONICAL

onae \ō-nē\ see ONY¹

onah \ō-nə\ see ONA

onal \ōn-ᵊl\ clonal, tonal, zonal • atonal, azonal, bizonal, coronal, hormonal • baritonal, ecotonal, microtonal, polyclonal, polytonal, semitonal

onald \än-ᵊld\ Donald, Ronald • MacDonald

onant \ō-nənt\ see ONENT

onas \ō-nəs\ see ONUS²

onative \ō-nət-iv\ conative, donative

onc \äŋk\ see ONK¹

once¹ \äns\ see ANCE²

once² \əns\ see UNCE

onch¹ \äŋk\ see ONK¹

onch² \änch\ see AUNCH¹

oncha \äŋ-kə\ see ANKA

oncho \än-chō\ honcho, poncho, rancho

onchus \äŋ-kəs\ bronchus, rhonchus

onco \äŋ-kō\ bronco, Franco

ond¹ \änd\ blond, bond, fond, frond, Gond, pond, rand, sonde, wand, yond • abscond, Armand, ash-blond, beau monde, beyond, despond, fishpond, Gironde, gourmand, haut monde, junk bond, millpond, neoned, pair-bond, respond • allemande, bottle blond, correspond, demimonde, Eurobond, income bond, savings bond, solar pond, Trebizond, Trobriand,

vagabond, Walden Pond
• back of beyond, radiosonde, slough of despond, strawberry blond—*also* -ed *forms of verbs listed at* ON[1]

ond² \ōⁿ\ *see* ON²

ond³ \ȯnt\ *see* AUNT[1]

onda \än-də\ Fonda, Lahnda, Rhonda, Rhondda, Wanda
• Golconda, Luganda, Rwanda, Uganda • anaconda

ondam \än-dəm\ *see* ONDOM[1]

ondant \än-dənt\ *see* ONDENT

onday \ən-dē\ *see* UNDI

ondays \ən-dēz\ *see* UNDAYS

ondda \än-də\ *see* ONDA

onde \änd\ *see* OND[1]

ondeau \än-dō\ *see* ONDO

ondel \än-dᵉl\ fondle, rondel

ondent \än-dənt\ fondant
• despondent, respondent
• corespondent, correspondent

onder¹ \än-dər\ bonder, condor, maunder, ponder, squander, wander, yonder, zander
• absconder, responder, transponder—*also* -er *forms of adjectives listed at* OND[1]

onder² \ən-dər\ *see* UNDER

ondly \än-lē\ *see* ANLY[1]

ondness \än-nəs\ *see* ANNESS

ondo \än-dō\ condo, Hondo, Kwando, rondeau, rondo, tondo • forzando, glissando, lentando, parlando, scherzando, secondo,

sforzando • allargando, rallentando, ritardando
• accelerando

ondom¹ \än-dəm\ condom, quondam

ondom² \ən-dəm\ *see* UNDUM

ondor \än-dər\ *see* ONDER[1]

ondrous \ən-drəs\ *see* UNDEROUS

ondyle \än-dᵉl\ *see* ONDEL

one¹ \ōn\ blown, bone, clone, cone, crone, drone, flown, groan, grown, hone, Joan, known, loan, lone, moan, Mon, mown, none, own, phone, pone, prone, Rhône, roan, Saône, scone, sewn, shone, shoon, shown, sone, sown, stone, throne, thrown, tone, zone • agon, aitchbone, alone, atone, backbone, Bastogne, bemoan, Big Stone, birthstone, Blackstone, bloodstone, bluestone, bondstone, Boulogne, breastbone, bridge loan, brimstone, brownstone, call loan, calzone, Capone, capstone, cell phone, cheekbone, chinbone, cogon, cologne, Cologne, colon, colón, Colón, condone, copestone, corn pone, curbstone, cyclone, daimon, dapsone, debone, depone, dethrone, dial tone, disown, Dordogne, downzone, dripstone, drop zone, drystone, earphone, earth tone, end zone, enthrone, estrone, fieldstone, firestone, Firestone, flagstone, flowstone, flyblown, footstone, freestone, free zone, full-blown, gallstone, gemstone,

Gijón, Gladstone, goldstone, gravestone, greenstone, grindstone, hailstone, halftone, handblown, hard stone, headphone, headstone, hearthstone, high-flown, hip bone, homegrown, hormone, hornstone, impone, ingrown, inkstone, in stone, intone, jawbone, jewel tone, keystone, León, leone, life zone, limestone, lodestone, long bone, Maidstone, milestone, millstone, misknown, moonstone, mudstone, nose cone, oilstone, orgone, outgrown, outshown, ozone, pay phone, peptone, pinbone, pinecone, piñon, pipestone, postpone, potstone, propone, Ramon, redbone, red zone, rezone, rhinestone, sandstone, shade-grown, shinbone, Shoshone, siltstone, snow cone, soapstone, splint bone, strike zone, T-bone, tailbone, thighbone, time zone, toadstone, tombstone, touchstone, touch-tone, tritone, trombone, turnstone, twelve-tone, two-tone, Tyrone, unknown, unthrone, war zone, well-known, whalebone, wheel-thrown, whetstone, windblown, wishbone, Yangon • acetone, allophone, altar stone, anglo-phone, anklebone, barbitone, Barbizon, baritone, Bayamon, bombardon, brain hormone, buffer zone, Canal Zone, cannon bone, chaperon, cherrystone, cinder cone, cobblestone, coffin bone, collarbone, comfort zone, cornerstone, cortisone, crazy bone, crumple zone, curling stone, cuttlebone, demand loan, diaphone, Dictaphone, ecotone, epigone, fracture zone, francophone, free-fire zone, frigid zone, frontal bone, funny bone, gramophone, growth hormone, hammerstone, herringbone, hold one's own, holystone, homophone, hydrophone, ice-cream cone, ironstone, isochrone, kidney stone, knucklebone, leading tone, leave alone, let alone, lithopone, marrowbone, megaphone, mellophone, methadone, microphone, microtone, minestrone, monotone, Mount Mayon, neutral zone, on one's own, overblown, overflown, over-grown, overthrown, overtone, Picturephone, plant hormone, polyphone, prednisone, provolone, quarter tone, rotenone, rottenstone, sacaton, saxophone, semitone, sex hormone, shacklebone, shatter cone, silicone, sousaphone, speakerphone, stand-alone, stepping-stone, telephone, temperate zone, temporal bone, thunderstone, Torreón, torrid zone, traffic cone, twilight zone, undertone, vibraphone, xylophone, Yellowstone • accident-prone, anticyclone, Asunción, Bois de Boulogne, bred-in-the-bone, close to the bone, Concepción, Darby and Joan, eau de cologne, enterprise zone, fire-and-brimstone, foundation stone, mesocyclone, metallophone,

Nuevo León, progesterone, radiophone, Rosetta stone, sine qua non, strawberry roan, testosterone, videophone • philosopher's stone, Ponce de León, Sierra Leone • radiotelephone

one² \ō-nē\ see ONY¹

one³ \än\ see ON¹

one⁴ \ən\ see UN

one⁵ \ȯn\ see ON³

onean \ō-nē-ən\ see ONIAN¹

oned¹ \ōnd\ boned, stoned, toned • cologned, earth-toned, high-toned, pre-owned, rawboned, rhinestoned, two-toned • cobblestoned—*also* -ed *forms of verbs listed at* ONE¹

oned² \än\ see ON¹

oneless \ōn-ləs\ boneless, toneless

onely \ōn-lē\ lonely, only, pronely • eyes-only

onement \ōn-mənt\ atonement, cantonment, dethronement, disownment, enthronement, postponement • Day of Atonement

oneness \ən-nəs\ dunness, doneness, oneness • rotundness

onent \ō-nənt\ sonant • component, deponent, exponent, opponent, proponent

oneous \ō-nē-əs\ see ONIOUS

oner¹ \ō-nər\ boner, cloner, donor, droner, groaner, honer, loaner, loner, moaner, owner, stoner, toner, zoner • condoner, deboner, dethroner, intoner, landowner, shipowner • telephoner

oner² \ȯn-ər\ see AWNER¹

onerous \än-ə-rəs\ onerous, sonorous

ones \ōnz\ jones, Jones, nones • bare bones, bare-bones, Burne-Jones, sawbones • Davy Jones, lazybones, make no bones, roll the bones • skull and crossbones—*also* -s, -'s, *and* -s' *forms of nouns and* -s *forms of verbs listed at* ONE¹

onest \än-əst\ honest • dishonest • Hinayanist, Mahayanist

oney¹ \ō-nē\ see ONY¹

oney² \ən-ē\ see UNNY

oney³ \ü-nē\ see OONY

ong¹ \äŋ\ Chang, Fang, gong, hong, Huang, prong, Shang, Tang, tong, yang • Anyang, barong, Da Nang, dugong, Guiyang, Hanyang, Heng-yang, Hong Kong, kiang, Mah-Jongg, Malang, Mekong, Padang, ping-pong, sarong, satang, Shenyang, Wuchang, Zhejiang, Zhenjiang • billabong, Chittagong, Liaoyang, Pyong-yang, Semarang, scuppernong, Sturm und Drang, Vietcong, Wollongong • ylang-ylang

ong² \ȯŋ\ bong, dong, gong, long, prong, song, strong, thong, throng, tong, wrong • agelong, along, Armstrong, art song, barong, belong, biltong, birdsong, chaise longue, daylong, ding-dong, diphthong, dugong, endlong, erelong, fight song, folk song, furlong, Geelong, Haiphong, headlong, headstrong, Hong Kong, hour-long, kampong, lifelong, livelong, Mekong, monthlong, Nanchang, nightlong, oblong, oolong, part-song, Ping-Pong, plainsong, prolong, sarong, Shandong, shout song, sidelong, singsong, so long, souchong, swan song, theme song, torch song, weeklong, work song, yard-long, yearlong • all along, before long, billabong, Chittagong, come-along, come along, cradlesong, drinking song, evensong, get along, go along, Palembang, run along, scuppernong, sing-along, siren song, string along, summerlong, tagalong, Vietcong • Lapsang suchong

ong³ \əŋ\ see UNG¹

ong⁴ \ùng\ see UNG²

onga \äŋ-gə\ conga, panga, tonga, Tonga • Kananga, Khatanga, malanga, mridanga, pa'anga • Alba Longa, chimichanga, Rarotonga, Zamboanga • Bucaramanga

onge \ənj\ see UNGE

onged \óŋd\ pronged, thonged, wronged • multipronged—*also* -ed *forms of verbs listed at* ONG²

onger¹ \əŋ-gər\ hunger, monger, younger • fearmonger, fellmonger, fishmonger, ironmonger, newsmonger, phrasemonger, scaremonger, warmonger, whoremonger, wordmonger • costermonger, fashionmonger, gossipmonger, rumormonger, scandalmonger

onger² \ən-jər\ see UNGER¹

ongery \əŋ-grē\ hungry • fellmongery, ironmongery

ongful \óŋ-fəl\ wrongful, songful

ongin \ən-jən\ see UNGEON

ongish \óŋ-ish\ longish, strongish

ongo \äŋ-gō\ bongo, Congo, congou, drongo, Kongo, mongo • Belgian Congo, Niger-Congo, Pago Pago

ongous \əŋ-gəs\ see UNGOUS

ongue¹ \əŋ\ see UNG¹

ongue² \óŋ\ see ONG²

ongued \əŋd\ lunged, tongued • sharp-tongued, smooth-tongued • leather-tongued, silver-tongued, triple-tongued

ongy \ən-jē\ see UNGY

onhomous \än-ə-məs\ see ONYMOUS

oni \ō-nē\ see ONY¹

onia¹ \ō-nē-ə\ bignonia, clintonia, Estonia, Franconia, Ionia, Laconia, Livonia, mahonia, Pannonia, paulownia, Polonia, Slavonia, Snowdonia, tithonia, valonia, Wallonia, zirconia • Amazonia, Babylonia, Caledonia, Catalonia, catatonia, Cephalonia, heliconia, hypertonia, myotonia, Macedonia, Patagonia • New Caledonia

onia² \ō-nyə\ doña, Konya, Sonia • ammonia, begonia, Bologna, Estonia, Franconia, Laconia, Livonia, pneumonia, Polonia, Slavonia, tithonia, valonia • anhedonia, Babylonia, Caledonia, Catalonia, Cephalonia, heliconia, Macedonia, Patagonia • double pneumonia, New Caledonia, walking pneumonia

onial \ō-nē-əl\ baronial, colonial • antimonial, ceremonial, Dutch Colonial, matrimonial, patrimonial, testimonial

onian¹ \ō-nē-ən\ Zonian • aeonian, Antonian, Baconian, Bergsonian, Bostonian, Capetonian, chelonian, Clactonian, demonian, Devonian, draconian, Estonian, Etonian, favonian, Franconian, Galtonian, Gibbonian, Gladstonian, gorgonian, Gorgonian, Houstonian, Ionian, Jacksonian, Johnsonian, Jonsonian, Laconian, Livonian, Miltonian, Newtonian, Nixonian, Oxonian, Petronian, plutonian, Samsonian, Shoshonean, Slavonian, Wilsonian • Amazonian, Apollonian, Arizonian, Babylonian, calypsonian, Catalonian, Chalcedonian, Ciceronian, Edmontonian, Emersonian, Galvestonian, Hamiltonian, Jeffersonian, Macedonian, Madisonian, Oregonian,

parkinsonian, Patagonian, Tennysonian, Washingtonian

onian² \ō-nyən\ Zonian • Bostonian, Estonian, Franconian, Galtonian, Houstonian, Johnsonian, Jonsonian, Laconian, Livonian, Miltonian, Newtonian, Nixonian, Slavonian • Amazonian, Arizonian, Babylonian, Caledonian, Calydonian, Catalonian, Ciceronian, Edisonian, Edmontonian, Emersonian, Galvestonian, Jeffersonian, Macedonian, Madisonian, Oregonian, parkinsonian, Patagonian, Tennysonian, Washingtonian

onic \än-ik\ chronic, chthonic, conic, dornick, phonic, sonic, tonic • Aaronic, aeonic, agonic, atonic, benthonic, bionic, boronic, Brittonic, Brythonic, bubonic, Byronic, canonic, carbonic, colonic, cryonic, cyclonic, daimonic, demonic, draconic, dystonic, euphonic, gnomonic, hadronic, harmonic, hedonic, hydronic, iconic, ionic, Ionic, ironic, laconic, Masonic, Miltonic, mnemonic, moronic, neutronic, photonic, phytonic, planktonic, platonic, plutonic, pneumonic, Puranic, pythonic, sardonic, Saronic, sermonic, Slavonic, subsonic, symphonic, synchronic, tectonic, Teutonic, transonic, zirconic • avionic, catatonic, cosmogonic, diachronic, diatonic, disharmonic, electronic, embryonic, epigonic, hegemonic, histrionic, homophonic, Housatonic, hydroponic, hypersonic, infrasonic, inharmonic, isotonic, macaronic, megaphonic, microphonic, monophonic, monotonic, nonionic, nucleonic, pentatonic, pharaonic, philharmonic, plate-tectonic, polyphonic, quadraphonic, saxophonic, semitonic, skeletonic, Solomonic, supersonic, supertonic, telephonic, thermionic, ultrasonic • aimatronic, anticyclonic, architectonic, chameleonic, cardiotonic, electrotonic, geotectonic, Neoplatonic, oxymoronic, stereophonic

onica \än-i-kə\ Monica
• harmonica, japonica, Salonika, veronica, Veronica • electronica, glass harmonica, Santa Monica, Thessalonica

onical \än-i-kəl\ chronicle, conical, monachal, monocle • canonical, demonical, ironical

onicals \än-i-kəlz\ Chronicles • canonicals

onicker \ä-ni-kər\ see ONNICKER

onicle \än-i-kəl\ see ONICAL

onicles \än-i-kəlz\ see ONICALS

onics \än-iks\ onyx, phonics • bionics, cryonics, Ebonics, mnemonics, photonics, sardonyx, tectonics • avionics, electronics, histrionics, hydroponics, microphonics, nucleonics, plate tectonics, quadriphonics, radionics, supersonics, thermionics, ultrasonics • animatronics,

architectonics—*also* -s, -'s, *and* -s' *forms of nouns listed at* ONIC

onika \än-i-kə\ see ONICA

oniker \ä-ni-kər\ see ONNICKER

oning¹ \än-iŋ\ awning
• couponing—*also* -ing *forms of verbs listed at* ON¹

oning² \ō-niŋ\ de Kooning, jawboning, landowning—*also* -ing *forms of verbs listed at* ONE¹

onion \ən-yən\ see UNION

onious \ō-nē-əs\ Antonius, erroneous, euphonious, felonious, harmonious, Petronius, Polonius, Suetonius, symphonious • acrimonious, Apollonius, ceremonious, disharmonious, inharmonious, parsimonious, sanctimonious • unceremonious

onis¹ \ō-nəs\ see ONUS²

onis² \än-əs\ see ONUS¹

onish \än-ish\ donnish, monish • admonish, astonish, premonish • leprechaunish

onishment \än-ish-mənt\ admonishment, astonishment

onium \ō-nē-əm\ euphonium, harmonium, plutonium, zirconium • pandemonium, Pandemonium

onius \ō-nē-əs\ see ONIOUS

onja \ō-nyə\ see ONIA²

onjon \ən-jən\ see UNGEON

onjure \än-jər\ conjure, rondure

onk¹ \äŋk\ ankh, bonk, bronc, clonk, conch, conk, Franck, honk, Planck, plonk, wonk, zonk • honky-tonk

onk² \əŋk\ see UNK

onker \äŋ-kər\ conker, conquer, honker • honky-tonker

onkey¹ \äŋ-kē\ see ONKY

onkey² \əŋ-kē\ see UNKY

onkian \äŋ-kē-ən\ conquian • Algonkian

onky \äŋ-kē\ conky, donkey, wonky, yanqui

onless \ən-ləs\ see UNLESS

only \ōn-lē\ see ONELY

onment \ōn-mənt\ see ONEMENT

onn¹ \än\ see ON¹

onn² \ȯn\ see ON³

onna¹ \ȯn-ə\ donna, Donna, fauna, sauna • avifauna, megafauna, microfauna, prima donna

onna² \än-ə\ see ANA¹

onnage \ən-ij\ see UNNAGE

onne¹ \än\ see ON¹

onne² \ən\ see UN

onne³ \ȯn\ see ON³

onner \än-ər\ see ONOR¹

onnet \än-ət\ bonnet, sonnet • bluebonnet, Scotch bonnet, sunbonnet, warbonnet • English sonnet • bee in one's bonnet, Italian sonnet, Petrarchan sonnet

onnicker \ä-ni-kər\ donnicker, donniker, moniker

onnie \än-ē\ see ANI¹

onnish \än-ish\ see ONISH

onnor \än-ər\ see ONOR¹

onny¹ \än-ē\ see ANI¹

onny² \ən-ē\ see UNNY

ono¹ \ō-nō\ ono, phono • cui bono, kimono, pro bono • kakemono, makimono

ono² \ō-nə\ see ONA

ono³ \än-ō\ see ANO¹

onocle \än-i-kəl\ see ONICAL

onomer \än-ə-mər\ monomer • astronomer, comonomer

onomist \än-ə-məst\ agronomist, autonomist, economist, ergonomist, gastronomist, synonymist, taxonomist • Deuteronomist, home economist

onomous \än-ə-məs\ see ONYMOUS

onomy \än-ə-mē\ agronomy, antonymy, astronomy, autonomy, economy, eponymy, gastronomy, homonomy, metonymy, synonymy, taphonomy, taxonomy, toponymy • Deuteronomy, diseconomy, heteronomy, teleonomy

onor¹ \än-ər\ Bonner, fawner, goner, honor, pawner, spawner, wanner, yawner • dishonor, O'Connor • Afrikaner, court of honor, field of honor, Lipizzaner, maid of honor, marathoner,

point of honor, weimaraner
• Legion of Honor, matron of
honor, Medal of Honor

onor² \ō-nər\ see ONER¹

onorous \än-ə-rəs\ see ONEROUS

onquer \äŋ-kər\ see ONKER

onquian \äŋ-kē-ən\ see ONKIAN

ons¹ \änz\ see ONZE

ons² \ōⁿ\ see ON²

onsil \än-səl\ see ONSUL

onsin \än-sən\ see OHNSON

onson \än-sən\ see OHNSON

onsor \än-sər\ panzer, sponsor

onsul \än-səl\ consul, tonsil
• proconsul, vice-consul

ont¹ \ənt\ blunt, brunt, bunt,
front, grunt, hunt, Lunt, punt,
runt, shunt, strunt, stunt, want,
wont • affront, beachfront,
bowfront, breakfront, cold
front, confront, drag bunt, drop
front, fly front, forefront, home
front, housefront, lakefront,
manhunt, out-front, seafront,
shirtfront, shock front, shore-
front, still hunt, storefront,
swell-front, up-front, warm
front, wave front, witch hunt
• battlefront, oceanfront, polar
front, riverfront, waterfront
• occluded front, popular front,
scavenger hunt

ont² \änt\ see ANT²

ont³ \ónt\ see AUNT¹

on't \ōnt\ don't, won't

ontal¹ \änt-ᵊl\ pontil, fontal,
quantal • horizontal
• periodontal

ontal² \ənt-ᵊl\ see UNTLE

ontan \änt-ⁿ\ see ONTON

ontas \änt-əs\ see ONTUS

onte¹ \änt-ē\ see ANTI¹

onte² \än-tā\ see ANTE¹

onted \ónt-əd\ vaunted, wonted
• undaunted—*also* -ed *forms of
verbs listed at* AUNT¹

onter \ənt-ər\ see UNTER

onth \ənth\ month • billionth,
millionth, trillionth, twelvemonth
• gazillionth

ontian \änt-ē-ən\ Kantian,
Zontian • post-Kantian

ontic \änt-ik\ ontic • deontic,
gerontic, Vedantic
• endodontic, orthodontic
• anacreontic

ontil \änt-ᵊl\ see ONTAL¹

ontis \än-təs\ see ANTOS²

onto \än-tō\ see ANTO¹

ontra \än-trə\ contra, mantra,
tantra, yantra • per contra

ontre \ənt-ər\ see AUNTER¹

ontus \änt-əs\ Pontus
• Hellespontus, Pocahontas

onty \änt-ē\ see ANTI¹

onus¹ \än-əs\ Cronus, Faunus
• Adonis

onus² \ō-nəs\ bonus, clonus,
Cronus, Jonas, onus, slowness,
tonus • Adonis, colonus

ony[1] \ō-nē\ bony, coney, crony, phony, pony, stony, Toni, tony, Tony, yoni • baloney, Benoni, bologna, canzone, cow pony, Giorgione, Goldoni, Manzoni, Marconi, Moroni, Oenone, padrone, Shoshone, spumoni, tortoni, Zamboni • abalone, acrimony, agrimony, Albinoni, alimony, antimony, Berlusconi, cannelloni, ceremony, cicerone, colophony, hegemony, macaroni, mascarpone, matrimony, minestrone, Nakasone, one-trick pony, palimony, parsimony, patrimony, pepperoni, provolone, rigatoni, sanctimony, Shetland pony, testimony, zabaglione • phony-baloney • con espressione, conversazione, dramatis personae

ony[2] \än-ē\ see ANI[1]

onya \ō-nyə\ see ONIA[2]

onymist \än-ə-məst\ see ONOMIST

onymous \än-ə-məs\ bonhomous • anonymous, antonymous, autonomous, eponymous, homonymous, paronymous, pseudonymous, synonymous, theonomous

onymy \än-ə-mē\ see ONOMY

onyon[2] \ən-yən\ see UNION

onyx \än-iks\ see ONICS

onze \änz\ bonze, bronze, pons • long johns, Saint John's • Afrikaans—also -s, -'s, and -s' forms of nouns and -s forms of verbs listed at ON[1]

onzi \än-zē\ see ONZY

onzy \än-zē\ bronzy, Ponzi

oo[1] \ü\ see EW[1]

oo[2] \ō\ see OW[1]

oob \üb\ see UBE

oober \ü-bər\ see UBER

ooby \ü-bē\ booby, looby, ruby, Ruby

ooch[1] \üch\ brooch, hooch, mooch, pooch, smooch • capuche • scaramouch

ooch[2] \ōch\ see OACH

oocher \ü-chər\ see UTURE

oochy \ü-chē\ smoochy • Baluchi, Noguchi, penuche, Vespucci • Kawaguchi

ood[1] \ud\ good, hood, pud, rudd, should, stood, wood, would, yod • Atwood, aunthood, basswood, beefwood, bentwood, blackwood, boxwood, boyhood, brushwood, childhood, cordwood, corkwood, deadwood, do-good, dogwood, driftwood, Ellwood, Elwood, falsehood, fatwood, feel-good, firewood, for good, fruitwood, Gielgud, girlhood, godhood, greasewood, greenwood, groundwood, gumwood, hardwood, heartwood, ironwood, kingwood, knighthood, lancewood, logwood, maidhood, make good, manhood, matchwood, monkhood, monkshood, Mount Hood, no-good, pinewood, plywood, priesthood, pulpwood, redwood, rosewood, sainthood, selfhood, Sherwood, softwood, sonhood, springwood, statehood, stinkwood, Talmud, teakwood, torchwood, unhood, Wedgwood, whitewood, wifehood, wildwood, withstood, wormwood • adulthood, arrowwood, babyhood, bachelorhood, brotherhood, buttonwood, candlewood, cedarwood, cottonwood, fatherhood, geezerhood, hardihood, high priesthood, Hollywood, Isherwood, knock on wood, leatherwood, likelihood, livelihood, lustihood, maidenhood, motherhood, nationhood, neighborhood, orangewood, parenthood, personhood, puppyhood, Robin Hood, sandalwood, scattergood, servanthood, sisterhood, spinsterhood, toddlerhood, to the good, tulipwood, understood, widowhood, womanhood, yellowwood, zebrawood • blood brotherhood, grandparenthood, misunderstood, second childhood, unlikelihood, widowerhood

ood² \ōd\ see ODE

ood³ \üd\ see UDE

ood⁴ \əd\ see UD[1]

ooded¹ \əd-əd\ blooded • blue-blooded, cold-blooded, full-blooded, half-blooded, hot-blooded, pure-blooded, red-blooded, star-studded, warm-blooded—*also* -ed *forms of verbs listed at* UD[1]

ooded² \ud-əd\ hooded, wooded • soft-wooded

ooder¹ \üd-ər\ see UDER

ooder² \əd-ər\ see UDDER

ooding \ud-iŋ\ pudding • do-gooding, plum pudding, snow pudding, unhooding • cottage pudding, hasty pudding, Yorkshire pudding • Indian pudding

oodle \üd-ᵊl\ boodle, doodle, feudal, noodle, poodle, strudel • caboodle, canoodle, flapdoodle, paludal, toy poodle • timberdoodle, Yankee-Doodle

oodman \ud-mən\ goodman, woodman

oodoo \üd-ü\ doo-doo, hoodoo, kudu, voodoo • in deep doo-doo

oods \udz\ backwoods, case goods, dry goods, piece goods, soft goods, white goods, yard goods • bill of goods, damaged goods, piney woods • capital goods, consumer goods, Lake of the Woods, producer goods • deliver the goods—*also* -s, -'s, *and* -s' *forms of nouns and* -s *forms of verbs listed at* OOD[1]

oodsman \udz-mən\ woodsman • backwoodsman, ombudsman

oody¹ \üd-ē\ broody, Judy, moody, Rudy, Trudy

oody² \ud-ē\ cuddy, goody, hoody, woody • goody-goody

oody³ \əd-ē\ see UDDY[1]

ooer \ü-ər\ see EWER[1]

ooey \ü-ē\ see EWY

oof[1] \üf\ goof, hoof, kloof, poof, pouf, proof, roof, spoof, woof • aloof, behoof, bombproof, childproof, crushproof, disproof, fireproof, flameproof, foolproof, forehoof, germproof, greaseproof, heatproof, hip roof, leakproof, lightproof, moonroof, mothproof, pickproof, rainproof, reproof, rustproof, shadoof, shellproof, shockproof, skidproof, soundproof, stainproof, sunroof, Tartuffe, unroof, windproof, witloof • bulletproof, burglarproof, gable roof, gambrel roof, hit the roof, on the hoof, ovenproof, pilferproof, shatterproof, tamperproof, through the roof, veto-proof, warp and woof, waterproof, weatherproof • burden of proof, idiotproof, opéra bouffe

oof[2] \üf\ hoof, poof, roof, woof • forehoof, hip roof, moon roof, Tartuffe • cloven hoof, gable roof, gambrel roof, hit the roof, on the hoof, through the roof, warp and woof

oof[3] \ôf\ see OAF

oof[4] \üv\ see OVE[3]

oofah \ü-fə\ see UFA

oofer[1] \ü-fer\ proofer, roofer, twofer • flameproofer, mothproofer • waterproofer

oofer[2] \üf-ər\ hoofer, woofer • subwoofer

oofy \ü-fē\ goofy, kufi, spoofy, Sufi

ooga \ü-gə\ see UGA

ooge \üj\ see UGE[1]

ooger \ùg-ər\ see UGUR

oogie \ùg-ē\ bogey, boogie, noogie • boogie-woogie

oo-goo \ü-gü\ see UGU

ooh \ü\ see EW[1]

ooh-pooh \ü-pü\ hoopoe, pooh-pooh

ooi \ü-ē\ see EWY

ooist \ü-əst\ doest • tattooist, voodooist—also -est forms of adjectives listed at EW[1]

ook[1] \ùk\ book, brook, Brooke, chook, cook, Cook, crook, hook, look, nook, rook, schnook, shook, snook, stook, took • bankbook, betook, billhook, black book, blue book, boat hook, cant hook, caoutchouc, casebook, cash book, chapbook, checkbook, Chinook, closed book, codebook, cookbook, daybook, duck hook, e-book, forsook, fishhook, gang hook, good book, guidebook, handbook, hornbook, hymnbook, Innsbruck, jump hook, Kobuk, logbook, make book, match-book, mistook, Mount Cook, mouth hook, nainsook, nonbook, notebook, outlook, partook, passbook, Pembroke, phrase book, playbook, pothook, prayer book, prompt-book, psalmbook, retook, schoolbook, scrapbook, sketchbook, skyhook, song-book, sourcebook, studbook,

stylebook, textbook, trade book, unhook, white book, Windhoek, wordbook, workbook, yearbook
• Beaverbrook, bring to book, buttonhook, cock a snook, comic book, copybook, Domesday Book, donnybrook, gerenuk, grappling hook, inglenook, in one's book, Leeuwenhoek, off the hook, overbook, overlook, overtook, picture book, pocketbook, pocket book, pressure-cook, pruning hook, Sandy Hook, service book, statute book, storybook, talking book, tenterhook, undertook, Volapük
• audiobook, coloring book, commonplace book, gobbledygook, one fot the book, on one's own hook, ring off the hook, telephone book • by hook or by crook

ook² \ük\ see UKE

ooka \ü-kə\ yuca • bazooka, felucca, palooka, Toluca, verruca • Juan de Fuca, melaleuca

ookah \úk-ə\ hookah, sukkah

ooke \úk\ see OOK¹

ooker \úk-ər\ booker, cooker, hooker, Hooker, looker, snooker • good-looker, onlooker • pressure cooker

ookery \úk-ə-rē\ cookery, crookery, rookery

ookie \úk-ē\ bookie, brookie, cookie, cooky, hooky, rookie, rooky • fortune cookie, Takatsuki

ooking \úk-iŋ\ booking, cooking
• good-looking, onlooking
• forward-looking, solid-looking—*also* -ing *forms of verbs listed at* OOK¹

ooklet \úk-lət\ booklet, brooklet, hooklet

ooks¹ \üks\ deluxe, gadzooks —*also* -s, -'s, *and* -s' *forms of nouns and* -s *forms of verbs listed at* UKE

ooks² \úks\ Brooks, crux, looks, luxe, zooks • deluxe, gadzooks • hit the books, off the books, on the books • in one's good books, on tenterhooks—*also* -s, -'s, *and* -s' *forms of nouns and* -s *forms of verbs listed at* OOK¹

ooky¹ \ü-kē\ kooky, spooky • bouzouki, Kabuki, saluki, tanuki

ooky² \úk-ē\ see OOKIE

ool¹ \ül\ boule, boulle, buhl, cool, drool, fool, fuel, ghoul, gul, joule, mewl, mule, pool, Poole, pul, pule, rule, school, spool, stool, tool, tulle, you'll, yule
• air-cool, ampoule, babul, Banjul, befool, Blackpool, B-school, carpool, church school, cesspool, closestool, curule, dame school, day school, edge tool, Elul, faldstool, flake tool, footstool, gene pool, grade school, hangul, high school, home-school, Kabul, misrule, Mosul, old school, prep school, preschool, refuel, retool, self-rule, step stool, synfuel, tide

pool, toadstool, tomfool, trade school, uncool, unspool, vanpool, whirlpool • April fool, Barnaul, blow one's cool, boarding school, charter school, common school, cucking stool, cutty stool, dirty pool, ducking stool, fascicule, gallinule, grammar school, graticule, groupuscule, Hartlepool, Istanbul, kilojoule, lenticule, Liverpool, machine tool, magnet school, majuscule, middle school, minischool, minuscule, molecule, motor pool, normal school, nursery school, overrule, private school, public school, reform school, reticule, ridicule, summer school, Sunday school, training school, vestibule, wading pool • finishing school, junior high school, parochial school, primary school, senior high school, vestibule school • alternative school, biomolecule, correspondence school, divinity school, industrial school, Paraíba do Sul, secondary school • Mato Grosso do Sul, Rio Grande do Sul

ool² \ul\ see UL¹

oola \ü-lə\ see ULA

oole \ül\ see OOL¹

oolean \ü-lē-ən\ see ULEAN

ooled \üld\ bejeweled, unschooled • vestibuled—*also* -ed *forms of verbs listed at* OOL¹

ooler \ü-lər\ cooler, gular, ruler • carpooler, grade-schooler,

high schooler, homeschooler, preschooler, wine cooler • intercooler, middle schooler, ridiculer, watercooler

oolie \ü-lē\ see ULY

oolish \ü-lish\ coolish, foolish, ghoulish, mulish • pound-foolish

oolly¹ \ü-lē\ see ULY

oolly² \ul-ē\ see ULLY²

oom¹ \üm\ bloom, boom, broom, brougham, brume, combe, cwm, doom, flume, fume, gloom, glume, groom, Hume, khoum, loom, neume, plume, rheum, room, spume, tomb, toom, vroom, whom, womb, zoom • abloom, assume, backroom, ballroom, barroom, bathroom, bedroom, board-room, bridegroom, broadloom, chat room, checkroom, classroom, clean room, cloakroom, coatroom, consume, costume, courtroom, darkroom, dayroom, entomb, enwomb, exhume, foredoom, front room, great room, greenroom, guardroom, gun room, headroom, heirloom, homeroom, houseroom, illume, inhume, jibboom, Khartoum, legroom, legume, lunchroom, men's room, mudroom, mushroom, newsroom, perfume, playroom, poolroom, pressroom, presume, proofroom, push broom, relume, restroom, resume, salesroom, schoolroom, Scotch broom, sea room, showroom, sickroom, simoom, squad room, stateroom, stockroom, storeroom, strong room, subsume, sunroom, taproom, Targum, tearoom, throne room, toolroom, wardroom, washroom, weight room, whisk broom, white room, workroom • anteroom, baby boom, banquet room, birthing room, boiler room, checkerbloom, city room, coffee room, common room, counting room, cutting room, dyer's broom, elbow room, family room, impostume, Jacquard loom, keeping room, ladies' room, living room, locker-room, lumber room, miniboom, nom de plume, powder room, ready room, rumpus room, sitting room, smoke-filled room, smoking room, sonic boom, standing room, straw mushroom, tiring-room, waiting room, wiggle room, women's room, witches'-broom • composing room, lower the boom, master bedroom, recovery room, withdrawing room • emergency room, recreation room

oom² \ům\ see UM²

oomed \ůmd\ plumed, wombed • well-groomed—*also* -ed *forms of verbs listed at* OOM¹

oomer \ü-mər\ see UMER

oomily \ü-mə-lē\ doomily, gloomily • contumely

ooming¹ \ü-mən\ see UMAN

ooming² \ü-miŋ\ see UMING

oomlet \ům-lət\ boomlet, plumelet • baby boomlet

oomy \ü-mē\ bloomy, boomy, doomy, fumy, gloomy, plumy, rheumy, roomy, spumy • costumey

oon¹ \ün\ boon, Boone, coon, croon, dune, goon, hewn, June, loon, lune, moon, noon, prune, rune, shoon, soon, spoon, swoon, strewn, toon, tune • aswoon, attune, baboon, balloon, bassoon, Bethune, blue moon, buffoon, Calhoun, Cancún, cardoon, cartoon, cocoon, commune, doubloon, dragoon, festoon, fine-tune, forenoon, full moon, gaboon, gadroon, galloon, Gudrun, half-moon, harpoon, high noon, immune, impugn, jargoon, jejune, Kowloon, Kunlun, lagoon, lampoon, lardoon, Maine coon, maroon, monsoon, Neptune, new moon, oppugn, Pashtun, patroon, platoon, poltroon, pontoon, premune, puccoon, quadroon, raccoon, ratoon, repugn, rockoon, rough-hewn, saloon, Sassoon, shalloon, soupspoon, spittoon, spontoon, teaspoon, Torun, tribune, triune, tuchun, tycoon, typhoon, untune, Walloon • afternoon, apolune, barracoon, Brigadoon, call the tune, Cameroon, demilune, dessertspoon, greasy spoon, harvest moon, honeymoon, importune, macaroon, octoroon, opportune, pantaloon, perilune, picaroon, picayune, rigadoon, saskatoon, Saskatoon, silver spoon, tablespoon • autoimmune, barrage balloon, Courland

Lagoon, contrabassoon, double bassoon, inopportune, over the moon, runcible spoon, trial balloon

oon² \ōn\ see ONE¹

oona \ü-nə\ see UNA

oonal \ün-ᵊl\ see UNAL

oone \ün\ see OON¹

ooner \ü-nər\ crooner, crowner, lunar, pruner, schooner, sooner, swooner, tuner • cislunar, harpooner, lacunar, lampooner, oppugner • honeymooner, importuner, interlunar, prairie schooner, semilunar

oonery¹ \ün-rē\ buffoonery, lampoonery, poltroonery

oonery² \ü-nə-rē\ see UNARY

ooney \ü-nē\ see OONY

oonie \ü-nē\ see OONY

ooning \ü-niŋ\ nooning • ballooning, cartooning, cocooning, gadrooning—*also* -ing *forms of verbs listed at* OON¹

oonish \ü-nish\ moonish • buffoonish, cartoonish • picayunish

oonless \ün-ləs\ moonless, tuneless, woundless

oons \ünz\ lunes, zounds • eftsoons • afternoons, loony tunes—*also* -s, -'s, *and* -s' *forms of nouns and* -s *forms of verbs listed at* OON¹

oony \ü-nē\ cluny, gooney, loonie, loony, Moonie, moony, muni, puisne, puny, spoony, swoony, Zuni • cartoony, Mulroney

oop \üp\ bloop, coop, coupe, croup, droop, drupe, dupe, goop, group, hoop, loop, loupe, poop, roup, scoop, sloop, snoop, soup, stoop, stoup, stupe, swoop, troop, troupe, whoop • age-group, blood group, closed loop, duck soup, ground loop, in-group, newsgroup, out-group, pea soup, playgroup, recoup, regroup, subgroup, T-group, toe loop, war whoop • alley-oop, bird's-nest soup, cock-a-hoop, focus group, for a loop, Guadalupe, Guadeloupe, hula hoop, nincompoop, open loop, paratroop, pressure group, supergroup, support group • alphabet soup, encounter group, knock for a loop, mock turtle soup • affinity group, primordial soup

o-op \üp\ see OOP¹

ooped \üpd\ looped—*also* -ed *forms of verbs listed at* OOP

oopee \ü-pē\ see OOPY

ooper \ü-pər\ blooper, cooper, Cooper, Cowper, duper, grouper, hooper, looper, scooper, snooper, stupor, swooper, super, trooper, trouper, whooper • moss-trooper, storm trooper • cabbage looper, party pooper, paratrooper, pooper-scooper, super-duper, warsaw grouper

ooping \ü-piŋ\ grouping • moss-trooping—*also* -ing *forms of verbs listed at* OOP

oopoe \ü-pü\ see OOH-POOH

oops \ùps\ oops, whoops

oopy \ü-pē\ croupy, droopy, groupie, Kewpie, loopy, snoopy, soupy, swoopy, Tupi, whoopee

oor¹ \ór\ see OR¹

oor² \ùr\ see URE¹

oorage¹ \ùr-ij\ moorage • sewerage

oorage² \òr-ij\ see ORAGE²

oore¹ \òr\ see OR¹

oore² \ùr\ see URE¹

oored \órd\ see OARD

oorer \òr-ər\ see ORER

oori \ùr-ē\ see URY¹

ooring¹ \òr-iŋ\ see ORING

ooring² \ùr-iŋ\ see URING

oorish¹ \ùr-ish\ boorish, Moorish, poorish

oorish² \òr-ish\ see ORISH¹

oorly \ùr-lē\ see URELY

oorman \òr-mən\ see ORMAN

oors \órz\ Bors, drawers, yours • Azores, indoors, outdoors • close one's doors, out-of-doors, underdrawers, withindoors, withoutdoors • Louis Quatorze, pallida Mors—*also* -s, -'s, *and* -s' *forms of nouns and* -s *forms of verbs listed at* OR¹

oorsman \órz-mən\ see OARSMAN

oort \òrt\ see ORT¹

oosa \ü-sə\ see USA¹

oose¹ \üs\ see USE¹

oose² \üz\ see USE²

ooser¹ \ü-sər\ see UCER

ooser² \ü-zər\ see USER

oosey \ü-sē\ see UICY

oosh¹ \üsh\ see OUCHE

oosh² \ùsh\ see USH²

oost \üst\ boost, juiced, Proust, roost • langouste • self-induced, Zlatoust—*also* -ed *forms of verbs listed at* USE¹

oosy \ü-zē\ see OOZY

oot¹ \ùt\ foot, put, root, Root, soot • afoot, barefoot, bigfoot, bird's-foot, birthroot, Blackfoot, board foot, claw-foot, clubfoot, cocksfoot, coltsfoot, crow's-foot, cube root, enroot, flatfoot, forefoot, hard put, hotfoot, input, kaput, on foot, outfoot, output, prop root, Rajput, redroot, shot put, snakeroot, splayfoot, square root, squawroot, taproot, throughput, trench foot, uproot, webfoot • acre-foot, arrowroot, athlete's foot, bitterroot, cajeput, candle-foot, dorsal root, fescue foot, fibrous root, gingerroot, hand and foot, orrisroot, pussyfoot, puttyroot, tenderfoot, underfoot

oot² \üt\ see UTE

oot³ \ət\ see UT¹

ootage¹ \üt-ij\ fruitage, rootage, scutage

ootage² \üt-ij\ footage, rootage

ooted¹ \üt-əd\ booted, fluted, fruited, muted, suited • abluted, deep-rooted, jackbooted, pantsuited, reputed, voluted —*also* -ed *forms of verbs listed at* UTE

ooted² \ut-əd\ footed • barefooted, clubfooted, deep-rooted, flat-footed, fiddle-footed, fleet-footed, four-footed, heavy-footed, light-footed, slow-footed, splayfooted, sure-footed, web-footed, wing-footed • cloven-footed—*also* -ed *forms of verbs listed at* OOT¹

ooter¹ \ut-ər\ footer, putter • shot-putter • pussyfooter

ooter² \üt-ər\ see UTER

ooth¹ \üth\ smooth, soothe

ooth² \üth\ booth, Booth, couth, crwth, routh, ruth, Ruth, scouth, sleuth, sooth, tooth, truth, Truth, youth • bucktooth, cheek tooth, dogtooth, Duluth, egg tooth, eyetooth, forsooth, half-truth, home truth, houndstooth, in truth, Kossuth, milk tooth, sawtooth, selcouth, sweet tooth, tollbooth, uncouth, untruth, vermouth • baby tooth, Isle of Youth, pivot tooth, snaggletooth, wisdom tooth • long in the tooth, moment of truth, permanent tooth, projection booth, telephone booth

oothe \üth\ see OOTH¹

oothed \ütht\ toothed • bucktoothed, gap-toothed, sawtoothed • saber-toothed, snaggletoothed

oothless \üth-ləs\ see UTHLESS

oothly \üth-lē\ soothly • uncouthly

oothy \ü-thē\ couthie, toothy

ootie \üt-ē\ see OOTY¹

ooting¹ \üt-iŋ\ footing • off-putting, war footing—*also* -ing *forms of verbs listed at* OOT¹

ooting² \üt-iŋ\ see UTING

ootle \üt-ᵊl\ see UTILE

ootless \üt-ləs\ bootless, fruitless, rootless

ootlet \üt-lət\ fruitlet, rootlet

oots \üts\ firstfruits, grassroots, slyboots, Vaduz • put down roots, shoot-the-chutes—*also* -s, -'s, *and* -s' *forms of nouns and* -s *forms of verbs listed at* UTE

ootsie \üt-sē\ footsie, tootsie

ooty¹ \üt-ē\ beauty, booty, Clootie, cootie, cutie, duty, fluty, fruity, hooty, rooty, snooty, sooty, tutti, zooty • agouti, clafouti, Djibouti • Funafuti, heavy-duty, persecutee, tutti-frutti

ooty² \ut-ē\ rooty, sooty, tutti

ooty³ \ət-ē\ see UTTY

oove \üv\ see OVE³

oover \ü-vər\ see OVER³

oovy \ü-vē\ groovy, movie
• B movie

ooze \üz\ see USE²

oozer \ü-zər\ see USER

oozle \ü-zəl\ see USAL²

oozy \ü-zē\ bluesy, boozy, choosy, floozy, newsy, oozy, schmoozy, Susie, woozy
• Jacuzzi

op¹ \äp\ bop, chap, chop, clop, cop, crop, drop, flop, fop, glop, hop, knop, lop, mop, op, plop, pop, prop, scop, shop, slop, sop, stop, strop, swap, top, whop • Aesop, airdrop, a pop, atop, backdrop, backstop, bakeshop, barhop, bebop, bed-hop, bellhop, benchtop, big top, blacktop, bookshop, carhop, cartop, cash crop, chop-chop, chop shop, clip-clop, click stop, clop-clop, closed shop, coin-op, cookshop, cooktop, co-op, cough drop, desktop, dewdrop, doorstop, doo-wop, dramshop, drop-top, dry mop, Dunlop, dust mop, eardrop, eavesdrop, ESOP, estop, field crop, flag stop, flue stop, f-stop, fire-stop, flattop, flip-flop, foretop, grogshop, gumdrop, hardtop, head shop, hedgehop, high-top, hilltop, hip-hop, hockshop, housetop, joypop, laptop, mail drop, maintop, milksop, name-drop, nonstop, one-stop, outcrop, palmtop, pawnshop, pipe stop, pit stop, pop-top, post-op, pre-op, pro shop, ragtop, raindrop, redtop, ridgetop, ripstop, rooftop, root crop, sharecrop, shortstop, skin-pop, slipslop, snowdrop, soursop, speed shop, stone-crop, strip-crop, sweatshop, sweetshop, sweetsop, tank top, teardrop, thrift shop, tiptop, treetop, trip-hop, truck stop, unstop, wineshop, workshop • agitprop, barbershop, beauty shop, belly flop, blow one's top, body shop, bucket shop, carrottop, channel-hop, coffee shop, countertop, cover crop, curly top, double-crop, double-stop, drag-and-drop, Ethiop, gigaflop, glottal stop, intercrop, island-hop, lollipop, machine shop, malaprop, mom-and-pop, mountaintop, open shop, overtop, photo op, rent-a-cop, Ribbentrop, set up shop, soda pop, standing crop, suction stop, table-hop, tabletop, techno-pop, teenybop, turboprop, union shop, whistle-stop, window-shop • Babel-thuap • comparison shop

op² \ō\ see OW¹

opa \ō-pə\ dopa, opa, opah
• Europa

opah \ō-pə\ see OPA

opal \ō-pel\ copal, nopal, opal, Opal • Simferopol
• Constantinople

ope \ōp\ cope, coup, dope, grope, holp, hope, Hope, lope, mope, nope, ope, pope, Pope, rope, scop, scope, slope, soap, stope, taupe, tope, trope

• aslope, boltrope, borescope, downslope, elope, fly dope, footrope, gantelope, glide slope, Good Hope, jump rope, manrope, myope, nightscope, North Slope, pyrope, sandsoap, skip rope, soft-soap, tightrope, towrope, upslope, white hope, wire rope • antelope, antipope, arthroscope, biotope, bronchoscope, bunny slope, calliope, cantaloupe, chronoscope, cryoscope, endoscope, envelope, episcope, epitope, Ethiope, fluoroscope, forlorn hope, gastroscope, gyroscope, horoscope, interlope, isotope, kinescope, microscope, misanthrope, periscope, phalarope, radarscope, slippery slope, sniperscope, snooperscope, spectroscope, stethoscope, telescope • Cape of Good Hope, colonoscope, electroscope, hagioscope, heliotrope, hope against hope, kaleidoscope, oscilloscope, pay envelope, stereoscope • continental slope

opean \ō-pē-ən\ see OPIAN

opee \ō-pē\ see OPI

opence \əp-əns\ see UPPANCE

openny \əp-nē\ threepenny, twopenny

oper \ō-pər\ coper, doper, groper, hoper, loper, moper, roper, sloper, soaper, toper • eloper, no-hoper, soft-soaper • interloper

opera \äp-rə\ see OPRA

opey \ō-pē\ see OPI

oph \ōf\ see OAF

ophagous \äf-ə-gəs\ coprophagous, esophagus, monophagous, necrophagous, phytophagus, sarcophagus, xylophagus, zoophagous • anthropophagous

ophagy \äf-ə-jē\ coprophagy, geophagy, monophagy, mycophagy • anthropophagy

ophe¹ \ō-fē\ see OPHY

ophe² \ōf\ see OFF²

opher \ō-fər\ see OFER

ophet \äf-ət\ see OFIT

ophie \ō-fē\ see OPHY

ophir \ō-fər\ see OFER

ophonous \äf-ə-nəs\ cacophonous, homophonous

ophony \äf-ə-nē\ cacophony, colophony, homophony, monophony, theophany • heterophony, stereophony

ophy \ō-fē\ Sophie, sophy, strophe, trophy

opi \ō-pē\ dopey, Hopi, mopey, ropy, soapy, topee, topi

opia \ō-pē-ə\ diplopia, dystopia, myopia, sinopia, utopia • cornucopia, Ethiopia, hyperopia, presbyopia

opian \ō-pē-ən\ Popian • Aesopian, cyclopean, dystopian, Salopian, Trollopian, utopian • cornucopian, Ethiopian

opic¹ \äp-ik\ topic, tropic • Aesopic, anthropic, Canopic, diplopic, ectopic, myopic, subtropic • arthroscopic, cryoscopic, endoscopic, Ethiopic, fluoroscopic, gastroscopic, gyroscopic, hygroscopic, isotopic, lycanthropic, macroscopic, microscopic, misanthropic, periscopic, philanthropic, presbyopic, semitropic, stethoscopic, stroboscopic, telescopic • hagioscopic, kaleidoscopic, laparoscopic, oscilloscopic, stereoscopic

opic² \ō-pik\ tropic • Canopic, diplopic, myopic • Ethiopic, hydrotropic, isotopic, presbyopic, psychotropic • heliotropic

opical \äp-i-kəl\ topical, tropical • anthropical, subtropical • microscopical, neotropical, philanthropical, semitropical

oplar \äp-lər\ see OPPLER

ople \ō-pəl\ see OPAL

opol \ō-pəl\ see OPAL

opolis¹ \äp-ə-ləs\ propolis • acropolis, cosmopolis, metropolis, necropolis, Nicopolis • Heliopolis, megalopolis

opolis² \äp-ləs\ see OPLESS

opolist \äp-ə-list\ monopolist • bibliopolist, oligopolist

opoly \äp-ə-lē\ choppily, floppily, sloppily • duopoly, monopoly, vox populi • oligopoly

oppa \äp-ə\ see APA¹

opped \äpt\ see OPT

oppel \äp-əl\ see OPPLE

opper \äp-ər\ bopper, chopper, copper, cropper, dropper, flopper, hopper, lopper, mopper, popper, proper, shopper, stopper, swapper, topper, whopper • bebopper, cartopper, clodhopper, eavesdropper, eyedropper, eyepopper, grasshopper, heart-stopper, hedgehopper, hip-hopper, improper, jaw-dropper, job-hopper, joypopper, leafhopper, name-dropper, rockhopper, sharecropper, showstopper, skin-popper, treehopper, woodchopper • come a cropper, table-hopper, teenybopper, window-shopper

oppery \äp-rē\ coppery, foppery

oppet \äp-ət\ moppet, poppet

oppily \äp-ə-lē\ see OPOLY

oppiness \äp-ē-nəs\ choppiness, floppiness, sloppiness, soppiness

opping \äp-iŋ\ hopping, sopping, topping, whopping • clod-hopping, eye-popping, heart-stopping, jaw-dropping, job-hopping, name-dropping, outcropping, showstopping, strip cropping • channel-hopping—also -ing forms of verbs listed at OP¹

opple \äp-əl\ popple, stopple, topple • estoppel

oppler \äp-lər\ Doppler, poplar

oppy \äp-ē\ choppy, copy, crappie, floppy, gloppy, hoppy, kopje, poppy, sloppy, soppy, stroppy • corn poppy, jalopy, okapi, serape • microcopy, Nahuel Huapí, photocopy • opium poppy

ops \äps\ chops, copse, Ops, tops • beechdrops, Cheops, cyclops, Cyclops, eyedrops, Pelops, pinedrops, sundrops • knockout drops, lick one's chops, muttonchops • from the housetops, triceratops—*also -s, -'s, and -s' forms of nouns and -s forms of verbs listed at* OP[1]

opse \äps\ see OPS

opsy \äp-sē\ dropsy • autopsy, biopsy, necropsy

opt \äpt\ Copt, knopped, opt, topped • adopt, close-cropped, co-opt, end-stopped • carrot-topped—*also -ed forms of verbs listed at* OP[1]

opter \äp-tər\ copter • adopter, helicopter, ornithopter

optic \äp-tik\ Coptic, optic • panoptic, synoptic • fiber-optic

optimist \äp-tə-məst\ optimist, Optimist • Soroptimist

option \äp-shən\ option • adoption, co-option, stock option • local option • open adoption

optric \äp-trik\ catoptric, dioptric

opulate \äp-yə-lāt\ copulate, populate • depopulate • overpopulate

opuli \äp-ə-lē\ see OPOLY

opulous \äp-yə-ləs\ see OPULACE

opus \ō-pəs\ opus • Canopus, Mount Scopus • magnum opus

opy[1] \ō-pē\ see OPI

opy[2] \äp-ē\ see OPPY

oque[1] \ōk\ see OKE

oque[2] \äk\ see OCK[1]

oque[3] \ōk\ see ALK

oquial \ō-kwē-əl\ colloquial • ventriloquial

or[1] \ȯr\ boar, Boer, Bohr, bore, chore, cor, core, corps, crore, door, drawer, floor, for, fore, four, frore, gnawer, gore, Gore, hoar, hoer, lore, Moore, mor, more, More, nor, o'er, oar, or, ore, poor, pore, pour, roar, sawer, score, shore, snore, soar, sore, splore, spoor, spore, store, swore, Thor, tor, tore, torr, war, whore, wore, yore, your, you're • abhor, adore, afore, and/or, as for, ashore, backdoor, bailor, bandore, Bangor, bedsore, before, bezoar, bookstore, box score, but for, call for, candor, captor, centaur, chain store, claymore, closed-door, cold sore, cold store, condor, Côte d'Or, decor, deplore, dime-store, done for, donor, down-pour, drugstore, Dutch door, encore, ephor, explore, Exmoor, eyesore, fall for, feoffor, fetor, Fillmore, first floor, flexor, folklore, footsore, forbore, foreshore, forswore, fourscore, French door, full-bore, Gabor, galore, Glen More, go for, ground floor, gun for, hard-core, hog score, ichor, ignore, implore, Indore, indoor, in for, inpour, inshore, in-store, Kotor, Lahore, lakeshore, lector, lee shore, Lenore, lessor, line score, look for, Luxor, memoir, mentor, Mysore, nearshore, Nestor, next-door, Numfor, offshore, onshore, outdoor, outpour, outsoar, outwore, phosphor, pledgor, psywar, rancor, rapport, raptor, raw score, Realtor, restore, rhetor, savior, seafloor, seashore, sector, seignior, Senghor, senhor, señor, sensor, settlor, Seymour, signor, smoothbore, s'more, soft-core, sophomore, stand for, stentor, stertor, storm door, Strathmore, stressor, stridor, subfloor, swear for, Tagore, take for, temblor, tensor, therefor, therefore, threescore, Timor, top-drawer, trapdoor, turgor, uproar, vendor, what's more, wherefore, wild boar, wiredrawer, woodlore, z-score • albacore, allosaur, alongshore, anaphor, anymore, Apgar score, archosaur, at death's door, at one's door, Baltimore, Bangalore, bargain for, Barrymore, brontosaur, canker sore, carnivore, carnosaur, close the door, Coimbatore, come in for, commodore, comprador, consignor, corridor, cuspidor, devisor, dinosaur, door-to-door, double door, Eastern shore, East Timor, Ecuador, either-or, Eleanor, elector, endospore, evermore,

except for, forest floor, franchisor, from the floor, furthermore, general store, go in for, gonopor, guarantor, Gwalior, hackamore, hadrosaur, hellebore, herbivore, heretofore, humidor, in line for, Koko Nor, komondor, Labrador, licensor, Lipitor, louis d'or, madrepore, Mangalore, man-of-war, manticore, matador, metaphor, meteor, micropore, millepore, Minotaur, mirador, more and more, Mount Rushmore, Mount Tabor, nevermore, not long for, omnivore, open-door, out-of-door, package store, parador, Perigord, petit four, picador, pinafore, piscivore, pompadour, Pompadour, predator, promisor, pterosaur, reservoir, saddle sore, sagamore, Salvador, semaphore, servitor, Singapore, standard score, stand up for, stegosaur, stevedore, stick up for, struggle for, superstore, sycamore, take the floor, Theodore, theretofore, to die for, troubadour, tug-of-war, two-by-four, uncalled-for, underscore, unlooked-for, vavasor, warrantor • air commodore, alienor, ambassador, ankylosaur, brachiosaur, Cape Bojador, conquistador, conservator, convenience store, Corregidor, department store, El Salvador, esprit de corps, foot in the door, forevermore, go to bat for, have it in for, hereinbefore, hold a brief for, ichthyosaur, insectivore, legislator, mixed metaphor, national seashore, plesiosaur, revolving door, San Salvador, toreador, tyrannosaur, Ulaan Baatar • administrator, caveat emptor, caveat lector, lobster thermidor, Polish Corridor, variety store

or² \ər\ see EUR¹

ora \ȯr-ə\ aura, bora, Cora, Dora, flora, Flora, hora, Laura, Lora, mora, Nora, sora, Torah • Andorra, angora, aurora, Aurora, bandora, begorra, camorra, fedora, gemara, Gomorrah, haftarah, Lenora, Masora, menorah, pandora, Pandora, remora, senhora, señora, signora, Sonora, Tambora, Zamora • Amadora, Bora-Bora, cyclospora, grandiflora, Juiz de Fora, Leonora, Simchas Torah, Tuscarora

orable \ȯr-ə-bəl\ horrible, pourable, storable • adorable, deplorable, ignorable, restorable

orace \ȯr-əs\ see AURUS

oracle \ȯr-ə-kəl\ coracle, oracle

orage¹ \är-ij\ barrage, borage, forage, porridge

orage² \ȯr-ij\ borage, floorage, forage, porridge, storage • cold storage

orah \ȯr-ə\ see ORA

oral¹ \ȯr-əl\ aural, chloral, choral, coral, floral, laurel, Laurel, moral, oral, quarrel, sorrel • aboral, amoral, auroral, balmoral, binaural, brain coral, Cape Coral, fire coral, immoral, mayoral, monaural, peroral, red coral, restoral, sororal • electoral

oral² \ȯrl\ see ORL²

oram \ȯr-əm\ see ORUM

orate \ȯr-ət\ see ORET

orative \ȯr-ət-iv\ explorative, pejorative, restorative

oray \ə-rē\ see URRY

orb \ȯrb\ forb, orb, sorb, Sorb • absorb, adsorb, desorb, resorb • reabsorb

orbate \ȯr-bət\ see ORBIT

orbeil \ȯr-bəl\ see ORBEL

orbel \ȯr-bəl\ corbeil, corbel, warble

orbet \ȯr-bət\ see ORBIT

orbit \ȯr-bət\ orbit • adsorbate

orc \ȯrk\ see ORK²

orca \ȯr-kə\ orca • Majorca, Minorca

orcas \ȯr-kəs\ Dorcas, orchis

orce \ȯrs\ see ORSE¹

orced \ȯrst\ see ORST¹

orceful \ȯrs-fəl\ see ORSEFUL

orcement \ȯr-smənt\ see ORSEMENT

orcer \ȯr-sər\ courser, forcer • discourser, enforcer • reinforcer—*also* -er *forms of adjectives listed at* ORSE¹

orch \ȯrch\ porch, scorch, torch • blowtorch, leaf scorch, sunporch • sleeping porch • carry a torch, carry the torch

orcher \ór-chər\ scorcher, torture

orchid \ór-kəd\ forked, orchid • cryptorchid, monorchid

orchis \ór-kəs\ see ORCAS

ord¹ \órd\ see OARD

ord² \ərd\ see IRD

ord³ \ór\ see OR¹

ordan \órd-ᵊn\ see ARDEN²

ordancy \órd-ᵊn-sē\ mordancy • discordancy

ordant \órd-ᵊnt\ mordant, mordent • accordant, concordant, discordant

orde \órd\ see OARD

orded \órd-əd\ see ARDED²

ordent \órd-ᵊnt\ see ORDANT

order \órd-ər\ boarder, border, corder, hoarder, order, warder • awarder, back order, close order, court order, disorder, gag order, in order, keyboarder, mail-order, on order, recorder, reorder, rewarder, sailboarder, short-order, skateboarder, snowboarder, stop order, suborder, surfboarder, third order, to order, transborder, wakeboarder, word order • flight recorder, holy order, in short order, law-and-order, made-to-order, major order, market order, minor order, money order, mood disorder, pecking order, standing order, superorder, tape recorder, wire recorder • eating disorder, panic disorder, restraining order

ordered \órd-ərd\ bordered, ordered • disordered, well-ordered—*also* -ed *forms of verbs listed at* ORDER

orders \órd-ərz\ Borders • marching orders, Scottish Borders—*also* -s, -'s, *and* -s' *forms of nouns and* -s *forms of verbs listed at* ORDER

ordial \órd-ē-əl\ exordial, primordial

ordid \órd-əd\ see ARDED²

ording¹ \órd-iŋ\ boarding, hoarding, lording • recording, rewarding, skateboarding • self-recording, tape recording, weatherboarding, wire-recording—*also* -ing *forms of verbs listed at* OARD

ording² \ərd-iŋ\ see ERDING

ordingly \órd-iŋ-lē\ accordingly, rewardingly

ordion \órd-ē-ən\ accordion, Edwardian • Kierkegaardian

ordon \órd-ᵊn\ see ARDEN²

ordure \ór-jər\ see ORGER

ordy¹ \órd-ē\ Geordie, Lordy • awardee

ordy² \ərd-ē\ see URDY

ore¹ \ór-ē\ see ORY

ore² \úr\ see URE¹

ore³ \ər-ə\ see OROUGH¹

ore⁴ \ór\ see OR¹

oreal \ór-ē-əl\ see ORIAL

orean \òr-ē-ən\ see ORIAN

oreas \òr-ē-əs\ see ORIOUS

ored \òrd\ see OARD

oredom \òrd-əm\ boredom, whoredom

orehead \òr-əd\ see ORRID

oreign¹ \är-ən\ see ARIN

oreign² \òr-ən\ see ORIN¹

oreigner \òr-ə-nər\ see ORONER

orem \òr-əm\ see ORUM

oreman \òr-mən\ see ORMAN

orence \òr-ən(t)s\ see AWRENCE

oreous \òr-ē-əs\ see ORIOUS

orer \òr-ər\ borer, corer, floorer, horror, pourer, roarer, scorer, schnorrer, snorer, soarer • abhorrer, adorer, corn borer, deplorer, explorer, ignorer, restorer • Sea Explorer—*also* -er *forms of adjectives listed at* OR¹

ores¹ \òr-əs\ see AURUS

ores² \òrz\ see OORS

oreson \òrs-ᵊn\ see OARSEN

orest \òr-əst\ see ORIST

orester \òr-ə-stər\ see ORISTER

oret \òr-ət\ floret • sororate

oreum \òr-ē-əm\ see ORIUM

oreward \òr-wərd\ see ORWARD

oreword \òr-wərd\ see ORWARD

orey \òr-ē\ see ORY

orf \òrf\ see ORPH

org¹ \òrg\ morgue • Alborg, cyborg, Seaborg, Vyborg • Helsingborg, Swedenborg

org² \òr-ē\ see ORY

organ \òr-gən\ gorgon, morgan, Morgan, organ • end organ, Glamorgan, hand organ, house organ, mouth organ, pipe organ, reed organ, sense organ • barrel organ, centimorgan, Demogorgon

orge \òrj\ forge, George, gorge • disgorge, drop-forge, engorge, Fort George, Lake George, Lloyd George, reforge • Karageorge, Royal Gorge • Olduvai Gorge

orger \òr-jər\ bordure, forger, gorger, ordure • drop forger

orgi \òr-gē\ see ORGY

orgia \òr-jə\ Borgia, Georgia • New Georgia, South Georgia

orgian \òr-jən\ Georgian • Swedenborgian

orgon \òr-gən\ see ORGAN

orgue \òrg\ see ORG

orgy \òr-gē\ corgi, porgy

ori \òr-ē\ see ORY

oria \òr-ē-ə\ gloria, Gloria, noria, scoria, Soria • aporia, centaurea, dysphoria, euphoria, Peoria, Pretoria, victoria, Victoria, Vitoria • Lake Victoria • phantasmagoria

orial \òr-ē-əl\ boreal, loreal, oriel, oriole • arboreal, armorial, auctorial, authorial, cantorial, censorial, corporeal, cursorial,

factorial, fossorial, manorial,
marmoreal, memorial, pictorial,
praetorial, proctorial, raptorial,
rectorial, sartorial, seignorial,
sensorial, sponsorial, tonsorial,
tutorial, uxorial, vectorial
• conductorial, consistorial,
curatorial, dictatorial, directorial,
editorial, equatorial, immemorial,
incorporeal, janitorial, monitorial,
monsignoral, natatorial,
piscatorial, preceptorial,
professorial, purgatorial,
reportorial, senatorial, territorial
• ambassadorial, combinatorial,
conspiratorial, gladiatorial,
gubernatorial, prosecutorial,
time immemorial

oriam \ór-ē-əm\ see ORIUM

orian \ór-ē-ən\ Dorian, saurian,
Taurean • aurorean, Azorean,
Gregorian, historian, Ivorian,
Nestorian, praetorian, stento-
rian, Victorian • dinosaurian,
Ecuadorean, hyperborean,
Labradorean, madreporian,
Oratorian, prehistorian,
Salvadorean, senatorian,
Singaporean, terpsichorean
• salutatorian, valedictorian

oriant \ór-ē-ənt\ see ORIENT

oriat \ór-ē-ət\ see AUREATE²

oric \ór-ik\ auric, choric, Doric,
toric • Armoric, caloric, clitoric,
dysphoric, euphoric, folkloric,
historic, phosphoric, plethoric,
pyloric • ahistoric, anaphoric,
cataphoric, diasporic, meta-
phoric, meteoric, noncaloric,
paregoric, prehistoric,

sophomoric • aleatoric,
phantasmagoric

orical \ór-i-kəl\ auricle
• historical, rhetorical
• ahistorical, allegorical, art
historical, categorical,
metaphorical, oratorical

orics \ór-iks\ see ORYX

orid \ór-əd\ see ORRID

oriel \ór-ē-əl\ see ORIAL

orient \ór-ē-ənt\ orient, Orient
• euphoriant

orin¹ \ór-ən\ chlorine, florin,
foreign, Lauren, Orrin, sporran,
warren, Warren • Andorran
• Cape Comorin, cyclosporine

orin² \är-ən\ see ARIN

orine \ór-ən\ see ORIN¹

oring \ór-iŋ\ boring, flooring,
roaring, shoring • inpouring,
longshoring, outpouring, rip-
roaring, wood-boring—also -ing
forms of verbs listed at OR¹

öring \ər-iŋ\ see URRING

oriole \ór-ē-əl\ see ORIAL

orious \ór-ē-əs\ aureus, Boreas,
glorious • arboreous, cen-
sorious, inglorious, laborious,
notorious, sartorius, uproarious,
uxorious, vainglorious,
victorious • meritorious

oris \ór-əs\ see AURUS

orish¹ \ór-ish\ boarish, poorish,
whorish • folklorish

orish² \ur-ish\ see OORISH¹

orist \ór-əst\ florist, forest,
Forrest • afforest, Black Forest,

deforest, folklorist, reforest
• allegorist • Petrified Forest
—*also* -est *forms of adjectives
listed at* OR¹

orister \ór-ə-stər\ chorister,
forester

ority \ór-ət-ē\ authority, majority,
minority, priority, seniority,
sonority, sorority • apriority
• exteriority, inferiority, interiority,
posteriority, superiority

orium \ór-ē-əm\ corium
• castoreum, ciborium,
emporium, pastorium,
scriptorium, sensorium,
triforium • auditorium,
cafetorium, crematorium,
in memoriam, moratorium,
natatorium, sanatorium,
sudatorium

ork¹ \ərk\ burke, Burke, chirk,
cirque, clerk, dirk, Dirk, irk, jerk,
kirk, Kirk, lurk, murk, perk,
quirk, shirk, smirk, stirk, Turk,
work, yerk, zerk • artwork, at
work, beadwork, berserk,
breastwork, brickwork, bridge-
work, brightwork, brushwork,
capework, casework, clockwork,
coachwork, de Klerk, ductwork,
Dunkirk, earthwork, falsework,
fieldwork, file clerk, firework,
flatwork, footwork, formwork,
framework, fretwork, frostwork,
glasswork, goldwork, Grand
Turk, grillwork, groundwork,
guesswork, hackwork, hand-
work, hauberk, headwork,
homework, housework, in work,
ironwork, knee-jerk, lacework,
legwork, lifework, make-work,
meshwork, millwork, network,
outwork, paintwork, patchwork,
piecework, presswork,
quillwork, rework, roadwork,
salesclerk, schoolwork,
scrollwork, scut work, Selkirk,
shellwork, slopwork, South-
wark, spadework, steelwork,
stickwork, stonework, stump
work, teamwork, timework,
topwork, town clerk, waxwork,
webwork, wheelwork, wood-
work, young Turk • Atatürk,
basketwork, bodywork,
busywork, cabinetwork, city
clerk, clean-and-jerk, crewel-
work, donkeywork, fancywork,
handiwork, hatchetwork,
journeywork, lacquerwork,
latticework, leatherwork,
masterwork, metalwork,
needlework, openwork, out of
work, overwork, paperwork,
piece of work, plasterwork,
right to work, shipping clerk,
social work, soda jerk, stated
clerk, trestlework, wickerwork,
wonderwork

ork² \órk\ cork, Cork, dork, fork,
pork, quark, stork, torque, York
• bulwark, Cape York, Clark
Fork, futhorc, New York, North
York, pitchfork, salt pork,
uncork, wood stork

orked¹ \órkt\ corked, forked
• uncorked

orked² \ór-kəd\ see ORCHID

orker¹ \ər-kər\ jerker, lurker,
shirker, worker • berserker,
caseworker, dockworker,
farmworker, field-worker,
glassworker, guest worker,
handworker, ironworker,

networker, outworker,
pieceworker, sex worker,
steelworker, tearjerker,
timeworker, wageworker,
woodworker • autoworker,
bodyworker, metalworker,
needleworker, social worker,
wonder-worker

orker[2] \ȯr-kər\ corker, forker,
porker, torquer • New Yorker

orkie \ȯr-kē\ see ORKY

orking \ər-kiŋ\ hardworking,
networking, tear-jerking,
woodworking • metalworking,
wonder-working—*also* -ing
forms of verbs listed at ORK[1]

orky \ȯr-kē\ corky, dorky, forky,
Gorky, porky, Yorkie

orl[1] \ərl\ see IRL[1]

orl[2] \ȯrl\ schorl, whorl • ceorl

orld \ərld\ burled, knurled,
whorled, world • dreamworld,
first world, fourth world, free
world, half-world, New World,
old-world, Old World, real-
world, third world • afterworld,
brave new world, demiworld, in
the world, microworld, nether-
world, otherworld, second
world, underworld • for all the
world, man of the world, out of
this world • on top of the
world—*also* -ed *forms of verbs
listed at* IRL[1]

orled \ərld\ see ORLD

orm[1] \ərm\ berm, firm, germ,
herm, perm, sperm, squirm,
term, therm, worm • affirm,
bagworm, bloodworm, book-
worm, budworm, confirm,

cutworm, deworm, dew worm,
earthworm, eelworm, flatworm,
glowworm, heartworm,
hookworm, hornworm,
inchworm, infirm, long-term,
lugworm, lungworm, midterm,
pinworm, ringworm, round-
worm, sandworm, screwworm,
short-term, silkworm, tapeworm,
tubeworm, webworm, wood-
worm • angleworm, armyworm,
caddis worm, disaffirm,
disconfirm, gymnosperm,
pachyderm, reconfirm
• angiosperm, echinoderm

orm[2] \ȯrm\ corm, dorm, form,
norm, storm, swarm, warm
• art form, aswarm, barnstorm,
brainstorm, by-form, by storm,
conform, deform, Delorme,
dust storm, firestorm, free-
form, hailstorm, ice storm,
inform, L-form, landform, life-
form, line storm, lukewarm,
perform, planform, platform,
postform, preform, rainstorm,
re-form, reform, sandstorm, slip
form, snowstorm, transform,
triform, waveform, windstorm
• chloroform, cruciform,
dendriform, dentiform,
disciform, fungiform, funnelform,
fusiform, land reform, letterform,
microform, multiform, noncon-
form, racing form, thunder-
storm, uniform, up a storm,
vermiform • cuneiform, dress
uniform, electroform, magnetic
storm, quadratic form
• electrical storm

ormable \ȯr-mə-bəl\ formable
• conformable, deformable,

performable, reformable,
transformable

ormal \ȯr-məl\ formal, normal
• abnormal, conformal,
informal, subnormal
• paranormal, semiformal,
supernormal

ormally \ȯr-mə-lē\ formally,
formerly, normally, stormily
• abnormally, informally,
subnormally • paranormally,
supernormally

orman \ȯr-mən\ corpsman,
doorman, foreman, Mormon,
Norman • longshoreman
• Anglo-Norman

ormance \ȯr-məns\
conformance, performance
• nonconformance

ormant \ȯr-mənt\ dormant,
formant • informant,
nondormant

ormative \ȯr-mət-iv\ formative,
normative • deformative,
informative, performative,
reformative, transformative

orme \ȯrm\ see ORM²

ormed \ȯrmd\ formed, normed
• deformed, informed,
malformed, unformed • well-
informed—*also* -ed *forms of
verbs listed at* ORM²

ormer¹ \ȯr-mər\ dormer, former,
swarmer, warmer • barnstormer,
benchwarmer, brainstormer,
conformer, heart-warmer,
informer, performer, reformer,
shed dormer, transformer
• nonconformer

ormer² \ər-mər\ see URMUR

ormerly \ȯr-mə-lē\ see ORMALLY

ormie \ȯr-mē\ see ORMY¹

ormily \ȯr-mə-lē\ see ORMALLY

orming \ȯr-miŋ\ brainstorming,
heartwarming, housewarming,
performing • habit-forming,
nonperforming—*also* -ing *forms
of verbs listed at* ORM²

ormist \ȯr-məst\ warmest
• conformist, reformist
• nonconformist

ormity \ȯr-mət-ē\ conformity,
deformity, enormity • dis-
conformity, multiformity,
nonconformity, unconformity,
uniformity

ormless \ȯrm-ləs\ formless,
gormless

ormon \ȯr-mən\ see ORMAN

ormy¹ \ȯr-mē\ stormy, dormie

ormy² \ər-mē\ see ERMY

orn¹ \ȯrn\ born, borne, bourn,
corn, horn, lorn, morn, mourn,
Norn, Orne, porn, scorn, shorn,
sworn, thorn, torn, warn, worn,
Zorn • acorn, adorn, airborne,
alphorn, althorn, baseborn,
bass horn, bicorne, bighorn,
blackthorn, blue corn, boxthorn,
broomcorn, buckthorn,
bullhorn, Cape Horn, careworn,
Christ's-thorn, Dearborn,
dehorn, dent corn, earthborn,
einkorn, field corn, firethorn,
firstborn, flint corn, foghorn,
foreborn, foresworn, forewarn,
forlorn, forworn, freeborn,
French horn, green corn,

greenhorn, hartshorn, hawthorn, Hawthorne, highborn, hulled corn, inborn, inkhorn, krumm-horn, leghorn, longhorn, lovelorn, lowborn, newborn, outworn, pod corn, popcorn, post horn, pronghorn, ramshorn, reborn, saxhorn, seaborne, self-born, shipborne, shoehorn, shopworn, shorthorn, skyborne, soilborne, staghorn, stillborn, stinkhorn, suborn, sweet corn, tick-borne, timeworn, tinhorn, toilworn, tricorne, trueborn, twice-born, twinborn, unborn, unworn, wayworn, wellborn, well-worn, wind-borne
• alpenhorn, barleycorn, Capricorn, cyberporn, English horn, Firth of Lorn, flügelhorn, foreign-born, Golden Horn, hunting horn, longicorn, Matterhorn, peppercorn, powder horn, saddle horn, unicorn, waterborne, waterworn, weatherworn, winterbourne
• Indian corn, John Barleycorn, Little Bighorn, Texas longhorn
• to the manner born, to the manor born

orn² \ərn\ see URN

ornament \ȯr-nə-mənt\ ornament, tournament

orne \ȯrn\ see ORN¹

orned \ȯrnd\ horned, thorned
• unadorned—*also* -ed *forms of verbs listed at* ORN¹

orner \ȯr-nər\ corner, scorner, warner, Warner • Cape Horner, dehorner, hot corner, suborner

• coffin corner, hole-and-corner, kitty-corner

ornery \än-rē\ see ANNERY¹

orney \ər-nē\ see OURNEY¹

ornful \ȯrn-fəl\ mournful, scornful

orning \ȯr-niŋ\ morning, mourning, warning
• aborning—*also* -ing *forms of verbs listed at* ORN

ornis \ȯr-nəs\ see ORNICE

ornment \ərn-mənt\ see ERNMENT

orny \ȯr-nē\ corny, horny, porny, thorny

oro¹ \ər-ə\ see OROUGH¹

oro² \ȯ-rō\ Coro, Moro
• Chamorro, Mindoro, Sapporo
• Río de Oro

oroner \ȯr-ə-nər\ coroner, foreigner, warrener

orough¹ \ər-ə\ borough, burgh, burro, burrow, curragh, furrow, ore, thorough • Gainsborough, Greensboro, Roxborough, Scarborough, Yarborough
• Edinburgh, kookaburra, Peterborough, pocket borough, rotten borough

orough² \ər-ō\ see URROW¹

orous \ȯr-əs\ see AURUS

orp \ȯrp\ dorp, gorp, thorp, Thorpe, warp • Australorp, Krugersdorp, octothorpe, Oglethorpe

orpe \ȯrp\ see ORP

orph \ȯrf\ corf, dwarf, morph
• allomorph, Düsseldorf, ectomorph, endomorph,

lagomorph, mesomorph, zoomorph • anthropomorph, gynandromorph

orphan \òr-fən\ orphan • endorphin

orpheus \òr-fē-əs\ Morpheus, Orpheus

orphic \òr-fik\ orphic • dimorphic, dysmorphic • allomorphic, anamorphic, biomorphic, ectomorphic, endomorphic, isomorphic, mesomorphic, metamorphic, polymorphic, pseudomorphic, zoomorphic

orphin \òr-fən\ see ORPHAN

orphrey \òr-frē\ orphrey, porphyry

orphyrin \òr-fə-rən\ see ARFARIN

orphyry \òr-frē\ see ORPHREY

orpoise \òr-pəs\ see ORPUS

orpor \òr-pər\ see ORPER

orps \òr\ see OR[1]

orpsman \òr-mən\ see ORMAN

orpus \òr-pəs\ corpus, porpoise • habeas corpus

orque \òrk\ see ORK[2]

orquer \òr-kər\ see ORKER[2]

orr \òr\ see OR[1]

orra[1] \är-ə\ see ARA[1]

orra[2] \òr-ə\ see ORA

orrader \är-əd-ər\ see ORRIDOR

orrah[1] \òr-ə\ see ORA

orrah[2] \är-ə\ see ARA[1]

orran[1] \är-ən\ see ARIN

orran[2] \òr-ən\ see ORIN[1]

orrence \òr-əns\ see AWRENCE

orrel \òr-əl\ see ORAL[1]

orrent \òr-ənt\ horrent, torrent, warrant • abhorrent, bench warrant, death warrant, search warrant

orrer \òr-ər\ see ORER

orres \òr-əs\ see AURUS

orrest \òr-əst\ see ORIST

orrible \òr-ə-bəl\ see ORABLE

orrid \òr-əd\ florid, horrid, torrid

orridge[1] \är-ij\ see ORAGE[1]

orridge[2] \òr-ij\ see ORAGE[2]

orridor \är-əd-ər\ corridor, forrader • Polish Corridor

orrie[1] \är-ē\ see ARI[1]

orrie[2] \òr-ē\ see ORY

orrier \òr-ē-ər\ see ARRIOR

orrin[1] \är-en\ see ARIN

orrin[2] \òr-ən\ see ORIN[1]

orris[1] \är-əs\ charas, Juárez, Maurice, morris, Morris, Norris, orris • Benares, Polaris

orris[2] \òr-əs\ see AURUS

orro \ò-rō\ see ORO[2]

orror \òr-ər\ see ORER

orrow[1] \är-ō\ borrow, claro, morrow, sorrow, taro • bizarro, Ignarro, Pissarro, Pizarro, saguaro, tomorrow • Catanzaro • Kilimanjaro, Mohenjo Daro

orrow[2] \är-ə\ see ARA[1]

orry[1] \är-ē\ see ARI[1]

orry² \ər-ē\ see URRY

ors \orz\ see OORS

orsal \or-səl\ see ORSEL

orse¹ \ors\ coarse, corse, course, force, gorse, hoarse, horse, Morse, Norse, source • clotheshorse, concourse, crash course, dark horse, dawn horse, dead horse, deforce, discourse, divorce, dray horse, endorse, enforce, extrorse, golf course, gut course, high horse, introrse, iron horse, midcourse, of course, Old Norse, one-horse, packhorse, perforce, post-horse, racecourse, racehorse, recourse, redhorse, remorse, resource, retrorse, sawhorse, sea horse, string-course, trial horse, unhorse, warhorse, wheelhorse, Whitehorse, workhorse • charley horse, Crazy Horse, cutting horse, harness horse, hobbyhorse, intercourse, minicourse, nonrecourse, outercourse, pommel horse, quarter horse, reinforce, rocking horse, saddle horse, stalking horse, telecourse, tour de force, Trojan horse, vaulting horse, watercourse • collision course, matter of course, obstacle course, par for the course, Przewalski's horse • Arabian horse, correspondence course, sexual intercourse

orse² \ərs\ see ERSE

orseful \ors-fəl\ forceful • remorseful, resourceful

orsel \or-səl\ dorsal, morsel • middorsal

orseman \or-smən\ horseman, Norseman

orsement \or-smənt\ deforcement, divorcement, endorsement, enforcement • reinforcement

orsen \ərs-ᵊn\ see ERSON

orser \ər-sər\ see URSOR

orset \or-sət\ corset, Dorset

orsey \or-sē\ see ORSY

orsion \or-shən\ see ORTION

orst¹ \orst\ forced, horst—*also* -ed *forms of verbs listed at* ORSE¹

orst² \ərst\ see URST

orsted \ər-stəd\ see ERSTED

orsum \or-səm\ dorsum, foursome

orsy \or-sē\ gorsy, horsey

ort¹ \ort\ bort, court, fort, forte, mort, Oort, ort, port, Porte, quart, short, skort, snort, sort, sport, swart, thwart, tort, torte, wart, wort • abort, airport, amort, aport, assort, athwart, backcourt, bellwort, birthwort, bistort, blood sport, Bridgeport, carport, cavort, cohort, colewort, comport, consort, contort, crosscourt, deport, disport, distort, downcourt, effort, escort, exhort, export, extort, fall short, figwort, forecourt, for short, free port, frontcourt, glasswort, Gosport, Gulfport, half-court, homeport, home port, in short, jetport, lousewort, lungwort, madwort, milkwort, mugwort, Newport, outport, passport, presort, purport, ragwort, report, resort, resort, retort, sandwort, seaport, sell short, Shreveport, spaceport, spearwort, spoilsport, Stockport, support, toothwort, transport • bladderwort, butterwort, davenport, heliport, hold the fort, lifesupport, liverwort, moneywort, nonsupport, of a sort, on report, pennywort, price support, Saint-John's wort, sally port, self-report, selfsupport, spiderwort, teleport, treaty port, ultrashort, worrywart • after a sort, annual report, containerport, pianoforte, the long and short, underreport • destroyer escort

ort² \ȯr\ see OR¹

ort³ \ərt\ see ERT¹

ortage \ȯrt-ij\ portage, shortage • colportage, reportage

ortal \ȯrt-ᵊl\ chortle, mortal, portal, quartile • immortal • portal-to-portal

ortar \ȯrt-ər\ see ORTER

ortative \ȯrt-ət-iv\ hortative, portative • assortative, exhortative

orte¹ \ȯrt\ see ORT¹

orte² \ȯrt-ē\ see ORTY

orted \ȯrt-əd\ warted • assorted, ill-sorted, purported • selfreported, self-supported—also -ed forms of verbs listed at ORT¹

orten \ȯrt-ᵊn\ quartan, shorten • foreshorten

orter \ȯrt-ər\ mortar, porter, Porter, quarter, snorter, sorter, thwarter • aborter, assorter, colporteur, distorter, exhorter, exporter, extorter, headquarter, importer, lambs-quarter, Newporter, reporter, resorter, ripsnorter, supporter, transporter • brick-and-mortar, court reporter • police reporter • athletic supporter—also -er forms of adjectives listed at ORT¹

orteur \ȯrt-ər\ see ORTER

orth¹ \ȯrth\ forth, Forth, fourth, north, North • bring forth, call forth, thenceforth • and so forth, back and forth, Firth of Forth

orth² \ərth\ see IRTH

orthful \ərth-fəl\ see IRTHFUL

orthless \ərth-ləs\ see IRTHLESS

orthy \ər-thē\ earthy, worthy • airworthy, blameworthy, crashworthy, Galsworthy, newsworthy, noteworthy, praiseworthy, roadworthy, seaworthy, trustworthy, unworthy • creditworthy

ortic \ȯrt-ik\ see ARTIC²

ortical \ȯrt-i-kəl\ cortical, vortical • neocortical

ortie \ȯrt-ē\ see ORTY

orting \ȯrt-iŋ\ sporting • nonsporting, ripsnorting • self-supporting—also -ing forms of verbs listed at ORT

ortion \ór-shən\ portion, torsion • abortion, apportion, contortion, distortion, extortion, proportion, retortion • disproportion, in proportion, proabortion, reapportion • antiabortion

ortionate \ór-shnət\ extortionate, proportionate • disproportionate

ortionist \ór-shnist\ abortionist, contortionist, extortionist

ortis \órt-əs\ fortis, mortise, tortoise • aqua fortis, rigor mortis

ortise \órt-əs\ see ORTIS

ortive \órt-iv\ sportive • abortive, contortive, extortive, supportive

ortle \órt-əl\ see ORTAL

ortly \órt-lē\ courtly, portly, shortly, thwartly

ortment \órt-mənt\ assortment, comportment, deportment, disportment

ortoise \órt-əs\ see ORTIS

orton \órt-ən\ Morton, Norton, Wharton

orts \órts\ quartz, shorts, sports • Cinque Ports, of sorts • boxer shorts, out of sorts, undershorts • Bermuda shorts, bicycle shorts—*also* -s, -'s, *and* -s' *forms of nouns and* -s *forms of verbs listed at* ORT[1]

ortunate \órch-nət\ fortunate • importunate, unfortunate

orture \ór-chər\ see ORCHER

orty \órt-ē\ forty, shorty, sortie, sporty, warty • mezzo forte • pianoforte

orum \ór-əm\ foram, forum, jorum, quorum • decorum, Mizoram • ad valorem, cockalorum, indecorum, Karakoram, variorum • pons asinorum, sanctum sanctorum, schola cantorum

orus \ór-əs\ see AURUS

orward \ór-wərd\ forward, foreword, shoreward • bring forward, fast-forward, flash forward, henceforward, look forward, put forward, set forward, small forward, straightforward, thenceforward • carryforward

ory \ór-ē\ Corey, corrie, dory, glory, Gorey, gory, hoary, Laurie, Lori, lorry, lory, nori, quarry, saury, sorry, story, Tory, zori • backstory, centaury, clerestory, fish story, ghost story, John Dory, Noyori, Old Glory, outlawry, satori, self-glory, short story, sob story, vainglory, war story • a priori, allegory, amatory, auditory, bedtime story, cacciatore, castratory, category, con amore, cover story, crematory, damnatory, decretory, desultory, dilatory, dormitory, excretory, expletory, feudatory, fumitory, Göteborg, gustatory, gyratory, horror story, hortatory, hunky-dory, inventory, Lake Maggiore, laudatory, lavatory, mandatory, migratory, minatory, monitory, Montessori, morning glory, nugatory, offertory, oratory, overstory, piscatory, precatory, predatory, prefatory, probatory, promissory, promontory, purgatory, repertory, Ruwenzori, signatory, statutory, sudatory, territory, transitory, understory, vibratory, vomitory, yakitori • accusatory, admonitory, adulatory, a fortiori, aleatory, ambulatory, amendatory, applicatory, approbatory, celebratory, circulatory, cock-and-bull story, combinatory, commendatory, compensatory, conciliatory, condemnatory, confirmatory, confiscatory, conservatory, consolatory, contributory, copulatory, cosignatory, declamatory, declaratory, dedicatory, defamatory, denigratory, depilatory, depository, derogatory, designatory, dispensatory, divinatory, escalatory, excitatory, exclamatory, exculpatory, excusatory, exhibitory, exhortatory, expiatory, expiratory, explanatory, explicatory, exploratory, expository, expurgatory, incantatory, incubatory, indicatory, inflammatory, informatory, innovatory, inspiratory, inundatory, invitatory, judicatory, laboratory, masticatory, masturbatory, memento mori, millefiori, modulatory, obfuscatory, obligatory, observatory, performatory, persecutory, predicatory, premonitory, preparatory, prohibitory, reformatory, regulatory, repository, retributory, revelatory, respiratory,

salutatory, stipulatory, supplicatory, transmigratory, undulatory • a posteriori, anticipatory, conciliatory, congratulatory, discriminatory, hallucinatory, improvisatory, viola d'amore

oryx \ór-iks\ oryx • Armorics
• combinatorics

orze \órz\ see OORS

os¹ \äs\ boss, doss, dross, floss, fosse, gloss, joss, Kos, Maas, os, pross, stoss, toss • Argos, bathos, benthos, bugloss, chaos, Chios, cosmos, Delos, demos, Ellás, emboss, en masse, Eos, epos, Eros, ethos, Hyksos, kaross, kudos, kvass, Lagos, Laos, Laplace, Lemnos, Lesbos, Logos, Madras, Melos, mythos, Naxos, Nepos, nol-pros, nonpros, Paros, pathos, Patmos, peplos, Pharos, pit boss, pothos, ringtoss, Samos, Skyros, straw boss, telos, topos, tripos • albatross, coup de grâce, demitasse, dental floss, extrados, gravitas, intrados, isogloss, omphalos, reredos, semigloss, Thanatos, underboss, volte-face
• microcosmos

os² \ō\ see OW¹

os³ \ōs\ see OSE¹

os⁴ \ós\ see OSS¹

osa¹ \ō-sə\ Xhosa • Formosa, mimosa, Reynosa, samosa
• curiosa, virtuosa • anorexia nervosa

osa² \ō-zə\ Rosa • mimosa, mucosa, serosa, Spinoza, sub rosa • curiosa, Santa Rosa, virtuosa, Zaragoza

osable¹ \ō-zə-bəl\ closable • disposable, opposable, reclosable, supposable • decomposable, superposable

osable² \ü-zə-bəl\ see USABLE

osal \ō-zəl\ hosel, losel, Mosel • deposal, disposal, proposal, reposal, supposal

osan \ōs-ᵊn\ see OSIN

osch \äsh\ see ASH²

oschen¹ \ō-shən\ see OTION

oschen² \ȯ-shən\ see AUTION

oscible \äs-ə-bəl\ see OSSIBLE

osco \äs-kō\ see OSCOE

oscoe \äs-kō\ Bosco, roscoe, Roscoe • fiasco

oscopy \äs-kə-pē\ arthroscopy, cryoscopy, endoscopy, fluoroscopy, microscopy, rhinoscopy, spectroscopy • colonoscopy, laparoscopy, retinoscopy, sigmoidoscopy

ose¹ \ōs\ close, dose, gross, os • arkose, Bose, Carlos, cosmos, crustose, cymose, dextrose, engross, erose, fructose, globose, glucose, jocose, lactose, maltose, mannose, morose, mythos, nodose, pappose, pathos, pentose, pilose, plumose, ramose, rhamnose, ribose, rugose, scapose, schistose, setose, spinose, strigose, sucrose, Sukkoth, triose, up close, vadose, verbose, viscose • adios, adipose, bellicose, calvados, cellulose, comatose, diagnose, grandiose, granulose, Helios, lachrymose, megadose, otiose, overdose, racemose, Shabuoth, tuberose, varicose, ventricose • inter vivos, metamorphose, religiose • inter alios

ose² \ōz\ brose, Broz, chose, close, clothes, cloze, doze, froze, gloze, hose, nose, pose, prose, rose, Rose • Ambrose, appose, arose, bedclothes, bluenose, brownnose, bulldoze, Burroughs, compose, depose, dextrose, disclose, dispose, dog rose, enclose, expose, foreclose, fructose, glucose, hardnose, impose, Montrose, moss rose, Mount Rose, musk rose, nightclothes, old rose, oppose, plainclothes, primrose, propose, pug nose, quick-froze, repose, rockrose, smallclothes, suppose, transpose, trunk hose, tuberose, unclose, uprose, viscose, wind rose • Berlioz, cabbage rose, cellulose, c'est autre chose, China rose, Christmas rose, compass rose, counterpose, damask rose, decompose, diagnose, discompose, famille rose, indispose, interpose, juxtapose, letters close, on the nose, panty hose, pettitoes, predispose, presuppose, pussytoes, recompose, shovelnose, superpose, support hose, swaddling clothes, thumb one's nose, underclothes • anastomose, evening primrose, follow one's nose, look down one's nose, metamorphose, overexpose, pay through the nose, photocompose, superimpose, underexpose, under one's nose • altar of repose—*also* -s, -'s, *and* -s' *forms of nouns and* -s *forms of verbs listed at* OW[1]

ose[3] \üz\ see USE[2]

osed \ōzd\ closed, nosed • bluenosed, composed, exposed, hard-nosed, opposed, pug-nosed, sharp-nosed, snub-nosed, stenosed, supposed, unclosed • indisposed, shovel-nosed, toffee-nosed, well-disposed—*also* -ed *forms of verbs listed at* OSE[2]

osee \ō-zē\ see OSY

osel \ō-zəl\ see OSAL

osen \ōz-ᵊn\ chosen, frozen • deep-frozen, quick-frozen • lederhosen

oser[1] \ō-zər\ closer, dozer, poser, proser • brownnoser, bulldozer, composer, discloser, disposer, exposer, imposer, opposer, proposer • decomposer, interposer

oser[2] \ü-zər\ see USER

oset[1] \ō-zət\ see OSIT[2]

oset[2] \äz-ət\ see OSIT[1]

oset[3] \äs-ət\ see OSSET

osey \ō-zē\ see OSY

osh[1] \òsh\ see ASH[2]

osh[2] \äsh\ see OCHE[2]

oshed[1] \äsht\ sloshed • galoshed—*also* -ed *forms of verbs listed at* ASH[1]

oshed[2] \òsht\ see ASHED[1]

oshen \ō-shən\ see OTION

osher \äsh-ər\ see ASHER[1]

osia \ō-shə\ see OTIA[1]

osible \ō-zə-bəl\ see OSABLE[1]

osier \ō-zhər\ see OSURE

osily \ō-zə-lē\ cozily, dozily, nosily, prosily, rosily

osin \òs-ᵊn\ boatswain • Formosan, pocosin, triclosan

osing \ō-ziŋ\ closing, nosing • disclosing, imposing, self-closing, supposing—*also* -ing *forms of verbs listed at* OSE[2]

osion \ō-zhən\ plosion • corrosion, displosion, erosion, explosion, implosion

osis \ō-səs\ gnosis • cirrhosis, hypnosis, kenosis, lordosis, meiosis, miosis, mitosis, narcosis, necrosis, neurosis, orthosis, osmosis, prognosis, psychosis, sclerosis, stenosis, thrombosis • brucellosis, cyanosis, dermatosis, diagnosis, halitosis, heterosis, keratosis, psittacosis, scoliosis, silicosis, symbiosis • apotheosis, autohypnosis, cystic fibrosis, pediculosis, psychoneurosis, reverse osmosis, tuberculosis • mononucleosis

osit[1] \äz-ət\ closet, posit
• composite, deposit, exposit, reposit • oviposit

osit[2] \ō-zət\ prosit, roset

osite \äz-ət\ see OSIT[1]

ositive \äz-ət-iv\ positive
• appositive, dispositive, expositive, postpositive, prepositive • contrapositive, diapositive, Rh-positive, seropositive

ositor \äz-ət-ər\ compositor, depositor, expositor • ovipositor

osius \ō-shəs\ see OCIOUS

osive \ō-siv\ plosive • corrosive, erosive, explosive, implosive, purposive • high explosive

osk \äsk\ bosk, mosque • kiosk

oso[1] \ō-sō\ proso • Lombroso, maestoso, rebozo • arioso, Castelrosso, furioso, gracioso, grandioso, mafioso, Mato Grosso, oloroso, spiritoso, vigoroso, virtuoso • concerto grosso

oso[2] \ō-zō\ bozo • Cardozo, rebozo • furioso, gracioso, grandioso, spiritoso, vigoroso

oso[3] \ü-sō\ see USOE

osophy \äs-ə-fē\ philosophy, theosophy • anthroposophy

osque \äsk\ see OSK

oss[1] \ós\ boss, cross, crosse, dross, floss, gloss, joss, loss, moss, Ross, sauce, stoss, toss
• across, backcross, brown sauce, bugloss, club moss, crisscross, duck sauce, emboss, Greek cross, hard sauce, Kinross, kouros, lacrosse, oakmoss, outcross, pathos, peat moss, pit boss, Red Cross, ringtoss, straw boss, tau cross, topcross, uncross, white sauce
• albatross, applesauce, at a loss, autocross, béarnaise sauce, Celtic cross, chili sauce, come across, cyclo-cross, dental floss, double-cross, for a loss, get across, hoisin sauce, Iceland moss, intercross, Irish moss, Latin cross, Maltese cross, Mornay sauce, moto-cross, Nantua sauce, Navy Cross, Northern Cross, papal cross, put across, reindeer moss, run across, semigloss, single cross, Southern Cross, Spanish moss, tartar sauce, underboss • Calvary cross, Geneva cross, John of the Cross, pectoral cross, Perth and Kinross, profit and loss, Saint Andrew's cross, sign of the cross, viper's bugloss, Worcestershire sauce
• stations of the cross, Victoria Cross

oss[2] \ōs\ see OSE[1]

oss[3] \äs\ see OS[1]

ossa \äs-ə\ see ASA[1]

ossable \äs-ə-bəl\ see OSSIBLE

ossal \äs-əl\ docile, dossal, fossil, glossal, jostle, tassel, throstle, warsle, wassail
• apostle, colossal, indocile

osse[1] \äs\ see OS[1]

osse[2] \äs-ē\ see OSSY[1]

osse[3] \ós\ see OSS[1]

ossed \óst\ see OST[3]

osser \ó-sər\ Chaucer, crosser, saucer, tosser • embosser • double-crosser, flying saucer

osset \äs-ət\ cosset, faucet, posset

ossible \äs-ə-bəl\ possible • cognoscible, embossable, impossible

ossic \äs-ik\ see OSSICK

ossick \äs-ik\ fossick • isoglossic

ossil \äs-əl\ see OSSAL

ossity \äs-ət-ē\ atrocity, callosity, ferocity, gibbosity, monstrosity, pomposity, porosity, precocity, velocity, verbosity, viscosity, zygosity • animosity, curiosity, generosity, grandiosity, luminosity, reciprocity, virtuosity • religiosity

ossly \ós-lē\ costly, crossly

osso \ō-sō\ see OSO[1]

ossos \äs-əs\ see OCESS

ossum \äs-əm\ blossom, passim, possum • opossum, play possum, sic passim

ossus \äs-əs\ see OCESS

ossy[1] \äs-ē\ Aussie, bossy, drossy, flossy, glossy, posse, quasi • dalasi, Kumasi, Likasi, Madrasi, sannyasi

ossy[2] \ó-sē\ Aussie, bossy, lossy, mossy

ost[1] \äst\ accost, sol-faist • Pentecost, teleost—*also* -ed *forms of verbs listed at* OS[1]

ost[2] \ōst\ boast, coast, ghost, host, most, oast, post, prost, roast, toast • almost, at most, bedpost, compost, crown roast, doorpost, endmost, foremost, French toast, gatepost, glasnost, goalpost, gold coast, Gold Coast, guidepost, headmost, hindmost, impost, inmost, king post, lamppost, midmost, milepost, Milquetoast, outmost, outpost, pot roast, provost, queen post, rearmost, rib roast, riposte, seacoast, signpost, Slave Coast, sternmost, sternpost, topmost, upcoast, upmost, utmost • aftermost, ante-post, at the most, Barbary Coast, bottommost, coast-to-coast, command post, easternmost, farthermost, fingerpost, furthermost, headforemost, hithermost, Holy Ghost, innermost, Ivory Coast, listening post, lowermost, melba toast, nethermost, northernmost, outermost, parcel post, rudderpost, southernmost, staging post, sternforemost, trading post, undermost, uppermost, uttermost, westernmost, whipping post • from coast to coast, give up the ghost, Malabar Coast, Mosquito Coast • from pillar to post

ost[3] \óst\ cost, frost, lost • accost, at cost, defrost, exhaust, hoarfrost, Jack Frost, prime cost, star-crossed • holocaust, hypocaust, Pentecost, permafrost—*also* -ed *forms of verbs listed at* OSS[1]

ost⁴ \ə̇st\ *see* UST[1]

osta \äs-tə\ costa, hosta, pasta, Rasta

ostal¹ \ōs-təl\ coastal, postal • bicoastal • intercostal

ostal² \äs-təl\ *see* OSTEL

ostasy \äs-tə-sē\ apostasy, isostasy

oste \ōst\ *see* OST[2]

ostel \äs-təl\ costal, hostel, hostile • youth hostel • intercostal, Pentecostal

oster¹ \äs-tər\ coster, foster, Foster, roster • impostor, piastre • Double Gloucester, herpes zoster, paternoster • bananas Foster

oster² \ȯs-tər\ foster, Foster, roster • Double Gloucester • bananas Foster

oster³ \ō-stər\ *see* OASTER

ostic \äs-tik\ Gnostic • acrostic, agnostic, prognostic • diagnostic

ostile \äs-təl\ *see* OSTEL

ostle \äs-əl\ *see* OSSAL

ostly¹ \ōst-lē\ ghostly, hostly, mostly

ostly² \ȯs-lē\ *see* OSSLY

ostomy \äs-tə-mē\ ostomy • colostomy • enterostomy, tracheostomy

oston \ȯs-tən\ Austen, Austin, Boston • Godwin Austen

ostor \äs-tər\ *see* OSTER[1]

ostral \äs-trəl\ *see* OSTREL

ostrel \äs-trəl\ austral, costrel, nostril, rostral • colostral

ostril \äs-trəl\ *see* OSTREL

ostrum \äs-trəm\ nostrum, rostrum • colostrum

osty \ō-stē\ ghosty, toasty

osure \ō-zhər\ closure, crosier, osier • composure, disclosure, disposure, enclosure, exclosure, exposure, foreclosure, red osier • discomposure, time exposure • autoexposure, overexposure, underexposure • indecent exposure

osy \ō-zē\ cozy, dozy, mosey, nosy, Osee, posy, prosy, rosy • ring-around-the-rosy

osyne \äs-ᵊn-ē\ Euphrosyne, Mnemosyne

osz \ȯsh\ *see* ASH[2]

oszcz \ȯsh\ *see* ASH[2]

ot¹ \ät\ aught, baht, blot, boite, bot, chott, clot, cot, dot, ghat, got, grot, hot, jat, jot, khat, knot, kyat, lot, Lot, lotte, Mott, motte, naught, not, plot, pot, rot, scot, Scot, Scott, shot, skat, slot, snot, sot, spot, squat, stot, swat, swot, tot, trot, watt, Watt, what, wot, yacht • à droite, Alcott, allot, a lot, ascot, a shot, Banat, bank shot, begot, besot, big shot, black rot, black spot, blind spot, bloodshot, bowknot, boycott, brown rot, buckshot, bullshot, cachepot, calotte, cannot, cheap shot, chip shot, Connacht, crackpot, Crock-Pot, culotte, dashpot, despot, dogtrot, dovecote, draw shot, dreadnought, drop shot, drylot, dry rot, dunk shot, ear rot, earshot, ergot, eyeshot, eyespot, feedlot, fiat, firepot, fleshpot, foot rot, forgot, foul shot, fox-trot, fusspot, fylfot, garrote, gavotte, grapeshot, G-spot, gunshot, half-knot, Hallstatt, have-not, highspot, hotchpot, hot pot, hotshot, ikat, jackpot, job lot, jog trot, jump shot, Kalat, Korat, kumquat, leaf spot, long shot, loquat, love knot, manat, marplot, mascot, moon shot, motmot, mug shot, nightspot, odd lot, one-shot, Pequot, Pol Pot, potshot, Rabat, red-hot, reef knot, ring spot, robot, root knot, root rot, Sadat, sandlot, set shot, sexpot, Shabbat, shallot, Shebat, sheepcote, slap shot, slingshot, slipknot, slungshot, snapshot, soft rot, soft spot, somewhat, split shot, square knot, stinkpot, stockpot, subplot, sunspot, sweet spot, sword knot, teapot, tin-pot, topknot, tosspot, try-pot, upshot, wainscot, warm spot, whatnot, white-hot, woodlot, wood shot, wrist shot • aeronaut, aliquot, angle shot, apparat, apricot, aquanaut, argonaut, astronaut, beauty spot, bergamot, booster shot, burning ghat, cachalot, Camelot, caveat, carry-cot, chamber pot, chimney pot, coffeepot, cosmonaut, counterplot, diddley-squat, doodley-squat, floreat, flowerpot, flying spot, follow shot, gallipot, granny knot, guillemot, Gujarat, hit the spot, honeypot, Hottentot, Huguenot, juggernaut, kilowatt, Lancelot, like a shot, like as not, lobster pot, megawatt, melting pot, microdot, monocot, monoglot, noble rot, Nouakchott, ocelot, on the spot, overshot, paraquat, parking lot, passing shot, patriot, Penobscot, pepper pot, peridot, piping hot, polka dot, polyglot, running knot, samizdat, sansculotte, scattershot, scot and lot, shoulder knot, single knot, Southern blot, stopper knot, surgeon's knot, terawatt, tie the knot, tommyrot, touch-me-not, tracking shot, turkey trot, underplot, undershot, Western blot, Willemstadt, Windsor knot, Wyandot, wyandotte • as like as not, by a long shot, compatriot, expansion slot, forget-me-not, Gordian knot, hit the jackpot, immunoblot, Inupiat, magnificat, overhand knot, penalty shot, requiescat, stevedore knot, true lover's knot, whether or not • all over the lot, combination shot • Johnny-on-the-spot

ot² \ō\ see OW¹

ot³ \ōt\ see OAT

ot⁴ \ȯt\ see OUGHT¹

ôt \ō\ see OW¹

ota \ōt-ə\ bota, flota, iota, quota, rota • biota, Carlota, Dakota, iota, Lakota, pelota, Toyota • Minnesota, North Dakota, Sarasota, South Dakota

otable \ōt-ə-bəl\ notable, potable, quotable

otal \ōt-ᵊl\ dotal, motile, scrotal, total • immotile, subtotal, sum total, teetotal • anecdotal, antidotal, sacerdotal

otalist \ōt-ᵊl-əst\ teetotalist • anecdotalist, sacerdotalist

otamus \ät-ə-məs\ see OTOMOUS

otany \ät-ᵊn-ē\ botany, cottony • monotony

otarist \ōt-ə-rist\ motorist, votarist

otary \ōt-ə-rē\ coterie, rotary, votary

otas \ō-təs\ see OTUS

otch \äch\ blotch, botch, crotch, hotch, klatch, notch, scotch, Scotch, splotch, swatch, watch • bird-watch, deathwatch, debauch, dogwatch, hopscotch, hotchpotch, Sasquatch, stopwatch, top-notch, wrist-watch • butterscotch, coffee klatch

otchet \äch-ət\ crotchet, rochet

otchman \äch-mən\ Scotchman, watchman

otchy \äch-ē\ blotchy, boccie, botchy, splotchy • hibachi, huarache, huisache, Karachi, vivace • mariachi

ote¹ \ōt-ē\ dhoti, floaty, loti, roti, throaty • Capote, cenote, coyote, chayote, peyote, quixote, sapote • achiote, Don Quixote

ote² \ōt\ see OAT

ote³ \ät\ see OT¹

otea \ōt-ē-ə\ protea, scotia

oted \ōt-əd\ see OATED

otem \ōt-əm\ see OTUM

oten \ōt-ᵊn\ see OTON

oter \ōt-ər\ see OATER

oterie \ōt-ə-rē\ see OTARY

oth¹ \ȯth\ broth, cloth, froth, moth, sloth, swath, troth, wroth • betroth, breechcloth, broadcloth, cheesecloth, clothes moth, dishcloth, drop cloth, facecloth, floorcloth, grass cloth, ground cloth, ground sloth, haircloth, hawk moth, hellbroth, loincloth, oilcloth, presscloth, sackcloth, sailcloth, scotch broth, silk moth, sphinx moth, sponge cloth, washcloth, whole cloth, wire cloth • behemoth, gypsy moth, kente cloth, luna moth, Ostrogoth, tablecloth, three-toed sloth, tiger moth, two-toed sloth

oth² \äth\ Goth, sloth, swath, troth • behemoth, Ostrogoth, Visigoth

oth³ \ōs\ see OSE¹

oth⁴ \ōt\ see OAT

oth⁵ \ȯth\ see OWTH

othal \ȯth-əl\ see OTHEL

othe \ōth\ clothe, loathe
• betroth, unclothe

othel \óth-əl\ brothel • betrothal

other¹ \əth-ər\ brother, mother, nother, other, rather, smother, tother • another, big brother, blood brother, den mother, each other, earth mother, foremother, godmother, grandmother, half brother, housemother, queen mother, soul brother, stepbrother, stepmother • Christian Brother • fairy godmother, surrogate mother • significant other

other² \äth-ər\ see ATHER¹

otherly \əth-ər-lē\ brotherly, motherly, southerly • grandmotherly

othes \ōz\ see OSE²

othesis \äth-ə-səs\ prothesis • hypothesis

othing \ō-thiŋ\ clothing, loathing • underclothing • wolf in sheep's clothing—also -ing forms of verbs listed at OTHE

otho \ō-tō\ see OTO¹

oti¹ \ōt-ē\ see OTE¹

oti² \ót-ē\ see AUGHTY

otia¹ \ō-shə\ scotia, Scotia • agnosia, Boeotia, dystocia • Cappadocia, Nova Scotia

otia² \ōt-ē-ə\ see OTEA

otiable \ō-shə-bəl\ see OCIABLE

otiant \ō-shənt\ see OTIENT

otic¹ \ät-ik\ Scotic • aquatic, biotic, chaotic, cirrhotic,

demotic, despotic, ergotic, erotic, exotic, hypnotic, kenatic, kyphotic, leprotic, lordotic, meiotic, mitotic, narcotic, necrotic, neurotic, Nilotic, osmotic, psychotic, quixotic, robotic, sclerotic, thrombotic, zygotic • abiotic, amniotic, anecdotic, asymptotic, bibliotic, embryotic, epiglottic, homeotic, Huguenotic, idiotic, melanotic, patriotic, posthypnotic, sansculottic, semiotic, symbiotic • antibiotic, antipsychotic, autoerotic, homoerotic, macrobiotic

otic² \ōt-ik\ lotic, photic • aphotic, aprotic, dichotic

otic³ \ót-ik\ see AUTIC

otica \ät-i-kə\ erotica, exotica

otice \ōt-əs\ see OTUS

otics \ät-iks\ orthotics, robotics • aeronautics, astronautics, semiotics • macrobiotics—also -s, -'s, and -s' forms of nouns listed at OTIC¹

otid \ät-əd\ see OTTED

otient \ō-shənt\ quotient • negotiant

otile \ōt-ᵊl\ see OTAL

oting¹ \ōt-iŋ\ see OATING

oting² \ät-iŋ\ see OTTING

otinous¹ \ät-nəs\ see OTNESS

otinous² \ät-ᵊn-əs\ see OTONOUS¹

otion \ō-shən\ Goshen, groschen, lotion, motion, notion, ocean, potion • Boeotian, commotion, demotion, devotion, emotion, in motion, Laotian, promotion, slow-motion, stop-motion • Arctic Ocean, Eliotian, locomotion, Nova Scotian, set in motion, Southern Ocean • Antarctic Ocean, Atlantic Ocean, Brownian motion, harmonic motion, Indian Ocean, Pacific Ocean, social promotion

otional \ō-shnəl\ motional, notional • devotional, emotional, promotional • unemotional

otis \ōt-əs\ see OTUS

otist \ōt-əst\ protist, Scotist • anecdotist

otive \ōt-iv\ motive, votive • emotive, promotive • automotive, locomotive

otl \ät-ᵊl\ see OTTLE

otle \ät-ᵊl\ see OTTLE

otley \ät-lē\ see OTLY

otly \ät-lē\ Atli, hotly, motley

otness \ät-nəs\ hotness, squatness, whatness

oto \ō-tō\ koto, photo, roto, Sotho • Basotho, con moto, de Soto, ex-voto, in toto, Kyoto, Lesotho, Mosotho, Sesotho • Hashimoto, Kumamoto, pars pro toto, telephoto, Yamamoto

otomous \ät-ə-məs\ dichotomous • hippopotamus

otomy \ät-ə-mē\ dichotomy, lobotomy • craniotomy,

hysterotomy, laparotomy, tracheotomy • episiotomy

oton \ōt-ᵊn\ croton, Jotun, oaten • Lofoten, verboten

otonous¹ \ät-ᵊn-əs\ rottenness • monotonous, serotinous

otonous² \ät-nəs\ see OTNESS

otor \ōt-ər\ see OATER

otorist \ōt-ə-rəst\ see OTARIST

otory \ōt-ə-rē\ see OTARY

ots \äts\ Graz, hots, lots, Scots, Spaatz, swats • age spots, ersatz, Galati • call the shots, Eastern Ghats, Western Ghats • connect-the-dots, hit the high spots—*also* -s, -'s, *and* -s' *forms of nouns and* -s *forms of verbs listed at* OT¹

otsk \ätsk\ see ATSK

otsman \ät-smən\ Scotsman, yachtsman

ott \ät\ see OT¹

otta \ät-ə\ see ATA¹

ottage \ät-ij\ cottage, plottage, pottage, wattage • Cape Cod cottage

ottal \ät-ᵊl\ see OTTLE

otte¹ \ät\ see OT¹

otte² \ȯt\ see OUGHT¹

otted \ät-əd\ knotted, potted, spotted • carotid, proglottid, unspotted • polka-dotted—*also* -ed *forms of verbs listed at* OT¹

ottement \ät-mənt\ see OTMENT

otten \ät-ᵊn\ cotton, gotten, gratin, ratton, rotten, shotten

• au gratin, begotten, forgotten, guncotton, ill-gotten, ungotten
• misbegotten, sauerbraten

ottenness \ät-ᵉn-əs\ see OTONOUS¹

otter \ät-ər\ blotter, cotter, daughter, dotter, knotter, otter, plotter, potter, Potter, Qatar, rotter, spotter, squatter, swatter, Tatar, totter, trotter, water • allotter, backwater, bathwater, blackwater, blue water, boycotter, branch water, breakwater, Clearwater, cold-water, cutwater, dewater, deepwater, dishwater, firewater, first water, floodwater, flyswatter, freshwater, garroter, globe-trotter, Goldwater, gray water, groundwater, headwater, high water, hold water, hot water, ice water, jerkwater, limewater, low water, make water, meltwater, pinspotter, rainwater, red water, rosewater, saltwater, sandlotter, sea otter, seawater, shearwater, slack water, springwater, still water, tailwater, tap water, tidewater, tread water, wastewater, white-water • above water, alma mater, casual water, Derwent Water, dura mater, heavy water, holy water, imperator, in deep water, milk-and-water, mineral water, pig water, polywater, quinine water, river otter, running water, soda water, Stabat Mater, teeter-totter, toilet water, tonic water, underwater, Vichy water • dead in the water, fish out of water,

hell or high water—*also* -er *forms of adjectives listed at* OT¹

ottery \ät-ə-rē\ lottery, pottery, Tatary, tottery, watery

ottic \ät-ik\ see OTIC¹

ottid \ät-əd\ see OTTED

ottie \ät-ē\ see ATI

otting \ät-iŋ\ jotting • globe-trotting, wainscoting—*also* -ing *forms of verbs listed at* OT¹

ottis \ät-əs\ glottis • clematis • epiglottis, literatus

ottische \ät-ish\ see OTTISH

ottish \ät-ish\ hottish, schottische, Scottish, sottish • sanculottish

ottle \ät-ᵉl\ bottle, dottle, glottal, mottle, pottle, ratel, throttle, wattle • atlatl, bluebottle, Nahuatl, squeeze bottle • Aristotle, at full throttle, epiglottal, spin the bottle, vacuum bottle • Quetzalcoatl

otto¹ \ät-ō\ see ATO¹

otto² \ȯt-ō\ see AUTO¹

ottom \ät-əm\ see ATUM¹

otty \ät-ē\ see ATI

otum \ōt-əm\ notum, scrotum, totem • factotum, teetotum

otun \ōt-ᵉn\ see OTON

oture \ō-chər\ see OACHER

otus \ōt-əs\ lotus, notice, Otis • Duns Scotus, Pelotas • Polygnotus

oty \ȯt-ē\ see AUGHTY¹

otyl \ät-ᵉl\ see OTTLE

ou¹ \ō\ see OW¹

ou² \ü\ see EW¹

ou³ \aů\ see OW²

oubled \əb-əld\ see UBBLED

ouble \əb-əl\ see UBBLE

oubler \əb-lər\ bubbler, doubler, troubler

oubly \əb-lē\ see UBBLY

oubt \aůt\ see OUT³

oubted \aůt-əd\ see OUTED

oubter \aůt-ər\ see OUTER²

ouc¹ \ü\ see EW¹

ouc² \ük\ see UKE

ouc³ \ůk\ see OOK¹

ouce \üs\ see USE¹

oucester¹ \äs-tər\ see OSTER¹

oucester² \ós-tər\ see OSTER²

ouch¹ \üch\ see OOCH¹

ouch² \üsh\ see OUCHE

ouch³ \əch\ see UTCH¹

ouch⁴ \aůch\ couch, crouch, grouch, ouch, pouch, slouch, vouch • avouch, debouch • casting couch, on the couch, retort pouch, scaramouch • studio couch

ouche \üsh\ douche, louche, ruche, squoosh, swoosh, whoosh • barouche, capuche, cartouche, debouch, farouche, kurus, tarboosh • amuse-bouche, scaramouch

ouchy¹ \əch-ē\ see UCHY

ouchy² \aů-chē\ grouchy, pouchy, slouchy

oud¹ \üd\ see UDE

oud² \aůd\ boughed, bowed, browed, cloud, crowd, loud, proud, shroud, stroud • aloud, becloud, do proud, enshroud, highbrowed, house-proud, Oort cloud, out loud, purse-proud, Red Cloud, Saint Cloud, unbowed • funnel cloud, mushroom cloud, overcloud, overcrowd, thundercloud, well-endowed • electron cloud • Magellanic Cloud—*also* -ed *forms of verbs listed at* OW²

ou'd \üd\ see UDE

ouda \üd-ə\ see UDA

oudy \aůd-ē\ see OWDY

oue \ü\ see EW¹

ouf \üf\ see OOF¹

ouffe \üf\ see OOF¹

oug \əg\ see UG

ouge¹ \üj\ see UGE¹

ouge² \üzh\ see UGE²

ouge³ \aůj\ gouge, scrouge

ough¹ \ō\ see OW¹

ough² \ü\ see EW¹

ough³ \aů\ see OW²

ough⁴ \äk\ see OCK¹

ough⁵ \əf\ see UFF

ough⁶ \óf\ see OFF²

ougham¹ \ōm\ see OME¹

ougham² \üm\ see OOM¹

oughed \aůd\ see OUD²

oughen \əf-ən\ see UFFIN

ougher \əf-ər\ see UFFER

oughie \əf-ē\ see UFFY

oughish \əf-ish\ see UFFISH

oughly \əf-lē\ see UFFLY

oughs \ōz\ see OSE[2]

ought[1] \ȯt\ aught, bought, brought, caught, dot, fought, fraught, ghat, lotte, naught, nought, ought, sought, taught, taut, thought, wrought • a thought, besought, Connacht, distraught, dreadnought, forethought, free thought, handwrought, high-wrought, in-wrought, onslaught, self-taught, store-bought, unsought, untaught, unthought • aeronaut, aforethought, afterthought, aquanaut, argonaut, astronaut, cosmonaut, juggernaut, overbought, overwrought, second thought

ought[2] \au̇t\ see OUT[3]

oughten \ȯt-ᵊn\ see AUTEN

oughty \au̇t-ē\ doughty, droughty, gouty, pouty, snouty, trouty

oughy[1] \ō-ē\ see OWY

oughy[2] \ü-ē\ see EWY

ouie \ü-ē\ see EWY

ouille \ü-ē\ see EWY

ouis[1] \ü-ē\ see EWY

ouis[2] \ü-əs\ lewis, Lewis, Louis, Luis • Port Louis, Saint Louis, San Luis

ouk \ük\ see UKE

ouki \ü-kē\ see OOKY[1]

oul[1] \ōl\ see OLE[1]

oul[2] \ül\ see OOL[1]

oul[3] \au̇l\ see OWL[2]

ould[1] \ōld\ see OLD[1]

ould[2] \u̇d\ see OOD[1]

oulder \ōl-dər\ see OLDER[1]

ouldered \ōl-dərd\ bouldered, shouldered • round-shouldered—also -ed forms of verbs listed at OLDER[1]

ouldest \u̇d-əst\ couldest, shouldest, wouldest • Talmudist

ouldn't \u̇d-ᵊnt\ couldn't, shouldn't, wouldn't

oule[1] \ü-lē\ see ULY

oule[2] \ül\ see OOL[1]

ouled \ōld\ see OLD[1]

oulee \ü-lē\ see ULY

ouleh[1] \ü-lə\ see ULA

ouleh[2] \ü-lē\ see ULY

ouli \ü-lē\ see ULY

oulie \ü-lē\ see ULY

ouling \au̇-liŋ\ see OWLING[2]

oulish \ü-lish\ see OOLISH

ou'll[1] \ül\ see OOL[1]

ou'll[2] \u̇l\ see UL[1]

oulle \ül\ see OOL[1]

oulli \ü-lē\ see ULY

oully \au̇-lē\ see OWLY[2]

oult \ōlt\ see OLT[1]

oulter \ōl-tər\ see OLTER

oum \üm\ see OOM[1]

oumenal \ü-mən-əl\ see UMINAL

oun[1] \aún\ see OWN[2]

oun[2] \ün\ see OON[1]

ounce \aúns\ bounce, flounce, jounce, ounce, pounce, trounce • announce, denounce, enounce, pronounce, renounce • dead-cat bounce, fluid ounce, mispronounce

ouncement \aún-smənt\ announcement, denouncement, pronouncement, renouncement

ouncer \aún-sər\ bouncer • announcer, denouncer, pronouncer, renouncer

ouncil \aún-səl\ see OUNSEL

ouncy \aún-sē\ bouncy, flouncy, jouncy • viscountcy • paramountcy

ound[1] \ünd\ stound, swound, wound • flesh wound—*also* -ed *forms of verbs listed at* OON[1]

ound[2] \aúnd\ bound, crowned, found, ground, hound, mound, pound, Pound, round, sound, stound, swound, wound • abound, aground, all-round, around, astound, background, black-crowned, bloodhound, boozehound, brassbound, break ground, campground, chowhound, clothbound, come round, compound, confound, coonhound, dachshund, deerhound, deskbound, dumbfound, earthbound, eastbound, elkhound, expound, fairground, fogbound, foot-pound, foreground, foxhound, gain ground, go-round, greyhound, half-bound, hardbound, hellhound, hidebound, high ground, homebound, horehound, housebound, icebound, impound, inbound, ironbound, lose ground, newfound, newshound, northbound, outbound, playground, pot-bound, profound, propound, rebound, redound, renowned, resound, rockbound, rock hound, scent hound, sight hound, sleuthhound, smooth hound, snowbound, softbound, southbound, spellbound, staghound, stone-ground, stormbound, strikebound, surround, to ground, top round, unbound, unround, unsound, well-found, westbound, wolfhound, year-round • aboveground, Afghan hound, all-around, basset hound, battleground, been around, belowground, bottom round, break new ground, breeding ground, bring around, cast around, common ground, cover ground, decompound, dumping ground, end around, fool around, get around, go around, hang around, horse around, in the round, jerk around, kick around, mess around, middle ground, muscle-bound, Nootka Sound, Norton Sound, off the ground, on background, on the ground, otter hound, outward-bound, paperbound, perfect-bound, proving ground, Puget

Sound, push around, quarter-bound, runaround, Scoresby Sound, screw around, shoot-around, sleep around, spiral-bound, staging ground, stand one's ground, steamship round, stick around, stomping ground, surround sound, turnaround, turn around, ultrasound, underground, weather-bound, work-around, wraparound • adhesive-bound, Albemarle Sound, cover the ground, down to the ground, English fox-hound, into the ground, Irish wolfhound, Kotzebue Sound, Long Island Sound, McMurdo Sound, merry-go-round, Port Royal Sound, Prince William Sound, Queen Charlotte Sound, run rings around, Russian wolfhound, Scottish deerhound, superabound, thick on the ground, thin on the ground, three-quarter-bound • happy hunting ground, Mississippi Sound, run circles around, theater-in-the-round, throw one's weight around —*also* -ed *forms of verbs listed at* OWN²

oundal \aún-dᵊl\ poundal, roundel

oundary \aún-drē\ see OUNDRY

ounded \aún-dəd\ bounded, grounded, rounded • con-founded, unbounded, unfounded, well-founded, well-grounded, well-rounded—*also* -ed *forms of verbs listed at* OUND

oundel \aún-dᵊl\ see OUNDAL

ounder \aún-dər\ bounder, flounder, founder, grounder, hounder, pounder, rounder, sounder • all-rounder, backgrounder, compounder, confounder, dumbfounder, expounder, propounder, rebounder, tenpounder, typefounder, year-rounder • echo sounder, undergrounder

ounding \aún-diŋ\ grounding, sounding • astounding, high-sounding, resounding, rock-hounding, typefounding —*also* -ing *forms of verbs listed at* OUND²

oundless¹ \ün-ləs\ see OONLESS

oundless² \aún-ləs\ boundless, groundless, soundless

oundlet \aún-lət\ see OWNLET

oundling \aún-liŋ\ foundling, groundling

oundly \aúnd-lē\ roundly, soundly • profoundly, unsoundly

oundness \aún-nəs\ roundness, soundness • profoundness, unsoundness

oundry \aún-drē\ boundary, foundry

ounds¹ \ünz\ see OONS

ounds² \aúnz\ hounds, zounds • inbounds • Barren Grounds, hare and hounds, out-of-bounds • by leaps and bounds—*also* -s, -'s, *and* -s' *forms of nouns and* -s *forms of verbs listed at* OUND²

oundsel \aún-səl\ see OUNSEL

oundsman \aúnz-mən\ see OWNSMAN

ounge \aúnj\ lounge, scrounge • chaise lounge • cocktail lounge

ounger¹ \aún-jər\ lounger, scrounger

ounger² \əŋ-gər\ see ONGER¹

ounker \əŋ-kər\ see UNKER

ounsel \aún-səl\ council, counsel, groundsel • King's Counsel, Queen's Counsel • city council, privy council

ount¹ \änt\ see ANT²

ount² \aúnt\ count, fount, mount • account, amount, blood count, demount, discount, dismount, high-count, miscount, point count, recount, remount, seamount, surmount, viscount • bank discount, body count, cash discount, catamount, charge discount, no-account, on account, paramount, rediscount, Rocky Mount, take the count, tantamount, trade discount, undercount • bring to account, call to account, checking account, drawing account, expense account, hold to account, income account, on no account, savings account, suspense account • on one's own account, Sermon on the Mount, take into account

ountable \aúnt-ə-bəl\ countable, mountable • accountable, demountable, discountable, surmountable

• insurmountable, unaccountable

ountain \aúnt-°n\ fountain, mountain • transmountain • cat-a-mountain, drinking fountain, soda fountain

ountcy \aún-sē\ see OUNCY

ounter \aúnt-ər\ counter, mounter • bean counter, discounter, encounter, lunch counter, recounter, rencounter • Geiger counter • over-the-counter, under-the-counter

ountie \aúnt-ē\ see OUNTY

ounting \aúnt-iŋ\ mounting • accounting, and counting • cost accounting—also -ing forms of verbs listed at OUNT²

ounty \aúnt-ē\ bounty, county, Mountie • viscounty

oup¹ \ōp\ see OPE

oup² \ü\ see EW¹

oup³ \üp\ see OOP¹

oupe¹ \ōp\ see OPE

oupe² \üp\ see OOP¹

ouper \ü-pər\ see OOPER

oupie \ü-pē\ see OOPY

ouping \ü-piŋ\ see OOPING

ouple \əp-əl\ see UPLE¹

ouplet \əp-lət\ see UPLET¹

oupous \ü-pəs\ see UPUS

oupy \ü-pē\ see OOPY

our¹ \ór\ see OR¹

our² \úr\ see URE¹

our³ \aúr\ see OWER²

our⁴ \är\ see AR³

our⁵ \ər\ see EUR¹

oura \ùr-ə\ see URA

ourable \ȯr-ə-bəl\ see ORABLE

ourage \ər-ij\ courage
• demurrage, discourage,
Dutch courage, encourage

ourbon¹ \ər-bən\ see URBAN¹

ourbon² \ùr-bən\ see URBAN²

ource \ȯrs\ see ORSE¹

ourceful \ȯrs-fəl\ see ORSEFUL

ourcing \ȯr-siŋ\ outsourcing
—also -ing forms of verbs listed
at ORSE¹

ourd \ȯrd\ see OARD

ourde \ùrd\ see URED¹

ou're¹ \ȯr\ see OR¹

ou're² \ü-ər\ see EWER¹

ou're³ \ùr\ see URE¹

ou're⁴ \ər\ see EUR¹

oured \ȯrd\ see OARD

ourer¹ \ȯr-ər\ see ORER

ourer² \ùr-ər\ see URER¹

ourer³ \aùr-ər\ flowerer, scourer,
showerer • deflowerer,
devourer—also -er forms of
adjectives listed at OWER²

ourg¹ \ùr\ see URE¹

ourg² \ərg\ see ERG

ourge¹ \ərj\ see URGE

ourge² \ȯrj\ see ORGE

ourger \ər-jər\ see ERGER

ouri \ùr-ē\ see URY¹

ourier¹ \ùr-ē-ər\ courier
• couturier, couturiere, vaunt-
courier

ourier² \ər-ē-ər\ see URRIER

ouring¹ \ȯr-iŋ\ see ORING

ouring² \ùr-iŋ\ see URING

ourish \ər-ish\ currish, flourish,
nourish • amateurish

ourist \ùr-əst\ see URIST

ourly \aùr-lē\ dourly, hourly,
sourly • half-hourly

ourn¹ \ȯrn\ see ORN¹

ourn² \ərn\ see URN

ournal \ərn-ᵊl\ see ERNAL

ournament \ȯr-nə-mənt\ see
ORNAMENT

ourne \ȯrn\ see ORN¹

ourney¹ \ər-nē\ Bernie, Ernie,
ferny, gurney, journey, tourney
• attorney • district attorney

ourney² \ȯr-nē\ see ORNY

ourneyer \ər-nē-ər\ journeyer,
vernier

ournful \ȯrn-fəl\ see ORNFUL

ourning \ȯr-niŋ\ see ORNING

ournment \ərn-mənt\ see
ERNMENT

ours¹ \ȯrz\ see OORS

ours² \ärz\ see ARS

ours³ \aùrz\ ours • after-hours,
all hours, small hours, Three
Hours • Forty Hours, Little
Hours • to the showers—also
-s, -'s, and -s' forms of nouns

and -s *forms of verbs listed at*
OWER[2]

ours[4] \ūr\ see URE[1]

ourse \órs\ see ORSE[1]

oursome \ór-səm\ see ORSUM

ourt[1] \órt\ see ORT[1]

ourt[2] \úrt\ see URT[1]

ourth \órth\ see ORTH[1]

ourtier \ór-chər\ see ORCHER

ourtly \órt-lē\ see ORTLY

oury \aur-ē\ see OWERY

ous[1] \ü\ see EW[1]

ous[2] \üs\ see USE[1]

ousa[1] \ü-sə\ see USA[1]

ousa[2] \ü-zə\ see USA[2]

ousal \aú-zəl\ housel, spousal,
tousle • arousal, carousal,
espousal

ousand \aúz-ᵉn\ see OWSON

ouse[1] \üs\ see USE[1]

ouse[2] \aús\ blouse, chiaus,
chouse, douse, gauss, Gauss,
grouse, house, Klaus, Laos,
louse, mouse, scouse, souse,
spouse, Strauss • alehouse,
almshouse, baghouse,
bathhouse, Bauhaus, big
house, birdhouse, black
grouse, blockhouse, boat-
house, book louse, bughouse,
bunkhouse, call house,
cathouse, chophouse, clean
house, clubhouse, cookhouse,
courthouse, crab louse, crack
house, deckhouse, deer
mouse, degauss, delouse,
doghouse, dollhouse,
dormouse, espouse,
farmhouse, field house, field
mouse, firehouse, flophouse,
full house, fun house, gashouse,
gatehouse, glasshouse, great
house, greenhouse, grind
house, guardhouse, guest-
house, hash house, head louse,
henhouse, hothouse, house
mouse, icehouse, in-house,
jailhouse, joss house, keep
house, lighthouse, lobscouse,
longhouse, madhouse,
Manaus, milk house, nuthouse,
outhouse, penthouse, pest-
house, playhouse, poorhouse,
ranch house, rest house,
roadhouse, roughhouse,
roundhouse, row house, ruffed
grouse, safe house, sage
grouse, sandgrouse, school-
house, sea mouse, smokehouse,
springhouse, statehouse, steak
house, storehouse, teahouse,
third house, titmouse, tollhouse,
Toll House, town house, tract
house, tree house, warehouse,
washhouse, wheelhouse,
White House, whorehouse,
Wodehouse, wood louse,
workhouse • barrelhouse,
bawdy house, boardinghouse,
body louse, cat and mouse,
clearinghouse, coffeehouse,
countinghouse, country house,
customhouse, halfway house,
house-to-house, jumping
mouse, kilogauss, Lévi-Strauss,
manor house, meetinghouse,
Mickey Mouse, milligauss,
motherhouse, on the house,
open house, opera house,
overblouse, packinghouse,

pilothouse, pocket mouse, porterhouse, powerhouse, rooming house, shotgun house, slaughterhouse, sporting house, station house, sucking louse, sugarhouse, summerhouse, tiring-house, tower house, treasure-house, Westinghouse • bring down the house, garrison house, man of the house, settlement house, tenement house • disorderly house

ouse³ \aùz\ blouse, bowse, browse, douse, dowse, drowse, house, mouse, rouse, spouse, touse • arouse, carouse, delouse, doss-house, espouse, rehouse, roughhouse, warehouse—*also* -s, -'s, *and* -s' *forms of nouns and* -s *forms of verbs listed at* OW²

ouse⁴ \üz\ see USE²

ousel \aù-zəl\ see OUSAL

ouser \aù-zər\ houser, mouser, schnauzer, trouser, wowser • carouser, espouser, warehouser • rabble-rouser

ousin \əz-ᵊn\ see OZEN¹

ousing \aù-ziŋ\ housing, rousing • rabble-rousing—*also* -ing *forms of verbs listed at* OUSE³

ousle¹ \ü-zəl\ see USAL²

ousle² \aù-zəl\ see OUSAL

ousse \üs\ see USE¹

ousseau \ü-sō\ see USOE

oust¹ \aùst\ Faust, joust, oust, roust—*also* -ed *forms of verbs listed at* OUSE²

oust² \üst\ see OOST

ouste \üst\ see OOST

ousy¹ \aù-zē\ see OWSY

ousy² \aù-sē\ mousy • Ferdowsi

out¹ \ü\ see EW¹

out² \üt\ see UTE

out³ \aùt\ bout, clout, doubt, drought, flout, glout, gout, grout, knout, kraut, lout, out, pout, rout, route, scout, shout, snout, spout, sprout, stout, tout, trout • ablaut, about, act out, all-out, back out, bailout, bail out, bat out, bawl out, bear out, beat out, blackout, black out, blissed-out, blot out, blowout, bombed-out, bow out, Boy Scout, breakout, break out, breechclout, bring out, brook trout, brownout, brown trout, bugout, bug out, burnedout, burnout, burn out, butt out, buyout, buy out, call out, campout, cash out, cast out, catch out, checkout, check out, chill out, churn out, clappedout, clear out, closeout, close out, come out, cookout, copout, cop out, crank out, Cub Scout, cutout, cut out, devout, die out, dig out, dimout, dine out, dishclout, dish out, dole out, downspout, draw out, dropout, drop out, dry out, dugout, eelpout, eke out, en route, fade-out, fake out, fallout, fall out, farm out, farout, fill out, find out, fink out, fish out, flake out, flameout, flame out, flat-out, flunk out, foldout, force-out, foul out, freak-out, freaked-out, freeze out, full-out, get out, Girl Scout, give out, go out, grind out, gross-out, gross out, groundout, handout, hand out, hangout, hideout, holdout, hold out, horned pout, ice-out, iron out, kick out, knockout, knock out, lake trout, layout, lay out, leg out, let out, light out, lights-out, line out, lockout, lock out, lookout, look out, lose out, mahout, make out, max out, misdoubt, miss out, no doubt, nose out, opt out, pan out, pass out, payout, phaseout, phase out, pick out, pig out, pitchout, played out, play out, printout, print out, prove out, psych-out, pullout, pull out, punch out, putout, put out, rain out, rainspout, readout, read out, redoubt, redout, rollout, roll out, rub out, rubout, rule out, run out, sack out, salt out, Sea Scout, sea trout, sellout, sell out, setout, set out, shakeout, shake out, shell out, shoot-out, shout-out, shutout, shut out, sick-out, side-out, sign out, sit out, sleep out, smoke out, sold-out, spaced-out, space out, speak out, spell out, spinout, spin out, stakeout, stake out, standout, stand out, star route, step out, stick out, stop out, straight-out, stressed-out, stretch-out, strikeout, strike out, strung out, swear out, sweat out, takeout, take out, talk out, tap out, tapped out, tease out, thought-out, throughout, throw out, time-out, trade route, trot out, tryout, try out, tune out, turnout, turn out, umlaut, veg out, wait out, walkout, walk out, washed-out, washout, wash out, watch out, way-out, wear out, weird out, whacked-out, whiteout, wideout, wigged-out, wimp out, wiped out, wipeout, wipe out, without, workout, work out, worn-out, write out, zone out, zonked-out • all get-out, autoroute, bring about, brussels sprout, Cape Lookout, carryout, carry out, cast about, come about, coming out, cutthroat trout, diner-out, down-and-out, duke it out, Eagle Scout, falling-out, figure out, follow out, gadabout, get about, go about, golden trout, gut it out, gutter out, hammer out, have it out, hereabout, how about, infield out, inside out, just about, knockabout, layabout, long-drawn-out, muster out, odd man out, out-and-out, put about, rainbow trout, report out, roundabout, rouseabout, roustabout, runabout, rural route, sauer-kraut, set about, speckled trout, spit it out, stirabout, talent scout, thereabout, turnabout, walkabout, water-spout, water sprout • beat one's brains out, day in day out, eat one's heart out, knock-down drag-out, last-in first-out, reckon without, stick one's neck out • let it all hang out, technical knockout, throw one's weight about

oute[1] \üt\ see UTE

oute² \aut\ see OUT³

outed \aut-əd\ snouted
• undoubted—*also* -ed *forms of verbs listed at* OUT³

outer¹ \üt-ər\ see UTER

outer² \aut-ər\ doubter, flouter, grouter, outer, pouter, router, scouter, shouter, spouter, touter • come-outer • down-and-outer, out-and-outer—*also* -er *forms of adjectives listed at* OUT³

outh¹ \üth\ see OOTH²

outh² \auth\ mouth, routh, scouth, south • bad-mouth, Deep South, goalmouth, loudmouth, New South, poormouth, trench mouth • blabbermouth, cottonmouth, hand-to-mouth, motormouth, mouth-to-mouth, potty mouth, run one's mouth, word-of-mouth • down in the mouth • from the horse's mouth • put one's foot in one's mouth

outherly \əth-ər-lē\ see OTHERLY

outhey \au-thē\ see OUTHY

outhful \üth-fəl\ see UTHFUL

outhie \ü-thē\ see OOTHY

outhly \üth-lē\ see OOTHLY

outhy \au-thē\ mouthy, Southey

outi \üt-ē\ see OOTY¹

outing \aut-iŋ\ outing, scouting —*also* -ing *forms of verbs listed at* OUT³

outish \aut-ish\ loutish, snoutish, stoutish

outre \üt-ər\ see UTER

outrement \ü-trə-mənt\ see UTRIMENT

outs \auts\ bean sprouts
• hereabouts, ins and outs, on the outs, thereabouts, whereabouts—*also* -s, 's, *and* -s' *forms of nouns, and* -s *forms of verbs, listed at* OUT

outy \aut-ē\ see OUGHTY

ou've \üv\ see OVE³

ouver \ü-vər\ see OVER³

oux \ü\ see EW¹

ouy \ē\ see EE¹

ouyhnhnm \in-əm\ see INIM

ouzel \ü-zəl\ see USAL²

ov¹ \äf\ see OFF¹

ov² \of\ see OFF²

ova \ō-və\ nova • Canova, Jehovah, Markova, Moldova, pavlova, Pavlova, Rendova, zelkova • bossa nova, Casanova, Czestochowa, Kemerovo, supernova, Tereshkova

ovable \ü-və-bəl\ movable, provable • approvable, disprovable, immovable, improvable, removable

ovah \ō-və\ see OVA

oval \ü-vəl\ approval, removal • disapproval, on approval

ovat \əv-ət\ see OVET

ove¹ \əv\ dove, glove, love, of, shove • above, all of, as of, at love, dream of, foxglove, free love, hereof, in love, kid-glove, kind of, make love, out of, ringdove, rock dove, Sainte-Beuve, self-love, short of, thereof, tough love, truelove, whereof, white-glove • afoul of, ahead of, all kinds of, all sorts of, because of, become of, boxing glove, by dint of, by means of, by way of, courtly love, dispose of, get wind of, hand in glove, have none of, in back of, in case of, in face of, in front of, in lieu of, in light of, in place of, inside of, in spite of, instead of, in terms of, in view of, ladylove, light-o'-love, make fun of, make light of, make much of, make sport of, make use of, mourning dove, on pain of, on top of, outside of, puppy love, roman-fleuve, turtledove, unheard-of, well-thought-of • alongside of, apropos of, at the hands of, break the back of, by virtue of, hereinabove, in advance of, in behalf of, in default of, in favor of, in the face of, in the light of, in the name of, in the teeth of, in the wake of, make the most of, on account of, on behalf of, on the heels of, platonic love, push comes to shove, regardless of • at the mercy of, in defiance of, irrespective of

ove² \ōv\ clove, cove, dove, drove, fauve, grove, hove, Jove, mauve, rove, stove, strove, throve, trove, wove • alcove, behove, cookstove, mangrove, woodstove • Franklin stove, Garden Grove, interwove, treasure trove • potbellied stove

ove³ \üv\ groove, move, prove, you've • approve, behoove, commove, disprove, improve, remove, reprove • disapprove, microgroove, on the move, tongue-and-groove

ovel¹ \äv-əl\ grovel, novel • dime novel • antinovel, graphic novel, Yaroslavl'

ovel² \əv-əl\ grovel, hovel, shovel • steam shovel • pick-and-shovel, power shovel

ovement \üv-mənt\ movement • improvement • Oxford movement, pincer movement • rapid eye movement

oven¹ \əv-ən\ oven, sloven • Dutch oven • beehive oven, toaster oven • convection oven, microwave oven

oven² \ō-vən\ cloven, coven, woven • Beethoven, handwoven, plain-woven • interwoven

over¹ \əv-ər\ cover, glover, hover, lover, plover, shover • bedcover, break cover, discover, dustcover, gill cover, ground cover, hardcover, re-cover, recover, slipcover, softcover, uncover, windhover • blow one's cover, first day cover, undercover

over² \ō-vər\ clover, Dover, drover, Grover, over, plover, rover, stover, trover • allover, all over, bind over, blow over, boil over, bowl over, changeover, chew over, comb-over, come over, crossover, cross over, cutover, flashover, flopover, flyover, get over, give over, go over, hand over, hangover, Hannover, Hanover, holdover, hold over, in clover, kick over, knock over, layover, lay over, leftover, lie over, look over, makeover, make over, mess over, moreover, once-over, Passover, pass over, pick over, popover, pullover, pull over, pushover, put over, red clover, Rickover, rollover, roll over, runover, run over, sea rover, slipover, spillover, stopover, strikeover, sweet clover, takeover, take over, talk over, throw over, tide over, turnover, turn over, voice-over, walkover, walk over, warmed-over, watch over, wingover, work over • carryover, carry over, crossing-over, going-over, paper over, Strait of Dover • over and over

over³ \ü-vər\ groover, Hoover, louver, mover, prover • earth-mover, improver, maneuver, prime mover, remover, reprover, Vancouver • disap-prover, people mover

over⁴ \äv-ər\ see AVER¹

overly \əv-ər-lē\ loverly • Sir Roger de Coverley

overt \ō-vərt\ covert, overt • tail covert, wing covert

overy \əv-rē\ discovery, recovery • self-discovery

ovet \əv-ət\ covet, lovat

ovey \ə-vē\ covey • lovey-dovey

ovian \ō-vē-ən\ Jovian • Chekhovian, Markovian, Pavlovian, Varsovian • Nabokovian

ovie \ü-vē\ see OOVY

ovo \ō-vō\ Provo • ab ovo, de novo • Porto-Novo

ovost \äv-əst\ see AVIST

ovsk \ôfsk\ Petrovsk, Sverdlovsk • Brest Litovsk • Dnepropetrovsk, Petropavlovsk

ow¹ \ō\ beau, blow, bow, bro, Chou, crow, do, doe, dough, floe, flow, foe, fro, froe, frow, glow, go, grow, ho, hoe, jo, Jo, joe, Joe, know, lo, low, mho, mot, mow, no, No, O, oh, owe, Po, Poe, pow, pro, rho, roe, row, Rowe, schmo, sew, shew, show, sloe, slow, snow, so, sow, stow, Stowe, strow, though, throe, throw, toe, tow, trow, whoa, woe, yo • aglow, ago, airflow, airglow, air show, alow, although, archfoe, argot, a throw, backflow, backhoe, bandeau, Baotou, barlow, bateau, below, bestow, big toe, bon mot, Bordeaux, bravo, by-blow, cachepot, callow, caló, Carlow, cash flow, chapeau, chateau, Chi-Rho, cockcrow, Cocteau, cornrow, corn snow, crossbow, Darrow, Day-Glo, dayglow, death row, Defoe, de trop, deathblow, deco, down-bow, dumb show, elbow, escrow, fencerow, flambeau, floor show, flyblow, fogbow, forego, foreknow, forgo, freak show, free throw, Freneau, Fuzhou, galop, game show, Gâteau, genro, gigot, Glasgow, Glencoe, go-slow, Gounod, Guangzhou, gung ho, guyot, Hadow, hallo, Hangzhou, Hankow, Harrow, heave-ho, hedgerow, heigh-ho, hello, hollo, horse show, hullo, ice floe, ice show, inflow, in tow, Io, jabot, jambeau, Jane Doe, jim crow, Jinzhou, Joe Blow, Jiaozhou, John Doe, Juneau, Hounslow, kayo, KO, Kwangchow, Lanzhou, lie low, light show, longbow, low blow, Luchow, macho, mahoe, maillot, mallow, manteau, Marlowe, Marot, marrow, matelot, merlot, Meursault, minnow, Miró, misknow, Moho, mojo, Monroe, morceau, Moreau, morrow, Moscow, mucro, mudflow, Murrow, nightglow, no-no, no-show, nouveau, oboe, outflow, outgo, outgrow, oxbow, Paot'ou, peep show, Pernod, picot, Pinot, plateau, pronto, Quanzhou, quiz show, rainbow, Rameau, red snow, reflow, regrow, repo, reseau, road show, rondeau, rondo, roscoe, Roseau, rouleau, Rousseau, sabot, Saint-Lô, salchow, scarecrow, self-sow, serow, shadblow, Shantou, sideshow, skid row, ski tow, Soho, so-so, sound bow, sourdough, stone's throw, sunbow, Suzhou, tableau, Taizhou, talk show, tiptoe, Thoreau, tone row, tonneau, trade show, trousseau,

Trudeau, uh-oh, unsew, up-bow, upthrow, van Gogh, wallow, Watteau, Wenzhou, Wicklow, widow, willow, windrow, windthrow, winnow, Winslow, Wuzhou, Xuzhou, Yalow, yarrow, Zhangzhou, Zhengzhou, Zhuzhon, Zibo
• acid snow, afterglow, aikido, alpenglow, Angelo, apropos, art deco, art nouveau, audio, Baguio, Bamako, barrio, bay window, Bergamo, bibelot, Bilbao, black widow, blow-by-blow, body blow, bone marrow, bordereau, Borneo, bow window, buffalo, Buffalo, bungalow, Bushido, buteo, calico, cameo, cachalot, cembalo, centimo, CEO, chassepot, cheerio, Cicero, Clemenceau, cogito, comedo, comme il faut, Comoro, counterflow, Cupid's bow, curaçao, Curaçao, curassow, curio, daimyo, danio, dataflow, Delano, Diderot, do-si-do, domino, dynamo, embryo, entrepôt, Erato, escargot, Eskimo, extrados, fabliau, folio, French window, fricandeau, furbelow, gigolo, golden glow, go-no-go, grass widow, guacharo, hammer throw, hammertoe, haricot, heel-and-toe, hetero, high and low, HMO, Holy Joe, horror show, Idaho, in a row, indigo, in escrow, in the know, Jericho, kakapo, Kosciuszko, Lake Tahoe, latigo, little toe, long-ago, Longfellow, Maceió, Maginot, Manchukuo, Mario, massicot, medico, Mexico,

mistletoe, modulo, Monaco, Navajo, NCO, nuncio, oleo, olio, on tiptoe, overflow, overgrow, overthrow, ovolo, Pamlico, Papago, paseo, patio, peridot, picaro, piccolo, Pierrot, Point Barrow, polio, pomelo, pompano, portico, PPO, Prospero, proximo, quid pro quo, radio, raree-show, ratio, Richard Roe, Rochambeau, rococo, rodeo, Romeo, rose window, round window, saddlebow, Sapporo, sapsago, Scapa Flow, Scipio, Scorpio, semipro, show window, sloppy joe, so-and-so, SRO, standing O, status quo, stereo, stop-and-go, studio, subito, tallyho, tangelo, Taranto, tic-tac-toe, TKO, to-and-fro, Tokyo, tombolo, touch-and-go, touraco, tournedos, tremolo, tuckahoe, tupelo, UFO, ultimo, undergo, undertow, Veneto, vertigo, vibrio, video, virago, vireo, Zhangjiakou, zydeco • Antonio, Arapaho, arpeggio, at one's elbow, bocaccio, bull's-eye window, carrion crow, centesimo, clock radio, con spirito, continuo, curculio, D'Annunzio, DMSO, Etobicoke, Eustachio, ex nihilo, fantastico, fellatio, Fernando Póo, finocchio, fortissimo, Geronimo, get-up-and-go, go with the flow, Guantánamo, herein-below, home video, in dubio, intaglio, in utero, in vacuo, laminar flow, lancet window, La Rochefoucauld, lentissimo, locus in quo, lothario, magnifico, malapropos, Medicine Bow,

medicine show, milesimo, New Mexico, oregano, Ozark Plateau, picture window, politico, portfolio, presidio, prestissimo, punctilio, pussy willow, Querétaro, Quintana Roo, Rosario, quo warranto, Sarajevo, scenario, simpatico, sound-and-light show, status in quo, talk radio, tennis elbow, turbulent flow, Verrocchio • ab initio, archipelago, braggadocio, dog and pony show, duodecimo, ex officio, generalissimo, glory-of-the-snow, impresario, internuncio, oratorio, Paramaribo, pianis-simo, Punch-and-Judy show, rose of Jericho, variety show

ow² \aù\ bough, bow, brow, Chao, chiao, chow, ciao, cow, dhow, Dou, dow, Dow, Frau, hao, how, howe, Howe, jow, Lao, Liao, Mao, mow, now, ow, plow, pow, prau, prow, Rao, row, scow, slough, sough, sow, Tao, tau, thou, vow, wow, Yao • Aargau, allow, and how, ant cow, as how, avow, Belau, Bissau, bowwow, Breslau, cacao, cahow, Callao, cash cow, chowchow, chow chow, Cracow, Dachau, Davao, Donau, endow, enow, erenow, eyebrow, Fouchou, gangplow, Haikou, Hankow, hausfrau, haymow, highbrow, hoosegow, jiao, Jungfrau, know-how, kowtow, Kraków, landau, lowbrow, luau, Lucknow, Macao, mau-mau, meow, Moscow, nohow, Palau, powwow, Qing-dao, sea cow,

snowplow, somehow,
Spandau, Zwickau • anyhow,
carabao, cat's meow, curaçao,
Curaçao, disallow, disavow,
disendow, here and now, Hu
Jintao, Krakatau, middlebrow,
Mindanao, sacred cow, simple
vow, solemn vow • crème
de cacao, Guinea-Bissau,
Marianao • holier-than-thou,
Oberammergau

ow³ \ȯv\ see OFF²

owa \ō-və\ see OVA

owable¹ \ō-ə-bəl\ knowable,
sewable, showable
• unknowable

owable² \au̇-ə-bəl\ plowable
• allowable • disavowable

owage \ō-ij\ flowage, stowage,
towage

owal¹ \ō-əl\ see OEL

owal² \au̇l\ see OWL²

owan¹ \ō-ən\ see OAN¹

owan² \au̇-ən\ Gawain, gowan,
rowan, rowen

oward¹ \ȯrd\ see OARD

oward² \au̇rd\ see OWERED

owd¹ \üd\ see UDE

owd² \au̇d\ see OUD²

owdah \au̇d-ə\ see AUDE³

owder \au̇d-ər\ chowder, powder
• black powder, gunpowder,
tooth powder • chili powder,
curry powder, five-spice
powder, smokeless powder,
take a powder, talcum

powder—*also* -er *forms of
adjectives listed at* OUD²

owdown \ō-dau̇n\ blowdown,
lowdown, showdown,
slowdown, throw down

owdy \au̇d-ē\ cloudy, dowdy,
howdy, rowdy • cum laude,
pandowdy • magna cum laude,
summa cum laude

owe \ō\ see OW¹

owed¹ \ōd\ see ODE

owed² \au̇d\ see OUD²

owedly \au̇-əd-lē\ allowedly,
avowedly

owel \au̇l\ see OWL²

oweling \au̇-liŋ\ see OWLING²

owell¹ \au̇l\ see OWL²

owell² \ō-əl\ see OEL

owen¹ \au̇-ən\ see OWAN²

owen² \ō-ən\ see OAN¹

ower¹ \ȯr\ see OR¹

ower² \au̇r\ bower, cower, dour,
dower, flour, flower, gaur,
giaour, glower, Gower, hour,
lower, our, plower, power,
scour, shower, sour, Stour,
tour, tower, vower • avower,
cornflower, deflower, devour,
embower, empower, firepower,
Great Stour, half hour, H hour,
man-hour, mayflower, moon-
flower, off-hour, pasqueflower,
Peshawar, repower, rush hour,
safflower, sunflower, wallflower,
watchtower, wildflower,
willpower • air power, bell-
flower, bell tower, black power,
brainpower, coffee hour,

coneflower, credit hour, disk flower, fire tower, foamflower, Glendower, graham flower, great power, happy hour, horsepower, manpower, quarter hour, ray flower, sea power, starflower, state flower, strawflower, war power, whisky sour, world power, zero hour • Adenauer, candlepower, cauliflower, conning tower, cooling tower, Devils Tower, disempower, disendower, Eisenhower, eleventh hour, flower power, gillyflower, golden shower, hydropower, ivory tower, kilowatt-hour, minitower, motive power, overpower, passionflower, person-hour, police power, Schopenhauer, semester hour, staying power, superpower, sweet-and-sour, thundershower, trumpet flower, virgin's bower, waterpower, water tower, will to power, womanpower • balance of power, canonical hour, martello tower, sidereal hour

ower³ \ō-ər\ see OER⁴

owered \aürd\ coward, flowered, Howard, powered, towered • high-powered • ivory-towered, superpowered, underpowered—*also* -ed *forms of verbs listed at* OWER²

owerer \aür-ər\ see OURER³

owerful \aür-fəl\ flowerful, powerful • all-powerful

owering \aü-riŋ\ lowering, towering • nonflowering—*also* -ing *forms of verbs listed at* OWER²

owery \aür-ē\ bowery, cowrie, dowry, floury, flowery, kauri, lowery, Maori, showery

owff \aüf\ howff • langlauf

owhee \ō-ē\ see OWY

owie \aü-ē\ Maui, zowie

owing \ō-iŋ\ see OING¹

owl¹ \ōl\ see OLE¹

owl² \aül\ bowel, cowl, dowel, foul, fowl, growl, Howell, howl, jowl, owl, prowl, rowel, scowl, towel, trowel, vowel, yowl • avowal, batfowl, barn owl, barred owl, beach towel, befoul, elf owl, embowel, horned owl, night owl, peafowl, screech owl, seafowl, tea towel, wildfowl • cheek-by-jowl, disavowal, disembowel, guinea fowl, jungle fowl, on the prowl, roller towel, snowy owl, spotted owl, Turkish towel, waterfowl • throw in the towel • neither fish nor fowl

owland \ō-lənd\ lowland, Poland, Roland

owledge \äl-ij\ college, knowledge • acknowledge, foreknowledge, misknowledge, self-knowledge

owler¹ \ō-lər\ see OLLER

owler² \aü-lər\ fowler, Fowler, growler, howler, prowler, scowler • wildfowler • waterfowler

owless \ō-ləs\ see OLUS

owline \ō-lən\ see OLON

owling¹ \ō-liŋ\ see OLLING

owling² \aù-liŋ\ cowling, fouling, growling, howling, toweling • wildfowling • antifouling, biofouling, waterfowling—*also* -ing *forms of verbs listed at* OWL²

owlock \äl-ək\ see OLOCH

owly¹ \ō-lē\ see OLY¹

owly² \aù-lē\ foully, growly, jowly

owman¹ \ō-mən\ see OMAN

owman² \aù-mən\ bowman, cowman, plowman

ow-me \ō-mē\ see OAMY

own¹ \ōn\ see ONE¹

own² \aùn\ Braun, brown, Brown, clown, crown, down, Down, drown, frown, gown, lown, noun, town • back down, Baytown, bear down, blowdown, boil down, boomtown, breakdown, break down, Bridgetown, bringdown, bring down, call down, Cape Town, cast down, Charlestown, clampdown, clamp down, climb down, closedown, comedown, come down, cooldown, countdown, count down, count noun, cow town, crackdown, crack down, crosstown, cry down, cut down, downtown, drawdown, draw down, dress down, dropdown, dumb down, embrown, facedown, fall down, first down, Freetown, Georgetown, George Town, get down, ghost town, godown, go down, half crown, hand down, hands-down, hoedown, hold down, hometown, hull down, Jamestown, keep down, knockdown, knock down, lay down, letdown, let down, lie down, live down, lockdown, look down, lowdown, markdown, mark down, mass noun, meltdown, melt down, midtown, new town, nightgown, North Down, nutbrown, pastedown, pat down, pay down, phase down, pipe down, play down, plunk down, pronoun, pull-down, pull down, pushdown, put-down, renown, rubdown, rundown, scaledown, set down, shakedown, shake down, shire town, shoot down, showdown, shutdown, shut down, sit-down, slap down, slowdown, Southdown, splashdown, splash down, stand-down, stare down, stepdown, stop down, strike down, stripped-down, sundown, swansdown, take down, talk down, tank town, tea gown, tear down, throw down, thumbs-down, tie-down, topdown, touchdown, touch down, trade down, turndown, turn down, uncrown, uptown, Von Braun, wash down, wear down, weigh down, wet down, wind down, write-down, write down, Youngstown • Allentown, broken-down, button-down, Charlottetown, Chinatown, common noun, dressing-down, dressing gown, eiderdown, Germantown, go to town, hand-me-down, Oxford down, proper noun, reach-me-down, shantytown, simmer down, Spanish Town, thistledown, Tinseltown, trickle-down, Triple Crown, tumbledown, up and down, up-and-down, upside down, Vandyke brown, verbal noun, water down, watered-down • bring the house down, company town, Geneva gown, keep one's head down, let one's hair down, man-about-town, nervous breakdown, put one's foot down, with one's pants down

ownded \aún-dəd\ see OUNDED

ownding \aún-diŋ\ see OUNDING

owned[1] \ōnd\ see ONED[1]

owned[2] \aúnd\ see OUND[2]

owner[1] \ō-nər\ see ONER[1]

owner[2] \ü-nər\ see OONER

owner[3] \aú-nər\ browner, crowner, downer, frowner • downtowner, sundowner

owness \ō-nəs\ see ONUS[2]

ownia \ō-nē-ə\ see ONIA[1]

ownie \aú-nē\ see OWNY

owning[1] \ō-niŋ\ see ONING[2]

owning[2] \aú-niŋ\ Browning —also -ing forms of verbs listed at OWN[2]

ownish \aú-nish\ brownish, clownish

ownsman \aúnz-mən\ gownsman, groundsman, roundsman, townsman

owny \aú-nē\ brownie, browny, downy, townie

owper \ü-pər\ see OOPER

owry \aúr-ē\ see OWERY

owse \aúz\ see OUSE[2]

owser \aú-zər\ see OUSER

owson \aúz-ᵊn\ thousand • advowson

owster \ō-stər\ see OASTER

owsy \aú-zē\ blousy, blowsy, drowsy, frowsy, lousy, mousy

owth \ōth\ both, growth, loath, loth, oath, quoth, troth • betroth, ingrowth, old-growth, outgrowth, upgrowth • inter-growth, overgrowth, second growth, undergrowth • Hippocratic oath

owy \ō-ē\ blowy, Chloe, doughy, joey, Joey, showy, snowy, towhee • echoey • kalanchoe

owys \ō-əs\ see OIS[3]

ox \äks\ box, cox, fox, Fox, Knox, lox, ox, pax, phlox, pox • aurochs, bandbox, black box, boom box, boondocks, Botox, call box, cowpox, detox, dough box, dreadlocks, firebox, Fort Knox, gearbox, glove box, gravlax, gray fox, hatbox, hotbox, icebox, in-box, jewel box, jukebox, kit fox, live-box, lockbox, mailbox, matchbox, musk ox, out-box, outfox, pillbox, poor box, postbox, press box, red fox, redox, saltbox, sandbox, saucebox, skybox, smallpox, snuffbox, soapbox, sound box, squawk box, strongbox, sweatbox, swell box, swift fox, toolbox, unbox, voice box, volvox, workbox, Xerox • arctic fox, ballot box, bobby socks, chatterbox, chicken pox, chocolate box, dealing box, ditty box, equinox, flying fox, journal box, miter box, music box, orthodox, Orthodox, paradox, pepperbox, pillar-box, ready box, sentry box, service box, shadowbox, shadow box, silver fox, Skinner box, stuffing box, tinderbox, window box, witness-box • dialog box, econobox, Greek Orthodox, heterodox, homeobox, idiot box, jack-in-the-box, Pandora's box, penalty box, unorthodox • dementia praecox, Eastern Orthodox, neoorthodox, safe-deposit box—*also -s, -'s, and -s' forms of nouns and -s forms of verbs listed at* OCK[1]

oxen \äk-sən\ oxen
• Niedersachsen

oxer \äk-sər\ boxer, Boxer
• kickboxer • bobby-soxer

oxie \äk-sē\ see OXY

oxin \äk-sən\ coxswain, tocsin, toxin • dioxin • aflatoxin, antitoxin, biotoxin, mycotoxin, neurotoxin

oxswain \äk-sən\ see OXIN

oxy \äk-sē\ boxy, doxy, foxy, moxie, oxy, poxy, proxy
• epoxy • orthodoxy, Orthodoxy • heterodoxy, unorthodoxy • neoorthodoxy

oy \ȯi\ boy, buoy, cloy, coy, foy, goy, hoy, joy, Joy, koi, oy, ploy, poi, Roy, soy, toy, troy, Troy • ahoy, alloy, Amoy, annoy, bad boy, ball boy, batboy, B-boy, beachboy, bellboy, bell buoy, best boy, big boy, bok choy, borzoi, boy toy, busboy, callboy, carboy, charpoy, choirboy, convoy, cowboy, decoy, deploy, destroy, doughboy, employ, enjoy, envoy, flyboy, footboy, Hanoi, hautbois, highboy, homeboy, houseboy, killjoy, Khoikhoi, Leroy, life buoy, linkboy, lowboy, McCoy, newsboy, old boy, pak choi, pageboy, page boy, playboy, plowboy, po'boy, postboy, potboy, Quemoy, Rob Roy, Saint Croix, Savoy, schoolboy, sepoy, stock boy, tallboy, tatsoi, teapoy, Tolstoy, tomboy, travois, viceroy • Adonai, altar boy, attaboy, breeches buoy, bullyboy, cabin boy, Charleroi, chorus boy, copyboy, corduroy, good old boy, hoi polloi, Illinois, Iroquois, maccaboy, mama's boy, Niterói, office boy, overjoy, paperboy, poster boy, pretty boy, redeploy, reemploy, roaring boy, sonobuoy, teddy boy, Tinkertoy, water boy, whipping boy • delivery boy, drugstore cowboy, Helen of Troy, hobbledehoy, paduasoy, superalloy

oya \ȯi-ə\ see OIA

oyable \ȯi-ə-bəl\ deployable, employable, enjoyable
• unemployable

oyal¹ \ī\ see ILE¹

oyal² \óil\ see OIL

oyalist \ói-ə-ləst\ loyalist, royalist

oyalty \óil-tē\ loyalty, royalty
• disloyalty, viceroyalty

oyance \ói-əns\ buoyance, joyance • annoyance, chatoyance, clairvoyance, flamboyance

oyancy \ói-ən-sē\ buoyancy
• chatoyancy, flamboyancy

oyant \ói-ənt\ buoyant
• chatoyant, clairvoyant, flamboyant

oyce \óis\ see OICE

oyd \óid\ see OID¹

oyden \ói-dᵉn\ Boyden, Croydon, hoyden

oydon \ói-dᵉn\ see OYDEN

oyed \óid\ see OID¹

oyen \ói-ən\ doyen, Goyen
• Iroquoian

oyer \óir\ coir, foyer, moire
• annoyer, destroyer • tank destroyer

oyes \óiz\ see OISE²

oying \óiŋ\ see AWING

oyle \óil\ see OIL

oyless \ói-ləs\ joyless, Troilus

oyment \ói-mənt\ deployment, employment, enjoyment

• redeployment, self-employment, subemployment, unemployment
• underemployment

oyne \óin\ see OIN¹

oyo¹ \ói-ō\ boyo • arroyo

oyo² \ói-ə\ see OIA

o-yo \ō-yō\ see OLLO²

oyster \ói-stər\ see OISTER

oz¹ \əz\ see EUSE¹

oz² \óz\ see AUSE¹

oz³ \ōz\ see OSE²

oza \ō-zə\ see OSA²

oze \ōz\ see OSE²

ozen¹ \əz-ᵉn\ cousin, cozen, dozen • first cousin • baker's dozen, cater-cousin, daily dozen, kissing cousin, second cousin • a dime a dozen

ozen² \ōz-ᵉn\ see OSEN

ozenage \əz-ᵉn-ij\ see OUSINAGE

ozer \ō-zər\ see OSER¹

ozily \ō-zə-lē\ see OSILY

ozo¹ \ō-sō\ see OSO¹

ozo² \ō-zō\ see OSO²

ozy \ō-zē\ see OSY

ozzer \äz-ər\ rozzer • alcazar

ozzle \äz-əl\ Basel, Basil, nozzle, schnozzle

u

u¹ \ü\ see EW¹

ua¹ \ü-ə\ skua • great skua, Karlsruhe, lehua, Manua, Quechua • Timucua

ua² \ä\ see A¹

uable \ü-ə-bəl\ chewable, doable, suable, viewable • accruable, construable, renewable, reviewable, unchewable, undoable • nonrenewable, unreviewable

ual \ü-əl\ see UEL¹

uan \ü-ən\ bruin, ruin, Siouan, yuan • Ryukyuan

uancy \ü-ən-sē\ see UENCY

uant \ü-ənt\ see UENT

uart \ürt\ see URT¹

ub \əb\ bub, blub, chub, club, cub, drub, dub, flub, grub, hub, nub, pub, rub, schlub, scrub, shrub, slub, snub, stub, sub, tub • bathtub, book club, brew pub, flubdub, glee club, health club, hot tub, hubbub, key club, nightclub, redub, war club, washtub, yacht club • billy club, Christmas club, country club, jockey club, overdub, service club, syllabub • Beelzebub

uba \ü-bə\ Cuba, juba, scuba, tuba, Yuba • Aruba, saxtuba, Tshiluba

ubal \ü-bəl\ Jubal, nubile, ruble, tubal

uban \ü-bən\ see EUBEN

ubbard \əb-ərd\ cupboard • Mother Hubbard

ubber \əb-ər\ blubber, clubber, drubber, dubber, grubber, lubber, rubber, scrubber, slubber, snubber, tubber • foam rubber, landlubber, nightclubber • money-grubber

ubbery \əb-rē\ blubbery, rubbery, shrubbery

ubbily \əb-ə-lē\ bubbly, chubbily, grubbily

ubbin \əb-ən\ dubbin, nubbin

ubbing \əb-iŋ\ drubbing, rubbing, slubbing • land-lubbing—*also* -ing *forms of verbs listed at* UB

ubble \əb-əl\ bubble, double, Hubble, nubble, rubble, stubble, trouble • abubble, redouble, soap bubble, undouble • body double, borrow trouble, daily double,

double-double, hubble-bubble, on the double, triple-double

ubbled \əb-əld\ bubbled, doubled, rubbled, stubbled, troubled • redoubled, untroubled

ubbler \əb-lər\ see OUBLER

ubbly¹ \əb-lē\ bubbly, doubly, nubbly, stubbly

ubbly² \əb-ə-lē\ see UBBILY

ubby \əb-ē\ bubby, chubby, clubby, cubby, grubby, hubby, nubby, Rabi, scrubby, shrubby, snubby, stubby, tubby

ube \üb\ boob, cube, lube, rube, tube • blowtube, boob tube, Danube, flashcube, haboob, j'adoube, jujube, test tube • bouillon cube, breathing tube, down the tube, hypercube, inner tube, speaking tube • cathode-ray tube

uben \ü-bən\ see EUBEN

ubens \ü-bənz\ Rubens—*also -s, -'s, and -s' forms of nouns listed at* EUBEN

uber \ü-bər\ Buber, cuber, goober, tuber

uberance \ü-brəns\ exuberance, protuberance

uberant \ü-brənt\ exuberant, protuberant • overexuberant

uberous \ü-brəs\ see UBRIS

ubic \ü-bik\ cubic, pubic • cherubic

ubile \ü-bəl\ see UBAL

ubious \ü-bē-əs\ dubious, rubious

ubis \ü-bəs\ pubis, rubus • Anubis

uble \ü-bəl\ see UBAL

ublic \əb-lik\ public • go public, make public, republic • notary public • banana republic

ubman \əb-mən\ clubman, Tubman

ubric \ü-brik\ Kubrick, lubric, rubric

ubrious \ü-brē-əs\ lugubrious, salubrious • insalubrious

ubris \ü-brəs\ hubris, tuberous

ubtile \ət-ᵊl\ see UTTLE

ubus \ü-bəs\ see UBIS

uby \ü-bē\ see OOBY

uca \ü-kə\ see OOKA

ucal \ü-kəl\ ducal, nuchal • archducal

ucan \ü-kən\ glucan, kuchen, Lucan • interleukin

ucat \ək-ət\ see UCKET

ucca¹ \ü-kə\ see OOKA

ucca² \ək-ə\ see UKKA

uccal \ək-əl\ see UCKLE

ucci \ü-chē\ see OOCHY

ucco \ək-ō\ see UCKO

uccor \ək-ər\ see UCKER

uccory \ək-rē\ see UCKERY

ucculence \ək-yə-ləns\ see UCULENCE

uce \üs\ see USE¹

uced \üst\ see OOST

ucement \ü-smənt\ inducement, seducement, traducement

ucence \üs-ᵊns\ nuisance • translucence

ucer \ü-sər\ juicer, looser, sprucer • adducer, Bull Mooser, inducer, lime-juicer, producer, reducer, seducer, traducer, transducer • introducer, reproducer

uch¹ \ich\ see ITCH

uch² \ük\ see UKE

uch³ \əch\ see UTCH¹

uchal \ü-kəl\ see UCAL

uche¹ \ü-chē\ see OOCHY

uche² \üch\ see OOCH¹

uche³ \üsh\ see OUCHE

uchen \ü-kən\ see UCAN

ucher \ü-chər\ see UTURE

uchin \ü-shən\ see UTION

uchsia \ü-shə\ see UTIA

uchy \əch-ē\ duchy, smutchy, touchy • archduchy, grand duchy

ucia \ü-shə\ see UTIA

ucial \ü-shəl\ crucial, Trucial • fiducial

ucian \ü-shən\ see UTION

ucible \ü-sə-bəl\ crucible • deducible, educible, inducible, producible, protrusible, reducible • irreducible, reproducible • irreproducible

ucid \ü-səd\ deuced, lucid • pellucid, Seleucid

ucifer \ü-sə-fər\ crucifer, Lucifer

ucity \ü-sət-ē\ abstrusity, caducity

ucive \ü-siv\ see USIVE

uck¹ \ək\ buck, Buck, chuck, cluck, cruck, duck, guck, huck, luck, muck, pluck, puck, Puck, ruck, schmuck, shuck, snuck, struck, stuck, suck, truck, Truk, tuck, yech, yuck • amok, awestruck, blackbuck, black duck, bushbuck, Canuck, cold duck, dead duck, dumbstruck, dump truck, fire truck, fish duck, fly-struck, hand truck, hard luck, Kalmuck, lame-duck, light-struck, moonstruck, mukluk, muktuk, potluck, reedbuck, roebuck, sawbuck, shelduck, stagestruck, starstruck, sunstruck, unstuck, upchuck, woodchuck • geoduck, Habakkuk, horror-struck, Keokuk, Koyukuk, ladder truck, megabuck, motortruck, muckamuck, nip and tuck, pass the buck, Peking duck, pickup truck, planet-struck, push one's luck, sitting duck, thunderstruck • high-muck-a-muck

uck² \ùk\ see OOK¹

ukar \ək-ər\ see UCKER

ucker \ək-ər\ bucker, chukar, chukker, ducker, mucker, plucker, pucker, shucker, succor, sucker, trucker, tucker • bloodsucker, goatsucker, hog sucker, sapsucker, seersucker, shark sucker • bib and tucker

uckery \ək-rē\ puckery, succory

ucket \ək-ət\ bucket, ducat, tucket • gutbucket, lunch-bucket, Nantucket, Pawtucket, rust bucket • kick the bucket • drop in the bucket

uckle \ək-əl\ buccal, buckle, chuckle, knuckle, suckle, truckle • Arbuckle, bareknuckle, parbuckle, pinochle, swashbuckle, turnbuckle, unbuckle, white-knuckle • honeysuckle

uckled \ək-əld\ cuckold, knuckled • bare-knuckled —also -ed forms of verbs listed at UCKLE

uckler \ək-lər\ buckler, knuckler, truckler • swashbuckler

uckling \ək-liŋ\ duckling, suckling • swashbuckling • ugly duckling—also -ing forms of verbs listed at UCKLE

ucko \ək-ō\ bucko, stucco

uckold \ək-əld\ see UCKLED

uckoo \ü-kü\ cuckoo • Maluku, seppuku

ucks \əks\ see UX[1]

uckus \ük-əs\ ruckus, Sukkoth

ucky \ək-ē\ ducky, lucky, mucky, plucky, sucky, yucky • Kentucky, unlucky • happy-go-lucky

uco \ü-kō\ juco • pachuco, Temuco • osso buco, Pernambuco

ucre \ü-kər\ euchre, lucre

uct \əkt\ duct • abduct, adduct, bile duct, conduct, construct, deduct, destruct, eruct, induct, instruct, obstruct, reluct, subduct • aqueduct, deconstruct, reconstruct, self-destruct, usufruct, viaduct —also -ed forms of verbs listed at UCK[1]

uctable \ək-tə-bəl\ see UCTIBLE

uctance \ək-təns\ conductance, inductance, reluctance

uctible \ək-tə-bəl\ conductible, constructable, deductible, destructible • indestructible, ineluctable, nondeductible, reconstructible

uctile \ək-tᵊl\ see UCTAL

ucting \ək-tiŋ\ ducting • nonconducting • semiconducting—also -ing forms of verbs listed at UCT

uction \ək-shən\ fluxion, ruction, suction • abduction, adduction, conduction, construction, deduction, destruction, eduction, effluxion, induction, instruction, obstruction, production, reduction, seduction, subduction, transduction • coproduction, deconstruction, introduction, liposuction, mass production, reconstruction, reproduction, self-destruction

uctive \ək-tiv\ adductive, conductive, constructive, deductive, destructive, inductive, instructive, obstructive, productive, reductive, seductive • deconstructive, nonproductive, reconstructive, reproductive, self-destructive, unconstructive, uninstructive, unproductive • counterproductive

uctor \ək-tər\ abductor, adductor, conductor, constructor, destructor, eductor, inductor, instructor, obstructor • deconstructor, nonconductor, reconstructor • semiconductor, superconductor

uctress \ək-trəs\ conductress, instructress, seductress

uculence \ək-yə-ləns\ succulence, truculence

ucy \ü-sē\ see UICY

ud[1] \əd\ blood, bud, crud, cud, dud, flood, fud, Judd, mud, rudd, scud, spud, stud, sudd, thud • at stud, bad blood, blue blood, coldblood, disbud, earbud, full-blood, half-blood, hotblood, leaf bud, lifeblood, new blood, oxblood, pure-blood, redbud, rosebud, shed blood, smell blood, sweat blood, warmblood • dragon's blood, flesh and blood, flower bud, in cold blood, in the bud, superstud • stick-in-the-mud

ud[2] \üd\ see UDE

ud[3] \u̇d\ see OOD[1]

uda \üd-ə\ Buddha, Gouda, Judah • Barbuda, Bermuda, Neruda, remuda • barracuda, Buxtehude • Gautama Buddha

udable \üd-ə-bəl\ excludable, extrudable, includable • ineludible

udah \üd-ə\ see UDA

udal \üd-ᵊl\ see OODLE

udas \üd-əs\ Judas • Santa Gertrudis

udd[1] \u̇d\ see OOD[1]

udd[2] \əd\ see UD[1]

udded \əd-əd\ see OODED[1]

udder \əd-ər\ budder, flooder, judder, rudder, shudder, udder

uddha \üd-ə\ see UDA

uddhist \üd-əst\ see UDIST[1]

uddie \əd-ē\ see UDDY[1]

udding[1] \əd-iŋ\ budding, studding—also -ing forms of verbs listed at UD[1]

udding[2] \u̇d-iŋ\ see OODING

uddle \əd-ᵊl\ buddle, cuddle, fuddle, huddle, muddle, puddle, ruddle • befuddle

uddly \əd-lē\ cuddly, Dudley, muddly, studly

uddy[1] \əd-ē\ bloody, buddy, Buddy, cruddy, cuddy, duddie, muddy, ruddy, study • brown study, case study, work-study • buddy-buddy, course of study, fuddy-duddy, understudy

uddy[2] \u̇d-ē\ see OODY[2]

ude[1] \üd\ brood, crowd, crude, dude, feud, food, hued, Jude, lewd, lude, mood, nude, oud, pood, prude, pseud, rood, rude, shrewd, snood, stewed, 'tude, who'd, wood, wud, you'd • allude, blood feud, collude, conclude, delude, denude, elude, etude, exclude, extrude, exude, fast-food, Gertrude, health food, include, intrude, junk food, nonfood, obtrude, occlude, plant food, postlude, preclude, prelude, protrude, quaalude, seafood, seclude, subdued, transude, unglued • altitude, amplitude, aptitude, attitude, certitude, comfort food, consuetude, crassitude, desuetude, devil's food, finger food, finitude, fortitude, frankenfood, gratitude, habitude, hebetude, interlude, lassitude, latitude, longitude, magnitude, mansuetude, multitude, negritude, platitude, plenitude, promptitude, pulchritude, quietude, rectitude, seminude, servitude, solitude, turpitude, vastitude • beatitude, correctitude, decrepitude, disquietude, exactitude, inaptitude, incertitude, ineptitude, infinitude, ingratitude, inquietude, natural food, senectitude, similitude, solicitude, vicissitude • dissimilitude, inexactitude • verisimilitude

ude² \üd-ə\ see UDA

udel \üd-ᵉl\ see OODLE

udence \ü-dᵉn(t)s\ prudence, Prudence, students • imprudence • jurisprudence

udeness \üd-nəs\ see UDINOUS

udent \üd-ᵉnt\ prudent, student • day student, imprudent, nonstudent • jurisprudent

udents \ü-dᵉn(t)s\ see UDENCE

uder \üd-ər\ brooder, Tudor • concluder, deluder, excluder,

extruder, intruder, obtruder, preluder—*also* -er *forms of adjectives listed at* UDE¹

udge¹ \əj\ bludge, budge, drudge, fudge, grudge, judge, kludge, nudge, sludge, smudge, trudge • adjudge, begrudge, forejudge, misjudge, prejudge

udge² \üj\ see UGE¹

udgeon \əj-ən\ bludgeon, dudgeon, gudgeon • curmudgeon

udgie \əj-ē\ see UDGY

udging \əj-iŋ\ drudging, grudging—*also* -ing *forms of verbs listed at* UDGE¹

udgy \əj-ē\ budgie, kludgy, pudgy, sludgy, smudgy

udi \ü-dē\ see OODY¹

udible \üd-ə-bəl\ see UDABLE

udie \ü-dē\ see OODY¹

udinous \üd-nəs\ crudeness, lewdness, nudeness, rudeness, shrewdness • altitudinous, hebetudinous, multitudinous, platitudinous, plenitudinous, pulchritudinous, rectitudinous

udis \üd-əs\ see UDAS

udish \üd-ish\ dudish, prudish

udist¹ \üd-əst\ Buddhist, feudist, nudist—*also* -est *forms of adjectives listed at* UDE¹

udist² \üd-əst\ see OULDEST

udity \üd-ət-ē\ crudity, nudity

udley \əd-lē\ see UDDLY

udly \əd-lē\ see UDDLY

udo \üd-ō\ judo, kudo, pseudo, scudo • escudo, Matsudo, menudo, testudo • O altitudo

udor \üd-ər\ see UDER

udsman \udz-mən\ see OODSMAN

udu \üd-ü\ see OODOO

udy[1] \ü-dē\ see OODY[1]

udy[2] \əd-ē\ see UDDY[1]

ue[1] \ü\ see EW[1]

ue[2] \ā\ see AY[1]

ued \üd\ see UDE

ueful \ü-fəl\ rueful • pantofle

ueghel \ü-gəl\ see UGAL

ueil \əi\ Arauil • Argentueil

uel[1] \ü-əl\ crewel, cruel, dual, duel, fuel, gruel, jewel, Jewel, Jewell, newel, Newell • accrual, eschewal, refuel, renewal, synfuel • biofuel, diesel fuel, fossil fuel, Pantagruel

uel[2] \ül\ see OOL[1]

uely \ü-lē\ see ULY

uement \ü-mənt\ see EWMENT

uence \ü-əns\ affluence, confluence, congruence, effluence, influence, pursuance, refluence • incongruence

uency \ü-ən-sē\ fluency, truancy • affluency, congruency, nonfluency

ueness \ü-nəs\ see EWNESS

uenster \ən-stər\ see UNSTER

uent \ü-ənt\ fluent, suint, truant • affluent, confluent, congruent, effluent, influent • incongruent

uer \ü-ər\ see EWER[1]

uerdon \ərd-ᵉn\ see URDEN

uerile \ur-əl\ see URAL

ues \üz\ see USE[2]

uesman \üz-mən\ see EWSMAN

uesome \ü-səm\ gruesome, twosome

uesy \ü-zē\ see OOZY

uet \ü-ət\ bluet, cruet, peewit, suet • conduit, intuit

uette \et\ see ET[1]

uey \ü-ē\ see EWY

ufa \ü-fə\ loofah, tufa • opera buffa

uff \əf\ bluff, buff, chough, chuff, cuff, duff, fluff, gruff, guff, huff, luff, muff, puff, rough, ruff, scruff, scuff, slough, snuff, sough, stuff, tough, tuff • breadstuff, cream puff, dyestuff, earmuff, enough, feedstuff, foodstuff, french cuff, greenstuff, handcuff, hang tough, hot stuff, kid stuff, outbluff, Pine Bluff, rebuff, small stuff • blindman's buff, call one's bluff, oeil-de-boeuf, off-the-cuff, overstuff, powder puff, strut one's stuff, up to snuff

uffa \ü-fə\ see UFA

uffe[1] \üf\ see OOF[1]

uffe[2] \uf\ see OOF[2]

uffed \əft\ buffed, chuffed, ruffed, tuft • candytuft—*also* -ed *forms of verbs listed at* UFF

uffel \əf-əl\ see UFFLE[1]

uffer \ˈəf-ər\ bluffer, buffer, duffer, puffer, rougher, snuffer, stuffer, suffer • candlesnuffer, stocking stuffer—*also* -er *forms of adjectives listed at* UFF

uffet \ˈəf-ət\ buffet, tuffet

uffin \ˈəf-ən\ muffin, puffin, roughen, toughen • MacGuffin • English muffin, ragamuffin

uffish \ˈəf-ish\ huffish, roughish

uffle¹ \ˈəf-əl\ duffel, muffle, ruffle, scuffle, shuffle, snuffle, truffle • kerfuffle, reshuffle, unmuffle

uffle² \ü-fəl\ *see* UEFUL

uffled \ˈəf-əld\ truffled • unruffled—*also* -ed *forms of verbs listed at* UFFLE¹

uffler \ˈəf-lər\ muffler, shuffler, snuffler

uffly \ˈəf-lē\ bluffly, gruffly, roughly, ruffly, toughly

uffy \ˈəf-ē\ chuffy, fluffy, huffy, puffy, scruffy, snuffy, stuffy, toughie

ufi \ü-fē\ *see* OOFY

ufous \ü-fəs\ doofus, rufous, Rufus

uft \ˈəft\ *see* UFFED

ufti \ˈəf-tē\ mufti, tufty

ufty \ˈəf-tē\ *see* UFTI

ufus \ü-fəs\ *see* UFOUS

ug \ˈəg\ bug, chug, Doug, drug, dug, fug, hug, jug, lug, mug, plug, pug, rug, shrug, slug, smug, snug, thug, trug, tug, ugh, vug • bear hug, bedbug, billbug, debug, earplug, firebug, fireplug, goldbug, humbug, june bug, lovebug, nondrug, sea slug, smart drug, spark plug, stinkbug, throw rug, unplug, wall plug • antibug, antidrug, chugalug, date rape drug, doodlebug, gateway drug, jitterbug, ladybug, lightning bug, litterbug, mealybug, orphan drug, prayer rug, pull the plug, scatter rug, shutterbug, sulfa drug, superbug, toby jug, water bug, wonder drug • designer drug, miracle drug, prescription drug • oriental rug

uga \ü-gə\ ruga, yuga • beluga, Cayuga, Kaluga, sastruga, sevruga, suruga, Tortuga, Vetluga • Chattanooga

ugal \ü-gəl\ Brueghel, bugle, frugal, fugal, fugle, kugel • conjugal • centrifugal

ugar \u̇g-ər\ *see* UGUR

uge¹ \ˈüj\ huge, kludge, Lodz, scrooge, scrouge, stooge • deluge, refuge • calcifuge, centrifuge, febrifuge, subterfuge, vermifuge

uge² \üzh\ Bruges, luge, rouge • deluge, gamboge, refuge • Baton Rouge • après moi le déluge

ugel \ü-gəl\ *see* UGAL

uges \üzh\ *see* UGE²

uggaree \əg-rē\ *see* UGGERY¹

ugger¹ \əg-ər\ bugger, chugger, hugger, lugger, mugger, plugger, rugger, slugger, tugger • Bhavnagar, debugger,

Jamnagar, Srinagar, tree hugger • hugger-mugger

ugger[2] \ug-ər\ see UGUR

uggery[1] \əg-rē\ buggery, puggaree, snuggery, thuggery • humbuggery, skulduggery

uggery[2] \ug-rē\ see UGARY

ugget \əg-ət\ drugget, nugget

uggie \əg-ē\ see UGGY

uggish \əg-ish\ sluggish, thuggish

uggle \əg-əl\ guggle, juggle, smuggle, snuggle, struggle

uggler \əg-lər\ juggler, smuggler, struggler

uggy \əg-ē\ buggy, druggie, druggy, fuggy, luggie, muggy, vuggy • beach buggy, dune buggy, swamp buggy • baby buggy, horse-and-buggy

ugh[1] \əg\ see UG

ugh[2] \ü\ see EW[1]

ughes \üz\ see USE[2]

ugle \ü-gəl\ see UGAL

ugli \ə-glē\ see UGLY

uglia \ül-yə\ see ULIA

ugly \əg-lē\ smugly, snugly, Ugli, ugly • plug-ugly

ugn \ün\ see OON[1]

ugner \ü-nər\ see OONER

ugric \ü-grik\ tugrik, Ugric • Finno-Ugric

ugrik \ü-grik\ see UGRIC

ugu \ü-gü\ fugu, goo-goo

ugur \ug-ər\ booger, bugger, sugar • blood sugar, brown sugar, cane sugar • maple sugar

uhe \ü-ə\ see UA

uhl \ül\ see OOL[1]

uhr[1] \ər\ see EUR[1]

uhr[2] \ur\ see URE[1]

ührer \ur-ər\ see URER[1]

ui[1] \ā\ see AY[1]

ui[2] \ē\ see EE[1]

uice \üs\ see USE[1]

uiced \üst\ see OOST

uiceless \ü-sləs\ see USELESS

uicer \ü-sər\ see UCER

uicy \ü-sē\ goosey, juicy, Lucy, sluicy, sprucy • Brancusi, Watusi • acey-deucey, Arginusae, loosey-goosey

uid \ü-id\ Clwyd, druid, fluid

uidable \īd-ə-bəl\ see IDABLE[1]

uidance \īd-ᵊns\ see IDANCE

uide \īd\ see IDE[1]

uided \īd-əd\ see IDED

uider \īd-ər\ see IDER[1]

uidon \īd-ᵊn\ see IDEN

uiker \ī-kər\ see IKER

uild \ild\ see ILLED

uilder \il-dər\ see ILDER

uilding \il-diŋ\ see ILDING

uile \īl\ see ILE[1]

uileless \īl-ləs\ see ILELESS

uiler \ī-lər\ see ILAR

uilleann \i-lən\ see ILLON

uilt \ilt\ see ILT

uimpe \amp\ see AMP[3]

uin[1] \ü-ən\ see UAN

uin[2] \ən\ see UN

uin[3] \a[m]\ see IN[4]

uing \ü-iŋ\ see OING[2]

uint \ü-ənt\ see UENT

uir \ûr\ see URE[1]

uirdly \ûr-lē\ see URELY

uis \ü-əs\ see OUIS[2]

uisance \üs-[e]ns\ see UCENCE

uisard \ī-zərd\ see ISORED

uise[1] \üz\ see USE[2]

uise[2] \īz\ see IZE

uiser \ü-zər\ see USER

uish \ü-ish\ see EWISH

uisne \ü-nē\ see OONY

uiste \is-tē\ see ICITY[2]

uit[1] \ü-ət\ see UET

uit[2] \üt\ see UTE

uitable \üt-ə-bəl\ see UTABLE

uitage \üt-ij\ see OOTAGE[1]

uite \üt\ see UTE

uited \üt-əd\ see OOTED[1]

uiter \üt-ər\ see UTER

uiterer \üt-ər-ər\ fruiterer, pewterer

uiting \üt-iŋ\ see UTING

uitless \üt-ləs\ see OOTLESS

uitlet \üt-lət\ see OOTLET

uitor \üt-ər\ see UTER

uitous \ü-ət-əs\ circuitous, fortuitous, gratuitous

uits \üts\ see OOTS

uittle[1] \üt-[e]l\ see UTILE

uittle[2] \ət-[e]l\ see UTTLE

uity[1] \ü-ət-ē\ acuity, annuity, circuity, congruity, fatuity, fortuity, gratuity, tenuity, vacuity • ambiguity, assiduity, conspicuity, contiguity, continuity, exiguity, incongruity, ingenuity, perpetuity, perspicuity, promiscuity, superfluity • discontinuity

uity[2] \üt-ē\ see OOTY[1]

uk[1] \ük\ see UKE

uk[2] \ùk\ see OOK[1]

uk[3] \ək\ see UCK

ukar \ə-kər\ see UCKER

uke \ük\ cuke, duke, fluke, gook, juke, kook, Luke, nuke, Nuuk, puke, snook, souk, spook, suq, tuque, uke, yeuk, zouk • archduke, Baruch, blood fluke, caoutchouc, chibouk, Chinook, Dubuque, Farouk, grand duke, Kirkuk, Mamluk, peruke, rebuke, Seljuk, Shilluk • antinuke, Heptateuch, Hexateuch, liver fluke, Pentateuch

uki[1] \ü-kē\ see OOKY[1]

uki[2] \ù-kē\ see OOKIE

ukka \ək-ə\ chukka, pukka, yucca • felucca, Molucca

ukkah \ùk-ə\ see OOKAH

ukker \ək-ər\ see UCKER

ukkoth \ùk-əs\ see UCKUS

uku \ü-kü\ see UCKOO

ul¹ \ùl\ bull, Bull, full, pull, shul, wool, you'll • armful, bagful, bellpull, brimful, bulbul, cageful, canful, capful, carful, cheekful, chestful, chock-full, cupful, drawerful, earful, eyeful, fistful, forkful, glassful, handful, houseful, in full, jarful, John Bull, jugful, lapful, leg-pull, mouthful, mugful, outpull, pailful, panful, pipeful, pit bull, plateful, potful, push-pull, rackful, roomful, sackful, scoopful, shelfful, skinful, spadeful, spoonful, stageful, steel wool, stickful, tankful, tinful, topful, trainful, trayful, truckful, trunkful, tubful • barrelful, basinful, basketful, bellyful, bucketful, closetful, cock-and-bull, demand-pull, dipperful, gardenful, harborful, Irish bull, Istanbul, ladleful, pitcherful, platterful, satchelful, shovelful, Sitting Bull, tableful, teacupful, teaspoonful, thimbleful, tumblerful • dyed-in-the-wool, tablespoonful

ul² \ül\ see OOL¹

ul³ \əl\ see ULL¹

ula \ü-lə\ Beulah, doula, Fula, hula, moola, pula, Tula • ampulla, Missoula, tabbouleh • Ashtabula, Lobengula, Pascagoula • San Pedro Sula

ular \ü-lər\ see OOLER

ulcent \əl-sənt\ see ULSANT

ulcer \əl-sər\ see ULSER

ulch \əlch\ cultch, gulch, mulch

ule¹ \ü-lē\ see ULY

ule² \ül\ see OOL¹

ulean \ü-lē-ən\ Boolean, Julian • Acheulean, Apulian, cerulean, Friulian, Herculean

uled \üld\ see OOLED

ulep \ü-ləp\ see ULIP

uler \ü-lər\ see OOLER

ules \ülz\ gules, Jules—also -s, -'s, and -s' forms of nouns and -s forms of verbs listed at OOL¹

ulet \əl-ət\ see ULLET¹

uley¹ \ü-lē\ see ULY

uley² \ùl-ē\ see ULLY²

ulf \əlf\ golf, gulf, Gulf • engulf • Beowulf

ulgar \əl-gər\ see ULGUR

ulge \əlj\ bulge • divulge, indulge • overindulge

ulgence¹ \əl-jəns\ divulgence, effulgence, indulgence, refulgence • self-indulgence • overindulgence

ulgence² \ùl-jəns\ effulgence, refulgence

ulgent \əl-jənt\ fulgent • indulgent

ulgur \əl-gər\ bulgur, vulgar

ulhas \əl-əs\ see ULLUS

uli \ùl-ē\ see ULLY²

ulia \ül-yə\ Julia, Puglia • Apulia

ulie \ü-lē\ see ULY

ulip \ü-ləp\ julep, tulip • mint julep

ulish \ü-lish\ see OOLISH

ulity \ü-lət-ē\ credulity, garrulity, sedulity • incredulity

ulk \əlk\ bulk, hulk, skulk, sulk, yolk

ulky \əl-kē\ bulky, sulky

ull¹ \əl\ cull, dull, gull, hull, Hull, lull, mull, null, scull, skull, stull, trull • annul, Choiseul, mogul, numskull, pas seul, seagull • aleph-null, herring gull, Issyk Kul, laughing gull, monohull, multihull, Sitting Bull, Solihull

ull² \ùl\ see UL¹

ulla¹ \ü-lə\ bulla, mullah • ampulla

ulla² \ü-lə\ see ULA

ulla³ \əl-ə\ see ULLAH¹

ullage \əl-ij\ sullage, ullage

ullah¹ \əl-ə\ Gullah, mullah, nullah, Sulla • medulla • ayatollah

ullah² \ùl-ə\ see ULLA¹

ullan \əl-ən\ see ULLEN

ullard \əl-ərd\ see OLORED

ullate \əl-ət\ see ULLET¹

ulle \ùl\ see OOL¹

ullein \əl-ən\ see ULLEN

ullen \əl-ən\ mullein, stollen, sullen • Lucullan

uller¹ \ùl-ər\ fuller, puller • wire-puller

uller² \əl-ər\ see OLOR¹

ulles \əl-əs\ see ULLUS

ullet¹ \əl-ət\ culet, cullet, gullet, mullet • cucullate • dodge a bullet • magic bullet, silver bullet

ullet² \ùl-ət\ bullet, pullet

ulley \ùl-ē\ see ULLY²

ullion \əl-yən\ cullion, mullion, scullion • slumgullion

ullis \əl-əs\ see ULLUS

ullitt \ùl-ət\ see ULLET²

ullman \ùl-mən\ fulmine, Pullman

ullus \əl-əs\ Dulles • Agulhas, Catullus, Lucullus, portcullis, Tibullus • Cape Agulhas

ully¹ \əl-ē\ cully, dully, gully, sully

ully² \ùl-ē\ bully, fully, gully, muley, puli, pulley, woolly

ulmine \ùl-mən\ see ULLMAN

ulp \əlp\ gulp, pulp • insculp, wood pulp

ulsant \əl-sənt\ pulsant • convulsant, demulcent

ulse \əls\ dulse, pulse • avulse, convulse, expulse, impulse, repulse

ulser \əl-sər\ pulser, ulcer

ulsion \əl-shən\ pulsion • avulsion, compulsion, convulsion, emulsion, evulsion, expulsion, impulsion, propulsion, repulsion, revulsion • jet propulsion, self-propulsion

ulsive \əl-siv\ compulsive, convulsive, emulsive, expulsive, impulsive, propulsive, repulsive, revulsive • anticonvulsive

• electroconvulsive, obsessive-compulsive

ult \əlt\ cult • adult, consult, exult, incult, indult, insult, occult, penult, result, subcult, tumult • anticult, cargo cult, catapult, difficult, unadult • antepenult

ultancy \əlt-ᵊn-sē\ consultancy, exultancy

ultant \əlt-ᵊnt\ consultant, exultant, resultant

ultch \əlch\ see ULCH

ulter \əl-tər\ consultor, insulter, occulter

ultery \əl-trē\ see ULTRY

ultor \əl-tər\ see ULTER

ultry \əl-trē\ sultry • adultery

ulture \əl-chər\ culture, multure, vulture • subculture • agriculture, apiculture, aquaculture, aviculture, counterculture, floriculture, horticulture, mariculture, microculture, monoculture, permaculture, silviculture, turkey vulture, viniculture

ulty \əl-tē\ see ALTI[1]

ulu \ü-lü\ lulu, Sulu, Zulu • KwaZulu • Bangweulu, Honolulu

ulunder \əl-ən-dər\ see OLANDER

ulva \əl-və\ ulva, vulva

ulvar \əl-vər\ see ULVER

ulver \əl-vər\ culver, vulvar

uly \ü-lē\ bluely, boule, coolie, coolly, coulee, duly, ghoulie,

Julie, muley, newly, puli, ruly, stoolie, Thule, truly, tule • Bernoulli, Grand Coulee, guayule, patchouli, tabbouleh, unduly, unruly, yours truly • douroucouli • ultima Thule

um¹ \əm\ bum, chum, come, crumb, cum, drum, dumb, from, glum, gum, hum, lum, mum, numb, plum, plumb, rhumb, rum, scrum, scum, slum, some, strum, sum, swum, them, thrum, thumb, yum • alum, aplomb, bass drum, bay rum, beach plum, become, benumb, bolt from, degum, dim sum, dumdum, dum-dum, eardrum, far from, green thumb, hail from, ho-hum, how come, humdrum, income, in sum, off plumb, outcome, pond scum, side drum, snare drum, sour gum, steel drum, subgum, succumb, sweet gum, therefrom, to come, Tom Thumb, tom-tom, wherefrom, yum-yum • apart from, aside from, beat the drum, bubblegum, chewing gum, kettledrum, kingdom come, on the bum, out of plumb, overcome, rule of thumb, sugarplum, Tweedledum, zero-sum • baba au rhum, far be it from, hop-o'-my-thumb, walk away from

um² \ùm\ broom, cum, groom, Qom, room • back room, backroom, ballroom, barroom, bathroom, bedroom, board room, boardroom, chat room, checkroom, classroom, cloakroom, coatroom, courtroom, darkroom, front room, headroom, homeroom, lunchroom, men's room, mushroom, push broom, rec room, restroom, schoolroom, stateroom, sunroom, Targum, washroom, weight room, workroom • anteroom, breathing room, common room, dining room, drawing room, dressing room, elbow room, family room, ladies' room, locker room, sitting room, smoke-filled room, standing room, waiting room, wiggle room • mare librum

um³ \üm\ see OOM[1]

uma \ü-mə\ duma, luma, pneuma, puma, struma, Yuma • Exuma, Ruvuma, satsuma • Ancohuma, Montezuma, Petaluma

umage \əm-ij\ see UMMAGE

uman \ü-mən\ blooming, crewman, human, lumen, Newman, numen, rumen, Truman, Yuman • acumen, albumen, albumin, bitumen, cerumen, ichneumon, illumine, inhuman, nonhuman, panhuman, prehuman, subhuman • antihuman, catechumen, protohuman, superhuman

umanist \ü-mə-nəst\ see UMENIST

umanous \ü-mə-nəs\ see UMINOUS

umb \əm\ see UM[1]

umbar \əm-bər\ see UMBER[1]

umbed \əmd\ green-thumbed, unplumbed—also -ed forms of verbs listed at -UM[1]

umbel \əm-bəl\ see UMBLE

umbency \əm-bən-sē\ incumbency, recumbency

umbent \əm-bənt\ decumbent, incumbent, procumbent, recumbent • anti-incumbent, superincumbent

umber¹ \əm-bər\ cumber, Humber, lumbar, lumber, number, slumber, umber • call number, cucumber, encumber, outnumber, prime number, renumber • disencumber, sea cucumber • atomic number, 800 number, serial number

umber² \əm-ər\ see UMMER

umbered \əm-bərd\ numbered • unnumbered • unencumbered —also -ed forms of verbs listed at UMBER[1]

umberland \əm-bər-lənd\ Cumberland • Northumberland

umberous \əm-brəs\ see UMBROUS

umbery \əm-brē\ ombre, slumbery

umbing \əm-iŋ\ see OMING

umble \əm-bəl\ bumble, crumble, fumble, grumble, humble, jumble, mumble, rumble, scumble, stumble, tumble, umbel • rough-and-tumble

umbler \əm-blər\ bumbler, fumbler, grumbler, humbler, mumbler, rumbler, stumbler, tumbler

umbling \əm-bliŋ\ rumbling, tumbling—also -ing forms of verbs listed at UMBLE

umbly[1] \əm-blē\ crumbly, grumbly, humbly, mumbly, rumbly

umbly[2] \əm-lē\ comely, dumbly, dumly, numbly

umbness \əm-nəs\ dumbness, glumness, numbness • alumnus

umbo \əm-bō\ gumbo, jumbo, umbo • Colombo • mumbo jumbo

umbra \əm-brə\ umbra • penumbra

umbral \əm-brəl\ see UMBRIL

umbria \əm-brē-ə\ Cumbria, Umbria • Northumbria

umbril \əm-brəl\ tumbril, umbral • penumbral

umbrous \əm-brəs\ cumbrous, slumberous

ume \üm\ see OOM[1]

umed \ümd\ see OOMED

umedly \ü-məd-lē\ consumedly, presumedly

umelet \üm-lət\ see OOMLET

umely \ü-mə-lē\ see OOMILY

umen \ü-mən\ see UMAN

umenist \ü-mə-nəst\ humanist, luminist • ecumenist, illuminist, phillumenist • secular humanist

umer \ü-mər\ bloomer, Bloomer, boomer, groomer, humor, roomer, rumor, Sumer, tumor • consumer, costumer, exhumer, perfumer, presumer, schussboomer • baby boomer, gallows humor, out of humor

umeral \üm-rəl\ humeral, humoral, numeral • Roman numeral • Arabic numeral

umerous \üm-rəs\ see UMOROUS

umerus \üm-rəs\ see UMOROUS

umey \ü-mē\ see OOMY

umf \əmf\ see UMPH

umi \ü-mē\ see OOMY

umice \əm-əs\ see UMMOUS

umid \ü-məd\ humid, tumid

umin[1] \əm-ən\ cumin, summon

umin[2] \ü-mən\ see UMAN

uminal \ü-mən-ᵊl\ luminal, noumenal, ruminal • cacuminal

uminate \ü-mə-nət\ acuminate, aluminate, illuminate

umine \ü-mən\ see UMAN

uming \ü-miŋ\ blooming • consuming • everblooming, time-consuming, unassuming —*also* -ing *forms of verbs listed at* OOM[1]

uminist \ü-mə-nəst\ see UMENIST

uminous \ü-mə-nəs\ luminous, numinous • albuminous, aluminous, bituminous, ceruminous, leguminous, quadrumanous, voluminous

umma \əm-ə\ gumma, momma, summa

ummage \əm-ij\ rummage, scrummage • West Brumage

ummary[1] \əm-rē\ see UMMERY[2]

ummary[2] \əm-ə-rē\ see UMMERY[1]

ummate \əm-ət\ see UMMET

ummel \əm-əl\ see OMMEL[2]

ummell \əm-əl\ see OMMEL[2]

ummer \əm-ər\ bummer, comer, drummer, gummer, hummer, mummer, plumber, rummer, slummer, strummer, summer • latecomer, incomer, midsummer, newcomer • overcomer, snow-in-summer, up-and-comer • Indian summer —also -er forms of adjectives listed at UM[1]

ummery \əm-ə-rē\ flummery, mummery, summary, summery • Montgomery

ummet \əm-ət\ grummet, plummet, summit • consummate

ummie \əm-ē\ see UMMY

ummit \əm-ət\ see UMMET

ummock \əm-ək\ hummock, stomach

ummon \əm-ən\ see UMIN[1]

ummoner \əm-nər\ see UMNAR

ummous \əm-əs\ gummous, hummus, pomace, pumice

ummox \əm-əks\ flummox, hummocks, lummox, stomachs

ummus \əm-əs\ see UMMOUS

ummy \əm-ē\ chummy, crummie, crummy, dummy, gummy, mommy, mummy, plummy, rummy, scummy, slummy, tummy, yummy • gin rummy

umnar \əm-nər\ summoner, Sumner • columnar

umner \əm-nər\ see UMNAR

umness \əm-nəs\ see UMBNESS

umnus \əm-nəs\ see UMBNESS

umor \ü-mər\ see UMER

umoral \üm-rəl\ see UMERAL

umorous \üm-rəs\ humerus, humorous, numerous, tumorous • innumerous

umous \ü-məs\ brumous, humus, spumous • posthumous

ump \əmp\ bump, chump, clomp, clump, comp, crump, dump, flump, frump, grump, hump, jump, lump, mump, plump, pump, rump, schlump, slump, stump, sump, thump, trump, tump, ump, whump • air pump, broad jump, heat pump, high jump, long jump, mugwump, no-trump, outjump, ski jump, speed bump, sump pump, tub-thump • bungee jump, callithump, overtrump, prime the pump, quantum jump, vacuum pump • dowager's hump, hop skip and jump

umper \əm-pər\ bumper, dumper, jumper, lumper, plumper, pumper, stumper, thumper • BASE jumper, broad jumper, high jumper, long jumper, show jumper, ski jumper, smoke jumper, tubthumper • Bible-thumper, bungee jumper, puddle jumper • bumper-to-bumper

umph \əmf\ bumf, humph • galumph, harrumph

umpish \əm-pish\ dumpish, frumpish, lumpish, plumpish

umpkin \əŋ-kən\ see UNKEN

umple \əm-pəl\ crumple, rumple

umply \əm-plē\ crumply, plumply, rumply

umps \əms\ dumps, mumps • goose bumps—*also* -s, -'s, *and* -s' *forms of nouns and* -s *forms of verbs listed at* UMP

umption \əm-shən\ gumption • assumption, consumption, presumption, resumption, subsumption

umptious \əm-shəs\ bumptious, scrumptious, sumptuous • presumptuous

umptive \əm-tiv\ assumptive, consumptive, presumptive • heir presumptive

umptuous[1] \əm-chəs\ sumptuous • presumptuous

umptuous[2] \əm-shəs\ see UMPTIOUS

umpus \əm-pəs\ see OMPASS[2]

umpy \əm-pē\ bumpy, clumpy, dumpy, frumpy, grumpy, humpy, jumpy, lumpy, stumpy

umulous \ü-myə-ləs\ see UMULUS

umulus \ü-myə-ləs\ cumulous, cumulus, tumulus

umus \ü-məs\ see UMOUS

umy \ü-mē\ see OOMY

un[1] \ən\ bun, done, Donne, dun, fen, foehn, fun, gun, hon, Hun, jun, maun, none, nun, one, pun, run, shun, son, spun, stun, sun, sunn, ton, tonne, tun, won • A-1, air gun, begun, big gun, blowgun, Bull Run, burp gun, chaconne, Chang-chun, Chaplin, dry run, earned run, end run, finespun, first-run, flashgun, fordone, forerun, godson, grandson, handgun, hard-won, have done, hired gun, home run, homespun, inrun, long run, milk run, outdone, outgun, outrun, popgun, pressrun, redone, rerun, sea-run, short run, shotgun, six-gun, speargun, spray gun, squirt gun, stepson, stun gun, top gun, trial run, undone, V-1, well-done, Xiamen, zip gun • Acheron, Algonquin, allemande, all-or-none, antigun, Balzacian, Bofors gun, Browning gun, Gatling gun, give the gun, hit-and-run, jump the gun, kiloton, machine-gun, machine gun, megaton, midnight sun, one-on-one, one-to-one, on the run, overdone, overrun, pellet gun, radar gun, ride shotgun, riot gun, run-and-gun, Sally Lunn, scattergun, smoking gun, squirrel gun, tommy gun, twenty-one, underdone, underrun, water gun • alexandrine, son of a gun, submachine gun, under the gun, under the sun

un[2] \ün\ see OON[1]

un[3] \ùn\ Fushun, Lushun, tabun

una \ü-nə\ Buna, Cunha, kuna, Luna, Poona, puna, tuna • Altoona, Jamuna, kahuna, lacuna, laguna, mizuna, vicuña, Yamuna • Tristan da Cunha

uña¹ \ü-nə\ see UNA

uña² \ün-yə\ see UNIA

unal \ün-ᵊl\ communal, jejunal, lagoonal, monsoonal, tribunal

unar \ü-nər\ see OONER

unary \ü-nə-rē\ unary • buffoonery, festoonery, lampoonery, poltroonery, sublunary • superlunary

unate \ü-nət\ unit • lacunate, tribunate

unc \ənk\ see UNK

uncan \əŋ-kən\ see UNKEN

unce \əns\ dunce, once—also -s, -'s, and -s' forms of nouns and -s forms of verbs listed at ONT¹

unch \ənch\ brunch, bunch, crunch, hunch, lunch, munch, punch, scrunch • big crunch, box lunch, free lunch, keypunch, milk punch • counterpunch, one-two punch, out to lunch, planter's punch, ploughman's lunch, pull a punch, rabbit punch, sucker punch • beat to the punch, eat someone's lunch

unche \ənch\ see UNCH

uncheon \ən-chən\ luncheon, puncheon, truncheon

uncher \ən-chər\ cruncher, luncher, muncher • cowpuncher, keypuncher • counterpuncher, number cruncher

unchy \ən-chē\ bunchy, crunchy, punchy, scrunchy

uncial \ən-sē-əl\ uncial • quincuncial • internuncial

uncle \əŋ-kəl\ nuncle, uncle • carbuncle, caruncle, Dutch uncle, furuncle, granduncle, great-uncle, peduncle, say uncle

unco¹ \əŋ-kō\ bunco, junco, unco

unco² \əŋ-kə\ see UNKAH

unct \əŋt\ trunked • adjunct, conjunct, defunct, disjunct —also -ed forms of verbs listed at UNK

unction \əŋ-shən\ function, junction, unction • adjunction, cofunction, compunction, conjunction, disjunction, dysfunction, expunction, injunction, malfunction, subjunction • extreme unction

unctional \əŋ-shnəl\ functional, junctional • conjunctional, dysfunctional, nonfunctional

unctious \əŋ-shəs\ compunctious, rambunctious

uncture \əŋ-chər\ juncture, puncture • conjuncture, disjuncture • acupuncture, lumbar puncture

uncular \əŋ-kyə-lər\ avuncular, carbuncular, peduncular

unculus \əŋ-kyə-ləs\ homunculus, ranunculus

und¹ \ənd\ bund, fund, gunned • dachshund, defund, hedge fund, obtund, refund, rotund, secund, slush fund, trust fund • cummerbund, orotund,

overfund, pudibund, rubicund, sinking fund, underfund
• mutual fund—*also*-ed *forms of verbs listed at* UN[1]

und[2] \und\ bund • dachshund

und[3] \unt\ see UNT[1]

und[4] \aund\ see OUND[2]

unda \ən-də\ Munda, Sunda
• osmunda, rotunda
• barramunda, floribunda

undae \ən-dē\ see UNDI[1]

undant \ən-dənt\ abundant, redundant • nonredundant
• overabundant, superabundant

unday \ən-dē\ see UNDI[1]

undays \ən-dēz\ Mondays, Sundays, undies—*also* -s, -'s, *and* -s' *forms of nouns listed at* UNDI[1]

undem \ən-dəm\ see UNDUM

under \ən-dər\ Bandar, blunder, funder, plunder, sunder, thunder, under, wonder
• asunder, down under, go under, hereunder, plow under, snow under, thereunder
• knuckle under, steal one's thunder • build a fire under

underous \ən-drəs\ plunderous, thunderous, wondrous

undi \ən-dē\ Monday, sundae, Sunday • Whitmonday, Whitsunday • barramundi, Bay of Fundy, jaguarundi, Mrs. Grundy, salmagundi
• coatimundi

undies \ən-dēz\ see UNDAYS

undity \ən-dət-ē\ fecundity, jocundity, profundity, rotundity
• moribundity, orotundity, rubicundity

undle \ən-dᵊl\ bundle, rundle, trundle • unbundle

undness \ən-nəs\ see ONENESS

undum \ən-dəm\ corundum • ad eundem, Carborundum

undy \ən-dē\ see UNDI[1]

une \ün\ see OON[1]

uneau \ü-nō\ see UNO

uneless \ün-ləs\ see OONLESS

uner \ü-nər\ see OONER

unes \ünz\ see OONS

ung[1] \əŋ\ brung, bung, clung, dung, flung, hung, lung, mung, pung, rung, slung, sprung, strung, stung, sung, swung, tongue, tung, wrung, young, Young • among, bee-stung, black lung, brown lung, cliff-hung, far-flung, forked tongue, hamstrung, high-strung, iron lung, Kaifeng, low-slung, unstrung, unsung, well-hung, with young • adder's-tongue, Aqua-Lung, bite one's tongue, double-hung, double-tongue, egg foo yong, farmer's lung, hold one's tongue, mother tongue, triple-tongue, overhung, overstrung, underslung

ung[2] \uŋ\ Jung, Kung, Sung
• Antung, Bandung, Dandong, Dadong, Hamhung, Tatung, Zigong • Nibelung
• geländesprung
• Götterdämmerung

ungal \ən-gəl\ see UNGLE

unge \ənj\ grunge, lunge, plunge, sponge • expunge • take the plunge

unged \ənd\ see ONGUED

ungeon \ən-jən\ donjon, dungeon, spongin

unger[1] \ən-jər\ grunger, lunger, plunger, sponger • expunger

unger[2] \əŋ-gər\ see ONGER[1]

ungible \ən-jə-bəl\ fungible • inexpungible

ungle \əŋ-gəl\ bungle, fungal, jungle, pungle • asphalt jungle

ungo \əŋ-gō\ fungo, mungo

ungous \əŋ-gəs\ fungous, fungus • humongous

ungry \ən-grē\ see ONGERY

ungus \əŋ-gəs\ see UNGOUS

ungy \ən-jē\ grungy, spongy

unha \ü-nə\ see UNA

uni \ü-nē\ see OONY

unia \ün-yə\ petunia, vicuña

unic \ü-nik\ eunuch, Munich, Punic, runic, tunic

unicate \ü-ni-kət\ tunicate • excommunicate

unich \ü-nik\ see UNIC

union \ən-yən\ bunion, grunion, onion, ronyon, trunnion • Paul Bunyan

unis \ü-nəs\ see EWNESS

unish[1] \ən-ish\ Hunnish, punish

unish[2] \ü-nish\ see OONISH

unit \ü-nət\ see UNATE

unitive \ü-nət-iv\ punitive, unitive • nonpunitive

unity \ü-nət-ē\ unity • community, disunity, immunity, impunity • importunity, opportunity

unk \əŋk\ bunk, chunk, clunk, drunk, dunk, flunk, funk, gunk, hunk, junk, monk, plunk, punk, shrunk, skunk, slunk, spunk, stunk, sunk, thunk, trunk • bohunk, chipmunk, debunk, Podunk, preshrunk, punch-drunk, quidnunc, slam dunk • countersunk, cyberpunk, hic et nunc, steamer trunk • Saratoga trunk

unkah \əŋ-kə\ punkah, unco

unkard \əŋ-kərd\ bunkered, drunkard, Dunkard, hunkered

unked \əŋt\ see UNCT

unken \əŋ-kən\ Duncan, drunken, pumpkin, shrunken, sunken

unker \əŋ-kər\ bunker, Bunker, clunker, Dunker, flunker, hunker, junker, lunker, plunker, punker, younker • debunker, spelunker

unkie \əŋ-kē\ see UNKY

unkin \əŋ-kəm\ see UNCAN

unks \əŋs\ hunks • quincunx —also -s, -'s, and -s' forms of nouns and -s forms of verbs listed at UNK

unky \əŋ-kē\ chunky, clunky, donkey, flunky, funky, gunky, hunky, Hunky, junkie, junky, monkey, punkie, punky, skunky, spunkie, spunky • grease monkey

unless \ən-ləs\ runless, sonless, sunless

unn \ən\ see UN

unnage \ən-ij\ dunnage, tonnage • megatonnage

unned \ənd\ see UND[1]

unnel \ən-ᵊl\ funnel, gunnel, gunwale, runnel, trunnel, tunnel • wind tunnel • carpal tunnel

unner \ən-ər\ cunner, gunner, runner, scunner, shunner, stunner, tonner • base runner, forerunner, front-runner, gunrunner, race runner, roadrunner, rumrunner, shotgunner, stretch runner • machine gunner

unnery \ən-rē\ gunnery, nunnery

unness \ən-nəs\ see ONENESS

unning \ən-iŋ\ cunning, running, stunning • baserunning, gunrunning, hand running, rum-running • blockade-running, in the running • hit the ground running, out of the running —also -ing forms of verbs listed at UN[1]

unnion \ən-yən\ see UNION

unnish \ən-ish\ see UNISH[1]

unny \ən-ē\ bunny, funny, gunny, honey, money, punny, runny, sonny, sunny, tunny • blood money, dust bunny, mad money, pin money, prize money, seed money, smart money, unfunny • Ballymoney, even money, for one's money, funny money, on the money, pocket money, spending money • run for one's money

uno \ü-nō\ Bruno, Juneau, Juno, uno • numero uno

unster \ən-stər\ Muenster, punster

unt¹ \unt\ dachshund, Dortmund • exeunt

unt² \ənt\ see ONT[1]

untal \ənt-ᵊl\ see UNTLE

unter \ənt-ər\ blunter, bunter, chunter, grunter, hunter, punter, shunter • confronter, foxhunter, headhunter, pot-hunter, white hunter, witch-hunter • bounty hunter, fortune hunter

unting \ənt-iŋ\ bunting • foxhunting, head-hunting, pothunting, witch-hunting —also -ing forms of verbs listed at ONT[1]

untle \ənt-ᵊl\ frontal, gruntle • confrontal, disgruntle • contrapuntal

unty \ənt-ē\ punty, runty

unwale \ən-ᵊl\ see UNNEL

unx \əŋs\ see UNKS

uny \ü-nē\ see OONY

unyan \ən-yən\ see UNION

uoth \ü-əs\ see EWESS

uoy¹ \ü-ē\ see EWY

uoy² \öi\ see OY

uoyance \ü-əns\ see OYANCE

uoyancy \ȯi-ən-sē\ see OYANCY

uoyant \ȯi-ənt\ see OYANT

up \əp\ cup, dup, hup, pup, scup, sup, tup, up, yup • act up, add up, backup, back up, balls-up, ball up, bang-up, bear up, beat-up, beat up, belt up, bid up, blowup, blow up, bone up, bound up, breakup, break up, bring up, brush up, buck up, buildup, build up, built-up, bulk up, bung up, buy up, call-up, catch-up, chalk up, change-up, checkup, chin-up, choose up, clam up, cleanup, clean up, close-up, close up, cock-up, come up, cough up, crack-up, cry up, curl up, cutup, cut up, death cup, dial-up, dial up, dig up, doll up, do up, draw up, dream up, dress up, dried-up, drive-up, drum up, dry up, dustup, eggcup, eyecup, faceup, face up, fed up, feel up, fetch up, fill-up, fill up, fix up, flare-up, foul-up, foul up, frame-up, fry-up, fry up, gang up, gear up, getup, get up, giddap, give up, go up, grade up, grown-up, grow up, hand up, hang-up, hang up, hard up, heads-up, hepped up, het up, hiccup, hitch up, holdup, hold up, hole up, hookup, hook up, hopped-up, hot up, hung up, hyped-up, jack-up, jam-up, juice up, keep up, kickup, kick up, kingcup, knock up, lash-up, lay-up, lead-up, leg up, letup, let up, lie up, line up, linkup, lit up, lockup, lookup, look up, louse up, made-up, makeup, make up, markup, matchup, mix-up, mixed-up, mock-up, mop-up, muck up, mug up, nip-up, one-up, pass up, pasteup, pay up, pickup, pick up, pileup, pinup, pipe up, play up, pop-up, post up, prenup, press-up, pull-up, pump up, punch-up, push-up, put-up, rack up, rake up, ramp up, re-up, ring up, roll up, roundup, round up, rub up, run-up, scaleup, scare up, screwup, screw up, send-up, setup, set up, sew up, shack up, shake-up, shape-up, shape up, shook-up, shoot up, show up, shut up, sign up, sit-up, size up, slap-up, slipup, slip up, smashup, souped-up, soup up, speak up, speedup, spiffed-up, spit up, stack up, stand-up, start-up, steam up, step up, stepped-up, stickup, stick up, stink up, strike up, stuck-up, sum up, sunup, tag up, take up, talk up, tart up, teacup, tear up, throw up, thumbs-up, tie-up, top up, toss-up, touch-up, trade up, trumped-up, tune-up, turn up, use up, wait up, wake up, walk-up, warm-up, washed-up, washup, windup, wised-up, workup, work up, wrap-up, write-up • belly-up, belly up, bottom-up, buckle up, bundle up, buttercup, butter up, buttoned-up, cover-up, cover up, cozy up, double up, dummy up, fancy up, follow-up, giddyup, gussy up, higher-up, hurry up, lighten up, live it up, loosen up, loving cup, measure up, mix it up, open up, pick-me-up, pony up, power up, runner-up, seven-up, shoot-'em-up, stirrup cup, suck it up, suction cup, summing-up, up-and-up, wickiup, winding-up • from the ground up, Johnny-jump-up, sunny-side up

upa \ü-pə\ pupa, stupa • chalupa

upas \ü-pəs\ see UPUS

upboard \əb-ərd\ see UBBARD

upe \üp\ see OOP[1]

upel \ü-pəl\ see UPLE[2]

upelet \ü-plət\ see UPLET[2]

uper \ü-pər\ see OOPER

upi \ü-pē\ see OOPY

upid \ü-pəd\ Cupid, stupid

upil \ü-pəl\ see UPLE[2]

uple[1] \əp-əl\ couple, supple • decouple, quadruple, quintuple, sextuple, uncouple

uple[2] \ü-pəl\ cupel, duple, pupil, scruple • quadruple, quintuple, sextuple

uplet[1] \əp-lət\ couplet • quadruplet, quintuplet, sextuplet

uplet[2] \ü-plət\ drupelet • quadruplet

uplicate \ü-pli-kət\ duplicate • quadruplicate, quintuplicate, sextuplicate

upor \ü-pər\ see OOPER

uppance \əp-əns\ threepence, twopence • comeuppance

upper \əp-ər\ crupper, scupper, supper, upper • Last Supper, Lord's Supper, stand-upper • builder-upper, fixer-upper

uppie \əp-ē\ see UPPY

upple[1] \üp-əl\ see UPLE[3]

upple[2] \əp-əl\ see UPLE[1]

uppy \əp-ē\ buppie, cuppy, guppy, puppy, yuppie • hush puppy, mud puppy

upt \əpt\ abrupt, bankrupt, corrupt, disrupt, erupt, irrupt • developed, incorrupt, interrupt—*also* -ed *forms of verbs listed at* UP

upter \əp-tər\ corrupter, disrupter • interrupter

uptible \əp-tə-bəl\ corruptible, eruptible, irruptible • incorruptible, interruptible

uption \əp-shən\ abruption, corruption, disruption, eruption, irruption • interruption

uptive \əp-tiv\ corruptive, disruptive, eruptive, irruptive • interruptive, nondisruptive

upus \ü-pəs\ lupus, upas

uq \ük\ see UKE

uque \ük\ see UKE

ur[1] \or\ see OR[1]

ur[2] \ur\ see URE[1]

ur[3] \ər\ see EUR[1]

ura \ur-ə\ crura, dura, durra, Jura, Kura, pleura, sura, surah • Agoura, bravura, caesura, datura, Madura, tamboura, tempura • aqua pura, Arafura,

Bujumbura, sprezzatura, tessitura • acciaccatura, appoggiatura, bella figura, Bonaventura, coloratura, Estremadura, fioritura • camera obscura

urable \ùr-ə-bəl\ curable, durable, thurible • endurable, incurable, insurable, nondurable, perdurable, procurable • unendurable, uninsurable

uracy \ùr-ə-sē\ curacy • obduracy

urae \ùr-ē\ see URY[1]

urah \ùr-ə\ see URA

ural \ùr-əl\ crural, jural, mural, neural, pleural, plural, puerile, rural, Ural • caesural, subdural • commissural, epidural, extramural, intramural, semirural • caricatural

uralist \ùr-ə-ləst\ muralist, pluralist, ruralist

uran \ü-rən\ see URIN[2]

urance \ùr-əns\ durance • assurance, endurance, insurance • coinsurance, health insurance, life insurance, reassurance, reinsurance, self-assurance

urate \ùr-ət\ curate, turret • indurate, obdurate • barbiturate

urative \ùr-ə-tiv\ curative, durative

urb \ərb\ see ERB

urban \ər-bən\ bourbon, Bourbon, Durban, rurban, turban, turbine, urban, Urban • exurban, nonurban, steam turbine, suburban, wind turbine • interurban

urber \ər-bər\ Berber, Ferber, Thurber • disturber

urbia \ər-bē-ə\ Serbia • exurbia, suburbia

urbid \ər-bəd\ turbid, verbid

urbine \ər-bən\ see URBAN[1]

urbit \ər-bət\ burbot, sherbet, turbot • cucurbit

urble \ər-bəl\ see ERBAL

urbot \ər-bət\ see URBIT

urcate \ər-kət\ see IRCUIT

urch \ərch\ birch, church, Church, curch, lurch, merch, perch, search, smirch • besmirch, Christchurch, research, strip-search, unchurch • antichurch

urchin \ər-chən\ birchen, urchin • sea urchin

urchly \ərch-lē\ churchly, virtually

urcia \ər-shə\ see ERTIA

urd[1] \ùrd\ see URED[1]

urd[2] \ərd\ see IRD

urdane \ərd-ᵉn\ see URDEN

urden \ərd-ᵉn\ burden, guerdon, lurdane, verdin • disburden, unburden • beast of burden, overburden, white man's burden

urder \ərd-ər\ see ERDER

urderer \ərd-ər-ər\ murderer, verderer

urdle \ərd-ᵉl\ curdle, girdle, hurdle • engirdle

urdu \ər-dü\ see ERDU

urdum \ərd-əm\ see IRDUM

urdy \ərd-ē\ birdie, curdy, sturdy, wordy • hurdy-gurdy, Mesa Verde, Monteverdi

ure¹ \ur\ Boer, boor, bourg, cure, dour, ewer, fewer, lure, moor, Moor, Moore, Muir, poor, pure, Ruhr, sewer, skewer, spoor, stour, sure, tour, Tours, your, you're • abjure, adjure, Adour, allure, amour, Ashur, assure, brochure, ceinture, cocksure, coiffure, conjure, contour, couture, demure, detour, dirt-poor, endure, ensure, Exmoor, faubourg, for sure, Fraktur, grandeur, gravure, guipure, hachure, immure, impure, insure, inure, kultur, land-poor, langur, ligure, manure, mature, mohur, obscure, parure, perdure, procure, rondure, secure, siddur, tambour, tandoor, tenure, Uighur, unmoor, unsure, velour, velure • amateur, aperture, armature, blackamoor, carrefour, carte du jour, coinsure, commissure, confiture, connoisseur, coverture, cubature, curvature, cynosure, embouchure, epicure, filature, forfeiture, garniture, geniture, green-manure, haute couture, immature, insecure, ligature, manicure, nonsecure, overcure, overture, paramour, pedicure, plat du jour, portraiture, prelature, premature, quadrature, reassure, Reaumur, reinsure, saboteur, sepulture, sequitur, signature, simon-pure, sinecure, soup du jour, tablature, temperature, to be sure, troubadour, vavasour, white amur, Yom Kippur • candidature, caricature, discomfiture, distemperature, divestiture, entablature, entrepreneur, expenditure, imprimatur, investiture, literature, miniature, musculature, nomenclature, non sequitur • primogeniture

ure² \ur-ē\ see URY¹

urean \ur-ē-ən\ see URIAN

ureau \ur-ō\ see URO

ured¹ \urd\ gourd, gourde, Kurd, urd • assured, steward • off one's gourd, self-assured • out of one's gourd, underinsured —also -ed forms of verbs listed at URE¹

ured² \ərd\ see IRD

urely \ur-lē\ buirdly, poorly, purely, surely • cocksurely, demurely, impurely, maturely, obscurely, securely • immaturely, insecurely, prematurely

urement \ur-mənt\ allurement, immurement, inurement, procurement, securement

uren \ur-ən\ see URIN²

ureous \ur-ē-əs\ see URIOUS

urer \ur-ər\ curer, führer, furor, furore, juror, lurer, tourer • abjurer, assurer, insurer, manurer, procurer, tambourer • coinsurer, reinsurer—also -er *forms of adjectives listed at* URE[1]

urety[1] \ur-ət-ē\ see URITY

urety[2] \urt-ē\ see URTI

urey \ur-ē\ see URY[1]

urf \ərf\ kerf, scurf, serf, surf, turf • enserf, windsurf • Astroturf, bodysurf, channel surf, surf and turf

urfy \ər-fē\ Murphy, scurfy, turfy

urg \ərg\ see ERG

urgative \ər-gə-tiv\ see URGATIVE

urge \ərj\ dirge, merge, purge, scourge, serge, splurge, spurge, surge, urge, verge • converge, deterge, diverge, emerge, immerge, resurge, submerge, upsurge • demiurge, dramaturge, reemerge, thaumaturge

urgence \ər-jəns\ see ERGENCE

urgency \ər-jən-sē\ see ERGENCY

urgent \ər-jənt\ urgent • assurgent, convergent, detergent, divergent, emergent, insurgent, resurgent • preemergent • counterinsurgent

urgeon \ər-jən\ burgeon, sturgeon, surgeon, virgin • tree surgeon • plastic surgeon

urger[1] \ər-gər\ burger, burgher, turgor • cheeseburger, hamburger, Limburger • Luxembourger, veggie burger

urger[2] \ər-jər\ see ERGER

urgery \ərj-rē\ see ERJURY

urgh[1] \ər-ə\ see OROUGH[1]

urgh[2] \ər-ō\ see URROW[1]

urgh[3] \ərg\ see ERG

urgher \ər-gər\ see URGER[1]

urgic \ər-jik\ see ERGIC

urgical \ər-ji-kəl\ surgical • liturgical, theurgical • demiurgical, dramaturgical, metallurgical

urgid \ər-jəd\ turgid • synergid

urgle \ər-gəl\ burgle, gurgle

urgor \ər-gər\ see URGER[1]

urgy \ər-jē\ clergy • theurgy • dramaturgy, metallurgy, thaumaturgy

uri \ur-ē\ see URY[1]

urial[1] \ur-ē-əl\ curial, urial, Uriel • manurial, mercurial, seigneurial, tenurial • entrepreneurial

urial[2] \er-ē-əl\ see ARIAL

urian \ur-ē-ən\ durian, Hurrian • Arthurian, Asturian, centurion, Etrurian, Ligurian, Manchurian, Masurian, Missourian, Silurian • Canterburian, epicurean, holothurian, Khachaturian

uriance \ur-ē-əns\ see URIENCE

uriant \ur-ē-ənt\ see URIENT

urible[1] \ur-ə-bəl\ see URABLE

urible[2] \er-ə-bəl\ see ERABLE

uric \ur-ik\ uric • anuric, mercuric, purpuric, sulfuric, telluric • barbituric

urid \ur-əd\ lurid, murid

urie \ür-ē\ see URY[1]

uriel \ür-ē-əl\ see URIAL[1]

urience \ür-ē-əns\ prurience
• esurience, luxuriance

urient \ür-ē-ənt\ prurient
• esurient, luxuriant, parturient

urier[1] \er-ē-ər\ see ERRIER

urier[2] \ür-ē-ər\ see OURIER[1]

uriere \ür-ē-ər\ see OURIER[1]

urin[1] \ər-ən\ burin, murrain

urin[2] \ür-ən\ burin, Huron, urine

urine \ür-ən\ see URIN[2]

uring \ür-iŋ\ during, mooring, touring, Turing • alluring, enduring—also -ing forms of verbs listed at URE[1]

urion \ür-ē-ən\ see URIAN

urious \ür-ē-əs\ curious, furious, spurious • incurious, injurious, luxurious, penurious, perjurious, sulfureous, uncurious, usurious

uris \ür-əs\ see URUS

urist \ür-əst\ jurist, purist, tourist
• manicurist, pedicurist
• caricaturist, chiaroscurist, miniaturist—also -est forms of adjectives listed at URE[1]

urity \ür-ət-ē\ purity, surety
• futurity, impurity, maturity, obscurity, security • immaturity, insecurity, prematurity • Social Security

urk \ərk\ see ORK[1]

urka \ər-kə\ burka, charka, circa, Gurkha • mazurka

urke \ərk\ see ORK[1]

urker \ər-kər\ see ORKER[1]

urkey \ər-kē\ see ERKY

urkha[1] \ür-kə\ see URKA[2]

urkha[2] \ər-kə\ see URKA[1]

urki \ər-kē\ see ERKY

urky \ər-kē\ see ERKY

url \ərl\ see IRL[1]

urled \ərld\ see ORLD

urlew \ərl-ü\ curlew, purlieu

urlieu \ərl-ü\ see URLEW

urlin \ər-lən\ see ERLIN

urling \ər-liŋ\ curling, hurling, sterling—also -ing forms of verbs listed at IRL[1]

urlish \ər-lish\ churlish, girlish

urly \ər-lē\ burley, burly, curly, early, girlie, hurly, knurly, pearly, squirrely, surly, swirly, twirly, whirly • hurly-burly

urman \ər-mən\ see ERMAN

urmity \ər-mət-ē\ see IRMITY

urmur \ər-mər\ firmer, murmur, termer, wormer • infirmer

urn \ərn\ Bern, burn, churn, curn, earn, erne, fern, kern, learn, pirn, quern, spurn, stern, tern, terne, turn, urn, yearn
• adjourn, astern, attorn, casern, concern, discern, downturn, epergne, eterne, extern, heartburn, Hepburn, intern, in turn, inurn, kick turn, lucerne, Lucerne, nocturn, nocturne, outturn, return, sauternes, secern, sojourn, star turn, stem turn, step turn,

sunburn, unlearn, upturn, U-turn, windburn • about-turn, Arctic tern, Comintern, in return, on the turn, out of turn, overturn, slash-and-burn, taciturn, to a turn, unconcern • at every turn, from stem to stern • point of no return

urnable \ər-nə-bəl\ burnable, turnable • discernible, returnable • indiscernible, nonreturnable

urnal \ərn-ᵊl\ see ERNAL

urne \ərn\ see URN

urned \ərnd\ burned, durned • concerned, sunburned, unearned, unlearned, well-turned, windburned—*also* -ed *forms of verbs listed at* URN

urner \ər-nər\ burner, earner, turner • discerner, returner • afterburner

urnery \ər-nə-rē\ see ERNARY

urney \ər-nē\ see OURNEY¹

urnian \ər-nē-ən\ see ERNIAN

urnish \ər-nish\ burnish, furnish • refurnish

urnt \ərnt\ see EARNT

urnum \ər-nəm\ sternum • laburnum, viburnum

uro \ùr-ō\ bureau, duro, euro, Euro • enduro, maduro • in futuro, politburo, travel bureau, weather bureau • chiaroscuro

uron \ùr-ən\ see URIN²

uror \ùr-ər\ see URER¹

urore \ùr-ər\ see URER¹

urous \ùr-əs\ see URUS

urp \ərp\ burp, chirp, perp, slurp, stirp, twerp • Antwerp, usurp

urphy \ər-fē\ see URFY

urplice \ər-pləs\ see URPLUS

urps \ərps\ see IRPS

urr \ər\ see EUR¹

urra¹ \ùr-ə\ see URA

urra² \ər-ə\ see OROUGH¹

urrage \ər-ij\ see OURAGE

urragh \ər-ə\ see OROUGH¹

urrain \ər-ən\ see URIN¹

urral \ər-əl\ see ERRAL

urrant \ər-ənt\ see URRENT

urray \ər-ē\ see URRY

urre \ər\ see EUR¹

urred \ərd\ see IRD

urrence \ər-əns\ concurrence, conference, deterrence, incurrence, occurrence, recurrence, transference • reoccurrence

urrent \ər-ənt\ currant, current, weren't • concurrent, crosscurrent, decurrent, deterrent, excurrent, incurrent, noncurrent, occurrent, recurrent, rip current, susurrant • countercurrent, undercurrent, supercurrent

urrer \ər-ər\ see ERRER

urret \ùr-ət\ see URATE

urrey \ər-ē\ see URRY

urrian \ùr-ē-ən\ see URIAN

urrie \ər-ē\ see URRY

urrier \ər-ē-ər\ courier, currier, furrier, hurrier, worrier—*also -er forms of adjectives listed at* URRY

urring \ər-iŋ\ furring, shirring, stirring—*also -ing forms of verbs listed at* EUR[1]

urrish \ər-ish\ see OURISH

urro[1] \ər-ə\ see OROUGH[1]

urro[2] \ər-ō\ see URROW[1]

urrow[1] \ər-ō\ borough, burgh, burro, burrow, furrow, Murrow, thorough • Marlborough • interborough, pocket borough

urrow[2] \ər-ə\ see OROUGH[1]

urry \ər-ē\ blurry, burry, curry, flurry, furry, dhurrie, gurry, hurry, Moray, Murray, murrey, scurry, slurry, spurrey, surrey, Surrey, whirry, worry • hurry-scurry, in a hurry

ursa \ər-sə\ see ERSA

ursal \ər-səl\ see ERSAL[1]

ursar \ər-sər\ see URSOR

ursary \ərs-rē\ bursary, cursory, mercery, nursery • day nursery • anniversary

urse \ərs\ see ERSE

ursed \ərst\ see URST

ursement \ər-smənt\ see ERCEMENT

urser \ər-sər\ see URSOR

ursery \ərs-rē\ see URSARY

ursion \ər-zhən\ see ERSION[1]

ursionist \ərzh-nəst\ see ERSIONIST

ursive \ər-siv\ see ERSIVE

ursor \ər-sər\ bursar, cursor, mercer, nurser, purser, worser • converser, disburser, disperser, precursor, rehearser, reverser, traverser

ursory \ərs-rē\ see URSARY

urst \ərst\ burst, cursed, durst, erst, first, Hearst, thirst, verst, worst, wurst • accursed, airburst, Amherst, at first, athirst, bratwurst, cloudburst, downburst, emersed, face-first, feetfirst, groundburst, headfirst, knockwurst, outburst, starburst, sunburst • liverwurst, microburst, wienerwurst—*also -ed forms of verbs listed at* ERSE

ursus \ər-səs\ see ERSUS

ursy[1] \ər-sē\ see ERCY

ursy[2] \əs-ē\ see USSY

urt[1] \u̇rt\ yurt • Erfurt, Frankfurt • Betancourt

urt[2] \ərt\ see ERT[1]

urtain \ərt-ən\ see ERTAIN

urtal \ərt-əl\ see ERTILE

urtenance \ərt-ən-əns\ see ERTINENCE

urtenant \ərt-nənt\ see IRTINENT

urter \ərt-ər\ see ERTER

urtesy \ərt-ə-sē\ see OURTESY

urther \ər-thər\ further, murther

urti \u̇rt-ē\ surety • Trimurti

urtium \ər-shəm\ nasturtium, sestertium

urtive \ərt-iv\ see ERTIVE

urtle \ərt-ᵊl\ see ERTILE

urton \ərt-ᵊn\ see ERTAIN

urture \ər-chər\ see IRCHER

uru \u̇r-ü\ guru, kuru • Nauru

urus \u̇r-əs\ urus • Arcturus,
mercurous, sulfurous
• Epicurus, eremurus, sui juris
• tinea cruris

urve \ərv\ see ERVE

urved \ərvd\ see ERVED

urviness \ər-vē-nəs\ see ERVINESS

urvy \ər-vē\ curvy, nervy, scurvy
• topsy-turvy

ury¹ \u̇r-ē\ curie, Curie, fleury,
fury, houri, Jewry, jury, Kure,
Urey • Bhojpuri, de jure, grand
jury, Missouri, tandoori • lusus
naturae

ury² \er-ē\ see ARY¹

urze \ərz\ see ERS

urzy \ər-zē\ see ERSEY

us¹ \əs\ bus, buss, crus, cuss,
fuss, Gus, Huss, muss, plus,
pus, Russ, suss, thus, truss, us
• airbus, concuss, cost-plus,
discuss, nonplus, percuss,
railbus, school bus, surplus,
untruss • autobus,
blunderbuss, Gloomy Gus,
harquebus, microbus, minibus,
motor bus, omnibus, overplus,
trolleybus • eleven-plus

us² \ü\ see EW¹

us³ \üs\ see USE¹

us⁴ \üsh\ see OUCHE

us⁵ \üz\ see USE²

usa¹ \ü-sə\ Coosa, Sousa
• Azusa, medusa, Medusa
• Appaloosa, barbirusa, Gebel
Musa, Jebel Musa, Siracusa,
Tallapoosa, Tuscaloosa

usa² \ü-zə\ Sousa, Susa
• medusa, Medusa • Arethusa

usable \ü-zə-bəl\ fusible,
losable, usable • abusable,
diffusible, excusable, infusible,
protrusible, reusable, trans-
fusible, unusable • inexcusable,
irrecusable, nonreusable

usae \ü-sē\ see UICY

usal¹ \ü-səl\ streusel • occlusal,
recusal

usal² \ü-zəl\ foozle, fusil, ouzel,
snoozle, streusel • accusal,
bamboozle, occlusal, perusal,
refusal

usc \əsk\ see USK

uscan \əs-kən\ buskin, Ruskin,
Tuscan • Etruscan, molluscan

uscat \əs-kət\ see USKET

uscle \əs-əl\ see USTLE

uscular \əs-kyə-lər\ muscular
• corpuscular, crepuscular,
majuscular

uscule \əs-kyül\ crepuscule,
groupuscule, majuscule,
opuscule

use¹ \üs\ Bruce, crouse, crus,
cruse, deuce, douce, goose,
juice, loose, Luce, moose,
mousse, noose, nous, puce,
rhus, ruse, Russ, schuss,
Seuss, sluice, spruce, truce,
use, Zeus • Aarhus, abstruse,

abuse, adduce, Arhus, Atreus, blue spruce, bull moose, burnoose, caboose, Cayuse, Cepheus, ceruse, charmeuse, chartreuse, Chartreuse, conduce, couscous, cut loose, deduce, diffuse, disuse, educe, effuse, excuse, fair use, footloose, hang loose, induce, Lanús, misuse, mixed use, mongoose, Morpheus, negus, obtuse, Orpheus, papoose, Peleus, Perseus, prepuce, produce, profuse, Proteus, Purus, recluse, red spruce, reduce, refuse, retuse, reuse, Sanctus, seduce, slip noose, snow goose, Tereus, Theseus, traduce, transduce, turn loose, unloose, vamoose • Belarus, Betelgeuse, calaboose, charlotte russe, cook one's goose, fast and loose, flag of truce, introduce, mass-produce, Mother Goose, multiuse, Odysseus, overuse, Prometheus, reproduce, self-abuse, Syracuse, Typhoeus, widow's cruse • Canada goose, hypotenuse • Sancti Spiritus

use² \üz\ blues, booze, bruise, choose, cruise, cruse, Druze, flews, fuse, Hughes, lose, Meuse, muse, news, ooze, Ouse, roose, ruse, schmooze, snooze, trews, use, whose • abuse, accuse, amuse, Andrews, bad news, bemuse, berceuse, chanteuse, charmeuse, chartreuse, coiffeuse, confuse, contuse, danseuse, defuse, diffuse, diseuse, disuse, effuse, Elbrus, enthuse, excuse, ill-use, incuse, infuse, j'accuse, masseuse, misuse, perfuse, peruse, recluse, recuse, refuse, reuse, short fuse, suffuse, Toulouse, transfuse, vendeuse • Betelgeuse, circumfuse, disabuse, interfuse, mitrailleuse, Newport News, overuse, p's and q's, Santa Cruz, Syracuse, Veracruz, widow's cruse • Goody Two-shoes, hypotenuse

used \üzd\ used • confused • underused—also -ed forms of verbs listed at USE²

useless \ü-sləs\ juiceless, useless

user \ü-zər\ boozer, bruiser, chooser, cruiser, doozer, loser, muser, schmoozer, snoozer, user • abuser, accuser, amuser, diffuser, end user, excuser, infuser, misuser, nonuser, peruser, refuser • battle cruiser, cabin cruiser, multiuser

ush¹ \əsh\ blush, brush, crush, Cush, flush, gush, hush, lush, mush, plush, rush, shush, slush, squush, thrush, tush • airbrush, broad-brush, bull rush, bulrush, bum-rush, bum's rush, four-flush, gold rush, hairbrush, hot flush, hush-hush, inrush, nailbrush, onrush, paintbrush, sagebrush, scrub brush, song thrush, straight flush, toothbrush, uprush, wood thrush • bottlebrush, hermit thrush, Hindu Kush, royal flush, underbrush

ush² \ùsh\ bush, Bush, Cush, mush, push, shush, squoosh, swoosh, tush, whoosh • ambush, bell push, cost-push, rosebush, spicebush, thornbush • beauty bush, burning bush, Hindu Kush, sugar bush • beat around the bush

ushable \ə-shə-bəl\ crushable, flushable

usher¹ \əsh-ər\ blusher, brusher, crusher, gusher, musher, rusher, usher • four-flusher, gold rusher—*also* -er *forms of adjectives listed at* USH¹

usher² \ùsh-ər\ pusher • ambusher, pen pusher • pencil pusher

ushi \ùsh-ē\ see USHY²

ushing \əsh-iɳ\ onrushing, toothbrushing, unblushing —*also* -ing *forms of verbs listed at* USH¹

ushu \ü-shü\ Kyushu, wushu • Kitakyushu

ushy¹ \əsh-ē\ brushy, gushy, mushy, plushy, rushy, slushy

ushy² \ùsh-ē\ bushy, cushy, mushy, pushy, sushi

usi \ü-sē\ see UICY

usian \ü-zhən\ see USION

usible¹ \ü-sə-bəl\ see UCIBLE

usible² \ü-zə-bəl\ see USABLE

usic \ü-zik\ music • Tungusic

usie \ü-zē\ see OOZY

usil \ü-zəl\ see USAL²

using \əs-iɳ\ busing, trussing • antibusing—*also* -ing *forms of verbs listed at* US¹

usion \ü-zhən\ fusion • affusion, allusion, Carthusian, collusion, conclusion, confusion, contusion, delusion, diffusion, effusion, elusion, exclusion, extrusion, illusion, inclusion, infusion, intrusion, Malthusian, obtrusion, occlusion, perfusion, prelusion, profusion, prolusion, protrusion, reclusion, seclusion, transfusion, Venusian • Andalusian, circumfusion, disillusion, interfusion, malocclusion • foregone conclusion • optical illusion

usionist \üzh-nəst\ fusionist • diffusionist, exclusionist, illusionist, perfusionist

usity \ü-sət-ē\ see UCITY

usive \ü-siv\ abusive, allusive, amusive, collusive, conclusive, conducive, delusive, diffusive, effusive, elusive, exclusive, extrusive, illusive, inclusive, intrusive, obtrusive, occlusive, preclusive, prelusive, protrusive, reclusive, suffusive • all-inclusive, inconclusive, nonexclusive, nonintrusive, unobtrusive

usk \əsk\ brusque, busk, cusk, dusk, husk, musk, rusk, tusk • subfusc

usker \əs-kər\ busker, husker, tusker • cornhusker

uskie \əs-kē\ see USKY

uskin \əs-kən\ see USCAN

usky \əs-kē\ dusky, husky, muskie, musky

usly \əs-lē\ pussley, thusly

uso \ü-sō\ see USOE

usoe \ü-sō\ Rousseau, trousseau, whoso • Caruso • Robinson Crusoe

usque \əsk\ see USK

uss[1] \us\ puss, Russ, schuss, wuss • chartreuse, sea puss, sourpuss • glamour-puss, octopus, platypus

uss[2] \üs\ see USE[1]

uss[3] \əs\ see US[1]

ussant \əs-ənt\ mustn't • discussant

ussate \əs-ət\ see USSET

usse \üs\ see USE[1]

ussel \əs-əl\ see USTLE

ussell \əs-əl\ see USTLE

usset \əs-ət\ gusset, russet • decussate

ussia \əsh-ə\ Prussia, Russia • Belorussia

ussian \əsh-ən\ see USSION

ussing \əs-iŋ\ see USING

ussion \əsh-ən\ Prussian, Russian • concussion, discussion, percussion • Belorussian, repercussion

ussive \əs-iv\ jussive, tussive • concussive, percussive • antitussive, repercussive

ussle \əs-əl\ see USTLE

ussley \əs-lē\ see USLY

ussy \əs-ē\ fussy, gussy, hussy, mussy, pursy, pussy

ust[1] \əst\ bust, crust, dost, dust, gust, just, lust, must, musth, rust, thrust, trust, wast • adjust, adust, august, blind trust, bloodlust, brain trust, combust, degust, disgust, distrust, encrust, entrust, in trust, leaf rust, mistrust, moondust, piecrust, robust, sawdust, stardust, unjust, upthrust • angel dust, antirust, antitrust, baby bust, bite the dust, cosmic dust, counterthrust, dryasdust, living trust, readjust, unitrust, upper crust, wanderlust —*also* -ed *forms of verbs listed at* US[1]

ust[2] \əs\ see US[1]

ust[3] \üst\ see OOST

ustable \əs-tə-bəl\ see USTIBLE

ustard \əs-tərd\ bustard, custard, mustard • cut the mustard—*also* -ed *forms of verbs listed at* USTER

usted \əs-təd\ busted • disgusted • maladjusted, well-adjusted—*also* ed *forms of verbs listed at* UST[1]

uster \əs-tər\ bluster, buster, cluster, Custer, duster, fluster, luster, muster, thruster, truster • adjuster, ballbuster, blockbuster, brain truster, clotbuster, combustor, crop duster, deluster, gangbuster, lackluster, pass muster, sodbuster, trustbuster • antitruster, baby buster, broncobuster, filibuster, knuckle-duster

ustful \əst-fəl\ lustful, thrustful, trustful • disgustful, distrustful, mistrustful

usth \əst\ see UST[1]

ustian \əs-chən\ see USTION

ustible \əs-tə-bəl\ trustable • adjustable, combustible • incombustible

ustin \əs-tən\ Justin • Augustine

ustine \əs-tən\ see USTIN

ustic \əs-tik\ fustic, rustic

ustion \əs-chən\ fustian • combustion

ustive \əs-tiv\ adjustive, combustive • maladjustive

ustle \əs-əl\ bustle, hustle, muscle, mussel, Russell, rustle, trestle, tussle • corpuscle, crepuscle, Jack Russell, outhustle, outmuscle

ustn't \əs-ᵊnt\ see USSANT

ustom \əs-təm\ custom, frustum • accustom • disaccustom

ustor \əs-tər\ see USTER

ustrious \əs-trē-əs\ illustrious, industrious

ustule \əs-chül\ frustule, pustule

ustum \əs-təm\ see USTOM

usty \əs-tē\ busty, crusty, dusty, fusty, gusty, lusty, musty, rusty, trusty

usy \iz-ē\ see IZZY

ut[1] \ət\ but, butt, cut, glut, gut, hut, jut, mutt, nut, putt, rut, scut, shut, slut, smut, soot, strut, tut, ut, what • abut, all but, beechnut, blind gut, brush cut, buzz cut, catgut, chestnut, clean-cut, clear-cut, cobnut, cockshut, crew cut, crosscut, doughnut, foregut, groundnut, haircut, jump cut, kick butt, locknut, lug nut, Meerut, midgut, offcut, peanut, pignut, pine nut, precut, putt-putt, rebut, recut, rotgut, rough cut, sackbut, shortcut, somewhat, tut-tut, uncut, walnut, wing nut, woodcut • antismut, betel nut, brazil nut, butternut, coconut, congregate, hazelnut, intercut, Lilliput, lychee nut, Nissen hut, occiput, overcut, scuttlebutt, undercut, uppercut • director's cut, open-and-shut

ut[2] \ü\ see EW[1]

ut[3] \üt\ see UTE

ut[4] \u̇t\ see OOT[1]

uta \üt-ə\ Baruta, Ceuta, likuta, valuta • barracouta

utable \üt-ə-bəl\ mutable, scrutable, suitable • commutable, computable, disputable, immutable, imputable, inscrutable, permutable, statutable, transmutable • executable, incommutable, incomputable, indisputable, irrefutable, prosecutable, substitutable

utage \üt-ij\ see OOTAGE[1]

utal \üt-ᵊl\ see UTILE

utan \üt-ᵊn\ cutin, gluten, Luton, mutine, Newton, Putin, rutin, Teuton • Laputan, rambutan, Rasputin • highfalutin

utant \üt-ᵊnt\ mutant • disputant, pollutant

utative \üt-ət-iv\ mutative, putative • commutative, imputative, transmutative

utch[1] \əch\ clutch, crutch, cutch, dutch, Dutch, grutch, hutch, much, scutch, smutch, such, touch • and such, as much, as such, a touch, nonesuch, retouch, soft touch, so much, too much • a bit much, common touch, double-clutch, double Dutch, Midas touch, overmuch, pretty much, such and such

utch[2] \uch\ butch, putsch

utcher \əch-ər\ scutcher • retoucher

utchy \əch-ē\ see UCHY

ute \üt\ boot, bruit, brut, brute, bute, Bute, butte, chute, cloot, coot, cute, flute, fruit, glout, glute, hoot, jute, Jute, loot, lute, moot, mute, newt, pood, root, Root, rout, route, scoot, scute, shoot, snoot, soot, suit, suite, toot, tout, ut, Ute • acute, astute, Asyût, bear fruit, beetroot, Beirut, birthroot, bloodroot, breadfruit, butut, cahoot, Canute, catsuit, cheroot, choucroute, clubroot, commute, compute, confute, crapshoot, cube root, deaf-mute, depute, dilute, dispute, dry suit, elute, en route, enroot, flight suit, folkmoot, freeboot, galoot, grapefruit, G suit, hardboot, hip boot, hirsute, imbrute, impute, jackboot, jackfruit, jumpsuit, kashruth, lawsuit, long suit, lounge suit, minute, nonsuit, offshoot, outshoot, Paiute, pantsuit, permute, playsuit, pollute, pursuit, reboot, recruit, refute, repute, salute, sans doute, seaboot, Silk Route, snowsuit, solute, spacesuit, sport-ute, square root, star fruit, star route, statute, strong suit, sunsuit, sweat suit, swimsuit, take root, taproot, to boot, tracksuit, trade route, transmute, tribute, uproot, volute, wet suit, zoot suit • absolute, Aleut, arrowroot, Asyût, attribute, autoroute, bandicoot, bathing suit, birthday suit, bitterroot, bodysuit, boilersuit, bumbershoot, business suit, comminute, constitute, contribute, convolute, counter-suit, Denver boot, destitute, disrepute, dissolute, evolute, execute, follow suit, gingerroot, hot pursuit, institute, involute, kiwifruit, leisure suit, malamute, overshoot, parachute, passion fruit, persecute, point-and-shoot, prosecute, prostitute, qiviut, resolute, restitute, revolute, run-and-shoot, rural route, subacute, substitute, troubleshoot, undershoot • electrocute, forbidden fruit, Hardecanute, hyperacute, Inuktitut, irresolute, reconstitute, redistribute, telecommute

uted \üt-əd\ see OOTED[1]

utee \üt-ē\ see OOTY[1]

utely \üt-lē\ cutely, mutely • acutely, astutely, minutely • absolutely, dissolutely, resolutely • irresolutely

uten \üt-ᵊn\ see UTAN

uteness \üt-nəs\ cuteness, glutenous, glutinous, muteness, mutinous • acuteness, astuteness, diluteness, hirsuteness, minuteness • absoluteness, destituteness, dissoluteness

utenist \üt-ᵊn-est\ lutenist, Teutonist

utenous \üt-nəs\ see UTENESS

uteous \üt-ē-əs\ beauteous, duteous, gluteus, luteous

uter \üt-ər\ cooter, neuter, fluter, hooter, looter, pewter, rooter, router, scooter, shooter, souter, suiter, suitor, tooter, tutor • accoutre, commuter, computer, confuter, crapshooter, diluter, disputer, freebooter, hip shooter, jump shooter, peashooter, polluter, recruiter, refuter, saluter, sharpshooter, six-shooter, square shooter, straight shooter, trapshooter, two-suiter, uprooter, zoot-suiter • coadjutor, executor, instituter, motor scooter, persecutor, prosecutor, prostitutor, troubleshooter • microcomputer, minicomputer, telecommuter —also -er forms of adjectives listed at UTE

utes \üts\ see OOTS

uteus \üt-ē-əs\ see UTEOUS

uth¹ \üt\ see UTE

uth² \üth\ see OOTH²

uther¹ \ü-thər\ Luther, Reuther, Uther

uther² \ə-thər\ see OTHER¹

uthful \üth-fəl\ ruthful, truthful, youthful • untruthful

uthless \üth-ləs\ ruthless, toothless

uti \üt-ē\ see OOTY¹

utia \ü-shə\ fuchsia • minutia, Saint Lucia, Yakutia

utian \ü-shən\ see UTION

utic \üt-ik\ maieutic, scorbutic, toreutic • hermeneutic, parachutic, propaedeutic, therapeutic

utical \üt-i-kəl\ cuticle • hermeneutical, nutriceutical, pharmaceutical

uticle \üt-i-kəl\ see UTICAL

utie \üt-ē\ see OOTY¹

utiful \üt-i-fəl\ beautiful, dutiful

utile \üt-ᵊl\ brutal, footle, futile, rootle, tootle, utile • inutile • Kwakiutl

utin \üt-ᵊn\ see UTAN

utine \üt-ᵊn\ see UTAN

uting \üt-iŋ\ fluting, luting, suiting • hip-shooting, sharpshooting, trapshooting—also -ing forms of verbs listed at UTE

utinous¹ \üt-ᵊn-əs\ glutinous, mutinous

utinous² \üt-nəs\ see UTENESS

utiny \üt-ᵊn-ē\ mutiny, scrutiny

ution \ü-shən\ Lucian • ablution, Aleutian, capuchin, Confucian, dilution, elution, locution, pollution, solution • absolution, allocution, attribution, comminution, consecution, constitution, contribution, convolution, destitution, devolution, diminution, dissolution, distribution, elocution, evolution, execution, exsolution, institution, involution, lilliputian, persecution, prosecution, prostitution, resolution, restitution, retribution, revolution, Rosicrucian, substitution • antipollution, circumlocution, coevolution, electrocution, final solution, green revolution, irresolution, joint resolution, maldistribution, reconstitution, redistribution

utionary \ü-she-ner-ē\ ablutionary • elocutionary, evolutionary, illocutionary, revolutionary, substitutionary

utionist \ü-shnest\ devolutionist, elocutionist, evolutionist, revolutionist

utish \üt-ish\ brutish, Jutish, Vutish

utist \üt-est\ chutist, flutist • absolutist, parachutist—also -est *forms of adjectives listed at* UTE

utive \üt-iv\ dilutive, pollutive • absolutive, constitutive, persecutive, substitutive

utl \ü-tᵊl\ see UTILE

utland \et-lend\ Jutland, Rutland

utlass \et-les\ cutlass, gutless

utler \et-ler\ butler, Butler, cutler, sutler

utless \et-les\ see UTLASS

utlet \et-let\ cutlet, nutlet

utment \et-ment\ hutment • abutment

utney \et-nē\ chutney, gluttony • Ascutney

uto \üt-ō\ Bhutto, Pluto, putto • Basuto, cornuto, Maputo, tenuto • sostenuto

uton \üt-ⁿ\ see UTAN

utor \üt-er\ see UTER

utriment \ü-tre-ment\ nutriment • accoutrement

uts \ets\ see UTZ

utsch \uch\ see UTCH²

utsi \üt-sē\ see UZZI²

utsy \et-sē\ gutsy, klutzy

utt \et\ see UT¹

uttack \et-ek\ see UTTOCK

uttal \et-ᵊl\ see UTTLE

utte \üt\ see UTE

uttee \et-ē\ see UTTY

utter¹ \et-er\ butter, clutter, cutter, flutter, gutter, mutter, nutter, putter, scutter, shutter, splutter, sputter, strutter, stutter, utter • abutter, aflutter, haircutter, leaf-cutter, price-cutter, rebutter, stonecutter, unclutter, woodcutter • bread and butter, cookie-cutter, paper cutter

utter² \ut-er\ see OOTER¹

uttery \et-e-rē\ buttery, fluttery, spluttery

utti¹ \üt-ē\ see OOTY¹

utti² \üt-ē\ see OOTY²

utting \út-iŋ\ see OOTING[1]

uttish \ət-ish\ ruttish, sluttish

uttle \ət-ᵊl\ cuittle, scuttle, shuttle, subtile, subtle
• rebuttal, space shuttle

utto \üt-ō\ see UTO

uttock \ət-ək\ buttock, Cuttack, futtock

utton \ət-ᵊn\ button, glutton, mutton, Sutton • hot-button, keybutton, push-button, unbutton • belly button, leg-of-mutton, on the button, panic button

uttony \ət-nē\ see UTNEY

utty \ət-ē\ butty, gutty, jutty, nutty, puttee, putty, rutty, slutty, smutty

utum \üt-əm\ scutum, sputum

uture \ü-chər\ blucher, future, moocher, suture • wave of the future

uty \üt-ē\ see OOTY[1]

utz \əts\ futz, klutz, lutz, nuts
• blood-and-guts, spill one's guts—also -s, -'s, and -s' forms of nouns and -s forms of verbs listed at UT[1]

utzy \ət-sē\ see UTSY

uu \ü\ see EW[1]

uvial \ü-vē-əl\ fluvial, pluvial
• alluvial, colluvial, diluvial, eluvial, exuvial

uvian \ü-vē-ən\ alluvion, diluvian, Peruvian, vesuvian, Vesuvian
• postdiluvian • antediluvian

uvion \ü-vē-ən\ see UVIAN

uvium \ü-vē-əm\ alluvium, colluvium, effluvium

ux[1] \əks\ crux, flux, lux, tux
• afflux, aw-shucks, big bucks, conflux, deluxe, efflux, influx, redux, reflux • Benelux, megabucks—also -s, -'s, and -s' forms of nouns and -s forms of verbs listed at UCK[1]

ux[2] \üks\ see OOKS[2]

uxe[1] \üks\ see OOKS[1]

uxe[2] \üks\ see OOKS[2]

uxe[3] \əks\ see UX[1]

uxion \ək-shən\ see UCTION

uy \ī\ see Y[1]

uygur \ē-gər\ see EAGER

uyot \ē-ō\ see IO[2]

uyp \īp\ see IPE

uz[1] \üts\ see OOTS

uz[2] \üz\ see USE[2]

uze \üz\ see USE[2]

uzz \əz\ see EUSE[1]

uzzi[1] \ü-zē\ see OOZY

uzzi[2] \üt-sē\ Tutsi • Abruzzi

uzzle \əz-əl\ guzzle, muzzle, nuzzle, puzzle • crossword puzzle, jigsaw puzzle

uzzler \əz-lər\ guzzler, muzzler, puzzler • gas-guzzler

uzzy \əz-ē\ fuzzy, muzzy, scuzzy

y

y¹ \ī\ ai, ay, aye, bi, Bligh, buy, by, bye, chai, chi, cry, die, dry, dye, eye, fie, fly, fry, guy, Guy, hi, hie, high, Huai, i, I, lie, lye, my, nigh, phi, pi, pie, ply, pry, psi, rye, scythe, sei, shy, sigh, sky, Skye, sly, spry, spy, sty, Tai, Thai, thigh, thy, tie, try, vie, why, wry, wye, xi, Y • Abbai, aby, agley, air-dry, Alai, ally, Altai, anti, apply, assai, awry, aye-aye, Bacchae, Baha'i, banzai, barfly, bee fly, Belgae, belie, bigeye, big lie, birds-eye, black eye, blackfly, black tie, blow-dry, blowby, blowfly, blue-sky, Bo Hai, Bottai, bone-dry, bonsai, botfly, Brunei, buckeye, bugeye, bulls-eye, bye-bye, canaille, catchfly, cat's-eye, Chennai, chess pie, Chiang Mai, cockeye, cockshy, come by, comply, cow pie, crane fly, cream pie, cross-eye, deadeye, decry, deep-fry, deep-sky, deerfly, defy, Delphi, deny, descry, do by, dong quai, drip-dry, drachmai, drive by, drop by, dry eye, dry fly, Dubai, elhi, Eli, espy, face fly, firefly, fish-eye, flesh fly, flyby, fly high, forby, freeze-dry, frogeye, fruit fly, gadfly, gallfly, get by, GI, glass eye, go by, good-bye, greenfly, grisaille, gun-shy, Haggai, Hawkeye, heel fly, hereby, hermae, hi-fi, hog-tie, horn fly, horsefly, housefly, imply, jai alai, July, Karzai, Kasai, Katmai, Kaui, Kenai, knee-high, korai, lanai, Lanai, lay-by, lay by, Lehigh, let fly, Levi, lie by, litae, magpie, mai tai, mao-tai, Masai, mayfly, medfly, Menai, mind's eye, Moirai, mooneye, Mumbai, my eye, nearby, necktie, nilgai, nisi, Ögödei, outbuy, outbye, outcry, outfly, outvie, oxeye, pad thai, Panay, panfry, Parcae, piece-dye, pigsty, pinkeye, Po Hai, pop eye, Popeye, pop fly, porkpie, potpie, put by, Qinghai, quasi, rabbi, rebuy, red-eye, rely, reply, retry, rib eye, ride high, rocaille, rough-dry, run dry, Sakai, sand fly, saw fly, sci-fi, screw eye, semi, Sendai, serai, set by, shanghai, Shanghai, sheep's eye, shoofly, stonefly, shut-eye, Sinai, sky-high, small-fry, sockeye, stand by, standby, stir-fry, string tie, supply, swear by, swing-by, terai, test-fly, thereby, tie-dye, titi, tongue-tie, Transkei, twist tie, two-ply, untie, vat dye, Versailles, walleye, watcheye,

437

well-nigh, whereby, whitefly, white tie, wild rye, wise guy, worms-eye, yarn dye • abide by, Adonai, alibi, alkali, amplify, apple-pie, argufy, assegai, azo dye, basify, beautify, bias-ply, bolo tie, butterfly, by-and-by, by the bye, caddis fly, calcify, certify, Chou En-lai, citify, clarify, classify, coalify, cockneyfy, codify, college try, cottage pie, crucify, cut-and-dry, cut-and-try, cutie-pie, DIY, damnify, damselfly, dandify, deify, densify, dignify, dobson-fly, do-or-die, dragonfly, dulcify, eagle eye, edify, evil eye, falsify, fancify, fortify, frenchify, fructify, gasify, Gemini, gentrify, glorify, glutei, goggle-eye, goldeneye, gratify, Haggai, harvest fly, hexerei, high and dry, hip and thigh, Hokusai, hook and eye, horrify, hoverfly, humble pie, Iceni, junior high, justify, kiss good-bye, lazy eye, lignify, liquefy, lithify, Lorelei, lullaby, Madurai, magnify, Malachi, mallei, Maracay, minify, misapply, modify, mollify, Molokai, Mordecai, mortify, Mount Katmai, Mount Sinai, multi-ply, multiply, mummify, mystify, nazify, nitrify, notify, nuclei, nullify, occupy, old school tie, Olduvai, on standby, on the fly, ossify, overbuy, overdry, overfly, overlie, pacify, Paraguay, passerby, peccavi, petrify, pilei, PPI, preachify, prettify, private eye, prophesy, protei, purify, putrefy, qualify, quantify, ramify, rarefy, ratify,

RBI, reapply, rectify, reify, res gestae, resupply, robber fly, runner's high, Russify, samurai, sanctify, satisfy, scarify, schwarmerei, seeing eye, semidry, senior high, set store by, shepherd's pie, shoofly pie, signify, simplify, sine die, solei, Spanish fly, specify, speechify, stratify, stultify, stupefy, superhigh, sweetie pie, Tenebrae, terrify, testify, tie-and-dye, tigereye, Trans Alai, tsetse fly, tumble dry, typify, uglify, ultradry, ultrahigh, underlie, unify, Uruguay, Veneti, verify, versify, vilify, vinify, vitrify, vivify, weather eye, Windsor tie, xanthene dye, yuppify, zombify • acetify, acidify, ammonify, aniline dye, a priori, beatify, bourgeoisify, commodify, complexify, cross-multiply, decalcify, decertify, declassify, demystify, denazify, desanctify, desertify, detoxify, Dioscuri, disqualify, dissatisfy, diversify, electric eye, electrify, emulsify, esterify, exemplify, facetiae, Gorno-Altay, hang out to dry, Helvetii, humidify, identify, indemnify, intensify, misclassify, money supply, objectify, oversupply, personify, preoccupy, prequalify, prespecify, reliquiae, reunify, revivify, rigidify, sacrifice fly, saponify, see eye to eye, solemnify, solidify, syllabify, transmogrify, turn a blind eye, undersupply, vox populi, water supply • a fortiori, caravanserai, corpus delicti, deacidify, dehumidify, ex hypothesi, misidentify, modus vivendi, nolle prosequi, oversimplify • amicus curiae, curriculum vitae, in the blink of an eye, modus operandi

y² \ē\ see EE¹

ya \ē-ə\ see IA¹

yable \ī-ə-bəl\ see IABLE¹

yad \ī-əd\ dryad, dyad, naiad, pleiad, Pleiad, sayyid, triad • Umayyad • hamadryad, jeremiad

yan \ī-ən\ see ION¹

yant \ī-ənt\ see IANT

yatt \ī-ət\ see IET

ybe \īb\ see IBE¹

ybele \ib-ə-lē\ Cybele • amphiboly, epiboly

yber \ī-bər\ see IBER

ybia \i-bē-ə\ see IBIA

ycad \ī-kəd\ cycad, spiked

ycan \ī-kən\ see ICHEN¹

yce \īs\ see ICE¹

ych¹ \ik\ see ICK

ych² \īk\ see IKE²

yche \ī-kē\ see IKE¹

ychnis \ik-nəs\ see ICKNESS

ycia \ish-ə\ see ITIA¹

ycian \ish-ən\ see ITION

ycin \īs-ᵊn\ see ISON¹

ycle¹ \ī-kəl\ cycle, Michael • cell cycle, life cycle, recycle, song cycle, two-cycle • business cycle, Calvin cycle, carbon cycle, epicycle, Exercycle, hemicycle, kilocycle, megacycle, motorcycle, unicycle, vicious cycle, Wanne-Eickel

ycle² \ik-əl\ see ICKLE

ycler \ik-lər\ see ICKLER

yd \ü-id\ see UID

yde \īd\ see IDE¹

ydia \i-dē-ə\ see IDIA

ydian \id-ē-ən\ see IDIAN

ydice \id-ə-sē\ see IDICE

ydney \id-nē\ see IDNEY

ye \ī\ see Y¹

yeable \ī-ə-bəl\ see IABLE¹

yed \īd\ see IDE¹

yer \īr\ see IRE¹

yeth \ī-əth\ see IATH¹

yfe \īf\ see IFE¹

yfed \ər-əd\ see OVED

yg \ig\ see IG

ygamous \ig-ə-məs\ see IGAMOUS

ygamy \ig-ə-mē\ see IGAMY

ygia \ī-jə\ see IJAH

ygian \i-jən\ Phrygian, pidgin, pigeon, smidgen, stygian, wigeon • clay pigeon, religion, rock pigeon, stool pigeon, wood pigeon • callipygian, Cantabrigian, get religion, homing pigeon, irreligion • carrier pigeon, passenger pigeon

ygiene \ī-jēn\ see AIJIN

ygma \ig-mə\ see IGMA

ygnus \ig-nəs\ see IGNESS

ygos \ī-gəs\ see YGOUS

ygous \ī-gəs\ gigas • azygos • hemizygous, homozygous, steatopygous

ygrapher \ig-rə-fər\ see IGRAPHER

ygraphist \ig-rə-fəst\ see IGRAPHIST

ygyny \ij-ə-nē\ see IGINE

ying \ī-iŋ\ crying, flying, lying, trying • high-flying, low-lying, outlying, undying • nitrifying, terrifying, underlying—*also* -ing *forms of verbs listed at* Y

yke \īk\ see IKE²

yked \īkt\ see IKED¹

yl \ēl\ see EAL²

ylan \il-ən\ see ILLON

ylar \ī-lər\ see ILAR

yle \īl\ see ILE¹

ylem \ī-ləm\ see ILUM

yler \ī-lər\ see ILAR

ylet \ī-lət\ see ILOT

yley \ī-lē\ see YLY

yli \ē-lē\ see EELY

ylic \il-ik\ see ILIC

ylie \ī-lē\ see YLY

yling \ī-liŋ\ see ILING¹

yll \īl\ see ILE¹

ylla \il-ə\ see ILLA²

yllable \il-ə-bəl\ see ILLABLE

yllary \il-ə-rē\ see ILLARY

yllic \il-ik\ see ILIC

yllis \il-əs\ see ILLUS

yllium \il-ē-əm\ see ILIUM

yllo¹ \ē-lō\ see ILO²

yllo² \ī-lō\ see ILO¹

ylum \ī-ləm\ see ILUM

ylus \ī-ləs\ see ILUS

yly \ī-lē\ dryly, highly, maile, Philae, riley, shyly, slyly, smiley, spryly, Wiley, wily, wryly • life of Riley

ym \im\ see IM¹

yma \ī-mə\ Chaima, cyma

yman \ī-mən\ see IMEN

ymathy \im-ə-thē\ see IMOTHY

ymbal \im-bəl\ see IMBLE

ymbol \im-bəl\ see IMBLE

yme \īm\ see IME¹

ymeless \īm-ləs\ see IMELESS

ymen \ī-mən\ see IMEN

ymer \ī-mər\ see IMER¹

ymic¹ \ī-mik\ thymic • enzymic

ymic² \im-ik\ gimmick, mimic • bulimic • acronymic, antonymic, eponymic, homonymic, matronymic, metonymic, pantomimic, patronymic, synonymic, toponymic

ymical \im-i-kəl\ see IMICAL

ymie \ī-mē\ see IMY

ymion \im-ē-ən\ see IMIAN

ymity \im-ət-ē\ see IMITY

ymmetry \im-ə-trē\ see IMETRY

ymn \im\ see IM[1]

ymp \imp\ see IMP

ymph \imf\ lymph, nymph

ymric \im-rik\ Cymric, limerick

ymus \ī-məs\ see IMIS

ymy \ī-mē\ see IMY

yn \in\ see IN[1]

ynah \ī-nə\ see INA[1]

ynast \ī-nəst\ see INIST[1]

ynch[1] \inch\ see INCH

ynch[2] \iŋk\ see INK

yncher \in-chər\ see INCHER

ynd \īnd\ see IND[1]

yndic \in-dik\ see INDIC

yne \īn\ see INE[1]

yness \ī-nəs\ see INUS[1]

ynia \in-ē-ə\ see INIA

ynic \in-ik\ see INIC[2]

ynical \in-i-kəl\ see INICAL

ynn \in\ see IN[1]

ynne \in\ see IN[1]

ynth \inth\ see INTH

ynthia \in-thē-ə\ see INTHIA

ynx \iŋs\ see INX

yon \ī-ən\ see ION[1]

yone \ī-ə-nē\ see YONY

yony \ī-ə-nē\ bryony • Alcyone

yp \ip\ see IP

ypal \ī-pəl\ typal • disciple
• archetypal, prototypal

ype \īp\ see IPE

yper \ī-pər\ see IPER

ypey \ī-pē\ see IPY

yph \if\ see IFF

yphen \ī-fən\ hyphen, siphon

yphic \if-ik\ see IFIC

yphony \if-ə-nē\ see IPHONY

ypic \ip-ik\ typic • philippic
• allotypic, biotypic, ecotypic,
genotypic, holotypic,
monotypic, phenotypic,
polytypic

yping \ī-piŋ\ see IPING

ypo \ī-pō\ hypo, typo

ypress \ī-prəs\ cypress, Cyprus,
viperous

yprus \ī-prəs\ see YPRESS

ypse \ips\ see IPS

ypso \ip-sō\ see IPSO

ypsy \ip-sē\ gypsy, Gypsy, tipsy

ypt \ipt\ see IPT

yptian \ip-shən\ see IPTION

yptic \ip-tik\ cryptic, diptych,
glyptic, styptic, triptych, tryptic
• ecliptic, elliptic • apocalyptic

ypy \ī-pē\ see IPY

yr \ir\ see EER[2]

yra \ī-rə\ Ira, Lyra, Myra, naira
• bell-lyra, Corcyra, Elmira,
Elvira, hegira, hetaera, palmyra,
Palmyra • spirogyra

yral \ī-rəl\ see IRAL

yrant \ī-rənt\ see IRANT

yre \īr\ see IRE[1]

yreal \ir-ē-əl\ see ERIAL

yria \ir-ē-ə\ see ERIA[1]

yriad \ir-ē-əd\ see ERIOD

yrian \ir-ē-ən\ see ERIAN[1]

yric[1] \ī-rik\ pyric • oneiric • panegyric

yric[2] \ir-ik\ see ERIC[2]

yrical \ir-i-kəl\ see ERICAL[2]

yrie[1] \ir-ē\ see EARY

yrie[2] \ī-rē\ see IARY[1]

yril \ir-əl\ see ERAL[1]

yrist \ir-əst\ see ERIST[1]

yrium \ir-ē-əm\ see ERIUM

yrna \ər-nə\ see ERNA

yro[1] \ī-rō\ biro, Cairo, gyro, Gyro, tyro • enviro • autogiro

yro[2] \ir-ō\ see ERO[3]

yron \ī-rən\ see IREN

yros \ī-rəs\ see IRUS

yrrh \ər\ see EUR[1]

yrrha \ir-ə\ see ERA[2]

yrrhic \ir-ik\ see ERIC[2]

yrrhus \ir-əs\ see EROUS

yrse \ərs\ see ERSE

yrsus \ər-səs\ see ERSUS

yrtle \ərt-əl\ see ERTILE

yrup \ər-əp\ see IRRUP

yrupy \ər-ə-pē\ see IRRUPY

yrus \ī-rəs\ see IRUS

ysail \ī-səl\ see ISAL[1]

ysch \ish\ see ISH[1]

yse \īs\ see ICE[1]

ysh \ish\ see ISH[1]

ysia[1] \ish-ə\ see ITIA

ysia[2] \izh-ə\ see ISIA

ysian[1] \is-ē-ən\ Piscean • Odyssean • Dionysian

ysian[2] \ish-ən\ see ITION

ysian[3] \izh-ən\ see ISION

ysian[4] \ī-sē-ən\ see ISCEAN[1]

ysical \iz-i-kəl\ physical, quizzical • nonphysical • metaphysical

ysis \ī-səs\ see ISIS

ysm \iz-əm\ see ISM

ysmal \iz-məl\ dismal • abysmal, baptismal • cataclysmal, catechismal, paroxysmal

yson \īs-ən\ see ISON[1]

yss \is\ see ISS[1]

yssal \is-əl\ see ISTLE

yssean \is-ē-ən\ see YSIAN[1]

ysseus \ish-əs\ see ICIOUS[1]

yssum \is-əm\ see ISSOME

yssus \is-əs\ see ISSUS

yst \ist\ see IST[2]

ystal \is-təl\ see ISTAL

yster[1] \is-tər\ see ISTER

yster[2] \ī-stər\ see EISTER[1]

ystery \is-trē\ see ISTORY

ystic \is-tik\ see ISTIC

ystical \is-ti-kəl\ see ISTICAL

ystine \is-tən\ see ISTON

ysus[1] \ē-səs\ see ESIS

ysus[2] \ī-səs\ see ISIS

yta \īt-ə\ see ITA[1]

yte \īt\ see ITE[1]

yterate \it-ə-rət\ see ITERATE

ytes \īt-ēz\ see ITES

ythe[1] \ī\ see Y[1]

ythe[2] \īth\ see ITHE[1]

ythia \ith-ē-ə\ Scythia • forsythia • stichomythia

ythian \ith-ē-ən\ Pythian, Scythian

ythy \i-thē\ see ITHY

ytic \it-ik\ see ITIC

ytical \it-i-kəl\ see ITICAL

ytics \it-iks\ see ITICS

yting \īt-iŋ\ see ITING

ytis \ī-təs\ see ITIS

ytton \it-ᵊn\ see ITTEN

yve \īv\ see IVE[1]

yx \iks\ see IX[1]

yxia \ik-sē-ə\ see IXIA

yxie \ik-sē\ see IXIE

yze \īz\ see IZE